1918

1918

A VERY BRITISH VICTORY

PETER HART

Weidenfeld & Nicolson

LONDON

This book is dedicated to all the men
who served in the British Army in 1918.

First published in Great Britain in 2008
by Weidenfeld & Nicolson

1 3 5 7 9 10 8 6 4 2

© Peter Hart 2008

A CIP catalogue record for this book
is available from the British Library.

ISBN 978 0 297 84652 9

Typeset at The Spartan Press Ltd,
Lymington, Hants

Printed and bound at Mackays of Chatham plc,
Chatham, Kent

All photographs supplied by the Imperial War Museum

Weidenfeld & Nicolson

The Orion Publishing Group Ltd
Orion House
5 Upper Saint Martin's Lane
London, WC2H 9EA

An Hachette Livre UK Company

The Orion Publishing Group's policy is to use papers that
are natural, renewable and recyclable products and made
from wood grown in sustainable forests. The logging and
manufacturing processes are expected to conform to the
environmental regulations of the country of origin.

www.orionbooks.co.uk

Contents

	List of Maps	vii
	Preface	1
1	Of Mice and Men	11
2	The Best-laid Schemes	33
3	21 March 1918	64
4	Retreat to the Somme	106
5	Desperate Measures	141
6	Turning the Tide	176
7	Battle for Flanders: 9 April 1918	220
8	Battle on the Aisne: 27 May 1918	264
9	Planning for the 'All Arms Battle'	301
10	The Black Day: Amiens, 8 August 1918	317
11	Advance to the Somme	362
12	With Our American Friends at the Front	403
13	Breaking the Hindenburg Line	420
14	Germany Falling	464
15	This is the End: 11 November 1918	495
	Acknowledgements	517
	Notes to the Text	522
	Index	541

List of Maps

1   The Western Front, 1918   8

2   The XVIII defences, March 1918   41

3   The German attack, 21 March   76

4   The German attack, 22 March   109

5   The German attack, 23 March   121

6   The German attack, 24 March   143

7   The German attack, 25 March   164

8   The German attack, 26 March   179

9   The Lys Offensive, April 1918   223

10 The Aisne, May–June 1918   267

11 Attack on the French lines, 9 June 1918   297

12 The British advance, August–September   365

13 The American attack, September 1918   417

14 Breaking the Hindenburg Line   427

15 Advance to victory, October–November 1918   467

Preface

IN MANY WAYS 1918 was the most awful and tragic year of the Great War. The scale of the fighting on the Western Front exceeded anything that had gone before. It was continental warfare on an epic scale as the huge citizen armies of the Central Powers and the Allies faced each other head-on in the final battles that would decide the war. It was a year when the Allies for a time appeared close to defeat, when they had their backs to the wall, when it seemed that all might be lost. But it was also the year that resulted in the ultimate *British* victory, greater than Waterloo or Trafalgar in both its overall scale and the end results. For the only time in world history the British Army could lay a realistic claim to being the dominant military force.

Yet this amazing achievement has been almost forgotten. In the years since, the battered victors have been besmirched by a sustained campaign of vilification. Any legitimate acclaim is drowned out by a strange retrospective defeatism that at the time the majority of soldiers would surely have rejected out of hand. Despite being miserable, frightened and at times let down by the failures of their High Command, amongst the soldiers themselves there was undeniably a collective determination to 'see it through'. Even celebrated war poets, such as Siegfried Sassoon and Wilfred Owen, abandoned their pacifism and returned to the fray as they saw the war boiling up to its final crescendo. At heart they were soldier-poets rather than just poets.

There is a story here that must be told, an analysis that must be made. For too long the 'History of the Great War' has had a strangely unfinished look. Historians pore over the Battles of Mons and Ypres in 1914; they vigorously comment on the Battles of Second Ypres and

Loos in 1915; they examine and argue at interminable length over the Battles of the Somme and Jutland in 1916; they feast upon the horrors of Third Ypres and the Passchendaele Ridge in 1917; they even gloatingly record the 'dark days' of the German offensives of 1918 with much extravagant praise for the brilliant 'new' German tactics that forced back the British Army. Yet there is a strange silence over the end results of the self-same battles of spring 1918. The Allies may have fallen back in the face of the German hammer-blows, but they stood firm, stuck together and, as long as the accursed fog stayed away, they inflicted murderous casualties on the advancing Germans – although all at considerable cost to themselves. Following this, buoyed up by the promise of massive American reinforcements, the Allies launched into a 100-day advance to victory that still beggars belief and which was duly acclaimed throughout the 1920s. But many later commentators, blinkered by their hatred – not a lightly chosen word – of Field Marshal Sir Douglas Haig, originating in his command record in 1916 and 1917, seek to brush over this ultimate triumph. For them it was self-evident that the Germans were beaten by the naval blockade, beaten by the Americans, beaten by the 'real men' (Australians or Canadians), beaten by 'enemies within' – beaten by anybody and everybody but the combined efforts of the British and French Armies that had actually battered down the iron door to Germany. They blame Haig for the tragedies of Somme and Passchendaele, and refuse to admit that he could ever have triumphed. These are the real revisionists, tearing away at the prevailing orthodoxy of the post-war years, building their case on the quicksand of politicians' memoirs, stirred with heart-rending personal accounts that naturally reflect the very real horror of any war, and all underpinned by the 'evidence' of a few gifted poets howling their despair at the moon. This heady brew has become the new 'orthodoxy', but says far more about our own era than it does about the reality of 1918.

And the truth? Well it is still a matter of opinion, but the current consensus amongst military historians is that the earlier view was essentially on the right track. Throughout the Great War the British generals often made mistakes; sometimes committed outright blunders costing thousands of lives. They took unnecessary risks, they missed opportunities and they resolutely followed blind alleys. All of this is undeniable. Yet given the appalling problems posed by modern warfare in 1914–18, where artillery ruled the battlefield in an unholy trinity with layered trench lines and sputtering machine guns, it is unlikely that anyone could have done better. The British simply did not have enough guns, the right kind of ammunition or the trained gunners to fire them. The Germans constantly mutated their defensive tactics, creating new problems and new challenges for the British generals and their troops to overcome. Although there was an overall learning curve for the Allied High Command, a far better analogy is that of a 'learning big dipper' with the occasional terrifying descent to disaster as a previously successful tactic was exposed by a sudden change in the layout of German defences or self-inflicted blunders engendered by over-confidence.

When all is said and done, Haig and his generals learnt a great deal from the long, grim years of 1915–17. The culmination of all this experience was the 'All Arms Battle'. Here were the infantry: well armed with light Lewis machine guns and rifle grenades, deploying sophisticated tactics that minimised losses. In immediate support were the heavy Vickers machine guns banded together to provide lethal firepower in attack or defence, the light and heavy mortars hurling high explosives, deadly thermite or poisonous gas canisters. Concealing them were dense smoke barrages that mimicked the fog, which at times seemed to be at the beck and call of the Kaiser. Trundling along into action alongside the infantry were the heavy tanks to crush the wire and assault German strongpoints, behind them came the supply tanks bringing forward huge quantities of ammunition, then there were the lighter tanks and armoured cars held ready to push through and cause chaos in the rear areas in the event of a rupture in the German lines. Aircraft flew above them, now not just photographing or carrying out artillery observation functions, but diving to spray machine-gun fire and small bombs to harass and disrupt the German Army every step of the way. Aerial bombing had progressed to such a level that it was not only used to kill on, or near, the battlefield, but also to try and sever the German strategic rail communications that were needed to bring up reinforcements. Behind everything there was the artillery: truly, as the Royal Artillery motto suggests, the guns were *ubique* – everywhere – on the Western Front. Within the whole murderous conglomeration that was the All Arms Battle they were still the supreme weapons system.

The sheer power and complexity of the artillery bombardments seemed beyond human comprehension. The guns were the first of the weapons successfully added to the infantry bedrock of the 'All Arms' equation. At the beginning of the war there had been no widespread conception within the Royal Artillery of deploying massed guns, of indirect fire, of prolonged barrages or of suppression rather than destruction of the opposition forces. They had the wrong kind of guns, a preponderance of field artillery rather than medium or heavy guns, firing the wrong kind of ammunition, shrapnel rather than high explosive shells. There were shocking shortages of ammunition of all kinds. Overall standards of accuracy were regrettably low and the study of the technical side of gunnery was considered *infra dig* – something best left to the Royal Garrison Artillery. The battles of 1916 had taught the Royal Artillery a great deal and their emerging experts had attained a mastery of their profession by 1917. Target acquisition had become a multi-faceted process. The reconnaissance aircraft of the Royal Flying Corps provided pinpoint photographs that uncovered concealed batteries, machine-gun posts and headquarters. In addition the new methods of flash spotting and sound ranging could locate any active German battery to within a matter of yards. The science of gunnery was understood: both the theory and practice had been mastered. New young officers had by then thoroughly learnt their trade and could prepare the most complex bombardments, while the gun detachments they commanded had reached a pitch of perfection that only long practice could achieve. En masse they could take on the German batteries head to head and defeat them to establish a domination of the whole battlefield area. When the British infantry went 'over the top' the gunners would create a 'creeping barrage', moving just in front of the troops as they attacked across No Man's Land and forcing the German garrison to keep its head well down until it was too late for effective resistance. Then, when the attack had succeeded, the gunners would lay down lethal standing barrages that effectively curtained off the whole area, thwarting any chance of a successful German counter-attack. The guns ruled the battlefield with a hail of steel splinters and high explosives.

The guns were also the main delivery system for poisonous gas. This weapon of war has aroused an overwhelming horror, despite the fact that it was at that stage one of the more benign battlefield weapons. The main intent was to incapacitate, either by the effects of the gas itself or by forcing the opposing soldiers to wear respirators that vastly restricted their vision, hearing and ability to breathe. It left men stumbling around, cut off in their own little worlds and unable to undertake any prolonged physical activity. Serious exposure to gas could kill and certainly ruined victims' lungs – there would be a harvest of death in the bronchial wards of hospitals long after the war – but it was not in itself a major battlefield killer. Another impact of gas warfare was deeply psychological: it deprived soldiers of the elementary ability to breathe in safety and gas masks gave everyone a terrifyingly alien appearance. Gas, consequently, was regarded as an inhuman weapon even amidst the horrors of modern warfare.

In the end the Germans had no answer to the All Arms Battle. After their attacks had manifestly failed to rupture the British line the 'worm' turned and launched a major counter-attack on 8 August. This was the beginning of the end. After the Germans stemmed the initial break-through, the focus of Allied attacks swiftly shifted to other sectors of the Western Front. They never allowed the Germans to settle, regain balance or establish a strong line all along the front. The Allied dominance in *matériel* was such that the guns did not have to be painstakingly moved: there were enough guns and ammunition stacked all along the front to back up an attack almost anywhere. This was impossible in previous years. It wasn't *only* a matter of tactics; it was also the merciless application of superior resources. Time and time again the reeling German divisions were turfed out of their defensive positions. Whatever obstacles they put in front of the advancing Allies were overcome in grand style. There was no let up in the pounding until the German Army was falling apart at the seams. From top to bottom its morale was comprehensively undermined. The Germans knew there was no stopping the Allied advance.

To deny the proud record of the British Army in the battles of 'the Hundred Days' in 1918 is to pour scorn on and diminish the capabilities and achievements of the men themselves. These were not helpless victims, marched to the slaughter by incompetent generals: they were soldiers tried to the very limits of their being, fed up to the back teeth and scared witless a lot of the time, but generally willing to endure to play a part in the greatest series of victories ever won by the British Army. Those stunning victories were their collective achievement. It is worth noting that during the offensives the British captured 188,700 prisoners and some 2,840 guns; the far larger combined French, American and Belgian forces took 196,800 and 3,775 respectively. But war is a collective business and the German Army lost 385,500 prisoners and 6,615 guns. No army could withstand that kind of punishment, especially when at the same time hundreds of thousands of fresh young American soldiers were added to the Allied cause. The Germans were well beaten by 11 November.

Could the German Army have continued to fight into 1919? Perhaps it could; it was, after all, less than two months away, but it would have been to no real end. The army was outnumbered on the battlefields – there were simply no young Germans left to join the colours – while the German economy had been brought finally to its knees by the combination of the grinding pressures of total war and the stringent blockade of the Royal Navy. Their dreams of holding back the Allies on the line of the River Rhine were just that. The German Army would have been blasted aside by the untrammelled power of the Allied guns, the soldiers gassed in their thousands by the deadly new gases emerging from the laboratories of the chemists, and undermined from within and without by the spectre of violent revolution.

It was of course sad, tragic even, that so many men should die with the end of the war so close. For many these tragic late losses have come to be symbolised by the death of the hapless Wilfred Owen, killed while bravely leading his men into action across the Sambre River on 4 November. His family got the dreaded telegram even as the local church bells pealed out their Armistice celebrations just a week later. He was just one of many who did not live to see the vast geopolitical changes caused by the war, the avalanche of change that would sweep away a whole way of life. In the wake of the 'war to end wars' life would never be the same, never safe again.

Peter Hart
August 2008

Map 1 The Western Front, 1918

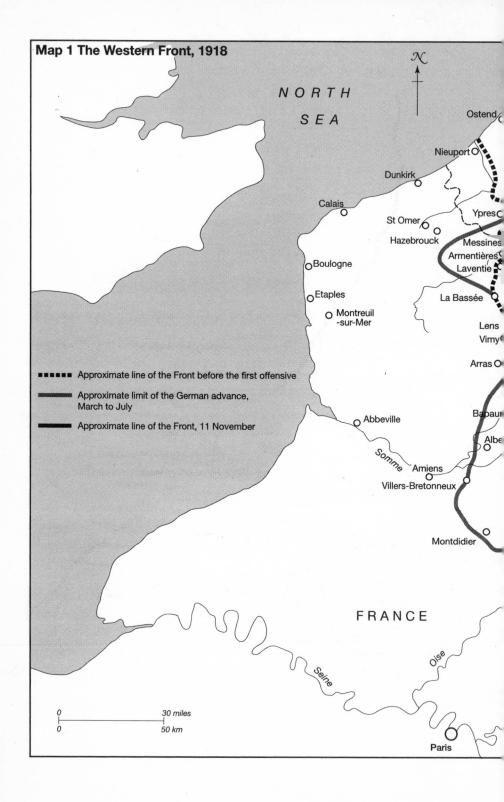

NORTH

SEA

Ostend

Nieuport

Dunkirk

Ypres

Calais

St Omer

Hazebrouck

Messines

Armentières

Laventie

Boulogne

La Bassée

Etaples

Lens

Montreuil -sur-Mer

Vimy

Arras

■■■■■ Approximate line of the Front before the first offensive

▬▬▬ Approximate limit of the German advance, March to July

▬▬▬ Approximate line of the Front, 11 November

Bapaume

Albert

Abbeville

Somme

Amiens

Villers-Bretonneux

Montdidier

FRANCE

Oise

Seine

| 0 | | 30 miles |
| 0 | | 50 km |

Paris

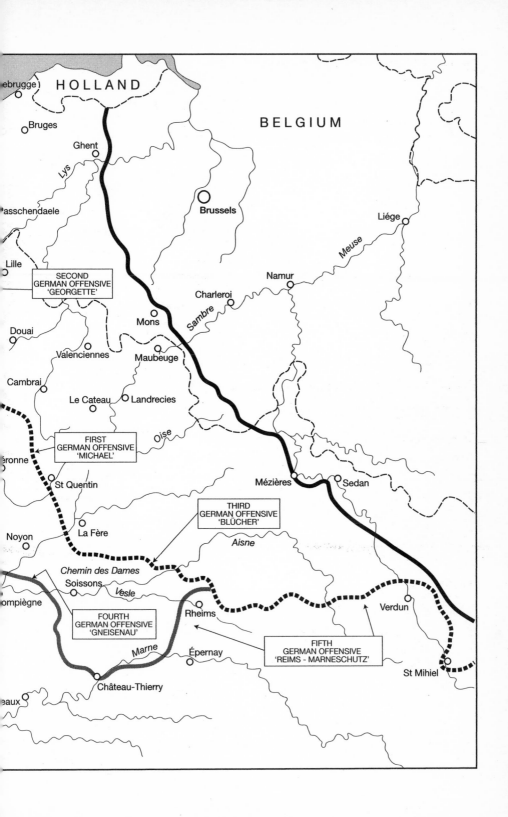

CHAPTER ONE

Of Mice and Men

IN 1917 AN EARTH-SHATTERING event occurred that would dominate the Great War on the Western Front over the next year. Without a doubt it was the collapse of the Russian Empire that allowed the German offensives in March 1918 and all the mayhem that followed. The Russian Army had fought hard in the early years of the war, but excessive casualties had drained its strength and willpower to breaking point. The Revolution and subsequent toppling of the Tsar in March 1917 was not in itself too much of a surprise, but it was soon evident that the advent of the reformist government led by Alexander Kerensky was not sufficient to stem the deep-rooted socialist and revolutionary pressures boiling up in Russia. In these circumstances the decision by Kerensky to launch an offensive against the Germans in July 1917 was an utter disaster. Afflicted by a combination of defeatism, pacifism and revolutionary ideals, the troops simply failed to advance. In a sense the Kerensky offensive was a brutal form of self-selection that duly slaughtered those left in the Russian Army who were still willing to fight. It left Russia helpless before her enemies both military and political. The Germans had allowed the Bolshevik leader Vladimir Lenin to pass through their territory and with the Soviet Revolution in November 1917 the Russian bear was finally brought down and out of the war, although the formal peace treaty would take several more months to negotiate.

The German High Command was well aware of the likely benefits of a total Russian collapse. By late 1917, although Kaiser Wilhelm II still nominally ruled Germany, Field Marshal Paul von Hindenburg and his chief of staff Quartermaster General Erich Ludendorff were effectively in charge. As the German state was dominated increasingly by the requirements of fighting a total war it was all but inevitable that their influence had spread to all sectors of government and society. Together they had to find the solution to the greatest enduring German strategic problem, the nightmare that had tormented their generals ever since the formation of the German Empire: war against Russia to the east, and Britain and France to the west, dividing German military strength and resources. Troops could be moved from west to east and vice versa, but neither could be ignored for long without inviting disaster. The removal of Russia and the Eastern Front meant they could concentrate all their armies and resources in a single direction – to crush the British and French Armies on the Western Front. For Ludendorff, this was the decisive moment of the war.

> Owing to the breakdown of Russia the military situation was more favourable to us at New Year 1918 than one could ever have expected. As in 1914 and 1915, we could think of deciding the war by an attack on land. Numerically we had never been so strong in comparison with our enemies.[1]
>
> Quartermaster General Erich Ludendorff, General Headquarters, Imperial German Army

Certainly, the Germans desperately needed something to break the deadlock of the Great War. They may have been fighting a military 'draw' but their economy was in a truly parlous state by 1917. The war was cripplingly expensive, the voracious demand for men was denuding industry and agriculture of workers and the iron band of the Royal Navy blockade was preventing both the import of vital raw materials and the income-generating export of produce. The economic consequences of global war were gradually rendering ordinary life almost impossible in Germany. There was a serious food shortage and the permitted ration fell to a level below that necessary to sustain basic human health, never mind happiness. It was inevitable that there would be a shortage of imported raw materials given the blockade, but gnawing labour shortages and the gradually failing transport infrastructure meant that there were problems distributing even theoretically plentiful resources like coal. Strikes to secure more food became ever-more commonplace and there was considerable social unrest centred on the burgeoning agitation for peace. It was only the conquest of Romania with its oil supplies that kept Germany going. There was very little long-term hope here for the German High Command: the war had to end soon or Germany would be condemned to outright defeat.

Yet there was worse to come: 6 April 1917 also saw the entry of a new element into the overall strategic situation when the United States of America entered the war. German diplomacy, an oxymoron, had lamentably failed to counter the British efforts to draw the Americans into the war on the grounds of the unrestricted campaign waged by German submarines. America had not figured large in the calculations of European generals in the eighteenth and nineteenth centuries, but generations of mass immigration had built a new superpower across the Atlantic. The regular American Army might be laughably small, but America's huge population and vast industrial capacity made its military potential evident. America may have been an unknown quantity, but it could no longer be ignored.

> I felt obliged to count on the new American formations beginning to arrive in the spring of 1918. In what numbers they would appear could not be foreseen; but it might be taken as certain that they would balance the loss of Russia; further, the relative strengths would be more in our favour in the spring than in the late summer and autumn, unless, indeed, we had by then gained a great victory.[2]
> Quartermaster General Erich Ludendorff, General Headquarters, Imperial German Army

And there was the nub. The temptation before the German High Command was almost irresistible. There was a brief six-month window of opportunity during which the Allies would be weak. Whatever Ludendorff planned to do, he would have to do soon, before the window was slammed shut and the predictable course of the war was restored; a course that could only lead to defeat for Germany.

All over the United States a new army was gathering. Hundreds, thousands, hundreds of thousands, millions of men were all determined to play their part in what they had become convinced was their fight. Amongst the thousands was one young man who enlisted in a state of mind that could be regarded as typical of his contemporaries.

I have decided to go to Plattsburg to the training camp, if I can get in. I thought for a couple of days that I wouldn't, but when I found that I hadn't any real excuse or reason to give myself, I gave up trying to find one. Nobody here knows any more about the war than you do: one says five years, another ninety days, etc. If Russia breaks, it will be twenty years. I don't know. I don't see how people can think the war will end soon; Germany has ten million men under arms at the present time, and it is not divided. From a military standpoint it will take five years. The economic pressure will make it less, I am sure. But less than two years is out of the question. Whatever it is, it is up to me to be there, and I wouldn't be your son if I didn't.[3]

Kenneth Walser

If the Germans allowed the American Army to gather its forces to join the battle on the Western Front, then all their extra divisions from the Eastern Front would avail them nothing. It was now or never for the Germans. The British and French had to be defeated before the summer of 1918 or the Great War was lost.

THE ALLIED HIGH COMMAND was also uncomfortably aware of the grim possibility of a Russian collapse. As early as May 1917, the British Chief of Imperial General Staff, General Sir William Robertson, warned the War Cabinet, led by Prime Minister David Lloyd George, of the looming consequences.

We should be prepared for the worst, namely that the Central Powers will be free to concentrate their forces against their remaining enemies. It must be assumed that the whole of the German Army on the Eastern Front will be available for operations in the West.[4]

General Sir William Robertson, Imperial General Staff, London

There was a definite message here. For Robertson was a 'Westerner'. As such he believed implicitly that to win the war the British Empire must concentrate all resources possible on the Western Front where it faced the German Army, rather than be distracted by campaigns in the Middle East and around the fringes of the main battle. For Robertson the aggressive campaigns being waged at the behest of the 'Easterners' in Palestine, Salonika, Mesopotamia and even Italy were diversions from the main battlefield where the war would be decided. The 'Easterners' were largely politicians who sought to avoid the appalling casualties on the Western Front; they therefore formed a strategy based on knocking away the 'props' of the German Empire, rather than confronting it head-on. Yet there was no easy route to Berlin through Palestine, Salonika, Mesopotamia or Italy. Geographical imperatives rendered such ideas nothing but fantasies. The end result was the deployment of hundreds of thousands of British troops in the most appalling conditions that ranged from arid deserts to precipitous mountains. Here they were wracked by diseases from dysentery to malaria while fighting Turks, Bulgarians and Austrians who were never likely to send troops to support the Germans on the Western Front, but who were thus given plenty of opportunity to kill British troops. Robertson explicitly warned his political masters that the imminent collapse of Russia meant that such distractions and any further wasteful deployment of troops, always strategically dubious, would be rendered positively dangerous. In particular, he recommended the disengagement from Salonika, truly a campaign that was going nowhere, and the reduction of other commitments to the minimum force required to defend essential interests.

Although Robertson had made the strategic position crystal clear, he still failed to convince Lloyd George as to the seriousness of the situation that loomed before them. Let there be no mistake: Lloyd George was utterly committed to winning the war. This was no wilting politician unwilling to take the war to his country's enemies, but he simply could not reconcile his personal beliefs as to the conduct of the war with the methods advocated and employed by his senior generals and military advisers. He genuinely believed that the war could be won in Salonika, Italy or Palestine – anywhere, in fact, but the Western Front, where he believed the lives of thousands were being thrown wastefully away to no end. As such, his nemesis was the British commander-in-chief on the Western Front, Field Marshal Sir Douglas Haig.

Throughout the war Haig was the ultimate Westerner. He knew that the German Army *was* the Central Powers: defeat it and you win the war. Unfortunately, this was by no means easy. Germany might be suffering from the effects of the blockade, but it was a huge country, rich in natural resources and with an enormous underlying economic strength that often tempted neutrals to collaborate in supplying raw materials. But above all the German Army was a colossus, its strength measured in millions and with a strong sense of national identity that promoted a high morale. To beat it there was a bloody requirement to kill millions of well-armed, well-led, well-equipped men; defeat had to be smashed down the collective German throat, anything less would merely encourage an ever more desperate resistance.

Douglas Haig was a man almost entirely foreign to 'modern' tastes. Born on 19 June 1861, after a privileged Victorian education he passed through the Royal Military College Sandhurst, to be commissioned into the 7th Hussars in 1885. His regimental service culminated in his attendance at the newly established Staff College at Camberley in 1896. His first experiences of active service took place in the Sudan and during the Boer War, where he impressed his superiors as a competent officer and the pace of promotion began to increase. Haig had a gift for sheer hard work, rigorously applying himself to the task at hand, and he undoubtedly excelled in several staff and administrative appointments, including his responsibility for much of the spadework required in creating the Territorial Army in 1908. His reward was promotion to lietenant general and the plum command of the two divisions based at Aldershot that would form the I Corps when the British Expeditionary Force (BEF) was mobilised on the declaration of war on 4 August 1914.

Haig's early experiences in the opening battles of the war, when he served under the overall command of Field Marshal Sir John French, were often traumatic as he and all the other British commanders were brought face to face with the sheer scope of the problems of modern continental warfare on the Western Front. Nevertheless, Haig was still seen as a safe pair of hands, promoted first to general as the commander of the First Army and then ultimately to commander-in-chief of the BEF on the fall of Sir John French in December 1915.

Thus it was that in 1916 it was Douglas Haig who controlled the destinies of hundreds of thousands of young men when Britain fought its first-ever, real continental-scale battle as it attacked on the Somme on 1 July 1916 – a date truly never forgotten. He was forced by the requirements of his French Allies to commit his New Army and Territorial divisions into action, long before he considered them ready, in order to switch German attention from their murderous attritional offensive on the French at Verdun. His armies learnt many of the complex fighting skills of modern war on the bloody battlefields of the Somme, but they suffered excruciating losses in doing so. Yet Haig was firmly convinced that the five months of hell suffered by the Germans on the Somme coupled with their equally awful ordeal at Verdun had drained the German Army.

If the British Army had a doctrine then it was best exemplified by the Field Service Regulations, a deceptively simple document that contained the basic tenets that would guide most of the British senior commanders throughout the war. The nature of the war they were fighting and the method of introducing new weapons were both presaged in the FSR whereby any battle would go through stages: initial contact, the wearing-out battle, securing fire supremacy and the advance to victory. As new weapons were added to the mix they were harnessed to secure the all-important fire supremacy. The length of the 'battle' was unexpected but Haig always saw the fighting on the Western Front as, in effect, one long, drawn-out battle with the phases of combat measured in years rather than hours: 1914 and 1915 had seen the initial manoeuvring for position and the first clash of battle, 1916 had seen the wearing-out process of indeterminate length before one side began to fold and he was confident that the decisive stroke could be dealt in 1917.

It was in accordance with such beliefs that the Allies had sought to hammer home their advantage in 1917, but everything went wrong for them in that truly benighted year. The waters had been muddied early on by the accession of a new commander-in-chief of the French Army. General Robert Nivelle was a man blessed with a rare, but dangerous, combination of both military skills and articulacy. He soon had both British and French politicians eating out of his hand as he sketched out how he would win the war at a stroke in April 1917. Lloyd George at last had found a general he could do business with and, in fact, Haig was briefly suborned under Nivelle's overall direction, as British troops were once again required to sacrifice themselves in the French interest at the diversionary Battle of Arras. When the Nivelle offensive in the

Aisne area was an utter failure the French Army suffered a disastrous collapse in morale, leading to several serious outbreaks of mutiny – suddenly Nivelle was yesterday's man and General Henri-Philippe Pétain was made the French commander-in-chief charged with rebuilding his shattered army. Born on 24 April 1856, Pétain had always had a cautious approach to warfare, maintaining that the increased firepower of modern warfare had rendered attack a dangerous option. These were not popular views in a France obsessed with the spirit of the offensive and at the start of the war he was still only a colonel with retirement staring him in the face. The brutal realities of the fighting in the Great War had saved his career as it gave a new value to his cautious realism, and he was rapidly propelled to the command of the Second Army before fighting a grim determined battle in defence of Verdun for which he had been widely acclaimed a hero. Pétain would take no chances with the lives of his battered *poilus*.

In the summer of 1917, once again independent of French control, Haig took the chance to launch his long-cherished major offensive in Flanders. Although the offensive started well with the Battle of Messines in June 1917, the unseasonable wet weather conditions during the main assault severely hampered operations, while the new German defence-in-depth techniques tested British tactical acumen to the limit. Eventually the doctrine of 'bite and hold' emerged as the only feasible assault method: massed artillery barrages would both destroy and suppress the German defences, allowing the infantry to seize the front-line system, before hastily consolidating and beating back any German counter-attacks assisted by further massed artillery barrages. The system worked well in itself, but it was intrinsically limited in what it could realistically achieve and for all the painstaking preparations and careful planning, casualties were still high. The German artillery and machine guns could never be entirely subdued by the weapons deployed by the British Army in the summer of 1917.

Even when Haig finally admitted that the Germans had survived in Flanders, there was still time for one more assault on the Germans in 1917. The Battle of Cambrai launched on 20 November was of crucial importance for it marked the next development of the All Arms Battle. At first sight it seemed that the tanks, used en masse for the first time, offered a partial solution to many of the most stubborn tactical problems of trench warfare. They could crush the German barbed wire without the necessity of a telltale preliminary bombardment. Their steel plating offered a partial protection to the crews from rifle or machine-gun fire, allowing them to bring their 6-pounder guns or machine guns into action at close range to eradicate German strongpoints. There were, however, two important hampering factors: the tanks were still too slow and mechanically unreliable, and secondly, they may have been just about bullet-proof but they were emphatically not immune to the German artillery. The tank was not a war-winning weapon on its own – it was part of the greater whole.

When the early tanks had duly revealed their limitations on the Somme, there was much thought given by the High Command as to how best to fit them into the All Arms Battle, but this was often compromised by the natural desire to win the battle at hand. Thus tank doctrine was being hammered out at the same time as the tanks were being used ad hoc in the various offensives made by the British Army in 1916 and 1917. But by November 1917 the British Army had a very good idea of what it could expect and, just as importantly, not expect from its massed Mark IV tanks. The ability of the tanks to crush the thickest barbed wire and their role as trouble-shooters in dealing with pillboxes or machine guns was thoroughly established. It was to be these abilities that allowed the next great step in artillery techniques to bear full fruit.

For Cambrai was also a great *artillery* battle. The gunners and their surveyors had completely overhauled the way the guns were able to operate on the Western Front. The old inaccurate maps had been replaced with newly surveyed maps accurate on the ground to within a matter of mere feet. It was self-evident that if the position of both a gun and its target could be established with such a degree of accuracy – then the range between them could be accurately calculated. A field gun firing at some 6,500 yards was not a pinpoint weapon, but it did create a 'beaten zone', which was the target area in which shells could reasonably be expected to fall. Guns could never be entirely accurate, but by 1917 great long strides had been taken in understanding the factors that affected where the shells landed.

One of the key steps was in fully understanding the importance of meteorological corrections. Early in the war there was much foolish resistance by the less technically competent of the Royal Artillery officers to such concepts, which were often seen as purely theoretical, emanating from the 'eggheads' at the Woolwich Royal Military Academy, and hence of no relevance to 'practical gunnery'.

> The senior subaltern said, 'I'm going to the Major', he was along in his dugout, 'to ask him if I can put the meteor corrections on the guns!' When he got there, the Major, who was a regular, mark you, an Irishman, he said, 'My boy, this is war, this is practical stuff! Forget all that nonsense they taught you at "The Shop"! If it's cold cock her up a bit!'[5]
>
> Second Lieutenant Murray Rymer Jones, Royal Artillery

Such caricature 'stick in the mud' figures were partly responsible for the inaccuracy of the preliminary barrages on the Somme. They were helped along by the inexperienced gun detachments, barely trained officers and the huge variations in the quality of the shells, which together made the artillery barrages far less effective than they should have been.

By 1917 the Royal Artillery as a whole had moved onwards and upwards. The meteorology data for wind direction and strength, air temperature and barometric pressure were all seen as vital and the corresponding adjustments were made to the guns to allow for their effects on the flight through the air of a shell. It was also realised that the guns themselves varied in their characteristics not only in comparison to each other but also over the length of their own lives as the barrel rifling became worn. Guns were calibrated and fired in test conditions, so that any adjustments necessary from the norm could be carefully noted and included in the calculations for that gun. When they moved into their new gun positions the gunners could determine their position on the map to within 5 yards, while if they were targeting a German battery then with the help of reconnaissance aircraft, flash spotters and sound ranging they could identify their opponents' position with a similar level of accuracy. After the gunners had finished their complex trigonometrical calculations they could fire with reasonable confidence that the shells would fall in close proximity to the target. They could never guarantee a direct hit with an individual shell, but there were a lot of guns and an awful lot of shells – in the end the odds were in their favour. This meant that the previous painful necessity for individually registering every gun onto its intended target before the barrage opened was no longer required. Guns could be brought up in secrecy and their battery positions carefully camouflaged to conceal them from any prying German aerial observation. As the tanks could brush aside the barbed wire without the necessity for a long barrage, it was evident that the factor of surprise had been reintroduced to the complex equation of modern warfare.

When the barrage opened on 20 November the hundreds of tanks rolled slowly forwards, followed in their tracks by the grateful infantry, sheltered from the worst of the usual storm by the hurricane of shells crashing down on the German defences. All seemed well until the tanks moved beyond the range of their own field artillery barrage. As the cavalry missed their chance, if it ever truly existed, to exploit the breakthrough, the tanks then found themselves helpless before the German field guns and their attack broke down in considerable confusion. There were insufficient reserves to exploit the success of the first day and, in any case, although the British had broken *into* the German defensive system, they still had not actually broken *through*. The German response to the British success at Cambrai was murderously effective and in itself marked a whole new development in German tactics as they premiered some of their own attacking options: carefully orchestrated artillery barrages and what have become known as stormtrooper tactics. Although the British regarded German methods as being dominated by the philosophy of infiltration, at this stage it seems that the German stormtrooper idea was more to secure a tight co-ordination of infantry support weapons: light machine guns, hand grenades and light mortars to establish a firepower domination seeking always to locate an unprotected flank. Both of these tactics would be seen in full flow on the Western Front in the spring of 1918. The British first-day gains were soon swept aside – the German Army was still strong, still developing its killing power and still a dreadful enemy. The overall lesson of Cambrai is surely that the hitherto static nature of the war was at last changing. New weapons were coming to deadly fruition; old weapons were being used in new ways. Together they would bring a new dimension of death and destruction to war on the Western Front.

*

AND WHAT of the individual soldiers who made up the teeming hundreds of thousands of men under Haig's command? The 'happy warriors' of 1914 had long gone and there was an overwhelming sense of depression throughout the BEF. This was not unnatural; these men had been through some of the most dreadful experiences that could be imagined. Many had joined with totally false expectations of what war was like, created by a combination of upbringing, patriotism, propaganda, religious fervour and, above all, ignorance. Well, they knew now.

> War is the most ruthless system of organised murder that the animal 'man' has invented, and the most horrible. Wars are fought by young men, inexperienced and impressionable, to whom in large part the thing is seen in the light of an adventure. Indeed, it is in some degree an adventure, and no adventure is worth calling such without a degree of risk to life and limb. But its results are so ghastly that inevitably there comes a time when war ceases to be an adventure and the young regard it cynically, disillusioned and disenchanted. I do not suppose any generation ever marched to war with the stars in their eyes as my generation did, but after the Somme and the even worse slaughter at Third Ypres there were no more stars. We continued to fight, and I think we fought well – as the British soldier has always fought. No one in his senses who has seen war at close quarters would claim that the British soldier never broke and ran – there are things that no human being can be expected to endure and one of these is concentrated shell fire.[6]

> Lieutenant Richard Dixon, 251st Siege Battery, 53rd Brigade, Royal Garrison Artillery

The physical and emotional effects of warfare on the Western Front were almost unbearable to the average man. It was not only the shells, the sense-shattering explosions, the deadly shrapnel whirring through the air to deadly effect and the random mayhem brought by the *minenwerfer* shells, but also the seeping horror of poisonous gas, the lives snuffed out in a moment by the unseen sniper's bullet, the brutal necessity of attacking across No Man's Land in the face of the scything machine guns and the unspeakable horrors of close combat, where a life could splutter out feebly amidst the deafening crash of bombs and the sudden glitter of sharpened bayonets. It was *all* of these and something more. For these men were not professional soldiers; most had only joined for the duration of the war and for no longer. Now they faced the complete and utter loss of their personal freedom: the private soldier was the lowest of the low within a rigid army hierarchy of rank that sometimes seemed to stifle any residual intellect and initiative.

> Once I was young and handsome and laid claim to an intelligence that permitted me to hold intercourse with beings fashioned just a little lower than the angels. I was almost human in my actions and tastes. I was said by some to possess a 'temperament' (whatever that may be). I claimed a little originality and considered myself someone. I washed twice or three times a day. And wore clothes that might have been said to fit. But behold me now – I am become a portion of Canada's gift to the empire. I am a full private in the army – I have not even a name. How have the mighty fallen![7]
>
> Private Herbert D'Alton Bolster, Canadian Corps

Then there were the underlying physical discomforts, the dull monotony of a diet that reduced eating to a necessity not a pleasure, the biting cold, the sweltering heat, the incessant rain, the revulsion caused by lice, rats and maggots – life in the trenches of the Great War was always a grievous trial and this, too, certainly had an impact on morale.

> Perhaps you would like to know something of the spirit of the men out here now. Well, the truth is (and as I said before I'd be shot if anyone of importance collared this missive) every man Jack is fed up almost past bearing, and not a single one has an *ounce* of what we call patriotism left in him. No one cares a rap whether Germany has Alsace, Belgium or France *too* for that matter. All that every man desires now is to get done with it and go home. I may add that I too have lost pretty nearly all the patriotism that I had left, it's just that thought of you all over there, you who love me and trust me to do *my* share in the job that is necessary for your safety and freedom. It's just *that* that keeps me going and enables me to 'stick it'.[8]
>
> Corporal Laurie Rowlands, 15th Battalion, Durham Light Infantry, 64th Brigade, 21st Division

One of the most damaging elements clawing away at morale was the absence of any foreseeable end to the troops' ordeal. Germany seemed as strong as ever, the most implacable of all enemies. Time and time again the troops had been promised victory, there had been new dawns a-plenty, but nothing seemed to crack the German resistance.

It seemed as if the war would last for ever, each year bringing new weapons, greater intensity, more men, more guns, greater slaughter – until one side should reach the end of its resources and the war end through sheer exhaustion and universal insanity.[9]

Lieutenant Kenneth Mealing, R Anti-Aircraft Battery, 61st Division

Increasingly the new recruits were not enthusiastic at the prospect of serving 'King and Country'. Only conscription had secured their presence in the army and only a draconian disciplinary structure kept some of them in line. The acceptable physical and mental standards were also steadily deteriorating. Few had any remaining illusions of what they would be facing when they had completed their training and were drafted to the front. It was particularly hard for their families, who were reluctant to let their children go to war.

I was on my six days' leave, which meant I was going overseas. My mother, without being told, knew I was off to France. The last day she followed me round the house until it was time for me to go. I got to the front door and she was crying and holding me round my knees – I was forced to drag her to the front gate.[10]

Private Reginald Backhurst, 8th Battalion, Royal West Kent Regiment, 72nd Brigade, 24th Division

Yet, despite all the casualties, the awful privations and constant fear, some of the men still managed to look on the bright side of life. They stoically endured all the humiliations and discomforts of trench life to discern a silver lining even amidst their bleak surroundings.

Bye the bye, I reported to the medical officer the other day and found I had scabies, however, I got some sulphur ointment from him and have managed to get a hot bath daily and using the ointment I think I'll be pretty well rid of it before we go into the line. Did I tell you that when we were in the line last, every morning at stand-to just breaking day, a skylark would be soaring and singing away, in No Man's Land, the heavy gun firing, machine-gun fire etc. made no difference, our skylark was always there singing at the break of day.[11]

Captain James Evans, 5th (Western Cavalry) Battalion, 2nd Brigade, 1st Canadian Division

The prevailing mood, though, was one coloured by exhaustion and an underlying depression. They were now reluctant soldiers, with few illusions left, but they were still sticking out. Such then were the men of the British Army that would have to face the greatest, most dest-ructive onslaught ever launched in the history of war. Ready or not the Germans were coming.

WHILE THE BRITISH HIGH COMMAND was thoroughly aware of the new threats facing it on the Western Front and its men gritted their teeth ready for the trials to come, there was a vital third factor in the equation – the British civilian political establishment as represented by Lloyd George. Here there was a problem: Ludendorff had the support of his government; indeed, he and Hindenburg almost were the government. This was by no means the situation facing Haig. Lloyd George, as we have seen, had a fundamental difference of opinion with his generals over the conduct of the war and as 1917 wore on he was increasingly determined to establish some, indeed any, kind of authority over Haig. Yet as the Liberal leader of a coalition Cabinet working side by side with Conservative ministers, Lloyd George lacked the political support to take the drastic step of dismissing Haig outright. For the moment if he was to get his way he could only rely on persuasion and the art of politics, in both of which he was an accomp-lished master. It proved to be a close-run thing. Lloyd George side-stepped all established military protocol by inviting Haig's failed predecessor Field Marshal Lord French and the foremost military 'outsider' Lieutenant General Sir Henry Wilson to comment direct to the War Cabinet on the various options to be considered for action in 1918. Both men were somewhat embittered and naturally used the opportunity to attack both Haig and Robertson while putting forward their own idiosyncratic ideas. They finished up by suggesting the estab-lishment of a Supreme War Council consisting of the prime ministers and a senior military representative of each of the Allies to direct the war. The attraction of this was fairly obvious to Lloyd George, whose twitching political antennae could sense a way round the wall of the British military establishment. Robertson, on the other hand, was scathing at the prospect.

> Advice given by others, although they may be professionals, is often without value and may be positively mischievous. Such advice poses as being expert, whereas the person who gives it can seldom possess the information on which to base a reliable opinion, and as he is not responsible for the execution of his proposals his outlook is quite different from that of the person who has the responsibility. I frequently told ministers that if I were not CIGS I could produce half a dozen different plans for winning the war, quickly, and at small cost, but as it was I had but one plan, and that a hard one to carry out – the defeat of the German armies on the west front.[12]
>
> General Sir William Robertson, Imperial General Staff, London

Robertson was not a compromiser by nature: as far as he was concerned he did his duty as he saw it and saw no reason to bend to the dictates of fashionable thought.

As Lloyd George manoeuvred for position with one eye on the creation of a Supreme War Council, it is no surprise that the Prime Minister increasingly took the French side at the existing inter-Allied conferences trying to coordinate operations. Haig had already found himself briefly subjugated beneath Nivelle in early 1917, but in late 1917 he found that his political leaders had allowed the French to press home their claim that the British should take control over more of the Western Front. On the surface this proposal seemed only fair. After all, the French held 350 miles with 972 battalions in contrast to the British 100 miles held with 806 battalions. Yet some miles were distinctly harder to hold than others. Much of the French line was quiescent, under little or no threat and occupied by minimal troops living a 'live and let live' lifestyle that did not actively challenge the Germans facing them. As a result nearly half the German divisions on the Western Front were facing the British sector. Here the Germans were harried from pillar to post by a policy of unending trench raids and harassing artillery fire, which soon provoked a response in kind from the

Germans who were rarely chary of accepting a bellicose challenge. Haig protested at taking over more of the line, but the pass had already been sold and soon it was only a matter of negotiation between the British and French High Commands to try and sort out the exact scale of the handover. The end result was that another swathe of the front line between St Quentin and the Oise River was to be handed over to British control in January 1918.

Naturally, the French were pleased with the progress of these negotiations and saw very real advantages to involving Lloyd George more closely in matters of grand strategy. When he proposed the concept of a Supreme War Council they were therefore supportive and after an intensive period of diplomacy with the Americans and Italians an outline structure was agreed upon. While there were naval, economic and diplomatic committees established as part of the overall council, one crucial element was the creation of a permanent Allied General Staff. Lloyd George had made it a condition that the national chiefs of staff were not to be involved and thus with one bound he was rendered partially free of the dogged Robertson. Instead, Lieutenant General Sir Henry Wilson was selected to accompany the Prime Minister and give military advice in conference: a man that neither Haig nor Robertson regarded highly. It was not that Wilson was stupid – he emphatically was not – but his undoubted taste for political intrigue often clouded his judgement. As such he was an ideal foil for Lloyd George. The Supreme War Council was to prove an anomaly, for although the idea of proper coordination of the efforts of the Allied powers was sound, the politicians' motivation of evading responsible advice from the proper military channels was not. As Robertson later claimed, 'The real object of ministers was not so much to provide effective unity of military command as to acquire for themselves a greater control over the military chiefs.'[13]

The initial meetings of the Supreme War Council and associated bodies at Versailles resembled little more than talking-shops. Issues, concepts and plans that had long been under prolonged consideration by the military authorities were raised and debated as if they were something new. It was also evident at an early stage in the proceedings that there was a heavy Easterner bias towards seeking an end to the war by destroying Germany's allies rather than facing the prime enemy direct. Rather than concentrate their scarce resources to face the imminent German challenge on the Western Front, the emphasis was increasingly on seeking a decision elsewhere. Despite the obvious danger of the situation the Allies met only infrequently and, amidst the sterile debates, even useful concepts like the formation of an Allied General Reserve over and above the usual national army reserves soon stagnated. The idea was widely accepted, but predictably bitter disputes soon arose over both the source and command of the divisions that would form such a reserve. All sides were more or less intransigent, national interests dominated, decisions were delayed and nothing concrete emerged.

There was a further problem for the increasingly beleaguered Haig when the War Office revealed on 3 November 1917 that the reinforcements that Haig was relying on to top up and maintain his divisions in the line in 1918 would be totally inadequate for that purpose. The War Office foresaw that the current deficit of 75,000 men would expand to 259,000 by late 1918. Haig's horrified staff feared it might rise as high as a 460,000 shortfall. In essence the cause was simple: Lloyd George wanted to retain a huge number of soldiers at home in Britain to prevent Haig 'misusing' them on the Western Front. Haig's concerns were intensified and indeed confirmed when control of Britain's manpower was assigned to a Cabinet committee in December 1917. This *political* body was required to determine the relative priorities of the army, navy, industry, agriculture and munitions for manpower, the raw material of war, in 1918. The army had asked for some 615,000 men to maintain its formations in the field. Without any direct military involvement it was inevitable that the civilians followed the political imperatives of their master, Lloyd George. They considered the army's requests excessive for what would, at least in the early part of 1918, be a defensive campaign on the Western Front. As a result only 200,000 men were made available for the army and half of these were not fully fit. Such parsimony placed the BEF in a desperate situation. There either had to be fewer divisions – perhaps as many as fifteen less – or a complete root and branch restructure to reorganise each division with only nine, as opposed to the then twelve, battalions.

Haig continued to protest vigorously at these potentially crippling manpower restrictions but he found himself baulked at every turn by what to him was obviously specious reasoning: copious drafts were still required on other fronts, the 'homeland' had to be protected whether there was a realistic threat or not, many of the young recruits were ineligible for service on the Western Front as being under 19 years old, and finally – and here was the real crux of the matter – Lloyd George considered that if troops were sent to France they would be 'wasted' on indecisive operations that offered no hope of winning the war.

> Hundreds of thousands of men were still retained under arms in England – kept there partly from a ridiculous fear of a German invasion, and partly because the Cabinet actually did not desire to trust Haig with any more men, blaming him for all that 1917 had cost the British. This seems both a weak and an unjust attitude for Mr. Lloyd George and his colleagues to have taken up. The battles of 1917 had been fought with the knowledge and consent of the Cabinet and at the particular demand of the French.[14]
>
> General Sir Hubert Gough, Headquarters, Fifth Army

When it came to the crunch there was nothing that Haig could do. The government controlled the levers, indeed the whole mechanism, that deployed reinforcements to the front. In the end he had no choice but to reorganise his divisions onto the reduced scale of nine battalions. So it was that the British began to tear apart the divisions, brigades and battalions that over the past four years had made up the British Expeditionary Force. Working relationships forged in the heat of battle were dissolved at the stroke of a pen and some 134 infantry battalions disappeared from the BEF. As the Germans and French had already organised their divisions on this basis there was nothing wrong per se with the idea of a reorganisation; it was the motivation, the rushed execution and, above all, the excruciating timing that caused consternation at GHQ. While the Germans finalised their plans for Armageddon on the Western Front, Haig was engaged in shuffling a seriously reduced hand and had simply no option but to throw his troops onto the defensive for the first time since 1915.

Haig's attitude to politicians was fairly typical amongst senior officers of his generation. Their cultural mindset was such that they had an idealised perception of the soldier – in their eyes an imperturbable, incorruptible force standing in contrast to the tarnished morality of many in civilian life. One officer of Haig's cavalry escort from the 17th Lancers, a shy man himself, was at first hugely intimidated by the prospect of long rides with the 'chief'. But in the end he quickly found himself won over and, indeed, brought into the great man's confidence.

> Rode with the 'chief' for the first time and my terror somewhat abated. He asked about the new horses, the changes in the troop, etc. He asked me if I had intended always being a soldier when at Varsity and said after a pause, 'I always think it's a fine clean life a soldier's – not like a politician's or even a parson's. We soldiers can at least always afford to be honest!'[15]
>
> Major Ian Hedley, 17th Lancers, General Headquarters, BEF

Haig was hardly always strictly 'straight' in his dealings with his military rivals earlier in the war, but in his struggles with the Prime Minister he was dealing with a prince of politicians. And Lloyd George had by no means finished with his Machiavellian schemes. Although he realised he still had insufficient support within the Cabinet for a direct attack on Haig himself, he could start to chip away at his supporters of which Robertson and the Minister of War Lord Derby were most obvious targets. Robertson fell first. The Prime Minister's solution was typically cunning: he approached Henry Wilson and offered him Robertson's post of CIGS, but then offered Robertson the poisoned chalice of Permanent Military Representative to the Supreme War Council. Robertson was in a quandary – he earnestly believed that Lloyd George as prime minister had every right to seek a replacement CIGS, but he could not support the creation of this alternative stream of advice from outside the existing military establishment, even if it was he himself that was taking up the post and giving the advice.

> Lord Derby had already told me that the Prime Minister could not 'get on' with me. After that there was nothing more to be said, and I said nothing except to ask when it was desired I should hand over my duties to my successor. The question of taking up the new post at Versailles was on a different plane. On the principle that a soldier should obey orders, put personal considerations aside, and do the best for his country wherever he may be sent, my first impulse was to accept the

post, but after careful reflection I resolved that I could be no party to a system which established a dual authority for the military direction of the war. Whether I stayed in London or went to Versailles could make no difference to the pernicious arrangement which created two separate military advisors.[16]

General Sir William Robertson, Imperial General Staff, London

Lloyd George announced Robertson had 'resigned' and he was duly replaced by General Sir Henry Wilson in February 1918.

On the surface Wilson was an awful choice as CIGS and a serious long-term threat to Haig, who relied on solid support from Robertson back in London. Yet in selecting his man Lloyd George had forgotten the nature of his 'beast'. Once Wilson had the position he craved he soon went 'native' in a manner that must have infuriated his political master. Most ironically of all, he almost immediately insisted that as CIGS *he* must control Lieutenant General Sir Henry Rawlinson, who was appointed the Permanent Military Representative at the Supreme War Council. Within weeks Wilson was effectively a Westerner and had established a working relationship with Haig, who in any case by late March 1918 was far too busy with the German Army to much care who was in office as CIGS.

Lloyd George was also manoeuvring to secure the removal of another Westerner and Haig supporter in the Minister of War, Lord Derby, whom he planned to replace with Lord Milner. These political coups did not go unnoticed in France, especially amongst those close to Haig's headquarters. Yet there was nothing that they could do and their resentment was obvious – indeed, at times overstated.

Lloyd George is trying to sacrifice 'Wullie' and Derby, and if he succeeds I suppose the 'chief' must go before long. Then we get H. Wilson and Milner, and God knows whom as commander-in-chief. Obviously he's aiming at one thing, 'David Lloyd George first president of the British Republic!' God help England![17]

Major Ian Hedley, 17th Lancers, General Headquarters, BEF

IN THE FINAL ANALYSIS the dire situation of the BEF on the Western Front in the spring of 1918 was caused by an unresolved clash between the British civilian prime minister and the British commander-in-chief on the Western Front. The situation was complicated by the fact that both were undoubtedly the best fitted for the job at hand. There was no alternative to Lloyd George that would have a tithe of his drive, his commitment to the British cause or his ability to win through whether at home or amongst the 'nest of vipers' lurking around the conference table of the Allies. His qualities as a civilian leader were unquestioned. Acting for him were specially selected men who had rapidly recast the overall economy and reorganised Britain's shaky heavy industries for the colossal task of munitions production on an unprecedented scale. No, it was Lloyd George's shaky grasp of military issues that was seriously at fault. If he genuinely disagreed with the prevailing military orthodoxy to the extent that he was willing to undermine the defence of the Western Front in the face of an imminent German offensive, then perhaps he should have bitten the bullet, sacked Haig and ridden out the political storm. In the end he did not dare take this step as he lacked the support to secure the objective without triggering a crisis that might well end his premiership. Lloyd George believed, with justification, that that would be a disaster for his country. Then again, perhaps Haig should have made the proper reinforcement and concentration on the Western Front a resignation issue as commander-in-chief. But there was no real alternative to Haig either – and he, too, was well aware of the fact. All the generals who were senior enough to be realistically considered for the post were cast from exactly the same mould and endorsed the same Westerner policies: some clearly lacked the spark of talent to take the step to the highest level of command and others were just plain incompetent and not serious options. As such Haig could not threaten resignation – he saw it as his duty to soldier on and accept Lloyd George's interference. Like it or not both men were locked together for the duration.

CHAPTER TWO

The Best-laid Schemes

THE GERMANS WERE PLANNING to end the war in 1918 and the scale of the resources and planning they allotted to the Western Front clearly matched the serious requirements of that aspiration. Although some troops were of necessity retained on the Eastern Front to keep an eye on the Russians during the protracted peace negotiations, the bulk of their divisions were soon transferred by rail across to the Western Front. By the spring of 1918 the Germans could deploy some 192 divisions along the 468 miles of the Western Front in contrast to only 156 British and French divisions. This was clearly a great opportunity for the Germans, but their first major decision had to be whether to attack the British, the French, or both. This conundrum was the subject of a meeting with the staffs of the various German Army Groups operating on the Western Front held at Mons on 11 November 1917. Ludendorff presided. At this stage the choice lay between a blow against the British in Flanders directed at the Channel ports or an attack on the French at Verdun. Already Ludendorff's preference was to attack the British, whom he rightly considered to be the driving force behind the Allies in 1918. Beat the British, and the French would collapse; beat the French, and the British might well fight on. Nevertheless, no final decision was taken and the planning continued without at that stage ruling anything out.

The methodical German staff officers of the army groups up and down the Western Front were kept busier than ever drawing up and polishing various plans to meet every eventuality that might occur on the Western Front in 1918. These schemes and the preparations that they entailed would not only serve an additional purpose of disguising the real intentions of the Germans when the final decision was made, but would allow Ludendorff the flexibility to change his point of attack as required once the offensive had commenced.

Three of the schemes concerned assaults on the British Army. The first, designated Operation George, was for an attack in Flanders, smashing through the British lines in the Lys River sector near Armentières and lungeing straight for the crucial rail junctions, followed by the Channel ports of Dunkirk and Calais. However, it was evident that the low-lying, wet terrain in Flanders was not compatible with the requirement for an early spring start – there was a fear that the attack would literally bog down in the mud. A second scheme, Operation Michael, was drawn up for an attack to break through the British lines in the southern Arras and Somme areas. Once through the attackers would leave a flank guard to absorb any reaction from the French to the south before turning north and rolling up the British line towards Arras and beyond. Thirdly, there was Operation Mars, a direct assault on the British lines around the Arras front; this option was never much favoured by the German High Command as the difficulties in assaulting the steep slopes of Vimy Ridge were evident.

The attacks planned against the French were variously codenamed: 'Archangel', hitting south of the Oise River; 'Hector' and 'Achilles' were for attacks in the Reims area; 'Roland' revisited the old Champagne battlefields; the twins 'Castor' and 'Pollux' were invoked for possible pincer attacks either side of Verdun; while finally 'Strassburg' and 'Belfort' were being prepared for the southern extremities of the Western Front.

The wide variety of plans and preparations gave great flexibility to the German High Command, but it is also perhaps indicative of a certain amount of strategic vacillation that with so much at stake the plans had not yet been finalised as it moved into 1918. The final decision was only taken by Ludendorff on 21 January, leaving just two months to go before the ultimate launch date of 21 March 1918. In the end Ludendorff went with his own gut instincts and therefore the British Army would indeed be the target. Once this had been decided upon, as Flanders was too wet and Arras too difficult, the die was cast for Operation Michael.

It was an awe-inspiring scheme almost terrifying in its scale. Three massively reinforced German armies would attack on a nearly 60-mile front. In the north the Seventeenth Army under General Otto von Below would attack south of the River Scarpe, pushing in towards Bapaume and pinching out the north side of the Flesquières Salient. In the centre the Second Army commanded by General Georg von der Marwitz would pinch out the southern side of the salient and drive on to Péronne. Finally the Eighteenth Army commanded by General Oskar von Hutier would attack either side of St Quentin, moving to take up a flank-guard position extending along the River Somme and Crozat Canal to the natural junction with the existing German line in the La Fère sector. This would protect the flank and rear of the Seventeenth and Second Armies as they smashed their way through the British lines, aiming first for Albert and then sweeping north to roll up the whole British line. Just in case any further nails needed hammering in Operation Mars would then be unveiled, striking against Arras several days after the offensives had started. Nor had Operation George been forgotten: preparations for this would continue so that it could be launched as a second hammer-blow once Flanders had dried out in early April.

For Ludendorff the problem was how to break into, and then through, the British lines; after that events would to some extent look after themselves. He saw the battles as a tactical problem and his overarching strategic objectives remained somewhat sketchy, other than to exploit any breakthrough as best as possible. One more point should be made: there was nothing of the 'bite and hold' in the German plans; this was truly a do-or-die enterprise designed to put Britain out of the war. Anything less than complete success would leave the overall German strategic situation unchanged – their temporary superiority of numbers on the Western Front would soon be reversed by the arrival of the Americans and Germany would be doomed to defeat.

Once they had made their decision the Germans were determined to conceal their intentions for as long as possible to secure an element of tactical surprise. This was far easier said than done. They needed to move almost half their total artillery into just one relatively short section of the line and on top of that move up the millions of shells that they would require. Then they had to move up the sixty-three divisions that would be joining the 'usual' eleven in the line. All of this had to be done without alerting the British. The Germans certainly spared no efforts to conceal their immense build-up and used the cloak of night to the maximum effect. The bulk of the guns were moved into pre-prepared, concealed positions only over the last ten days. The stupendous numbers of shells had already been brought up and dumped near by. Finally, the actual assault divisions were only brought into the front line on the penultimate night. But the best obfuscation of their intentions was the simple fact that in preparing for all their other planned offensives the Germans had ensured that the British could not be quite sure what was the real danger and what was a mere diversion.

Despite their hitherto defensive stance on the Western Front the German Army had developed a variety of new offensive tactics. At the centre of these, as one would expect, was a determination to make the most effective use of its artillery. The sheer scale of the artillery concentration took the breath away: along the attack frontage there were 6,608 guns in total. To this could be added 3,534 heavy trench mortars. But this would not be an exercise just of brute force. The army's foremost artillery specialist was brought in to oversee the artillery bombardment. Oberstleutnant Georg Bruchmüller had achieved a formidable reputation after the triumph inspired by his methods during the Battle of Riga in September 1917. His aim was to suppress the defenders, to prevent the artillery and machine guns from firing, and to cow the defending infantry so that they were incapable of a coherent opposition. Preparation was at the heart of his methodology – the guns were carefully calibrated and brought up covertly to reduce or eradicate the necessity to register their targets. Aerial photography could identify the British batteries and machine-gun posts, the communication lines and signal centres, the command centres – the muscles, nerves and brains of the British defence. When the time came the bombardment would be fired in carefully controlled phases designed to play upon different types of targets and by constantly switching between them promote additional chaos and confusion in the British lines. A plethora of gas shells was of particular importance, designed to incapacitate and render helpless the bulk of the defenders, but particularly the British artillery. When the German infantry were ready to emerge the German version of the creeping barrage, advancing in bounds just ahead of the infantry, would be fired. The assault troops were warned that their only safety was to stay as close to the barrage as possible and that the British infantry, taking shelter, would not be annihilated by the barrage hence they must hit them hard before they could emerge from their dugouts.

By 1918 the German Army had invested considerable time and effort in developing its infantry stormtrooper assault tactics in the manner that had been premiered on the Western Front in its counter-attack at Cambrai on 30 November 1917. All soldiers were to undergo special training in these new tactics, but in addition many infantry battalions were sieved to extract all their fittest and most experienced soldiers who then were formed into special stormtrooper units. Armed mainly with rifles, light machine guns and stick hand grenades but accompanied by flamethrowers and light mortars, they received intensive training in infiltration. They would attack across No Man's Land, moving quickly on the heels of the creeping artillery barrage, sweeping through the British lines, bypassing any centres of resistance and penetrating as deep as possible with the ultimate aim of overrunning the British artillery batteries before they even knew they were under threat. Behind them would come the heavily armed support troops, surrounding any centres of resistance. Finally, the ordinary infantry would occupy the captured trenches, checking all dugouts were clear and finally overrunning any remaining British redoubts with the assistance of forward artillery units. The stormtroopers were concentrated into eighteen battalions, one attached to each army, but there were also small detachments at battalion, regimental and divisional level. All designated attack divisions were put through assault training, practising over mock-up trench sections. To add further menace to the storm-troopers feeling their way forward on the ground there were special ground-attack aircraft units – the *Schlachtstaffeln* – flying tough two-seaters armoured against ground fire and carrying machine guns and small bombs. Pilots were trained to skim just above the advancing troops, attacking any pockets of resistance, disrupting the movement of British reserves and raking the hordes of troops retreating in disarray. All in all the German offensive tactics were a potent mix: a devastating bombardment, ruthless elite stormtroopers marauding across the battlefield, low-flying aircraft harrying the defenders from the skies and massed infantry to complete the job by utterly overwhelming any remaining resistance.

Other than the concept of elite trained units these methods were not that dissimilar to the attack tactics used by the British in 1917, but the British Army had never been on the receiving end of such an attack. The Germans planned a rude awakening for it in 1918.

NO BRITISH COMMANDER in history had ever faced such a challenging concentration of forces as Haig had to face in 1918. The much-vaunted Napoleonic artillery and massed columns of Austerlitz and Waterloo were inconsequential compared with the destructive capacity and manpower that the Germans were deploying. Haig could not be strong everywhere: somehow, somewhere, something had to give. It was a tremendous responsibility, but the obdurate, inarticulate Haig was a man who above all knew his own mind and in making his decision as to how he should dispose his divisions along the 126-mile British sector of the Western Front he was guided by his clear sense of strategic priorities. In the north, stretching from the Belgian Front to just north of Armentières, was the Second Army under General Sir Herbert Plumer. Flanders was strategically vital for the same reasons that had already generated the copious bloodshed of the First, Second and Third Battles of Ypres: here the Channel ports and crucial rail links lay just behind the British front, vulnerable to the smallest advance by the Germans. Haig could not conceive of any economy of effort or resources in this sector. Plumer had twelve divisions to cover 23 miles of front, with the possible opportunity of shortening the front by 3 miles if he abandoned under pressure the 'sacrificial ground' of the Passchendaele Ridge bought at such cost in the later stages of the 1917 offensive. To the south lay the front of the First Army, commanded by General Sir Henry Horne, stretching 33 miles from Armentières to Gavrelle. Horne deployed some fourteen divisions to cover the tactically significant Vimy and Lorette Ridges, won at a ferocious cost in blood earlier in the war. Not far behind his lines were economically significant coalfields. Here, too, there was no room for skimping. Next in line was General Sir Julian Byng's Third Army with fourteen divisions to cover just 28 miles from Gouzeaucourt to Gavrelle in front of Arras. Byng also had the option of shortening his line if pressed by abandoning the Flesquières Salient created in the recent Battle of Cambrai. Finally,

General Sir Hubert Gough's Fifth Army was responsible for 42 miles of front from Gouzeaucourt to Barisis. Some of this was partially covered by the meanderings of the Oise River, but nevertheless it was a daunting responsibility for just twelve divisions supported by three weak cavalry divisions. However, Haig reasoned that behind the Fifth Army there was plenty of room to allow a controlled retreat before any significant strategic objective could be attained by the Germans. The crucial railway centre at Amiens was the closest objective of real value and that lay a good 40 miles behind the lines. Haig had paltry reserves of just eight divisions, which were duly apportioned in pairs behind each of his four armies. In effect he had no strategic reserve capable of making a difference once battle was engaged.

As early as December 1917, Haig had begun the long process of converting the BEF from an offensive to a defensive force when his headquarters issued a memorandum to guide his armies in the correct application of the new defensive techniques. These introduced the radical concept for the British Army of defence in depth, which had been largely gleaned from a study of German methods over the last year. The British Army had always fought in lines; indeed, the Napoleonic Wars had come to be symbolised by the French columns being thrown back from some benighted ridge or other by the 'thin red lines' of British battalions. Now every defensive position was to be organised in depth.

The main zone of resistance was the Battle Zone, which was to be some 3,000 yards deep and sited to take maximum advantage of the terrain. It was usually constructed in two or three lines, with redoubts intended to focus resistance. The bulk of these defences were not permanently occupied, but the allocated troops would move forward from their camps to occupy their allotted positions whenever danger threatened. As the memorandum explained:

> The Battle Zone will consist of strong successive systems of defence. Diagonal switch lines, supporting points and defended localities must be constructed within the Battle Zone, with a view to preventing the enemy from spreading outwards and rolling up the position, should he succeed in temporarily penetrating the defences. The more important localities in the Battle Zone will be permanently garrisoned.[1]
>
> General Headquarters, BEF

Plans for the employment of both the garrison troops and the reserves in defensive fighting and counter-attacks were to be prepared and the troops properly trained in their role. This was to be the main battle-ground when the attack came, where the Germans were to be stopped in their tracks. But there were two more zones of defences. The first was the Forward Zone, originally known as the Outpost Zone. This line was often based around the original front-line defence systems and had a specific purpose in mind.

> The Forward Zone will be organised for defence in depth and will be sufficiently garrisoned and strengthened to guard against surprise, to break up the enemy's attacks and compel him to expend large quantities of ammunition, and employ strong forces for its capture. The backbone of the defence in this zone will be machine guns skilfully concealed in combination with wire entanglements.[2]
> General Headquarters, BEF

The Forward Zone usually consisted of three lines based on the old linear system, but these were rarely held continuously, instead relying on isolated outposts, with small redoubts in the old third line. The priority in locating these positions was in establishing interconnecting fields of machine-gun fire and the intention was that the raw firepower of assorted Vickers machine guns, Lewis guns and trench mortars would replace the old reliance on massed Lee Enfield rifles.

But this was not all. Some 4–8 miles behind the main Battle Zone was to be a Rear Zone, prepared for defence: 'Arrangements will be made by GHQ in conjunction with Armies to have this defensive zone reconnoitred and the projected defences spit-locked.'[3] This sounded jolly impressive, but all spit-locked really meant was that the position of the intended trenches would be roughly marked out by turning over the turf on the ground. Indeed, the instructions tacitly admit this by omitting reference to the Rear Zone in discussing the defensive tactics to be employed.

> The troops allotted to the defence of the Forward Zone will do all in their power to maintain their ground against every attack. Garrisons of works and localities will hold their defences at all costs, and local reserves will counter-attack immediately, without waiting for orders,

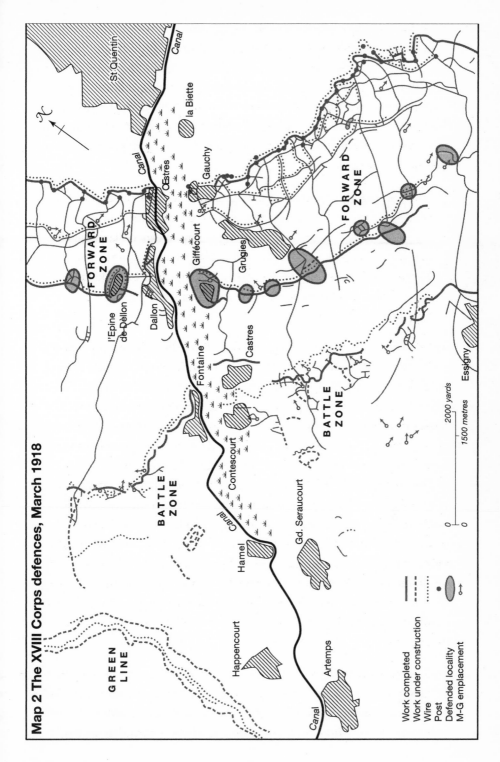

Map 2 The XVIII Corps defences, March 1918

St Quentin

Canal

Canal

la Biette

Gauchy

Ostres

FORWARD ZONE

Giffécourt

Grugies

l'Epine de Dallon

Dallon

Fontaine

Castres

BATTLE ZONE

Contescourt

Canal

Gd. Seraucourt

Hamel

Essigny

2000 yards

1500 metres

BATTLE ZONE

Happencourt

Artemps

Canal

GREEN LINE

Work completed
Work under construction
Wire
Post
Defended locality
M-G emplacement

should the enemy succeed in penetrating the defences. Should the efforts of these troops fail to maintain or re-establish the line, it is for the higher commander to decide whether he will employ any of his general reserves to regain the lost ground. Unless the enemy's attack is weak, and his lodgement on a narrow front, the value of the ground to be recaptured will seldom be worth the cost involved. The Battle Zone, being the ground on which it has been decided to give battle should the enemy attack in strength, must be maintained. Should the enemy succeed in penetrating this zone, and the immediate counter-attacks of local reserves fail to dislodge him, a deliberate counter-attack must be launched at the first possible moment. Unless the penetration is on a narrow front and only at one place, time will be necessary before a deliberate counter-attack is launched, in order that thorough prepa-rations may be made, including possibly the coordination of two or more attacks. The deliberate counter-attack should, when the enemy has expended his strength in the attack, not only aim at re-establishing the Battle Zone; arrangements should also be made to exploit the success, and inflict defeat upon him.[4]

General Headquarters, BEF

At the heart of these infantry defensive plans were the combination of barbed wire and machine guns, which had served the Germans so well over the previous two years in the face of British attacks.

Machine guns should be distributed in depth and sited for flanking fire so as to form impassable belts of fire, and by breaking up any enemy attack to prepare the way for the counter-attack. Concealment of machine-gun positions must be one of the first considerations; for this it will frequently be advisable to site them in low-lying, well-hidden places, providing the field of fire obtainable is satisfactory.[5]

General Headquarters, BEF

The artillery was also to be laid out in depth. In an offensive role the batteries were naturally all as close to the front line as was feasible in order to extend their penetration as far as possible into the German lines. In defence this was not necessary and many batteries were held back in the Battle Zone ready for the real fight. Batteries left in the Forward Zone were to be given all-round barbed wire protection to prevent them being too quickly overrun. A complex system of silent batteries, roving gun sections and dummy gun positions was introduced to avoid all the guns being swiftly targeted, neutralised and destroyed in the opening German bombardment. Camouflage and concealment from German eyes in the sky was an obvious priority.

As a result of these instructions the reduced strength of the BEF was in effect committed to a huge engineering construction programme stretching from end to end of the British line. This involved staggering amounts of labour: thousands upon thousands of miles of barbed wire had to be laid, criss-crossing not only along the front but between the outposts and strongpoints. Hundreds of reinforced concrete pillboxes were needed to shelter the machine-gun teams, while copious deep dugouts were needed to accommodate troops in relative safety and to protect all the unit headquarters. Communications of all kinds had to be improved whether they were multiple telephone lines, roads, rail or light Decauville railway lines. And, of course, trenches beyond number had to be dug. Not spit-locked and airily sketched out on staff officers' maps, but dug deep into the ground to a depth of over 6 feet, with parapet and parados, a firestep, bays and endless winding communications trenches. Gun emplacements had to be carved out of the ground for the thousands of guns. It was a truly mammoth task. The question was whether they had enough time and enough men to do the work.

While the men on the ground sweated there was a desperate need for the British High Command to locate where exactly the Germans planned to attack. The first priority of the British intelligence department at GHQ was to build up an accurate German order of battle, recording which divisions were in the line or reserve. A great deal of valuable information could be gleaned by tracking all their movements in and out of the line. In particular, concentrations of force could be located, an obvious sign of an imminent attack. A vital source of this information was the regular raids across No Man's Land, which harvested the raw materials of intelligence: prisoners, captured official documents and ordinary correspondence.

By 1918 interrogation had been developed into a fine art. Prisoners were placed in cells where unbeknownst to them their conversations could be overheard. They endured lengthy sessions with interviewers who would be their new best friend, or brutally intimidating, as seemed most effective. Their confidence was frequently undermined by interrogators pretending to already know everything they were told, thereby implying that any further effort to maintain secrecy was futile. Another increasingly useful form of intelligence was wireless listening sets that monitored all German signal activity. Even changes in the pattern of German wireless transmissions could be informative whether by the number of messages or the number of wireless stations transmitting. Belgian and French spies were also employed behind the German lines, mainly to gather details of German troop movements, which were then despatched by carrier pigeon or wireless. All these different forms of intelligence were used to check on each other. Thus if sources indicated a new division or corps had moved into the line then a raid would be 'commissioned' to check on the accuracy or otherwise of the statement.

One crucial means of identifying the build-up of the raw materials essential for an offensive was in the hands of the pilots and observers of the Royal Flying Corps (RFC). The German preparations were so intense that they could not *all* be concealed from the RFC. Daily photographic reconnaissance missions were flown over the German lines, bringing back the plate-glass negatives that could later be blown up and examined in detail by eagle-eyed photographic interpreters to discover vital intelligence all but invisible to the naked eye. The Germans may have been preparing on more than one front, but the sheer weight of the intelligence gleaned from these missions gradually told its own story in reports of new airfields, ammunition and supply dumps; prisoner-of-war cages; new gun positions; improvements to the road and rail networks; additional billet huts; and the gradually increased rail traffic bringing supplies and troops to the front. As a result, by late January 1918, Major General John Salmond, the officer commanding the RFC on the Western Front was able to discern that the German attack would be launched in the general area facing the British Third and Fifth Armies to the south of the British front.

It should not be forgotten that the British High Command was also well aware that the Germans had a clear geographical imperative pushing them towards an attack in the south. Flanders might be strategically vital but the British, too, grasped that the muddy ground conditions made it an unfeasible location for an early spring offensive. They could see that if the Germans wanted to make best use of their time before the Americans arrived en masse then their first attack at least must be south of Arras. This was further confirmed when British intelligence sources also revealed that General Otto von Below, fresh from his victory at the Battle of Caporetto in Italy, had been appointed to command the Seventeenth Army facing the British Third Army. When it was realised that the victor at Riga, General Oskar von Hutier, had been appointed to command the German Eighteenth Army opposing the Fifth Army, there was an accumulation of clear signs that the Germans intended to attack between Arras and the Somme.

It was not so simple for Haig: true, the likely point of danger had been discerned, but what if *this* was the diversion? What if the Germans intended after all to attack in northern France or Belgium? If he denuded the north of his front to reinforce Byng and Gough in the south then there would be no chance to retrieve the situation in Flanders if the attack came there. The loss of the Channel ports would be disastrous – better to maintain the concentration in the north and be certain.

The greatest amount of pressure in the early months of 1918 undoubtedly fell on the relatively youthful shoulders of Lieutenant General Hubert Gough commanding the Fifth Army in the Somme area. Gough was born on 12 August 1870 and was thus only 47 at this, the apex of his career. His army service had not been particularly noteworthy before he attracted attention commanding a mobile column during the Boer War. His career was almost derailed when his Irish Unionist sympathies embroiled him deep in the Curragh Incident of March 1914. War probably saved his career and he climbed the ranks in quick-fire succession to become a general at the tender age of 44. He was seen as one of Haig's favourite generals mainly because of his bright, 'can-do' attitude but his reputation was badly hit by his stumbling performance in the Battles of the Somme, Arras and Third Ypres. Overall he seemed to be a general whose natural confidence verged on blind optimism and who lacked the ability to carry out the all-important graft and attention to detail needed in preparing a full-scale offensive. His natural sense of humour was also held to be little more than arrogant sarcasm by many who served under him.

If the Germans did attack Gough then it was obvious he would have to stand alone for several days before significant assistance could be guaranteed. In particular, he knew that the French would be unlikely to move their reserves until they were absolutely sure that there was no lingering threat to their own front. Gough fully appreciated the difficulty and the scale of the task that lay before him and was not shy about passing his views to Haig about the likely effect of the imminent German offensive.

> The more recent German attacks (i.e. Verdun February 1916, Riga, the attack on Italy) have been characterised by a short bombardment of up to about six hours, and the most strenuous efforts to obtain surprise. These efforts I cannot be sure of defeating; consequently in his initial attack the enemy might find me disposed as at present, with the equivalent of eight divisions in line on a 40-mile front; this would naturally go far towards ensuring him success, especially in view of the state of my defences.[6]
>
> General Sir Hubert Gough, Headquarters, Fifth Army

His arguments were well made, but Haig had a wider duty beyond the boundaries of the Fifth Army sector. He had to look at the whole of the British Front and Gough's protests were heard, but not acted upon. Haig was never a man for turning once he had made up his mind.

Having made his point, Gough reluctantly accepted his dire situation and he began the process of a root and branch reorganisation of his defences in accordance with the recently issued tactical defence plans. The obvious course was to use whatever labour could be amassed to build a defence line to the west of the devastated area that had been deliberately razed by the Germans in their retreat to the Hindenburg Line in March 1917. Indeed, in the Fifth Army area there was much to be said for falling back to a new defence line along the Somme River. This would hand the problem fairly and squarely back to the Germans who would then themselves have to cross a wilderness before they could launch an attack on defensive lines protected by a substantial river. Unfortunately, tactical imperatives stood in direct opposition to the effect on morale of freely surrendering ground won at such horrendous cost. Generals may understand that ground was immaterial compared with the importance of tactical position and overall requirement of efficiently killing German soldiers, but what about their politician masters and the public? What would they think? There was another problem. The endemic culture of the British Army forbade retreat; the very word was shunned in favour of euphemisms such as 'retirement' or 'tactical withdrawal'. The history of almost every regiment was adorned with proud fights to the last man. It was difficult to change this mindset.

> The British Army has certain shibboleths, one of which, and it has cost the lives of scores of thousands of soldiers, is that when you are attacked in overwhelming force you mustn't run away. The French, who are much more logical than we, and who consider results and not prestige, invariably run away under such circumstances, and when the right moment comes run back again and deliver a counter-attack.[7]
>
> Captain Charles Miller, 2nd Battalion, Royal Inniskilling Fusiliers, 109th Brigade, 36th Division

The result of the deliberations was a compromise: the Fifth Army would fight east of the Somme in its present position, but if pressed too hard it was prepared to fall back to a loosely defined 'Emergency Line' along the Somme River. This merely added another layer of defences that the Fifth Army was supposed to complete before the Germans attacked.

In the final analysis it was evident that there was simply not enough labour to do all the work that had to be done: manpower shortages existed at every level and labour too had been earmarked according to the strategic priorities of GHQ. The various types of manpower available were the British Labour Battalions, usually made up of men who were not fit enough for front-line service; units of Indian, Chinese and Italian labour; and German prisoners of war who were not allowed to work near the front. Gough's Fifth Army eventually received some 48,000 men but most of them were working on the roads, railways, depots, ammunition dumps and camps – leaving less than 9,000 available for work on the actual defences. This prioritisation may seem perverse, but without logistic support the troops at the front could not exist for long. The communications across the 1916 battlegrounds and the areas devastated by the Germans prior to their retreat in March 1917 had not yet been restored, never mind brought up to the standard required by an army at war.

All these conflicting logistical priorities left little spare capacity to actually dig the trenches and fortifications that were needed if the zones marked on staff maps were to have any reality on the ground. In the end, as may have been predicted, the ordinary infantrymen had to carry out the bulk of the work in addition to taking their turn in the line.

> The whole thing was done with a minimum of delay and the troops in reserve just behind the line had to come up to the trenches nightly and work on the strongpoints. Of course this was tremendously hard work. What it meant was that my battalion would hold the line for four days, and then go into reserve for four days; but every night of the four days in reserve we had to march to the trenches and work. At the beginning, however, the men stuck this well and cheerfully. I remember giving a lecture to my company on the subject of this new idea in defence and noticing their interest. Everyone knew by then that in all probability we were in for a very bad time, but at least this much more elastic type of defence did give us a better chance of holding on and fighting back.[8]
>
> Captain Charles Miller, 2nd Battalion, Royal Inniskilling Fusiliers, 109th Brigade, 36th Division

In the siting of the defences there were the usual conflicts between local commanders and their superiors. The colonels and their company officers who were required to defend the strongpoints in the Forward Zone had an obvious imperative to protect themselves as best they could. Yet there was a substantial amount of intervention by senior officers, sometimes operating from a different defensive agenda, but perhaps often meddling almost for the sake of it. Captain Miller was undoubtedly a fairly cynical officer, but he considered that the well-meaning but catastrophic intrusion of their gallant brigadier wrecked the Inniskillings' efforts to prepare a serious resistance.

> We had already started to dig the strongpoints in the sites selected by the colonels, when the brigadier chose to inspect them, and of course, decided to alter the positions. We started all over again, but there were lots of other 'brass hats' who had to have their say in the matter, and time and time again the position of the strongpoints was changed. The appalling and crass stupidity of it all! Putting up barbed wire entanglements at night-time is a hard enough job in itself, but we reached the point where we had to uproot the entanglements that we had previously erected on abandoned sites, cart them off and erect them on

new sites, which is simply Herculean labour. And all this had to be done on the nights when we supposed to be resting. The result was chaotic. In the first place, the men were tired to death; in the second place, since the position of the strongpoints was constantly being changed it was impossible to organise a regular drill by which every man knew his strongpoint and got there in the quickest possible time when ordered to do so; lastly, instead of being deeply dug, strongly revetted and wired it was quite obvious that when the moment came to use them the strongpoints would hardly be strong enough to keep out a well-aimed snowball.[9]

Captain Charles Miller, 2nd Battalion, Royal Inniskilling Fusiliers, 109th Brigade, 36th Division

Unfortunately, this was by no means an isolated incident. The situation in the Fifth Army sector was a world away from the perfectly sound theoretical position laid out in the GHQ memorandum. The problem was that although the Forward Zone could be regarded as the least important zone, until the defences there were in place troops could not be released to build and occupy the Battle Zone defences. Thus the Forward Zone attracted a great deal of the attention of everyone concerned. As a result, while it was more than evident that much work still needed to be done on the Battle Zone, the so-called Rear Zone remained a pure figment of the imagination. Generally known as the 'Green Line', at the time of the German assault it still was nothing more than a single spit-locked trench, which may have been an imposing 7 feet wide but was a much less adequate 12 inches deep! Noticeboards indicated the future sites of machine guns. In the Fifth Army sector the further Emergency Line was meant to be under preparation along the Somme River, incorporating a bridgehead in the Mont St Quentin sector. This, too, was a fantasy.

Meanwhile, the supporting engineer units were carefully briefed as to their role in the defence works. The sappers had a specialist role and although their responsibilities were great they found themselves per-force devoting much of their time to siting and laying out the redoubts being constructed at the back of the Forward Zone. One sapper officer later described the care and attention that went into creating one of these redoubts.

It was called Ellis Redoubt after our officer commanding who sited it. It lay on the banks either side of a small valley that led into St Quentin and consisted of various cunningly concealed machine guns built in deep dugouts in the sides of the banks, and the entrance to these dugouts was by means of a carefully camouflaged trench. The whole object of the machine guns was to come as a surprise and to bring close-range fire on an attacking party when they least expected it. With this in view the utmost trouble was taken to conceal any signs of our work, most of it done at night. The remainder of the redoubt consisted of trench posts mutually supporting each other and which could bring enfilade fire on an attacking party. Very special care was taken with the barbed wiring, which was run out in the form of rays that converged towards the redoubt forming pockets commanded by machine guns. We were all convinced that when the time came our redoubt would hold its own.[10]

Lieutenant Robert Petschler, 201st Field Company, Royal Engineers, 30th Division

One new concern for the British engineers was the prospect of being attacked by German tanks. In fact, the Germans had completely missed the boat with regard to developing an effective tank. Design work had been begun in late 1916 but the resulting offering, the A7V, was a disappointment. It was a large oblong box shape weighing some 30 tons. Armed with no less than six machine guns and a front mounted 5.7-cm gun it needed a crew of eighteen to take it into battle. Grossly underpowered it could reach an optimistic top speed of about 3 mph across country. The A7V was not a success and only about twenty ever got into service. The bulk of the tanks available to the Germans were patched up, captured British tanks of which they had about seventy-five.

The British were not sure where exactly the Germans stood with regard to tanks, but they had to proceed on the grounds that they would be deployed in the great attack. After a detailed survey of the ground they plotted routes and localities where they thought that any marauding German tanks must pass through. Here they laid large numbers of anti-tank mines. This was a weapon that was not yet fully understood as was found by Captain John March in somewhat farcical circumstances.

We moved up to a sunken road near Revelon for intensive wiring of support lines. In this area, on our previous visit, we had sown a minefield between the front and support lines, but while we were out some ass decided that it was too dangerous to keep mines fused, and took all the fuses and detonators away. As it happened, we had no time to put them back![11]

Captain John March, 90th Field Company, Royal Engineers, 9th Division

Having deployed tanks themselves, the British were keenly aware that the German Army was likely to have its own tanks by this time. This was something that they feared and they sought to counter it using what the Tank Corps had already recognised from bitter experience at Cambrai would be the most potent tank destroyer – the artillery. Single field guns were therefore covertly moved forward and carefully concealed within 2,000 yards of the front-line outposts.

These guns were never to open fire till the enemy's infantry advanced, so as to ensure their presence remaining a secret. About eight of these guns per corps were placed in these forward positions – a total of over thirty.[12]

General Sir Hubert Gough, Headquarters, Fifth Army

There was, however, no real understanding of the possible use of the Tank Corps in a defensive battle. Tank-versus-tank duels or battles were not yet a reality and their employment against attacking infantry was still problematic.

Tanks were still too new an arm to have a code of tactical instructions for all occasions, and so far we had no experience of their use in defence. It was in Fifth Army that their employment in this capacity was first worked out. The tanks were placed in sections of two or three attached to the counter-attack troops, and were moved into position concealed from the air close to these troops.[13]

General Sir Hubert Gough, Headquarters, Fifth Army

Many of the Tank Corps were dismayed at the deployment of their tanks in 'penny packets'. They coined their own sarcastic description of the policy.

We were moved up to near the front line in small parties. We had sections of four tanks dotted about in various concealed positions close to the line, within half a mile in some cases. It was part of my job to go round and visit these detachments, which was fairly exciting work because the approaches were overlooked by the Germans. The idea was that when the Germans arrived the tanks would start out and, as somebody described it, 'emerge like savage rabbits' and go into the Germans. They had absolutely no conception of using these valuable fighting machines to lead a coherent force in a counter-attack. It was imposed on us, that was why we were so 'savage'. The thing was simply ridiculous.[14]

Major Mark Dillon, 2nd Tank Battalion, Tank Corps

The policy was, in fact, already under review as the offensive loomed and at the last minute in early March it was decided that the tanks would be held back in battalion groups some miles behind the front ready for deployment in numbers in a coordinated counter-attack role.

Out of the line, infantry troops practised for their role in the coming battle with ceaseless exercises. They had been fighting in trenches for the best part of four years but now there was something new in the air. The British Army still intended to fight based in trenches and redoubts but there was now a need for counter-attacks operating in open warfare conditions. One battalion training for this new role was the 7th Somersets, which was to be held back in reserve at the village of Freniches.

We would be put into the line or sent up as reinforcements wherever the enemy attacked fiercest and wherever we should be wanted the most. We would therefore be taken by bus or train and then would have a long march to where the enemy had broken through. Of course, we would be fighting in open country and not in trenches. During this 'rest', therefore, we were hard at work training the men in open warfare and its tactics, getting the men used to long route marches and in every way getting the men fit. We had physical training, squad, platoon and company drill, instruction in the Lewis gun, bombing and shooting, practise in digging in with entrenching tools, and last of all battalion drill, battalion attacks and route marches. Whilst on route marches, we practised suddenly scattering in all directions on the alarm of hostile aircraft and small bodies of men were told off to get the Lewis gun firing and snipers to snipe at the aircraft. We also practised getting ready to march off at a moment's notice.[15]

Captain George McMurtrie, 7th Battalion, Somerset Light Infantry, 61st Brigade, 20th Division

As can be imagined the Royal Artillery was crucial to all the British plans for a successful defence. Even before the battle started it could make its presence felt with long-range heavy artillery reaching deep behind the German lines to interfere with any preparations that had been identified by the RFC reconnaissance missions.

Aeroplane photos showed that he was strengthening bridges and erecting new ones, and also collecting large dumps of ammunition behind his lines. These were called 'maggots' in orders and 'Comic Cuts' because this is what they looked like in the photos. We had orders to do destructive shoots on these bridges by day with aeroplane observation and to harass them by night to prevent them repairing them. Also we used to strafe his dumps by night and succeeded in blowing quite a few up. In order to mislead the Hun as to the amount of artillery we had, we used to trail a gun round the countryside at night and poop off from odd spots, so that his sound rangers would pick up guns firing from new places every night. I really don't know that it did much good, except to amuse the men who called it the 'circus gun'![16]

Second Lieutenant L. R. Ward, 113th Siege Battery, Royal Garrison Artillery

All too aware of the devastating power of their guns there is no doubt that many of the young British artillery officers were somewhat blasé, never believing that there was a real threat. For Lieutenant Brian Bradnack of the 122nd Siege Battery the whole proceedings bore the hallmarks of a French farce from the moment that they arrived.

Coming as we did from a part of the line where the war had been taken desperately seriously, much too seriously in fact, it seemed to us that here there was a conspiracy afoot to prevent anyone taking anything seriously. It began on the day of our arrival, when all troops were instructed to pretend they were French, as we were taking over the sector from the French. The line troops were issued with French helmets and we gunners were directed to disguise our nationality by substituting for our peculiar and perpetual artillery activity, the policy of masterly inactivity unless greatly provoked, which was always practised by the French artillery.[17]

Lieutenant Brian Bradnack, 122nd Siege Battery, 66th Brigade, Royal Garrison Artillery

Such scepticism was also the general mood evident amongst the officers of the 111th Siege Battery in their gun positions and dugouts close to the village of Épéhy.

There was no doubt that those at headquarters 'had the wind up'. From time to time 'Comic Cuts' even fixed the date when the offensive was to begin – but these proved false alarms. In spite of these warnings and predictions of terrible things to come, I don't remember feeling particularly worried or alarmed and I don't think others in the battery were either. I think one somehow consoled oneself by thinking those at headquarters were unduly anxious, and anyhow, if they felt so sure as to what the enemy intended, surely they were making all necessary and adequate precautions to frustrate those intentions, and the enemy would soon find out it was hopeless to attempt anything of the sort – or if they did, they would get it in the neck. In the meantime, life in the battery went on very smoothly and comfortably. Rations were good, whisky was plentiful, there was a battery car available and the officer commanding was very generous in allowing officers the use of it for jaunts behind the lines.[18]

Lieutenant Edward Allfree, 111th Siege Battery, Royal Garrison Artillery

Yet by and large, whatever they may have thought of the seriousness of the threat, the self-same officers carried out the required precautions in a reasonably conscientious manner. There was a professionalism about the Royal Artillery that would not have been present two years earlier.

The Major had prepared a close-range map. This comprised the ground lying between the battery position and our own front-line trenches and was marked off in squares. Each of these squares was given a distinctive letter or number. The necessary angle from the aiming point and the elevation for the guns was then worked out for each target and a list made, the idea being that in the event of the Hun breaking through, an officer could take this close-range map to the high ground in front of the battery. On seeing the Huns swarming over the particular patch of ground represented on the map by, say, 'Target C', all he would have to do would be to telephone back to the section commander on the guns, 'Target C!' The section commander would at once shout out the necessary orders for the switch and elevation of the guns and a 6-in shell would be falling on the target within a very few seconds.[19]

Lieutenant Edward Allfree, 111th Siege Battery, Royal Garrison Artillery

The concept of defence in depth was new to the Royal Artillery and many of the officers believed that they were wasting their time digging reserve gunpits and dugouts miles behind their normal battery positions.

A lot of our time was taken up with constructing a reserve battery position close to Clastres. We thought that was a rather poor joke to play on us as Clastres was a good mile beyond Montescourt, and we had to march our digging parties there daily for three weeks or more on their flat feet – and that on our 'off duty' days too. Moreover the ground was hard chalk and frosty withal, and took a good deal of working. But still even that was a joke and we entered into the spirit of it as best we could. We dug with great vigour and camouflaged with some care. No amount of camouflage could possibly hide the enormous heap of chalk, or those lorry tracks from the little lane, from the glasses and cameras of the German airmen who appeared now and then – well, why worry? Anyhow it was almost out of range of the line, would never be used and it was a stupid place for corps to have selected. But it was all part of the game, and if corps liked it, we didn't mind![20]

Lieutenant Brian Bradnack, 122nd Siege Battery, 66th Brigade, Royal Garrison Artillery

The idea of rapidly abandoning the forward positions under duress was simply untenable. How, after all, could the Germans get as far as the gun line? The infantry machine guns, the barbed wire and above all the massed power of the British guns would take care of them long before that.

The NCOs in the forward section received their emergency orders in polite silence, except for Sergeant Upton, an old regular, who had been detailed to take charge of a covering party of fifty riflemen, to keep off the Boche if necessary while we were pulling out. He complained loudly that if the so-and-so Boche were coming over the top he wanted to be fighting with his gun and not mooning about with a pack of rifles –

why, wasn't it just at times like this when we wanted sergeants for guns? What was the sense of leaving any gun, let alone *his*, to a blinking corporal? The rest, I think, thought the whole thing a waste of time.[21]

Lieutenant Brian Bradnack, 122nd Siege Battery, 66th Brigade, Royal Garrison Artillery

The shortage of manpower in the BEF was most evident when it came to properly garrisoning the line. The brigades given the task of holding the Forward Zone found it difficult to cope with the requirements imposed on them. In many cases the frontage they were responsible for was simply too wide to hold in any meaningful strength. The situation as perceived by Brigadier General Stanley of 89th Brigade was threatening in the extreme.

One battalion was holding the whole brigade front. It could not be considered anything else than a lightly held outpost line. They had a few posts out in front, about six in all, and each of these posts consisted of about six men. Behind this we had a series of other posts, and again, behind these, a couple of strongpoints. This absorbed two companies of the battalion. Then there was one company which was detailed for counter-attacking purposes, and the fourth, and last was responsible for the garrison and upkeep of a redoubt called Epine de Dallon. Here also was situated the battalion headquarters. For any further defence one had to go back to what was called the Battle Zone – a distance of some 2 or 3 miles back. This was a series of posts and strongpoints, which had been dug within the last month, and in our case was to be manned by the remaining two battalions at our disposal. I might say that the division had two brigades, each of them holding a sector, whilst the third brigade was in corps reserve. From this it will be seen, therefore, that if the enemy attacked in sufficient strength, there was no possibility of helping the battalion that was holding the line.[22]

Brigadier General F. C. Stanley, 89th Brigade, 30th Division

The sheer physical distance between the outpost line and the Battle Zone meant that there would not be time to send help from there and, even if help was sent, in doing so the already thinly held Battle Zone defences would be fatally weakened. The reality was that the men in the Forward Zone would be left to fend for themselves. Luckily for Brigadier Stanley, on 17 March his 89th Brigade was moved out of the line and took up a reserve role. It would not therefore be caught in the front line when the blow fell. His men, however, were then put to work improving the Battle Zone defences.

Ironically, the gallant Brigadier Stanley seems to have had a close escape from the careless hands of one of his more unruly soldiers, although, unsurprisingly, this amusing incident did not merit mention in his subsequent history of the 89th Brigade.

We would sally out in the morning after breakfast and try to complete the digging of the reserve trenches. One of our platoons had become a little disgruntled: they weren't actually mutinous but they hadn't completed their task. We would dig for an hour and a half, then have quarter of an hour's rest. They suddenly decided that rest shouldn't be wasted so we had to spend that doing respirator drill or rapid loading and unloading of rifles. Few of the troops had ever fired a rifle at the enemy. In trench warfare you never saw an enemy. We were given an order that the troops had to find a safe bank and fire 25 rounds apiece into it, firing and unloading. The supply of dummy cartridges ran out so they said, 'Well you'll have to use live ones boys, but just be careful!' One of our madmen must have had his rifle at a high elevation, he pulled his trigger as a kind of *feu de joi* and the round went off into the distance. There was nobody near, but about ten minutes later a staff officer came up on a horse, 'Who was firing live rounds, the Brigadier nearly got hit?'[23]

Corporal Edmund Williams, 19th Battalion, King's Liverpool Regiment, 89th Brigade, 30th Division

By early on 19 March the last few remaining pieces of the intelligence jigsaw were placed in front of the High Command and fell neatly into place. There was no longer any doubt as to where the German first blow would fall: the Somme front *was* the target.

A German artillery NCO captured west of Bony, an aeroplane pilot brought down near Ly-Fontaine, infantry prisoners captured southwest of Villers-Guislain, and Alsatian deserters from a trench mortar battery south of St Quentin, all told the same story, each in his own way – in some cases, it is true, quite unwittingly. The sources of information were not only independent, but the prisoners were of widely differing types: and the news they gave, corroborating many other indications, completed the last links in the chain of evidence gradually forged during the preceding weeks.[24]

Intelligence Officer Lieutenant Colonel F. S. G. Piggott, Headquarters, Fifth Army

Gough sought permission from General Headquarters to move up his two army reserve divisions in readiness so that he could respond quickly to any threatened breakthrough.

> We knew we were to be attacked in overwhelming force. We knew our line was dangerously thin, and that the fighting which the difficult and delicate role of a delaying action and the *manoeuvre en retraite* imposed on us must involve a prolonged struggle, and it was important to spare the troops as much hustle and fatigue as possible. Moreover, all the lessons of war, both in attack and defence, had taught us how important it was, once your action was decided on, to close up the supports and reserves behind the line. The 20th Division was 15 miles behind the front of the XVIII Corps, and I wanted to move it up 5 to 8 miles further northward, to Ham and north of it. In addition, I wished to move the 50th Division at least a day's march and bring it across to the east side of the Somme – as it was more than 25 miles behind the front – and I asked authority of General Headquarters for these moves. These steps were in my opinion most urgent, almost vital. The Chief of Staff said that it was not sound to move reserves before the situation was clear, that to move them up would be to tie them down.[25]

General Sir Hubert Gough, Headquarters, Fifth Army

The different principles of war clashed, as of course they often do. Gough's plans were frustrated by the General Headquarters staff, who were determined to retain their overall flexibility to reinforce vital points as revealed in the actual fighting rather than by prejudging the situation. As is so often the case in such situations both sides were right and both sides were wrong. It was all a matter of perspective. This, however, did not help Gough.

AS THE GERMAN troops moved into the line they were understandably ambivalent about the attack that lay before them. Any major offensive on the Western Front was an extremely dangerous enterprise for the men no matter how well prepared they may have been. And like the British 'Tommies' they had been at war for too long to have retained any enthusiasm for the fray. War was something to be endured.

> We were taken back behind the front lines and we were trained for attack. It was a hard time for us because the food was scarce; we felt the blockade. We hoped for victory in our attack, we were convinced that we could see it through to get a fair peace. We didn't want to want to conquer foreign lands but we wanted to keep what we had and hoped for a fair peace.[26]
>
> Hartwig Pohlmann, 36th Division, Imperial German Army

The soldiers were not fools and they had plenty of correspondence from their families telling them of the day-to-day struggle for existence that represented life in Germany. But they had also been buoyed up by the same prospects that had cheered Ludendorff. They knew that for just a few months they had a fighting chance to win the war.

> Our superiors and the newspapers assured us that big events were approaching. As far as we were told there were only 30,000 Americans in France, most of them inexperienced soldiers. There were more Americans to come, but then we had hundreds of submarines that controlled the seas. Now that the whole Eastern Army had been transferred to the West, a million men strong, it seemed to us that the next offensive would bring victory and peace.[27]
>
> Unteroffizier Frederick Meisel, 371st Infantry Regiment, 43rd Ersatz Brigade, 10th Ersatz Division, Imperial German Army

As the troops moved up, they could see the enormous scale of the preparations, could see that everything possible was being done to guarantee victory when the moment came. Of course, most of the ordinary soldiers still did not know exactly when they would be going 'over the top', they only knew it would be soon.

> The big offensive is now ready. All the villages near the front are full of troops. Troop movement is on a massive scale; all roads leading to the front have been repaired. Everywhere one sees that things are going to

happen in the next few days. Although there are no civilians, the place is very busy. With so many soldiers here, they have to sleep out of doors. Absolutely everywhere is crammed with troops. Enemy aeroplanes are constantly on the move, a sign that the offensive will soon begin, and rumour has it that this should begin on 19 March.[28]

Signaller Edwin Kühns, 1047th Telephone Unit, Imperial German Army

The assault troops had all moved up the night before 21 March. They had laid up concealed all day, now they had nothing to do but wait or try to sleep as the last few hours and minutes trickled away to Zero Hour.

About three o'clock I went out of my dugout to look round. The night was silent, nothing was to be heard and there was a clear night with stars shining and glittering. I thought, 'These are the same stars that my family at home are looking at!' I went down into my dugout to have a bit of sleep.[29]

Hartwig Pohlmann, 36th Division, Imperial German Army

The German Army was all set for the greatest offensive in military history.

THE BRITISH, TOO, were as ready as they could be, given that they could hardly ask for the postponement they so desperately craved. Even those who had never really believed that the German assault was truly imminent began to realise that the moment was nigh. For all the false alarms, for all the manifold frustrations of trying to achieve impossible tasks with too few men and not enough time, the mood was gradually changing.

A new element began to make its appearance in the atmosphere. The spirit of make-believe and the practical joke idea actually persisted right up to the eve of the great offensive, but by then it had been gradually ousted into the position of junior partner in our emotional Joint Stock Company by a new spirit, an eerie sensation of something uncanny about. As it does not become even amateur soldiers to be dominated by this suspicious questioning state of mind, it was perhaps natural for us unconsciously to attempt to banish our uneasiness by an extra emphasis on the note of the practical joke. Comicality gradually developing into creepiness, partially explained the peculiarly muddled state of mind in which we received word at last that we might expect a big attack on 21 March. The warning of the attack chimed in with the eeriness of the atmosphere, and would account for many of the queer things we had noticed, but yet we could not quite throw off the idea that everything in our sector was being run as a play-game and a joke, so that we went to bed on 20 March only half-convinced that a real battle was on the verge of beginning, and still half-believing that someone's leg was being pulled on a rather extensive scale.[30]

Lieutenant Brian Bradnack, 122nd Siege Battery, 66th Brigade, Royal Garrison Artillery

Late on the night of 20 March the final intelligence briefings or, more accurately given the circumstances, warnings were beginning to trickle forward to the men of the Third and Fifth Armies. The news came in various forms, but the import was the same: the Germans would be coming over next day.

We were having supper on the mess when a despatch messenger arrived from corps with a roll of maps. The Colonel took them, opened them and put them on the supper table. We had a look at them, they were maps of the front line in our area. The signal officer said to the Colonel in quite a jovial voice, 'What are all those little black dots, Sir?' The Colonel said to him very grimly, 'Those are German guns in the open, my boy, they were spotted by the RFC a couple of hours ago!' That brought home to us that the German offensive was very imminent. When we went to bed we felt quite certain that something was going to happen next morning.[31]

Captain Arthur Behrend, 90th Brigade, Royal Garrison Artillery

There was very little dressing up of the situation in the messages received by the units who had the grim task of holding the Forward Zone, just a stark indication of what seemed likely to happen. The men holding the strongpoints knew their place in the scheme of things and it was by no means a reassuring prospect. Death, wounds and capture seemed to form the limits of their world, certainly as far as the lugubrious Captain Miller was concerned.

About midnight I got a chit from Farnham to the effect that it was a certainty that the attack would come on the 21st or the 22nd, that there was to be no question of retreat, and that the main battle would be fought at a point some 3 miles behind us. He wished me good luck, and I returned his wishes because I liked Farnham very much, and it seemed to me that this was likely to be the end of our acquaintance. I then got my four platoons into their strongpoints, taking all my men out of the front line and this was accomplished easily and successfully. It was a dead still and rather chilly night. I myself was in the strongpoint allotted to company headquarters. I had with me a subaltern and a full platoon. My strongpoint consisted of about 150 yards of trench with one deep and very spacious dugout quite capable of holding us all and protecting us from the effects of shell fire; but a death-trap if the enemy infantry got in before we could get out of it. At each end of the trench there was a strong 'stop' with a certain amount of cover for riflemen. There was one fairly strong belt of wire running in a half-circle right round the front of the strongpoint and ending about 20 yards wide of the two 'stops' at each end of the trench. Had that wire been thicker and stronger it would have been a much more formidable little place for a frontal attack. Of course, by rights, the wire should have been all round it. I had time to make a visit to one of the points occupied by my platoons. I hated the look of it: a couple of dugouts, hastily made and inadequately wired, and I wished I had disobeyed orders and put them into one of the previously discarded strongpoints. There was, however, no time to alter dispositions and I wished them good luck.[32]

Captain Charles Miller, 2nd Battalion, Royal Inniskilling Fusiliers, 109th Brigade, 36th Division

There was a strange atmosphere up and down the threatened front that night. Private James Brady of the 43rd Field Ambulance, RAMC was ensconced in a first-aid post in a quarry just behind the line in the Battle Zone at Essigny.

After an evening meal of bully and mash I felt a bit heady, caused by the accumulative pollution of fumes from primus stove and oil lamps, plus heavy smoking by residents. Andy Chapman and I went upstairs for a breath of fresh air. The night was chilly and pitch-black except for the occasional display of Very lights from the forward trenches half a mile up the road. In the distance we could hear the loud rumble of German transport trundling up to their front-line positions from the direction of St Quentin and there were the intermittent flashes of enemy light guns as they slung over a couple of whizz-bangs – just for the hell of it![33]

Private James Brady, 43rd Field Ambulance, Royal Army Medical Corps, 14th Division

Worried by the alarms, the freely circulating rumours and the all-pervading sense of tension, Colonel Bernard Prior of the 9th Norfolks spent the whole night touring his front-line posts, checking for himself that whatever might be about to happen the Norfolks would be ready for it.

I went some way out into No Man's Land and obtained the impression that this was no longer a false alarm. I don't quite know what gave me this impression. In the Boche lines there was a stillness which, at the same time, was not a complete silence, just as if a large number of men were already in position, waiting in intense excitement, and speaking to each other in whispers.[34]

Lieutenant Colonel Bernard Prior, 9th Battalion, Norfolk Regiment, 71st Brigade, 6th Division

The machine-gunners that were so crucial to the defence plans obsessively checked and rechecked their Vickers guns, cleaning and oiling all moving parts; laying out the ammunition belts; changing the water and ensuring they had a full complement of spare parts to hand in case of a stoppage. Many were confident that it was well within their powers to dish out to the Germans a dreadful vengeance for all they had suffered at the hands of their Maxim machine-gunners over the past three years. Then they waited in the dark.

All guns were ready for action. I caressed the grip of my trusty Vickers and felt a grim kind of satisfaction when I thought of the deadly stream of lead I should soon be directing on the oncoming Boche.[35]

Private David Polley, 189th Machine Gun Company, 189th Brigade, 63rd (Royal Naval) Division

The British knew when the Germans were coming and they knew where the blow would strike. The only question was whether they could stop them?

CHAPTER THREE

21 March 1918

FOG! A simple, small word, but a natural phenomenon that rendered the carefully crafted British defensive plans all but useless on 21 March 1918. By sheer misfortune it was the first really foggy morning of the spring to boot. The mist seemed to rise up from the ground in the early evening of the previous night, gradually swelling to fill up the dark valleys and softly cover the rows of barbed wire. The world closed in on the isolated British outposts, as they were blanketed by a fog so thick that it left some of the worst affected sectors with a visibility of just 10 yards. Their pre-planned fields of machine-gun fire in the front line were still valid, but it would have to be unaimed fire sprayed in the general direction of a threat. The artillery would have to fire on their SOS lines but without any corrections or coordinates for new targets from their blinded forward observers. Targets of opportunity would pass unobserved and unmolested as the stormtroopers went about their grim business.

The British sent out a few patrols on the final night – there were even some minor raids – but in the circumstances these could achieve next to nothing. The very few German prisoners that were taken were more than willing to confirm the imminence of an attack and indeed their obvious desperation to be taken back out of the danger zone and out of artillery range spoke volumes about what was to come. Up and down the British line the troops began taking up their battle positions and some of the batteries began a general harassing fire in an attempt to disrupt any German final preparations.

Still the massed German guns waited in silence. The barrage was to start at 0440. They had spent the previous weeks moving up the artillery, camouflaging battery positions and secretly bringing forward the huge quantities of ammunition that would be required by the 6,608 guns. Now they were ready. Leutnant Herbert Sulzbach was with his battery in the ruins of the St Quentin suburbs.

> The darkness begins to lift, very, very slowly; we stand at the guns with our gas masks round our necks, and the time until 4.40 crawls round at a dreadfully slow pace. At last we're there, and with a crash our barrage begins from thousands and thousands, it must be from tens of thousands, of gun barrels and mortars, a barrage that sounds as if the world were coming to an end. For the first hour we only strafe the enemy artillery with alternative shrapnel, Green Cross and Blue Cross. The booming is getting more and more dreadful, especially as we are in a town between the walls of houses. I often have to make a break in my fire control duties, since I just can't carry on with all the gas and smoke. The gunners stand in their shirtsleeves, with the sweat running down and dripping off them. Shell after shell is fired.[1]
>
> Leutnant Herbert Sulzbach, 63rd Field Artillery Regiment, Imperial German Army

The German gunners swung into their long-practised drill. Every single member of the gun detachments and command post teams had a distinct role, and the accuracy of their fire was all-important if the barrage was to have the designed impact.

> I had to direct the guns, using my tables to adjust for strength and direction of wind. The barrage started all at one time. A terrific intensity. Normally we used to protect our ears by holding our hands against the ears when the gun was discharged. This time that was pretty impossible. The effect was that for a few days afterwards I was almost deaf![2]
>
> Feldwebel Walter Rappolt, 2nd Battery, 406th Artillery Battalion, 1st Guards Foot Artillery Regiment, Imperial German Army

So the field artillery guns barked out staccato messages that melded into a thunderous cacophony, while from far behind the front lines came the deep-bellied roar of the heavy artillery. One such mammoth 38-cm gun was located close to the billet of telephonist Edwin Kühns in the Cambrai sector.

A devastating bang! The first shot was fired. A huge fireball lit up the sky – a 14-cwt shell flew towards Bapaume – 4-cwt of gunpowder is needed for one shot and it travels 54 kilometres. All billets within a radius of 400 metres have to be evacuated. We, too, were without a roof over our heads. As everywhere was occupied we moved back into our place where all the windows had been blasted out and even bits of wall had fallen down. At every shot we thought the place was going to collapse.[3]

Signaller Edwin Kühns, 1047th Telephone Unit, Imperial German Army

The bombardment unleashed by the Germans was truly terrifying. If it was indeed an orchestral piece – the *feuerwalzer* as Colonel Bruchmüller would have it – it was laid on with a heavy baton.

The hurricane broke loose. A curtain of flames was let down, followed by a sudden impetuous tumult such as was never heard, a raging thunder that swallowed up the reports even of the heaviest guns in its tremendous reverberations and made the earth tremble. This gigantic roar of annihilation from countless guns behind us was so terrific that, compared with it, all preceding battles were child's play. What we had not dared to hope came true. The enemy artillery was silenced, put out of action by one giant blow.[4]

Leutnant Ernst Jünger, 73rd Hanoverian Fusiliers Regiment, Imperial German Army

Individual guns fired up to 600 shells; in just five hours they collectively fired an incredible 1.16 million shells and during the whole day they would fire in the region of 3.5 million shells into the Third Army and Fifth Army lines.

The first phase seemed to particularly concentrate on their opposite numbers in the British artillery gun lines. Batteries were absolutely deluged with gas and high explosive shells. The effects were over-whelming.

From in front there came the dim report of one 77-mm gun, which burst a few hundred yards in front of us, a moment's silence and then from all round, from above and below it seemed, one tremendous whistle. Before the shells landed we knew – it was the attack. Followed by a deafening crash, as I don't know how many shells burst at once and squibs of flame spurted up everywhere. A hoarse bellow of 'SOS!', followed almost at once by an answering bellow from a sergeant, quite indecipherable though he was only 15 yards away. As I doubled towards him, he shouted in my ear, 'Picket . . . lamps . . . gone!' For five minutes we tried to go on, without aiming, but just firing, and in that five minutes, I think, we collected our wits again. It was no good. A shell burst had covered each gun in muck: everything seemed lost or buried or blown away. We returned to the dugouts to wait – for what?[5]

Lieutenant Brian Bradnack, 122nd Siege Battery, 66th Brigade, Royal Garrison Artillery

Stuck in their dugouts the men could hear the shells raining down all around their gun positions. They were hardly safe in their dugouts but they knew that their chances of survival were poor if they went outside. Yet duty called.

As I dressed in the dark I said to myself, 'Well, I'd better put on my best tunic because whether we're killed or not, the probability will be that one will be either wounded or captured and there is no good being captured in an old tunic.' I had a look up and down the sunken road and everything was at sixes and sevens.[6]

Captain Arthur Behrend, 90th Brigade, Royal Garrison Artillery

Lieutenant Bradnack found himself effectively trapped in his battery command post, accompanied by an extremely scared technical assistant who had constantly to be dissuaded from running away. Bradnack himself was none too happy as the shells crashed down all around them and he began to experience a nagging perception of personal victimisation.

One gun I could hear above all others: quite a small one, but the gun that is aiming absolutely directly at you, you can always hear. While it was yet afar off, the shell was audible, nearer and nearer – 'Plop!' Short! Again: nearer and nearer, 'Whoosh! Plop!' Just over! How long would it go on for? How long would one's luck hold?[7]

Lieutenant Brian Bradnack, 122nd Siege Battery, 66th Brigade, Royal Garrison Artillery

It seems unbelievable that he could detect a particular shell within that crazy Germanic symphony of destruction, but many officers had developed the ability to track the flight of shells. They had had plenty of practice.

Heavy slow howitzer shells would go wandering along, on and on and on, until suddenly the pace seems to accelerate, coming down with a whoosh. Then one hears a thud and c-r-r-ump of the burst and knows that someone's happy little home is probably disintegrating about his ears, as like the Jabberwock, they 'Whiffled through the tulgy wood and burbled as they came!' There was always a thrill in listening to them; a thrill that was even greater though of a different quality when they happened to be travelling in one's direction.[8]

Second Lieutenant John Fleming, 'U' Battery, 16th Brigade, Royal Horse Artillery

Lieutenant Allfree initially felt safe enough in his dugout behind a carefully positioned double gas curtain, but he was soon ordered up to the 6″ howitzer positions to check on his gun teams who had managed to get into action. They, too, were having severe problems with the fog and the smothering gas clouds that billowed around them as they fired on their SOS night lines at pre-selected targets. The Germans were using a mixture of gases including Blue Cross, Green Cross and Yellow Cross. The Blue Cross was the German pièce de résistance, a truly deadly weapon – if it had worked properly. It contained an arsenic-based compound that acted as a powerful sternutator on the respiratory system – in other words it irritated the nasal and respiratory passages to cause coughing, sneezing and sometimes vomiting. It was, in fact, not really a gas at all, but an inert powder that could pass straight through the British gas mask. When the sneezing, choking, vomiting victim tore off his mask in an effort to breathe he would then be exposed to the deadly Green Cross shells that contained phosgene, a lung irritant sixteen times more lethal than the chlorine gas used in 1915. It was fortunate indeed for the British gunners that the German Blue Cross shells were one of the biggest failures of the war as the detonation of the shell on landing proved inadequate to properly disperse the powder as a fine cloud in the atmosphere. As such it fell to the ground and had a minimal effect. Far more dangerous was the menace of the Yellow Cross mustard gas. Exposure to this unpleasant substance severely burnt the skin and had a terrible effect on the eyes. The eyeballs were inflamed, the eyelids swelled up and soon the victim was blind, helpless and in great pain. Although the effects were only temporary, lasting up to ten days, the sufferers had to be removed from the field of battle. It was an insidious gas that took some time to disperse and thereby rendered areas virtually impassable for long periods. That morning, Allfree could only be sure that whatever the gases were, swirling all around him, they would be severely injurious to his health.

> I adjusted my box respirator over my face, groped my way up the dark steps, crept under the first gas curtain, adjusted it behind me, then under the second and so found myself outside in the sunken road. It was still almost dark and there was a thick mist. Shells were falling everywhere. It was a perfect hell – no other words can describe how utterly beastly it was. I felt my way up the sunken road towards the guns. The eyepieces of the respirator got fogged immediately and you could see nothing. I eventually found myself at the guns. The layers were experiencing the utmost difficulty in laying the guns, as they could not see the lamps on the aiming pickets owing to the mist. They had got their respirators off their faces in order to see better, retaining the nose clip and mouthpiece. I sent a man out with an electric torch to lay on, but even this could only be seen with difficulty. So I went to the map room and took the magnetic bearing of the target they were firing on, then armed with a prismatic compass, I laid the guns as accurately as I could. I should not like to vouch for the accuracy of the fire, but the great thing was to get some shells over.[9]
> Lieutenant Edward Allfree, 111th Siege Battery, Royal Garrison Artillery

Second Lieutenant Cyril Dennys of the 212th Siege Battery was moving up to take up his designated position as the forward observation officer in the Bois d'Holnon at the front of the Battle Zone facing St Quentin when he was caught in the barrage. He was walking forwards with his signaller when they encountered a field artillery colonel and his subaltern.

> I said to the Colonel, 'It's pretty nasty this morning, isn't it?' He said, 'Yes it is, but you know I don't think it can go on very long at this rate – I mean there must be some limit to the ammunition they've got!' Just at that point there was a very loud crash in the air caused by the burst of a high explosive shell, probably a 5.9″, we called them 'woolly bears', and great eddies of greasy black smoke. I didn't like the look of this; then there came another, closer and we all got down. I couldn't see anything

69

for mud, dust and smoke. When I could see again, I couldn't see the Colonel at all, but the subaltern was lying on his back. I looked at him and I thought, 'He's been hit!' I put my hand under his head and in effect I put my hand into his brains, which were out. A fragment had come through the front of his head and taken his brains away at the back. I thought he was dead already but he wasn't, he was still breathing. 'What do I do now?' Just leaving him isn't very good, on the other hand it was quite clear that even if he could have been got to an advance dressing station he had only minutes to live.[10]

Second Lieutenant Cyril Dennys, 212th Siege Battery, Royal Garrison Artillery

To stay would probably have been the easier option, but Dennys rightly felt that he had no real excuse to avoid carrying on up to his observation-post duty. He duly abandoned the dying man but never forgot the man he left to die alone that day.

The initial German barrage was also intended to have a devastating effect on the entire British communication system. Shells crashed down on the headquarters of companies, battalions, brigades and divisions with a gay abandon. They smashed up the wireless stations and soon most of the telephone lines were severed – no matter how deeply they had been buried the larger shells seemed to sniff them out to expose them to destruction. The almost comic trials of one ordinary Royal Engineer signaller attached to the 1/7th Londons could well stand for the general experience of the vast majority of signallers. Signaller Bert Chaney discovered to his utter horror that all his careful 'failsafe' preparations had been rendered useless by a combination of the German bombardment, the mist and the eternal problems of working with dumb animals.

One by one our telephone lines were smashed. We endeavoured a number of times to repair them, going out into the barrage, creeping down communication trenches trying to find the ends of the wires, but in that mist and in that barrage it was a hopeless task, and we had to get back to our dugout thankful to be in one piece. Looking across in the direction of our visual communication system on the mound we saw that it was impossible to see anything: the Aldis lamps were unable to penetrate the mist, even the telescope did not help. Dashing down into the dugout I scribbled two similar coded messages on the special thin paper, screwed them up and pushed them into the little containers that clip onto the pigeon's leg. I and one of my boys, each carrying a pigeon, crept up the steps and pushing the gas blanket to one side, threw our birds into the air and away they flew. We watched them as they circled round a couple of times and then they swooped straight down and settled on top of our dugout. We retrieved them and tried once more, but those birds refused to fly. So down into the dugout again and another message was written and put into the small pouch attached to the dog's collar. Leading it to the entrance, I gave it a parting slap on the rump, at the same time shouting firmly, 'Home boy! Allez!' I watched it for a minute or two as it trotted off, then dropped the gas blanket back. Even while we were still sighing with relief a wet nose pushed the blanket aside and in crawled the dog, scared out of its wits. All our efforts could not budge him, we pushed and shoved him, pulled him by the collar to get him moving, but he just lay down, clamped his body firmly to the ground and pretended to be asleep. He was a lot smarter than we were. All we could do was swear a lot and give him a kick. So ended all our wonderful preparations for keeping communications going during the attack.[11]

Signaller Bert Chaney, 1/7th Battalion, London Regiment, 140th Brigade, 47th Division

They did send signals via their new earth-buzzer system, indeed they endlessly repeated them in the forlorn hope that someone might still be listening. It was not until much later that they found out that the signallers at the other end had already been killed or captured.

Of course, Gough heard the rumble of the bombardment way back at Fifth Army headquarters and knew that the moment of truth had arrived. The first question he had to determine was the extent of the attack.

I was awakened by the roar of a bombardment, which, though it sounded dully in my room in Nesle, was so sustained and steady that it at once gave me the impression of some crushing, smashing power. I jumped out of bed and walked across the passage to the telephone in my office and called up the General Staff. On what part of our front was the bombardment falling? The answer came back almost immediately, 'All four corps report heavy bombardment along their front.'[12]

General Sir Hubert Gough, Headquarters, Fifth Army

Gough's last hope of an effective response had been that the Germans would attack only part of his front, which might have allowed him the flexibility of moving troops from unthreatened sectors to help reinforce those that had come under the German hammer. It had proved a stillborn hope as his whole thin khaki line was facing assault. But there was worse to follow when he finally noticed that even the elements had united with the Germans against him.

> I looked out of my window, and in the morning light I could see that there was a thick fog, such as we had not yet experienced during the whole of the winter. We were getting into spring, and it was extra-ordinary to have so dense a fog at this date. I threw myself back on my bed and went to sleep for an hour.[13]
>
> General Sir Hubert Gough, Headquarters, Fifth Army

Although the slumbering Gough claimed an impressive detachment from events, he knew that, for him at least, the die was cast. Until the German infantry actually attacked and the pattern of the battle became clearer there was very little else he could do. As a general his work had been undertaken in the months that preceded the German attack. The question was simple: was it enough? Haig and Pétain still had decisions to make, for the Germans had also fired diversionary bombardments along the fronts of the First Army and on the French occupying the Champagne area. These threats had to be properly assessed, before they could be perceived for what they really were. The French in particular were naturally desperately concerned that the Germans might be intending a mighty follow-up thrust for Reims or Verdun. That, of course, was the whole intention of the Germans – to distract and divert attention from the real battle until it was too late.

At the front the men in the Forward Zone were cut off in a cloud of uncertainty. With their communications broken, they could only tell what was happening by logging the changes in the tumultuous sound of the barrage sweeping around them, desperately trying to judge exactly when the Germans would launch their attack out of the mist. The longer the bombardment raged on, the more the tension grew. When dawn came at 0600, the mist still persisted along the whole line, but it was distinctly worse in the south on the Fifth Army front, especially near the valleys of the Oise and St Quentin Canal. Here the fog would endure almost undiluted until about 1300. Further north on the Third Army front things were far better, although it still lasted there until around 1000. The Germans had cut some of the British wire with their bombardment, but their engineers and infantry used the cover of fog to creep out unobserved to cut more channels through the wire. The main assault was timed to commence at 0940.

The German infantry had not gone unscathed from the British artillery firing on their fixed SOS lines. After all, even in the fog the Royal Artillery knew where the German front line was located. The company of Leutnant Ernst Jünger had suffered serious casualties and indeed one of his NCOs had had his leg severed immediately in front of him. As the moment drew nigh he and his men edged out into No Man's Land.

> The great moment had come. The fire lifted over the first trenches. We advanced. The turmoil of our feelings was called forth by rage, alcohol and the thirst for blood as we stepped out, heavily and yet irresistibly, for the enemy's lines. And therewith beat the pulse of heroism – the godlike and the bestial inextricably mingled. I was far in front of the company, followed by my servant and a man of one year's service called Haake. In my right hand I gripped my revolver, in my left a bamboo riding cane. The overpowering desire to kill winged my feet. Rage squeezed bitter tears from my eyes.[14]
>
> Leutnant Ernst Jünger, 73rd Hanoverian Fusiliers Regiment, Imperial German Army

The fog was all around them and they had to feel their way across No Man's Land. It was by no means easy for the Germans, who in the mad confusion of the battlefield soon had little or no idea of where they were. But they knew they had to go forward.

> I was afraid, how can this attack go in such a fog? Nevertheless we had to attack and the only way to find the direction was to take a compass in your hand and go straight on. The ground was very rough and we had to creep through barbed wire. Everyone knew that they had to go straight on and soldiers that had lost their own companies followed officers of other companies. Soon I had soldiers of several companies of my regiment following me. Suddenly we heard some guns firing behind us. So we turned around and came from behind to a British battery that

was firing barrage fire. They didn't know that we had broken through. One of our men laid his hand on the shoulder of the British officer and said, 'Cease fire!' They were surprised to see us coming from behind.[15]

Hartwig Pohlmann, 36th Division, Imperial German Army

The preambles were over: as the German infantry went forward the battle proper had begun. Preceding them was their creeping barrage, moving forwards in bounds just over 300 yards in front of them. It was a tactic borrowed from the British designed to cover the period of nakedness in No Man's Land, suppressing return fire and allowing them to sweep over the defences before the defenders could recover. The stormtroopers were on their way, their rifles slung over their backs, using showers of grenades to clear their path. Covered by the fog they felt their way forward, avoiding all British strongpoints and penetrating ever deeper, finding their way to the coveted gun batteries. Behind them came the supporting waves of infantry.

ON THE RIGHT of the Fifth Army front was the III Corps (58th, 18th and 14th Divisions) under the command of Lieutenant General Sir Richard Butler. His force sat astride the Oise valley, which the French had assured Gough was impassable. Unfortunately the 'marshes' proved to be somewhat illusionary, while the Oise River and Canal were all but dry that spring. The necessity to cover this sector stretched the already thin line and Butler's three divisions were to be faced by seven divisions of the German Eighteenth Army. As insufficient work had been done on the defences they were extremely exposed.

When the attack developed on the front of the 173rd Brigade of the 58th Division just south of the Oise they found themselves all but helpless. Their front covered some 5,000 yards and the outposts were scattered hundreds of yards apart. In this sector the Germans varied their time of assault and began their attack as early as 0610. Whenever the blow fell, the isolated company commanders in the front line had not the slightest clue of what was going on and could do little to counter the German assault.

At 7 a.m., the mist was so thick that we could not see 10 yards. All phone communication was cut and we couldn't see the visual lamps on account of the mist. At 7.05 a.m. a heavy barrage fell on my sector and lasted an hour. Immediately it lifted I went to my battle headquarters at the keep. At 8 a.m. I received a note from the battalion on my left, saying that their right had been driven in. I moved a platoon to cover my left flank. I sent two runners to battalion headquarters but discovered later that they were captured. A few minutes later a runner came from Mr Gibson (my right platoon commander) saying that he was being attacked from the front and south and north – at the same time hostile machine guns opened up on the keep from the rear. From this I gathered that, taking advantage of the thick mist, the enemy had succeeded in getting through the gaps in our line and encircled our posts. I had no news from the centre post (Mr Dixon) and runners were unable to get through.[16]

Captain Maurice Harper, 2/2nd Battalion, London Regiment, 173rd Brigade, 58th Division

Some of the outposts and redoubts fought on, but the Germans moved between them leaving any pockets of resistance to the men that followed.

Next in line to the south were the 18th and 14th Divisions who found it impossible to hold back the mighty rush of the German offensive. Here, too, desperate deeds were done: some became famous, while others lacked witnesses and the heroic defenders perished anonymously. Of course, many surrendered after only a token fight when they realised it was hopeless. As the casualties mounted it was not only the 'front line' infantry that suffered.

One group of men were the stretcher bearers and medical orderlies of the Royal Army Medical Corps and they were well aware that they would soon be rushed off their feet. One of them, Private James Brady of the 43rd Field Ambulance, was in a forward-post deep dugout hacked out of the face of a lime quarry near Essigny. There were three compartments: one for the medical officer, another with two-tier wire bunks for the men and a middle part that might be described as the kitchen/cookhouse/lounge – with nothing except empty ammunition boxes to sit on.

We awoke to the thunder of a thousand guns and the shattering crash of a storm of shells upstairs. The place was in darkness and the gas

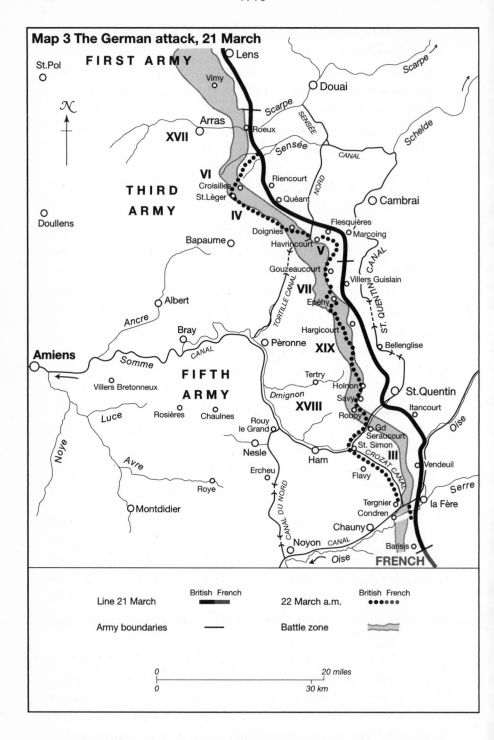

Map 3 The German attack, 21 March

FIRST ARMY

St.Pol

Lens

Vimy

Douai

Scarpe

Arras

XVII

Roeux

Scarpe

SENSÉE

Sensée

CANAL

Schelde

THIRD

Doullens

ARMY

VI

Croisilles

St.Lèger

IV

Riencourt

Quéant

NORD

Cambrai

Flesquières

Marcoing

Doignies

Havrincourt

V

Bapaume

Gouzeaucourt

Villers Guislain

TORTILLE CANAL

VII

Epéhy

ST. QUENTIN CANAL

Albert

Ancre

Hargicourt

Bellenglise

Bray

CANAL

Pèronne

XIX

Amiens

Somme

FIFTH

Villers Bretonneux

Tertry

Holnon

St.Quentin

Itancourt

Luce

Rosières

Chaulnes

ARMY

Dmignon

XVIII

Savy

Roupy

Rouy

le Grand

Gd

Seraucourt

Oise

Nesle

St. Simon

III

Vendeuil

Ercheu

CROZAT CANAL

Flavy

Serre

Avre

Roye

CANAL DU NORD

Tergnier

Condren

la Fère

Montdidier

Chauny

Barisis

Noye

Noyon

CANAL

FRENCH

Oise

Line 21 March	British French	22 March a.m.	British French
Army boundaries	——	Battle zone	

0   20 miles

0   30 km

curtain already hung in shreds. A shower of dirt descended on my face. Scared stiff we all tumbled out of our bunks, scrabbled round for tin hats and respirators, looking at the roof, now showing signs of bulging ominously in parts, in spite of being 20 feet underground. I remember hoping that the French sappers who had built our underground home had done a good job of it. Like the rest I dreaded being buried alive.[17]

Private James Brady, 43rd Field Ambulance, Royal Army Medical Corps, 14th Division

To leave their dugout at this point would have been suicide. But as the shells crashed down their chances appeared none to good even if they stayed where they were.

An almighty crash and a cloud of dust: the front entrance of the dugout had been blown in by a direct hit – obviously a 5.9″. Instantly the place was engulfed in choking fumes and everybody started to cough. All we could do was wait for the dust to settle. Again I felt that horrible, nerve-sapping fear of being buried alive grip my bones. It took me some minutes to recover. Tension was universal and I suggested a game of solo, cleared the table and sorted the cards. The game started, I taking a seat on an upturned ammo box at the foot of the stairs, so that by tipping backwards I could see up the stairs through the tattered gas curtains to the grey mists. Cunningham was still gibbering in the corner – he had a wife and three kids back home in Northampton. Andy Chapman sat on his bunk looking sadly pensive.[18]

Private James Brady, 43rd Field Ambulance, Royal Army Medical Corps, 14th Division

This was not *sangfroid*. Their game was a desperate effort to keep their minds off what was going to happen next. While they played, the barrage began to lift and move deeper into the British lines. They guessed that this meant the German assault was underway but that was all they knew. Unbeknownst to them the outposts just in front of them were fighting bravely, particularly around the village of Urvillers, which held out until 1600, but infiltration tactics rendered such resistance all but irrelevant. The Germans soon managed to slip through the boundary between the 14th Division and the 36th Division to the north. They exploited this gap, feeding in troops behind the British outpost line and swooping down quickly to the south, cutting behind the 14th Division and liaising with other small columns that had squeezed their way between the outposts. Private James Brady and his nervous comrades would not be safe much longer in their dugout.

To the north of the III Corps was the XVIII Corps (36th, 30th and 61st Divisions) commanded by Lieutenant General Sir Ivor Maxse. These three divisions held a frontage of just over 9 miles across the valley of the upper reaches of the Somme looking across to the town of St Quentin and were faced by fourteen German divisions. As we have seen, their forward defensive positions had had considerable work, not all of it fruitful, and the end result was not entirely in accordance with the BEF defensive guidelines. The former front line was not occupied by small posts that would fall back if attacked, but contained a line of redoubts designed to actively resist the German advance. Unfortunately, these redoubts were an obvious temptation for units to fight it out in the Forward Zone, which exposed the garrisons to destruction, rather than the originally intended delaying tactics prior to the *real* resistance in the Battle Zone.

The Germans swirled onwards towards the line of redoubts, which they reached within twenty minutes. Here they were meant to have been slaughtered by the artillery, but the British gunners were both blinded by the fog and suffering the after-effects of the severe pounding they had taken from the German guns. In the few minutes before the first Germans arrived Captain Charles Miller of the 2nd Royal Inniskilling Fusiliers found himself in a real quandary. He had never had the remotest confidence in the strongpoint occupied by his men and, as the shells had rained down, he was convinced that timing would be everything if he and his men were not to be caught like rats in a trap. But his senses were in turmoil: deafened by the shell explosions and blinded by the fog he found it extremely difficult to find rational grounds on which to make a judgement.

> One consideration was paramount, and that was that we must not be caught in the deep dugout when the enemy got into our bit of trench. I burnt my maps and papers and then put myself on the top stair of the dugout with the men behind me ready to dash out the moment the barrage seemed to lift at all. The noise was terrific, but I came to the conclusion that either there was some flaw in their battery work and our position was not getting its full share or else the barrage was

beginning to move forward – it was impossible to tell which! The night was alive with noise and explosions everywhere, but I thought it advisable to get out into the trench. The first thing I did was to send one party to the 'stop' at one end of the trench and I took a party to the 'stop' at the other end. I had hardly got there before I saw my first German. He was just at the point where the wire ended outside the 'stop'. It would have been impossible to know whether he was German or British on account of the mist, but the shape of his helmet was unmistakable. He disappeared into the mist again before I had time to fire, but was followed by another and another, and we proceeded to shoot them as fast as they appeared. What had happened was obvious: the attacking Germans had come on the semi-circular belt of wire that surrounded our post. They could not see that it was comparatively weak and therefore were feeling their way round it. Groping their way through the murk they hardly knew from where they were being shot.[19]

Captain Charles Miller, 2nd Battalion, Royal Inniskilling Fusiliers, 109th Brigade, 36th Division

For the moment the advantage lay with the defenders even though when Miller rushed along to the other 'stop' at the far end of his trench he found the same situation, as his men sniped at the ghostly figures scuttling past in the mist.

I had no illusions: it was obvious that they were through and advancing in vast numbers – as soon as the mist rose we should get what was coming to us. As a matter of fact the first attackers were into the trench long before the mist lifted. I was so occupied with the flanks that I barely saw them before they appeared out of the mist and leapt down into the trench. In a moment we were all mixed up in hand-to-hand fighting. I had two men coming at me with their bayonets, one of whom I think I shot with my revolver, while a sergeant standing just behind me shot the other at point-blank range with his rifle barrel over my shoulder. But almost at the same second a German stick bomb came whistling into the trench from the parapet right into the bunch of us, and killed or wounded practically the whole lot of us – English and German alike. Whether it was actually this bomb or a bayonet stab that gave me the wound in my neck I don't know – it might have been either. For a moment we were clear but there was a nasty little shambles round us – Sergeant Adcock, who had just saved my life, having his head blown off. There was a tremendous hubbub further down the trench and on my way there I got into a private duel with a German carrying a flamethrower. I got the best of that and then came into another shambles. There again we had settled them for the moment, but a lot of our men were out too. I felt awfully weak and discovered that a river of blood was flowing from my neck. I tried to bandage it, but the bandage wouldn't hold. In my giddiness I realised that the sun was getting up, which meant the end of us. Before they attacked again they brought up some trench mortars and knocked seven bells out of us – then swarmed into the trench. By that time there were only a handful of us left on our feet and all I suppose wounded. I got another wound from a stick bomb, which put a bit of metal into my thigh. Before I collapsed I tried to give the surrender signal, and hope I succeeded thereby in saving a few lives. We had done our best.[20]

Captain Charles Miller, 2nd Battalion, Royal Inniskilling Fusiliers, 109th Brigade, 36th Division

Some of the redoubts did hold out for a considerable time, but Miller in a sense was right – in doing so the numbers killed and wounded were certainly increased. The men that chose to fight to the last were incredibly brave, but their nuisance value to the Germans was localised.

The most famous of these last-ditch stands was that of the 16th Manchesters under the command of Lieutenant Colonel Wilfrith Elstob at what would become known as Manchester Hill, just outside the outskirts of St Quentin. Elstob was a 29-year-old former school-teacher who had been granted a commission in the 16th Manchesters on its formation in September 1914. Soon he was in command of a company and he had already won a Military Cross and been slightly wounded during the successful assault on Montauban on 1 July 1916. Elstob took over the command of the battalion after the death of its colonel in action in October 1916. More heavy fighting followed at Arras and Ypres in 1917 and, indeed, for a few months Elstob was acting brigadier in command of the 90th Brigade. Although he was young he had acquired a wealth of experience and a reputation for fearlessness under fire. When briefing his men before moving into the trenches he made his position crystal clear:

It must be impressed upon all troops actually allotted to the defence of any position, whether in the outpost system or the main battle position, that so far as they are concerned there is only one degree of resistance and that is to the last round and to the last man. Here we fight and here we die.[21]

Lieutenant Colonel Wilfrith Elstob, 16th Battalion, Manchester Regiment, 90th Brigade, 30th Division

He further remarked on seeing the band going back down the lines, 'Those are the only fellows that will come out alive.'[22]

Manchester Hill was a small hillock that offered a good field of fire in several directions. It also covered the main St Quentin–Savy road. Behind it was the Brown Quarry, which offered good protection from German shells and was hence filled with various dugouts. The 16th Manchesters were spread out on either side of the hill but the Manchester Hill Redoubt itself was garrisoned by 'D' Company and the battalion headquarters. They had been well wired in and the trenches were studded with machine-gun posts and bomb stops. But here, as elsewhere, all this had been rendered redundant by the fog. When it became evident that the attack was coming Elstob moved his headquarters from the quarry into their dugout on the hill and prepared to fight to the last.

The German attack began at about 0900 when a scream told the story of a sentry being bayoneted by the approaching stormtroopers. The fight that followed has passed into legend. The Colonel seemed to be everywhere, inspiring his men to keep up their resistance long after hope had gone. Although the phone lines were cut, an underground cable rendered a 90th Brigade headquarters staff officer an aural witness.

At about eleven o'clock Colonel Elstob informed me that the Germans had broken through and were swarming round the Redoubt. At about 2 p.m. he said that most of his men were killed or wounded, including himself; that they were all getting deadbeat, that the Germans had got into the redoubt and hand-to-hand fighting was going on. He was still quite cheery. At 3.30 he was spoken to on the telephone and said very few were left and that the end was nearly come. After that no answer could be got.[23]

Anon Staff Officer, Headquarters, 90th Brigade, 30th Division

By the end Elstob had been wounded three times, fighting not only with his revolver but also grabbing a rifle and bayonet and flinging bombs alongside his men. Private Horace Hardman was apparently one of the last to see Elstob alive after being sent to his deep dugout at the rear of the redoubt.

> We remained there for about half an hour; then the commanding officer went up to see how things were. He came back wounded in the head, but after having the wound dressed he carried on, being a fearless kind of man. Then the wires of communication were broken by the Germans and I was therefore told to go down to the front line to see if there was anything to report. On getting part way I heard a sound of shouting coming down the trench. I had no rifle with me, but had two bombs, so I waited to see who it was coming down. It was the Sergeant Major from the front line, who told me that all the men in the post had been taken prisoners. I reported this to the CO, who then gave orders for all to stand to and hold the Manchester Redoubt to the last man. He then went out with his revolver, and we were firing and bringing up bombs. We managed to hold the redoubt until 3 p.m.; then Jerry seemed to come from all directions. The CO's last words were, 'Here goes the gallant Sixteenth!' Then he was shot through the head. We were taken prisoners.[24]
>
> Private Horace Hardman, 16th Battalion, Manchester Regiment, 90th Brigade, 30th Division

Wilfrith Elstob was awarded the honour of a posthumous VC, but he has no known grave. The battalion history refers proudly to the fact that of 168 men who went into action with him only seventeen survived. This is, however, something of a misnomer – only seventy-three of the 16th Manchesters have been identified as dying on that day, of which only about half can have been on Manchester Hill*. The rest fought as long as they could, which for most men, in contrast to the truly indomitable Elstob, meant until there was no longer any hope, at which point they quietly surrendered. This amounted to three-quarters of the battalion. Of all the last-ditch fights carried out in the Forward

* I am indebted to the work of M. Middlebrook, *The Kaiser's Battle* (London: Allen Lane, 1978), p.333.

Zone redoubts the story of the 16th Manchesters has always attracted the most attention, but in reality it was not that much different from the general pattern. There were great deeds of courage, but in the end few men fought to the death, nor were there many sensible reasons for them to do so. The Germans had already broken through; indeed, in many sectors they were already assaulting the Battle Zone.

Behind the 16th Manchesters, tucked away in the Brown Quarry, were Lieutenant Robert Petschler and his party of sappers and stray elements of both infantry and gunners. They had been meant to get back to safety as quickly as possible but had been caught in their dugouts by the bombardment. The minutes became hours, but still the shelling continued. Every so often wounded men seeking sanctuary joined them in the dugout and brought the unwelcome news that the Germans were inside the redoubt and within 1,000 yards of the quarry.

> We dressed their wounds as best we could by the light of a few candles and laid them on stretchers. The dark of the tunnels, the moaning of the wounded men and the sound of the shells bursting on top made the tunnel a ghastly place. Soon after ten o'clock a gunner found his way into the tunnels and said he had come from his battery, which was only about 600 yards away in the wood. He had volunteered to deliver a message to his headquarters in Savy village, but owing to the shelling it had taken him several hours to reach the short distance to our tunnels. He said all the guns had been knocked out, their ammunition blown up, most of the men were wounded and there was only one officer left. This battery, which I had heard firing intermittently, must have been captured soon after. About eleven o'clock another wounded man arrived who had come from Manchester Redoubt and said that the Germans were attacking the redoubt and that it was nearly surrounded.[25]
>
> Lieutenant Robert Petschler, 201st Field Company, Royal Engineers, 30th Division

Their situation had moved inexorably from grim to desperate. Noticing a marked diminution in the shelling in the direction of Savy, Petschler decided that the Germans must have captured it and that if they wanted to avoid capture they must leave the 'safety' of the dugouts and make a break for it. Issuing careful instructions he shepherded his flock out into the maelstrom.

I waited outside until all the men were out and then rushed up to the front to lead the way. The unfortunate wounded we had to leave behind in the tunnels as it was impossible to take them. A shell burst amongst us and we came under machine-gun fire. Some of the men showed signs of exhaustion and when the shell scattered them they disappeared into shell holes and a trench close by. I shouted at them to follow on. Many shells burst within a few feet of us and many times lumps of shrapnel would scream past but just miss. Unfortunately, the barrage commenced to creep forwards with us and we also came within the range of the heavier guns. It was a foggy morning and the most you could see was about 60 yards ahead. We did not know where the gaps in the wire were and often had to scramble through belts of high wire entanglements that were as much as 20 to 30 feet deep – all our clothes were in ribbons. Most of the men had discarded their packs and equipment. Presently, to my relief, we entered the Battle Zone trenches.[26]

Lieutenant Robert Petschler, 201st Field Company, Royal Engineers, 30th Division

Nearby was Lance Corporal Harry Hopthrow who was responsible for a relay station transmitting wireless and power-buzzer signals from the front-line positions, including the 16th Manchesters. As the German bombardment increased in vigour the men moved their wireless equipment and cables down into a deep sap dug into the side of Savy Quarry.

We had a grenade trap at the bottom. We were down in the sap and we always kept a chap on top and he obviously didn't know quite what was going on and he came down and said, 'My word we're doing well today, there's a lot of prisoners gone by!' This didn't quite ring true, so one of us went up to look and we found that the 'prisoners' were all carrying bayonets, in other words they were the German main force. They were on the road that was 200 to 300 yards from the place where we were inside the quarry. We kept communications, we didn't send many messages, this sort of thing was badly organised. Nobody came along to look at us and then a white dog appeared. Where it came from I don't know. He came running towards us. That prompted two or three German soldiers to come towards us as well. When you knew you were being captured what you had to do was to send a message, 'ZZZ'.

I made a general call to all stations and sent, 'ZZZ'. We saw them coming and we set to and destroyed our instruments. They came and took over, came down the sap and sat down with us – very little communication, because we hadn't each other's language. There was no question of resistance; there were five of us and battalions of Germans going by. We offered them some spare food and cigarettes. Those three chaps were on to a very good thing – they were getting out of the war, they'd got a bunch of prisoners, they could always say that was why they were down there![27]

Lance Corporal Harry Hopthrow, Signal Service, Royal Engineers, 30th Division

Early that evening as they still sat in the sap they heard shells crashing around them. By this time the usual waifs and strays had collected together in Hopthrow's dugout, still guarded by the nervous Germans who had no intention of going anywhere till it was safer outside.

We suggested it was theirs and the warrant officer shook his head and said, 'No it's yours!' Sure enough it was! A heavy trench mortar bombardment from the 17th Manchesters. Very shortly afterwards they came over and they just reached the end of the quarry – just reached us! They arrived, they got on top of the ridge at the edge of the quarry. As soon as they realised our troops were on top the Germans threw their arms on the table. We didn't bother about them, it was getting dusk and I decided it was time we were getting out. I led the four of us, none of the others came; we made a dash for it. Some small arms fire, not aimed fire, but we got through it.[28]

Lance Corporal Harry Hopthrow, Signal Service, Royal Engineers, 30th Division

FOR THE ARTILLERY up and down the Fifth and Third Army fronts the position was by then even more desperate. Since the bombardment had begun they had been under near continuous fire, which ranged from a full-blooded bombardment to harassing fire. But as it got lighter and visibility improved a little, more and more British batteries managed to struggle into some kind of action. There were still severe problems to be overcome. All the artillery lines of communication – to its own observers, to its headquarters and to the surrounding units – had been broken. This was made worse by the loss of its aerial observation. One of the key roles of the Royal Flying Corps was to provide detailed artillery observation via wireless sets located with the batteries. Unfortunately, in the dense fog the aircraft rarely got off the ground. The few that did found it impossible to work out what was happening in the lingering mists. The front line was constantly moving and the gunners were left to guess where it might be based, as much on rumours from passing troops as on any concrete evidence.

> About 7 a.m. a murky sort of light began to creep through, just in time to save the remnants of our self-respect. It being possible to see, we got out, made some show of setting up new aiming pickets and scraped the guns as clear of soil as we could. Then we started firing on trench targets, full tilt. Having something to do, and being able to see, pulled everyone together and we were soon firing three rounds to the minute from each gun. The most heartening thing of all was the sound of one of our 60-pounders, which opened fire just about the time we did, its whip-crack being audible above everything. Then in a few moments, a shell from our rear section passed overhead and the men shouted good luck to it as it went. They chalked messages on their own shells for Jerry – we soon had to slow the rate of fire as the guns got so hot. Their tails were well and truly up.[29]
>
> Lieutenant Brian Bradnack, 122nd Siege Battery, 66th Brigade, Royal Garrison Artillery

When the Germans attacked, every gun that could opened up. It was a tradition of the Royal Artillery always to respond to appeals from the infantry, whether attacking, or as in this case, desperately defending.

> 'SOS lines, gun fire!' was shouted from our battery command post and we realised that the German infantry were out of their trenches and advancing. I sat beside the gun barrel and each time the gun was loaded I checked the dial sight and angle of sight bubble, then fired the gun. This action lasted until most of the ammunition was expended. The gun barrel was hot, and Grey, who had been setting the range in the No. 2 seat, and I were spattered in black oil. I was almost deaf. Apparently it was all of no avail as the sergeant shouted, 'Prepare to move!'[30]
>
> Gunner Percy Creek, 'A' Battery, 104th Brigade, Royal Field Artillery

When Second Lieutenant Cyril Dennys eventually got to his forward observation post he was delighted to find that, against all the odds, it was not only intact but still had a well-buried cable telephone line leading directly back to the guns.

> I saw grey figures, obviously German, going to and fro in Dum and Dee Copses. This struck me as a target worth having and I phoned through to brigade and said that I could see German infantry massing in these copses. I think they were preparing to make an attack on one of the surviving redoubts. The brigade turned all the surviving guns that we had onto the two copses. There was a most gratifying sight from my point of view – flashes, then large bursts of smoke and debris. When the smoke cleared away I could see no more German infantry at all; I hoped that I had got them, I was really feeling rather vindictive. I'd been frightened in the morning and it was time I frightened somebody else![31]
>
> Second Lieutenant Cyril Dennys, 212th Siege Battery, Royal Garrison Artillery

Lieutenant Allfree found that the close-range map so carefully prepared by his major began to be called into urgent use as the Germans punched through the British outpost lines and came under direct observation from the Major's position on the ridge just in front of the guns.

> Presently a target came through from the Major. I looked up the line and elevation on my list – may have made some slight correction for the error of the day – gave the guns the switch from zero line and the order, 'First charge, elevation 10 degrees!' and fired. It represented an alarmingly short range with a 6″ howitzer. Corrections and other targets came through, but soon my difficulty was to get a sufficiently low elevation on the guns to hit the targets and yet to clear the bank in front of the guns. I am afraid the rounds, for the most part, went over the Huns whom the Major could see swarming over. And so the Huns continued to advance, we continued to fire and the outlook was anything but rosy.[32]
>
> Lieutenant Edward Allfree, 111th Siege Battery, Royal Garrison Artillery

The most ominous sign for the gunners was the sight of the infantry falling back past the gun positions. It was apparent that things must be going very badly indeed in front of them.

No guns were firing from our side. Up the road, past our guns, hurried about a dozen infantry boys. 'Come on, come on!' they shouted, 'Nothing can stop the bastards!' They looked wild as they passed. We stayed and fired a round or two. As far as we could find out all lines to our battery had been cut. The last order was to continue firing. This was from our officer down the dugout – we never saw him after that! Half a dozen more infantry passed us. They stopped for a couple of minutes. They said they had fired until the machine guns were red hot. They had slaughtered wave after wave of Germans but still they came on.[33]

Bombardier William Pressey, 315th Battery, Royal Field Artillery

The infantry stories may or may not have been true, but the fact that they were retreating in confusion was certainly evident. Up and down the line the batteries found themselves increasingly isolated and vulnerable to being overrun. Thus 111th Siege Battery was soon warned by its forward observation post that the Germans were feeling their way round its flanks and would soon completely encircle it. Fortunately, soon afterwards, the battery was ordered to pull out and retire to the prepared position at the rear. The horses came dashing up, and the gunners had begun harnessing up the guns when there was an added contribution to the general prevailing chaos.

To add to our discomfort a Boche aeroplane came sweeping down low over the battery, the black cross on the bottom of the lower plane showing up very distinctly. He flew backwards and forwards two or three times, rattling his machine gun at us; causing us to take cover under the bank and anything that presented any sort of cover. Then he made off in search of other game. He was evidently enjoying himself immensely. He must have seen much to cheer his soul today – many a tempting target.[34]

Lieutenant Edward Allfree, 111th Siege Battery, Royal Garrison Artillery

This was a common occurrence as the visibility improved for the well-trained *Schlachtstaffeln* two-seaters skimming above the trenches, whose pilots were taught to seek out exactly such tempting targets. The gunners were not amused when they found that in addition to shell fire they had to put up with such gnat-like attentions. Some even plotted a revenge of sorts.

In the afternoon a Jerry plane flew over us a couple of times. We kept quiet and lay still beside the guns. No shells were being fired from our side at all and we thought everybody had left us. On the plane's next visit he sprayed round us with his machine guns, and although the bullets cut the ground up and pranged off the steel gun shield, he didn't hit one of us. We all had rifles and I had a revolver too. I said, 'Get the rifles ready, chaps, and we'll surprise him next time!' 'Here he comes!' shouted the cook. And just like cowboys shooting at Indians through wagon wheels, we waited for him to dive. It was a novelty for our boys to use rifles: some had never used one before. Rifle bolts being slid back and forth, shots of ours, his shots, and the noise of his engine made a terrifying couple of minutes. Whether we hit him we never knew, but he didn't come back again.[35]

Bombardier William Pressey, 315th Battery, Royal Field Artillery

With great difficulty Pressey's guns were eventually pulled out by their horses.

Meanwhile, an accident in moving off had comprehensively broken one team's harness and a howitzer would clearly have to be left behind. This was always a sensitive issue to any Royal Artillery officer as the guns were his regimental 'colours'. Tame surrender of the guns was not usually considered an option, but in this case higher authorities intervened.

Orders had been received that guns were not to be destroyed, should it be found necessary to leave them, as it was hoped that it might be possible to retake them again very soon. Therefore, Haley, the gunner artificer, was given orders to let the oil out of the buffer and the air out of the recuperator. While he was doing this, the Major had seized a pickaxe and was bashing the vital parts of the air compressor pump, to prevent it being used for refilling the recuperator. We were now satisfied that the Hun would not be able to fire the gun, but to make a complete job of it, the Major ordered Haley to remove the breech block and drop it down the officers' latrine.[36]

Lieutenant Edward Allfree, 111th Siege Battery, Royal Garrison Artillery

A few hours later they had to make another retreat. On this occasion the officer of the 111th Siege Battery engaged in a piece of unprincipled legerdemain that must have caused fury amongst the other batteries in his brigade.

> Major Penrose of 245th Battery, with perhaps a certain amount of foresight and cleverness had arranged for horse teams to come and pull his guns out. Leigh, while waiting for our FWD lorries, which did not turn up, saw the horse teams come up. They would have to pass our guns to get to 245th Battery's guns. He at once stopped the drivers and asked them if they were looking for some 6″ howitzers. They replied they were. 'Oh, good!' says Leigh, 'Here they are!' and he introduced them to our guns, which were soon hitched up and off they went. Result: 245th lost all their guns, but one! Further result: 245th Battery much annoyed with 111th Battery! Leigh, of course, said he was very sorry and that he did not know the teams were for them. If they had not lost their guns, we should have lost ours. As I am sure guns were more effective in the hands of 111th than in the hands of 245th Battery, it was really for the good of the Allied cause![37]
>
> Lieutenant Edward Allfree, 111th Siege Battery, Royal Garrison Artillery

To add insult to injury, the sole remaining gun of the benighted 245th Battery was handed over to the 111th Battery to replace the gun it had been forced to leave behind at Épéhy. It was probably logical, but the 245th must have really hated the sheer cheek and opportunism of the insouciant Major Leigh.

Many batteries found themselves engulfed as the Germans swirled around them. The general lack of communications meant there was no way of disseminating the warnings of the German approach. Lieutenant Brian Bradnack and the 122nd Siege Battery stuck to their guns until about 1600 – and then found it was too late to move.

> There was hardly a thought of moving our guns: instead we waited for the counter-attack, which we had been led to expect would be provided. It was on his own initiative that the Major did eventually give the order to pull out – just twenty minutes too late! Just as we got our first gun near the road, an advanced German machine gun opened fire at almost point-blank range, knocking out Sergeant Upton in the first burst. The only thing to do, we did rapidly: melt away into the

undergrowth and in short rushes running for the rear after we had sunk the breech blocks in a pond nearby.[38]

Lieutenant Brian Bradnack, 122nd Siege Battery, 66th Brigade, Royal Garrison Artillery

In this way hundreds of British guns were lost in the chaotic retreat.

TO THE NORTH OF the XVIII Corps came the XIX Corps (24th Division and 66th Division) under the command of Lieutenant General Herbert Watts. These two divisions found themselves facing nine German divisions. Here again the forward posts were soon over-run and an account from Private Reginald Backhurst of the 8th Royal West Kents gives an idea of the confusion pervading that morning in the vulnerable outposts in No Man's Land. As the bombardment moved away from them, towards the rear, the men realised the German attack would be following hard on the coat-tails of the shells.

The corporal said we must get back to our front line. We got out of the trench and ran to find the openings in our wire – we were forced to run in a zigzag fashion about 120 yards. When we got to our front line the machine-gunners were cleaning the gun and soon had it firing again. There was no target to fire at, but firing into the mist might do some damage. The corporal said, 'Where is your rifle?' I had to say I had left it at the outpost. He then said, 'You must go and get it!' I stood for a while thinking about it. The corporal had given me other things to carry; that must have been the reason for me forgetting my rifle. 'I must go!' I thought. So out of the trench I got and ran as hard as I could. I got back and nearly into the trench when a terrific blast shot me into the air. I felt my legs still running, but they weren't touching the ground. I fell into the trench, felt myself all over: I could see no blood, felt no pain and in a short time I was OK.[39]

Private Reginald Backhurst, 8th Battalion, Royal West Kent Regiment, 72nd Brigade, 24th Division

There were some pockets of desperate resistance but the 24th Division Forward Zone was nevertheless soon overrun. Far more common was the fate of Private Backhurst and his companions. When they discovered the Germans had surrounded them, their corporal led the way down into a dugout. Here they hid hoping for the best as the Germans overran their trench.

> The Germans were soon at the top throwing hand grenades down. Two of our party were wounded. After this it seemed to get much quieter and no noises were coming from the top. The corporal said he would go to the top and see if there was a chance to get back to our lines. He wanted another to go with him. They almost got to the top when rifle fire brought them stumbling down – the corporal wounded. Soon more grenades came down. By this time we had found a recess or two leading off the passage. We took shelter in them and the blasts went by. After a while the Germans shouted down, 'Come up with your hands up!' We realised it was no use staying down there so we went up the steps into the trench. I was now 19 years old, but when I saw the young German troops they must have been at least two years younger. They were sitting on both sides of the trench and we were pushed and punched along the trench.[40]
>
> Private Reginald Backhurst, 8th Battalion, Royal West Kent Regiment, 72nd Brigade, 24th Division

Their neighbours in the 66th Division had a similar fate. Sergeant Joe Fitzpatrick of the 2/6th Manchesters was with a support line Lewis gun team covering a communication trench winding back from the front line. They, too, were swiftly taken prisoners after a token resistance.

> I said, 'Come on, get ready!' Two officers came along, I think they were as drunk as lords, myself, because they were waving their revolvers and singing, 'Here's the Boche! Here's the Boche! The Boche is here!' I thought, 'You silly buggers!' They went up the front. I was waiting and waiting. Jerry must have come past the front line and I looked right and left and I saw them swooping down the valley! The Lieutenant sent an order, 'Tell Sergeant Fitz to bring twenty men up!' I got about a dozen and says, 'Come on with me!' I'm walking up this communication trench and my brain's working all the time, I said to myself, 'You're a silly bugger leading the way!' So I said to the runner, 'Run on and tell him we're coming!' He hadn't gone half a minute before he came running back: no tin hat, no rifle, 'They're here, Sergeant! They're here!' I looked and I saw this head, so I let go with my rifle, 'BANG!' I looked round and they'd scarpered! I don't blame them really! I ran

back and I got behind my Lewis gun team and I'm saying, 'Keep the bastards there – keep on that opening!' I've got my rifle and bayonet in my left hand and 'BANG!' I thought I'd lost all my fingers on my left hand. My nose hit the floor, I rolled into the trench, got my phial of iodine, broke it, smeared it over and put a bandage on it. I turned round, I picked a rifle up and I got firing away to my left. No need to take aim! You only had to fire straight at them! I must have done about 100 rounds; changed the rifle when it was white hot! I looked behind me and he's coming back up the valley, I thought, 'Well we're buggered here! We've had it, we've had our chips!' I turned to the left and I saw a Jerry officer 30 yards away, the other side of the wire. I always carried my cap up my shirt so I threw my helmet away, put me cap on and discarded my equipment and I walked through the wire.[41]

Sergeant Joe Fitzpatrick, 2/6th Battalion, Manchester Regiment, 199th Brigade, 66th Division

Neither the 24th nor the 66th Divisions were able to stop the Germans sweeping through with such speed that they were engaging the Battle Zone by 1100.

Next in line to the north, were the VII Corps (16th, 21st and 9th Divisions) under the command of Lieutenant General Sir Walter Congreve, who was responsible for defending the front line that had formed after the Battle of Cambrai in 1917. The corps was faced by ten German divisions. On the 16th Division front the Germans attacked slightly ahead of schedule, breached the forward defences and had the Battle Zone under attack as early as 0930. The 21st Division did slightly better and a particular fight developed around and to the north of the town of Peizière. A sterling defence was also made of the Vaucelette Farm Redoubt, which although in the Forward Zone had been specifically designated for serious defence. For all that it was only a couple of hours before the Germans overwhelmed the division.

BY NOON, all along the Fifth Army front, the Germans were hammering against the Battle Zone. This boded ill, for although the Forward Zone was not really meant to be held, shortage of resources, coupled with the still ingrained reluctance to give up ground, meant that it had by far the best prepared defences of the three zones facing the Germans. The next phase of the battle would be crucial. Yet the German advance formations had lost some significant advantages: the mists were fast fading away, which exposed them to the British machine-gunners and the fire of the Royal Artillery. They were also moving beyond the range of the bulk of their own field artillery and trench mortars. The German heavy guns were still part of the equation, but for any massed artillery support the troops would have to wait until the guns could be brought up. One consolation was that the Royal Artillery was not able to oppose them as effectively as usual. The battlefield was strewn with retreating British troops, falling back in no kind of order and the existence of pockets of British resistance made it difficult to organise any intensive artillery support without the risk of killing their own men.

As the hordes of German troops fell on the Battle Zone the fighting was intense but in some sectors the British line was unable to withstand the pressure. The worst affected area was on the III Corps front where the villages of Benay and Essigny lay on the Essigny Plateau in front of the Crozat Canal. The 14th Division was simply unable to hold on as the Germans burst through and swirled around it to seize the high ground. For Private James Brady and his comrades in their first-aid post dugout behind Essigny the end was sudden.

> There came an unholy 'BANG!' in the stairway, showering the dugout with acrid smoke and dust. I guessed it was a hand grenade – and I was right! Lucky for me the thing had exploded halfway down the stairway otherwise I would have caught the full blast. Then there was a com-motion upstairs and a guttural voice screamed, 'Come up Tommy! *Raus! Raus!*' Simultaneously a revolver cracked out, the bullet slapping into a sandbag inches from my foot. We filed upstairs, our hands held high above our heads, to be greeted by a group of youngsters looking grim and threatening, bayonets fixed, rifles shoulder slung, each with a hand grenade swinging from his right hand. Some had pistols. My tongue felt like a dried frog.[42]
>
> Private James Brady, 43rd Field Ambulance, Royal Army Medical Corps, 14th Division

As they finally emerged from the dugout the fog had largely cleared on the higher ground of Essigny Plateau and an amazing vista of the battle unfolded before them.

With our hands stretched high above our heads to indicate to oncoming German troops that we were prisoners, we marched forwards towards the German positions, fascinated by the great panorama of battle unfolding before us on the flat plains in front of St Quentin. As far as the eye could see in the thinning mist were vast waves of German soldiers trudging forward over what until a few hours before were the British front-line trenches. Behind them came the scores of small field guns, tended by boy soldiers seemingly barely out of their teens, youngsters with flamethrowers, canisters and hoses at the ready, engineers, signallers, field guns dragged by retching mules, heavier 5.9s on tractors, ammo limbers and gun carriages. Finally, a bewildering display of observation balloons soaring 50 feet in the air attached to tractors and ready to ascend to 1,000 feet if a halt should be called. And all the time the German guns thundered as they continued to pound away at our rear positions. Occasionally a single wayward shell from back beyond our lines whistled over to explode with pitiful ineffectiveness on open ground.[43]

Private James Brady, 43rd Field Ambulance, Royal Army Medical Corps, 14th Division

Although they were prisoners they still had a duty of care to the wounded and were more than willing to assist in picking up the copious numbers of British wounded that littered the battlefield. The sights they saw were as gruesome as they were heart-rending.

There were large numbers of wounded lying about waiting to be picked up by German stretcher bearers and here we readily gave assistance. We found a young private of the Somersets slumped on the roadside, both legs badly shattered and weak from loss of blood. Fashioning a stretcher out of a broken door we carried him for miles, his broken legs dangling over my shoulders as I walked in front, until we reached a German aid post just outside St Quentin. I went across to help another chap I found lying on his side, his left arm crooked round the front of his belly. When I opened his torn shirt his entrails gushed out. I called a doctor, but as we stood there helpless, he died. I took his name and address from his pay book and wrote to his mother after the war – to tell her how peacefully her son had died.[44]

Private James Brady, 43rd Field Ambulance, Royal Army Medical Corps, 14th Division

Amongst the Germans pouring forwards in tens of thousands were the gunners commanded by Leutnant Herbert Sulzbach.

> The limbers come up and we reach our finest hour when Leutnant Knauer gives the order, 'To the front – limber up!' We move through St Quentin at a trot and the British are hardly firing. Everything has gone brilliantly, the sappers have already thrown bridges across the British trenches, the whole supply column is working successfully. We move forward in the second line of advance. The first prisoners are coming though, well-built chaps, with very good uniforms and equipment, all thorough-going 'Tommies' walking along cheekily with a fag in their mouths.[45]
>
> Leutnant Herbert Sulzbach, 63rd Field Artillery Regiment, Imperial German Army

By the end of the day the Germans had cleared the Forward Zone and had made serious inroads into the Battle Zone of the III and XIX Corps of the Fifth Army, although they had not been able to push on far in the XVIII Corps area. Unfortunately, the fall of the Essigny Plateau to the south and the Omignon valley to the north thereby exposed both of the XVIII Corps flanks. When the reports came in Gough had no choice but to order a general retirement of the whole of the III Corps to a line tucked behind the Crozat Canal. The neighbouring XVIII Corps was consequently forced to 'bend back' to maintain a continuous line by withdrawing behind the Somme River along the short sector that ran from near the junction with the Crozat Canal to reconnect with the Battle Zone lines at Roupy. Gough had already ordered forward his immediate reserves but these were proving sadly inadequate in number. And since the 20th and 50th Divisions had been held back well to the west of the Somme it would take them some considerable time to march to the front. At the end of the day the Fifth Army was in crisis.

THE GERMAN PLAN in the Third Army area to the north was reasonably simple: they intended to launch attacks deep into each shoulder of the Flesquières Salient with the intention of pinching it out and dooming all the troops inside it. While their infantry assaults were thus geographically limited, the opening barrage was emphatically not and spread itself liberally right along the Third Army front. This added to the confusion and, as intended, helped mask the German intentions. The only real difference was that the Flesquières Salient itself would be completely saturated with the pernicious mustard gas to generally impede the defenders.

The V Corps (47th, 63rd and 17th Divisions with 19th Division in reserve), commanded by Lieutenant General Sir Edward Fanshawe, which was charged with holding the salient, was only attacked by a series of raids and feint attacks but had to undergo a thorough drenching with mustard gas shells. By the end of the day the corps had suffered over 3,000 casualties. Its continued safety depended on the successful resistance of the VII Corps of the Fifth Army to the south and its neighbours in the IV Corps to the north. As the VII Corps was falling back its situation was already looking grim.

Unfortunately, the IV Corps (51st and 6th Divisions with 25th Division in reserve) commanded by Lieutenant General Sir Montague Harper fared little better. The German troops drove through the Forward Zone before crashing deep into the Battle Zone. The fighting was often of a touch and go nature, as was found by Captain Douglas Wimberley of the 51st Battalion, Machine Gun Corps. His Vickers guns were truly formidable weapons that could whip up a storm of bullets and he managed to hold off the attacks with just a handful of men.

I started running towards my nearest guns and just at that moment the whole of the mist rolled away, almost like a curtain and I saw more Germans than I had ever seen before in my life. They really rather reminded me of men coming away from a football match. I got to my two guns and I found that my machine-gun officer was busy firing one of them. I had nothing else to do and no communications so I decided to fire the other gun myself. We had a most excellent hidden emplacement, a belt-filling machine and a dugout behind us. In the dugout the spare numbers were able to keep filling the belts of the machine guns. I started shooting, firing long bursts of 15 or 20 rounds. I couldn't see the strike of my bullets, but I could soon see when my bullets were effective because wherever I fired the Germans lay down and did not move at all. But, of course, we were in an empty trench in the Corps line and for perhaps 500 yards on either side of us there was nobody at all. I went on firing belt after belt and soon the reserve battalion came up from the back, a place called Velu, and occupied the trench. I must say that when they arrived I felt a great deal better.[46]

Captain Douglas Wimberley, 51st Battalion, Machine Gun Corps, 51st Division

Wimberley had held back the attack in his immediate sector but, as elsewhere, the Germans' malleable persistence enabled them to move round until his machine-gunners had no choice but to fall back.

To the north was the VI Corps (59th, 34th and 3rd Divisions with 40th Division in reserve) commanded by Lieutenant General Sir Aylmer Haldane. In the 59th Division sector the Germans smashed their way right through to the very rear of the Battle Zone – they were almost through. The German attack was not without subtlety for the Germans were intent on funnelling troops into this gap before driving south into the exposed southern flank of the 34th Division. Here the experiences of Captain Robert Johnston in command of a company of 16th Royal Scots located in Tunnel Trench near Croisilles were characteristic. At first he was fortunate in that most of the barrage fell on the artillery positions and other targets located well behind the front line. Some of his men even had time for moments of studied whimsy.

In one of the lulls I observed a sentry peering out into No Man's Land with some intensity. 'What is it?' I asked him. 'I'm thinking, Sir,' he said, 'that it's a fine soft growing morning for the crops!'[47]

Captain Robert Johnston, 16th Battalion, Royal Scots, 101st Brigade, 34th Division

When no attack came Johnston stood down his men at 0800 leaving double sentries to warn them if the Germans attacked. The visibility had reached about 50 yards and was slowly getting better. The battle seemed to be raging on their right flank but Johnston was aware that their turn would come soon enough.

Just after 9 or 9.30 a.m., we saw Boche in fair numbers coming down the hill out of the mist towards us and a few had reached our front line. There was no need to give fire orders. Rapid fire was opened by rifles and Lewis gunners – the noise was deafening. The enemy just disappeared, going down into the cover of the shell craters. Several times the attack seemed to get going again, but inevitably stopped before reaching our old front line.[48]

Captain Robert Johnston, 16th Battalion, Royal Scots, 101st Brigade, 34th Division

A second lull followed, broken by a shower of mortar bombs crashing down all around Tunnel Trench, and soon the men could hear the ominous sound of German hand grenades. By this time both his flanks were exposed and the Germans were using the time-honoured tactics of employing bomb and bayonet to creep along Tunnel Trench towards Johnston's men. Then suddenly the Germans launched a last desperate frontal attack.

At a critical stage in battle the British soldier is not a silent man. Cursing and blaspheming, the Jocks were exposing themselves reck-lessly and they fired round after round at the enemy. When a Lewis gunner near me was hit, I took over the gun and began spraying the Boche some 150 yards away. That attack died away, but it was no time to relax as the noise of exploding grenades on our right was steadily becoming nearer.[49]

Captain Robert Johnston, 16th Battalion, Royal Scots, 101st Brigade, 34th Division

It was all to no avail for Johnston was soon receiving reports that the Germans were not only attacking his bombing blocks to the left and right, but had also been sighted in the trenches behind their position. There was nothing left to do but make a sprint for safety, heading towards the nearby quarry where their battalion headquarters were located.

At the agreed time everyone leapt from his shell hole or trench and made his way in a ragged line over the top towards the support line and the quarry some 800 yards or so from Tunnel Trench. I was going fast and probably one of the first to jump down into a damaged part of the support trench where several shells had demolished the parapet. Then up the other side and off downhill going strongly for the quarry. Vaguely I saw two Germans near me in the support trench and I fired a couple of rounds from my revolver in their general direction. Looking over my shoulder I could see my Jocks coming along in the right direction but spread over an area of 200 yards. Some thirty or forty were fairly close to me. We could hear some machine-gun fire, but it didn't seem to be aimed at us. Still, feeling very exposed on that open hillside, we dashed towards the quarry and safety. Battalion headquarters had been located in it, on and off, all winter. The quarry had a steep face on the side nearest the trenches and the entrance was on the Fontaine–Croisilles road. I turned the corner with a thankful heart – but to my utter horror, confusion and amazement, what faced me was not the battalion headquarters personnel, but a German battery of light artillery with the men dismounted standing to their horses, obviously under cover and awaiting orders. My heart literally jumped into my mouth, the hairs on the back of my neck rose up in fright and I was quite unable to utter a sound. Instinctively I turned off at full speed across the road into the brushwood, mud and craters of the Sensée stream a few yards away, where the willows gave me cover from view.[50]

Captain Robert Johnston, 16th Battalion, Royal Scots, 101st Brigade, 34th Division

With the thirty or so men in his immediate vicinity he burst through and ran up onto Henin Hill. Those who were unable to keep up the cracking pace he set were killed or captured.

In this maze of old trenches on Henin Hill, opposite the entrance to the quarry, we found dozens of soldiers of many regiments all lost in the chaos of battle. There were no officers so far as I could see. No one knew where the Germans were. The loss of their leaders had bewildered the soldiers, who were in good heart, requiring only leaders. Our first task was to open fire on any Germans visible at the rather narrow entrance to the quarry only 200 yards off, and this was soon done. We could not see the guns or horses. I was exercising command through my company sergeant major and various sergeants from a point midway up the hill, when a salvo of enemy shells hit our trench. It killed one man near me, and hit me in the knee. I thought my leg had gone and was unwilling to look at it. However, I was soon bandaged and lay helpless in the bottom of the trench attended by a stretcher bearer – who had no stretcher![51]

Captain Robert Johnston, 16th Battalion, Royal Scots, 101st Brigade, 34th Division

Despite the tight situation Captain Johnston was eventually rescued when darkness fell and carried back to the casualty clearing station.

From north of the River Scarpe there were no infantry attacks but the bombardment stretched right up along the rest of the Third Army line in front of Arras, all along the First Army front in the Béthune area and into the Second Army front around Ypres. Although not as intensive as the 'real' bombardment it was still a concerted barrage. The German effort was staggering in its scale and achievement. By including the whole of the British front, with further diversionary barrages on the French front, the Germans forced a delay on the Allied High Command as they struggled to assess the situation.

UP AND DOWN the Fifth Army and Third Army fronts there was chaos and confusion. The army commanders moved forward their reserve divisions to bolster the sagging sectors of the Battle Zone. For Gough it was apparent that the situation was already one of extreme danger. Other British divisions were earmarked to come to his rescue, but they would take time to get from their current location with First and Second Armies. Meanwhile, Gough's first request to his French neighbours for assistance was for the moment stymied, as the French commander-in-chief Henri Pétain was still concerned that this was just a diversion before a pile-driver attack was launched on his own front. It was not until nearly midnight that Pétain would order his reserves to start moving to the British Fifth Army front – and this would only commence after noon on 22 March. The German diversionary bombardments on the French had borne their fruit.

The reserves were desperately needed to fill gaps that had opened and where necessary make counter-attacks to recapture key tactical features. Despite previous planning or briefings there was great confusion amongst the reserve formations at all levels of command. In many cases there was a dull disbelief that the Germans could have broken through.

Just one of many such reserve formations was the 17th King's Royal Rifle Corps (KRRC) of the 39th Division. Its troops had spent the night well behind the lines at Sorel-le-Grand.

Last night, after a jovial evening in our mess, we went to bed in a wooden hut, with a dim notion of the possibilities of the morrow, but with no special preparations for a 'stand to'. It is 4.30 a.m. of the 21st when we are awoken by a crashing bombardment, and its intensity leaves no room for doubting its purpose. With a feeling of suppressed excitement we are out of bed and dressing quickly, amid a round of chaff and banter. Shrapnel is already bursting heavily over the village and the word is passed to assemble in the valley on the football field, which is almost 'dead' ground. Here we fall in by platoons in the darkness only to find that fourteen of our men have already been hit in the huts by shrapnel.[52]

Second Lieutenant Frank Warren, 17th Battalion, King's Royal Rifle Corps, 117th Brigade, 39th Division

The German bombardment was designed to reach deep behind the front and they were not the only reserve unit surprised to be under fire from heavy shells crashing down that morning.

Our peace was shattered by a tremendous explosion, too near to be ignored. Some humorist blew a few notes on what seemed to be a hunting horn, and we were all outside *tout suite* into an impenetrable mist to discover a large crater made by the shell, which had just missed our hut and had uprooted a tree.[53]

Trooper Arthur Bradbury, Royal Scots Greys, 2nd Cavalry Division

To add to the confusion, despite the mist some of the German aircraft were abroad, their crews risking their lives in appalling flying weather, but taking full advantage of the surprise they could cause by bursting out of nowhere on unsuspecting troops. Their most important targets were the British observation balloons.

A whirring, humming sound – a Boche aeroplane. Four or five more appear out of the mist above the sausage balloon. One hovers, dives with a hail of machine-gun tracer bullets that leave a trail of white smoke. Missed! By Jove! But the balloon is doomed! Another aeroplane banks and seemingly hovers a moment right above its prey, it swoops and turns. There is a thin trail of smoke, then a burst of black fumes and slowly the balloon descends – a mass of flames.[54]

Second Lieutenant Frank Warren, 17th Battalion, King's Royal Rifle Corps, 117th Brigade, 39th Division

For the ordinary soldiers there was a whirlpool of gossip, guesswork and unbridled optimism. The stories came from nowhere, generated by wishful thinking or just a desire to keep talking rather than think of the matter at hand – the likelihood that they would all be fighting for their lives before the day was through.

> There are big rumours of British offensives at Passchendaele, at Lens and where not? The French, 'Have made a big push at Verdun!' So does rumour feed the tired 'Tommy'. All the morning up to midday, the ground has throbbed and quivered with the heavy artillery. Amid it all the larks are singing overhead![55]
>
> Second Lieutenant Frank Warren, 17th Battalion, King's Royal Rifle Corps, 117th Brigade, 39th Division

Eventually the orders came to start moving forward. Many of the soldiers had little idea of where they were going or what they were to do when they got there.

IN THE FINAL ANALYSIS it is evident that the German Army had succeeded in delivering a tremendous blow to the British line on 21 March. The huge concentration of divisions had surged forwards with every advantage given by the foggy conditions. Their successes that day were real and there is no doubt that the British were in severe trouble – especially on the Fifth Army front. The British had badly mishandled their defence of the Forward Zone. They had not really grasped the concept of defence in depth and by both accident and design still fatally over-weighted the Forward Zone. In effect this merely exposed their forward troops to far higher casualties than would have been the case if they had thinned out the garrison and relied on machine guns tucked away in reinforced concrete pillboxes in the German mould. But the British had not had the time, the labour or the resources for such a radical undertaking after taking the ground over from the French barely three months before. The troops may have done better but for the most part it is fair to say that they were unmanned by a combination of the ferocious German bombardment and the blanketing fog, which tore away at their discipline. Many took shelter in dugouts and only emerged when taken prisoner. Even those who fought on certainly did not fight to the last round and the last man. Hopelessly encircled the more enlightened officers realised that further resistance was all but futile, as they had already been bypassed in the fast-moving battle.

The German gains measured from 2,500 yards to 8,000 yards, and all along the line the Forward Zone had been lost. In a sense that was to be expected in a deep defence system, but the breakthrough of the Battle Zone on Essigny Plateau was far more serious. The shortage of troops had left the Battle Zone units tied to a 'passive' defensive role based on occupying what trenches had been completed. The German pattern of a reactive and mobile defence, reliant on strong counter-attacks, was impossible as there were simply not the British troops available. They could only stand and fight; so stand and fight they did.

The casualties on both sides were horrendous. The British suffered some 38,500 casualties, of which not less than 21,000 were prisoners of war and around 7,500 were killed. Over forty battalions had been all but destroyed and over 500 guns had been captured. The Germans had retaken 98½ square miles and some forty-six French villages that they had abandoned under duress in 1917. However, the German Army had also suffered its own grievous losses. Despite the apparent success of the infiltration of the stormtroopers, there were many cases of crude German attack tactics, where tight-packed mass formations stumbled into concentrated machine-gun or artillery fire. By the end of the day the Germans had suffered anywhere between 35,000 to 40,000 casualties, of which around 10,000 to 11,000 were dead. The German Army had undoubtedly achieved a great success on 21 March but it had failed to break through the Battle Zone along most of the front attacked. Nor indeed had it pinched out the Flesquières Salient as intended. But the German pincers still gripped, and the V Corps front line was partially pulled back from the tip of the salient to an Intermediate Line based solidly on the formidable defences of the old German Hindenburg Line between Havrincourt and Hermies. The V Corps was safer on this line, but it still occupied a salient because the units on either side had fallen back even further. The situation here, then, was still in doubt.

Ludendorff reacted to results of the day's fighting by pursuing narrow, tactical rather than strategic considerations: he had never really had a plan for success, more a list of aspirations to be followed as seemed most appropriate. Now, as he realised that von Hutier's Eighteenth Army had advanced the furthest, he decided to reinforce success. Instead of trying to break through and then thrusting in a north-western direction to roll up the British line around Arras as planned, he would reinforce the Eighteenth Army attack to the west, thereby skewing the weight of the whole offensive further south. This was to mark a sea change in Ludendorff's perspective of the battle.

There is no doubt that whatever the British Army could have done the Germans would probably have achieved great things on 21 March. They had invested so much destructive power and so many resources in their offensive that they were almost bound to break through some-where along the line. But the scale of the disaster inflicted on the Fifth Army was certainly exacerbated by the activities of British politicians. The bulk of the blame can be laid squarely on the thin shoulders of Lloyd George. His restriction of manpower resources to Haig and the Western Front had a bitter harvest that day. The British line stretched for some 126 miles, longer than ever before, and it had never been held by so few men and guns per mile of front. Haig and his generals could see this at a glance. Yet Lloyd George had been deaf to their pleas and as a result Haig had been forced to make the hard choices that politicians could evade. He had concentrated his troops to defend the strategic necessities in Flanders and northern France; in consequence, Gough and the Fifth Army had to fend for themselves until the reserves could arrive. That night Haig wrote a letter to the CIGS, Sir Henry Wilson, which summed up the day, at least as far as the British commander-in-chief was concerned.

> This morning at 4 a.m. the enemy started his attack on the wide front we expected. It is hardly necessary to urge the CIGS (for I have repeatedly done so) to insist on the Government producing men for drafts![56]
>
> Field Marshal Sir Douglas Haig, General Headquarters, BEF

The message was clear: this was not Haig's fault, it was the interference in military matters by Lloyd George and his political allies that had brought them to the brink of defeat on the Western Front. Now other men were paying for this interference with their lives.

CHAPTER FOUR

Retreat to the Somme

BEFORE DAWN ON 22 MARCH the British completed their withdrawal of the III Corps front to behind the Crozat Canal and the neighbouring 36th Division of the XVIII Corps behind the Somme River. This involved the destruction of numerous bridges of all shapes and sizes ranging from mighty railway bridges to the humble footbridge. The Crozat Canal was some 30–40 feet across and would be a valuable aid to defence especially given the total inadequacy of the Rear Zone Green Line defences in this sector. During the night the British troops fell back relatively unmolested as the Germans conspicuously declined to obey Ludendorff's directive that they were to press home their attacks overnight.

The Royal Engineers prepared for the destruction of the bridges. As early as January 1918 men had inspected every bridge along the front, assessed the explosives required and placed the requisite charges and fuses under a waterproof cover, ready if needed. Unfortunately, it had not been realised that decisions about when to blow the charges had to be made on the spot by relatively junior officers rather than by higher authorities who were further back at the end of uncertain communications and who had no means of judging the local situation. As a result of the confusion that arose several bridges were not blown up.

The most spectacular incident occurred at the substantial steel-girder bridge at Tugny. Here the Germans were hard on the heels of the 36th Division troops and were pushing across the bridge when the time fuse of the detonating charge unaccountably failed. The sapper officer in charge was Second Lieutenant Cecil Knox and without any apparent hesitation he ran forward under heavy rifle and machine-gun fire, struggled under the bridge where he tore off the failed time fuse and lit the instantaneous fuse. He was well aware of the personal risk he was taking. As a trained civil engineer in his peacetime profession, Knox knew exactly what would happen and just how low his chances of survival were. But miraculously, when the bridge blew up, he survived unscathed and the remnants of the bridge tumbled into the water. He would be awarded the VC for this near suicidal action.

Yet this was only part of a much larger-scale retirement that Gough planned for the Fifth Army. In the absence of any French reinforcements and given the paucity of his own reserves, Gough had decided that the only way to survive over the next few days was by conducting an organised retirement rather than being forced to fight a potentially disastrous, decisive battle trying to hold a brittle front.

> It was now evident that the German attack was so serious that I could not hope to fight it out successfully in the Battle Zone, but must carry out a delaying action, which would aim at saving the Army from complete annihilation, but which would enable it at the same time to maintain an intact, though battered and thin, line in face of the German masses until such time as the British and French Commands could send up sufficient troops to hold the ground.[1]
> General Sir Hubert Gough, Headquarters, Fifth Army

With this firmly in mind he issued his orders to his corps commanders on 22 March:

> In the event of serious hostile attack corps will fight rearguard actions back to forward line of Rear Zone (Green Line), and if necessary to rear line of Rear Zone. Most important that corps should keep close touch with each other and carry out retirement in complete cooperation with each other and corps belonging to Armies on flanks.[2]
> General Sir Hubert Gough, Headquarters, Fifth Army

The Emergency Line ran on the maps, but nowhere else, from Chauny on the Oise River, across to the town of Ham on the Somme River, along the west bank of the Somme to Péronne where there was to be a bridgehead defending the Péronne crossing. Then the line struck out towards Bapaume before finally connecting to the rock of the Arras defences. This was all very well, but if the Green Line was all but a work of fiction sketched out on the ground, then the Emergency Line some 3,000–5,000 yards further back was nothing but pure fantasy. Nevertheless, if there was to be an ordered withdrawal then units had to have some sort of framework to cling to as they fell back. As such the notational Emergency Line would at least serve to mark out where they should be making their next stand.

This was not the kind of battle where an army commander had much chance of shining as a great military leader. He was too remote, forced to issue orders that were little more than broad brush-strokes sketching out what should be done, but the real decisions had to be made far closer to the scene of the fighting. Gough could not intervene in any meaningful manner even should he have wished to do so. This left the senior officers all along the threatened front in a severe quandary. They were meant to act in concert: as battalions, brigades, divisions and corps, but the situation was such that the whole carefully assembled communications system that linked them together was under impossible strain. The German bombardment had cut most of the telephone lines and it was tempting for senior officers to drive or ride off to find out what was happening for themselves. Yet they perforce were then leaving their own headquarters empty. This in turn made it difficult, if not impossible, for junior officers to contact them. When the situation became desperate, decisions simply had to be taken by officers acting almost in isolation. Even when they took the plunge to withdraw, then there was still the problem of not only informing the battalions under their command, but also informing neighbouring formations that they were about to have their flanks exposed and, of course, passing the bad news of what they were doing on to the relevant divisional and corps staff.

The British commanders were doing all they could to sort out the chaos, but when dawn came on 22 March their defensive plans were cursed by another severe ground mist further confusing the issue. Soon it was apparent that they were once more under serious attack. On the right, in the III Corps sector, after hard fighting the Germans managed to breech the Crozat Canal Line to create a valuable bridgehead from Tergnier to Quessy. To the north the XVIII, XIX and VII Corps also came under heavy attack and began a series of rearguard actions.

On the XVIII Corps front, the men of the 19th Battalion, King's

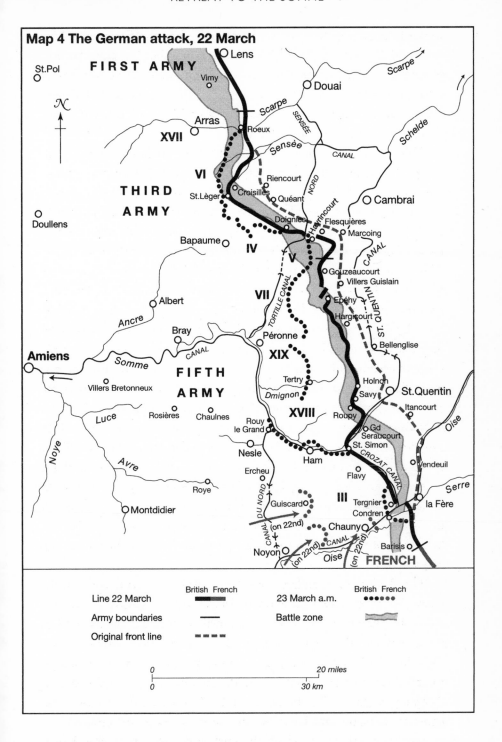

Map 4 The German attack, 22 March

FIRST ARMY

St.Pol

Lens

Vimy

Douai

Scarpe

Scarpe

SENSÉE

Arras

Roeux

Sensée

CANAL

Schelde

XVII

THIRD
ARMY

VI

St.Lèger

Croisilles

Riencourt

Quéant

Doignies

Havrincourt

Flesquières

Cambrai

NORD

Marcoing

Doullens

Bapaume

IV

V

Gouzeaucourt

Villers Guislain

Albert

VII

Epéhy

Hargicourt

CANAL

ST. QUENTIN

Ancre

Bray

CANAL

Péronne

TORTILLE CANAL

Bellenglise

Amiens

Somme

FIFTH

XIX

Holnon

St.Quentin

Villers Bretonneux

ARMY

Tertry

Savy

Itancourt

Luce

Rosières

Chaulnes

Dmignon

XVIII

Roupy

Oise

Rouy
le Grand

Gd
Seraucourt

Noye

Avre

Nesle

St. Simon

CROZAT CANAL

Vendeuil

Ham

Serre

Ercheu

Flavy

Roye

III

Tergnier

la Fère

CANAL DU NORD

Guiscard

Condren

Montdidier

(on 22nd)

Chauny

CANAL

Barisis

Noyon

(on 22nd)

Oise

(on 22nd)

FRENCH

	British French		British French
Line 22 March	▬▬	23 March a.m.	●●●●●●
Army boundaries	—	Battle zone	〰〰〰
Original front line	▬ ▬ ▬		

0   20 miles

0   30 km

Liverpool Regiment of General Stanley's 89th Brigade were in Corps Reserve when they were ordered forward to make an attack on the pivotal village of Roupy at 0115 on 22 March.

> Fall out the NCOs. We all fell out and the officer said our orders were: 'The Germans had penetrated the defence zone at the little village of Roupy, between St Quentin and Ham. We are to counter-attack it. The attack will take place at 0115 hours from the direction of the cemetery!' We sat in a shallow trench in a thick darkness, the mist was only just beginning to form. By this time we had become fatalistic. Any feelings that you had were subordinated. I can only liken it to when I played cricket in the good old days and before going in to bat you sat and shuffled a bit in the pavilion. I was nervous in the pavilion but once I got to the wicket in the middle the game was on and I was no longer nervous. This was the same – only a little more dangerous![3]
>
> Corporal Edmund Williams, 19th Battalion, King's Liverpool Regiment, 89th Brigade, 30th Division

Unfortunately, the promised barrage turned out to be a couple of desultory rounds from the widely scattered field artillery guns. The men were issued with two extra bandoliers of ammunition by the regimental sergeant major before going over the top.

> We got up in the darkness, with the dark line of the roadside hedging preventing us from either seeing or being seen from Jerries front. We got into our own low barbed wire hidden in the dead grass, we filed out as quiet as we could; then came out in line. We started to move, more than 300 yards, as we got nearer and nearer, waiting for a machine gun to open up so that I could hit the earth as quickly as possible and not be mown down! No machine gun opened up. We advance this 300 yards in the dark; not a shot! We passed the grey walls of the cemetery and came on to the ruins of Roupy. Jerry was not there! He had got in there early on, but he was not going to stick his neck out, so he just left it empty.[4]
>
> Corporal Edmund Williams, 19th Battalion, King's Liverpool Regiment, 89th Brigade, 30th Division

Corporal Williams and his men grabbed what sleep they could, for it was obvious that the dawn would bring a vicious reaction from the

Germans. When they discerned that the Germans were moving about somewhere in the mists in front of them, they took up what defensive positions they could in a random combination of trenches with no defensive cohesion. At about 0630 the German attacks began.

> We all lined the trench. I found myself firing rapid rounds as fast as I could into the mists, while my little brother was firing his Lewis gun. The machine gun in Roupy was enfilading us quite severely. Some of the bullets were coming into the trench just behind me. A runner went back to see what was to be done and to get some reinforcements; that runner never came back. There we were stuck high and dry. Our Lewis gun and rapid fire was enough to deter their advance. When the rapid fire had ceased I remained looking over the parapet into the mist with my rifle in front of me. A silhouette form got up and started to run from right to left. I thought, 'Allow 1 yard for every 100 in front and aim low!' I squeezed the trigger and the gentleman somersaulted and vanished. This was a game to win.[5]
>
> Corporal Edmund Williams, 19th Battalion, King's Liverpool Regiment, 89th Brigade, 30th Division

There was a halt in the proceedings while the Germans regrouped and slowly the fog cleared. Further attacks were repelled, but it was evident that other units were falling back and that the Germans were slowly encircling them.

> I congratulated myself on what a nice day it was to die on! We were all bunched together. There was a hiss of a bullet and one of the younger recruits fell down and died in the bottom of the trench. 'Don't bunch; spread out!' So we spread out. We were firing at snipers firing from the cemetery walls. I had the earth knocked up by my left ear once! I emptied my magazine at a bunch that were coming along the wide open trench trying to debouch from Roupy, but they didn't make any headway. I had only 25 rounds left. I'd known I was running short, I'd fired the two bandoliers, I'd fired all the rest of it! I must have fired that day between 200–300 rounds. At one point I found my fingers burning with the hot oil oozing from underneath the wood casing – the barrel gets pretty hot! The Lewis gun had jammed. My brother had gone somewhere or other, we were an isolated group. I was trying to pick my

shots. About 4 or 5 yards down the trench there were three other people and Corporal Dick Williams. I heard a clatter and a voice say, 'There's poor old Dick got it!' I looked round and saw that he was lying towards me with the top of his head off. That was my last vision before something hit me between the eyes, like a sledgehammer and I dissolved into unconsciousness. This was the end.[6]

Corporal Edmund Williams, 19th Battalion, King's Liverpool Regiment, 89th Brigade, 30th Division

A ricochet bullet had glanced across his forehead and knocked him senseless. He remained unconscious for some time. When he came to, although he was still bleeding profusely from his wound, his hard skull remained intact.

I came to paralysed, breathing shallowly. There was a little gap in the haze and sunlight. I could see the blood dripping down from the end of my nose into the clay, but I couldn't move. At the edge of the haze was a pair of boots. He said, 'You're not dead!' He pulled me to my feet and he got a field dressing, put it on me, bound it up, handed me my tin hat and said, 'You lucky beggar!' Now I'd come back I'd have to be killed all over again! I'd lost my rifle and I staggered down the trench.[7]

Corporal Edmund Williams, 19th Battalion, King's Liverpool Regiment, 89th Brigade, 30th Division

Williams was ordered to try and make his way back to the British lines, but he had little idea of what was really happening.

The concussion had rendered me out of this world; I didn't know what I was doing, not in control. With great reluctance I got out of the trench, the bullet storm going both ways. I got down and crawled and I even went down flat on my stomach because the bullets were coming down so low. I was crawling along in the sunshine.[8]

Corporal Edmund Williams, 19th Battalion, King's Liverpool Regiment, 89th Brigade, 30th Division

It was not long before he was picked up by a German patrol: for him the war was well and truly over. As they were marched back, joining the thousands of other prisoners in captivity, Williams had only one thought on his mind.

I kept saying, 'Have you seen my brother?' Nobody had found him and I was getting very tired and I lay down and had forty winks. Just lying down on the floor with my head on one of the blocks of masonry. When you're that tired you don't mind where you flop. I was wakened at daylight, the bloke said, 'Your brother's in the next room!' As I went out and came out one door, he came out by the other entrance, we looked at each other and said, 'What the hell are you doing here?' It was a feeling of peace; my anxiety was over – he was alive and he was here – what more could I want?[9]

Corporal Edmund Williams, 19th Battalion, King's Liverpool Regiment, 89th Brigade, 30th Division

Desperate little actions like the counter-attack at Roupy were going on up and down the fragmenting line. There was some heavy fighting, but in the end there was simply no holding the Germans.

The British gunners, too, were fighting back when and wherever they could but all their carefully laid plans were undermined by the lack of communications. Ad hoc arrangements were all that could be managed.

At 11.30 one of our RE8 contact planes, the first we had seen since the commencement of the battle, flew over the battery and dropped a streamer with a message that read, 'SOS north end of Jeancourt'. This target we got on to at once, passing the word along to Q Battery meanwhile, who also opened fire, with the result that in a few minutes the plane came buzzing back with another message, 'Good shooting! You are getting into them well!'[10]

Second Lieutenant John Fleming, 'U' Battery, 16th Brigade, Royal Horse Artillery

The gunners were still killing Germans right enough, but there were so many that they just seemed to keep on coming. Sometimes, golden opportunities to catch the Germans in the open enabled them to take a savage toll, but in the bedlam that surrounded the retreat batteries frequently found themselves being threatened. Gunner William Pressey had already almost been overrun in his forward position the previous day, but now his 315th Battery once again found itself in imminent danger of being overwhelmed. Timing was all-important in these matters. The gunners must fire as long as they could to support the infantry and fend off the Germans, but on the other hand they must give the horses, gun limbers and wagons, that were kept in a place of relative safety about a mile behind their gun positions, time to get forward when the moment finally came. Any mistake would be fatal and the margin for error was minute.

Suddenly the order, 'Prepare to limber up!' Up to us galloped the gun teams, with gun limbers of course. Before they reached us shells began to fall around us: a sergeant went down screaming, drivers were fighting their horses, some men were attending to the sergeant and men were struggling with the guns so that they could be hooked to the limbers quickly. It was a hellish few minutes. There were shouted orders and quite a little panic – coupling up one gun after another and holding the wounded onto the limbers. One gun was shooting while the others got away. This was No. 6 gun and firing it was Corporal Teesdale the 'chippy'. 'Come on!' He shouted, 'There they are, let the bastards have it!' He was never too brave but he had Dutch courage this time for he was half drunk. He kept on shooting until the Major ordered him to limber up. The drivers of that gun team didn't think much of his action, as they were waiting to couple up and each time he fired the team twisted and turned, wanting to get away. One gunner screamed out, 'There they are the bastards!' And away he ran towards them. Above his head he waved, not a rifle, but a spade. We screamed at him to come back, but he only looked back at us once and, waving his spade, ran on. According to his mates he had had a lot of rum the night before and had not recovered.[11]

Bombardier William Pressey, 315th Battery, Royal Field Artillery

Off they careered, the gunners clinging desperately to the gun limbers, hanging on for grim death to avoid being tossed off as they bounced across the rough ground with their frantic drivers whipping up their excited horses to gain every possible fraction of speed. Once more they were lucky; *most* of them had escaped. Corporal Teesdale was awarded the Military Medal for his actions in firing the gun on his own. The fate of the lunatic gunner was unknown and Pressey never saw him again.

As on the first day, on many occasions retreat was simply impossible. Thus it was for the five remaining 60-pounders of the 113th Siege Battery. The guns had already been pulled back to their rear positions into their pre-prepared gunpits and they were ready to make a long stand in the Soyècourt-Vermand sector. It was not to be.

By 3 p.m. the Hun were so close (within rifle range of the position) that we could not depress our guns enough to be able to put the range on. By a great effort we managed to get one gun out of the pit and into action in the open, but by this time the infantry were falling back through our guns to a trench in the rear of our position, so that there was nothing for it but to go. Fortunately there were some GS wagons up with ammunition, so we unhooked these teams and managed to get the one gun that was out of its pit away. We accordingly blew up the other four.[12]

Second Lieutenant L. R. Ward, 113th Siege Battery, Royal Garrison Artillery

The far superior numbers of the Germans enabled them to feel for the exposed flanks, constantly pushing forwards and forcing the outflanked British back even where they appeared to be doing well.

By 5 p.m. our attention was rudely drawn to our own front and we were soon firing in good earnest to cover Nobecourt Farm. The Huns seemed to come on, however, despite our efforts, and about 5.45 p.m. we spotted masses of men on the Vraignes/Nobecourt road. It could not be seen if these were our troops or not, so Darby rode forward to reconnoitre. He soon came back with the news that they were Germans and that our own infantry were rapidly falling back on us in a disorganised state. We packed up at once and slipped quietly back to a crest where we dropped into action and gave the Huns about 15 rounds per gun over open sights, the range being about 1,500 yards. The shooting must have told frightfully on the mass of men on the road, our shrapnel seeming to burst right among them, each shell being rewarded by a chunk of the target disappearing from sight. I still have a vivid mental picture of the dark mass of men against the afterglow on the skyline and the white woolly dots of the shrapnel bursting upon it. Each shell left a gap as though a tooth had been drawn. A minute having been sufficient to clear the road completely, we then limbered up and trotted quietly back out of sight to avoid reprisals.[13]

Second Lieutenant John Fleming, 'U' Battery, 16th Brigade, Royal Horse Artillery

As the battered units got back to the Green Line it was soon apparent that the scratched-out line was not really tenable. One of the brigadiers of the 50th Division, which had been moved up to behind the XIX Corps to help hold the line, succinctly summed up the prognosis for the next day as he examined the reports intermittently arriving from divisional headquarters, neighbouring brigades and his own struggling battalions.

> It was quite obvious that with very large enemy masses dug in within assaulting distance of the Green Line, with the paucity of troops holding the line, with practically no reserves, local or divisional, and with masses of guns that the enemy would be able to bring to bear at dawn or shortly after, that any chance of maintaining the line even for a few hours the following day was more than problematical. It was therefore necessary to withdraw some little distance behind the Green Line during the night, leaving the Lewis guns and snipers to the last moment to make the enemy think the line was still held.[14]
>
> Brigadier General Hubert Rees, Headquarters, 150th Brigade, 50th Division

As presaged by Gough's orders that morning it was evident that the division would have to keep going backwards to the imaginary Emergency Line at the back of the Rear Zone, where at least the very real flowing waters of the Somme would force the Germans to think twice before making a difficult river crossing under fire. Soon, however, it was more than apparent that there was no chance of clinging onto the Péronne bridgehead.

The British withdrawal had been carried out reasonably well, although some of the long ingrained habits of trench warfare died hard. Rather than occupy a position, opening fire as soon as possible even at long range to slow down the German advance before moving, preferably by cover of night to a new position, they tended to defend each position to the last minute, often opening fire only at short range in the approved manner of trench warfare. By staying in the same positions overnight they allowed the German artillery to register its targets the day before, which meant that the morning mists were an irrelevance to the gunners when the time came for them to open fire as they already knew the exact location and range of the British positions and could fire 'blind'. If the British had moved overnight the Germans also would have been hampered by fog as they strove to locate the new rearguard positions.

One of the peculiarities of the German infiltration methods was that while all this was going on, some of the outposts surrounded in the first day's fighting were still grimly holding to the bitter end deep into 22 March. Their position was hopeless and the only question that often remained was what that end would be. Captain Maurice Harper's men of the 2/2nd Londons had repulsed numerous attacks, but it was obvious that the game was up.

Our ammunition had got very low and the men were thoroughly exhausted. At 5 p.m. a British plane came over us and dropped two bombs on us. This had a great effect on the men, making them think that we were quite deserted and beyond help. At 6 p.m. I called together my officers and sergeant majors and we had a council of war. The result was that we concluded that we were evidently miles behind the German front line, that all the posts on our flanks had gone, we could not communicate with anyone, we were outnumbered 50 to 1 and that it would be best under the circumstances to give in, rather than sacrifice the men's lives. At this moment about 500 Germans were observed, on the road across the marshes. We opened on them with Lewis guns at 1,500 yards range and inflicted many casualties. The enemy were now observed in great numbers on all sides of us and many machine guns opened fire from all quarters. They were evidently going to attack in force. If we were to give in it was now or never. Very reluctantly therefore I gave orders for a white flag to be put out. When this had been done, the enemy ceased fire and called out to us to come out. An officer was called for and I went out to meet the enemy. I was armed, but dropped my revolver as I advanced. A German private, who would have bayoneted me, was stopped by an NCO and I was told to call my men out. They came, with their hands above their heads – the most heart-rending sight it has ever been my lot to witness.[15]

Captain Maurice Harper, 2/2nd Battalion, London Regiment, 173rd Brigade, 58th Division

The Germans had stood by the unwritten rules of war as Harper and his men surrendered before the final overwhelming assault went in.

But, in the circumstances, they were indeed lucky to be prisoners and not dead.

THE THIRD ARMY had a quieter day of it on 22 March. Yet the position of the V Corps divisions occupying what remained of the Flesquières Salient was still causing considerable concern to Byng. There was a very real reluctance to abandon ground won at such cost the previous year at the Battle of Cambrai. Yet sentiment has no place in the effective conduct of modern warfare and there is no doubt that the hesitation in evacuating the salient was foolish. Although the British had retired from the tip of the salient, the German advance on either side had rendered them, if anything, even more exposed to disaster, especially as during the day the retirement of the VII Corps of the Fifth Army further exposed the south face of the salient. This would be the real battleground of the day. Under heavy German pressure Byng ordered the retirement of the V Corps right back to the front line of the Battle Zone for the coming night of 22/23 March. However, even this would leave it in a salient, as the Germans had pushed in far beyond that on either side of these new positions. The German tactics were working, but they were finding the opposition far more dangerous than on the Fifth Army front.

On the northern flank of the salient the Germans battered away until they finally broke through in the Vaulx-Vraucourt sector in the late afternoon. It was here that Leutnant Ernst Jünger and his men of the 73rd Hanoverian Fusiliers were forcing their way forwards alongside many other units. Jünger had been ordered to attack a British-held line of trenches but fearing the consequences of a frontal assault across No Man's Land had decided to wait until the line was rolled up from the south. Only then would he take his company forwards.

Now we saw straight in front of us the curved flight and the white bursts of German stick-grenades. This was the moment we waited for. I gave the word to advance. We reached the enemy line without encountering much fire, and jumped in, eagerly welcomed by a storm troop of the 76th Regiment. Headway was slowly made in bombing along the trench. The enemy artillery soon found out, unfortunately, that we were obstinately eating into their lines. We were pretty sharply shelled with shrapnel and light shells, but the reserves who were streaming up to the trench over the open caught the worst of it. We did our utmost to clear the trench of the enemy so that we could take cover from the artillery fire. The Vraucourt Line was still being dug and many stretches of it were only marked out by the removal of the turf. When we rushed these pieces, we had all the fire in the neighbourhood concentrated on us. In the same way we had the enemy under our fire when they crossed these spots as they gave way before us, so that these short stretches of ground were soon heaped with bodies.[16]

Leutnant Ernst Jünger, 73rd Hanoverian Fusiliers Regiment, Imperial German Army

Under this kind of pressure, a significant gap opened up at Vraucourt that threatened the integrity of the whole line north of the Flesquières Salient. Fortunately, a battalion of tanks had been lying up near by in Velu Wood. When the call came the twenty-five heavy tanks of the 2nd Battalion, Tank Corps rumbled forward between Morchies and Vaulx-Vraucourt at about 1700. The counter-attack seems to have caused considerable confusion amongst the German infantry and for the moment stemmed their progress. Yet from the perspective of a young officer inside one of the tanks it was a tough afternoon's work that shook him to the very core.

We met small parties of the infantry on the retreat. They looked dazed and in the exaggerated way of men in those conditions, they told us that there were no longer any organised bodies of men fighting in the front. From the rallying point we received orders to drive down into a valley that faced us and into which large numbers of the enemy were advancing. We had no idea if any infantry would follow us in support of the counter-attack, but the odds were against this, since as far as we could see, none were available. From that time on all was confusion and we had to make our own decisions in the light of the circumstances prevailing. The only orders we were given were to the effect that there were stacks of Boche waiting for us and that we were to, 'Get into them!' As we moved over the bluff and into the valley, we were met with a hail of bullets from an enemy largely unseen. The inside of the tank was full of sparking and flying splinters of steel from the con-centrated fire, the like of which we had not encountered before. We must have gone forward half a mile with our guns firing, when we came up against a sunken road. At this point the valley swung left and having crossed the road to move up the forward slope, a German battery of field guns suddenly appeared. They unlimbered and started to fire at us over open sights. I thought this was too much and since we had no ammunition for our 6-pounder guns left, I thought it was time to go home. When we turned to retrace out steps, we saw tanks galore knocked out and a number of them on fire. As we recrossed the sunken road, we received a direct hit, which fortunately missed the traction, but seriously wounded two rear gunners. On the way back we picked up many survivors of knocked out tanks and when we finally limped back to our start point, we were bursting at the seams with men – many of them wounded.[17]

Lieutenant George Thompson, 2nd Battalion, Tank Corps

Of the twenty-five tanks committed to the attack only nine managed to return and the battalion suffered 70 per cent losses amongst the tank crews. The situation remained grim with the Germans pressing forward on either side of the salient even as the V Corps withdrew. The question now was whether the V Corps would be able to escape from what was still effectively the Flesquières Salient that night, before it was too late.

SATURDAY, 23 MARCH 1918 would prove a key day in determining the ultimate success or failure of the German offensive. That afternoon Ludendorff reported to a conference attended by both the Kaiser and Hindenburg, and he also entirely jettisoned the existing plans for the offensive. The idea of rolling up the British line to the north had now been all but abandoned – his eyes were firmly fixed on driving a wedge between the French and British Armies by pushing with the Eighteenth and Second Armies towards Noyon–Montdidier–Amiens. This in turn meant that he would be directly attacking the French as well as the British. Meanwhile, the Seventeenth Army would be required to attack simultaneously north-west, west and south-west – a dizzying and ludicrous prospect. The whole axis of the attack had changed decisively from the push to the north-west with a flank guard

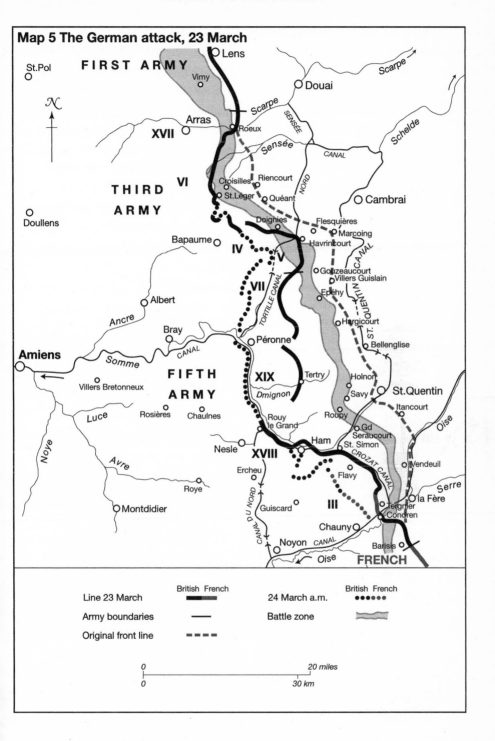

Map 5 The German attack, 23 March

Line 23 March — British French
Army boundaries —
Original front line - - - -

24 March a.m. — British French •••••
Battle zone

0 — 20 miles
0 — 30 km

along the Somme River to a general charge to the south-west – a ninety-degree change in focus. This was planning on the hoof at its worst and at face value represented a disastrous degree of over-confidence. Worst of all it was neither tactically nor strategically sound.

It was this change in the priorities of the German offensive that helped ensure the survival of the V Corps in the Flesquières Salient. Had Ludendorff properly reinforced the Seventeenth Army on 22 March, and in doing so kept his eye on the overall aim of pinching out the salient, then he may well have been successful. As it was, the 47th and 63rd Divisions were still in severe danger throughout 23 March and had begun a steady retirement, successively leapfrogging back.

As part of this process the men of the 1/23rd Londons found themselves occupying the Metz Switch Line, which circled the town of Metz and connected to Havrincourt Wood in the north. Amongst their officers was Captain George Brett, who was acting in a supernumerary capacity as third in command of the battalion. They had spent the previous day improving their trenches in expectation of an imminent German attack. Soon after dawn Brett had been made aware of German patrols probing for gaps in their defences and it was also evident that they had found the weakness they desired.

> The Germans kept up a constant pressure while they worked their way round our undefended right. Looking south, we saw more and more of their troops moving westwards. As the morning progressed we saw them marching in formed bodies, showing that no resistance was being met. Nearer to us their patrols remained uncertain and moved warily among the old trenches, having found that any overt movements attracted a hail of rifle and machine-gun fire. I was in the difficult position of knowing that we were to withdraw sometime and having to decide whether to risk casualties by counter-attacking. I decided not to attack unless failure to do so would jeopardise our withdrawal.[18]
>
> Captain George Brett, 1/23rd Battalion, London Regiment, 142nd Brigade, 47th Division

Eventually orders came for him to pull back and Brett managed to disengage relatively smoothly using a sunken lane and thick hedges to cover the battalion's withdrawal. It was to his men's credit that they managed to take with them all their wounded. Even so a further tragedy struck as they marched back in column to the relative safety of the Green Line in the Ytres sector some 2 miles further back.

> One solitary shell of large calibre came whistling through the air and burst just behind us, practically wiping out the rear platoon. I went back the few paces to where the men and bits of men lay and have never forgotten one poor fellow who, with blood pouring down his face and dreadful wounds in his body, pointed to my pistol holster and said, 'Put me out, Sir, please.' I could only tell him the doctors would be with us soon. Indeed, our medical officer and a party of stretcher bearers were on the spot very quickly and they did what they could to help those still alive.[19]
>
> Captain George Brett, 1/23rd Battalion, London Regiment, 142nd Brigade, 47th Division

The situation was exceptionally serious, for the right flank of the 47th Division was almost totally exposed to the Germans who were starting to cut in from the south. That night there was much evidence of widespread confusion as the Germans bit deep into the British lines, driving in from the direction of Fins and Equancourt. No one seemed to know what was going on. Private Roland Fisher of the 1/24th Londons had a particularly disturbing experience.

> We saw further on some huge burning shell dumps. They presented a magnificent spectacle, though somewhat frightening, sending aloft vast masses of flame some 200 feet into the black sky, and from which sprang all kinds of roaring explosions, with yellow, pink, red, blue and green flames. Out of these infernos hissed nose-caps and fragments of shells, which came tearing towards us. To our consternation, the officer in charge led us straight in that direction, and we were told to sit down on the ground, not 300 yards away from the dumps. But now came the greater surprise – another dump suddenly exploded 100 yards from us with a mighty, thunderous roar, which was followed by what seemed to be all the old iron in existence showering upon us. Scraps hit the ground all around us.[20]
>
> Private Roland Fisher, 1/24th Battalion, London Regiment, 142nd Brigade, 47th Division

Meanwhile, late on the evening of 23 March, the 1/23rd Londons were occupying another thin defence line stretching from Ytres. Major Thomas Hargreaves and Captain George Brett were sent with a dozen signallers and runners to take control of the situation on the right flank resting on the village of Léchelle and covering the main divisional retirement route through the village of Bus. Having found the remnants of 'C' Company Brett then settled down for a much-needed rest in a nearby farmhouse at a bend in the road leading into Léchelle itself. Unfortunately, there was no sign of anyone to their right – the flank was open. Worse was to befall them when orders for the next retirement failed to reach the isolated little force and their battalion withdrew without them.

I went down to the cellar, where there were some wire bunks. I loosened my belt, lay down and went straight off to sleep. How long I slept I have no idea, but I was awakened by Hargreaves shouting down the stairs, 'George, George, come up! Germans all around us!' I jumped up at once and went to get my steel helmet from near the bottom of a flight of stairs leading up to the road outside. As I got there I saw in the moonlight two Germans, one in the attitude of throwing something down. I abandoned the helmet and leapt round a corner when the grenade exploded behind me. Upstairs I found that we were being fired on from all the outbuildings encircling us. Our men were replying vigorously at the rifle flashes. One side was in complete darkness, but the other was well lit by the moon. The bright side seemed quiet and Hargreaves and I went to investigate. We were seen at once and a shower of bullets came at us from the barns on that side, Hargreaves being struck in the leg by a splinter off a wall. The men were in two rooms of the house and continued to fire at flashes and any hint of movements. After a bit I suggested to Hargreaves that we had better try to break out before the Germans got too strong for us. He agreed and I asked if he could run. He said he could and I went round all the men, told them that at a signal they were to follow me through the door into the yard, out through the gateway leading onto the road, turn left and run as fast as they could. They were not to wait to help any casualties. When all were ready, I threw open the door and charged out. It was only a few paces to the gateway and when I had nearly got there, two Germans came from the right round the corner of the building, one close behind the other. They were as much surprised as I was, but I grabbed the muzzle of the first man and prevented him from shooting or using his bayonet. I was poking his face with my revolver and it seemed quite an appreciable time before it occurred to me that if I pressed the trigger, the struggle would be over. I did so and then shot the second man in the chest. I jumped over their bodies and into the road, turning left. As I did so four shots were fired from a ditch on the far side. I felt a bullet hit my right arm and pass, I thought, into my chest. I was aware of a great clatter as men behind me fell with their rifles into the road. As I was falling three thoughts went through my head: a) the noise of my pistol sliding across the road; b) I'd read in stories about a red-hot searing pain through the lungs; and c) I'd better get away before they had the time to reload. The last thought ruled and I had scarcely touched the ground before I was up and haring along the road as if blue devils were after me. Then at about 50 yards, out of the darkness stepped four Germans, each with his rifle resting on my tummy – why none of them pressed his trigger, I shall never guess.[21]

Captain George Brett, 1/23rd Battalion, London Regiment, 142nd Brigade, 47th Division

This small party of 1/23rd Londons has been credited with delaying the Germans just long enough to prevent them closing the gap at Bus through which the 47th Division would escape that night. In the desperate skirmish Major Thomas Hargreaves was killed – he has no known grave. The wounded Brett had fought his last battle and was a prisoner of war.

A similar fate befell Sergeant Lewis Wells, who was in charge of the observers and snipers attached to the 1/22nd Londons. As such he was equipped with a variety of telltale specialist equipment including a telescopic rifle, prismatic compass and telescope, while in the further-ance of his duties he had the carbon copy reports of his snipers tucked away in his kitbag. For obvious reasons snipers were not popular with the Germans, or indeed with anyone else, and it was thus more than a little unfortunate that Wells lost touch with his unit and found himself trapped behind German lines. He and another sergeant decided to try to make their way towards Étricourt.

We saw lights ahead of us in the valley where a railway line crosses the road. We could also hear the rumble of army wagons and were very pleased we had come that way, as we knew that at that spot there was a large canteen and we concluded that the stores were being packed ready for retirement. Just by the level crossing was a sentry box and by the glow of a cigarette we could see that it was occupied. My friend went up to the sentry and said, 'Say, chum, can we get to Étricourt along the railway?' We got the biggest shock of the night for, instead of a 'Tommy', out stepped a 'Fritz'! We then saw Germans all over the place. We were properly caught. A good deal of jabbering took place and while this was going on I managed to drop my telescopic rifle behind the sentry box. We were then marched to a dugout to await the coming of an officer. My prismatic compass and binoculars went as souvenirs, for which I was very thankful; as I did not want to explain them to anybody in authority owing to tales I had heard of the German way with snipers. It did not help our self-respect to learn that we had been taken prisoners by artillerymen. After a time an officer arrived and he ordered us to march in front of him as he rode on horseback and we preceded him thus as far as Fins where his headquarters was a farmhouse. On the way, under cover of darkness, I managed leaf by leaf to dispose of the carbon copies of my sniper's reports for the past few weeks, which I had in a book in my haversack and which had not been searched. I was now more content, as I had got rid of most of the incriminating matter connecting me with the most unpopular part of an enemy's force![22]

Sergeant Lewis Wells, 1/22nd Battalion, London Regiment, 142nd Brigade, 47th Division

By the end of the night the 47th Division had managed to withdraw through the narrow bottleneck; it was still in an exposed position but the situation had eased a little. The Germans had failed in their attempt to pinch out the Flesquières Salient.

BACK ON THE FIFTH ARMY FRONT on the night of 22 March, Gough ordered his chief engineer Major General Grant to ensure that there were responsible officers at every bridge that the advancing Germans could feasibly use to cross the Somme River. Even quite junior officers had to be given the authority to blow the bridges without prevarication if the German infantry were on the point of capturing the bridges.

It was obvious that unless some such arrangement was made there would be a risk of premature firing, or firing not taking place at all. I saw the general staff officer and chief engineer VII Corps at about 12.30 a.m. on the night of 22/23 March. I was informed that everything was ready, and parties standing by at each bridge. I asked that officers should be at each bridge empowered to fire the charges without having to wait for messages that might never reach them. I then proceeded to Headquarters XIX Corps at Villers Carbonnel, and saw the Corps Commander and the Brigadier General General Staff, and pressed for similar arrangements if not already made.[23]

Chief Engineer Major General P. G. Grant, Headquarters, Fifth Army

It was, of course, utterly vital that the Somme River and Canal front be secured, especially as the defences on the western side were rudimentary in the extreme. The orders passed down the various channels of command and reached Brigadier F. C. Stanley, who had completely lost touch with his brigade, which in its capacity as the XVIII Corps reserve had already been thrown piecemeal into the battle. He was tasked with defending the town of Ham on the Somme, although he was given no troops. Stanley duly rushed round siting trenches, but all too soon realised that it was hopeless, 'There was little more that could be done for the good reason that there was nobody to do it with, and no time to do it in.'[24] The troops on the ground were little more than the flotsam and jetsam that had come to rest at Ham.

Nobody knew anybody – there was no such thing as a battalion. We were a nondescript pile of all sorts of regiments. Bits and pieces, anybody at all: sanitary people, cooks, everybody – they're all in it.[25]

Sergeant Ernest Bryan, 19th Battalion, King's Liverpool Regiment, 89th Brigade, 30th Division

Despite the paucity of troops on the ground, the one thing Brigadier Stanley made sure of was that the bridges were ready for demolition. Lieutenant Robert Petschler was one of the engineer officers called into Stanley's headquarters.

I had to report to General Stanley for special orders. I set off at once to the headquarters, which were in Ham, and found them busy packing up preparing to depart. I saw the General and he gave me personal orders about the blowing up of one of the bridges:

Your only duty is to blow up No 4 Bridge in the event of the enemy being in possession of the bridgehead – i.e. that there are none of our troops who can prevent him getting over.

Two things are most important:

(i) That the enemy should not cross by the bridge;

(ii) That it is not blown up unnecessarily.

You are personally responsible for the carrying out of these orders.

Brigade Major, 89th Infantry Brigade

The bridge had to be left to the last, as it was the main line of retreat. It spanned the canal at Ham on the main road.[26]

Lieutenant Robert Petschler, 201st Field Company, Royal Engineers, 30th Division

This was a real case of 'damned if you do' and 'damned if you don't'. The understandably worried Petschler rushed off to his bridge, which he found had already been prepared for demolition. Conscious of his responsibility, he carefully checked the charges. It was as well that he did so, for all was not as it should be.

The bridge consisted of a double roadway, each roadway hung from two steel lattice girders. There were sixteen charges of guncotton in all, designed to cut each girder in two places. I found that there was a small footbridge near the main bridge that was made of very heavy baulks of timber, but it had been overlooked and was not prepared for demolition. As it would have enabled troops to cross, we at once set out to destroy it, and after great effort managed to dislodge the timbers and drop them into the canal. The canal was almost dry in places and was passable for determined men, although without the bridge it would be impossible for transport to pass.[27]

Lieutenant Robert Petschler, 201st Field Company, Royal Engineers, 30th Division

This bridge, which spanned the Somme Canal, was a temporary construction built to replace the original bridge destroyed by the Germans during their retreat in 1917. The canal was a far greater obstacle than the river, being 58 feet wide and about 6 feet deep, while the river meandered in several channels and was only 4 feet deep at most. Meanwhile, the Germans had commenced a heavy shelling of Ham. Huge shells came crashing down out of the blue every ten minutes or so. Whole houses were smashed to smoking mounds of rubble and scattered debris. In the midst of wholesale destruction Petschler had to remain calm and collected.

> I ran out my firing leads from the bridge to the archway of a house about 50 yards away and carried my exploder – the firing device – to a handy spot close by. Every thirty minutes or so I tested the leads to make sure they were still intact. The roads were now crowded with transport and guns that were retiring, and all these had to pass over my bridge. They came in endless streams for hours on end and I soon found I had to act as traffic controller. All through the night the traffic still streamed over my bridge and I began to wonder whether it would all get away. The sound of rifle firing came nearer.[28]
>
> Lieutenant Robert Petschler, 201st Field Company, Royal Engineers, 30th Division

A few troops occupied trenches in front of Ham and snipers were posted about the streets to harass the Germans if or when they should break through. That night was tense, with matters not helped by German aircraft launching a night bombing raid on the town. There were no thoughts of sleep.

> I heard one or two loud explosions and realised that some of the other bridges were being blown. The traffic began to dwindle and about four o'clock had ceased altogether. It was now getting quite light but there was a heavy mist that prevented objects more than 100 yards away from being seen. The sound of machine-gun and rifle fire was now very close and the wounded were more frequent. I began to fear that the Germans would pass on the flanks and encircle the town thus effecting its capture. As I only had three men with me, I posted them out as sentries to the best advantage where they could see all round – that is so far as the mist would allow them![29]
>
> Lieutenant Robert Petschler, 201st Field Company, Royal Engineers, 30th Division

All along the Somme the same scenes were being played out. As the engineer officers sweated over their responsibilities the position for the troops retreating towards the bridges was equally desperate. There was a desperate need to get across the bridges before the sappers blew the charges, but at the same time their rearguards had somehow to hold back the Germans long enough to allow their comrades to get back over the bridge. If the Germans were allowed to get their machine guns or field artillery up and in position to cover the river crossings then there would be a massacre.

> We, on the high ground, were converging on two country roads that led to bridges over the river. We could see feverish activity and guessed the Royal Engineers were preparing to blow them up. The bridges and roads were crowded with retreating troops. Progress was so slow and congestion so great, that we were all consumed with anxiety as to whether we would get across before the bridges were blown. We were uncomfortably near the end of the queue. When we halted on the top of the hill leading to the river, I was with 'A' Section. Feeling an urgent call from nature, I stepped into a copse, did what I wanted to and went back. I could not find A Section! I concluded that they had gone on down towards the bridges, so I followed on the crowded road. No chance of catching up. Our group was about the last over the bridge before it was demolished by the REs. After a bit I found 151st Company, and was ordered to go to the commanding officer by the company sergeant major. It seemed my turning up needed a lot of explaining and it could have been very serious for me. It seemed that after I had slipped off to the copse, 'A' Section and its four guns, plus some infantry support, had been ordered to about turn, and find good positions to fire and hold up Jerry in order to give more time for the evacuation over the bridges. I had heard heavy firing and seemingly the improvised rearguard did a good job. Few of that rearguard survived – of about thirty machine-gun men only about half a dozen got back to 151st Company by swimming the river or getting across broken girders when darkness fell. A nasty blow and how easily I could have been one of them. Luckily the CO accepted my story.[30]

Private William Parkin, 151st Machine Gun Company, 151st Brigade, 50th Division

Back at Ham, Lieutenant Petschler was still weighed down by his responsibility: afraid of being encircled or surprised before he could carry out his mission, frightened at the same time of blowing the bridge too soon and dooming men to capture on the other side of the canal.

> The position was now desperate. The stragglers got fewer and in smaller parties, and I continually asked NCOs or officers if there were more to follow and the answer was, 'No, not many!' The machine-gun

fire was very intense and occasional bullets passed over the bridge. In the distance I saw an officer leading about a platoon of men. When he approached he said he was the last of the infantry. I began to be very much on the alert. I called in my sentries and waited. The officer came running back and said that his commanding officer ordered the bridge to be blown up. I did not do it immediately and waited for at least a quarter of an hour. Then I heard a tremendous burst of cheering – it was the Huns entering the town. Bullets were flattening themselves on the walls and road near me. Through the mist I thought I saw a movement and then it was unmistakable – a small party of Huns were rushing for the bridge. I waited until they just set foot on the bridge and then pressed down the handle of the exploder for all I was worth. Up went the bridge with a terrific crash and it was quite some minutes before the pieces stopped falling.[31]

Lieutenant Robert Petschler, 201st Field Company, Royal Engineers, 30th Division

Petschler finally blew the bridge at 0800 on the morning of 23 March. Unfortunately, the results were less than satisfactory. There was an impressive explosion, but when debris had stopped falling the gap blown was inadequate, especially as the debris was substantial and itself had fallen into the canal. It was evident that the gap would soon be bridged and indeed would do little to stop infantry getting across the rubble and twisted girders, but there was nothing more that Petschler could do. This kind of problem was common as the bridges did not simply vanish on demolition but rather fell into the river or canal beneath them.

THE GERMANS MANAGED to force several passable crossings during the day and once again the British front line was fragmenting, as the troops had little more than hastily scratched out trenches. Troops manning the Somme west bank were increasingly forced to throw out flank guards to counter real or imagined German incursions threatening to cut them off, encircle them and pin them back against the river. This in essence was the threat facing the 7th Somerset Light Infantry – as part of the 61st Brigade it had been attached to the 36th Division –

which now found the Germans swirling round its right flank, having broken through all along the Crozat Canal on the III Corps front. Captain George McMurtrie was at the battalion headquarters.

> A great fight was going on. Huns attacked us and for about an hour we kept shooting at them and kept them at bay. The CO was shot through the neck by a rifle bullet, and Berry, who was next to me firing away, got up to look over the bank, over which we were shooting. He got a bullet right through the head and was killed instantly, falling on top of me with a groan. I was very upset to see him killed. I now had to take command of battalion headquarters. Ammunition was given out and the Germans were gradually working round us and threatening to surround us at any minute. I considered it would be a waste of life to hold on any longer, having done all we could to delay the enemy for as long as possible. A great many men had already been killed or wounded and I decided it was time to withdraw.[32]
>
> Captain George McMurtrie, 7th Battalion, Somerset Light Infantry, 61st Brigade, 20th Division

Meanwhile, the position in the VII Corps sector to the north was also of increasing concern. Troops were occupying the Green Line between Hamel and Equancourt and it was their responsibility to maintain the link between the XIX Corps on their right, which was busy falling back across the Somme to the Emergency Line, and the V Corps on the right of the Third Army, which had just evacuated the Flesquières Salient. The Germans were surging forwards intent on widening the crack between the armies into an unreachable chasm. The VII Corps position was increasingly untenable and early on the morning of 23 March, with considerable reluctance, Lieutenant General Congreve issued the necessary orders for his divisions to fall back.

Once again there was a requirement for rearguards to cover the retirement of the majority of the troops. A typical action was fought by the men of the 17th King's Royal Rifle Corps who were dug in on the blunt nose of a hill looking down on the village of Longavesnes. It was a far cry from the serried layers of trenches they had occupied in the Ypres Salient. Their line was by no means continuous and they had no barbed wire defences. This naturally afforded the officers a great deal of concern as they awaited the all but inevitable German attack. To their intense relief, at first at least, they found that the dreaded fog was absent.

> Soon the Boches can be seen massing in the village of Longavesnes. Our field guns have seen them too, and begin to sprinkle shrapnel over the solid ranks. Through my field glasses I can see the foremost skirmishers creep forward in twos and threes. Gradually they mass under cover of a protecting bank. Now the sun appears. And with it a few puffs or whisps of mist. Quickly this spreads and settles down over all. Once again our advantage has gone and we are to fight after all in an enveloping fog.[33]
>
> Second Lieutenant Frank Warren, 17th Battalion, King's Royal Rifle Corps, 117th Brigade, 39th Division

The Germans could now gather ready for the assault, cloaked in invisibility. To fire their rifles was a waste of ammunition. Warren's company was moved forward from reserve to reinforce the front line ranged along the bank of a road.

> In the thick mist we cannot see 20 yards ahead, and it is difficult to know what is actually happening. A tank comes lumbering out of the mists and squats down, snorting and spitting bullets, just behind us. Enemy machine guns are playing down the valley and bullets ricochet merrily from the armoured sides of the tank. I walk up to this tank. A shutter opens in front and a white face appears at the open port hole. It is the officer in charge, whose appearance is made the more curious by protective spectacles made up of tiny dangling chains, forming a shiny fringe, to ward off splinters from the eyes. Two more tanks come galumphing through the mist, one cruising madly in the wrong direction. I stand up and question the officer, who owns that he has waltzed round so many times that he hasn't an earthly notion where he is. 'What can he best do?'[34]
>
> Second Lieutenant Frank Warren, 17th Battalion, King's Royal Rifle Corps, 117th Brigade, 39th Division

To his credit Warren seems to have told him without recourse to the temptations of vulgarity. The 17th King's Royal Rifle Corps eventually found that it was to fall back on Péronne just in front of the Somme River. What Warren and his fellow officers would later jokily refer to as the 'Péronne Handicap' had begun. The fog was still so bad that they set their course by compass as if for a night march. Units in all sizes, shapes and general conditions were falling back on Péronne. Many avoided the roads, aware that the German heavy artillery had them taped and were well capable even in the fog of searching for prey up and down the roads, bringing havoc to the long trails of men marching back. It was a testing time for all of them and some proved themselves beyond general expectations.

> A man in 'A' Company, a great strong hulking fellow, but an inveterate gambler, one who grouses loudly whenever he is not otherwise employed. When Freer was hit, stretcher bearers were needed, and Péronne was 8 miles away. Our Scotsman – for such he was – was there unasked and helped to carry his officer those 8 long miles – and without a murmur![35]
>
> Second Lieutenant Frank Warren, 17th Battalion, King's Royal Rifle Corps, 117th Brigade, 39th Division

When the fog at last lifted, it was just in time to allow enfilading German guns to sight their prey and redouble their efforts to slaughter the retiring troops.

As they fell back there was increasing traffic congestion of all sorts. The roads were soon blocked and *everyone* seemed to have a legitimate priority – the result was gridlock where often nobody could move. It was of course a bad situation for the infantry, but at least they had the option of cutting across country. For the heavy artillery units roads were a simple necessity and there seemed a real threat of traffic jams delivering hundreds of guns to the pursuing Germans. The 111th Siege Battery sent Lieutenant Allfree ahead by motorcycle with sidecar along to select the next gun positions. He located a reasonable spot about a mile from Mont St Quentin and then waited, scanning the unending nose-to-tail traffic for a sign of his battery with ever increasing concern. At last it came into view.

> I spotted the guns approaching in the stream of traffic. I stopped them, and in stopping them stopped everything else behind them, which had to wait while we pulled the guns right across the road and manhandled them into the selected position. After the usual heaving on drag-ropes,

unlimbering, unloading 100-lb shells and laying out lines of fire by compass bearing from the map, the guns were ready for action. The guns were given some line and elevation, and soon were barking again – firing on the roads we had so recently passed over. Meanwhile, the traffic streams along the road – retreating, ever retreating. One wonders how near the beastly Huns are getting. Nothing seems to hold them up.[36]

Lieutenant Edward Allfree, 111th Siege Battery, Royal Garrison Artillery

When the men of the 17th KRRC reached Péronne they could not understand why the inviting defensive possibilities offered by Mont St Quentin, the hill seemingly purpose-built to defend Péronne, were being ignored. But to their surprise the retreat continued without stopping. There simply was not time to sort out a coherent defence from the disordered units falling back. The Germans were too close behind and would be on top of the rear formations well before they had time to dig trenches.

Here we see the British 'Tommy' at his irrepressible best. Tired and worn, he pauses for a rest. Some bright spirit lights upon a quarter- master's store filled with all manner of change of raiment. Lo! The Boches are but 2,000 yards away and coming on fast. But 'Tommy' strips himself stark naked and shouts with glee as he dons clean vest, shirt, pants, socks and whatnot! One man has an armful of clean towels, which he doles out to every man that passes. I gladly accept the offer of a pair of new socks, and a boon they prove, for my feet are already blistered and painful.[37]

Second Lieutenant Frank Warren, 17th Battalion, King's Royal Rifle Corps, 117th Brigade, 39th Division

Back went the 17th KRRC, harried continually by the onrushing Germans. Once again it was required to provide a rearguard, this time focused tightly on the bridge across the Somme.

We skirt Péronne and halt, on the deep sunken road that runs north and south, to form a bridgehead guard. The village of Allaines is all ablaze, and the oncoming of the Boches is to be traced in the smoke columns that darken the sky. There are masses of our transport and artillery limbers parked on the gentle slopes towards Cléry. Now the

Boche heavy artillery has got the range. The fall of heavy shells among the struggling mass of horses and men is one of the wickedest sights of the day. Most of the limbers gallop clear away, but scores of smashed carts, wheels and many a fallen horse repay the Boche for their ghastly efforts. We are wondering what our defence of the bridgehead might mean, when – a rending zoom and fragments of bridge fly 100 to 200 feet into the air, all falling nearly on the same spot. Our work is done for the time being.[38]

Second Lieutenant Frank Warren, 17th Battalion, King's Royal Rifle Corps, 117th Brigade, 39th Division

The traffic on the roads to the Cléry-sur-Somme sector was frustrating beyond measure and terrifying at the same time.

The stream of traffic moved so slowly – at times coming to a standstill for minutes on end, to allow other traffic to come in from other roads. There were several streams of traffic converging on the village. First one stream was held up to let another come on, and then that one was allowed to go on while the other was held up. There were traffic controls doing their best to regulate the traffic in this way. It was a hell of a crush. There was just a block of traffic, miles in length. It seemed absolutely hopeless to expect ever to get on. And now, on the face of the ridge just behind us, appeared some of our tanks, creeping across country and occasionally firing at something. What I dreaded and every moment expected, was to see the Hun cavalry swooping down on us. But this did not happen. I don't think the enemy could have had any cavalry, or he must have used it on an occasion such as this. What a haul he could have had! But he *had* got aeroplanes. Three of the beastly things appeared: swooping down low over the road and with machine guns rattling they flew up and down. They were also dropping bombs. I leapt lightly down a shell hole – a fairly deep one – and crouched against that side of the crater that afforded most protection. As the aeroplane passed over me, so I passed to the other side of the shell hole. I heard the bullets going, 'Zip! Zip! Zip!' into the ground. They were so low as to induce some officers to shoot at them with revolvers, but of course this was a futile thing to do.[39]

Lieutenant Edward Allfree, 111th Siege Battery, Royal Garrison Artillery

As every minute passed the troops knew that the Germans behind them were surely getting closer. If the German artillery got near enough to open an aimed fire onto the tightly packed road then there would be a massacre.

> At last the stream is moving again and I jump onto the front of an FWD lorry drawing one of our guns. We go about 20 yards, stop again and wait, wait, wait. Every minute seems an hour. You are powerless to do anything. There is nothing for it but to sit stolidly and patiently there – wondering how near the enemy is getting and whether those aeroplanes will return, perhaps flocks of them next time? We move again. Are we really off this time? No – another stop! And now parties of infantry pass us – retiring. This really does look cheerful – we shan't even have any infantry between us and the Hun soon! Ah, the lorry in front of us is moving again. [40]
>
> Lieutenant Edward Allfree, 111th Siege Battery, Royal Garrison Artillery

So the endless grind went on as inch by inch and yard by yard they crawled up the road.

As the British fell back there were additional complications to bear in mind. Normally a battery was at the sharp end of a great logistical pyramid that kept it functioning without much thought from the likes of Lieutenant Allfree and his fellow officers. Thousands of heavy shells, fuel and oil for the lorries, food for the men, all these had been taken for granted. But now they were on their own and if they ran out of anything vital – like petrol – then they would be in even worse trouble than they already were.

> This was quite a stressful time for the Army Service Corps officer attached to the battery. On him devolved the duty of keeping the battery supplied with ammunition, which was no easy job. We left most of our shells behind at each position. And as all the forward ammunition dumps were now in the hands of the enemy, it probably meant going many miles back to procure more, with the chance of finding the battery gone from the spot he had left it in, with perhaps some difficulty in finding it. The battery quartermaster sergeant was also kept busy in much the same way in supplying the battery with rations. He sometimes had to go far afield with his rations lorry and pick up the battery

again wherever it happened to be. He managed on the whole rather well. I do not remember that we were ever really short of food, though we might not always have the time or opportunity for a proper meal. I expect the German soldiers fared much worse: they were getting further and further from their bases and we were getting nearer to ours. It must have been an enormous undertaking keeping those German hordes fed.[41]

Lieutenant Edward Allfree, 111th Siege Battery, Royal Garrison Artillery

Meanwhile, Lieutenant Warren and his party of men were feeling their way back along a rough track across the low marshes of the Somme River towards the sanctuary of the Cléry bridges. Here they were once again found by German aircraft, that screamed down to pounce on them. There was no real breathing space for these unwilling entrants in the 'Péronne Handicap'.

Perhaps a dozen Boche aircraft take up the running and we scurry in ignominious flight to re-form under cover at the front of the slope leading towards the bridges at Cléry. Several of the men have been hit by machine-gunners in the aeroplanes, mostly leg wounds. There is an uncomfortable feeling about standing in the open under aeroplane fire, but except against massed targets, the effect of the fire is merely distracting.[42]

Second Lieutenant Frank Warren, 17th Battalion, King's Royal Rifle Corps, 117th Brigade, 39th Division

Unfortunately, there were plenty of massed targets for the German aircraft skimming with malicious intent above the battlefield. As the men approached the bridge they found that the Germans had managed to get a field gun into position to cover through open sights the Cléry bridge across the Somme River.

We can see the gunners at work, but cannot hit back, for they are out of the range of rifle fire. At present they are firing about two shots to the minute. We draw into a covering chalk pit to examine their methods and the best escape. Soon they turn their attentions to the plank bridges that span the streams, under which the current is flowing swiftly. We watch others run the gauntlet of shots. One shell skims the heads of two tall men and fall 'plonk' in the water 10 yards beyond. The next shell bursts in the bank, and a man doubles up – badly hit. Quickly, we realise that a direct hit on the bridge will mean that we have to swim for it! The next shell pitches amongst some men clustered in a corner under the lea of a cliff that we are hugging. There is no time to lose! We make our dash – safely as it proves.[43]

Second Lieutenant Frank Warren, 17th Battalion, King's Royal Rifle Corps, 117th Brigade, 39th Division

Warren and his men moved across the valley to cross the Somme Canal bridge. His 'A' Company was just seventy-five strong as it moved towards the tiny hamlet of Buscourt, but he found that on this, their longest day, they still had work to do.

It is growing dark as we are led off to line a trench for the defence of the canal should the enemy attempt to follow up his success. A series of explosions just as darkness comes on tells the tale of the blowing up of the Cléry bridges, all built with wooden beams, and the glare from the burning timbers seems to show that the destruction is complete. 'Fritz' has done well this day, but must be just as played out as we are.[44]

Second Lieutenant Frank Warren, 17th Battalion, King's Royal Rifle Corps, 117th Brigade, 39th Division

By the late afternoon most of the retreating British units had got back across the Somme. As part of the efforts to prevent the Germans from crossing, the 199th Brigade of the 66th Division had deployed two battalions to hold the west bank facing the Bristol Bridge leading across into Péronne during the afternoon of 23 March. Most of the rest of the bridges had already been blown, but this had been preserved to allow for the retreat of the 16th Division. The troops found that in one sense there was too much of a good thing.

The 5th and 6th Manchesters were given the job of holding the bridge from the town of Péronne, where the wine was running in the gutters as the French tried to get rid of it. We crossed the bridge and dug in on the west bank guarding the bridge. I shall never forget that night. In spite of the efforts of the French, the German advance had been so rapid that they had not been able to destroy all their stocks completely and the Germans were soon roaring drunk, singing and shouting, and by midnight setting fire to buildings all over the town.[45]

Private P. R. Hall, 2/6th Battalion, Manchester Regiment, 199th Brigade, 66th Division

The question now was whether the battered British battalions could stop the Germans on the Emergency Line along the Somme.

CHAPTER FIVE

Desperate Measures

IT WAS ON THE THIRD DAY that Haig and General Head-quarters chose to intervene in the conduct of the battle. They had watched with considerable concern as the Fifth Army fell back, abandoning the Forward Zone, the Battle Zone and the Green Line at the front of the Rear Zone. Now the Fifth Army was clinging to the Emergency Line at the back of the Rear Zone. Haig felt that the running had to stop; that this was the time to make a concerted attempt to hold the line – with the assistance of the meandering Somme river valley and the canal it should be able to make a fist of the defence. At 1700 on 23 March he therefore issued unequivocally stern orders to Gough.

> Fifth Army must hold the line of the Somme River at all costs. There must be no withdrawal from this line. It is of the greatest importance that the Fifth Army should effect a junction with the French on their right without delay. The Third and Fifth Armies must keep in closest touch in order to secure their junction and must mutually assist each other in maintaining Péronne as the pivot.[1]
>
> General Headquarters, BEF

These orders caused considerable angst at the Fifth Army head-quarters. The Somme was, after all, only a small proportion of a battlefield that stretched from Noyon in the south, right up to Croisilles in the north on the Third Army front. While the river and canal were an obvious assistance to defence, if the defending battalions fought to the end on its banks, then when the flanking formations were forced back they would soon be surrounded and annihilated. As to the question of maintaining links with the French, this was of course the British intention – the question was whether the French would keep in touch with them or retreat to the south-west with the aim of covering Paris. And of course, Gough intended to keep in touch with Byng and the Third Army. In truth, this was not a terribly helpful interjection from GHQ and without reserve divisions to match the dry exhortations it was meaningless.

Meanwhile, Haig had met the French Commander-in-Chief Pétain to discuss the vital issue of cooperation between their two great armies. Without French help the British would never hold the German onslaught – and Haig knew it. But even more importantly the Allies must stick together and not allow the Germans to get between the two armies.

> General Pétain arrived about 4 p.m. He has arranged to put two armies under General Fayolle on my right, to operate in the Somme Valley and keep our two armies in touch with one another. The basic principle of cooperation is to keep the two Armies in touch. If this is lost and the enemy comes in between us, then probably the British will be rounded up and driven into the sea! This must be prevented even at the cost of abandoning the north flank.[2]
>
> Field Marshal Sir Douglas Haig, General Headquarters, BEF

Better that the link between the British Third and Fifth Armies be at risk rather than the greater threat of a split from the French.

ON SUNDAY, 24 MARCH the Fifth Army bestirred itself to the task of holding what was left of the line along the Somme. On average the troops had fallen back between 4 and 6 miles during the previous day. They had been ordered to hold the Somme Line without fail, but in reality had already failed: the Germans had broken through the Crozat Canal and swept across the Somme up to and including Ham. The integrity of the line was thereby shattered as the Germans pushed up from the south. Gough's divisions had been expended in the fighting. All his reserves thrown into the fight and the battalions strung along what remained of the line were severely under-strength, ravaged by casualties and further undermined by the effects of exhaustion inevitable after three days of near-continuous fighting.

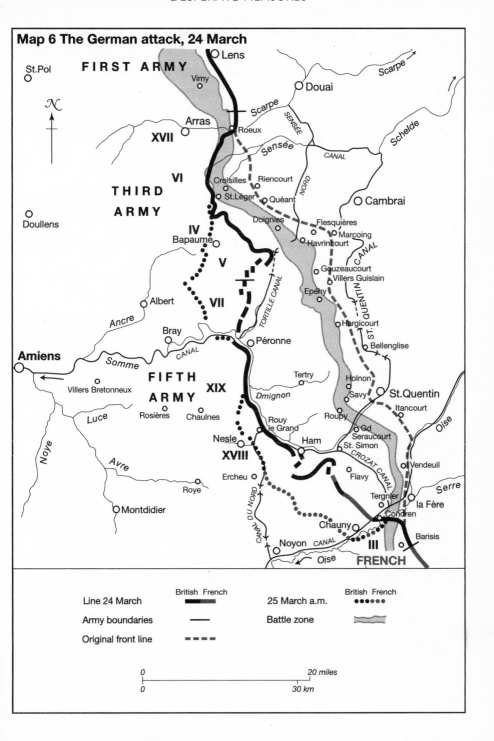

Map 6 The German attack, 24 March

St.Pol

FIRST ARMY

Lens

Vimy

Scarpe

Douai

N

Arras

XVII

Roeux

Scarpe

SENSÉE

Sensée

CANAL

Schelde

Doullens

THIRD ARMY

VI

Croisilles

Riencourt

St.Léger

Quéant

NORD

Cambrai

IV

Bapaume

Doignies

Flesquières

Marcoing

Havrincourt

V

Gouzeaucourt

Villers Guislain

TORTILLE CANAL

Epéhy

ST. QUENTIN CANAL

Albert

Ancre

VII

Hargicourt

Bellenglise

Bray

Péronne

CANAL

Somme

Amiens

FIFTH ARMY

XIX

Tertry

Dmignon

Holnon

Savy

Roupy

St.Quentin

Itancourt

Villers Bretonneux

Luce

Rosières

Chaulnes

Rouy le Grand

Oise

Nesle

Ham

Gd Seraucourt

St. Simon

XVIII

Noye

Avre

Ercheu

Roye

CANAL DU NORD

Flavy

CROZAT CANAL

Vendeuil

Serre

Tergnier

la Fère

Montdidier

Condren

Chauny

Barisis

III

Noyon

CANAL

Oise

FRENCH

	British	French		British	French
Line 24 March	▬▬▬	▨▨▨	25 March a.m.	●●●●	○○○○
Army boundaries	▬		Battle zone	▨▨▨	
Original front line	▬ ▬ ▬				

0   20 miles

0   30 km

Typical of these troops were the 2/6th Manchesters trying to hold the line near the Bristol Bridge just south of Péronne. All was relatively quiet at first, but as the Germans got a grip of the situation they began to bring more and more of their artillery into action, pounding the west bank, trying to weaken the defences that they had already registered the previous afternoon. The result was a terrible trial for the men of the 2/6th Battalion.

Somehow we held on to this bridgehead, resisting every attack and under heavy artillery bombardment and, worse still, large numbers of trench mortars from the troops in the town on the opposite bank. Not only *minenwerfers*, but the very heavy ones we called 'flying pigs', which on landing dug in deep before exploding and thus produced a large crater. One of these exploded just in front of the parapet, killing two other men in the same bay with shock and flying metal from the bomb itself. Although I was nearer to it than they were, it just pushed the parapet on top of me, burying me face downwards with only my left hand showing when rescuers came running from the next bay. They saw the hand moving and that I was alive and shouted for stretcher bearers. The first to arrive scraped away a small channel through to my face hoping to give me a chance to breathe, but the loose sand from the broken sandbags above me was still trickling down as fast as they moved it and it threatened to smother me. The next fifteen minutes were quite the worst I remember, because I was quite helpless and held down as if in a vice by the weight of the sandbags. I wanted them to remove two or three from the top of my head and shoulders, but they said that if they did so then the whole 5 or 6 feet of sandbag wall would slide forward and crush me. One of them knelt on the floor scraping away as much as he could of the loose sand still trickling onto my face every time they shifted another bag. When the wall had been reduced to 2 or 3 feet they freed my right arm and decided to pull me forwards. Two of them took hold and pulled, while two others braced themselves against the sandbags to hold up the remainder of the wall. It did slide, but only up to my waist and they soon freed my legs, which were numb and bruised, but not seriously hurt.[3]

Private P. R. Hall, 2/6th Battalion, Manchester Regiment, 199th Brigade, 66th Division

Holding the line was clearly going to be a painful business and the whole experience did not presage well for the men's chances next morning on 25 March. They were already in deep trouble and it was evident that the Germans would have all night to move up more artillery and prepare a renewed assault.

Further south, along the banks of the Somme at Béthencourt, another young officer was making life or death decisions. In front of him was a stepping-stone crossing that was viable for determined troops. The men of the 2nd East Lancashires had dug hasty trenches, but with constant rumours swirling around that the Germans had managed to cross the river on either side of them, panic was very near to the surface. But Second Lieutenant Harold Mellersh was resolved that he and his men would stand their ground until it was definitely established that they had been outflanked.

> I stood in the waist-high trench, scanning the scene in front with my field glasses, when a shell landed almost on top of me. They always said that the shell that got you, you did not hear coming – and they were right! With no warning I heard the explosion, like a thousand doors slamming. For the moment I think I was senseless. Then my brain began to work. I was dead! No, I wasn't. I began to yell. It seemed to me, rightly or wrongly, that no noise came out of my mouth at all. Then I came at least partly to my senses. My field glasses had been blown out of my hands, and my tin hat off my head. As I looked at my hands, which were black, they began to ooze blood; my face and one knee were in the same condition. I think that paradoxically its very nearness saved me, that and the luck that none of the shell-case fragments but only the blast came my way.[4]
>
> Second Lieutenant Harold Mellersh, 2nd Battalion, East Lancashire Regiment, 25th Brigade, 8th Division

In that crushing detonation all thoughts of heroic resistance were smashed out of him. The Lieutenant Mellersh who was meekly led back as a casualty by his servant was a very different person from the confident and determined soldier of just seconds before.

The situation further south along the front was even more desperate due to the threat of the Germans sweeping round the crossing forced at Ham. By this stage there were only faint grounds for optimism. On the right the French had taken over operational command of the III Corps in conjunction with the French V Corps, which had managed to move up some units. Despite this the British were still bearing the brunt of the fighting and the French units at first merely seemed to be joining in the retreat. Perhaps their best hopes were the French troops moving up behind them to create support lines.

There was certainly nothing here to cheer up Captain McMurtrie of the 7th Somersets, who had already been forced back in desperate circumstances from the all-embracing arms of the German advance when his battalion was almost destroyed. After falling back the remnants had been attached to the 7th Duke of Cornwall's Light Infantry and told to hold its left flank. On the morning of 24 March they found themselves in an all too familiar situation – enveloped in thick fog and enfiladed by German machine guns firing down from nearby high ground.

> We stuck this out till about 11 a.m., when ammunition and bombs began to run out. We were all very, very hungry having had no rations the night before. I received a verbal message by a runner from the Colonel to the effect that my party was to cover the withdrawal of the rest. Almost immediately they started withdrawing and after they had got clear I gave orders to withdraw too. I was determined not to let the men start running, for once they did in such a situation it was impossible to hold them. I had my revolver out and anyone who tried to run I immediately threatened to shoot. This stopped all running but it was the worst hour I have ever been through. The enemy was lining the right ridge and pouring a deadly fire into us, shells and shrapnel were bursting everywhere. German aeroplanes started flying over us and firing into our midst. Men were dropping everywhere, some were wounded and calling out for help, others were dying and groaning in their pain. It was a ghastly situation. Second Lieutenant Butler was killed. The Colonel had given me no place where we were to withdraw and so I steered a course straight to our rear. The end was very near and soon we ran bang into a huge number of German artillery and transport and were captured. A German on a horse came up and led me to believe that he wanted my revolver. He took it and fired a round into the ground. I had heard of the awful treatment by the Germans of their prisoners and so thought this German was trying my revolver in order to shoot me. I waited, but nothing happened. I was told to take the rest of

my kit off and then being very thirsty, got my water bottle out, filled it from a stream and at last got a drink – the first one for 24 hours.[5]

Captain George McMurtrie, 7th Battalion, Somerset Light Infantry, 61st Brigade, 20th Division

There were problems along the Somme Line but to the north of the Fifth Army front there were also increasing stresses and strains tearing apart the exhausted divisions of the VII Corps. Torn between the necessity to maintain a link with the Somme Line and at the same time trying to connect with the right of the Third Army, they were stretched far too thinly. When they were pushed hard by the advancing Germans, they soon gave way. They simply did not have the time or the men to prepare the kind of defensive positions that might have held up the Germans for long.

The experiences of Captain John March of the Royal Engineers were typical of the general air of chaos and panic.

Very early we were ordered to go back to the top of the hill to the east of Combles and there establish a line to which the infantry could in due course fall back. We found a line of trenches, dug some two years before, which ran in the right direction and suited our purpose well. The infantry then being in retreat towards us, but scattered over the countryside, I posted the sappers, some 150 strong, in a long line to intercept and direct them to the new position. I also posted out in front of the new line two of our own Lewis gun crews, in old pillboxes, to engage the enemy until our troops were established and organised in the line. With great relief, I then sought out the senior infantry officer in the 3-mile-long front and handed the command over to him. I then collected my scattered sappers reinforced by stragglers from sister companies into a close group in my vicinity, where I could keep an eye on them. By about noon we were being heavily attacked from the front and there were ominous sounds to our left, where the hill curved around to our rear and into the village of Combles. We had no difficulty in fighting off the frontal attacks, but our forward Lewis gun teams were obviously overrun, as we heard no more of them. Soon after noon written orders arrived for withdrawal to a line some 3 miles back on the other side of the valley in which Combles lay. It entailed crawling out of the trench and up the hill the 100 yards or so to the rear, after which movement would be easier. I was near the commanding officer when he gave his orders and knowing how tired the troops were, I knew they would not crawl, but just get out and walk, and that would be just what the German gunners wanted. So I sent orders to the sappers to stay put until I gave the word, and that they must get out in twos and threes and *crawl*. The infantry moved to their orders as I had expected and were received with heavy fire, which caused many casualties. I held on until quiet reigned again, and the Germans were in the open and advancing; then gave the order for 15 rounds rapid fire, followed by a stealthy retreat. It worked beautifully and our men had no casualties. When they had all gone, Cawthra and I, with one man, followed. But when we had crawled about 20 yards we got fed up and decided to walk to the crest. At once they were on to us with a machine gun and Cawthra got a nice 'Blighty' wound in the thigh. I helped him over the crest and into cover.[6]

Captain John March, 90th Field Company, Royal Engineers, 9th Division

March had lost touch with his men but on descending into Combles he found plentiful evidence of what had befallen them from the corpses scattered about the village streets. The Germans had been thrown back but it was obvious that their next attempt would be successful. There was no one left to fight them.

I advanced cautiously, revolver in hand, feeling very frightened and lonely, past groups of dead Germans and Scots, until I reached the big marquee. With great caution I entered and found it empty, except for rows of beds and a long row of trestle tables down the centre piled high with medical stores, heaps of blankets and a lot of petrol tins under. 'Ah!' thought I, 'Some medico had a bit of sense and left it easy for me to destroy!' I opened a petrol tin and poured its contents over the blankets, took a newspaper, made a long torch, lit it and put it to the blankets. They refused to burn, so I opened another tin, smelt and tasted the contents and found it was water! By this time I was quite jittery and my wits forsook me! I crept out, even forgetting that I could as easily destroy the whole by just setting fire to the canvas of the tent with a heap of newspapers. So the Germans got a fully equipped hospital![7]

Captain John March, 90th Field Company, Royal Engineers, 9th Division

*

THE THIRD ARMY spent much of 24 March in a systematic retirement so that it could maintain some kind of contact with the fast-retiring left of the Fifth Army. As it withdrew its path took it straight back across the 1916 battlefields of the Somme. Units retired, took up defensive positions in the old trench lines, held on for as long as they could, until they were once again outflanked and back they went again.

> To our rear, against the evening sky, rose a long hill with outrunning spurs. Up it, along two or three tracks in the direction of Gueudecourt, trailed black streams of men and limbers; up the sides half a dozen tanks were puffing, they carried wounded on top and were making the best speed they could away from the enemy pursuit. At the foot of the hill a damaged tank had been set on fire and was burning. A 9.2-in gun was being drawn along slowly by a light tractor. All around was evidence of utter confusion and surprise. For the first time since the beginning, one's heart sank and one began to fear that morale might be giving and that we might be getting a harder knock than we could stand.[8]
>
> Second Lieutenant Gilbert Laithwaite, 10th Battalion, Lancashire Fusiliers, 52nd Brigade, 17th Division

As Laithwaite surveyed the depressing scene he saw further evidence of panic alongside the track running west from Le Transloy.

> By the side of the track was a great heap of papers. I turned them over: they were the whole battalion records of a regular battalion – the 2nd Royal Fusiliers from the 2nd Division. There were orders dating back to 1914; sets of all the secret books, pamphlets, battalion diaries and papers; new army books lying beside the large black record box just as they had been tossed out. There were no maps. No efforts had been made to destroy all this. All along the track were masses of clothing: sets of silk pierrot suits from some divisional concert troops, music, a dump of damaged boots, old khaki tunics, socks, equipment – littered for half a mile. When we saw it we could not help saying, 'Whatever will the Boche think when he sees this – he'll think he has us on the run and broken us.'[9]
>
> Second Lieutenant Gilbert Laithwaite, 10th Battalion, Lancashire Fusiliers, 52nd Brigade, 17th Division

Yet for all these disasters and mishaps, even here the Germans were still suffering severe casualties whenever they inadvertently exposed themselves to the still potent weapons of their enemies. Thus Captain Francis Whaley of the 15th Hampshires saw clear evidence that not all German attack tactics were sophisticated. Overnight his unit had occupied a line along the Bihucourt–Biefvillers Ridge between Bapaume and Achiet-le-Grand.

> Over the skyline and down the slope came line upon line of German infantry, as though in some ceremonial march past, perhaps six or ten men deep and shoulder to shoulder. Along the ridge, of which I could see about a quarter of a mile of frontage, I reckoned to be watching the best part of a brigade – a wonderful target for our guns, if any. Then as though in answer to prayer, came the bang and swish of shells over-head. High explosive and shrapnel from two or three batteries began to plaster the forward slope. The thick, well-aligned ranks seemed to waver, break up and disintegrate. Clumps of men and single figures broke away and began to run down the slope into dead ground or scatter like disturbed ants. In a minute or so the drama was over. The ridge was once more deserted. The gunfire slackened and died.[10]
>
> Captain Francis Whaley, 15th Battalion, Hampshire Regiment, 122nd Brigade, 41st Division

When the Germans renewed their attack the Hampshires were once again rescued by one of the other arms – this time the Tank Corps, who came to the assistance of the infantry at considerable cost to itself.

> A tank came suddenly into view from behind the wood. Cruising on a parallel course between attackers and defenders it began to turn its guns on the former. Two or three times it went backwards and forwards until suddenly it stopped in a flurry of smoke and flame. Three of its crew began to run for safety, but were shot down.[11]
>
> Captain Francis Whaley, 15th Battalion, Hampshire Regiment, 122nd Brigade, 41st Division

Their sacrifice had done the trick: the German attack once again broke down and the Hampshires were left undisturbed for the rest of that long day.

Meanwhile, the 8th Battalion, Tank Corps had been sent into action south-east of Bapaume to help to cover the withdrawal of the 2nd Division near Haplincourt Wood. Amongst the troops was Private George Brown, a Lewis gunner from Manchester, in a tank commanded by Lieutenant Henderson. They had gone into the attack knowing little or nothing of what was going on around them. When their engine broke down they were forced to evacuate their tank and make a run for it. This was the prelude to disaster for the crew who soon found themselves trapped behind the German lines. The next few days would prove a traumatic experience for Private George Brown and his companion Private Stan Allen.

> There appeared only one route to escape, that was alongside of a farm building. Allen, Boylett and me were together. First Boylett was hit, he fell dead at my side; three holes were in his helmet. Next I was hit by a single bullet. I still ran on having seen a shell hole about 10 yards away. I dived into it and a few seconds later Allen dropped beside me and said, 'I've been hit.' I said, 'So have I.' He was wounded in his leg. A bullet had ripped through my back into my chest and through my tunic. We were both very lucky in having wounds that with ordinary care would not prove fatal.[12]
>
> Private George Brown, 8th Battalion, Tank Corps

They took shelter in a dugout tunnel and found themselves trapped there for two days, listening to the German voices of troops passing by. At midnight on the second night they finally plucked up the courage to try and escape their predicament.

> We started walking until we came to a sunken road. We heard the sound of horses coming along the road. Lay down and watched them pass. It was a convoy of Germans, five or six wagons. Once they had gone we crossed the road onto the fields again. Now we needed a drink so we searched around, found some equipment, took off the water bottle, and found some water in a hole. We obtained only a drop, we both drank some, it was horrible. So we were in a bad way, lay down again in another shell hole, fell asleep. Soon Allen awoke and said, 'George, I'm very cold, let's move on.' We started walking and it was beginning to become daylight. Then we saw some bell tents, we walked downhill towards them, not knowing whether they were occupied by

German or English troops. We soon found out. Walking through the lines and listening we heard voices, German voices. Walking back up the hill two German soldiers were walking towards us. They were only about 30 yards at the point where we crossed. We could not get away quickly enough, so I said to Allen, 'Don't turn round and don't run!' It was now just breaking dawn when we reached the top of the hill and just escaped from a dangerous situation. We lay down in a shell hole and, realising there were German troops in the same field, we fell asleep still in need of food and drink. Probably it was the extreme cold that wakened me at that moment, but looking up I saw a German soldier stood on the edge of the shell hole. I do not know who was most surprised, him or me. I nudged Allen and said, 'Here is a German soldier, stand up and don't panic!' We told the German we were wounded and had no food or drink since Sunday morning. Then seeing a comrade some distance away, he shouted to him that he had found two Englanders asleep. The other Germans came running up to us. Then to our surprise they put their arms around us and down the hill again to a field kitchen where we were surrounded by a large number of friendly looking German soldiers. They gave us soup, coffee, bread and jam. Later an officer came and asked us how we came to be there when our front line was 20 kilometres away. We told him, but he did not believe us and stormed away angrily. Next thing that happened, we were taken to a first-aid post where our wounds were dressed by a medical orderly who spoke good English. He said to me, 'You have been very lucky, the bullet missed your lung and you should be all right!'[13]

Private George Brown, 8th Battalion, Tank Corps

In the course of the retreat, it was a perverse fate that sent the 47th Division right back past the brick-dust remnants of the village of Flers and the infamous stumps of High Wood where it had had so many grim experiences two years earlier. In the increasing confusion an amorphous gaggle of troops had congregated around the retreating headquarter staff of the 142nd Brigade under the command of Brig- adier General Vivian Bailey. They were just north of Delville Wood.

The sun was sinking behind High Wood. The brilliant light was fully on us, but ahead lay the deep shadow from the rising ground. After an interval there loomed white on our left the hewn face of a quarry. Emerging from the opening was a black column of men, almost invisible against the gloom. This column we approached rapidly, until when we were within a short distance, there came a hullabaloo of voices, a crash of rifle fire, and the men of our force lay scattered on the ground. There were three of us only who stood there unwounded. We were surrounded immediately by a swarm of Germans in threadbare uniforms, whose bodies stank to high heaven with sweat. While some knelt beside the casualties, a group of others sidled the three of us against the hard mud bank of the road and confiscated our arms. A hefty youth with a quantity of soft down on his chin and cheeks seemed prepared to shoot us one by one out of hand. While his finger pressed on the trigger and I gazed into the black orifice of the muzzle of his rifle, a sergeant passed between us saying, '*Nicht!*' I looked round me. Captain Peel, the brigade major, lay dead and General Bailey was wounded, while all along the road lay still bodies.[14]

Corporal William Hahn, 1/21st Battalion, London Regiment, 140th Brigade, 47th Division

Brigadier General Vivian Bailey was one of 146 British generals wounded during the war. As Corporal Hahn and the other survivors were escorted back across the old battleground, they had a perfect view of the advancing German Army.

We toiled up steep slopes of turf and over old trench lines choked with purple weeds, sighting vistas of wooden crosses with many recent dead lying unburied amongst them. Through the weird sunlit country, frieze after frieze of Germans advanced confidently. Some of the men capered and staggered as they came along, and one of our officers remarked that they had been at the dumps and were 'tight'. They certainly seemed to be. A string of reeling machine-gunners at one point quite affectionately proposed that the Germans with us should lie down while we provided targets for a little practice! Apprehensively our warders herded us on. They had, of course, had no tender feelings for us, but they were stone cold sober and realised that accidents might happen from rum-saturated marksmanship![15]

Corporal William Hahn, 1/21st Battalion, London Regiment, 140th Brigade, 47th Division

*

AS THE RETREAT continued there was no doubt that the discipline of both the Fifth and Third Armies was being tested to the very limits. Threatened with imminent destruction from all sides, harried from pillar to post, half starved, exhausted beyond all measure, the troops were inevitably prone to some disciplinary lapses when temptation reared its head. One obvious source of temptation was the abandoned stores and canteens that they passed en route.

> The columns marched up the hill to Maricourt, or what was left of it, and to our surprise suddenly came upon scattered units of the famous 51st Highland Division, in groups of ten or twelve with walking wounded among them, very battle-stained, but in high humour for they had evidently helped themselves to abandoned YMCA stores. They carried in their arms a varied assortment of articles: shirts, socks, pants, bottles of wine, tins of beer, cases of whisky, boxes of cigarettes, cigars. The officers were not immune either! Some of the Scots had drunk too much and gave voice to their favourite ditties as they ambled or staggered by. From their unwashed weary faces and bedraggled kilts it was obvious to our curious gaze that continuous fighting and lack of sleep had taken their toll, hence no one could begrudge them this demonstration of elation now that tension was relaxed as they streamed down the hill from the vicinity of Hardecourt. Andy Swanson hailed a tall lean Highlander, who carried a Lewis gun over his left shoulder and a pile of cigarette tins under his right arm, with a fancy shawl under his tin hat that added a comic touch, 'Where's the auction, Mac?' The Scot relieved himself of the gun for a moment and jerked his thumb over his shoulder, 'Yon storeman told us to help ourselves before they fired the canteen and we couldn't leave this loot to the bastard Germans!'[16]

> Private Edward Williamson, 17th Battalion, Royal Scots, 106th Brigade, 35th Division

With far less justification there were also many cases of pillaging from civilian property. Shops were tempting targets, but ordinary houses were raided too. However the men might try and excuse it or dress it up, it was still looting, the same crime that would have got them the death penalty from the Duke of Wellington just over a century earlier.

We travelled a couple of miles through a small town, full of cafés, shops and houses. We had stayed a night just outside this town on our way up a couple of months ago. We had gone into an *estaminet* and the owners had charged us about double for all wines – a bottle of champagne was out of the question. It was said the Americans and Canadians had been there and having five or six times our pay could afford their outrageous prices. We put up with *vin blanc* or *vin rouge* as we didn't like the weak French beer. Now all the houses were empty and this hotel too. We stopped for a few minutes near and down into the cellar went all our spare boys. We ran out with our arms full of bottles of every description, even champagne. We ran to the half-empty ammunition wagons, dropped lids, and soon wherever a shell had been taken out there was now in its place a bottle of wine. The awaiting drivers were given a bottle to get on with, while we went back for more. By the time we moved off my gun team had perhaps thirty bottles of wine with us. It seemed our officers either didn't know what was going on, or didn't care.[17]

Bombardier William Pressey, 315th Battery, Royal Field Artillery

In an atmosphere where everyone realised they could be dead any day soon, there was a definite dilution in the respect due to authority. Some of the men had certainly had criminal experience of one sort or another before joining the colours. They, too, began to take advantage whenever they could.

An Irish lad, Barney Hughes, one of the runners under my charge, in addition to ransacking the stores came across an officer's valise that he went through and found a revolver in a case, in which there was also about 200 francs in notes. Very soon after taking possession of these, the owner came up and asked him if he had seen anything of the revolver and case, to which Barney replied in the negative. The officer did not appear to be convinced of his innocence and returned again later to question him, but no satisfaction was obtained beyond the statement that Barney would commence to look for the missing article and if he found it would return it immediately to its owner. The runner then got the 'breeze up' and after talking the matter over with us, decided to throw the revolver into a trench and later accidentally 'find it', which programme was duly carried out. The case was returned to the officer who tendered his sincere thanks to Barney along with a 20 franc note for himself![18]

Sergeant Stanley Bradbury, 51st Battalion, Machine Gun Corps, 51st Division

There was also an increasing desperation for food: under the incredible strain of the confused retreat the supply system at times began to fall apart. When hungry enough the men would baulk at almost nothing and if they were in lush farming country then there was plenty of temptation all around them.

In one considerable village we scattered a flock of sheep, evidently all abandoned in extreme haste. These unfortunate sheep seemed inclined to move out with the troops and I could see in the eyes of my fellow troopers a hungry look, in spite of the stringent penalties against looting. We halted briefly on the hilly slopes above the village and witnessed the slaughter of a sheep by two of our troopers, who used their bayonets. This unlucky animal was summarily divided and tied to our saddles, which dripped with blood as we rode. We contrived to get some of it cooked when we halted for the night.[19]

Trooper Arthur Bradbury, Royal Scots Greys, 2nd Cavalry Division

The presence of numerous abandoned sheep and cattle was by no means unusual. The whole farming infrastructure of Picardy was falling apart following the departure of the French farmers.

About midnight we passed through the town of Roye, which was quite deserted except for hundreds of cows and young calves that were roaming about the streets having been abandoned by their owners. The sappers led some of these cows along with them and on the halts frequently milked them, but the poor beasts ultimately became so exhausted that we turned them loose to graze in a field, and no doubt they were soon captured by the Germans.[20]

Lieutenant Robert Petschler, 201st Field Company, Royal Engineers, 30th Division

There may have been cows all around, but a young staff captain of the 23rd Brigade came back from leave to find that a 'terrible loss' had bereft his unit during his absence.

The brigade had already suffered heavily and everyone was gloomy. One of the first casualties had been the brigade headquarters cow. She was acquired in 1915 and served with the 23rd Infantry Brigade for three years. During all that time she gave milk, often in the most depressing situations. All through the time we were at Passchendaele she stood in mud and never saw grass, but she continued to give milk. Her 'man' was from the Devons, a thorough yokel who could manage her like a horse. All our mess servants came from the Devons and they knew how to make Devonshire cream – that was what we use to do with her milk, drinking tinned milk the while in our tea. She was at once a boon and a distinction and was much mourned. She and her faithful man were killed by a shell near Villers-Carbonnel and fortunately it was instantaneous.[21]

Captain Philip Ledward, Headquarters, 23rd Brigade, 8th Division

It seems strange to read these tributes to the demise of a mere cow with the death of a man mentioned only in passing.

Of course, in the chaotic circumstances of the retreat it is natural that there were outbreaks of utter panic often associated with rumours of German uhlans and associated fifth-column activities. Rumours and false alarms festered even in areas that, for the moment at least, were well behind the British front line.

News travelled like lightning through the lines that the German cavalry had broken through and was approaching the village. Almost immediately from every point which the eye could see there came galloping scores of horses and mules drawing every kind of conveyance imaginable, in addition to thousands of men running. Evidently panic had caught well hold of everybody. Our own officers, instead of behaving like officers, soon caught the same fever and instructions were issued for everything to be thrown into the limbers as quick as possible and to move off irrespective of turn or order, but as soon as they were ready. Each driver therefore had the 'wind up' immediately and without even waiting to get properly loaded and fastened up, they galloped off across the fields.[22]

Sergeant Stanley Bradbury, 51st Battalion, Machine Gun Corps, 51st Division

In this manner, panic spread from one unit to another. Captain Westmacott, a staff officer of the 24th Division who had managed to find his first bed in ages, had just managed to get off to sleep when his rest was rudely disturbed by one such mass flight.

At 9.30 p.m. a battery rattled through at a fast trot, followed by a mob of transport galloping and men of labour units running and yelling that that the uhlans were among them. This put the wind up the civilians and they all ran out screaming that it was a rout. Chevalier (GSO3) and I got into a car and went round and quieted things down, finding the same story everywhere. A small officer with a dark moustache had ridden through on a motorcycle shouting that the line was broken and the uhlans were behind him. I am certain this man was a German agent. In the end this thing had a good result, as people were so ashamed of themselves that they did not stampede later on, when they would have had plenty of excuse.[23]

Captain Thomas Westmacott, Headquarters, 24th Division

There were also tragic cases of men snapping under the strain with awful consequences. Here was a complicated mixture of utter fatigue, the lacerating effects of heavy responsibility and, of course, man's natural fear under fire.

We had a very close call at divisional headquarters as a shell fell in our courtyard, but fortunately did not explode. Walker, the Commander Royal Engineers, went off his head and climbed up a tree with a rifle, with which he opened fire on Germans and British alike, until he was shot by one of our own people.[24]

Captain T. H. Westmacott, Headquarters, 24th Division

One hard-pressed senior officer, Brigadier General Hubert Rees of the 150th Brigade, was almost desperate in his concern for the safety and wellbeing of his men who had been scattered to the four winds during the last few days. Two of his battalions had been placed under the orders of Brigadier R. Haig of 24th Brigade, 8th Division and he went to check on their welfare, although he had been assured that they had been placed in an old casualty clearing station with a bed each for the night. He was in for a rude surprise.

We eventually reached 24th Brigade headquarters at Marchélepot at 4 a.m., 25 March, when I was informed that the two battalions, which I had imagined were in billets, were already in assembly trenches waiting to make an attack north of Licourt, as the Brigadier said, 'To straighten out my line'. I was so completely taken aback I didn't know what to do, so for the time being, went back to the western exit of Marchélepot, where my brigade headquarters were established, leaving a cyclist orderly to bring messages of any developments. On thinking it over, I came to the conclusion that I ought to protest against these battalions being used for attack except in the case of the most vital necessity, because it was impossible to believe that he could have understood the tremendous physical strain which they had undergone, or that 8th Division headquarters understood it either, if they asked them to attack without most urgent reasons. On top of a 30-mile march and continuous fighting, after a halt of less than twelve hours during the day at Belloy, they had marched from 2.30 p.m. to 9 p.m., from Belloy to Marchélepot and were completely exhausted on arrival, requiring, in fact, half-hour halts during the later stages in order to get them in at all. After an hour's halt in Marchélepot they had been sent on to their assembly positions. One can only add that, as I had not been consulted, the two most exhausted battalions were used for the attack. I protested to the 8th Division most strongly on the telephone and asked permission to return to Foucaucourt, where I hoped to be able to do something, at least, get the attack postponed. The attack was to take place at 9 a.m. I was refused permission. General Haig then spoke and told them that I considered that he ought to have relieved his battalions holding the line with his own battalions. I never made any such suggestion and told him so as he was talking on the telephone.[25]

Brigadier General Hubert Rees, Headquarters, 150th Brigade, 50th Division

Rees was obviously seething. Conflicting duties to their men, their higher formations, neighbouring units and the fraught military situation all competed for attention. And of course the two brigadiers were both themselves suffering from exhaustion and the severe stress that was inevitable in such dire circumstances.

As his officers and men struggled to hold the line there was little that Gough could do to help them. The normal communications were disjointed and unreliable, and his reserves were already spent. He could not even continue his policy of carrying out a deliberate retreat in stages, for he had been ordered by Haig to hold the Somme Line. Gough was well aware that the Somme Line could not be held, that it

was already hopelessly compromised, but orders were orders and he
must try his best.

> It was evident that we could not go on forever, and that if the divisions
> and battalions were not 'nursed', and if they were exposed too long to
> the onslaught of superior numbers, there would be a complete break.
> The officers and men were playing their part in this desperate game
> splendidly, and I had to play mine too; this was to see, as far as I could,
> that units were not exposed to annihilation or to complete exhaustion,
> that flanks were not permanently exposed, nor gaps left too long
> unfilled. To continue the retreat was therefore still the right course to
> pursue, as it was the only one that could ensure keeping the line intact.
> But I did not mean to give up the line of the Somme if I could help it;
> indeed General Headquarters had issued orders that it was to be held
> 'at all costs'.[26]

General Sir Hubert Gough, Headquarters, Fifth Army

Haig's General Headquarters had its own worries. The willing
cooperation of the French was utterly essential if the situation was to
be stabilised. But late in the evening of 24 March Haig had a most
disturbing meeting with Pétain. From a very early stage it was apparent
that their analysis of the situation reflected very different priorities – a
chasm of intent that could doom the Allies to defeat.

> Pétain struck me as very much upset, almost unbalanced and most
> anxious. I explained my plans and asked him to concentrate as large a
> force as possible about Amiens astride the Somme to cooperate on my
> right. He said he expected every moment to be attacked in Cham-
> pagne, and he did not believe that the main German blow had yet been
> delivered. He said he would give Fayolle all his available troops. He
> also told me that he seen the latter today at Montdidier, where the
> French reserves are now collecting, and had directed him in the event
> of the German advance being pressed still further, to fall back south-
> westwards to Beauvais in order to cover Paris. It was at once clear to
> me that the effect of this order must be to separate the French from the
> British right flank and to allow the enemy to penetrate between the two
> armies. I at once asked Pétain if he meant to abandon my right flank.
> He nodded assent, and added, 'It is the only thing possible, if the enemy

compel the Allies to fall back still further.' From my talk with Pétain I gathered that he had recently attended a Cabinet meeting in Paris and that his orders from his government are 'to cover Paris at all costs'. On the other hand to keep in touch with the British Army is no longer the basic principle of French strategy. In my opinion, our Army's existence in France depends on keeping the British and French Armies united. So I hurried back to my headquarters at Beaurepaire Château to report the serious change in French strategy to the CIGS and Secretary of State for War.[27]

Field Marshal Sir Douglas Haig, General Headquarters, BEF

With Pétain and apparently the French government intent on maintaining the unity of the French armies and defending their capital, rather than on maintaining the liaison with the British Army, it was evident that something had to be done. Haig seems to have grasped immediately that this was the crunch moment. The French and British had to work together in harmony and he was willing to do whatever was necessary to achieve that end.

ON THE MORNING of Monday, 25 March the Germans made another concerted thrust across the Somme near Péronne. Although it had been expected, that did not make it any easier to resist. The men of the 2/6th Manchesters were hit by a tornado of shells.

The Germans in the town increased their bombardment to an absolute crescendo during which our trumpeter was very seriously hurt. Before dying he propped himself up against the back of the trench, put his trumpet to his lips and put all he knew into playing the *Trumpet Voluntary*. The sound even penetrated the bombardment, the mortars stopped firing and the Germans started cheering. At first we thought they were showing their appreciation of the music, but as we looked round we saw that their troops had succeeded in crossing the river on both sides of us and were closing in behind us. The Germans in the town must have thought that it was one of their own trumpeters signalling that they were in possession of the bridge. Then the bombardment started again.[28]

Private P. R. Hall, 2/6th Battalion, Manchester Regiment, 199th Brigade, 66th Division

Clearly outflanked on both sides they had to make their escape up the ridge that lay behind their now useless defences. This left them very exposed to raking fire from the Germans who were now flooding unhindered across the river and exploring the exposed flanks of the 2/6th Manchesters.

We were fortunate in finding a dry gully running up the slope. The Germans were closing in on us from both sides and did not see us until we reached a culvert under a road that was blocked with debris. Then there was no alternative but to dash out, across the road and dive into the gully again. An enemy machine gun got onto us and about one in four of our men were killed in that dash across the road. I had stopped about 120 yards back to bandage a wounded man who had to be left behind. I gave him my water bottle and followed the others. When I came to the pile of dead on the road, the machine gun had stopped firing thinking that we were all across, so I made a dash and the gun opened up again just as I dived into the gully on the other side. It seemed obvious that they would be able to cut off my retreat, because I was out of breath and weak from the lack of food. Then I realised I was receiving covering fire from somewhere on top of the ridge. It took the Germans by surprise and made them hesitate, so I kept staggering on hoping to get through before they recovered. Just then a whizz-bang shell burst alongside me and I was knocked out. Both our men and the Germans saw me fall and thought I was dead. I became conscious again when a bullet struck the ground and spattered my face with gravel. I scrambled to my knees and a voice said, 'He's alive!' I looked round and saw a group of 17th Lancers sheltering behind their dead horses. One of them asked if I could crawl and when I said I could, told me to get quickly behind the horse with him as they were going to retreat in a few minutes. When I got there he told me I had been unconscious for two hours. They had charged over what they thought was my dead body, and the horses had avoided stepping on me, but they had been driven back, had regrouped and charged again. But the Germans had brought up machine guns and shot the horses from under them, so now they were going to retire and fight as infantry on the way back.[29]

Private P. R. Hall, 2/6th Battalion, Manchester Regiment, 199th Brigade, 66th Division

Up and down the Somme River and Canal there were similar scenes. What was left of the Somme Line was fast crumbling. At Brie, a little to the south, it was the turn of the 2nd Middlesex to be brushed aside in the German onslaught.

> Dawn broke and so did the silence of the night. Earth was turned into hell. Our task was to hold a bridge, which was not only under fire from our own battalion but also a detachment of the Machine Gun Corps. After four or five long hours had passed away our position became very hot, because not only were we under shells and rifle fire, but a big warehouse that was about 20 yards away from the end of our trench was set alight by the German gunners. Besides this, we had to cope with a German aeroplane that kept flying over our trench and firing a machine gun onto us. Also our own artillery was very bad and seemed to have the knack of firing their shells onto us! Jerry meant to stop at nothing and, after losing many men, crossed the bridge and drove us out of our trench.[30]
>
> Private Frederick Curtis, 2nd Battalion, Middlesex Regiment, 23rd Brigade, 8th Division

They fell back, occupying various shell-hole positions until what remained of Curtis's platoon took up a dangerously exposed position on top of a ridge. There was no proper cover, the Germans were clearly engaged in vigorously outflanking them and the casualties were mounting quickly. After a while it all became too much for Private Curtis.

> After seeing many of my pals and my officer drop down beside me, I thought it my best plan to get off this ridge. However, the task was not so easy as I thought. I managed it eventually, running from one shell hole to another, hearing the bullets cutting up the grass between my feet and trying to dodge a few shells. My next place of shelter was in a small dugout alongside a sunken road where I found four or five other fellows.[31]
>
> Private Frederick Curtis, 2nd Battalion, Middlesex Regiment, 23rd Brigade, 8th Division

All along the British front units were fragmenting: divisions were arbitrarily split up into brigades and rushed into action, brigades were losing track of whole battalions, the battalions were fragmenting into companies, the companies lost all cohesion and fell into their constituent platoons, the platoons became mere sections and soon all that

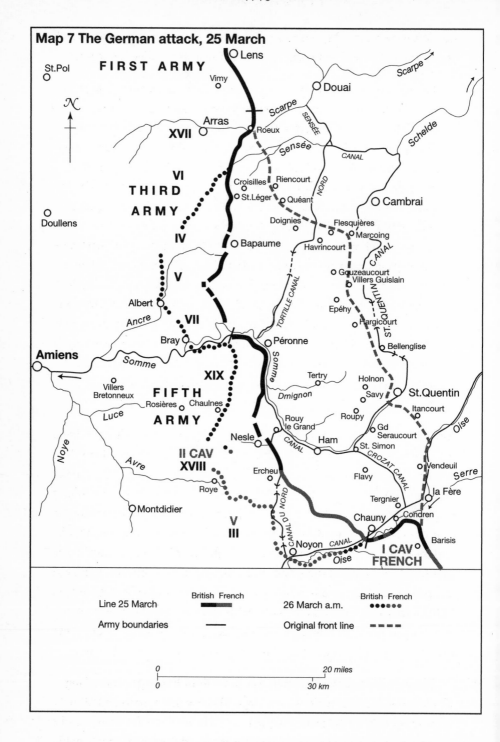

Map 7 The German attack, 25 March

St.Pol

FIRST ARMY

Lens

Scarpe

Vimy

Douai

$\mathcal{N}$

Scarpe

XVII

Arras

Roeux

Sensée

CANAL

Schelde

VI

THIRD

Croisilles   Riencourt

St.Léger   Quéant

NORD

Cambrai

ARMY

Doignies

Flesquières

Doullens

IV

Bapaume

Havrincourt

Marcoing

CANAL

V

Gouzeaucourt

Villers Guislain

ST. QUENTIN

Albert

VII

Epéhy

Ancre

Bray

Péronne

Hargicourt

Bellenglise

Amiens

Somme

Tertry

Holnon

St.Quentin

XIX

Somme

Dmignon

Savy

Itancourt

Villers

Bretonneux

FIFTH

Rosières   Chaulnes

Roupy

Oise

Luce

ARMY

Rouy
le Grand

Ham

Gd
Seraucourt

Nesle

CANAL

St. Simon

CROZAT CANAL

Vendeuil

II CAV

Noye

XVIII

Ercheu

Flavy

Serre

Avre

Roye

CANAL DU NORD

Tergnier

la Fère

Montdidier

V

Chauny

Condren

III

Noyon   CANAL

CANAL

I CAV

Barisis

Oise

FRENCH

	British	French			British	French
Line 25 March	▮▮▮	▦▦▦	26 March a.m.		●●●●●●	
Army boundaries	——		Original front line		─ ─ ─ ─	

0   20 miles

0   30 km

was left were isolated groups of just a few men making their way back across the battlefield as best they could. It was not a cheering sight.

> The road past our battery afforded some evidence of the fighting that was in progress in front of us. Wounded men continued to pass all day: the slightly wounded, glad of the opportunity to get out of the firing line, helping the badly wounded; men wounded in the legs supporting themselves by the shoulders of men wounded in the arms. Here and there, at rare intervals, a Hun prisoner under the escort of a perfectly good 'Tommy'. We spoke to some of them, but none had anything very cheering to relate. The general impression seemed to be that we were up against a hopeless task – that there would be no stopping them here – more reinforcements were needed. There were, on the other hand, some reinforcements brought up. Small detachments of dusty, tired-looking men, in charge of a young officer, passed the battery from time to time. Our men would give them a bit of a cheer and wish them luck. They would call back, 'That's the stuff to give 'em!' as a gun went off. It always seemed to cheer them a bit to find a battery in action and it certainly cheered us to see reinforcements being brought up![32]
>
> Lieutenant Edward Allfree, 111th Siege Battery, Royal Garrison Artillery

Amongst the reinforcements passing the battery may well have been the machine-gun crews of the 9th Battalion, Tank Corps. They had been brusquely detached from their Whippet tanks and sent forward as infantry to Maricourt, where it was hoped their extra firepower might help stem the German advance. On arrival they were pushed a couple of miles further forward into Trônes Wood – a name that for a while had been synonymous with disaster back in 1916. Once again the splintered remnants of the wood had a tactical significance for it offered the prospect of an uninterrupted view for German artillery observers right across the old Somme battlefields over which the British Army was now retreating. Amongst the machine-gunners sent forward were Private Herbert Thompson and his best pal, Private John Downing.

> Through field glasses we could see that a terrible struggle was taking place and our instructions were to get there with all speed and, if the position was still ours when we arrived, to help hold it at all costs until a certain hour in the evening when it was thought that our army would

be in a safe position. Our only means of approaching it, under the circumstances, was by means of an old German communication trench, which the Germans knew all about and were shelling for all they were worth, to prevent reinforcements being sent up. As a matter of fact, we were a sacrifice party, pure and simple, for if we got there, which was doubtful, it was not expected that we should get back. We started out at 8 a.m. and it was 11 a.m. before we reached the wood – stumps of battered trees. Most of the way we had crawled on all fours and our casualties were very heavy, the ammunition carrier who was assisting John and I being one of the first to go. The wood was still ours when we got there, though the sight that presented itself to us, I shall never forget. I couldn't describe it and I wouldn't if I could. Of the original number who held the position, only a few were left and the fighting had been terrible. A main road ran through the wood and it was in a trench on the opposite side of this road (the side nearest the Germans) that we found them, a mixed lot of dismounted Hussars, 17th Lancers and infantry. They were all in a pitiful condition and, like ourselves, thoroughly exhausted with their struggles. But for all that they greeted us with a cheer and for once in our lives at least we felt we were really and truly friends in time of need. We arrived just at the right moment, for no sooner had we taken up our positions than the Germans forced another attack and for the next two hours we were mighty busy. It looked a hopeless fight from the beginning as they came on in seemingly endless numbers, and at times came very near overwhelming us, but eventually they drew off again and we breathed freely once more. But not for long. They next tried to wipe us out with trench mortar bombs and shrapnel, they tried with machine-gun fire from aeroplanes, and then they launched another mass attack. Just at this time, two o'clock, while the attack was being prepared, we received an order to leave the position we were in, double back across the road and take up a position there, quickly. German bullets were flying round us in all directions as we scrambled across the road, John carrying the gun and I the ammunition. We reached the other side in safety and were in the act of changing over – that is, John giving me the gun to take my turn at firing while he handled the ammunition – when his end came with staggering suddenness. In the midst of the excitement, the sound of a bullet whizzing fearfully close told me instinctively that John was hit.

166

He swayed a little, we both released our grip on the gun and I caught him as he fell to the ground where I quickly undid the clothing at his throat. It was in vain, I tried to get him to speak to me; neither by sign nor sound did he signify that he knew what had happened to him. The bullet entered his right side behind his arm, passing in a slanting manner through his chest, came out on his left side in front of his left arm. I was certain then, as I am now, that his death was instantaneous. As I cease writing to think a little, I can see the scene so clearly. Bursting shells and shrieking bullets, little groups of men in crouching attitudes, apparently unconcerned with the little tragedy taking place a few yards from them, John lying on the beautiful green grass, and, except for a little jagged blood-smeared hole in the left side of his tunic, apparently sleeping and myself kneeling beside him with my eyes full of tears I couldn't check, as I realised he had gone and I had lost one of the kindest and bravest of chums. All this happened surprisingly quickly and scarcely had I realised that he was dead than the whistle blew and we were ordered back to the position we had just left. Theirs not to reason why, one's duty as a soldier is to obey orders, and automatically I sprang to my feet, grasped the gun in one hand and a case of loaded magazines in the other and joined in the scurry back again. Our temporary withdrawal had been a ruse to draw the Germans out of cover, break up their formation and render them easier for us to handle. The ruse was successful – we caught them in the open and inflicted severe losses on them. During this fighting, our officer, Mr Mecredy, an officer and a gentleman in every sense of the term, crawled up to me and asked where John was. I couldn't speak; I could only point across the way. He understood.[33]

Private Herbert Thompson, 9th Battalion, Tank Corps

They withdrew later that night; as far as they were concerned their task had been carried out. Private John Downing was left behind and today has no known grave. His death is commemorated on the Pozières Memorial.

During the fighting that day Brigadier de Pree found himself a strangely detached, but nevertheless interested witness to the free-flowing tactics adopted by the advancing German troops.

The front was covered by large patrols each carrying one or two light machine guns. The use of light signals by these patrols was most remarkable. They signalled each stage in their advance by sending up a Very light, with the result that the general effect given was the advance of a line of light signals going up as far as the eye could reach. There may have been some slight disadvantage in this, in that it showed their position to their enemy, but on the other hand it showed every man that he was supported on his right and left, and this was a far more decisive factor. The large patrols probed our front and if they found a gap, they at once passed through it and sent up a success signal. The troops in the rear at once moved to it and poured through the gap, and in a few minutes our flank was turned at that place. So far as could be seen the majority of the enemy's infantry on this part of the front had abandoned their rifles and simply acted as ammunition carriers to their numerous light machine guns. This seems to be borne out by the extraordinarily persistent volume of fire which they kept up from these guns. In no other way could it have been accomplished.[34]

Brigadier General H. D. de Pree, Headquarters, 189th Brigade, 63rd (Royal Naval) Division

In the end, Brigadier de Pree and his accompanying staff brigade major were extremely lucky to escape the fate of Brigadier Vivian Bailey when they encountered a marauding German patrol while riding late at night with their staff towards Englebelmer.

We rode towards the corner where the road turns out of Mesnil village towards Englebelmer, and as we reached it a party of men, evidently a German patrol, fired into us from the bank at about 5 yards range and began shouting. Fortunately no one was hit, and the party charged round the corner only to find themselves held up by a wire stretched across the road. We drove our horses into the wire and it gave, and our whole party clattered down the road.[35]

Brigadier General H. D. de Pree, Headquarters, 189th Brigade, 63rd (Royal Naval) Division

And so back they would have to go: outflanked and out-fought. Woods, villages and ridges that had taken months to capture in 1916 were surrendered in a matter of hours.

It was an infantryman's battle; even our divisional artillery joined us, often firing alongside us over open sights. Our Major General and his brigadiers were with us controlling his troops, Wellington-like. It was leapfrog in reverse: battalion went through battalion, company through company, but always a company, always a battalion standing facing the enemy ready to fight. So we came back to the Somme battlefield. Our General formed us in a square: his flanks in the air, he put out flanking battalions. In some six hours we came back over these old battlefields. We dropped into a trench we knew of old; we were back in the trench we had attacked from on 13 November 1916. Although we had not won, we had not been beaten.[36]

Sergeant Richard Tobin, Hood Battalion, 189th Brigade, 63rd (Royal Naval) Division

The 6″ howitzers of the 111th Siege Battery had been dropped into position in the yard of Bomfay Farm just off the main road and close to the village of Maricourt. Here the men had been ordered in no uncertain terms by a staff officer that they must stick it there to the last man and the last gun. There would be no further retreat. But good intentions and fine words do not make for comfortable bedfellows with military reality. In the end, their 'last stand' came to an ignominious end.

So the day wore on. We continued to fire, to work out fresh lines and elevations, and switch as fresh targets were given to us. The fight in front of us continued to rage, wounded continued to struggle back, and different reports and rumours reached us from time to time, till after tea, when the Major got the order to pull out at once and retire. We were given to understand that there was no time to be lost if we were to get away with the guns. So we were again pulling out and loading the lorries. So much for the 'no further retirement' order! We had been here a little over 24 hours.[37]

Lieutenant Edward Allfree, 111th Siege Battery, Royal Garrison Artillery

Over the next couple of days the staff officers at all levels of command truly had to earn their keep. When the usual rigid hierarchical system of military command broke down they were the glue that had to bind the army together. Someone had to be on the spot, taking control and making decisions. They might be the wrong decisions but someone had to do something or nothing would happen – and that could only be to the benefit of the onrushing Germans.

I motored forward to the great La Flaque Dump to hurry on the evacuation or destruction of its contents. It was a vast dump covering acres of ground, the Royal Engineers portion of it, chiefly timber and iron, had, of course, to be left, but the gun park, IOM works and ordnance stores were nearly cleared, and the ration dump was reduced to 50,000 rations instead of the million or so usually there. I tried to hasten the clearance of the gun park, but the labour company men who were loading the lorries were deadbeat. There was also 10,000 gallons of aeroplane petrol. We took as much as we could for our own private lorries, as it almost doubles their speed, but I fear the bulk of this dump had later to be set on fire.[38]

Major Neil Fraser-Tytler, Royal Artillery, Headquarters, Fifth Army

Guns of all calibres abounded in the gun parks and it was a desperate matter to try and get these huge lumps of unyielding steel, immobile at the best of times, back out of the reach of the Germans. The rear areas were scoured and any spare caterpillar tractors or lorries with sufficient power were hastily commandeered to tow the guns.

At night the Germans launched harassing bombing raids spattering their bombs across their targets. After all their daytime exertions the British found that sleep was rendered almost impossible as death and destruction fell from the skies.

We came in for one of the severest and most protracted bomb raids that has ever happened in France. Bombs are so much worse than shells. One can sleep with a feeling of perfect security when the Hun is pounding away with 5.9s at a battery 200 yards to a flank, but with bombs it is very different. There is always the eternal 'make and break' hum of the German machines, easily distinguished by ear from our own, the disgusting noise of the 'Archies' yapping like a pack of toy Schipperkes, then the final circle round with engine shut off, followed by four, six or eight bombs, according to their size. As bad luck would have it, just as the Colonel and Hills were standing outside my tent on their way to bed, a 120-lb bomb swished over the tent pole and burst exactly 4½ yards from the head of my camp bed. Hills and Davidson, our Colonel, were lucky to escape with their lives, the former being wounded in two places and Davidson in about twenty. The bill was a pretty heavy one, six officers and twenty-two men killed and wounded.

After we had got the worst case off to hospital I retired to my bed-bag, as sleeping head-on to such a crash does not improve one's walking or thinking powers. All the others retired to spend the night either sitting in the open fields or in some safer locality, but feeling disinclined to move from my wrecked tent I spent the night there. All night, until 3 a.m., with only short intervals between each raid, the bombs continued to fall. During these intervals gallant bands of would-be helpers regularly discovered me inside the remains of the tent, and invariably insisted that I must be a casualty, and frustrating their well-meaning efforts was somewhat trying to the temper.[39]

Major Neil Fraser-Tytler, Royal Artillery, Headquarters, Fifth Army

Come the dawn his tent proved to be a sorry sight, gaping holes abounded and the pole alone had been hit by some twenty-eight shell splinters.

The German bombing raids on the headquarters claimed the loss of many experienced, highly trained and skilled professional staff officers who were engaged in trying to bring order to the chaos of the retreat. There was also the general disruption to the sleep patterns and general morale of those who survived. Next morning they would be tired and the Germans would be back the next night and the nights following. Gradually men lost their edge and were either reduced to dull automatons or became semi-hysterical as they cracked under the pressure.

We were beginning to feel the strain of the past few days, for the lack of sleep pulls a man down quicker than most things. Nerves were almost at snapping point, but somehow we managed to keep almost cheerful and the sight of the cooker in full blast helped considerably. We were just about to draw our ration of precious liquid when along galloped a staff officer in the kind of rage into which 'Brass Hats' can work themselves. His face was purple and his eyes literally bulged. He harangued us thus, 'What the hell are you men doing? Can't you see the enemy advancing?' By all the laws of nature his vocal chords should have snapped with the sheer ferocity of his articulation, but they remained intact long enough for him to order us to move off as quickly as we could. We did not know who he was, but it is never wise to indulge in conversation with the 'Great Ones' who sport gold braid and red tabs. So we sorrowfully poured our tea in the ditch and bolted. This gentleman in a few seconds turned what had been more or less order into complete chaos![40]

Private David Polley, 189th Machine Gun Company, 189th Brigade, 63rd (Royal Naval) Division

If the staff officers were tired or drifting out of control, what of the men? Many were exhausted beyond reason and had little idea of what was happening to their platoon, never mind to the Third and Fifth Armies.

The majority of us were more or less stupid with fatigue. We noticed some barns where we halted and decided to make ourselves as comfortable as we could, but found everything locked. We were not, however, in the mood that is defeated by locked doors and very soon the locks were forced and we very thankfully lay our weary bodies on the straw and litter, to fall asleep almost immediately. The civilian population were still in residence, but were far from being friendly towards us. They were frightened and accused us of having let them down. This, I think you will agree, is not the ideal way of greeting tired troops. I am afraid that as a result we, in turn, were not as polite as we probably should have been. They would not do anything for us and sullenly refused to supply food.[41]

Private David Polley, 189th Machine Gun Company, 189th Brigade, 63rd (Royal Naval) Division

Five days of constant fighting, marching and sleeping rough had turned even the formerly gilded lily officers of the 16th Brigade, Royal Horse Artillery into a tramp-like state.

I was one of the most disreputable objects to be found in the fair land of France. I was filthy dirty and unshaven, '*Ça va sans dire*!' In addition I had lost one puttee and was wearing an old fleece lining torn in many places and loose oilskin overalls that came to just below the knee. Add to this the fact that my nose had been bleeding off and on during the day – I had started out without a handkerchief and had been employing an oily waste in my revolver holster for the purpose – and that my lips were still blistered and cracked with gas and you do *not* have the *beau ideal* of a Horse Artillery subaltern in a notoriously well-dressed battery.[42]

Second Lieutenant John Fleming, 'U' Battery, 16th Brigade, Royal Horse Artillery

The men didn't look like soldiers any more and soon they began to realise that they were no longer part of a great army. Their fate lay in the hands of their immediate officer or NCO; often whether they lived, died or became a prisoner lay in their own hands and depended on the smallest decision – whether to stand or run, which way to go at a turning, whether to push on or rest. Private Edward Williamson had lost touch with his battalion, the 17th Royal Scots, in all the confusion and was marching back with a group of randomly mixed soldiers from many different units.

Our small band gained a main road to be caught up at once in the confused mass of traffic that seemed endless, every branch of the service intent on squeezing into the smallest space available. There prevailed over everything else an urgency to keep moving and this resulted in a motion being reduced to a crawl and frequently to a full stop, creating frustration among officers and men alike. Infantry, transport, artillery, cars and lorries closely intermingled with cavalry, engineers, ambulances, field kitchens etc. It appeared more like a rout than an orderly withdrawal at this time, but in the early light of dawn it was impossible to get an accurate picture. After plodding along for some time with four of the Durhams, I obtained a lift on a gun limber with the connivance of the driver and an offer of a few 'smokes' as a bribe.[43]

Private Edward Williamson, 17th Battalion, Royal Scots, 106th Brigade, 35th Division

Under these circumstances some men not unnaturally began to take responsibility for their own survival, often in a manner prejudicial to good discipline or military order. When the orders appeared suicidal or wrong-headed then the men often edged away.

An officer and a mixed body of about twenty men held a trench and I joined them, recognising a man of my own regiment with whom I was slightly acquainted. They said they had fired off all their ammunition and the officer was apparently desirous of holding off the German Army with the bayonet. I looked at my friend, and he at me, and we decided against it! The officer gave no orders, I doubt whether he survived and we could but admire his optimistic courage.[44]

Trooper Arthur Bradbury, Royal Scots Greys, 2nd Cavalry Division

Yet within all the confusion, suffering and general despair there was evidence that the human spirit, or at least the priapic urges, can overcome most obstacles.

> If evidence of our high spirits and virility was needed I record the following for posterity. I was with a covering rearguard party and was passed by a small detachment of Gordon Highlanders. Hastening to catch up with my own unit, I surprised one of the kilted Jocks who had dodged his own column and was well and truly seducing a French girl in a pile of stones – and he had not even removed his pack![45]
>
> Sapper Frederick Cook, 78th Field Company, Royal Engineers, 17th Division

There was also one consolation for the British if they could have only known it. The German soldiers were also beginning to suffer from the incredible strains of the fast-moving campaign. As they moved inexorably forwards they could not help but see copious signs of the awful fighting that dragged at their nerves.

> We saw the remains of a German aeroplane, still in good shape. Underneath lay the pilot with just his underpants. All along the road were dead soldiers. At first, nearly all our soldiers; after that the English. In the ditches along the road these unfortunate souls are lying, their faces covered by a thick layer of dirt, the head bent slightly forwards, crouching, some still with their back packs and helmets. Nearly all of them had their shoes or boots taken away and the packs were rifled looking for valuables. We found shelter in dugouts that had been used by the English. These were half in the ground and the upper half covered in corrugated iron and sandbags round the sides. Of course, it was not very warm. We wandered round the fields and found dead bodies everywhere with weapons and clothing – especially blankets and trench coats, which we put on. Some of the bodies looked ghastly, for example, a German soldier whose eyes and cheeks had been gnawed by rats. Others were naked; others with broken skulls.[46]
>
> Signaller Edwin Kühns, 1047th Telephone Unit, Imperial German Army

The Germans were astonished by the copious stores they discovered. Although much had been destroyed, much still remained and it was a peek into another world for the deprived German soldiers. Huge depots, teeming with what to the Germans had become luxuries, canteens stuffed full of food and drink.

> We found large stores of food. Tins of corned beef, which I later heard were despised by the British, but we regarded them as a great delicacy! I emptied one or two of these tins. We also found a store of champagne and when we went forward I can recall myself running with a bottle of champagne at my mouth![47]
>
> Feldwebel Walter Rappolt, 2nd Battery, 406th Artillery Battalion, 1st Guards Foot Artillery Regiment, Imperial German Army

They had been told that the British were suffering awful privations and widespread shortages of food and resources from the effects of the U-boat campaign. But one thing was soon evident to any German soldier – the British soldier was in no danger of starving in the normal course of events.

CHAPTER SIX

Turning the Tide

TUESDAY, 26 MARCH 1918 was the day that would decide the future of the Anglo-French alliance. They would either pull together or fracture in the face of the excruciating German pressure. At noon the emergency conference convened at Haig's request met at Doullens. Various members of the British and French High Command attended: the Minister without Portfolio Lord Milner, the Chief of the Imperial General Staff General Sir Henry Wilson and Haig made up the main protagonists of the British team, while the French were represented by the Premier Georges Clemenceau, their President Raymond Poincaré, the Chief of General Staff Field Marshal Ferdinand Foch and their Commander-in-Chief Henri Pétain. It was a meeting of politicians and the military and as such it is fair to say that one could never expect a consistent account of what emerged from the proceedings. Everyone was in their own eyes at the centre of events; everyone bent everyone else to their will. But from the outside it seems likely that 'Tiger' Clemenceau was the dominant figure. Born on 28 September 1841, Clemenceau was already relatively old when he was appointed to the French premiership in November 1917, but the flame of his energy and drive seemed undimmed – put simply, he was the strong man of French politics. A staunch republican he was totally committed to the defeat of Germany and regarded backsliders seeking a negotiated peace with Germany as little more than traitors – like Lloyd George, he believed in total war. There is little doubt that Clemenceau wanted to use the dire British situation to establish a unity of command, under a French general of course – but he was irritated by Pétain's negativity and foresaw that if the French and

British Armies pulled apart on the battlefield then they would be defeated in detail.

Fortunately there was a ready-made alternative at hand – Ferdinand Foch was a man whose time had come. Born on 2 October 1851 he had carved out a pre-war career as the finest theorist at the French Staff College. Foch had a firm belief in the crucial importance of morale as a prerequisite to victory, which he allied to the importance of the offensive in securing victory. Although Foch had been influential as a military theorist he had not attained a particularly high rank at the onset of the war, being merely the commander of the XX Corps. As such he was unable to prevent his theories being twisted by many of his senior contemporaries into a veritable 'cult of the offensive', which reached its nadir in the hopeless Plan XVII offensives, as the French Army lunged recklessly for Alsace-Lorraine in August 1914. Since then his advance had been rapid. Commanding the Ninth Army he had performed great deeds during the Battle of the Marne, which he typified in his most famous quote, 'Hard pressed on my right. My centre is yielding. Impossible to manoeuvre. Situation excellent. I am attacking!' This might have reinforced perceptions of Foch as a head-less chicken of a general, but in reality there was far more to him than a witty aphorism. He only attacked after every preparation had been made, with a clear set of objectives and a reasonable likelihood of success. Like most generals in the Great War he had struggled in 1915 and 1916 with the complexities of trench warfare but had survived various ups and downs prior to his appointment as Chief of General Staff. Foch remained a beacon of positive thinking, and, as the Germans drove forwards, he drew great strength from his success four years before on the Marne in not dissimilar circumstances. He *knew* the Germans could be defeated; the Allies just had to be strong and stick together.

Haig's priority was simple: he needed French reinforcements and he needed them to commit to maintaining the link between the British and French Armies. Nothing else mattered. But Haig knew he could trust neither Wilson nor Milner to back him in any stand-off; he was well aware that they were in thrall to the absent Lloyd George. The meeting took place at the Hôtel de Ville just after noon. In retrospect the outcome was probably inevitable since the conference began with the sound of the guns rumbling in the background, which must have added a certain urgency to the proceedings.

> It was decided that Amiens must be covered at all costs. French troops are being hurried up as rapidly as possible and Gough has been told to hold on with his left at Bray. It was proposed by Clemenceau that Foch should be appointed to coordinate the operations of an Allied force to cover Amiens and ensure that the French and British flanks remained united. This proposal seemed to me quite worthless, as Foch would be in a subordinate position to Pétain and myself. In my opinion it was essential to success that Foch should control Pétain, so I at once recommended that Foch should control the actions of all the Allied Armies on the Western Front. Foch seemed sound and sensible, but Pétain had a terrible look. He had the appearance of a commander who was in a funk and had lost his nerve.[1]

> Field Marshal Sir Douglas Haig, General Headquarters, BEF

In the end, this was accepted by all sides. Haig knew that he could not get the unified command for himself; that was clearly an unrealistic proposition, as he did not even have the support of his own prime minister. But the situation was so desperate that Haig was willing to sacrifice his independence by accepting Foch in preference to Pétain, who had been found badly wanting under pressure. There has been considerable controversy as to who exactly instigated the final elevation of Foch to the role of Supreme Commander, but one way or another it was the work of Clemenceau, a true master of politics, who seems to have manoeuvred with considerable skill to ensure that it was the British who suggested what the French themselves wanted. Manipulated or not, there is no doubt that Haig fully accepted that it was a necessary step. At a second conference just a week later at Beauvais on 3 April, Foch was formally given the responsibility for the strategic direction of military operations by the French, British and American Armies on the Western Front. In some ways the sacrifice was not so great as the French had always been the senior partner in the alliance. Over the past two years Haig had consistently fallen in with the overall plans of the French commanders-in-chief and made the sacrifices required by his French Allies; he would continue to do so.

*

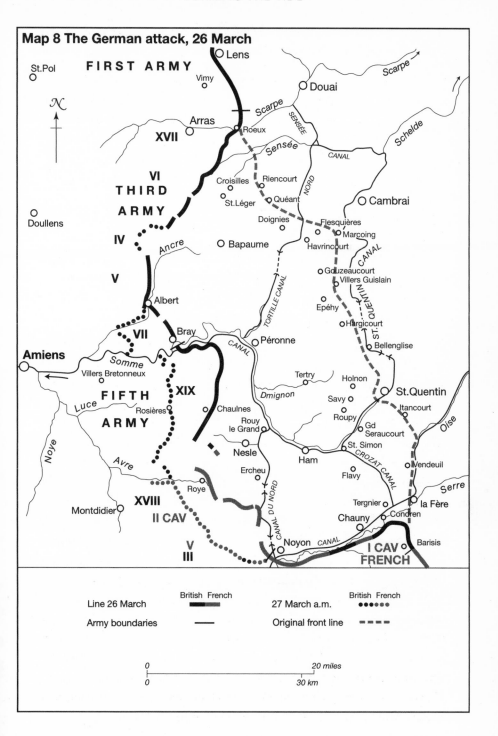

Map 8 The German attack, 26 March

FIRST ARMY

St.Pol

Lens

Vimy

Scarpe

Douai

N

Arras

Scarpe

Roeux

SENSÉE

Schelde

XVII

Sensée

CANAL

VI

THIRD

ARMY

Croisilles

Riencourt

Quéant

St.Léger

NORD

Cambrai

Doullens

IV

Doignies

Flesquières

Marcoing

Ancre

Bapaume

Havrincourt

V

Gouzeaucourt

Villers Guislain

Albert

Epéhy

CANAL

Bray

VII

Hargicourt

Péronne

ST. QUENTIN CANAL

Bellenglise

Amiens

Somme

Villers Bretonneux

Tertry

Holnon

FIFTH

Dmignon

Savy

St.Quentin

Luce

XIX

Itancourt

ARMY

Rosières

Chaulnes

Roupy

Oise

Rouy
le Grand

Gd
Seraucourt

Noye

Avre

Nesle

Ham

St. Simon

CROZAT CANAL

Ercheu

Flavy

Vendeuil

Roye

Serre

XVIII

Tergnier

la Fère

Montdidier

II CAV

Chauny

Condren

V

Noyon

CANAL

I CAV

Barisis

III

CANAL DU NORD

FRENCH

	British French		British French
Line 26 March	▬▬▬	27 March a.m.	●●●●●●
Army boundaries	———	Original front line	▬ ▬ ▬

0   20 miles

0   30 km

THE FIFTH ARMY LINE along the Somme had been irretrievably broken by the Germans by 26 March. Although the line of the Somme River was lost there were still men that had not been pushed back manning sections of the line near where the Somme swung round to the west. Naturally, their position was extremely perilous as the Germans swirled round behind them. Second Lieutenant Frank Warren and his men of 'A' Company, 17th King's Royal Rifle Corps had held the bank and the destroyed canal bridge at Feuillères without much incident throughout the previous day. But now they were comprehensively outflanked. The Germans were driving west, moving towards Cappy and Bray-sur-Somme with the obvious intent of cutting the remaining British defenders off and pinning them in a hopeless position with their backs to the river.

> Suddenly the word comes that the Boche are coming in force down both sides of the trench and that we must 'get out sharp' unless we are to be trapped. As second in command of the company it is my job to bring up the rear, and with Sergeant Williams I see that all the men have been roused and are clear of the trench. At length we get out on top under machine-gun fire and turn our steps towards a trench that seems to present a front to the oncoming Boches. But Fritz is coming on a bit too fast, and must be checked. I find Lieutenant Barber of 'D' Company beginning this good work with a section of men. Collecting eight or ten of our men, I join in the fun. Barber and I agree hastily to advance in alternate sections, in parade-ground style, each in turn giving covering fire to the other.[2]
>
> Second Lieutenant Frank Warren, 17th Battalion, King's Royal Rifle Corps, 117th Brigade, 39th Division

Nearby, the men of the 16th Rifle Brigade were undergoing a similar experience. They had no choice but to fall back, but the moment they left their prepared defensive positions it was difficult for anyone to co-ordinate their movements in the pandemonium of battle in the open.

> Sudden spatter of bullets apparently from nowhere. Increasing in volume. Something up. Officers alert. I look over the top of my bit of trench. Few figures running from canal bank across level – were they Fritzes? Impossible to see, however officers decide they were. We didn't

know whether they were some of our own men left on the canal bank now retiring, or not! However, the Lewis guns opened on them. Fusillade of bullets continued; spattering and ricocheting around us unpleasantly. I hear officer calling – wind up – 'What shall we do?' Order given to retire, but no rallying point given. Bad position: men cut up into small parties, not easy to communicate with each party, and difficult for officers and NCOs to keep control of men and situation. Waiting for the last man I follow. We cut along trench at top of ridge, under a continuous spatter of bullets. Then across a field of tall grass. Here come under direct machine-gun fire. Bullets whistle around. So fed up, chagrined at retreat, and generally disgusted, I refuse to run and walk along, escaping death or wound by sheer extraordinary luck. We get to a trench and line it. No officers to be seen.[3]

Stretcher Bearer Albert Cousins, 16th Battalion, Rifle Brigade, 117th Brigade, 39th Division

Much of the fighting was conducted in the open as small groups of men on both sides encountered each other almost at random. Speed of reaction and thought were crucial if they were to survive. They also needed a substantial slice of luck.

My men are firing at 400 yards, both sides lying or kneeling in roughish grass in the open. Several men on our side are 'winged', mainly by machine-gun bullets. The ground is dry and spurts of dust show me that our bullets are falling short. I say to Corporal Laurie, and the others, 'Put your sights up to 500 yards!' Corporal Laurie, who is a marksman, fires again, and a Boche, dropping his rifle, goes hopping off with a bullet in the leg! I say, 'Well done, Laurie! Give them another!' Ruefully he points to his right arm, and I see that he has got a bullet through the elbow. So I am afraid the Boche are quits with him at any rate![4]

Second Lieutenant Frank Warren, 17th Battalion, King's Royal Rifle Corps, 117th Brigade, 39th Division

They fell back, still frantically trying to avoid being pinned against the river. But the Germans were driving forwards hard in several different directions at once and the situation was hopelessly confused. No one knew what was happening.

The troops on our left have all come in on top of us. Next we see other troops on our right coming back fast. As the battalions get more and more mixed, order is fast disappearing. There is even a steady stream of stragglers flitting to the rear. One Scottish officer, revolver in hand, rallies these men. But the Boches can be seen coming round fast on both flanks: he has machine guns already in position. The men are mixed up in bewildered groups. Our men get mixed up with the crowd and I lose touch with them. Reluctantly we follow the fugitive stream, until we can reach a spot where we can re-form and regroup our men. It was a humiliating and exasperating half hour![5]

Second Lieutenant Frank Warren, 17th Battalion, King's Royal Rifle Corps, 117th Brigade, 39th Division

They finally managed to get reorganised under the cover of a solid series of defensive positions manned by the Gloucestershire Regiment. With due military discipline restored the men fell back to take up a line across the main Amiens road between Proyart and Framerville. Not far to the south of where Warren and the remnants of the 17th KRRC came to a halt were Private Curtis and the survivors of the 2nd Middlesex who had taken up positions in front of the railway line at Rosières-en-Santerre. When the Germans appeared late on the afternoon of 26 March they were initially caught in open ground and suffered heavy casualties.

We let him have it 'hell for leather' and a few prisoners were taken. During that night our commanding officer, Colonel Page, came round and complimented us on our fire, but our exaltations were short-lived, for when morning dawned again we were repaid in full. Our next move was over the parados at the rear of the trench and through the village. Many wounded men were crying out for help, but unfortunately it was not in our power to help them, as we were fagged out ourselves and had not a minute to spare. Our next position was in some old disused trenches with plenty of barbed wire in front of them. As the Boches came pouring out of the village our rifles took their toll. But before we realised it his snipers had managed to sneak round our flanks and take up very good positions. My mate, who was standing next to me in the fire bay caught one of their bullets and dropped dead at my feet. My, how it sickened me. Our next order was to fix bayonets, as Jerry had crept close up to the wire, but before we could use the cold steel we were ordered to evacuate the trench and to pass though a half-dug communication trench.[6]

Private Frederick Curtis, 2nd Battalion, Middlesex Regiment, 23rd Brigade, 8th Division

So the retreat went on. The speed of the German advance did not give them a chance to organise a defence line, not even to amass sufficient troops and machine guns to hold a village. And so they fell back, hoping each time to try and 'stick'. Yet it was to the British advantage that they had the space to retreat into. There was nothing of real strategic importance behind them until they got to Amiens. And although they were exhausted, the Germans were equally tired and suffering increasing supply problems as they pressed ever onwards away from their depots. Indeed, there were slight inklings that the German Army might also be suffering from the corrosive effects of open warfare on morale.

Scott is off duty and dozing, when he receives a whispered alarm of, 'Stand to!' from his sentry. Kneeling up he sees four figures in the darkness and thinks of our patrol, which is due to return. Suddenly he is all alert on hearing a hoarse whisper, '*Nicht schut! Nicht schut! Kamerad! Kamerad!*' And four Boches fully armed walk in with hands held high, overjoyed at the idea of going to England![7]

Second Lieutenant Frank Warren, 17th Battalion, King's Royal Rifle Corps, 117th Brigade, 39th Division

A more realistic idea of the friable nature of morale on *both* sides was perhaps evinced by the experience of Private William Parkin of the 151st Machine Gun Company. This was no tale of derring-do, but a story of exhausted men tested beyond their limits.

I was in a slit trench, dog-tired, when a body slipped down besides me – it was a Jerry! Frankly, I promptly gave myself up, only to realise that I had been asleep, then that he was alone, and then that he had come over to give *himself* up! I quickly recovered and became 'brave' once more as we sent him back under escort to our rear.[8]

Private William Parkin, 151st Machine Gun Company, 151st Brigade, 50th Division

As far as the British were concerned the Somme was no longer a north–south barrier but was now running from east to west, acting as the southern boundary of the Third Army. For the Third Army the situation was now beginning to solidify. As the advancing Germans tired, the British reserves began to get forward and play a real role in stemming the fading German advance. One of the key components of this was a regrouping of artillery units. This was perhaps typified by the arrival of the 310th Field Artillery Brigade, which been moved in from the Arras front to help reinforce the Bucquoy sector. Major Richard Foot of 'D' Battery found himself a splendid observation post and as his guns were dropped into position he quickly registered them on the obvious German approach routes. This boded ill for any advancing Germans and as their infantry pushed forward in dense columns they proved a splendid target for Foot's sweating gunners.

> As the sky began to lighten in the dawn of 26 March we were as ready for them as if we had been preparing for a day's practice shooting on Salisbury Plain. What a day that was! I could watch the German columns approaching one of my registered targets, and time the salvos of my own and other batteries, too, to arrive there with them. The smother of shell fire would disperse them: watching them reorganise, I could do the same to another column elsewhere, and then switch back to the first to break it up a second time. All day long they came on, and all day long we shifted our fire from one point to another across those valleys. They had plenty of other well-aimed opposition too: in fact Bucquoy became a new bastion of the British line that was never lost.[9]
>
> Major Richard Foot, 'D' Battery, 310th Brigade, Royal Field Artillery

Here, perhaps, was the real answer to the riddle of why the Germans weakened even as they pushed against the seemingly fragile British front line. The British were *not* toothless and, as we have seen, this kind of open warfare exposed the attacking German troops to sudden terrifying concentrations of fire that exacted a cruel toll in casualties. The German artillery, so deadly at the start of the battle, was now in a state of confusion: the communications linking it with the infantry and the German Air Service artillery observers had broken down, it was difficult for the gunners to register their targets in the confusions of open warfare and they were increasingly suffering from ammunition

1. Field Marshal Sir Douglas Haig (centre front) with his Army Commanders at Cambrai. Left to right behind him: General Sir Herbert Plumer, General Sir Julian Byng, General Sir William Birdwood, and General Sir Henry Horne with other senior officers. (IWM Q 9689)

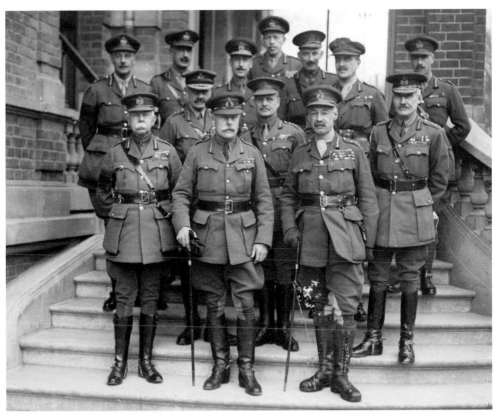

2. Kaiser Wilhelm II studying operational maps with Field Marshal Paul von Hindenburg (left) and General Erich Ludendorff (right). (Q 23746)

3. Lieutenant General Sir Hubert Gough, commander of the Fifth Army. (Q 35825D)

4. Lieutenant General Sir John Monash. (E(AUS) 2350)

5. General John Pershing and General Sir Arthur Currie. (CO 2602)

6. Field Marshal Ferdinand Foch and General Sir William Robertson. (Q 7629)

7. Four Canadian soldiers, sleeping and writing letters in the trenches near Willerval.
(CO 2533)

8. British Lewis gunners manning a barricade covering a bridge across the Lys Canal at Marquois on 13 April 1918. (Q 6612)

9. British soldiers lying dead on the battlefield at Songueval, March 1918. (Q 42245)

10. German infantry assault through the mist. (Q 47997)

11. German dead after the fighting at Villers Bretonneux, 26 April 1918. (E(AUS) 2434)

12. German soldier throwing hand grenade over a belt of barbed wire, May 1918. (Q 55020)

13. German troops working their way through the village of Pont-Arcy, 27 May 1918.
(Q 55010)

14. German reserves advancing, May 1918. (Q 55008)

15. German troops entrenched at Mont Kemmel, May 1918. (Q 47999)

16. Second Lieutenant Frank Warren of 17th King's Royal Rifle Corps. (HU 38679)

17. Gunners of the 51st Division posing at the entrance of their billet in an overturned water tower at Riencourt-les-Bapaume. (Q 8395)

18. Brigadier Hubert Rees meeting Kaiser Wilhelm II, 28 May 1918. (Q 108607)

shortages as the logistical arrangements stretched back across 30 or more miles of disrupted battlefield. The success in finally stemming the German advance at Bucquoy was symptomatic of a gradually improving situation on the Third Army front.

Yet, as always, as they handed out punishment, so the British continued to pick up a fair share of casualties from the German return fire. There were countless tales of courage from the wounded but what impressed Major Foot was the active determination of one officer to stay alive come what may.

> I came across a friend, an infantry officer, lying face downwards in a shell hole. I recognised him by his badges and thought he must be dead. I dropped in beside him and turned him over. He was alive, but unconscious. He had been hit in the right shoulder and his blood-stained tunic showed that he had lost a lot of blood. But he had saved his own life: with his left hand he had got hold of his revolver, pushed the barrel through the lanyard where it passed under his right shoulder strap, and turned and turned the heavy Colt round and round until the lanyard tightened on his wound and stopped the bleeding. He came to with a drink of water, recognised me and the first thing he said was, 'So the tourniquet did the trick!' A little later, before my stretcher bearers came to carry him away to hospital and recovery, he told me that when he was hit he lost consciousness; came to, after some unknown lapse of time, to feel the flow of blood and to realise that he might bleed to death. He thought out, as he lay, this one possible method at hand to stop the bleeding – then tightened and tightened the lanyard with his revolver barrel and his free hand, until he passed out again. Such is the inventiveness of the will to survive.[10]
>
> Major Richard Foot, 'D' Battery, 310th Brigade, Royal Field Artillery

ONE OF THE REASONS the German Army had difficulty moving troops and supplies across the battlefield was as a result of an often forgotten element of the British Army, which had more than proved its worth. Above the retreating troops there was a lot more than clouds: there were the teeming, buzzing aircraft of the RFC. They had been invaluable in their now well-established roles of photographic reconnaissance and artillery observation, although terribly handicapped by the dreaded fog that made flying either suicidally dangerous or simply useless. Whenever the aircrews could get off the ground, they flung caution to the four winds in a desperate effort to stem the German advance. The artillery cooperation functions of the two-seater corps machines may have been rendered all but impotent by the chaos on the ground, but the scouts still had their twin-machine guns and they tore into action, intervening directly in the ground fighting on a grand scale.

> We were all dragged quivering from our beds at 5 a.m., pushed into our machines, unwashed, unshaved and scantily fed, and sent down to an aerodrome near Bapaume to assist in trying to stop the Boche advance. This entails what is known as low strafing – that is going right behind the lines into enemy country, finding his transport, guns or men, and dropping bombs on them and emptying your guns into them in a long dive beginning at 3,000 feet and finishing up at 50 feet over them. At the time you are doing this, they of course are firing at you with field guns, anti-aircraft guns, machine guns, rifles etc. As they use a sort of green tracer, you can see their bullets coming up at you and hear them pierce the fabric of your machine with sharp little cracks – it gives you a very apprehensive feeling in a certain portion of your anatomy. You can't help wishing that the little leather cushion in your seat was made of steel or some other bullet-proof material. While being shot at you kick your rudder and fly as crookedly as possible, so as to be harder to hit from the ground.[11]
>
> Second Lieutenant Arthur Hollis, 1 Squadron, RFC

Ground fire may be laughably innocuous at an altitude of several thousand feet but when aircraft were skimming just above the trees in a hail of rifle and machine-gun fire it could be deadly. The pilots flew several missions a day: taking off, locating the enemy, strafing the field-grey columns until their guns were empty, then flying back to refuel and rearm. It was exhausting and there was an inexorable drain as the pilots were shot down one by one. It was the turn of Second Lieutenant Hollis on 26 March.

> It was a windy, cloudy, bumpy day. To begin with there were seventy or eighty machines working from this aerodrome and it was great to

hear the roar of their jolly big engines, to see each squadron take off like a flock of great birds, watch them pick up their formation in the air and disappear like black specks towards the Germans. Unfortunately, as the day progressed the machines returned in fewer numbers, as they got shot down. Every time one took off with a fresh load of ammunition and bombs, one wondered if the last landing was near. I survived until about 4.30 p.m., although I had been pretty well shot about. I had two bullet holes through my propeller, one of my tanks was shot through, and I had between thirty or forty bullet holes through my machine, but she was still flying beautifully.[12]

Second Lieutenant Arthur Hollis, I Squadron, RFC

Hollis took off on his last flight heading once more towards Bapaume accompanied by Lieutenant Harry Rigby and one other pilot with whom they soon lost contact. After bombing some German transport vehicles they spotted a particularly tempting target in the form of a large body of German infantry marching along a road just to the west of Bapaume.

I had just begun a long dive onto the German infantry on the road and had both guns going into them, when I heard Hun machines on my tail and saw tracer coming all round me. As it is fatal to fly straight in these circumstances, I immediately began a left-hand climbing turn to try and get above them, and had just seen they were black and white Albatros scouts when my elevator control wires were shot away. I realised with a sickening feeling that I was out of control, the nose of my machine dropped and I lost height, enabling three of them to get onto my tail. I was quite powerless.[13]

Second Lieutenant Arthur Hollis, I Squadron, RFC

Rigby had also been attacked and would recount his experiences post-war in a letter to Hollis. He reacted swiftly as the bullets zipped past his diving SE5a and he claimed to have shot one of his assailants down in flames before he was surrounded by an angry swarm of German scouts.

You were just to the east of me with three Huns on your tail. As I turned to try and help you, your wing went. I take it you were hit by an explosive bullet, at any rate the bottom right wing folded up and you started to spin. I could only watch you do a couple of turns, as I then had two Huns on my tail and one of your fellows was diving from the front. I gave him a burst as I did a climbing turn and nearly hit another fellow in a Pfalz. He dived and nearly hit an Albatros that had been on my tail. So that put two of them out of the scrap until they got height again. The next four or five minutes were rather hazy; although in them I knew why I was born. There was something about it made me feel as though I was living vividly. There was one trouble though and that was a horrible fed-up, sick feeling I had about your going down.[14]

Lieutenant Harry Rigby, I Squadron, RFC

However badly Rigby felt about the fate of his friend, it was as nothing compared with the emotions swirling through the mind of Hollis as his aircraft hurtled downwards.

Suddenly the control lever jumped from my hand because my bottom right wing had buckled up. My machine immediately began a terrific uncontrolled spin towards the ground. I knew it meant certain death, but shut off my engine and waited for it. I remember noticing my instruments and seeing that my altimeter read 2,500 feet and my speed indicator 180 mph. My childhood did *not* flit before my mind – I wish it had done – as I simply sat for those few seconds with a sickening feeling at the pit of my stomach each time the machine rushed into a fresh turn. What made it so bad was that I was absolutely powerless. I don't remember hitting the ground. I suppose I got such a dunt that the last two or three seconds were wiped from my memory. For me to have escaped death, it meant that the machine must at the last moment have stalled, or in some way lost its flying speed. Moreover, I crashed plumb in the middle of the German infantry I had been shooting up – and the astonishing thing is that they didn't finish me off.[15]

Second Lieutenant Arthur Hollis, I Squadron, RFC

The German soldiers probably thought poor battered, unconscious Hollis was dead, for they stripped his body of all valuables. But against all the odds Hollis woke up as a prisoner of war in a German field dressing station with nasty head injuries, three limbs immobile and a wound to his left foot. He had been lucky.

The scouts may have carried small Cooper bombs of 25 lb, but there were by this time fully fledged bomber squadrons flying over the battlefields by day and by night seeking out likely targets. Their bombs were laughably small by later standards, but everything is relative, and at the time it seemed more than enough to the Germans, especially if they got caught in the open at a bottleneck crossing beside one of the recently captured or rebuilt Somme bridges.

> The destructive power of bombs seemed to increase all the time. A British Handley Page bomber used bombs of 1,000 kilos. Bombs of 300 kilos were in daily use. Even the small 50 kilo bombs had destructive power equal to a 15 centimetre shell. A 12½ kilo bomb dropped on living targets moving on hard ground would burst into 1,400 pieces, each one sizzling parallel to the ground, and could cause very bad wounds.[16]
>
> Leutnant Fritz Nagel, Nr. 82 K Flak, Imperial German Army

The night-bombing squadrons continued to mirror the work of the day bombers concentrating their raids on the tactical requirements of the army. Night flying was still in its infancy so there was much preparation work to be done if the pilots were to have any chance of finding their targets. Second Lieutenant Hopkins was fortunate in that 83 Squadron had an extremely conscientious mapping officer who tried his very best to help the pilots locate their targets in the black nights.

> He used to go out with the machines at night, fly over sections that we operated in and come back with a whole picture of it in his mind. He'd get big sheets of the old blue sugar-bag paper and used that as a background to paint in the various landmarks: roads, railways, lakes, woods – that kind of thing. When we were given a particular objective in any area he'd bring out his sugar-bag paper, put it up on the wall and paint in the actual spot we were supposed to attack. As far as possible he would make it lifelike as to what the thing really looked like at night. We found this a great help because it was surprising how realistic these pictures were when we actually got over the spot.[17]
>
> Second Lieutenant J. C. F. Hopkins, 83 Squadron, RFC

Their bombs could never be really accurate but they brought the same kind of distress to the Germans that the German bombers had visited on Major Neil Fraser-Tytler and so many other exhausted British soldiers. The Germans, too, needed their sleep but were continually awoken by the drone of the British bombers and the thunderous crashes of their bombs. The morale effect of night bombing far out-weighed the actual physical damage and casualties inflicted.

More and more squadrons moved up; others flew sorties from their bases behind the other army areas. Soon up to a hundred aircraft at a time were skimming over the battlefield attacking the German infantry, swooping down on their artillery batteries, ripping into the long trans-port columns that wound along the few passable roads across the devastated battlefields. The RFC had come of age as a key part in the battlefield mix – aircraft were a key component in the All Arms Battle in their own right as opposed to being merely the handmaidens of the artillery.*

FOR FIVE TUMULTOUS DAYS the Third and Fifth Armies had fallen back, pivoting on the firm base of the intact Arras defences on the left of the Third Army. For the right of the Fifth Army this had involved falling back from the original front line at La Fère, right back some 30 hard miles to the town of Roye. This had opened up a potentially fatal gap along an east–west line, which had eventually been filled by a mixture of French divisions and the remnants of the British III Corps. These troops now passed under the control of the French Third Army under General Georges Humbert. Beside them was the still small French First Army of just two divisions commanded by General Marie Debeney. Next in line was the sad remnant of General Gough's Fifth Army, shrunk now to just the XVIII and XIX Corps. As a further indignity to Gough, Haig had decided that to unify command south of the Somme River the Fifth Army must be included with the afore-mentioned French First and Third Armies to form the Group of Armies of Reserve under the command of General Émile Fayolle. In truth there was little left of the Fifth Army, as the VII Corps on the north side of the Somme River had already been transferred to Byng's Third Army. The situation was indeed desperate, but there was still hope:

* The role of the RFC was vital but has been deliberately understated in this book as it is fully covered in the companion volume *Aces Falling: War Above the Trenches, 1918.*

the procession of French divisions reaching the area accelerated once Foch had begun to control the levers of power. There was no longer to be any doubt permitted: Amiens *would* be held and the unbroken front between the British and French Armies maintained at all costs.

Meanwhile, back across the English Channel the British government was horrified by the speed of the German advance. They had feared that Haig would waste men fighting on the Western Front but these losses were almost beyond pain. Between 21 March and 26 March it was estimated that the BEF had lost nearly 75,000 men, although in the chaotic circumstances no one could be really sure. All objections forgotten, the manpower suddenly became available: divisions were brought back from the backwaters of Italy, Palestine and Salonika; the age limits on active service were tweaked from 19 to 18½ and various soldiers on different forms of home service were released to fight. Over the next five months some 544,000 soldiers were despatched from one source or another to the Western Front. Suddenly what was impossible in January and February was perfectly feasible: now everyone was a Westerner.

In true fashion, the search now began for a scapegoat for the disaster that had befallen the British Army. Only one thing seemed predetermined in this search – that no one could blame Lloyd George or any member of his government. It soon became evident who was the popular choice as fall-guy: General Sir Hubert Gough. The Fifth Army had simply not fought well enough it was rumoured. Late on 26 March Gough was visited in his headquarters by the new Supreme Commander. Foch was brusque well beyond the point of rudeness and asked why Gough was at his headquarters and not with his troops in the fighting line. This was ludicrous for not only had Gough been ordered to meet him there but he would have been totally irrelevant at the front, unable in any way to control the battle away from his communications. Foch then asked Gough why his army was retiring – this, too, was purely rhetorical. Not unnaturally, Gough was distraught. Whatever his failings as a general he did not deserve to be blamed for the events of the previous five days. He had tried his best to warn Haig what was coming and he had done all he could to organise an elastic defence.

To the north of the Somme the Third Army was also falling back in conformity with the remnants of the Fifth Army on 26 March, although the pace had slowed as the front further north gradually stabilised. All of the original Somme battlefield from 1916 had now been surrendered and the troops were falling back towards and through Albert. There were terrible scenes in the old streets as the German aircraft tore into the vulnerable retreating columns of transport.

> The German airmen caught up with us as we entered Albert in bright moonlight. Swooping low they plunked bombs directly on our transport and marching men. This caused a horrible shambles of dead and dying men, horses and mules, trapped by the falling buildings and festooned with shattered telegraph wires over the living and the dead. As the dust settled the cries and groans of the men and animals in their death agonies became fainter. Over this inferno of horror the famous carved image of the Virgin hung precariously over the side of the church tower. We who were left alive set about pulling out our dead and wounded, clearing the street to allow the following transport to make a dash for safety. They galloped through, heedless of dead men and animals, as they hurtled their gun limber over all obstructions to gain a way out into the open country. At last a sudden quiet came over the stricken town and we were able to salvage about half of our animals and limbers. Smothered in dust and soaked in blood from lifting wounded into the only ambulance available – ignoring a doctor who at first refused to take those who obviously were on the way out. He was, of course, right in wanting to take only those who had a reasonable chance of recovering. I shall never forget the appealing look in the eyes of one of our sappers who was refused. I always look for his name on the war memorial on Torquay seafront when I am there.[18]
>
> Sapper Frederick Cook, 78th Field Company, Royal Engineers, 17th Division

As the British fell back, the town that had been their base during the Battle of the Somme was now in German hands and counter-attacks early next day were unavailing.

WHEN DAWN BROKE on the morning of Wednesday, 27 March the situation was still grim for the British troops south of the Somme River. Second Lieutenant Frank Warren and what remained of the 17th King's Royal Rifle Corps were still falling back; sometimes manning hedgerows, if they were lucky dropping into a ditch or taking over old trench lines, ripples in the earth left by the previous fighting in 1915 or 1916. In a battle of unfathomable complexity their story must stand for the experiences of thousands of young subalterns and the men under their command. Again and again they were outflanked: sometimes to the left, sometimes to the right and too often from both sides at once. They were well aware that casualties were inevitable every time they left the trenches or ditches to retreat – but to stay was to be cut off.

> I watch the bullets spurting on the track and road and I cross each in turn with a rare jerk! As I make my dash across the track I hear bullets – probably meant for me – strike the ground behind and past me, and I have that feeling of exultation that comes with a good miss! It is necessary to walk about on top of the trenches in order to shepherd our men in the right direction. Major Fairlie is engaged in the same work and when the immediate danger is past he remarks, 'That was a warm corner, Warren!' Happily few of our men are hit.[19]
>
> Second Lieutenant Frank Warren, 17th Battalion, King's Royal Rifle Corps, 117th Brigade, 39th Division

It was hard enough withdrawing under the noses of the Germans as infantry. But for the Royal Artillery it was near suicidal to try and get the guns out after a certain point was reached. Yet the gun teams tried their best and Warren watched one such scene of heroism with awe.

> We are drawing back upon a battery of field guns, which is still firing upon the advancing Boches. The Rifle Brigade and the Hertfordshires are now acting as rearguard, and we pass through them into the valley and up to the top of the ridge behind the guns, and settle down there to cover their withdrawal. The teams are drawn up ready to be hitched onto the guns. Suddenly a Boche gun is fired – from behind us! A shell pitches in the midst of a gun team, knocking out four of the horses. Instantly, our gun teams are galloped hell for leather down the hillside towards Morcourt. The guns are left! I gasp with astonishment as I say bitterly, 'The Royal Artillery used not to leave their guns.' But I was utterly wrong and spoke too soon. Some men remain with their guns and I imagine they are engaged in removing the breech blocks. Not a bit of it! The teams have run the gauntlet of rapid artillery fire, racing

and tearing down the steep slopes to shelter in 'dead' ground in the valley below. A pause. Suddenly up the slope come a team of horses. The Boche gun is watching but shoots too high or too low! It is breathless work for team and spectators. We can do nothing, but only look on. Artillerymen manhandle the gun down the slope to the team. In a few seconds away gallop the horses with the first of the guns and the Boches follow with a trail of shells, working their guns like mad. Saved! Number 1! So with the second, and on until more slowly the sixth and last leaves the slopes. We could cheer like blazes, for it was a fine piece of work and with all his shooting not a single shell from the Boches seemed to have told – since the first.[20]

Second Lieutenant Frank Warren, 17th Battalion, King's Royal Rifle Corps, 117th Brigade, 39th Division

The ups and downs of open warfare were clearly demonstrated moments later. As the Germans rushed forward in their keenness to capture the guns they ran into a deadly trap that cost them dearly.

From the slope towards the river on our left come racing two or three hundred Boches – running like a football crowd – full speed to capture the guns. In a dip in the ground they are lost to sight from us. But we can see what is hidden to them! Lying out in extended order in the brown soil of a ploughed field are fifty to sixty silent Munster Fusiliers. On come the Boche looking for an easy spoil. They are over the ridge, running and eager! There is a swelling burst of rapid fire from the Munster! Its effects are just out of our view, but ten minutes later twenty or thirty Boches straggle crestfallen over the lower slopes towards the river. They have been taught a severe lesson. Not long after, back came the Munsters with a grim smile on their faces![21]

Second Lieutenant Frank Warren, 17th Battalion, King's Royal Rifle Corps, 117th Brigade, 39th Division

The see-saw nature of fighting like this was almost dizzying. Within a short time the Germans facing Warren and his men had changed the whole balance of the situation by bringing up their machine-gunners and field artillery support. In fighting of this kind it was essential to gain fire superiority to try and suppress any possible response before emerging into the open. Their recent bloody nose had made them cautious.

On the ridge opposite us the Boches have now mounted some machine guns and give us an uncomfortable time with a steady 'Swish-Swish' or 'Sizz-Sizz' as the bullets skim the open ground where we lie. A corporal next to me was digging in quickly with his entrenching tool, making a small mound in front of him with his helmet in the centre. With bare hands I tear up the turfs and sods and follow his example. Fritz seems to be getting his own back for he has mounted a field gun and is at his favourite game of sniping with open sights on any of our men on the right who make themselves conspicuous.[22]

Second Lieutenant Frank Warren, 17th Battalion, King's Royal Rifle Corps, 117th Brigade, 39th Division

In the end, it was chaos: no matter how hard they tried, no matter how they attempted to stem the flow, nothing they attempted had any degree of permanence; every position taken up was just a temporary dam to the flood of German troops.

Meanwhile, the hapless Gough had been seeking to organise yet another notional rear line behind his fast-fragmenting front line. The latest line on his map was to be known as the Amiens Defence Line and its function was just that. The British had retired almost as far as they could without losing a strategically significant location, but Amiens, with its major railway junction, was central to Allied communications and it was vital that it be retained. The putative line lay about 15 miles in front of Amiens. For once it had some basis in reality for it was made up of the old French lines dating back to 1915. Unfortunately, some of the trenches and barbed wire had been removed in the intervening years, but it was a good place to start, for at least it had been sited with care, commanding good fields of fire. The problem Gough faced was that he had no divisions left to man the trenches and there were still gaps. Something had to be done and in desperation he resorted to scraping up spare men from every available source. Men normally proud of their status as 'almost non-combatants' found themselves thrust into what would be the next front line of the struggle.

The previous day Brigadier Rees had been ordered to report with his senior staff officer, Major Witts, to the Fifth Army headquarters at Villers-Bretonneux. When he got there he found that Major General George Carey had been placed in command of the force of miscellaneous troops that would bear the eponymous name 'Carey's Force' to occupy the line running from just south of Démuin, through Aubercourt, in front of Marcelcave, behind Warfusée and in front of Hamel to reach the Somme River at Sailly-le-Sec. As Rees inspected the line he found the situation was quite simply beyond desperation.

> This line had been sited, entrenched and wired by the French in 1914. A considerable portion of it still stood, but at a number of places, notably astride the main Amiens road in rear of Warfusée, the trenches had been filled in, the wire removed and the ground ploughed over. This line was now garrisoned by a number of units, most of whom were entirely untrained, such as engineering and mining companies, field survey companies, USA engineers, a Canadian railway construction battalion etc., strengthened by Lewis and Vickers gun teams from tank battalions and stray units, army and corps schools with their employed men and stragglers from the line.[23]
>
> Brigadier General Hubert Rees, Carey's Force

There were no effective means of communication or hierarchy of command in such a hotchpotch of small units and as a result everything had to be done on an ad hoc basis. Here an officer eager for responsibility could really make the difference.

> I could see no chance of the Fifth Army avoiding being rolled up from the left unless some troops were brought in to fill the gap. I told General Carey that our position would be attacked the following afternoon. I arranged that the GS wagons should go to the dump at Marcelcave where large quantities of wire were said to be, to draw wire and dump it along the line where gaps existed, early next morning. Soon after daybreak, Witts and I motored to Démuin and arranged for a loading party for the wire and distribution of wagons. We then went on to Marcelcave and found practically no wire available, but only tons of screw pickets. I then issued instructions that screw pickets were to be put out, even if wire was not immediately available![24]
>
> Brigadier General Hubert Rees, Carey's Force

The force got to work at once but the scale of the problem only truly became apparent on the morning of 27 March. There was a gap on the north flank of what had been the Fifth Army, between it and the Third

Army on the other side of the Somme River. With an air of barely controlled panic the British staff officers scoured the rear areas, desperately gathering together what men they could find. Small parties of disorganised parentless infantry, gunners without guns, transport drivers, storemen, sappers, officers' servants, cooks, bottle-washers: everyone was grist to their mill – there were too few troops for them to retain any degree of fussiness.

It was late afternoon when the red-hatted officer appeared and asked how much ammunition we had. 'None!' came the reply, whereupon the red-hat said, 'Parade as many men as you can spare with rifles and ammunition!' Soon all the gunners were paraded and were marched over open ground to an old trench to the right front of the gun site. The trench, which was overgrown with a covering of grass, was alive with a motley crew of men, many of them quite elderly – they were the sum of the Pioneer Corps. An officer with a red armband came along the trench and told us to load our rifles and apply the safety catch. He went on, 'You will be given the order to fire, but should you see any Germans moving along your front, shoot them!' I sat in that trench almost in despair. Only a few of the men had had any small arms training, even the gunners. I loaded many rifles and explained about the safety catch. It was real; yet it seemed unrealistic, but I knew I had to keep well in the rear if any firing started.[25]

Gunner Percy Creek, 'A' Battery, 104th Brigade, Royal Field Artillery

Creek had good reason for his despair. All along the makeshift line, men were being issued with rifles and placed on the qui vive in various ditches or trenches. By these means Brigadier Rees estimated that the force managed to gather about 3,580 men in total, but they were by no means 'fighting' troops. They were incapable of moving as a formed body and, of course, given their lack of experience or the bonding strength of a shared regimental tradition, were potentially extremely unreliable under fire, even when in decent trenches. To sum up, the improvised Carey's Force was deficient in almost everything necessary to mount a coherent defence.

Amongst the force was the signal section of the 1/7th London Regiment.

Every cook, batman, driver, messman, artilleryman, unmounted caval-ryman, any of the odds and sods who, though wearing uniform, had never used a rifle in their lives. What a bewildered lot they looked, lying there wondering what was going to happen next. They were given rifles and ammunition taken from the wounded as they passed through our lines. While we waited we passed the time giving a few lessons in loading and firing the rifle to those who needed it. We each made little piles next to us of the clips of cartridges for easy reloading, loaded up the magazine with nine cartridges and one in the breech, and waited.[26]

Signaller Bert Chaney, 1/7th Battalion, London Regiment, 140th Brigade, 47th Division

Chaney was exhausted and, as nothing seemed to be happening, he soon slumped down, more unconscious than asleep, in a ditch half full of water.

I was awakened with the shout of, 'Here they come!' A long way off could be seen an uneven line of men in grey uniforms, almost shoulder to shoulder, moving slowly, but steadily forward towards us. Suddenly everybody seemed to be firing and I added my quota to the din. At the beginning of the war I had been a first-class shot, but this day I found myself unable to really hold my rifle steady. I found myself jerking the trigger instead of squeezing it and blinked my eyes every time I fired a shot. God knows where my shots went, except in the general direction of the enemy. Some of our gang were shutting their eyes whenever they pressed the trigger, others were actually crying softly to themselves as they doggedly fired away without apparently taking aim, but there were others who determinedly took careful aim to make every shot count. They were the ones who helped to keep the line steady: cursing, shouting and sometimes cajoling those who had never been under fire before. Our shooting on the whole must have been good enough as line after line of advancing Germans were stopped.[27]

Signaller Bert Chaney, 1/7th Battalion, London Regiment, 140th Brigade, 47th Division

As Carey's Force dug itself deeper in and prepared for the next attack, Chaney, with his men, left it to try to find his battalion, with only an aching bruised shoulder as a memento of his unaccustomed stint as a rifleman. Collectively, the ramshackle conglomerations of men had taken their toll on the advancing Germans. But the situation was still precarious, with the staff officers moving up and down the line, acting as an intellectual fire brigade: identifying problems, suggesting solutions and occasionally directly intervening to rescue the situation.

> I went down to the left section about 2 p.m., motoring over the high ground east of Hamel. Here we found a party of thirty Lewis gunners, whose guns were being brought by lorry from Bois de Vaire which should have arrived and hadn't. It appeared possible that the lorry had gone up the road to Cerisy, with twenty Lewis guns and ammunition as a present for the enemy. We gave chase and caught the lorry about a mile up the Cerisy road.[28]
>
> Brigadier General Hubert Rees, Carey's Force

Nobody knew what was happening. They only knew that, come what may, they had to hold on.

ON THURSDAY, 28 MARCH, when all stood in the balance on the Somme, the Germans unveiled their next master stroke. Operation Mars was an attack by their Seventeenth Army on either side of the Scarpe River in front of Arras, with the intention of driving into the junction of the First and Third Armies. The tactics it employed were substantially the same but there was a massive difference in the state of readiness of the British defences and the density of the garrison manning them. The staff maps looked the same, but here the trenches, the belts of wire and the strongpoints existed on the ground as well as on the maps. The signs of imminent assault had been observed and the British knew the Germans were coming. When the massive preliminary bombardment opened up at 0300 on 28 March along the front held by the VI, XVII and XIII Corps, the British gunners manned their guns in the dark, determined to give of their best in defence of the infantry in front of them.

> The attack had come our way at last. The time of the assault was SOS time, when we would open defensive fire. All being alerted and the guns cleared ready for action, there was no more to be done but await events. All took cover again and waited. From the front line we could hear rolling up a reverberating and continuous succession of thuds. The

enemy had opened up with a trench mortar and artillery bombardment of our front line, terrific and appalling in its intensity. Meanwhile, high overhead through the upper darkness droned and whistled in a tremendous volume of sound an avalanche of shell, the dreaded back area barrage, shutting us off from the outer world with a curtain of flying steel. With our backs to this and our faces to the greying eastern skyline, we waited by our silent guns.[29]

Lieutenant John Capron, 109th Battery, 281st Brigade, Royal Field Artillery

Once again the German gunners played their practised score: gas shells deluged the British artillery batteries, communications were remorselessly targeted and the strongpoints of the Battle Zone hammered. Finally, after a severe pounding of the Forward Zone positions by the trench mortars, the German attack commenced at varying times between 0600 and 0730.

But now a jabber of machine guns swept up and a thousand star shells, red-green-red, the British SOS rush up and hang in the upper darkness. The Germans are over the top. Now it is our turn to join in with the response barrage. Until now we have only been under a desultory counter-battery fire but we are having to face a fiercer concentration – a determined blotting out. Faster and thicker whine down the shells, some well over, some short and some fearfully among us. The hideous energy, the dust and acrid reek, the blast and fury of each down rush makes us catch our breath – this is big stuff now! The ground heaves and seems to sway. It's a case of surviving – or not! How could the infantry have lived through a barrage such as now spouts around us? Yet, through the nearer tumult, fitfully comes and swells and fades, the sound of rifle fire. Heartened we slip and stumble perilously to and fro between gunpits and ammunition recesses, 'Come on 109s, the Londons are still there – give the bloody old Huns their rations!'[30]

Lieutenant John Capron, 109th Battery, 281st Brigade, Royal Field Artillery

The gunners were forbidden to take cover when firing in support of the infantry. But they were only flesh and blood, and it was predictable that some of them should begin to waver as the German shells crashed all around their gunpits.

Big shells were bursting, spraying earth and splinters all around the pit. We were keeping up a slow rate of support fire when Sergeant Harrison

200

cried in my ear, 'Should we take cover a little, Sir?' 'Wait a bit!' I said, but, without a word, he toppled forwards on his face and lay quite still. He was dead, killed instantaneously by a hideous great splinter. We dragged him clear and then, shaken, crawled to the central dugout to regain our nerve. But, 'No. 1 gun has stopped firing!' goes the word – that was the gun on the extreme right of the line. The Major calls to me to go and see why. Here, too, was tragedy, only worse, for Sergeant Minshall and the whole of that gun crew were dead – a direct hit. Other guns dropped out and casualties mounted. The day crawled past – no German helmets appeared upon our skyline and we still heard the ripple of rifle fire and stutter of machine guns billowing up from where our infantry must still be holding their ground. All honour to those Londoners![31]

Lieutenant John Capron, 109th Battery, 281st Brigade, Royal Field Artillery

Meanwhile, the German infantry troops were ready for their moment of truth, given confidence by the sheer power of the German bombardment.

We seemed to be inside a witch's cauldron. The firing of forward artillery and mortar groups thumped around and behind us and not too far ahead in the first English line the impact of all types of calibre raining down on them, especially the heavy mortar rounds. The enemy was so surprised that they only responded sparsely and slowly. We had no casualties at our exit positions, despite being packed as herrings in the tight trenches. No one remained behind, we were all on top of the trenches and as the battalion commanders gave the attack signal with their handkerchiefs at 7.20 everyone stormed forwards. The first and second enemy lines were overrun in closed formation.[32]

Oberleutnant Dose, Headquarters, 187th Infantry Regiment, Imperial German Army

The German infantry's initial success was hardly surprising, for many of the men in the British Forward Zone had been blown to hell as they and their posts were simply obliterated from the earth. Yet there was no mist this time and not too many men had been left as hostages to fortune in these forward outposts. Indeed, it had become policy to temporarily evacuate such outposts during barrages or at night. The

First Army in particular had preached the gospel of concentrating all available fighting resources back in the Battle Zone where the soldiers could really achieve something rather than sacrifice themselves to no real purpose. But there were still localised disasters where everything seemed to go wrong; where the artillery did not or, more likely, was unable to respond to the SOS calls of desperate infantry. Private Thomas Bickerton was part of a Lewis gun team holding positions in the Fampoux sector.

At daybreak we could see the Germans advancing down the valley. Our patrols had been withdrawn from the front line and, of course, we immediately let loose with everything we had got. I frantically filled magazines until my fingers could hardly move. We sent up our Very lights, but no artillery fire came. The artillery had been withdrawn and it appeared to us that we were going to be sacrificed. The Germans had broken through on our right and on our left, but owing to our commanding position we seemed to be able to hold them at bay. We sent back runners to battalion headquarters for instructions. The first two were either killed or taken prisoner, the third runner came back to tell us the Germans were cooking breakfast in our battalion head- quarters kitchen! By this time we were running very short of ammuni- tion and had started to dig up some that had been buried and, in consequence, was very dirty. This caused endless trouble on the Lewis gun. We suffered from separated cases, which meant that the gun had to be stripped. Our No. 1 was a first-class chap, he stuck at it until he was thoroughly exhausted and No. 2 took over – he became exhausted too. It is quite impossible to hold a Lewis gun forward against the rebound unless you are really feeling fit. It came to my turn and I'll admit that I couldn't stick it for long. The gun seized up, we stripped it down and put on a new barrel. By this time we were mentally and physically exhausted and wondering what the end would be – it was obviously very near. I went into the next firing bay to see if our platoon commander was there and he was sitting on the firestep in the corner with a revolver in his hand. I think he had shot himself rather than be taken prisoner. One of my comrades received a tiny piece of shrapnel through his jugular vein. He came to me and I put on a dressing, blood was spurting in a thin stream from the vein. The Germans were almost up to our trench and a corporal tied his white handkerchief to his bayonet and stuck it up over the trench. The Germans called on us to come out. Our No. 1 had stripped the gun and thrown the spare parts over the back before giving himself up. Those of us who were gunners had torn our Lewis gun badges off our jackets because we were afraid of what might happen to us. All arms had to be abandoned and we were instructed to run with our hands over our heads towards the German rear. I had not got far before I was pulled up by a German flourishing a dagger. Fortunately, I had the presence of mind to whip out my pocket wallet, which I thrust into his hand, and while he was looking at it, I ran on. Our heavy machine guns were still firing and my next encounter with a German was when one of them pulled me down into a shell hole. I wondered what was going to happen, but he was anxious that I shouldn't be shot! He indicated that we were both in danger from this machine gun. I quote both these instances to indicate the difference between the Germans: some good, some bad. Eventually we reached the first collecting station, a very crude barbed wire enclosure. Here we were addressed by a German intelligence officer, who informed us we'd been a damned nuisance and that we'd held up their advance for over three hours.[33]

Private Thomas Bickerton, 2nd Battalion, Essex Regiment, 12th Brigade, 4th Division

The 2nd Essex lost some 431 officers and men in this doomed fight, but it was an isolated disaster. In most areas the troops fell back before the Germans and took up the pre-prepared positions in the Battle Zone. As the Germans pushed forward they became aware of ever-increasing opposition and the last stand made by the likes of Bickerton and his comrades may well have been noticed by Dose.

Heavy machine-gun fire unexpectedly appeared at the left flank from Fampoux, causing severe casualties especially amidst the officers. The attack slowed down a bit, causing the accompanying barrage of fire to lose connection with the attack and it's purpose, covering the attacking infantry, was lost. In front of the Scots line, the English main position, the attack would be stopped, because the enemy infantry, protected by the cover of machine-gun fire from their Fampoux positions, resisted fiercely, driving our infantry into the trenches for cover, halting further development. The repeated attack in the afternoon also didn't succeed.

> The strong English infantry defensive actions were backed by their regrouped artillery batteries that were firing at their own well-known positions, now occupied and overfilled by us.[34]
> Oberleutnant Dose, Headquarters, 187th Infantry Regiment, Imperial German Army

This time there was no fog to blot out the British defenders' view of the advancing German infantry. Well dug in, with copious masses of barbed wire funnelling the Germans into their sights, they took a heavy toll of the German attackers. Without the successful suppression of the British artillery, machine guns and infantry, the German infiltration tactics were rendered all but irrelevant – there was little to infiltrate here other than a series of blind alleys. And the men being killed or wounded first were the elite stormtroopers, while the masses of infantry moving forward behind them were exceptionally tempting targets. When they did make progress and threaten to break through, the counter-attack arrangements worked reasonably smoothly. Few soldiers of the British Army in March 1918 could fire the 15 aimed rounds a minute of their predecessors of the 1914 Regular Army, but they took great pleasure in trying their best and, after all, they could hardly miss when firing at massed formations. Once again the German casualty figures were rocketing skywards.

Ludendorff certainly recognised failure when he saw it. Operation Mars was closed down and his attention turned to the possibility of launching the next attack on the Lys front to threaten the Channel ports directly. Meanwhile, he would have one last attempt to break through at Amiens. But there is no doubt that his plans, and his expectations, had been severely knocked off course by the stubborn British defence.

> In spite of employing extraordinary masses of artillery and ammunition, the attack of the Seventeenth Army on both banks of the Scarpe was a failure; it was fought under an unlucky star.[35]
> Quartermaster General Erich Ludendorff, General Headquarters, Imperial German Army

It is likely that Ludendorff was still mentally staggering from the effects of the death of his stepson, Leutnant Erich Pernert of the German Air Service. He had been reported missing from a mission flying over Nesle and a few days later Ludendorff had had the unpleasant task not only of identifying the recently exhumed corpse, but also of telling his wife that a second of her three sons was dead. She never properly recovered. The Great War had a way of striking home even in the most illustrious of households. But all that aside, the failure of the Seventeenth Army was *not* some piece of 'bad luck'. It was merely what happened when the much-vaunted German attack tactics encountered the British system of defence in depth, garrisoned with enough troops to operate the method properly and without a blanket of fog.

ON THE SOMME FRONT 28 March was also a significant day. The Germans continued to attack but they now faced arriving, fresh French divisions, who crashed into the counter-attack. However, the British near the Somme River were still in trouble and, as ever, individual units found themselves in desperate straits. Second Lieutenant Frank Warren for a while believed that the Germans were all around his unit, with no way out. It seemed hopeless, but then the RFC intervened to point the way back.

> We get an unexpected order dropped from a friendly aeroplane to the effect that there is a gap of 1,000 yards open in the enemy lines, and we are to get our men away in twos and threes as quickly as possible, south-west in the direction of Harbonnières. Immediately, a thin stream of men begins to bolt from the trench, according to orders, running the gauntlet of machine-gun fire from two quarters – the road to the south-east and the ridge to the east. When my men, who have waited their turn, are all clear I am cornered by an officer of the Gloucester Pioneers, who tells me to wait to give covering fire for the withdrawal of his men! Having had definite orders from my own company commander, I remind him that all my men have gone, and prepare for my quick dash to cover. I have been watching the flick of the machine-gun bullets in the dusty ground and have noted where the stream of fugitives is thickest. Then I make my bolt, keeping to the edge of the stream of men and running zigzag. The immediate zone of danger appears to be about 200 yards in depth and in passing through it I see several men slightly wounded but still able to push along more slowly than the rest. On the whole the machine gun fire cannot have

been very deadly, for we were leaving big gaps between our men as they stream out and the machine guns are fairly distant. I have picked up a rifle and 150 rounds of ammunition and in the midst of my flight stoop to pick up a spare tin of bully beef, so that I need not go hungry all day.[36]

Second Lieutenant Frank Warren, 17th Battalion, King's Royal Rifle Corps, 117th Brigade, 39th Division

Once again Warren and his men had escaped. But their ordeal was not over. Their retreat continued as they fell back to Ignaucourt. This was a pretty little village, previously untouched by the war, but it was now thrust into the combat zone.

'Brass hats' are just leaving the village in gorgeous motor cars; their rubber baths and other luxuries stacked on the roof call forth ironical cheers from the troops. Here too can be seen the most pitiful of all sights of war – the civilian population fleeing for their lives. The alarm has been given and the villagers have jumped up straight away to join the stream of refugees. Here is a table, neat and ready laid with coffee pot, loaf and butter as if for *déjeuner*. One family, bolder than the rest, is but now setting out westwards on its journey to safety. Madam with firm careworn face, framed with silvery hair, takes command, while Monsieur jabbers vociferously but ineffectually. A pretty girl of 16 has a rope over her shoulder hitched to the handcart bearing the treasured feather bed and a few household goods. Another rope is tied to the collar of a faithful dog.[37]

Second Lieutenant Frank Warren, 17th Battalion, King's Royal Rifle Corps, 117th Brigade, 39th Division

Back they fell. Battalions had been reduced to washed-out husks. Many had less than 100 men left under command as their strength was eroded away. By this time there is little doubt that Warren's men were reaching the end of their tether.

Our men are gaunt and weary, unwashed and with eight days' growth of beard, their lips raw and deeply chapped by the salted bully beef they have gnawed, and the coldness of the March winds. Most are limping painfully, for few have a change of socks with them or have had their boots off for eight days and nights. Over and over again we have been promised a relief that never comes, until a numbness of sensation has come over us all. They obey orders mechanically but sink fast asleep when opportunity offers.[38]

Second Lieutenant Frank Warren, 17th Battalion, King's Royal Rifle Corps, 117th Brigade, 39th Division

These men were not alone in their despair. The numbness that came with prolonged stress and total exhaustion began to undermine confidence and clawed at morale all along the British line. Soldiers need hope of ultimate victory to carry on, to make their sacrifice seem worthwhile.

We felt that the war was to all intents and purposes over, that there were no troops to support us and that the retreat would go on indefinitely. To understand this frame of mind it must be remembered that we had no news of what had been happening up and down the line, and that there was strong evidence to support the rumour that violent Hun attacks nearer the sea had met with success, in which case every man available would probably be employed in stemming his advance on Calais and the Channel ports. I suppose things couldn't have looked blacker. By then, however, depression had little effect on us: the only thing to do was just to go on plugging away till the end came, whatever that might be. It didn't really matter what it was. Hoarse, deaf, filthy and without hope, there had long since ceased to be much of an element of personal fear.[39]

Second Lieutenant John Fleming, 'U' Battery, 16th Brigade, Royal Horse Artillery

They had missed too many meals, lost too much sleep and even the simplest of tasks were increasingly beyond them.

I had a sudden almost complete blackout of mental powers. Hoare had given me orders to work out our position and lay out lines of fire on the map board – a relatively easy performance. All I could do was to sit on the ground, gazing at the map board and crying softly in rage at my incapacity. Hoare was most understanding, took the board from me and told me to take five minutes easy. With shaky fingers I opened a tin of bully and started eating. In a few minutes I was perfectly *compos mentis* and normal again. A weird and disconcerting experience.[40]

Second Lieutenant John Fleming, 'U' Battery, 16th Brigade, Royal Horse Artillery

Some men had gone beyond the point of no return. They were physically and mentally broken by their experiences.

As I pass a ruined cottage outhouse I hear a suspicious noise. I draw my pistol and challenge as I enter, only to find an obviously young, gentlemanly British officer cowering there, his nerves entirely gone. A pity, he must have been plunged into these last few days and just couldn't take it. I curtly ordered him to get up and grasp his forearm to steady him. He is trembling, crying and shaking. I partly drag him out and lead him along having pocketed my pistol. I held him firmly to help him gain control.[41]

Major Leonard Humphreys, 'A' Battery, 190th Brigade, Royal Field Artillery

The staff officers of the various divisional headquarters were still up to their eyes in hard, largely thankless graft. As red tabs they were the butt of everyone's jokes, but many soldiers would not have survived without their dedicated work. Traffic control, for instance, did not have a glamorous image but it was nonetheless utterly vital in this kind of situation.

In my opinion this was the most critical period of the whole retreat. If the enemy had slipped his cavalry and guns on the afternoon of the 28th, nothing could have saved us. I realised that there would be a block at the Castel bridge. From 4 p.m. till midnight we worked at the bridge. The saddest part of the whole thing was the stream of panic-stricken civilians flying before the Germans with farm wagons, peram-bulators and wheelbarrows crammed with their belongings. There was no panic among the troops, but it was a single-way bridge with a steep way up to it, upon which overloaded civilian carts kept sticking and holding up the traffic. Furious gunners kept coming and saying their guns *must* be got across before anyone else, and all the time it poured with rain and one had the sickening thought that the enemy might be on us at any moment. At last I had to turn all civilian traffic off the road to give free passage for the troops. One woman went on her knees in the mud in front of me and said, 'Monsieur, for the love of God let my wagons across the bridge!' But though I knew that the civilians would probably fall into the hands of the Germans I had to refuse, as it was vital to get the troops across first. Towards midnight about 500 men passed me on the bridge, deadbeat and hardly able to walk. I shouted out, 'What battalion is that?' and a man I knew answered out of the darkness, 'It is what is left of the 17th Brigade.'[42]

Captain Thomas Westmacott, Headquarters, 24th Division

It was a close-run thing but Westmacott had got the remnants of the division back across the river. In truth, he had divined a key point that undermined the whole of the German offensive. Where was the fast exploitation arm of the German Army? Tanks in 1918 were far too mechanically unreliable and too slow to take on such a role, but in any case the Germans had only ever had a few of their own in addition to various captured British machines. Cavalry were the only effective arm of exploitation, the only way of catching up and slaughtering retreating troops. That they were endemically vulnerable to machine-gun fire or barbed wire was true, but they were still ideal for riding down and spearing a helpless rabble for all that. The British were getting away because their infantryman could walk or run in retreat at roughly the same pace as his German counterpart could advance. How then could the Germans properly overhaul and drag down the retreating British, especially when the German infantry troops were just as prone to fatigue as the 'Tommies', even buoyed up as they were by apparent victory? Where were the German cavalry to hammer home the nail of victory? The answer was simple: the German cavalry divisions were still stationed on the Eastern Front, exploiting the opportunities of German victory over the new Soviet government of the Russians.

North of the Somme River the Third Army had a day of real stress. The Germans launched another huge attempt to break through, which the British Official Historian later compared with the original British assault on the Somme on 1 July 1916 – but on almost twice the scale. The death toll may not have matched that awful day, but as the Germans met stern resistance and achieved little of note there is no doubt that casualties would have been dreadfully high. The German divisions were slowly being exhausted by the constant fighting, which, rather than getting easier, was starting to get noticeably tougher. The British reserves were now being smoothly funnelled into the line and made an immediate impact, particularly the highly regarded Australian

Corps. The threat to the integrity of their lines had not yet been resolved but there was greater hope for the Allies.

Overall it was evident by the end of 28 March that the new Allied command arrangements were beginning to take effect as Foch got to grips with the fast-moving situation. Haig was certainly impressed by the new Supreme Commander. Their relationship would always be based on persuasion and consent, but it prospered because neither man sought to push too far beyond what was mutually acceptable. Foch ordered where Haig wanted to go; Haig suggested what Foch wanted to hear. Both avoided conflict.

> I think Foch has brought great energy to bear on the present situation, and has, instead of permitting French troops to retire south-west from Amiens, insisted on some of them relieving our troops and on covering Amiens at all costs. He and I are quite in agreement as to the general plan of operations.[43]
>
> Field Marshal Sir Douglas Haig, General Headquarters, BEF

But one other command change had now been forced upon Haig that day. General Hubert Gough was relieved of his command by General Sir Henry Rawlinson who took over the ashes of the Fifth Army as of 1630 on 28 March. His new command stood at little more than the XIX Corps, as by this time the suffering XVIII Corps had been pulled out of the line.

After the storm of the previous day, Good Friday 29 March was much quieter: the Germans paused to lick their wounds and the Allies gradually reorganised their lines ready for the next real thrust. The ragtag and bobtail rabble that was Carey's Force was still holding some kind of line across the way to Amiens. Some reserve cavalry units had been added to the rough mixture but the line remained fairly rudimentary. Although the Germans launched no major assault they actively patrolled, feeling for weak flanks to exploit. Brigadier Rees was still at the heart of the defence, responding as best he could to every new crisis, real or imagined.

> During the afternoon General Carey came to see me and while he was there a message came in from Major Chaffers to say that the enemy were working round his right flank, which was in the air, that hostile

cavalry patrols were to be seen at Marcelcave and that he considered his position untenable. I sent back a message ordering him to hold on at all costs. This message went astray and another message from Chaffers said that unless he had other instructions, he intended to retire on Villers-Bretonneux after dark. I therefore sent Major Playfair to relieve him and followed a little later myself. The situation was not satisfactory and touch between Major Chaffers and Major Hill's Yeomanry had not been satisfactorily established. I therefore ordered that the stragglers' company in reserve should dig a new trench south of the Amiens road, level with the support line and find touch with the Yeomanry. I went to find cavalry brigade headquarters near the Bois de Vaire and was practically arrested as a spy by a cavalry officer, who refused for a long time to believe in any bona fides.[44]

Brigadier General Hubert Rees, Carey's Force

Despite all the chaos, the confusion, the mistakes of omission and commission that must have been legion, Carey's Force struggled on until nightfall next day, when it was finally relieved and ceased to exist. But it, too, had done its job. Brigadier Rees was released from his attachment and rejoined his beloved 150th Brigade, which with the rest of the badly battered remnants of the 50th Division, were shortly afterwards moved to a quiet sector in northern France. Here they could rest at last.

BY SATURDAY, 30 MARCH 1918 the great German offensive finally seemed to be running out of steam. It was also the day when the exhausted Second Lieutenant Frank Warren finally stopped running. At first it was just another ridge line, another skirmish, another attempt to hold back the advancing Germans.

One of the men is crawling forward with his Lewis gun to gain a shell hole with a more commanding position. Suddenly I hear a thud and portions of him, as it seems, spurt in all directions! He doubles up convulsively and I fear the worst. A stretcher bearer rolls over and over to reach him and finds that the man's water bottle hanging in front of him has stopped a bullet fair and square, the water spurting out as I had noticed. He is badly winded and probably bruised but otherwise seems to be hurt but little![45]

Second Lieutenant Frank Warren, 17th Battalion, King's Royal Rifle Corps, 117th Brigade, 39th Division

But for Warren this was to prove one skirmish too many. How many thousands of bullets, hundreds of shells had been aimed in his direction and narrowly missed him? But now in a flash one found its mark.

Suddenly I am knocked spinning with a numbing blow on the back of the head. I fall instinctively, rather than by the force of the blow, and my first thought is that it is all over and I am dead. Then I hear someone calling, 'Warren's hit! Warren's down!' Several men come running round me, including Sergeant Page of 'C' Company who asks me if I have a shell dressing. I tell him, 'No!' and beg him not to let a crowd assemble or it will draw fire and someone else will be shot. By this time I find I can raise my head and tell the men, 'Oh, I am not too bad!' Sergeant Page dabs a shell dressing to the back of my head and secures it in position. I sit up and unbuckle my equipment, which with revolver, ammunition pouch, glasses, compass, haversack and water bottle is no mean weight. Blundell offers to come along with me as my servant and I gladly accept his services. I find I can now stand well, so wishing the men, 'Cheerio!' and with the parting words, 'Give them one for me!' I begin my journey off the field.[46]

Second Lieutenant Frank Warren, 17th Battalion, King's Royal Rifle Corps, 117th Brigade, 39th Division

He had more than done his bit.

Another soldier had been fighting hard for ten days when he, too, well and truly ran out of luck. Private Joseph Pickard of the 1/5th Northumberland Fusiliers was caught in the open by German artillery.

They started to 'harrow' the box, like harrowing a field, searching the box with shells. The first lot was all right and it was coming through the second time when I got hit. I remember seeing this big black cloud go up the side of the ditch. When I came to myself I was lying back up the road amongst a lot of dead Frenchmen. There was one Frenchman hit about the head; he was just like a pepper pot! I jumped straight up and went straight down again and I thought, 'Well the leg's away!' I found out where I was hit, tore the trousers down. I got me first-aid packet out and there was a lot of gauze, a little tube of stuff and a big safety pin – that was your first aid. I pulled the trousers down, I was hit underneath the joint of the leg and I tied it on there. The piece of shrapnel had cut the sciatic nerve, chipped both hip joints, smashed the left side of the pelvis and made three holes in the bladder. I knew there was something the matter with my face – I was bound to, I knew the blood was running. I never bothered about it. Well, I mean in a case like that you think whether you want to live and to hell with what you look like! I'd lost my nose – a right bloody mess. I thought, 'Well if I stop here its either a bullet or the bayonet!' The Germans wouldn't pick you up you know, couldn't afford it, they were trying to travel fast. I crawled down the road on my hands and knees. I saw a fellow I knew and I gave him a shout, a fellow called Craig from Darlington. He got two little fellows, two little Durhams, to come out. I was about head and shoulders above them. Somehow or other they got a stretcher and there was a Red Cross van pulled up near the bottom of the road. They carried us through the barrage a third time and I got into the wagon and the fellow said, 'You'll be all right now, chum!' The ambulance took me to an old farmhouse, the roof was blown off and everything else. I wanted a drink. Well they wouldn't give us any water – abdominal wounds, you see. They must have bandaged me there at this advanced clearing station. When I came round it was dark and I was lying on a stretcher. I didn't know what was the matter with us and it turned out there was a blanket over the top of us. I was left for dead! The old lady got the number of my grave and the King and Queen's sympathy! God! I got rid of this blanket and I saw a light, a storm lantern and I shouted out to an orderly. Two of them came down, picked the stretcher straight up and put us on a hospital train.[47]

Private Joseph Pickard, 1/5th Battalion, Northumberland Fusiliers, 149th Brigade, 50th Division

AS THE ORIGINAL UNITS were withdrawn from the line, new units filtered in and the arrival of the Australians generated considerable comment from some of the soldiers who had not yet encountered the 'Cobbers'. The Australians were an exotic mixture and, although up to a third were former British emigrants, they had adopted a manly persona that was as much in evidence behind the front as on the battlefield.

> In the village of Ribemont, some of the Australian troops paid us a visit, looted some wine shops and proceeded to dress up in borrowed plumes, even nightdresses and hats taken from the houses and shops nearby. They then mounted a large barricade, danced and sang ribald songs; all this in the bright moonlight with German shells falling all around and our troops engaged in a 'back to the wall' fight about three-quarters of a mile away. It was an eerie scene.[48]
>
> Lieutenant Godefroi Skelton, 205th Field Company, Royal Engineers

One incident contained so many examples of national stereotyping of both the British and Australians soldiers that one can only present it without comment.

> We found a girl's high school, with beautiful beds, girls' clothes, wigs, paint and powder. A number of the men were putting on wigs, trying on the clothes, lying on the beds in their filthy, lousy clothes and enjoying every minute of it. All at once, an Australian officer, who was drunk, dropped in on us. He shouted, 'Have you gone stark raving mad? Do you know that the Germans are only a quarter of a mile away, in full force, or are you just playing about, forgetting that there is a war on?' So saying, he fell, dead drunk, to the floor and was collected by his servant.[49]
>
> Driver Rowland Luther, 'C' Battery, 92nd Brigade, Royal Field Artillery

Many of the Australians harboured a dislike bordering on contempt for the soldiers of the 'Old Country'. Whether it arose from personal experience or the myths that originated from Gallipoli, they combined a splendidly high opinion of themselves with a willingness to believe the worst of the British. But the Australians did not win every bruising encounter with representatives of the 'Old Country'.

> I called out, 'Halt, who are you?' He said, 'Fucking Australian! Who the fucking hell are you?' So I realised he was drunk and I said, 'You realise you're talking to an officer?' and he told me to go and fuck myself! My troops were watching this and I wondered how to handle it. You can't say, 'Fall in two men, take his name and his number!' So I hit

him! I knocked him down! I can see him now sitting with his knees up and his head at the back. I never saw him again; I didn't want to! He probably had a vague idea he had been hit, that somebody had knocked him into the mud. It was the only thing to do![50]

Lieutenant Jim Davies, 9th Battalion, Royal Fusiliers, 36th Brigade, 12th Division

The animosity between the two sides perhaps reached its pinnacle when Australian Brigadier General Pompey Elliott reacted a little too sharply after a British officer was allegedly caught with a mess cart full of champagne on his way out of the village of Corbie. Even a fellow Australian officer, Captain Thomas Louch, was taken aback.

Pompey Elliot issued two remarkable orders to his brigade. The first was that any officer seen taking wine out of Corbie was to be publicly hanged in the market place; and the other that anyone spreading rumours or orders to retire was to be taken before the nearest commanding officer and, unless he could give a satisfactory account of himself, he was to be shot forthwith. It was all very reminiscent of the Red Queen in *Alice in Wonderland*. The men of his brigade were said to laugh at these things but others found them embarrassing.[51]

Captain Thomas Louch, Headquarters, 13th Brigade, 4th Australian Division,

Yet as a whole the men of the Australian Corps had achieved a wonderful reputation in their two years on the Western Front. Although they had been taken aback by the scale of the fighting after their previous experience in the relative backwater at Gallipoli, they had blossomed into a formidable fighting force and their presence would do much to stiffen and stabilise the British front.

AIDED BY the strong reinforcing divisions the Allies were gradually pulling together a firm defensive front. The Germans might still with great efforts bite small chunks out of the line but there was no longer any doubt that their offensive was slowly breaking down. Where were they going, what was being achieved? Their lack of direction or real strategic focus was now becoming evident and the ground they had gained was of very little military value. They seemed to be advancing merely for the sake of it.

While the British and French began to present a unified front there were also ever-increasing problems for the hard-pressed German supply arrangements behind the lines. Every mile of advance was another mile away from their original depots, while the British were moving closer to theirs. The Germans had to get all the supplies and munitions forwards across a battlefield that was more or less devastated. To add to their problems the inevitable bottlenecks at every surviving river crossing were mercilessly targeted day and night by the RFC. It looked like they were winning but that did not fill empty stomachs.

> The food got worse. On Easter Sunday we had nothing except half a loaf of bread per man. Everyone was miserable as they were so hungry. A comrade brought a joint of horsemeat from a horse that had been killed, which we had to roast. Horse meat is rather tough, but everyone liked it, even those who would never have eaten it if they had known beforehand.[52]
>
> Signaller Edwin Kühns, 1047th Telephone Unit, Imperial German Army

Late on 30 March Ludendorff accepted that he needed a period to reorganise and move up new forces if he was to make any more meaningful progress. For the moment there would be a real lull, although the after-shocks of fighting continued.

The problem with this break in the fighting was that it allowed time for the British to move in their reserves to replace the exhausted veterans of the March fighting. The men of the 315th Battery were certainly enlivened by the sight of the reinforcements.

> Suddenly someone shouted, 'Look over there – and over there, too!' On both sides of the road, stretching as far as you could see, were guns, guns and still more guns of all sizes. Oh, how our hearts leapt at the sight. Then from all directions ran soldiers, mainly artillerymen. They took off their hats, waving and cheering us as we passed. Oh it was just grand. 'Go and rest, boys', they shouted, 'and leave him to us!' Some of the boys shed tears at this. I don't think anyone noticed mine.[53]
>
> Bombardier William Pressey, 315th Battery, Royal Field Artillery

Now that it was almost over, back at GHQ Major Ian Hedley reviewed recent events from his limited but unique perspective of commanding the troop of 17th Lancers assigned to provide Haig's personal escort.

I have been very much impressed mainly by the various ways in which various people have taken it all. Some very cheerful, some up one day and down the next and some permanently much below zero. In the first class comes essentially the Chief who has been simply wonderful. The further the enemy has advanced the more cheerful he has appeared, 'Think how much worse it will be for them when we counter-attack and start to drive him back! Think how uncomfortable the enemy is on that old battlefield where *he* has no cover, *we* are in billets and *he* can't feed his men! How our RFC gives him hell day and night! How he has lost thousands upon thousands of men!' All the time thoroughly cheerful though the dreadful anxiety he must be going through would kill most men. His wonderful spirit spreads to others. The troop always ask the returning escort, 'How was the Chief?' 'Oh as cheerful as usual – even more so!' 'Then it's all right and let the Boche take Amiens if he can! It don't matter a bugger – it will be all right if the Chief's cheerful!' I've never conceived of a man so filled with magnetism.[54]

Major Ian Hedley, 17th Lancers, General Headquarters, BEF

The lull lasted until 4 April 1918 when once again the Germans lunged forwards to the south of the Somme River. A key objective was the town of Villers-Bretonneux, which guarded the approach to Amiens. A heavy bombardment fell along the front of the Fifth Army and the French First Army. There was much hard fighting but some of the battalions of the badly battered 14th Division were no longer up to the job of providing resistance to a serious attack. Second Lieutenant Walter Harris found the collapse of his unit a deeply depressing experience.

Our division, tired after its March battles, was in no mood to fight and for the first time I saw British troops retreating in disorder and individually leaving their trench without orders; for the first and only time I saw a British officer holding his own men with his revolver. I happened to be in a support trench, and all these men crowded into our trench for a time, but very soon, as the enemy attack developed, we were retiring again. I got separated from my unit and quite suddenly came on Australian headquarters. I told a captain that we had lost the front-line trenches and he said, 'They won't come any further, only over my dead body!'[55]

Second Lieutenant Walter Harris, 9th Battalion, Rifle Brigade, 42nd Brigade, 14th Division

The sight of British officers and men running in panic was not edifying and certainly did not improve the reputation of the British soldier with his Australian counterparts. Crucially, the Australians were still fresh troops and they would indeed recapture most of the lost ground. Although the Germans had taken another small step towards Villers-Bretonneux and Amiens the replacement of the 'blown' British divisions by the Australian Corps – the largest in the British Army – rendered the front far more secure.

Next day, on 5 April 1918, the Germans attacked again, this time north of the Somme River. Their aim was to expand their small bridgehead at Albert over the Ancre River, break through the lines south of Hébuterne and capture the British 'rock' of Bucquoy. This time the Germans were held, their gains too trivial to matter and their casualties unnerving. For the British it was the end of what had been an unparalleled ordeal.

JUDGED BY ITS OWN OBJECTIVES when all was said and done the German offensive had been a gigantic failure. Ludendorff had intended to win the war outright, before the Americans could join the fray, by breaking through the British lines and rolling them up to the north. In the end the results were almost exactly as had been predicted by the *éminence grise,* German staff officer Colonel Wetzell, way back in November 1917.

It must not be forgotten that in a successful offensive, the attacker will be forced to cross a difficult and shot-to-pieces battle area and will get gradually further away from his railheads and depots, and that, having to bring forward masses of artillery and ammunition columns, he will be compelled to make pauses which will give time to the defender to organise resistance. Too optimistic hopes should not be conceived, therefore, as regards the rapidity of the breakthrough attack on the Western Front. If our foes act only in a more or less planned and rapid manner, as we have done so far in spite of the most desperate situations, they also will succeed in bringing our offensive to a stop after a certain time.[56]

Colonel Wetzell, General Headquarters, Imperial German Army

The offensive had always had a somewhat vague strategic set of priorities and the success of the initial operations against the Fifth Army had distracted Ludendorff into a drive on Amiens intending to drive a wedge between the British and French Armies. In this too he had failed, although it had at times been a close-run thing. True, the Germans had taken a great wedge of land, totalling 1,200 square miles, but ground was irrelevant in the battles of the Great War unless it contained strategic objectives or features of great tactical significance. In reality all that had been gained was a 40-mile deep salient bulging uncomfortably into the Allied lines. A substantial area of this ground was a wasteland that the Germans themselves had created during their retreat the previous year to the security of the Hindenburg Line. This was the crux of the matter: the new front line was anything but secure. The German salient was vulnerable to attack from the French driving into the side from the south or British from the north. The Allies may not have been in a position to attack at that moment, but one thing was certain: when the Americans arrived they would seize their moment. The offensive had been intended to shatter the British; they were not shattered. No army in the world could lightly suffer the 178,000 casualties the British suffered from the beginning to the end of the Michael offensive. The French suffered a further 92,000 to make an Allied total loss of about 270,000. Yet the Germans themselves had lost 239,000 men. They had also expended huge amounts of resources that could never be recovered. Every one of the millions of shells fired into the Allied lines was digging into Germany's finite stock of raw materials. The Allies lost 1,300 guns, 200 tanks, over 2,000 machine guns and 400 aircraft but these were a statistical irrelevance. The Allied war machine was in full flow and their material losses were more than made good within a matter of mere weeks. The real issue was simple: the war went on and unless the Germans could force a decision before the summer they were going to lose.

CHAPTER SEVEN

Battle for Flanders: 9 April 1918

THE SOMME AND ARRAS spring offensives had failed. This time Ludendorff was determined to strike the decisive blow in Flanders, where there were genuine strategic targets just behind the British lines. The vital Hazebrouck rail centre was just 20 miles to the east of Armentières with its network of railways linking the Channel ports to all the key sectors of the northern front. Just 50 miles away, were Dunkirk and Calais, the capture of which would sever the BEF from the homeland. Thus an offensive in Flanders offered glittering prizes to the Germans and, now that the wet lowlands had dried out following a relatively dry early spring, the stage was set for the ultimate battle. Ludendorff dusted off the existing George plans and his staff duly came up with the scaled-down version of Operation Georgette, planned to commence on 9 April 1918. Seventeen divisions of the German Sixth Army would smash into the junction of the Second and First Armies between Armentières and La Bassée Canal, lunging forwards with little subtlety directly for the Hazebrouck rail complex and passing through Bailleul en route. Next day the German Fourth Army would attack along the Messines Ridge nearer Ypres, aiming for the relatively prominent feature of Mont Kemmel and thereby threatening encirclement of the whole Ypres Salient garrison.

Haig had never let his attention drift too far from Flanders. He knew what was at stake and recognised clearly that there was no room for manoeuvre, trapped as the British were in the narrow Belgian coastal plains. He still planned a flexible defence but here the Battle Zone *must* be held for there was almost nowhere else to run. However, notwithstanding the importance of Flanders, divisions had still been sent from his northern Second and First Armies to relieve the gigantic pressure on the faltering Third and Fifth Armies. Haig had shuffled and rotated his divisions as best he could, but the fact remained that of the fifty-six British divisions no less than forty-six had already been involved in the defensive battles. Indeed, many of the worst affected were now stationed in the very area where Ludendorff was planning to attack.

The British vulnerability was symbolised by the presence of a weak Portuguese corps in the Laventie sector of the tactically significant Lys valley. It had been stationed there for the winter months, when the sector was waterlogged, but it still had not been relieved now the valley was perfectly passable. A further sign of this endemic weakness was the willingness to consider evacuating the Ypres Salient, pulling back to a sensible flattened line of defence based on the low Pilckem Ridge running just in front of the town itself. No one wanted to evacuate all the ground they had fought so hard for during the Third Battle of Ypres just a few months before; in particular, they did not want to abandon the Passchendaele Ridge, which offered considerable potential as a vantage point from which to launch the next British offensive towards the German railway complex at Roulers. But in April 1918 the next British offensive still seemed a distant prospect: survival was all that mattered. For the moment they held onto their gains, although the precautionary preparations for withdrawal were well under way.

There was considerable confusion in the Allied High Command. As it stood awaiting the next German assault it was difficult for the intelligence services to get a grip on the situation. The main complication was that the Germans had prepared a splendid variety of offensive schemes up and down the line and it was still difficult to discern which was to be triggered next. Haig expressed his concerns for his northern front, but Foch had other priorities: he was watching the Germans like a hawk in the Somme area and still feared for the security of Amiens. Once again, if the British Army was attacked it would have to hold on until the French reserves could reach the scene. In the event, when the Germans did attack they were to be faced by just the 55th, Portuguese 2nd, 40th and 34th Divisions of the XI and XV Corps with the 50th and 51st Divisions earmarked as their reserves. All of these divisions other than the 55th and the Portuguese had been through the mill during the March battles and the new drafts had had no chance to bed down since.

One advantage possessed by the British in the Lys and Messines sectors was a comprehensive coverage with defence works. The area was chock-a-block with redoubts, machine-gun posts, pillboxes, deep dugouts, massive belts of barbed wire, switch lines and artillery gun positions prepared for all-round defence. There was no massive labour required here to convert the existing system into a deep-lying, three-zone defence system; in essence the existing lines and redoubts were just converted to their new roles. By now there was a greater understanding abroad in the British Army of the new defensive tactics and many more units had practised in the roles of either garrison or counter-attack troops.

When the German attack was launched on 9 April 1918, their basic tactics had not changed. The barrage first crashed out at 0415, moving through the usual carefully controlled phases to culminate in the infantry attack timed for 0845. Once again the battlefield was blanketed in a dense fog; once again the defenders were blinded as to the movements of the attacking troops across No Man's Land. When the stormtroopers emerged through the mists the Portuguese troops simply ran for their lives. Perhaps they were wise for they were facing no less than four German divisions. Much has been made of their headlong retreat, but they had long demonstrated their unwillingness for the fight. The ordinary Portuguese soldiers did not understand what their country was doing in the war in the first place, what business it was of their small country while the European superpowers slugged it out for supremacy. They had endured a miserable, long cold winter in their sodden trenches with the inevitable drip-drip of casualties to gnaw at their morale. Now, after the kind of bombardment that could strip any man of his senses, they were expected to resist a murderous assault emerging from right under their noses. It is hard to blame them for running.

The Germans in accordance with their principle pushed hard into the vacuum opening up in front of them. By 1000 they had overrun all the Forward Zone. Although, of course, there were a few exceptions to the general collapse of the Portuguese forces, the rout was more or less total.

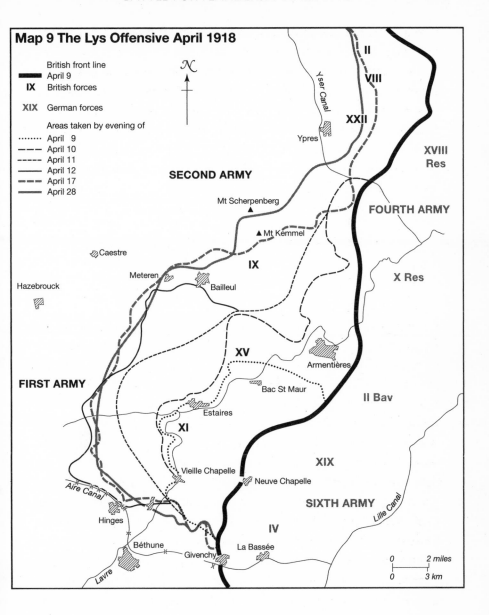

Map 9 The Lys Offensive April 1918

British front line
April 9
IX British forces

XIX German forces

Areas taken by evening of
.... April 9
– – – April 10
– – – – April 11
——— April 12
– – – April 17
▨▨▨ April 28

N

SECOND ARMY

II

VIII

XXII

Yser Canal

Ypres

XVIII Res

Mt Scherpenberg ▲

FOURTH ARMY

▲ Mt Kemmel

Caestre

IX

X Res

Meteren

Bailleul

Hazebrouck

Armentières

XV

Bac St Maur

II Bav

FIRST ARMY

Estaires

XI

Vieille Chapelle

XIX

Neuve Chapelle

Aire Canal

SIXTH ARMY

Lille Canal

Hinges

IV

Béthune

La Bassée

Givenchy

Lavre

0   2 miles
0   3 km

The Portuguese artillery and engineers did not retreat. I saw one artillery battery calmly sticking out one of the worst strafes I have ever seen. No one could have done better. The infantry were the delinquents, and in especial, the infantry officers who led the retreat. If the officer had not run I do not think the men would have done so. In one instance two British subalterns rallied a Portuguese battalion and got it to put up a good fight.[1]

Captain John Marshall, 468th Field Company, Royal Engineers, 46th Division

On the southern flank of the attack the Germans came up against a very different opposition in the soldiers of the 55th Division. They had been given a rest since their involvement in the Battle of Cambrai and they seem to have responded to the new challenge exceptionally well. Well dug in and trained to a peak of efficiency, not only did they hold their front against the three German divisions launched against them but they also pivoted back and provided an efficient defensive flank to prevent the Germans exploiting their breakthrough.

To the north of the Portuguese the 40th Division, who had been badly mauled in the March offensives, was not able to hold on. Its flanks were turned and it was soon tumbling back towards Fleurbaix. Major John Lyne of the 64th Brigade, Royal Field Artillery found that some of his guns, sent forward to supply close support for an intended infantry raid, were now in mortal danger of being overrun.

The Colonel was waiting for me on the bridge. He said, 'I've had no communication with the front line for the last twenty minutes and for all I know they already have been overrun by the German attack. So I can't give you any orders about going up to try and collect the guns. However, if you feel like going, I won't try to stop you but must leave it entirely to you!' For a couple of minutes I was in a difficulty. To leave the guns without making an attempt to get them away was unthinkable and yet, if they had been overrun, by trying to get them out I might sacrifice the whole of my battery and we would be quite useless for the future. I therefore put it to the drivers themselves and asked how many teams would volunteer to make this rather hazardous effort. Rather to my surprise every arm was raised and as there wasn't a minute to lose, we set off across the bridge at a gallop.[2]

Major John Lyne, 64th Brigade, Royal Field Artillery

Avoiding the main road, which was a natural magnet for German shells, they bumped hell for leather across open country towards the marooned guns. Although they avoided most of the shelling they still attracted a considerable smattering of rifle fire.

> I came across no retreating infantry who could give me an idea as to how far the advancing Germans had actually come and it was a great relief when I pulled into the field where the gun position was, to find my gunners still clustered round the guns and cheering our arrival. Actually they were on the point of destroying the guns as they had given up any hope of being able to get them away, since the Germans were already firing at them from some hedges a few hundred yards away. The rifle fire was as yet only some scattered shooting and it only took a few minutes to get the guns limbered up for departure.[3]
>
> Major John Lyne, 64th Brigade, Royal Field Artillery

Although he only had five gun teams and limbers one of the teams doubled up the guns to get away all Major Lyne's six guns. As soon as they were ready they galloped off as fast as they could. But when they got back to the bridge over the Lys at Bac St Maur they found there were no infantry anywhere in sight. Lyne saw at a glance that this was going to be death or glory stuff, something to tell the children about.

> The shelling by now was a good deal heavier. The village had had quite a pounding and there were several broken wagons and dead horses as we went through. We came to the bridge over the Lys and here I think I began to realise for the first time the queer trick fate was playing on me. It was as if I had dredged up from my long forgotten childhood memories of the episode of Lord Robert's son and the guns at Colenso, which had been one of my boyhood obsessions, and it was now unrolling like a sort of scenario for a novel by G. A. Henty or an adventure story for *Boy's Own Paper*, but of course, completely distorted as dreams are distorted when you try to recapture them in real life. All the ingredients were there: galloping horses, jingling harness and bursting shell. But instead of being a scenario of romantic endeavour and heroic achievement, what was actually happening was much more reminiscent of something from Fred Karno's army. The motley caval-cade that I was trying to lead to safety through the shattered streets of

Bac St Maur comprised one six-horse gun team towing a limber with two guns tied on with ropes, one six-horse team with another gun and limber with three wounded men tied on to prevent them being thrown off, two six-horse teams with guns and limbers but with the gunners from my forward gun riding bareback on the off-side horses because there was no space for them, and one gun and limber towed by a three-horse team. The whole circus fittingly rounded off by my senior subaltern, Foster, who for some reason I've never been able to fathom had taken his bedding roll to the forward gun position, and now appeared in a pair of blue-striped pyjamas tucked into gumboots and surmounted by a balaclava worn under his steel helmet. And so we clattered over the Bac St Maur bridge for the last time. Fortunately, perhaps, there were no onlookers to cheer us on or to contrast our manoeuvres, possibly unfavourably, with the King's Troop at the Royal Tournament.[4]

Major John Lyne, 64th Brigade, Royal Field Artillery

But they had not finished yet. Their orders had been to delay as long as was feasible the Germans in their attempts to get across the Lys. Unfortunately, the gun positions Major Lyne took up to cover the bridge were very exposed to the German artillery observers and it was not long before once again Lyne had to order up the gun teams. In the last moments their luck ran out as a shell landed right alongside one of his guns, wounding three of his crew.

I ran over to try and help the survivors of the crew to right it before the teams came up. While I was actually pushing on the wheel to straighten it, with my feet apart, I heard the next shell coming. And, if you are on the receiving end of a howitzer shell you can, once the remaining velocity drops below the speed of the sound, hear it on its way and often judge whether it is going to be near or far away. This shell was obviously going to be very close and while I was still pushing on the wheel, to my horror I saw it fall exactly between my feet. For a slice of eternity time stood still while I watched the hole between my feet and had time to wonder whether I should hear the explosion that was going to blow me apart, or whether death would be so sudden that I should know nothing. Well, I both heard and felt the explosion, but by some millionth defect in the fuse or the bursting charge, the shell, instead of bursting on impact must have burrowed its way 3 or 4 feet into the ground – because the explosion, when it came, was like a rumbling underground volcano that, while it nearly threw me off my feet, let not even a splinter of shell escape. I suppose no one can go through a war without remembering many narrow escapes or close shaves, but to actually see a miracle happen before your eyes and beneath your feet is probably more uncommon. I doubt if time will ever erase the memory of that slice of eternity, during which I actually watched death changing its mind at the last possible moment, disappear into a hole in the ground, leaving only a puff of smoke swirling harmlessly around my feet.[5]

Major John Lyne, 64th Brigade, Royal Field Artillery

When his thoughts had cleared he and his men once again managed to get the guns away. He had been more than lucky. *Boy's Own* exploits usually resulted in unmarked graves.

Meanwhile, the reserves of the 50th and 51st Divisions were ordered forward to block the hole in the line left by the Portuguese. At that point in time all that was covering the wide gap was a medley of men from the 11th Cyclist Battalion and the King Edward's Horse. The words 'déjà vu' were far too mild to encompass the feelings of Brigadier Hubert Rees of the 150th Brigade as he established a joint head-quarters with Brigadier Edward Riddell of the 149th Brigade in a rickety old building at Pont de Poivre and tried to work out what was happening. He had been ordered to hold bridgeheads on the west side of the Lys but they had already been lost. By the afternoon it was far more a matter of preventing the Germans from seizing the bridges and crossing the Lys River in force. Indeed, reports soon reached him that the Germans had succeeded in crossing the Bac St Maur bridge to his left, while the bridges in the town of Estaires were under increasing pressure by the early evening.

Not all of the men coming into action that day were old campaigners like Brigadier Rees. Many of them were new drafts who had only just arrived at the front. As such they were painfully inexperienced.

We had been marching for about four hours and were just having our fourth ten minutes rest, when we noticed a funny singing sound. On asking, one of the old 'uns informed us that it was a shell and that if we kept quiet we would hear it burst. A few seconds passed and we could hear a dull thud and boom, as this shell burst in a town about 3 or 4 miles away. I cannot explain what sort of feeling passed over me when I knew that a shell had actually passed over me and when I realised that we were getting near 'there'.[6]

Private Albert Bagley, 1/6th Battalion, Northumberland Fusiliers, 149th Brigade, 50th Division

When they set about digging fresh trenches the newcomers bent their back with a will. Then they stood-to and waited. It was at this point that Private Albert Bagley learnt another valuable lesson of practical soldiering – even if the Duke of Wellington may not have approved!

Some of the 'old sweats' must have got rather bored with this state of affairs, for I noticed that one by one they were disappearing over the parapet. A few minutes elapsed and they commenced to reappear, some with what appeared to be coloured tablecloths slung over their backs. On jumping back into the trench, they commenced to open their various bundles. To my surprise I saw they contained all manner of articles, such as knives, forks, spoons, loaves of bread, pink little cigarette packets, clocks, watches and pictures were amongst the curious collections. One of them informed me that they had informed these goods from houses a few yards in front of us. The cigarettes were eventually handed out to all of us – on receiving my share I was as pleased as punch![7]

Private Albert Bagley, 1/6th Battalion, Northumberland Fusiliers, 149th Brigade, 50th Division

At the end of the first day both sides could claim some success. The Germans had broken through and pushed forward up to, and in places over, the Lys River Line – a gain of up to 5½ miles in an area where there wasn't a mile to spare. Despite the best efforts of men like Major John Lyne they had also captured another 100 or so British guns. On the other hand, the British had managed to maintain a continuous line extending all the way round the German incursion, aided greatly by the heroic resistance of the 55th Division. Many felt that but for the dissolution of the Portuguese the front would have held firm and they would have repeated the triumph of the Third Army twelve days before at Arras. Nevertheless, Haig was deeply worried by the situation and immediately contacted Foch to request that the French take over more of the British line. Foch, however, was still determined to retain control of his reserves for as long as possible, fearing to commit them too early before the location of the 'decisive' battle could be definitely discerned. It was his view that Operation Georgette was just a diversion before the real battle began back in Picardy. He was confident that the British would hold out in the north; ironically, just like Gough before him, Haig must make do with his own reserves. As a result the 29th and 49th Divisions were despatched from the Second Army line in the Ypres area.

While his soldiers fought on the Western Front, Lloyd George was in political action on the Home Front. Stung by criticism of his policy in restricting the reinforcements required by Haig on the Western Front, he answered his detractors in the House of Commons – by sheer coincidence, on 9 April. The great politician was on excellent form as he batted off his critics, pointing out that the BEF was 'considerably stronger' on 1 January 1918 than it had been the previous years. He even had the statistics to prove it: a rise from 1,532,919 on 1 January 1917 to 1,750,892 a year later. He pointed to an increase of some 218,000 men. This may have stymied his critics in the Commons but the soldiers knew the truth. Lloyd George was blatantly manipulating the statistics to suit his political ends. Somehow he totally forgot to mention that the second figure included 335,454 men in the Labour Corps. This was a new organisation made up largely of labour drafts emanating from China, India and Africa. These corps were invaluable in the work they carried out behind the lines but they were emphatically not fighting soldiers capable of taking their place in the line when the Germans came over the top. When standing on the defensive the role of the infantry was paramount, yet the proportion of infantrymen in the global figure had shrunk from 59 per cent (904,422 men) in 1917 to 36 per cent (630,321 men) in January 1918. The new artillerymen, tank crews and RAF personnel were invaluable but the infantry divisions still had to be restocked. The moment passed, Lloyd George got away with his 'lies, damned lies and statistics' in Parliament, while on the same day on the Western Front the BEF paid the price for his mistakes. Although later challenged in the press with misleading the House he was always too politically wily for his bluff accusers and was never brought fully to book.

Next day, 10 April, marked the second stage of the Georgette offensive as the German Fourth Army extended the scope of the operation to encompass an assault on Armentières and attacks all along the Messines Ridge manned by the XI Corps of the Second Army. The bombardment started at 0245 and at 0515 four German divisions attacked the town of Armentières.

Our artillery had been firing all night with such tremendous force that it blew to pieces everything that meant defence, leaving only destruction and ugly shell holes filled with terrible-looking messes to tell of their marksmanship. When the rays of the sun grew brighter, they found us passing about a mile to the left of Armentières. Our artillery fire was engulfing it in a cloud of black and white smoke and dust, through which the flames shot out at times and I could readily distinguish houses crumbled to pieces. It was breathtaking, for one could not help but marvel at all this destruction. Before my eyes a big town was being wiped off the map. Someone remarked jokingly that, 'The girls of Armentières, *parlez vous*, would not love and kiss any more for souvenirs.'[8]

Unteroffizier Frederick Meisel, 371st Infantry Regiment, 43rd Ersatz Brigade, 10th Ersatz Division, Imperial German Army

The pleasant town of Armentières had always been dangerously close, just 2 miles from the front, but somehow civilian life had carried on regardless. When the Germans shells crashed down it was obvious that the civilians had to leave their homes and flee for their lives.

Many of the young mothers were carrying their babies. As the German shells burst, the mothers laid their babies down on the ground and lay on top of them to protect them from the blasts and flying metal. We helped them as much as we could to get out of the dangerous parts. The sight of these poor folks was terrible to see. Even we, who were used to seeing ghastly sights, were really shocked at 'man's inhumanity to man'. In a very short time we saw many of the children become motherless and many mothers childless.[9]

Sergeant John Stephenson, 1/6th Battalion, Duke of Wellington's Regiment, 147th Brigade, 49th Division

The fate of the French refugees was a side of warfare that few could stomach. There was almost nothing they could do to help, but every fibre of their civilised being cried out at their inaction. Major Lyne saw the civilians teeming back and found it difficult to maintain a soldierly detachment.

> The reddest horror of the battlefield grows smaller by comparison with what war brings to these poor inhabitants. People in England imagine that all the terrors of war are theirs when an air raid siren comes, and feel brave when they endure the discomfort of a night underground, but they have never seen the stark misery we saw. Things were so sudden, so hopelessly unexpected, and those who should have given warning had none ourselves. People would come weeping to us to know if they should go or stay, and we couldn't tell them. They looked to us for help we couldn't give them, they looked to us to stay the attack while they collected their few belongings and we couldn't do it. Once we passed a bedridden old lady pushed along in a wheelbarrow by a tottery old man, here a tired mother carrying a baby and dragging two weeping children, further on a poor old man who could go no more, his few poor goods beside him and gazing with pathetic eyes at the crowd flowing past. Here a little girl about 6 years old lay dead by the roadside where a shell had burst. We helped a little, those that we could, but it was so small the bit we could do; we who should have done so much.[10]
>
> Major John Lyne, 64th Brigade, Royal Field Artillery

Unteroffizier Meisel and his fellow machine-gunners of the 371st Infantry Regiment were involved in the attack on the Armentières railway station, closely supported as ever by the German artillery.

> From the station we were greeted with rifle and machine-gun fire. Here and there some of the men were hit and fell. Cries and groans were heard, orders shouted, the war was on again, taking its toll of victims. Before we had time to form ourselves again and return the fire, the whining sound of heavy German shells passed over our heads. A second later they crashed into the station, caving it in with loud bursts of fire and steel, ripping up the platform and twisting the rails out of position. A few more shells hit around the station, uprooting telegraph poles and sending steel splinters and shrapnel flying through the air. The shell fire ceased and we attacked. But in the debris life still existed, desperate

men defending a ruin. Bullets whistled from it and more familiar faces vanished. With fixed bayonets the station was stormed, to be met by a handful of Scottish infantry. Our Leutnant made gestures for them to surrender, but his good intentions were repulsed by a loud yell, 'Go to hell!', to be followed by several shots. Karl threw several hand grenades into their barricades, which exploded filling the ruins with smoke and dust, making the few shattered walls crack and fall, burying the defenders. Then we reached the station. Among piles of bricks and splintered planks lay bleeding and groaning men. Some lay stiff and cold, their bodies and faces covered with earth and blood. The place was littered with torn equipment, broken and twisted rifles and splintered furniture. On one of the cracked walls still hung the placard of the French railroad company, which ironically enough showed a beautiful seashore scene in the south of France.[11]

Unteroffizier Frederick Meisel, 371st Infantry Regiment, 43rd Ersatz Brigade, 10th Ersatz Division, Imperial German Army

As they rested after their violent exertions the German soldiers began to tend to the wounded.

We began to extricate human forms that showed signs of life. From our field flasks we gave them coffee and water to drink; then washed their faces and bandaged their wounds. Our hands, hard and sunburned as they were, must have felt to many of them as tender as the pitying hands of their loved ones, for they were kind hands. There was Leutnant Baunacker dressing the splintered arm of a young Scotsman, Karl picking up a bleeding man and carrying him like a baby. Soon everyone followed his example. Khaki-clad arms lay on grey-clad shoulders. Where was that hate they talked about in newspapers and at home – there was nothing of it here![12]

Unteroffizier Frederick Meisel, 371st Infantry Regiment, 43rd Ersatz Brigade, 10th Ersatz Division, Imperial German Army

The bedraggled British and Portuguese prisoners made their way slowly back to the German rear. Prisoners never look at their best, but their sheer numbers brought hope to the Germans

Heaps of prisoners came from the other side. They were in a rather desperate condition, very tired and worn out. They all said nothing else

but, 'The war is over for us and we don't want to go back any more!'
They were extremely friendly with us and we were extremely friendly
with them. We'd had enough of the war; and they'd had enough. We
had the feeling that if their army was in such a destitute condition the
war couldn't go on much longer.[13]

Gunner Paul Oestreicher, Imperial German Army

The 34th Division fell back towards the Lys River, for if its troops
stood and fought where they were it was evident that the Germans
would soon get round behind them from their incursions the previous
day. The division's neighbours in the IX Corps of the Second Army
were not up to the job of resisting the German onslaught. The 25th,
19th and 9th Divisions had lost most of their fighting strength on the
Somme and they certainly needed a little more than a couple of weeks
to make any kind of a recovery. One of the units facing the hammer-
blow was the 6th Wiltshires of the 19th Division. Once its neighbouring
brigade had pulled back it was left dreadfully exposed.

There was a good deal of intermittent machine-gun and rifle fire on the
right of my company, but we were in touch with our troops both on our
right and left and so far there was no suggestion that there was any
particular development. However, by midday visibility still being very
bad, the firing went on and as the mist lifted one occasionally saw signs
of movement to our right, where there seemed to be small parties of
Germans some distance away moving over open ground. It was very
difficult to see anything at all clearly. Early in the afternoon we realised
that contact with the troops on our right had broken and we manned a
communication trench at right angles to our original front line.[14]

Major Wilfred House, 6th Battalion, Wiltshire Regiment, 58th Brigade, 19th Division

They had actually been given orders to retire but these did not get
through to the 6th Wiltshires until 1630 that afternoon. It was far too
late. When they began to pull back the Germans deluged them with
heavy fire that seemed to come from all sides. As darkness began to fall
the Wiltshires slowly fragmented into small parties trying to make their
way back. Private Clarence Uren found himself trapped in a trench full
of water and under simultaneous fire from three German machine
guns.

The machine-gun fire was terrific and we were already wet through. The trench from which the fire was coming was about 100 yards away from us and kept up a hot fire along our parapet so that we could not raise a finger above it without being hit. It was now plain to us all that it was all up and we could not get out of the trap into which we had run. So Mr Knowles gave the order to the sergeant to hoist the white flag, which was done by handkerchief tied to a rifle. Fritz at once came out of his trench, called, 'Tommy!' to us and beckoned us across. We dumped our rifles and started across No Man's Land. Some of the first fellows did not take their equipment off and a machine gun was turned on us, hitting one fellow straight through the stomach. This put the wind up us properly, I thought they had got us out of cover and were going to do a dirty on us. But as soon as we had all dumped our stuff, the fire packed up and we crossed over to our captors, who turned out quite decent chaps.[15]

Private Clarence Uren, 6th Battalion, Wiltshire Regiment, 58th Brigade, 19th Division

Major Wilfred House was well aware that they were all but surrounded, but he was still determined to make an attempt to break out. The difficulty was trying to find a point of weakness in the German ring that was slowly tightening around them.

I had about twenty-five or thirty men with me and whenever we tried to move in the direction of what we thought might be our own lines we were heavily fired at. As darkness came on we could see by the Very lights that the Germans had got some way behind us. It seemed to me that the only thing was to form ourselves into groups of two or three men each and try to make our way through in the dark, which would confirm that they were moving in the right direction. I could only tell them what I believed to be the direction of the British line and advise them to watch the Very lights. I would move with a young officer called Findlay and we would set off as soon as it was really dark. We didn't know the ground very well, but I had the idea there was a stream running at right angles to the original front line. Findlay and I decided that we would make for the water and walk in it as being less likely to meet parties of Germans.[16]

Major Wilfred House, 6th Battalion, Wiltshire Regiment, 58th Brigade, 19th Division

They splish-sploshed along in the pitch darkness as quietly as they could, following the shallow stream bed for some two or three hours, judging their direction only by the twinkling of the Very lights that rather effectively marked out the British front line.

> We came to what seemed like a straight cobbled main road, which crossed the line of the stream, a sort of causeway. We had to cross over this road quietly and having done so lay down and listened. The only noise we heard at first was the sound of a man snoring very loudly 15–20 yards from us; in due course we heard men whispering in German. We realised that it must be an outpost of the German front line. We had no idea how many of them there were, or in which direction they were facing. I said to Findlay that we must get back across the road. When halfway across a Very light went up not far away and we realised that we must be silhouetted and lit up. We froze absolutely still and waited for the light to die down; then completed our trip across the road. By watching other Very lights we thought we knew how the German lines ran and decided to go further along than the outpost. We thought we must be more or less in No Man's Land and started to move more briskly. At this point my life was saved by the moon coming out from behind a bank of cloud and showing me that we were on the point of walking into a pond, or rather gravel pit – deep water! Again helped by Very lights we got round it. After a little time we heard voices – and they were foreign! Then we realised they were talking Welsh not German. We decided that we must walk boldly towards the voices and challenge them. They answered, 'Ninth Welsh!' so we got safely back to British lines![17]

Major Wilfred House, 6th Battalion, Wiltshire Regiment, 58th Brigade, 19th Division

They had been lucky. Most of the 6th Wiltshires were lost that night.

Yet overall the situation was still loosely under control: the Germans had failed to shatter the British line. While the Second Army had fallen back it had still maintained its cohesion and kept contact with the units on either side. To the north, on the First Army front, the 55th Division was still holding firm while the 50th and 51st Divisions had only been forced to retreat a further 1,000–2,000 yards from the impromptu line they had occupied along the west bank of the Lys and Lavre Rivers.

The problem was that as the British front line stretched to encompass the growing salient punched out by the Germans, the battalions were becoming stretched with it. Indeed, units were often so spread out that they had little sensation of the bigger picture. The arrival of the reserves was crucial: until they were reinforced the line could break at any time. The nearest source was the First Army where Major Philip Neame VC was engaged as a staff officer.

> One knew pretty well exactly how many divisions could be moved by rail in a given time, say in one day, two days, three days. When there was a real emergency and it was a case of moving four, five or six divisions from one part of the front 40 or 50 miles away to another part of the front where the Germans were starting to deliver a very heavy attack, you had to make quick decisions as to what was the quickest way of moving them, how many you could move by rail and how many had to go by road, depending on where they were billeted, or whether you had to take divisions out of the trench line and spread your troops more thinly. This required very complicated thinking and working out so as to get the maximum number of troops on the move as quickly as possible. The German long range shelling started on the railways that we were using, and they cut the railway line. We had a division moving by rail; in fact, part of it had already passed the place that was cut by their shelling. Fortunately, I was able to get reports to say that the shelling stopped at a certain time and we got engineer railway troops on at once to repair the damage. So the movement carried on, the line was repaired and the whole of that division got through and saved the situation.[18]

Major Philip Neame VC, Headquarters, First Army

Staff officers, too, could make the difference.

On 11 April Haig, that most undemonstrative of generals, felt the need to issue a special order of the day, an effort to inspire his men to greater resistance. Although the retreat was so far controlled, there was absolutely no room to spare if the Hazebrouck rail junction and the Channel ports were not to be fatally uncovered.

> Many amongst us now are tired. To those I would say that victory will belong to the side which holds out the longest. The French Army is moving rapidly and in great force to our support. There is no other

course open to us but to fight it out. Every position must be held to the last man: there must be no retirement. With our backs to the wall and believing in the justice of our cause each one of us must fight on to the end. The safety of our homes and the freedom of mankind alike depend upon the conduct of each one of us at this critical moment.[19]

Field Marshal Sir Douglas Haig, General Headquarters, BEF

It can be noticed in passing that Haig was undoubtedly stretching a point when he said the French were moving rapidly and in great force to their support. Foch was still resolutely obdurate, determined that the British must take the strain. But the overall tone certainly chimed in with the prevailing mood of desperate resistance.

That day the Germans had seemed to redouble their efforts against the 51st and 50th Divisions, driving straight for Hazebrouck. At 1130 Brigadier Rees received delayed orders to concentrate his 150th Brigade at Pont de la Trompe on a tributary of the Lys. Here they would find some sappers organising a new line of defences acting in conjunction with the newly arriving 29th Division, which was filling the gaping gap between the 50th and 40th Divisions. Rees moved forward accompanied only by his brigade major but soon found that circumstances were yet again tumbling out of control.

As I arrived I saw the Germans running towards us on the road and they promptly fired at us with a machine gun. On the right was a company of 29th Division Royal Engineers and away to their right again, I could see no signs of anyone. North of the road I heard there was a party of Durham Light Infantry and beyond them a reinforcement battalion. Moving out from the village I saw the Germans advancing in mass from Estaires. Three lines of men, at two paces interval or so, and behind them columns in artillery formation. It was a fine sight, but as I only saw a mere handful of men to stop them and the Huns were only 1,000 yards away the situation looked very precarious.[20]

Brigadier General Hubert Rees, Headquarters, 150th Brigade, 50th Division

As Rees rushed back to his headquarters at Vieux-Moulin to report events to 50th Division headquarters, the thin line duly collapsed behind him.

237

I set off to try and stop the rot. I brought a number of men to a standstill along a light railway to the north and then chased some more men going back north-west. On the next parallel road I found a couple of hundred men belonging to my brigade coming down from Doulieu and directed them to take up a position north of and astride the road. Some East Yorks I sent south of the road and some Durham Light Infantry to report to Colonel Spense, also south of the road. The situation south of the road looked very bad. Lines of men, not very many of them at that, were retiring on Vierhook. I galloped across country to try and stop them, under a fair amount of fire from rifles and machine guns at long range. At Vierhook I couldn't get past a battery, which were firing as hard as they could, but managed to scramble through a hedge to find General Martin rallying the men on the outskirts of the village. One of the houses was on fire and the place was under machine-gun fire. Not more than sixty men appeared to be available and the situation was getting desperate. In fact if the Germans had pushed home their attack, there was nothing to stop them.[21]

Brigadier General Hubert Rees, Headquarters, 150th Brigade, 50th Division

Fortunately for them the Germans did not press home their advantage and during the night reinforcements appeared to plug the wide gaps that existed in the tenuously formed British line.

Up and down the line for the next couple of days this was the nature of the fighting on the 50th Division front. Desperate men, clinging on as best they could, falling back, filtering in the newly arriving reinforcements that were inevitably soon chewed up in the intense fighting. A typical incident happened when the 149th Brigade of 50th Division was ordered forward to fill a gap astride the Estaires–Strazeele road. On their arrival just before daybreak on 12 April, the men of the 1/6th Northumberland Fusiliers were met with a hailstorm of fire from the houses and orchards of the nearby village of Neuf-Berquin.

So sudden and intense was the fire that our troops were compelled to lie flat on the road on which they were marching – there being no ditches or other cover available – and no movement could take place so long as the enemy machine guns were allowed to remain in position. I hastily collected some twenty men and advanced across an open ploughed field for 400 yards to the outskirts of the village. On reaching the first outbuildings I had only four men left, but by making our way through and around the houses we cleared the village of the enemy as far as the road junction – an advance of some 1,000 yards. Being such a small party and in danger of being captured we returned – with difficulty.[22]

Lieutenant Alex Thompson, 1/6th Battalion, Northumberland Fusiliers, 149th Brigade, 50th Division

In the confusion caused by this attack the rest of the battalion had managed to advance into tenable positions on either side of the road. Every skirmish, every battle, had a cost in human lives. Private Albert Bagley had already seen ample evidence of what a moment's hesitation, sheer bad luck or good German shooting could mean when one of his comrades was badly hit.

Poor boy! He was groaning something awful. Looking into his face I saw he was a boy called Phillips whom I knew fairly well while in training in England. Just then a corporal came up, and hearing the boy groaning, said, 'Come on lad, do you want the Jerries to get you, come on, buck up!' All he replied was, 'Oh mother, mother!' till he was calling at the top of his voice. His condition got worse, until at last he fell back – all over within two minutes of receiving the fatal bullet.[23]

Private Albert Bagley, 1/6th Battalion, Northumberland Fusiliers, 149th Brigade, 50th Division

They lifted him gently up and laid him under nearby hawthorn trees, covering him with a ground sheet. Private Edgar Phillips, the 25-year-old son of Edith Phillips of Stoke-on-Trent, has no known grave.

Once again the 149th Brigade and with it the 1/6th Northumberlands were gradually pushed back. As they retreated they took what shelter they could find or swiftly dug slit trenches some 18 inches deep with their entrenching tools. They may not have been deep but it was hard grafting work all the same. The fighting was episodic and difficult to piece together. Many men had little idea of where they were or what was happening around them. Withdrawals were often followed by small-scale counter-attacks to gain features that meant little or nothing to the ordinary soldier. As the troops charged forward in these affairs there was often no real guiding intelligence: just a sudden communal realisation amongst the survivors that they were not going to succeed.

The volume of firing got so fierce that at last flesh and blood could not stand against it any longer. As if by some instinct every man threw himself down flat, burying his face in the soil as best he could for protection. I was lying flat and wondered how long I would be like this, for the soil was sticking to my lips, and I felt a tickling sensation under my face. Raising my head as high as I dare, I saw that the tickling was caused by a beetle worming its way. Oh! How I wished then that I was a beetle, or at least could be so small. The bullets flying over my back, about a foot and a half from the ground brought me back to the reality of things.[24]

Private Albert Bagley, 1/6th Battalion, Northumberland Fusiliers, 149th Brigade, 50th Division

When troops broke it happened suddenly – men had screwed up their nerve to attack, so when they started to falter their self-control evaporated and they simply took to their heels.

An order was given to retire, as the Germans on our right flank were advancing in a circle and we were in danger of being surrounded – we had enough to do to watch those straight in front! Well, it took no second telling for our chaps to fall back as the strain of facing the machine-gun fire had almost upset all mental balance. It was through one or two bolting, as they did, that gave the others the idea that the game was up, and when a chap sees another fleeing, he doesn't see why he should stick it when the chap next is off! Instead of being a 'retire', it developed into a race of who could put the most distance between the Germans and ourselves in the least time. Of course, we did not run at first, but when you saw your own men going back like mad, it stood to common sense it was no good you trotting back then firing a few rounds, then back further, then firing again and so on – which is meant by 'retiring'. A lot of the chaps were taking their equipment off and throwing it away, thus enabling them to run faster. While jogging over the rough fields I reasoned out with myself that if a bullet was coming at me it may hit part of my equipment and thus perhaps lessen its bad intent on my poor body. I suddenly remembered that the rifle in my hand was useless, so dropped it, but of course that was justified.[25]

Private Albert Bagley, 1/6th Battalion, Northumberland Fusiliers, 149th Brigade, 50th Division

A couple of days later Bagley had another dreadfully close escape. He and a small party of the 1/6th Northumberland Fusiliers were left totally surrounded from all sides.

> All of our fellows were trying to settle in their own minds what was the best thing to do. I saw an officer crawling towards our hole, and as he passed the various posts he gave them instructions. He told us it was hopeless trying to do anything against the Jerries. We had to vacate our position, one at a time and make a dash for freedom.[26]
>
> Private Albert Bagley, 1/6th Battalion, Northumberland Fusiliers, 149th Brigade, 50th Division

As the men began carefully crawling away, the Germans spotted them and opened fire, but their flying bullets posed an equal threat to their own men creeping round behind the Fusiliers. In the resulting confusion several of Bagley's comrades decided that enough was enough.

> To my horror, I saw a lot of our men taking off their equipment and then jumping up, holding their hands up and advancing towards the excited Germans. I was not of the same mind. Getting out of the hole, I said to my pal, 'Come on, mate! I'm not sticking here, let's make a bolt for it!' and commenced to run down our line to the right – as that was the only possible 'exit'. The firing from the left was getting worse, so I intended to shelter at the next hole till it died down. On jumping in, I found a man lying, half in and half out of the hole. Looking closer I saw that he was an officer; also underneath him was another officer practically invisible. I was shocked to see the top man was no other than Lieutenant Waggott. His trench coat was badly torn and saturated with blood, but he was quite dead, which rather unnerved me, when I had been under him just the day before.[27]
>
> Private Albert Bagley, 1/6th Battalion, Northumberland Fusiliers, 149th Brigade, 50th Division

He burst out of his shallow hole and made another break for it. Once again the 'race' was on. In all, about a dozen men made the desperate dash for freedom.

> Running across ploughed fields is heavy work, but when fear possesses a person it adds speed to his feet. A few of the chaps behind overtook

me as I was getting short-winded. Walking for a short time to regain my
breath, I once more commenced to run with the intention of trying to
catch up to a group of six of seven, who had got further on while I was
walking. I had barely commenced to run, when I heard an awful
whistling, and knowing by the sound it was going to drop pretty close,
threw myself flat on the ground. Immediately there was a terrific
'BANG', and dust and earth filled the sky. As I got up to run again, to
my horror, the group of men had disappeared. Passing the spot where
the shell burst, there were only bits of clothing and patches of blood.
Looking behind me, instead of nine or ten men, there were only two or
three still running: All this time the bullets had been flying past close by,
others hitting the ground just in front of my feet.[28]

Private Albert Bagley, 1/6th Battalion, Northumberland Fusiliers, 149th Brigade, 50th
Division

It was a frantic run, with a real nightmarish feel about it, but Bagley
eventually reached relative safety in a well-made trench occupied by
troops still under discipline, including elements of the 235th Company,
Machine Gun Corps.

Sometimes there was no such happy ending. Thus it was when
Lieutenant Alex Thompson found himself completely cut off with a
small group of men. They were occupying slit trenches but had a poor
field of fire with a thick hedge in front of them that was soon occupied
by copious German troops supported by both machine guns and trench
mortars.

Our position seemed hopeless but I knew there were no troops in
reserve to our position so I issued an order that the position must be
held at all costs until further orders. Early in the morning, the 13th, the
enemy sent several aeroplanes over us and a concentrated bombardment was thus accurately directed on our positions. Infantry attacks
were driven back with heavy losses. After a very short time my last
remaining Lewis gun was destroyed by shell fire. I ordered all men to lie
flat in the shallow trench and one man only was instructed to keep
watch and pass the word along the trench when the next infantry
attackers were within 40 yards of our trench. When this happened all
the garrison opened rapid fire, the result being that the enemy imagined that we were more numerous than we really were, and each

time the enemy were driven back with heavy losses. These tactics of bluff were repeated throughout the day. Bombardments and infantry attacks continued throughout the whole day and so intense and accurate was the fire that even wounded men and stretcher bearers were shot down – not one wounded man left the trench without being killed.[29]

Lieutenant Alex Thompson, 1/6th Battalion, Northumberland Fusiliers, 149th Brigade, 50th Division

As the day wore on the Germans drove out neighbouring troops and they began to encircle Thompson's party. Things were looking more than desperate and men's lives depended on the decisions that Thompson made over the next few hours.

At 3.30 p.m. a large body of enemy infantry appeared on the road on high ground some 200 yards to our rear and these men gradually closed upon us. After firing in three different directions with the few men I had left, the Grenadier Guards on my right did the only thing possible in the circumstances and surrendered. I and the two remaining men with me (one wounded) then laid down our arms and left the trench full of dead. The two men who were with me were prepared to fight on for a few seconds longer, but it was obvious that no good purpose could be served by three more lives being lost when the position was already captured.[30]

Lieutenant Alex Thompson, 1/6th Battalion, Northumberland Fusiliers, 149th Brigade, 50th Division

Thompson was a prisoner, but other stragglers fought on. Private Albert Bagley at least had the chance to get a little of his own back as he watched the Vickers gun of the 235th Machine Gun Company spew into action when the Germans launched an attack from a hastily constructed trench some 100 yards in front of them.

Suddenly we were surprised to see the Germans mount their parapet and start towards us. Immediately we were on the alert, fingering our triggers and waiting for the officer to give us the word – but no sound from his lips. We were getting up to fever heat, wondering what was going to happen. Then the officer said, in a quiet voice, 'When I give the word, no one except the machine gun must fire.' This did not give much satisfaction, but it somehow broke the tension. When the Jerries were barely 50 yards away, the word came, and what a relief it was. The sergeant was working the Vickers gun, and he seemed very calm as he slowly turned the gun from left to right. I was amazed to see that almost every fourth man went down. Still they came on, and the gun slowly started its return journey. Still almost every fourth man was going down – it was as if watching some machinery working. The Jerries were still advancing, but somehow did not look quite so determined, and as the gun commenced again to mow from left to right, they seemed to waver. Then we could hear the officers ordering them to advance, at least I imagined so, from the tone of the voices. The Jerries then halted altogether, still the voices urged them on, when suddenly, as if by instinct, they all turned and commenced to bolt. At that we opened fire with our rifles to help them along, and it did make them move! Straight over their own trench they went, and on, getting smaller and less in numbers, till finally very few were left. Like children we cheered ourselves almost hoarse.[31]

Private Albert Bagley, 1/6th Battalion, Northumberland Fusiliers, 149th Brigade, 50th Division

As Bagley must have known from his bitter personal experiences over the last few days, the enjoyment of a panicked retreat depends almost entirely on being the beholder rather than the participant.

As they advanced the German troops were giving way to temptation and there was a considerable amount of looting. Meisel had pushed forward to the small town of Steenwerck halfway along the road between Armentières and Bailleul.

It was a German soldier's dream come true. The first thing we came to was a sweet shop filled with the choicest of chocolates and we hadn't seen sweets for three years. We looked through the big show windows in amazement at their contents. Rifle butts smashed the windows and doors in, broken glass filled the show cases. Ravenously we started in on the chocolates, filling our pockets and even throwing away a belt of machine-gun ammunition to refill the now empty box. We continued on to the next, a jewellery shop. Again glass splintered and doors were broken down. The store showed signs of having been emptied by the proprietor of everything of value. Only empty boxes, imitation jewellery, a few cheap watches and several large clocks had been left behind.

Fritz Gruen broke into the shop gleefully calling out, 'Leave that junk and come across the street!' On the other side of the street was a large grocery shop. Other soldiers had entered there already. The place was filled with hams, sausages, cans of delicacies and white bread. Duty was forgotten. More soldiers were piling in bringing with them bottles of wine and beer. Outside in the street whistles shrilled. The officers were trying to assemble their men again, but nobody paid any heed. Different regiments were arriving by now, but they, too, followed our example. Pretty soon the whole town was filled with men who, probably for the first time in long years, lost their discipline. They broke into houses, demolishing the interiors. They discovered a brewery and started rolling barrels of beer into the street, breaking them open with bayonets and spades to drink to their heart's content. Here and there arguments ensued, to be followed by fist fights. If the British could have returned they would have captured some of the very best German divisions without difficulty.[32]

Unteroffizier Frederick Meisel, 371st Infantry Regiment, 43rd Ersatz Brigade, 10th Ersatz Division, Imperial German Army

Meisel and his companions made themselves comfortable with their ill-gotten gains in a nearby cellar. A sign of things to come was the arrival of a new draft to replace the German casualties. Not only were they ominously young but they also brought unwelcome news from the home front.

Boys 17 years old that looked barely 15. We helped them to make themselves comfortable, set them behind the table and started to dish up the captured delicacies. The youngsters looked at the jam, the white bread, sardines and meats with unbelieving eyes and fell on the food like starving men. Hans had been in a hospital near Berlin and he told us about the conditions at home, saying that the people did not believe in a German victory any more. The babies were starving for lack of food and milk; the ammunition workers dissatisfied with their wages of 14 marks a day. Karl brought his fist down on the table, bursting out hotly, 'Fourteen marks a day, why that's half our monthly pay! Besides staying at home in safety and comfort and having all the women to themselves – and still they're not satisfied!'[33]

Unteroffizier Frederick Meisel, 371st Infantry Regiment, 43rd Ersatz Brigade, 10th Ersatz Division, Imperial German Army

Next morning the Royal Artillery began to drop its shells into Steenwerck.

> An explosion above our heads awakened us. Gripping our equipment, everybody scrambled up the steps and out into the street. It was the first shot fired by the British artillery into the town. Half of the house had been wrecked by the explosion and all of the windows broken. The body of the sentry, a young recruit that had come the night before, lay before the entrance to our cellar. His head had been smashed by shrapnel and his friends stared at his bloody and still smoking body horror-stricken. This was the first death they had seen in action. To them it was a terrible sight, but Karl and I were used to such horrors.[34]
>
> Unteroffizier Frederick Meisel, 371st Infantry Regiment, 43rd Ersatz Brigade, 10th Ersatz Division, Imperial German Army

They hastily evacuated the town and Meisel watched from the nearby open fields as the shells reduced the buildings to a smoking rubble.

While the British southern flank held firm, benefiting from the original success of the 55th Division, there was still a threat to the city of Béthune, which lay only 2 miles from the front. As the heavy shells crashed down the civilians fled in terror. Soon, the 468th Field Engineer Company of the 46th Division was ordered into the town to help prepare the defences. Its men were given a myriad of additional jobs, which ranged from digging trenches to repairing disrupted water supplies and other more unusual tasks.

> Doctor Foster and myself spent the best part of two days going round the town letting out dogs from premises – the owners of which had locked them up, leaving the dogs in charge, with the idea that they themselves would return in a day or two. We had several stiff climbs, up walls and trees to get at some of these animals – and then they generally received us as burglars in a most ungrateful manner. Doctor Foster rescued a parrot that called itself Coco. The bird bit him twice on the nose, so that he had to wear a bandage. It could swear beautifully![35]
>
> Captain John Marshall, 468th Field Company, Royal Engineers, 46th Division

Beneath the streets were copious cellars brimming with assorted wines and spirits.

Some looting undoubtedly took place. All the cellars were full of wine and though much was destroyed a good deal was drunk by our men. My fellows mixed port, vermouth, brandy, champagne and other liquids together, heated it in dixies and doled it out in mess tins. I contented myself with telling the men what the regulations were, but that, if broken, no man was to be 'tight', all drink was to be shared and none was to be taken except *after* the day's work. The consequence was that I never saw one of them the worse for liquor, though they had plenty.[36]

Captain John Marshall, 468th Field Company, Royal Engineers, 46th Division

On 11 April the Germans had forced their way into Merville and Nieppe as they pushed inexorably forward towards Bailleul, Méteren, Strazeele and, of course, their main objective, just behind the Fôret de Nieppe, Hazebrouck. Amongst the British reserves coming into the line was the 33rd Division. Lieutenant Colonel Graham Seton Hutchison of the 33rd Machine Gun Battalion sent his troops forward to defend Méteren. His tale, often told, has become symptomatic of this kind of last-ditch battle. His battalion had been rushed in by train but had none of the usual transport to carry the machine guns and ammunition boxes. Hutchison set up his headquarters in a farmhouse at Méteren and, after carrying out a personal reconnaissance, he was aware that the situation was desperate. He took a robust attitude to securing the necessary transport to get his men forward.

In Méteren there was an Army Service Corps motor lorry column. I requested the use of a lorry, but the officer refused it. I hit him on the head with the butt of my revolver, and instructed the driver Sharples, a splendid young fellow, to drive off. We halted at my farmhouse and within a few minutes half a company of machine-gunners, guns and ammunition complete had been packed into the lorry.[37]

Lieutenant Colonel Graham Seton Hutchison, 33rd Battalion, Machine Gun Corps, 33rd Division

They drove forward with Hutchison sitting with his adjutant Captain Harrison in the front cab. Hutchison was still wielding his revolver.

We drove straight on over the ridge on which stood the Hoegenmacker Mill, which became the fulcrum of the fighting, where we surprised in a ditch the advance guard of the enemy. From our seat beside the driver, Harrison and I loosed off our revolvers and killed the gun crew, all German stormtroops, and captured their machine gun.[38]

Lieutenant Colonel Graham Seton Hutchison, 33rd Battalion, Machine Gun Corps, 33rd Division

His men dropped into action, setting up eight machine guns to cover the approaches to Méteren. Meanwhile, Hutchison took action to stem the retreat of the infantry and bolster the meagre forces holding the ridge.

Masses of British infantry in complete disorder and often led on by the officers, were retiring on to Méteren. At the revolver point I halted one battalion of north country troops, commanded by a young major, and ordered them to turn about and occupy Hoegenmacker Ridge. Three times I gave my order and put it also into writing. Each time I was refused. Finally I gave the officer, whose men refused to accept any order except through one of their officers, two minutes in which to decide, with the alternative of being shot out of hand. At the end of these two minutes I struck him and the Regimental Sergeant Major said to me, 'That is what we have been waiting for all day, Sir!' He led the companies up to the ridge, though they proved but a feeble defence and leaked away in the night.[39]

Lieutenant Colonel Graham Seton Hutchison, 33rd Battalion, Machine Gun Corps, 33rd Division

It was evident that Colonel Hutchison was both determined and ruthless.

We discovered in the *estaminet* beside the mill a crowd of stragglers, fighting drunk. We routed them out, and with a machine gun trained on them sent them forward towards the enemy. They perished to a man. Then, as we ourselves left the inn, we found that the advancing Germans had infiltrated between our gun posts, and we came under machine-gun fire at close range. Why we were not immediately cut to ribbons passes my comprehension. We dropped on to the ground in a field, fortunately heavily furrowed by fresh ploughing, and while machine-gun bullets flicked past our ears and ripped the haversacks on our backs, we worked our way along the furrows as rapidly as possible, clawing at the earth as we travelled on our stomachs.[40]

Lieutenant Colonel Graham Seton Hutchison, 33rd Battalion, Machine Gun Corps, 33rd Division

Hutchison sent back the lorry and soon had his whole machine-gun battalion in action, spaced out all along the 3-mile ridge line. In the actions that followed over the next few days Hutchison was proud of his officers, proud of his men and, most of all, proud of himself.

The rapidity of the action; the extraordinary situation; the perfect discipline and drill; the setting of untouched farmhouses, copses and quietly grazing cattle; the flying civilians with their crazy carts piled high with household chattels and the retiring infantry behind; the magnificent targets obtained; and the complete grip of the situation by, and determination of, machine-gun commanders – this action takes the highest place of all time in the history of the Machine Gun Corps, and is an epic of the tenacity and grit of the British soldier, well led, with his back to the wall fighting against great odds.[41]

Lieutenant Colonel Graham Seton Hutchison, 33rd Battalion, Machine Gun Corps, 33rd Division

But others, too, appreciated the efforts of the 33rd Machine Gun Battalion and their eccentric commander who collectively managed to hold the Germans back for four days. They did not do so entirely on their own – they were manfully assisted by various infantry units – but here was a man and his unit making a real difference.

The pressure bore down relentlessly on Haig, who was getting un-characteristically testy.

He was told at breakfast that the division that had come up north to help us had arrived without guns or transport etc. He said, 'Indeed. They used to do that on the salient a lot. One would have thought three and a half years would have made a difference. It does make it rather *difficult to carry on a war of this sort!*'[42]

Major Ian Hedley, 17th Lancers, General Headquarters, BEF

One can imagine the increasing emphasis used to indicate Haig's irritation. He and all of his staff were also grimly aware that the

Germans were not Haig's only enemy. There were others manoeuvring against him back in London.

> They are now determined to remove the 'Chief' as soon as the first lull comes. This German advance serving as an excuse for making this murderous sacrifice, which was of course obviously decided long ago by the jealousy and fear of the smaller men who would rather see England beaten than themselves eclipsed by the Chief victorious. Now for the successor: the idea is 'Wullie', who, however, has not been approached on the subject yet and who may easily tell them to go to hell. Plumer, Byng and Allenby are in the running. While H. Wilson will take it if necessary, though he would rather not leave his present job where he is very happy! Ye Gods!! If Douglas Haig can hold the enemy he will be quite the biggest man in modern history, and even bigger when it is realised at home how he had not only to fight an enemy in front of him – the Boche – but also an enemy behind him – the politicians.[43]
>
> Major Ian Hedley, 17th Lancers, General Headquarters, BEF

Although the town of Bailleul fell on 15 April, the British stemmed the advance on Hazebrouck. As their reserves arrived, including divisions recalled from Italy, Palestine and Egypt, the Germans found the resistance significantly increasing until their progress slowed to a halt. Gradually stalemate set in, where as usual the advantage was with the defenders rather than the attackers, who had a disrupted battlefield behind them. The advantages of surprise soon diminished and as the exhausted British divisions were replaced or augmented by relatively fresh units the German casualties expanded exponentially. In the end Foch had relented, releasing a cavalry corps and two infantry divisions, but the battle had been largely fought and won by the British.

MEANWHILE, FURTHER NORTH the German success in retaking the Messines Ridge was increasingly threatening the viability of the whole Ypres Salient. Ypres was the word metaphorically carved into the heart of Douglas Haig. He had cemented his reputation back in November 1914 in the chaos of the First Battle of Ypres, so many lifetimes expended away. General Sir Hubert Plumer also had a huge emotional investment in the low ridges, splintered woods and swampy streams of the salient. His Second Army had been responsible for holding the salient since 1915; it had taken the Messines Ridge in June 1917 and been responsible for the last phases of Third Ypres, the battle for the benighted 'heights' of Passchendaele Ridge. Plumer and his Chief of Staff Brigadier Charles Harington met to discuss the worsening situation. Although Harington is a somewhat unreliable source, his account of the decisive meeting with Plumer has considerable emotional force that fairly reflects the seriousness of the moment.

> The Army Commander was with me standing at my desk examining the map. I knew what he was feeling about Passchendaele. We both knew the limit had been reached. We should have to come out. The risk was too great. No more help could come from anywhere. Méteren was in flames. Hazebrouck was threatened. At last I summoned up courage to say what I had feared for days. 'I think, Sir, you will have to come out of Passchendaele.' The effect was magic. My old Chief, always like a father to me, made one last bid. He turned to me and showed the most wonderful example of his bulldog tenacity that I had ever seen. I can hear it now, 'I won't!' It was indeed a plucky effort. The next moment I felt, and I have often felt it since, his hand on my shoulder, 'You are right, issue the orders.' He knew it all the time. He knew it was coming. We both did. We did not talk about it. He went off to his room.[44]
>
> Brigadier Charles Harington, Headquarters, Second Army

In fact, the prospect of withdrawal from the Ypres Salient had long been an option and thorough preparations had already been made. Troops had gradually been withdrawn until Passchendaele was only covered by a few isolated infantry posts and the bare minimum of field artillery guns. Although everything seemed quiet everyone was aware that the Germans might be biding their time, ready to strike during the evacuation to cause the maximum possible confusion and disruption. Captain Francis Whaley and his men of the 15th Hampshires were occupying one of the very most isolated outposts, situated beyond Passchendaele village itself. Whaley was a bitter man. He had served at Ypres during the 1917 Flanders offensive and he resented giving up the ground they had won at such dreadful cost just six months before.

As the hour of departure grew near, my economical mind deplored the wastage and capture of our trench stores: ammunition, bombs and so on. There seemed no quick way of disposal without telltale noise or other difficulties, so I made each man carry a small load in addition to his usual quota. In the course of distribution we unearthed an ammunition box, which was unexpectedly found to be full of small-size ration biscuits. My feelings of sorrow and bitterness at giving up the hard-won ground with which I had been so closely associated prompted my next action. Pushing a Mills bomb down among the biscuits, I wedged it securely so as then to withdraw the pin without releasing the lever, and left the box not too obviously in view. The least disturbance to the box must result in death or injury to nearly all the new occupiers of the post. Besides the immediate result, I reckoned that alarm and despondency might spread among the advancing Germans, making their progress more slow and cautious – as well as giving them a dose of their own medicine.[45]

Captain Francis Whaley, 15th Battalion, Hampshire Regiment, 122nd Brigade, 41st Division

Having left his deadly booby trap, Whaley groped his way back in the dark across a landscape rendered almost featureless by the attentions of the British and German artillery. He was soon hopelessly lost.

We came at last to the debris of Passchendaele church from which we had to make our way to the head of the duckboard track leading back to civilisation. Here disaster overtook us. I have always been poor at location and movement in the dark and after blundering about for what seemed a very long time, I finally found myself and the platoon back at the church. The ruins looked the same at all angles, so that I could hardly tell which way we were facing. An increasing number of enemy flares were rising on three sides of us and they seemed to draw nearer. Exhausted by the heavy going and with a feeling of near despair, I called a halt to consider the next move. Then, to our left front, the silence was broken by the sound of stumbling or squelching footsteps, together with the creak and clatter of equipment. What sounded like a large body of men was approaching from the direction of Germany. We immediately spread out and took up fire positions. There seemed nothing for it but to stay put and fight it out. But then we heard voices speaking in English. It was a neighbouring company of the Queens, considerably behind time. Joining up with them we finally struck the duckboard track.[46]

Captain Francis Whaley, 15th Battalion, Hampshire Regiment, 122nd Brigade, 41st Division

It was as well that they resumed a purposeful movement in the right direction for they were up against the clock. Also deep in the sacrificial ground was Lieutenant Robert Petschler of the 201st Field Company, Royal Engineers. After his frenetic experiences in the March retreat he had been moved to the Ypres Salient. Now he prepared to carry out a familiar duty.

On the 13th we got orders to prepare all bridges over the Steenbeek for demolition. I had twelve of these bridges to prepare. As an attack was expected all the time Bennett, Smith and I took it in turns to be always on the spot. At night-time we used to sleep in pillboxes close to the bridges. During the night our infantry withdrew to a new line behind the Steenbeek and at 5.30 a.m. we blew up all the bridges simultaneously. The 200th Field Company blew up all the pillboxes and the gunners blew up all their surplus ammunition that they could not remove. All these demolitions were made together and the whole area was ablaze.[47]

Lieutenant Robert Petschler, 201st Field Company, Royal Engineers, 30th Division

This was a very well-planned, organised affair compared with the haphazard panic and one-off decision-making process in blowing the bridges over the Somme River and Canal a month earlier. Everyone knew what they were doing and both the retirement and the demolitions were well controlled by a central guiding intelligence. The troops fell back to occupy the 'new line' on Pilckem Ridge.

With the evacuation of the salient the line solidified. The Germans tried again after a brief pause, attacking on 17 April 1918 all along the front from Dixmude in the north right down to Béthune. They achieved nothing but heavy casualties for their pains and another rather more prolonged lull followed. The real focus of the fighting had by now switched to a fight for Mont Kemmel, occasionally sarcastically referred to as the 'jewel' of the 'Belgian Alps', but nevertheless a dominating height of 510 feet in that flat wasteland. On 25 April the

Germans threw in seven fresh divisions against the three French divisions who had taken over the defence of Mont Kemmel. It was a natural stronghold, but it was a bad day for the French and, unaccountably, they were turfed out in short order by the assaulting Germans.

It is noticeable that the preliminary bombardment that commenced at 0230 was widely perceived by the French survivors as worse than anything at Verdun. Most of the artillery in support was effectively neutralised by the gas-shell bombardment and, when the assault came in at 0600 in conditions of thick impenetrable fog, the Germans swiftly overran the French trenches. By 0710 the Alpine Division was on top of Mont Kemmel and consolidating as fast as was humanly possible. They had taken some 6,000 dazed French prisoners.

The fighting in the Mont Kemmel sector held terrible memories for Unteroffizier Frederick Meisel, who had to be both lucky and brutally ruthless to survive his ordeal.

> Suddenly our artillery fire stopped. An awful silence followed the terrific noise. A whistle shrilled, bayonets were fixed. Another whistle signalled the descent into the valley. Not a sound, not a rifle shot could be heard from the opposite side. Crossing the valley we stopped to readjust ourselves and began to climb the hill before us. Now we discovered why it had been so quiet, for over this territory lay the silence of death. The shell holes were filled with ghastly and bloody messes; freshly built trenches had caved in burying the occupants. Stumbling over mutilated bodies we reached the summit.[48]
>
> Unteroffizier Frederick Meisel, 371st Infantry Regiment, 43rd Ersatz Brigade, 10th Ersatz Division, Imperial German Army

Then the French artillery began to pay them back in kind, covering the hillsides with masses of bursting shells.

> French shells began to hit to the right and left of us, leaving human forms writhing in agony. Our advance came to a stop and after hesitating a few minutes we drew back while the artillery fire followed us, ripping large gashes in our formation – soon the French drumfire engulfed us, the air was filled with gas and flying pieces of steel.[49]
>
> Unteroffizier Frederick Meisel, 371st Infantry Regiment, 43rd Ersatz Brigade, 10th Ersatz Division, Imperial German Army

With their young recruits sticking close to them, Unteroffizier Meisel and his sergeant took shelter in a deep shell crater.

> We automatically mounted the machine gun for action. Then like animals we burrowed into the earth as if trying to find protection deep in its bosom. Something struck my back where I carried my gas mask, but I did not pay attention to it. A steel splinter broke the handle of my spade and another knocked the remains out of my hand. I kept digging with my bare hands, ducking my head every time a shell exploded near by. A boy to my side was hit in the arm and cried out for help. I crawled over to him, ripped the sleeves of his coat and shirt open and started to bind the bleeding part. The gas was so thick now I could hardly discern what I was doing. My eyes began to water and I felt as if I would choke. I reached for my gas mask, pulled it out of its container – then noticed to my horror that a splinter had gone through it leaving a large hole. I had seen death thousands of times, stared it in the face, but never experienced the fear I felt then. Immediately I reverted to the primitive. I felt like an animal cornered by hunters. With the instinct of self-preservation uppermost, my eyes fell on the boy whose arm I had bandaged. Somehow he had managed to put the gas mask on his face with his one good arm. I leapt at him and in the next moment had ripped the gas mask from his face. With a feeble gesture he tried to wrench it from my grasp; then fell back exhausted. The last thing I saw before putting on the mask were his pleading eyes.[50]
>
> Unteroffizier Frederick Meisel, 371st Infantry Regiment, 43rd Ersatz Brigade, 10th Ersatz Division, Imperial German Army

Unteroffizier Meisel never had the chance to learn the name of that young recruit. This was the horrible reality of war. Following hard on the heels of the French barrage came the predictable counter-attack.

> Through the damp glasses of my mask I saw dim outlines of men appear and when they approached more closely I could distinguish French uniforms and dull blinking bayonets. Gruen threw himself behind the machine gun and I instinctively pointed the barrel of the machine gun into the mist towards the advancing enemy. His hands tightened themselves round the handles while his thumbs pressed on

the triggers. Flames spurted from the barrel of the guns and I saw the Frenchmen plunge headlong into the grass.[51]

Unteroffizier Frederick Meisel, 371st Infantry Regiment, 43rd Ersatz Brigade, 10th Ersatz Division, Imperial German Army

At last it was over. They were relieved and fell back. Of the draft of eight young lads they had received just a few days before, no less than four were now dead.

On the Allied side of the line, once the initial shock had died down, no one panicked and the reserves and counter-attack divisions soon stemmed the German advance. Although a surprise attack on 29 April captured a further height in the 'Belgian Alps' – Scherpenberg – lying between Mont Kemmel and Ypres, there was never really any more danger of the Germans rupturing the line. Once again the Germans had failed in their objectives. They had not taken the rail centre at Hazebrouck, and although it was now within reach of long-range guns it was not put out of action. Neither had they cut off the Second Army troops in the Ypres Salient and they had emphatically not gained the all-important Channel ports. In the end, all they had gained was land: another ugly salient bulging into the Allied lines and vulnerable to counter-attack at some point in the future. The British had not been thrown out of the war; the Americans were still coming. Ludendorff was running out of time and options.

AS A CODA to the Ypres operations there had been a brief flurry of activity on the Somme front. As Foch had suspected, Ludendorff had not forgotten that the tempting vista of the Amiens rail centre lay just 10 miles behind the front at Villers-Bretonneux and in late April the Germans made a renewed attempt to take the town.

The Australians had handed over the defence of Villers-Bretonneux to the 8th Division of the III Corps while they held the bulk of the Somme front to the north. From this time the Australian Corps would play a crucial role in the campaigns of 1918. Captain Philip Ledward, a staff officer serving with the 8th Division, left a sharp pen-picture of Major General John Monash commanding the 3rd Australian Division, reflecting his own prejudices no doubt, but nevertheless giving an indication of the sheer strength of the man.

We relieved the Australians, who had created a scandal by getting drunk in the grand manner and on a large scale on wine discovered in the town. I have vivid recollections of General Monash. He was a great bullock of a man, dark and florid, with a strain of Jewish blood, blazing black eyes and the kind of fierce vitality that one associates with wild animals. He made a great impression on me, for though his manners were pleasant and his behaviour far from rough, I have seen few men who gave me such a sensation of force. He was an able and, I should have judged, unscrupulous man, just bursting with the fighting spirit, a fit leader for the wild men he commanded.[52]

Captain Philip Ledward, Headquarters, 23rd Brigade, 8th Division

Monash had already been marked by Haig for command of the Australian Corps and despite a last-ditch anti-Semitic campaign launched by some elements within the Australian hierarchy he would duly take over at the end of May. John Monash was born on 27 June 1865 in West Melbourne, Victoria, Australia. He was of German Jewish origin and excelled at his academic studies before commencing a career as a civil engineer. At the same time he was a keen member of the Australian militia and attained the rank of colonel before the outbreak of war. War brought the usual promotion and he fought at Gallipoli with some distinction, although he also experienced failure during a chaotic night attack on Sari Bair in August 1915. On reaching the Western Front his planning skills, spectacular organisational abilities and general enthusiasm for the nitty-gritty detail of the grim trade of war increasingly impressed Haig who could recognize talent when he found it.

Ledward was ambivalent towards those 'wild men'. He clearly didn't like the Australians, but despite himself he admired them.

Remembering that the pick of the Australians were killed in Gallipoli, I have often wondered whatever they can have been like. It is my considered opinion that the Australians, even in 1918, were better in a battle than any other troops on either side. They were not popular. They had a contempt for Britishers to begin with – I myself heard the expression, 'Not bad for a Britisher!' used by one about some successful feat of British arms. They were untidy, undisciplined, 'cocky', not 'nice' enough for the taste even of 'Tommy Atkins'. But it seems indisputable that a greater number of them were personally indomitable, in the true sense of the word, than of any other race. I am glad they were on our side.[53]

Captain Philip Ledward, Headquarters, 23rd Brigade, 8th Division

The German attack on Villers-Bretonneux began on 24 April. Once again the 8th Division found itself in the thick of the fighting. Behind the lines the 2nd Middlesex medical officer, Captain Maberly Esler, and his stretcher bearers were badly exposed to the barrage.

First of all we were gassed heavily, we were down the valley and it got so full of gas that we had to clear out of it and we went and took up our position in some support trenches. The only place I could find as a first-aid post was a large quarry; it was some shelter from behind anyway. The sergeant and I went in one end of the quarry, there was a small cave. There was a much bigger cave in the other end where I put all the stretcher bearers, the stretchers and the drugs. Unfortunately, one of the shells fell short and hit the top of the quarry, buried all these fellows and killed them at once. Captain Toye came round to my shelter in the quarry and said, 'Where are all your stretcher bearers?' And I said, 'Under that lot', pointing to the pile of rubble. He said nothing more.[54]

Medical Officer Captain Maberly Esler, 2nd Battalion, Middlesex Regiment, 23rd Brigade, 8th Division

Captain Toye ordered Esler to pull back. On the way they ran into another terrifying German barrage. It was bad enough to make a man doubt his senses.

We started 180 strong, and we arrived with twenty-one the other end and so my chances of survival were nine to one against really. Of course I was frightened, but it was so like a nightmare that I thought it must *be* a nightmare, that such a thing couldn't be happening and that I'd wake up suddenly and find it was a dream. Oh, it was terrible, terrible. I remember a sergeant beside me, a shell went up and as the smoke cleared he was sitting with his two stumps waving in the air, his legs completely shot off. I said, 'Well, we'll take you to the side of the road.' He said, 'You're not going to leave me here?' I said, 'I'm afraid we can't do anything about it, we've got no stretcher bearers, we've got nothing to carry you with, we've got nothing to give you, we'll just put you out of the way of the tanks!' They were following us down the road. It was an awfully painful thing to have to do. The wounded who could walk were helped along: I had about five people clinging to me, one with a jaw blown away bleeding all over me. It was like a nightmare.[55]

Medical Officer Captain Maberly Esler, 2nd Battalion, Middlesex Regiment, 23rd Brigade, 8th Division

The 8th Division broke. It had barely had time to assimilate its new drafts and it simply had not had a chance to build up the resilience and *esprit de corps* within the ranks to resist this kind of pressure.

It certainly did not help the rattled men of the 8th Division that the Germans threw into the attack a few of their tanks, which provoked terror amongst the British troops who were sorely lacking in effective anti-tank training. However, it also triggered the first-ever tank versus tank fight when three German A7Vs clashed head-on with three British Mark IVs, of which two were female and one the male variety armed with two 6-pounder guns. The most famous account of the incident was left by Lieutenant Frank Mitchell, who was commanding the Mark IV male and had been ordered to hold the line at all costs. His crew were already suffering badly and were down to just four of the seven due to the effects of the German gas shells.

Suddenly, out of the ground 10 yards away, an infantryman rose, waving his rifle furiously. We stopped. He ran forward and shouted through the flap, 'Look out! Jerry tanks about!' and then as swiftly disappeared into the trench again. I informed the crew, and a great thrill ran through us all. Opening the loophole, I looked out. There, some 300 yards away, a round, squat-looking monster was advancing. Behind it came waves of infantry and further away to left and right crawled two more of these armed tortoises.[56]

Lieutenant Frank Mitchell, 1st Battalion, Tank Corps

This was a historic moment pregnant with possibilities for both sides. It would presage much of the future of armoured warfare, much as the clash between the ironclads *Monitor* and the *Merrimac* had attained fame during the American Civil War.

The 6-pounder gunners crouching on the floor, their backs against the engine cover, loaded their guns expectantly. We still kept on a zigzag course, threading the gaps between the lines of hastily dug trenches, and coming near the small protecting belt of wire, we turned left and the right gunner, peering through his narrow slit, made a sighting shot. The shell burst some distance beyond the leading enemy tank. No reply came. A second shot boomed out, landing just to the right, but again no reply. Suddenly, against our steel wall, a hurricane of hail pattered, and the interior was filled with myriads of sparks and flying splinters. Something rattled against the steel helmet of the driver sitting next to me and my face was stung with minute fragments of steel. The crew flung themselves flat on the floor. The driver ducked his head and drove straight on. Above the roar of our engine could be heard the staccato rat-tat-tat-tat of machine guns and another furious jet of bullets sprayed our steel side, the splinters clanging viciously against the engine cover. The Jerry tank had treated us to a broadside of armour-piercing bullets![57]

Lieutenant Frank Mitchell, 1st Battalion, Tank Corps

Meanwhile, the two female Mark IV tanks had been hit and were slowly making their way back. In reality it made little difference as their armament was of little use against the armoured sides of the German SK7s. Mitchell manoeuvred across a dip in the ground to get out of range and then once again turned to fight. His gunners had badly swollen eyes from the effects of the gas and it was almost impossible for them to get an accurate bead on their target as their Mark IV bucked and swayed across the broken ground. In the end Mitchell decided to slow down and take a risk in the hope of improving their accuracy of fire. This almost immediately brought results.

The left gunner, registering carefully, hit the ground right in front of the Jerry tank. I took a risk and stopped the tank for a moment. The pause was justified; a carefully aimed shot hit the turret of the German tank, bringing it to a standstill. Another roar and yet another white puff at the front of the tank denoted a second hit! Peering with swollen eyes through his narrow slit the elated gunner shouted words of triumph that were drowned by the roaring of the engine. Then once more with great deliberation he aimed and hit for the third time. Through a loophole I saw the tank heel over to one side and then a door opened and out ran the crew. We had knocked the monster out![58]

Lieutenant Frank Mitchell, 1st Battalion, Tank Corps

But he still had two more SK7s to contend with and he was by no means sanguine as he tried to locate them.

> The two great tanks were creeping forward relentlessly; if they both concentrated their fire on us at once we would be finished. We sprinkled the neighbourhood of one of them with a few sighting shells, when to my intense joy and amazement, I saw it go slowly backwards. Its companion did likewise and in a few minutes they both had disappeared from sight, leaving our tank the sole possessor of the field.[59]
>
> Lieutenant Frank Mitchell, 1st Battalion, Tank Corps

Meanwhile Villers-Bretonneux had fallen and the way to Amiens was open – but not for long. Once again the Australians were recalled to the line to retake Villers-Bretonneux using a pincer attack in conjunction with what remained of the 8th Division. During the planning for the counter-attack Brigadier Pompey Elliott once again behaved with a magnificent lack of tact and managed to thoroughly upset Major General William Heneker commanding the 8th Division.

> Heneker was highly regarded as a commander, but we did not see him at his best. He was justifiably disturbed and indignant because it had come to his notice that Pompey Elliott had issued an order that morning to the effect that any British troops seen withdrawing from the front were to be stopped and turned back; and that any who refused were to be shot. Elliott had the reputation of being a good fighting soldier; but he was an aggressive and erratic man. He criticised and quarrelled with everyone; and any officer who incurred his momentary displeasure was promptly put under arrest. This happened frequently to his battalion commanders and the members of his staff. No action ever followed, and after a suitable interval the officer concerned merely resumed his duty.[60]
>
> Captain Thomas Louch, Headquarters, 13th Brigade, 4th Australian Division

The attack went in at 2200 on the night of 24 April. The 13th and 15th Australian Brigades took the lead and it proved a bloody affair as they broke through and charged into the town. Many of the troops were aware that in a couple of hours it would be Anzac Day – 25 April, the third anniversary of the first landings at Anzac Cove, Gallipoli.

Whatever the reason, the Australians certainly took it out on the Germans that day.

> With a ferocious roar and the cry of, 'Into the bastards, boys!' we were down on them before the Boche realised what had happened. The Boche was at our mercy. They screamed for mercy but there were too many machine guns about to show them any consideration as we were moving forward.[61]
>
> Sergeant R. A. Fynch, 59th Battalion, 15th Brigade, 5th Australian Division

The Anzacs were fighting mad, overtaken by a dreadful primitive blood lust that fuelled the speed of their dash forward.

> There was a howling as of demons as the 57th, fighting mad, drove through the wire, through their enemy. The wild cry rose to a voluminous, vengeful roar. There was no quarter on either side. Bathed in spurting blood they killed and killed. Bayonets passed with ease through grey-clad bodies and were withdrawn with a sucking noise. Some found chances in the slaughter to light cigarettes, then continued the killing. Then, as they looked for more victims, there were cries of, 'There they go, there they go!' and over heaps of big, dead Germans they sprang in pursuit. One huge Australian advanced firing a Lewis gun from the shoulder, spraying the ground with lead. It is unlikely that any of the enemy escaped their swift, relentless pursuers. They were slaughtered against the lurid glare of the fire in the town. One saw running forms in the dark, and the flashes of rifles, then the evil pyre in the town flared and showed to their killers the white faces of Germans lurking in shell holes, or flinging away their arms and trying to escape, only to be stabbed or shot down as they ran. Machine-gun positions were discovered burrowed under haystacks, crammed with men, who on being found were smashed and mangled by bomb after bomb after bomb. It was impossible to take prisoners. Men could not be spared to take them to the rear.[62]
>
> Sergeant William Downing, 57th Battalion, 15th Brigade, 5th Australian Division

Two battalions of the 8th Division cleared the town itself but the real work had been done by the Australians. Afterwards came the reaction: these men were not natural killers, despite appearances on the morning of 25 April. One of the 5th Brigade officers, Lieutenant J. C. Christian of the 59th Battalion, noticed a heightened excitability and nervous tension amongst his men. As one of them said to him, 'I can't help thinking about that chap I bayoneted.'[63] Yet as a result of that madness, Villers-Bretonneux once again was denied to the Germans. The little splutter of excitement on the Somme died down and the German offensives – for the moment – were over.

THE MICHAEL AND GEORGETTE OFFENSIVES are often hailed as tactical successes but such praise misunderstands the very nature of the fighting in the Great War. Ground won did not mean tactical victory unless the ground gained granted a recognisable tactical advantage for the *next* battle. Large salients were vulnerable to being pinched out, as the Germans themselves had demonstrated in the cases of the Flesquières and Ypres Salients over the past two months. The statistics of the German achievements looked impressive: miles of France and Belgium had been overrun, they had taken more prisoners, captured more guns – but what had really changed? Since 21 March the British Army had suffered over 236,300 casualties. However, some 270,000 men had been despatched in drafts to the Western Front and six new American divisions had also reached the front. The writing was on the wall for the Germans.

CHAPTER EIGHT

Battle on the Aisne: 27 May 1918

SO FAR THE ALLIES had held the ring but they knew that it was by no means over. The Germans may have gone quiet in May 1918, but they were clearly still planning something. The balance of opinion amongst the Allied High Command was that the Germans would try again in the Somme region, striking again towards Amiens or Paris. There was no denying that the British Army had borne the strain and been badly battered in March and April so Foch approved a scheme to gain a little flexibility in the overall Allied order of battle. Tacitly accepting that the British front was far more active than the bulk of the French-held line, he approved the rotation of the worst-hit British divisions into one of the currently quietest sectors on the Chemin des Dames Ridge where they would be incorporated as the IX Corps into the French Sixth Army commanded by General Denis Duchêne. The divisions selected represented a roll-call of pain from the battles they had collectively endured on the Somme and Flanders: the 8th, 21st, 25th and 50th Divisions. They were stuffed full of inexperienced drafts, fresh troops it was true, but lacking the experienced NCOs and officers that could bind them together in action. The relieved French divisions would then form a General Reserve for deployment by Foch as and when required. This was eminently sensible and indeed there proved to be only one thing wrong with this plan – this area happened to be the very location chosen for the next German offensive.

Yet again Ludendorff was able to secure tactical surprise as he dusted off Operation Blücher, one of the alternative schemes prepared earlier in the year. This called for the German Seventh and First

Armies to smash into the French Sixth Army along the Chemin des Dames Ridge with the aim, at least in the first instance, of reaching the line of the Aisne River. The underlying intention was to draw in the Allied reserves before launching a new assault in Flanders, codenamed Operation Hagen and set to commence in July. Hagen was to achieve a complete breakthrough and overall victory. Once again the Germans began their meticulous preparations, moving in the divisions and all-important artillery that would provide the driving force for the offensive.

The pressing requirement for fresh blood for the stormtrooper formations was gradually stripping the normal German Army units of their best men. The stormtroopers had not originally been intended as an elite – all the divisions were meant to be retrained in the stormtrooper tactics. But the pressure of war meant that the existing trained stormtrooper units had to be restocked after each costly battle with fresh drafts taken from other formations. There was no time for anything else.

> Some days ago six men were transferred from our platoon: two to the infantry, four to the field artillery. Now all those under 35 years of age are to be called on, including me of course! We are expecting to be transferred in July. For me it is not a happy prospect as the younger ones are picked for the stormtroopers.[1]
>
> Signaller Edwin Kühns, 1047th Telephone Unit, Imperial German Army

There are arguments for the deployment of a small proportion of elite units where a special impact is required, but the German Army was falling into the trap of weakening the huge majority of its ordinary infantry divisions. When all its best men had been taken it would be left with a rather unprepossessing and militarily weak rump of nothing but the unfit and the old.

As usual the Germans took great precautions to conceal the imminent assault. And who proved to be in the front line where the German blow was struck? It was cruel luck, but once again the 'resting' 50th, 8th and 21st Divisions found themselves in the firing line when the German onslaught burst upon them.

*

BRIGADIER REES WAS still commanding what was left of his 150th Brigade. He had high hopes that the move south would give his exhausted men the chance to recuperate from their efforts over the previous two months. The 150th Brigade was by no means untypical of the 50th Division in that it had lost 1,133 men on the Somme and a further 1,091 on the Lys a couple of weeks later. In the meantime Rees had received assorted drafts from home, topped up with a few men detached from the 40th Division, until he had a brigade fighting strength of some 2,500 men. He hoped that this time the men would have time to rest and rebuild as they took up their positions on the Californie Plateau. This was a steep-sided bluff feature rising up from Craonne and continuing as the Chemin des Dames Ridge, which stretched 25 miles to Compiègne. In front of the ridge was the valley of the Ailette River while some 4 miles behind them was the Aisne River and the associated canal. Although considered a quiet front in 1918, the Chemin des Dames had in the past been one of the great slaughterhouses of the war, passing between French and German hands, until it had been finally captured at great cost by the French in 1917. Now it was being passed over to British custodianship for the first time.

The French, as you know, believe that every occasion should be celebrated by some repast of a ceremonial nature. After we had completed the takeover, the Brigadier General and his staff were bidden to lunch with the French in the heat of the day at the hottest time of the year, in a dugout that combined all the disadvantages of stuffiness and the sun seeping in through the open doorway. There we went through the usual menu, which was much heavier than any of us were used to, and the assortment of wines always felt by the French to be proper to a ceremonial occasion. The French colonel commanding the regiment gave an impassioned oration saying how pleased he was to hand over this bit of line to his English Allies and bade us remember that it had been won at the cost of hundreds of thousands of French lives during Nivelle's great offensive the spring before. That speech required a reply from my Brigadier who rose to his feet and in very halting and extremely bad French gave the French the assurance that their 'sacred ground' would not be left by the British except over their dead bodies. That ended the handover![2]

Captain Sydney Rogerson, Headquarters, 23rd Brigade, 8th Division

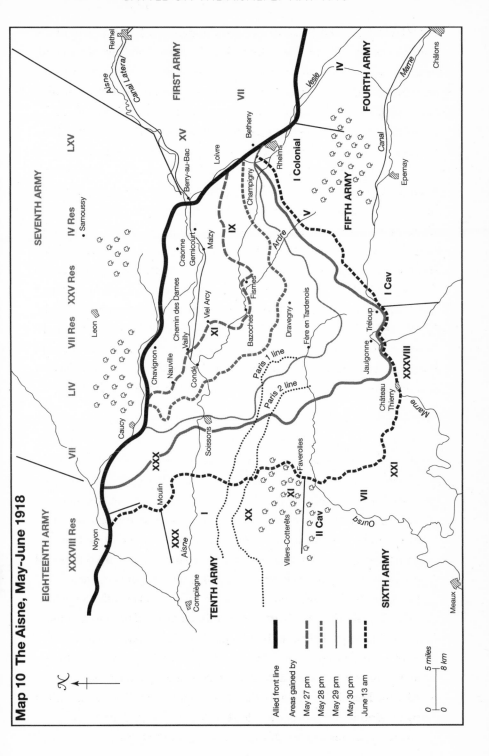

Map 10 The Aisne, May–June 1918

EIGHTEENTH ARMY

XXXVIII Res

SEVENTH ARMY

VII

LXV

IV Res

VII Res   XXV Res

LIV

FIRST ARMY

XV

VII

• Samoussy

Moulin

XXX
Aisne

XXX

I

Noyon

Compiègne

Soissons

Caucy

Chavignon •

Nauville

Condé

Leon

Chemin des Dames

Vailly

Viel Arcy

Craonne

Gemicourt

Malzy

XI

Berry-au-Bac

Loivre

IX

Rheims

Champigny

Betheny

I Colonial

FOURTH ARMY

IV

Châlons

Rethel

Aisne   Canal Lateral

Vesle

Marne

Epernay

Canal

FIFTH ARMY

V

I Cav

Fismes

Bazoches

Dravegny •

Fère en Tardenois

Tréloup

Jaulgonne

XXXVIII

Château
Thierry

Marne

Arcre

TENTH ARMY

XX

Paris 1 line

Paris 2 line

Favérolles

XI

II Cav

Villers-Cotterêts

VII

Ourcq

XXI

SIXTH ARMY

Meaux

Allied front line

Areas gained by

May 27 pm

May 28 pm

May 29 pm

May 30 pm

June 13 am

0   5 miles
0   8 km

N

General Duchêne commanding the French Sixth Army (and hence the British IX Corps) was simply determined, regardless of any concept of defence in depth, to hold onto the front lines running along the Chemin des Dames. This left the bulk of his forward troops terribly exposed to the devastating German artillery fire that could be expected as a matter of course when the Germans attacked. Even worse, if the line should break then a substantial portion of the retreating garrison would be trapped up against the Aisne River immediately behind it.

As the British soldiers took over from their French Allies it is unfortunate to report that their attitude was as parochial as ever and they missed no chance to poke fun at their gallant French allies. In this the selfsame Captain Sydney Rogerson was a notable culprit.

> We got some fun with the aid of Rogerson, a rather fatuous West Yorks officer who was attached to divisional headquarters, out of the French orders for the relief. The phrases *'en cas de bombardement on se couche'* and *'pas de manoeuvre deal lampes électriques'* lent themselves to subsequent quotation and became brigade jokes. The sector was renowned for its quietude. The French boasted that they had had three casualties in two months, and the trenches and dugouts were in wonderful condition. We had at brigade headquarters a splendid deep dugout *'en cas de bombardement'*, but we lived in quiet attractive little rooms at ground level.[3]
>
> Captain Philip Ledward, Headquarters, 23rd Brigade, 8th Division

For all their mockery, some aspects of their new trenches were far superior to anything the British were used to, especially the command posts, which were situated about a mile behind the front line. The headquarters of the 25th Brigade seemed reassuringly secure to Second Lieutenant Walter Harris who had been detached from his Rifle Brigade battalion to command a trench mortar battery.

> The best system of corridors and dugouts I had ever seen – it must have been a great effort by the French to make such a fine underground headquarters. Electric lighting installed in all passages and dugouts, some furniture for the comfort of senior officers, all gave an impression

that war was far away – even heavy shells exploding above only gave a muffled rumble.[4]

Second Lieutenant Walter Harris, 25th Light Trench Mortar Battery, 25th Brigade, 8th Division

Despite such secure physical conditions, it was evident that the convalescing divisions were in no shape to hold the line against any determined German assault.

> The commanders of the 50th Division were burdened with the further anxiety that they were fully aware that the division was not in a condition to take part in a great battle and required time to recuperate. The company officers were completely untrained, almost without exception. The simplest orders were misunderstood, while the frontage allotted to the division, some 11,000 yards, reduced the forces available for defence to a minimum.[5]

Brigadier General Hubert Rees, Headquarters, 150th Brigade, 50th Division

Furthermore, by Sunday 26 May it had become cruelly apparent that the Germans were planning something big. The more experienced officers began to notice the ominous signs mounting in the lines opposite them.

> We hadn't been there a week when we noticed that things were far too quiet. We began to be a little suspicious. Our little heaven began to show signs of a serpent entering into it. We noted that the Germans were doing no patrolling. When the German artillery had scored a direct or anything like a near hit on a gun emplacement, the shelling would stop. That could only mean they were calibrating new guns, as soon as they had got the range they would reserve it, note it in their books and use it when they had to open their bombardment. In other words we had a pretty shrewd idea that they were registering their targets. We noted that the enemy observation balloon behind Juvincourt was being run up and pulled down with great frequency, which seemed to confirm our suspicions there was good deal of observation of a special nature going on. The intelligence officer of the 24th Infantry Brigade had noticed the presence of a lot of black boards in the German lines, which we knew from previous experience to be used by

the Germans to guide their tanks and heavy vehicles over the navigable points of the trench.[6]

Captain Sydney Rogerson, Headquarters, 23rd Brigade, 8th Division

Predictably, the Germans had clung to that hoary old principle of war – always do what your enemy least wants you to. At 1400 on 26 May, Private William Parkin was ordered to accompany the commanding officer of the newly constituted 50th Battalion Machine Gun Corps to a IX Corps conference.

I had to hide myself at the back and take notes. I still remember that scene: all brigadiers were there from all four divisions, brigade majors and lots more. The corps commander got up and said he had some surprising news. Earlier that day information on good authority had come from British headquarters and the French that the Germans were massing heavy artillery and arms of all sorts opposite our front. He required all divisions and brigades to go on full alert and see that all the line trenches were adequately manned and so on and so forth. He concluded by frankly stating that if Jerry attacked, and if he managed to make any break in our position, it would rapidly become very, very serious, because he had been told that there were literally no troops behind his corps.[7]

Private William Parkin, 50th Battalion, Machine Gun Corps, 50th Division

As the intelligence firmed up during the day a message came from the French headquarters that the Germans intended to attack at dawn the very next day. In confirmation, reports began to pour from the observation posts in the Forward Zone that the roads to the rear of the German trenches were black with troops moving forward ready for the attack. In the line to the right of the 50th Division were the 8th Division and at the headquarters of the 23rd Brigade, under the command of Brigadier General George Grogan, the strain was tangible.

There was an ominous silence of the German guns all night, but ours kept banging away. Grogan made a pretence of going to bed, but I sat up reading Blackwood's magazine, with my watch on the table in front of me. It was a hot still night and the feeling of suspense and tension

was, speaking for myself, very acute. I haven't now the faintest notion
of what I was reading.[8]

Captain Philip Ledward, Headquarters, 23rd Brigade, 8th Division

In the same headquarters Captain Rogerson was making his final
preparations for the battle. Even his cheery nature was a little depressed
at the thought of what lay ahead of them.

We were a very miserable lot of people because we realised we were
going to be for it again. I packed up a pack with a bottle of whisky, a
pair of boots, a shirt and other things hoping by that that I would
preserve myself against tomorrow as far as I could.[9]

Captain Sydney Rogerson, Headquarters, 23rd Brigade, 8th Division

The final confirmation that the attack was due arrived late that
evening. Captain Hugh Lyon of the 6th Durham Light Infantry was
holding a sector of the front line with 'X' Company when he got the
note that indicated he and his men were all in deep trouble. He made
all the necessary preparations to defend their positions but at the same
time he took action to reduce the possible intelligence value to the
Germans when they were overrun – as appeared almost unavoidable.

At about 10.30 p.m. came the message that dispelled all doubts as to
the nature of the coming blow. I made a précis of it and sent it out to
platoon commanders. 'Prisoner states attack coming at 4 a.m.
Bombardment probably with gas at 1 a.m. Tanks may be used. Troops
must fire at infantry and not tanks. No fighting men to carry wounded.
Issue 50 extra rounds per man and inspect pouches. All Lewis gunners
over four per team to come to company headquarters at once. Destroy
all maps and important documents.' I wrote out my orders with my
signallers munching chocolates at my side and transferred my headquarters to the most accessible corridor of the dugout, leaving Wilson
behind to burn all my maps – which he did at imminent risk of
suffocation. All that was necessary to convert our already prepared
defensive measures into an active defence was done in about an hour. I
then went round the men, who seemed cheery and confident, and saw
that they understood their orders. I thought their cheeriness sufficiently

marked to mention to our headquarters and sent down a message, 'All serene; men as cheery as cuckoos!'[10]

Captain Hugh Lyon, 6th Battalion, Durham Light Infantry, 151st Brigade, 50th Division

Cheery or not, for many of his men there would be no dawn on Monday, 27 May once the German gunners got to work. The bombardment opened up as predicted at 0100. It followed the usual stages and pattern of fire as devised by Oberst Bruchmüller, stretching from Berry-au-Bac all along the 24 tortured miles to Chavignon, spraying shells at an unprecedented rate down on the French and British front. An incredible 3,719 German guns had been amassed and the effects were almost beyond comprehension.

At 1 a.m. exactly came the beginning of the German bombardment, following the fire of our guns as a roar of applause might follow a single speaker, drowning and obliterating it in a moment. I had a lance corporal at the head of my dugout who reported a great concentration of trench mortars and aerial torpedoes on the front line. I went out to him occasionally, but there was nothing else I could do till the time of the attack came. Our dugout was the target for one or two 'heavies', but was not damaged, though the concussion was considerable.[11]

Captain Hugh Lyon, 1/6th Battalion, Durham Light Infantry, 151st Brigade, 50th Division

As usual the shells reached back behind the front line, carefully picking out the various elements of command and control that the British and French forces would require when the assault came – as it must.

At 1 a.m. some forty or fifty shells burst simultaneously on my head-quarters and so began a bombardment of an intensity that I have never seen equalled in the war. Our own guns were smothered under it and very few were firing half an hour after it began. My telephone connection with the 4th East Yorks was destroyed almost at once, also all lines to the artillery. Luckily the buried lines to Colonel Thomson's headquarters on the Californie Plateau and to our most valuable observation post remained intact. These lines were practically my only means of communication, as runners could not get through to any headquarters unhurt.[12]

Brigadier General Hubert Rees, Headquarters, 150th Brigade, 50th Division

As the shells crashed down all around the 23rd Brigade headquarters it seems that there was an atmosphere of barely suppressed chaos.

> Brigadier Grogan ran out of his room with his boots in his hand and that look of consternation on his face which always appeared in moments of this kind – he used to look as if he were on the point of bursting into tears and I'm not sure that he wasn't either, for he was very emotional. He exclaimed, 'By George, it's true!' We called all the clerks, servants and runners and all of us went down into our deep dugout.[13]
>
> Captain Philip Ledward, Headquarters, 23rd Brigade, 8th Division

Present in the same dugout was Captain Sydney Rogerson who found little to amuse him as the highly tuned German barrage of shells rained down around them. It seems fair to say that all thoughts of his prior witticisms on the general subject of '*en cas de bombardement on se couche*' were driven from his mind.

> A thousand guns roared out their iron hurricane. The night was rent with sheets of flame. The earth shuddered under the avalanche of missiles, leapt skywards in dust and tumult. Even above the din screamed the fierce crescendo of approaching shells, ear-splitting crashes as they burst. All the time the dull thud, thud, thud of detonations and drum fire. Inferno raged and whirled round the Bois des Buttes. The dugouts rocked, filled with the acrid fumes of cordite, the sickly-sweet tang of gas. Timbers started: earth showered from the roof. Men rushed for shelter, seizing kits, weapons, gas masks, message pads as they dived for safety. It was a descent into hell.[14]
>
> Captain Sydney Rogerson, Headquarters, 23rd Brigade, 8th Division

Down in the dugout conditions soon became desperate. As if by some primeval instinct most men seemed to whisper rather than talk deep below ground level.

> Crowded with jostling, sweating humanity the dugouts reeked, and to make matters worse headquarters had no sooner got below than the gas began to filter down. Gas masks were hurriedly donned and anti-gas precautions taken – the entrances closed with saturated blankets, braziers lighted on the stairs. If gas could not enter, neither could the air. As a fact both did in small quantities and the long night was spent

40 foot underground, at the hottest time of the year, in stinking overcrowded holes, their entrances sealed up and charcoal burners alight drying up the atmosphere – suffocation rendered more complete by the gas masks with clip-on nostrils and gag in the teeth.[15]

Captain Sydney Rogerson, Headquarters, 23rd Brigade, 8th Division

Here again, in just a few words, was justification for the mixed barrage of high explosive and gas shells the German gunners were raining down on them. The gas was not to kill: it was to cause every possible form of nuisance to the key personnel of the British Army in carrying out their duties. Everything was made more difficult, everything was more uncomfortable; everything was more tiring and stressful.

The barrage went through its phases until the stormtroopers burst out of their trenches at 0340. All along the 8th and 50th Divisions' fronts the divisional, brigade, battalion and company headquarters had no idea what was going on. After receiving various confused reports Captain Lyon of the 1/6th Durhams emerged from his shallow front-line dugout to check for himself.

I had been reckoning on the customary pause before an infantry line can follow a barrage. But the German tactics here were to place their advance troops almost in the skirts of their barrage, thus giving the defence no time to recover. When I came out into the open I found to my dismay and surprise files of Germans immediately in front and level with our line on the right. I got down my few men as best I could to face these two fronts. The Germans were coming on leisurely, meeting with little or no resistance. The air was full of their planes, which went before them and swept the trenches with machine guns. A few tanks had broken through and were by now well behind us. The defence seems to have crumpled up completely: the intense bombardment, heavy beyond all precedent, split the defence into small isolated groups of sadly shaken men, who fell an easy prey to the first German line. A large number must have surrendered without any resistance. Our own position became almost at once untenable. A heavy machine-gun fire was opened on us from our left rear, showing that the enemy would soon be all round us, so I decided to get back while I could and withdrew my men as fast as possible.[16]

Captain Hugh Lyon, 1/6th Battalion, Durham Light Infantry, 151st Brigade, 50th Division

As he moved back he ran into the German barrage again. Even when he found his battalion headquarters it was in a state of confusion.

This kind of dilemma was being repeated up and down the line as individual commanders at every level found that with their telephone communications severed they had to decide what to do: stay in safety or risk it outside. Brigadier Edward Riddell commanding the 149th Brigade resolved to join the men in the trenches, but he did not get far.

> My brigade headquarters were at Centre D'Evreux about 300 yards north-east of the 151st Brigade headquarters. I decided to leave my own headquarters and join General Martin with a view to holding the trenches about our own headquarters as a last ditch. It was all hands to the pumps. Martin and I with Leathart of the gunners ran towards the 5th Northumberland Fusiliers. We had only gone a few yards when a shell burst on our left. I felt a terrific blow in my face and saw Martin roll over. I went to him. He was quite dead. I walked on half dazed, with a great hole in my face into which I could put my hand, but I did not feel much pain. I could not have my wound bound up as the bandage would have prevented me from giving orders.[17]
>
> Brigadier General Edward Riddell, 149th Brigade, 50th Division

Should they stay or should they go? Either way, it seemed they were damned. Captain Maberly Esler saw another commanding officer who believed it was his responsibility to join his men in the trenches, and damn the consequences.

> I was in a tunnel in the trenches with the Colonel and Hugh. In the ordinary way Colonel Page should have remained there and runners would have reported from companies every few minutes and he would have directed orders as circumstances required. But no! He must go out himself and visit every sector of the defence. I remember him saying, 'I must go and see what all this bloody row is about!' Turning to Hugh he said, 'You deal with reports as they come in, and I will deal with events as I find them.' As he made his exit from the tunnel his last words were, 'Phew! What a bloody smell of gas! Look after yourself, Esler!' This is the last I ever saw of him.[18]
>
> Medical Officer Captain Maberly Esler, 2nd Battalion, Middlesex Regiment, 23rd Brigade, 8th Division

In the chaotic fighting that ensued Lieutenant Colonel C. A. S. Page was taken prisoner but managed to survive the war. Back in the 'safety' of the dugout, Esler soon found himself in deep trouble.

> At about 4.30 a.m. the barrage lifted a bit. I said to Walsh, 'Curious thing, nobody has come in wounded! I will go out and see what is happening and will let you know whether the stretcher bearers are needed.' As I emerged into the open I smelt the early morning smell of mist and vegetation, superimposed by a pervading smell of cordite. Through the bushes emerged a few men with fixed bayonets and an officer with a revolver in his hand. From their helmets I recognised that they were Germans – and that they were making a bee-line for me. When the enemy break through they are excited and out to kill. If they see a man opposing them, they shoot or charge with a bayonet. If they see a dugout, they chuck a hand grenade in first before they investigate. As they came running the thought crossed my mind, 'The possibility of being exterminated by a shell has been present often, but I never thought of ending my life with a bayonet wound in my belly, and I don't like it one little bit!' All I could do was to shrug my shoulders and point to my Red Cross armlet. The officer recognised this at once and told his men not to kill. I pointed to my dugout and said, 'Red Cross!' so they did not chuck in their usual grenade.[19]
>
> Medical Officer Captain Maberly Esler, 2nd Battalion, Middlesex Regiment, 23rd Brigade, 8th Division

As he looked round at the corpses in the trenches, Esler had a strange reaction: he was too numb to feel any kind of sorrow at all.

> Two of our own officers were lying dead, aged I should think about twenty-five. As I looked at them, I thought, 'Well, worse could have happened to you: you have had a virile and, I hope, happy life up to date, you were killed instantly and so avoided all the possible troubles of an invalid life and, eventually, a failing old age.'[20]
>
> Medical Officer Captain Maberly Esler, 2nd Battalion, Middlesex Regiment, 23rd Brigade, 8th Division

Behind the front lines in their advanced dressing station the men of the 24th Field Ambulance soon found themselves completely isolated and rendered redundant by the rapid progress of the Germans. It was soon obvious to them that on this occasion at least their dressing station was far too far 'advanced'.

> About twelve slightly gassed men turned up and sprawled all over the floor. I got the gassed into some order – they promptly fell asleep and slept through it all. Barrage lifted later, on to the river, advancing quickly. 6.30 news that Germans were behind us, all around us! Two drivers volunteered to try to get back, machine guns in the road – impossible. 7.00–8.30 waiting. I tore up all letters of any use and unfortunately tore up three of yours, thought it better – wish I hadn't – something of you . . . Packing our pockets etc. etc. 8.30 bomb on dugout heralded Germans. All marched out – about twenty-five of us, three medical officers. The gassed left to be brought on later – when they woke up they would find themselves prisoners for we left them still asleep.[21]
>
> Medical Officer Captain Alan Boyle, 24th Field Ambulance, 8th Division

Boyle was taken back through the lines and subsequently encountered the captured Esler.

Meanwhile, Captain Lyon of the 1/6th Durhams had reported to his battalion headquarters that its front had been comprehensively broken. Their Colonel decided to gather together everyone he could and fall back in turn towards the brigade headquarters. En route Lyon was detached with twenty men to join a reserve company of the 1/5th Durhams in making another stand.

> Our way led along a most 'unhealthy' communication trench, which led right up to a little wooded hill, Butte de l'Edmonde, which formed the left of the line we were to hold. We could now distinguish rifle and machine-gun bullets, which sounded unpleasantly close. At one point, where we had to get out of the trench to cross a road, one or two of the men were hit. By now the front of the company had reached the top of the hill to find this already in the enemy's possession. Some were killed, some captured and the rest came helter-skelter down on top of my party in the rear. We turned with them to find the way back as bad as the way in. Men were being hit on every side now and an aeroplane flying low added to the hail of bullets. Some of the men crept into a dugout in spite of my language, and I found very few still with me.

When we came to the road I crossed it unhurt, but of the others who tried nearly all were wounded or killed. I saw two Germans through the trees about 20 yards to my right, and one took aim at me. I found some cover, where three or four men followed me – all but one wounded. By now I saw Germans all round the hill and looking up I saw half a dozen of them 10 yards away, shouting and raising their rifles. The wounded men were shouting at me to surrender, and indeed I saw nothing else for it – so I just stood up and in a minute we were prisoners.[22]

Captain Hugh Lyon, 1/6th Battalion, Durham Light Infantry, 151st Brigade, 50th Division

All along the British front the Forward Zone had been overrun and the infiltrating Germans were penetrating right through and pushing ever onwards.

At about 8 a.m. the Germans broke through and were all around us. I was in a trench with the sergeant and our officer, Lieutenant Pottle. He made an attempt to get out of the trench and was shot through the arm. We then made our way down the trench. There was rifle fire coming from all directions. He was losing a lot of blood and could hardly walk. We moved on a bit further and were suddenly surrounded by German troops. I was told to throw down my rifle, which I did, not wanting to be felled by bullets. One of the Germans attended to the officer and we were taken down the trench to join a party of more prisoners. My thoughts went back to when we were told of the Germans shooting all their prisoners and I began to wonder what was coming next. We were lined up, about 450 in all, and marched down to a road. Sure enough there was a German in position with a machine gun. I offered up a prayer and hoped for the best, but he was not there for us and we were taken over the ridge and back to the German lines. We were at once put to work digging graves and burying the dead. The Germans did not take any identifications and they were buried as they were, poor devils. The Germans were coming up the road in hundreds in army lorries. They were full of beans and on the sides of the lorries was written, 'On to Paris'. They were shouting at us and calling us English swine.[23]

Sapper Charles Taylor, 7th Field Company, Royal Engineers, 4th Division

Trapped deep in the underground warren of the 15th Brigade head-quarters Second Lieutenant Walter Harris was becoming increasingly desperate to find out what was happening to his trench-mortar teams. Yet the noise of copious numbers of shells bursting above them was a powerful disincentive.

> I sat waiting for a quiet period when I would make my way to the batteries in the front line, but that never came. Through that massive shelling came a runner. He reported to the Brigadier that the enemy occupied our front line. Shortly afterwards a message came through that all the mortar batteries had been knocked out; Second Lieutenant Honey, who had been in charge, was making his way back – he never turned up, nor did any of the crew. With the dawn the shelling ceased, but in its place came the crackling of machine-gun fire. At this time I got a message from the Brigadier to report at his dugout. He told me that the enemy were advancing, I was to go through the dugouts and collect all the men I could find. He said, 'Now, there is only one thing left, to stand and fight! Lead your men towards the front line and put up the best show you can!' I saluted and left him. I gathered about twenty men composed of cooks, clerks, runners, signallers and all those who are attached to brigade headquarters. As we made our way through the corridors towards the steps that led up to the top a bomb burst at the far end. I decided to go back and try another way up.[24]
>
> Second Lieutenant Walter Harris, 25th Light Trench Mortar Battery, 25th Brigade, 8th Division

Rushing back through the underground corridors of their headquarters dugout, Harris finally emerged to lead his motley crew into a trench.

> The whizz of bullets greeted us as the enemy swept the parapets and I knew he was not far away. We had only gone about 20 yards towards the front line, when, leading the way around a traverse, I ran straight onto a bayonet with a very small German behind it. He had the advantage of me and I immediately put my hands up. Almost at the same moment a whole crowd of Germans appeared above my head walking by the parapet. One of them lobbed a bomb into the men behind me – I saw the three next to me had escaped injury, but the remainder I never saw again. The Germans disarmed us, passed us along the trench for a short distance and then made us get out on

the top. Across the country as far as we could see were German infantry.[25]

Second Lieutenant Walter Harris, 25th Light Trench Mortar Battery, 25th Brigade, 8th Division

Meanwhile, at the headquarters of the 151st Brigade only minimal reports had reached Brigadier Rees. The deafening silence from other front-line units, neighbouring brigades and the French left him in an impossible command position. He had minimal information on which to base a rational plan. He knew from a rare surviving underground telephone line that the 5th Yorkshires on Californie Plateau were fighting hard, but the reports he was getting gave little hope that they could hold out for long.

> Colonel Thomson rang up to say that the counter-attack he had launched with his reserve company had been swept away and that he was fighting desperately round his headquarters. The Germans were also shooting him in the back from Craonne with a machine gun. I suggested that he might try and work along the edge towards the East Yorks. He was afraid it was hopeless and said, 'I'll say goodbye, General, I'm afraid I shall not see you again.' I said, 'Try to escape, the British Army can't afford to lose you.'[26]

Brigadier General Hubert Rees, Headquarters, 150th Brigade, 50th Division

When Thomson finally made a run for it after a desperate resistance, he was killed by the machine gun lurking in Craonne. Some of the guns of 'A' Battery, 250th Brigade, Royal Field Artillery were also marooned up on the Craonne Plateau in gun positions that had been taken over from a French howitzer. When the bombardment started Signaller George Cole was desperately trying to repair his fragmented telephone lines.

> Our line went back to headquarters and every time in action that was the first thing that went. Mark Carr and I went back to try and repair the line. You couldn't wait, you had to get out. We went out into the wood following the line through, he was knocking hell's bells out of the place, but we were plodding our way through, we had to get through to try and repair the line. We followed it so far, repaired one or two breaks, then away again – it was still out of commission. The

bombardment got worse and worse so we took shelter in a dugout for a time. When we came out the Germans were there, we had no rifles and he was standing there with a bomb in his hand, '*Komm Tommy*!' They'd come round both sides of the hill and we were prisoners.[27]

Gunner George Cole, 'A' Battery, 250th Brigade, Royal Field Artillery

But by then Rees himself was in severe danger as he set off back to Craonnelle accompanied only by his orderly.

After a look from the dugout entrance, I said to the orderly that he had better be prepared to run as he had never run before. I have never been through such a storm of shells. We got into a shallow trench about 300 yards from headquarters and lay there for a bit to try and find a lull for our next rush. I fancy I got gassed, as I couldn't go more than 20 yards afterwards without stopping. However, on nearing Craonnelle, we got out of it, the barrage lifting back. At the same time I was fired at by one or two riflemen from about 600 yards away towards Craonne. I saw lines of the enemy sweeping over the top of the Craonne Plateau in extended order and an attack formation pouring down the spur, where the 4th Yorks were, taking them from the French side in flank and from behind.[28]

Brigadier General Hubert Rees, Headquarters, 150th Brigade, 50th Division

His brigade was being overwhelmed. In the previous two German offensives, bad as they were, they had been reserve or support troops moving into the battle and then carrying out a fighting retreat. This time they were in the front line, right where the sledgehammer fell. This was very different: his brigade was facing annihilation. Now it was simply a question of whether Rees and his headquarters staff could escape.

We struck off across the valley for P. C. Terrasse. Half a mile further on, we found German infantry in fours marching down the Beaurieux road and nearer to P. C. Terrasse than we were. It was quite obvious that the battle with the French on our left had progressed much faster than ours. We eventually reached P. C. Terrasse and I found a few machine-gunners there and a considerable number of dead and wounded men. I was told that my brigade major, Captain Witts, was wounded and in a dugout at the end of the terrace. I rushed down there and got him out. When we came out an officer rushed up to say that the Germans were coming down the path 60 yards away. We then ran down into the wood and I stopped some 200 yards further on. I told Witts to go on, I felt I must stop and see whether there were any stragglers that could be collected. In almost all battles there are stragglers, but this time I saw none. After waiting a short time I saw large enemy patrols advancing through the wood on each side of us, so started back.[29]

Brigadier General Hubert Rees, Headquarters, 150th Brigade, 50th Division

The wounded Witts managed to escape after a series of adventures that included swimming the Aisne River. All Rees had left of his brigade was a single officer, a sergeant and his trusty orderly. They were now well behind the onrushing German front line and, dodging patrols, the party hit upon the edge of the woods with a German piquet stationed just 100 yards away. Between them and the Aisne River was a German artillery unit blazing away in fine style. There was nothing for it but to wait until dark before attempting to cross the Aisne.

After some consideration we decided that we had better get a log to help to ferry the party across and set off downstream to find one, or an unguarded bridge. Unfortunately, in crossing the road, we were seen by a man on horseback, who trotted up, shouting to us to halt. We ran into a barbed wire entanglement and struggled through it, while the man on the horse emptied his pistol into us, without effect. Running away on the other side, I thought we had come off rather well, but almost at once, we ran into a line of transport carts, right across our front. There was nothing left to be done then except ask the nearest man where his officer was. I was taken to the headquarters of the 231st German Division and, by the irony of fate, was examined in the room at Maizy that I had used as a headquarters some three weeks before.[30]

Brigadier General Hubert Rees, Headquarters, 150th Brigade, 50th Division

Rees had finally run out of luck. Yet there was one more astounding twist to his tale. He and two other staff officers were ordered to get into a car and without explanation were driven to Craonne.

I imagined that we were being taken to see some corps commander, thought it was deliberately humiliating and made a remark to this effect. The German staff officer with us overheard it and said, 'When you reach the top you will see His Imperial Majesty, the Kaiser, who wishes to speak to you!' When we approached, the Kaiser was apparently having lunch, but stepped forward onto a bank and told me to come and speak to him. He asked me numerous questions with regard to my personal history and having discovered I was a Welshman said, 'Then you are a kinsman of Lloyd George!' He asked no questions that I could not answer without giving away information and made no indirect attempts either. Presently he said, 'Your country and mine ought not to be fighting against each other, we ought to be fighting together against a third. I had no idea that you would fight me. I was very friendly with your royal family, with whom I am related. That, of course, has now changed and this war drags on with its terrible misery and bloodshed for which I am not responsible.' He added some further comments on the intense hatred of Germany shown by the French and then asked, 'Does England wish for peace?' 'Everyone wishes for peace!' I replied. He then, after a pause, said, 'My troops made a successful attack yesterday. I saw some of your men, who have been taken prisoner, they looked as if they had been through a bad hour. Many of them were very young.' I then said that I hoped my troops had fought well against him. He said, 'The English always fight well' and bowed to intimate that the interview was at an end. I withdrew.[31]

Brigadier General Hubert Rees, Headquarters, 150th Brigade, 50th Division

Second Lieutenant Walter Harris had a far more common, and much less exalted, experience as he walked miserably back across the battlefield as a prisoner of war. The habit of souveniring was universal amongst soldiers and few Germans could resist the temptation.

A couple of Germans ran out to me. One put his rifle to my head and I thought my time had come. The other knelt at my feet and started to unlace my boots – they were leather knee-boots and a fine pair. He had just unlaced one when an officer came up and spoke to him. The man immediately laced my boot up again and the rifle came down – they both saluted and marched away. The officer then said to me, 'Are you wounded?' in good English. I said, 'No'. He then pointed to a German lying wounded in a shell hole and said, 'Take your men and carry him back to the nearest dressing station!' This German was dead, so we carried a British Tommy instead![32]

Second Lieutenant Walter Harris, 25th Light Trench Mortar Battery, 25th Brigade, 8th Division

Whatever his rank, whatever had happened to him, the stigma of capture was something that each man had to deal with in his own way. Many wondered if they could have done more in the final moments before capture. Surrendering was a deeply personal decision made by every conscious unwounded prisoner and for many it gnawed away at their self-esteem.

The shame of that moment has proved ineffaceable. I suppose that every man taken in battle must feel that smart of indignation and remorse, for every such man has deliberately chosen life before freedom. And such a choice, even in the most desperate conditions, is a falling off from the ideal – so often in men's mouths – of 'resistance to the last shot and the last man'. For myself, I only know that it seemed inevitable, and that in similar circumstances I should almost certainly do the same again. It may be a taint of cowardice or merely an unheroic commonsense.[33]

Captain Hugh Lyon, 1/6th Battalion, Durham Light Infantry, 151st Brigade, 50th Division

Further back, Lieutenant John Nettleton was waiting for the 2nd Rifle Brigade to return to the transport lines. By the time he got the order to move back at daylight, rumours of the disaster afflicting the units in the front line were already rife.

There was only one road exit from the wood we were in. It was a dirt track that curved back from the back of the wood to join a main road in the valley below. The Boche had it taped and were dropping 5.9"s on it about one every minute or a little less. Our battalion transport were lined up just inside the wood and as soon as a shell had exploded the GS wagon or limber at the head of the line would dash out at full gallop to try and get past the danger point before the next shell arrived. It was very exiting, something like a Roman chariot race, with the horses made frantic by the explosions and the drivers lashing them through the smoke of one shell to get clear before the next.[34]

Lieutenant John Nettleton, 2nd Battalion, Rifle Brigade, 25th Brigade, 8th Division

Meanwhile, Captain Sydney Rogerson had found himself lost and for a while alone on the battlefield.

> Brigadier Grogan decided to evacuate the headquarters and he dashed up the stairs followed by me and said, 'Rogerson, you've reconnoitred the route to the river, lead on!' I dashed off down the trench, got about 200 yards and found nobody was following me. It was always my terror, although I didn't mind war or battle particularly, I was absolutely terrified if I found myself alone. So I doubled back to the headquarters, which was then roughly evacuated, except I stumbled across two Royal Artillery officers. I joined up with them and we decided we had to make our way back to the Bois de Juvincourt, which was the reserve headquarters – but we couldn't find our way! It was cross-country, which was a dreadful journey with a tin hat on, a pack on your back, a gas mask on your nose, stumbling and floundering in shell holes, barbed wire and whatnot. When we did find our way, there was no bridge to get across! There was nothing left for us to do but to stumble down the bank of the river to the bridge at Pontavert – where I found the Brigadier, who had decided it was no good going through the communication trench but had wandered slowly down the main road to the village. One of the artillery officers gallantly swam across the Aisne losing his false teeth in the effort![35]
>
> Captain Sydney Rogerson, Headquarters, 23rd Brigade, 8th Division

Once the remnants of the British forward troops had managed to get themselves back across the Aisne they paused to take stock. Several of the bridges along the Allied front had not been demolished or were still reasonably passable by the infantry and it was evident that the river would not be a serious obstacle to the Germans. To the left the French XI Corps had been thrown back in equal measure and there was great difficulty in establishing a coherent defensive line. As ever the Germans were feeling at the open flanks of the neighbouring divisions to widen the gap and generally add to the confusion.

In amidst the festering chaos units were able to retain their cohesion and fought it out to the end. Amongst these were the 2nd Devons who fought a much-acclaimed battle. They had been in reserve when the battle broke out but soon Captain Ulick Burke found himself putting his life on the line defending the bridge at Pontavert. That morning he watched as the retreating scraps of various Allied units fell back across the Aisne.

> Out of this haze, right on top of you appeared the Germans: you started shooting like hell. But unfortunately it turned out to be our gallant friends, the French fleeing in pyjamas and God knows what, I never saw such a rabble in my life, shouting and gesticulating – everything was finished! Then we had lots of Middlesex wounded coming back through us. They got over the river, back over the Pontavert bridge behind us. Then the West Yorks who were in support started coming back and they went through us. The order was to stay put as long as we could – we were not to retire! We stayed where we were. We were on two small hills. We shot and shot and shot till the fellows in the trenches could hardly hold their rifles. They killed thousands; I have never seen so many dead in front of our trenches. We were shooting at their artillery that was coming down, because they didn't stop – they went through us.[36]
>
> Captain Ulick Burke, 2nd Battalion, Devonshire Regiment, 23rd Brigade, 8th Division

The Lewis guns certainly cut a swath through the advancing Germans who continued to offer tempting targets as they came on en masse.

> We had two Lewis guns and these opened fire, sweeping down great numbers of Germans, while the men in the trenches maintained rapid fire continually at the waves and waves of the enemy who still continued to approach. In their front wave they had riflemen. These approached to within nearly 50 yards of our trenches and then took cover. From somewhere behind their first wave there was another that bombed us with rifle grenades, and, after this had continued for some time, during which we had suffered heavy casualties, the riflemen, who had been taking cover and getting ready for the assault, suddenly jumped up and rushed at us. The boys kept blazing away and this attack was beaten off, but they had hardly given a sign of falling back before the rifle grenades came falling among us, doing even greater damage than before. Then a third party of Germans attacked us, coming forward through the rifle grenadiers and the riflemen, and hurling stick bombs into our trench. There were hundreds of them,

and, though we took a heavy toll, they also had their revenge and our ranks were thinned out terribly.[37]

Corporal L. Leat, 2nd Battalion, Devonshire Regiment, 23rd Brigade, 8th Division

Soon the battalion had lost all cohesion and small groups of isolated Devons were left fighting on, many of them hopelessly cut off.

Lads were falling right and left, but I had a capital weapon in the Lewis gun, which I was firing steadily at the German hordes. I looked about and I seemed to be all alone. Still, I kept on firing at them. Then, when the enemy waves were about 100 yards away, things got a bit too warm, so I picked up the gun, ran back about 100 yards and had another go.[38]

Private Alexander Borne, 2nd Battalion, Devonshire Regiment, 23rd Brigade, 8th Division

The situation had moved beyond desperate but the Devons had been told to defend the Pontavert bridge and most of them seemed to have had no idea of retreating. Colonel Rupert Anderson-Morshead had been unequivocal, 'Your job for England, men, is to hold the blighters as much as you can, to give our troops a chance on the other side of the river. There is no hope of relief. We have to fight to the last!'[39] Even when the Germans had in effect bypassed them they continued the unequal struggle. The Colonel himself was killed but his men fought on regardless.

About five to twelve the Regimental Sergeant Major came to me and said that he couldn't locate any of the other companies. As far as we were concerned there were twenty-three of us; we had just about 200 rounds of ammunition left. They were coming on: I said, 'Right, three men go out and strip any of the dead you can find of their ammunition!' We went on firing until all the ammunition was gone. We held on till about half past twelve when the only ammunition left was 6 rounds in my revolver. Suddenly I said, 'Charge!' I was wounded in the legs – about nine machine-gun bullets up my legs – and they charged with the sergeant major. Twenty-three men charged against nearly 10,000 Germans. That finished us. We were soon picked up by the Germans and our wounds were dressed.[40]

Captain Ulick Burke, 2nd Battalion, Devonshire Regiment, 23rd Brigade, 8th Division

The Devons had finally ceased to slow up the German advance. It had been at a terrible cost. Their colonel lay dead and most of his officers and men were dead, wounded or lost into captivity.

Meanwhile, on the other side of the Aisne it was a moot point whether there were enough troops available to make use of the time the Devons had gained. Staff Captain Philip Ledward found Brigadier George Grogan of the 23rd Brigade in a field at the bottom of Roucy Hill. After some pleasant detached musings between them as to what the Emperor Napoleon Bonaparte might have done in such a situation, they rightly decided that the 'Great Man' wouldn't have started from there. They then began the serious business of trying to establish some kind of defence line on the hills facing the Aisne.

> On Roucy Hill had been gathered what remained, not of our brigade only, but of the 8th Division and it amounted I suppose to about 300 of all ranks. The 24th Brigade staff disappeared from the battle, the 25th Brigade staff was all killed, no battalion commander found his way back to us, and no senior officer of any kind. The 23rd Brigade staff was complete at this stage, but very few of our own troops were with us. I do not recall that a single officer or man of the Middlesex, except Lawson who was incapacitated, got back over the Aisne. General Heneker sent up orders to Grogan to take charge of the infantry of the division, and we never heard of, or from, the division again. Cope, Thompson, Millis and a few others had made a line of sorts on Roucy Hill and the men were digging in. I feel as if I should never forget the view of the plain up to and across the Aisne towards our old front line, for it was black with Germans. At that distance they looked like ants: small, busy and innumerable.[41]
>
> Captain Philip Ledward, Headquarters, 23rd Brigade, 8th Division

As the Germans pushed forward the fragments of British troops were forced further and further back from the river. Time after time they found their impromptu defensive positions swiftly outflanked by the Germans, compelling an equally rapid retreat if they were not to be captured. Amongst them was Private William Parkin, who had managed to get across a light railway bridge over the Aisne.

> We just broke cover and ran for the railway embankment. It was a short distance, but he got most of us. The chap running next to me dropped

with a shocking hit in the back of his head. I reached the foot of the railway and, as I jumped for the embankment, I felt such a blow on my left side that I felt sure a 6-in shell at least had hit me. Actually, it was only a machine-gun or rifle bullet. The blow completed my jump and literally threw me towards and over the embankment. I saw my tin hat go flying in the air. The bullet had cut the strap, caught the brim and away it went. The bullet had also chipped my jaw and I lost two good lower teeth. The embankment down which I was thrown gave me full cover from further enemy fire. I lay unconscious for what must have been a short space of time. Coming to, I felt no pain and all was quiet and peaceful. I was alone, perhaps the only survivor of my group. Jerry had evidently knocked off for tea! I felt my left hand fingers were poking into and hurting my right eye. Impulses to move it brought no response, so I angrily pushed my left hand away. Then – oh the pain! My left shoulder and neck were a ball of fire. I was staggered to see the left side of my tunic was smothered with blood and this seemed to be extending. I ditched my rifle, but I could not get out of my webbing equipment. Picking myself up, I set off down the hill for the village. Getting there, I met a couple of artillery chaps coming out from an *estaminet* cellar. Both were dead drunk. They said I was in a hell of a mess, but they got my web equipment off, then got out my field dressing and tied it round my throat. The iodine it contained made me scream with pain. They also got my arm into my tunic and buttoned it to form a sort of sling. They were good chaps. They then produced a bottle of champagne and gave me a hefty dose – it was a godsend![42]

Private William Parkin, 50th Battalion, Machine Gun Corps, 50th Division

After many more adventures, desperately attempting to stay one step ahead of the onrushing Germans, Parkin was eventually evacuated to safety although by then he was drenched from head to foot in blood. He was lucky to survive his traumatic experiences for the doctors found he had a nasty throat wound, shattered shoulder blade, smashed collarbone and, of course, his facial injuries.

Meanwhile, the remnants of the 8th Division had fallen back from Roucy Hill to Treslon Ridge. Here they were soon overrun and the same desperate game of leapfrog began.

Treslon Ridge was evacuated and I got a view of our troops running down the side of the ridge and across the valley towards the ridge I was on, then a few moments afterwards the Germans swarming over the ridge. I lay down and watched through my field glasses. I recall the swinging strides of a German machine-gunner as he came over the top, plumped his light machine gun down and began to fire it. The next thing his bullets were hitting the ground all round me, and for the first and only time in the war I was seriously frightened of bullets. At that moment Grogan came up and I had to stand up. He asked me why I was not mounted and told me to get my horse and stay on it! He was quite right too. That I had ever dismounted was clearly due to cold feet. For the next two hours I rode backwards and forwards about the ridge. The battle seemed in a way unreal. Grogan, who was 20 yards in front of us, was shot at at point-blank range by a German soldier whom we could see – he can't have been more than about 60 yards from our line and 40 yards from Grogan. Why the Germans did not pick us off one by one by deliberate aimed fire I simply can't imagine; nor why we didn't do ditto to them! The bullet went through the lower lip of his horse. Grogan, who was by this time hardly conscious of what he was doing, wheeled his horse around, cocking a snook at the German marksman and rode towards us calling out, 'Did you see that?' and laughing like anything. The German machine-gunners continued throughout to fire too high. Unending streams of bullets poured over our heads without doing any harm.[43]

Captain Philip Ledward, Headquarters, 23rd Brigade, 8th Division

Back they went. Time ceased to have any meaning and many of them had attained a dreamlike state where rational thought and decisions are rendered almost impossible.

Lieutenant John Nettleton had been unable to locate his unit but had been placed in command of odds and sods scraped together from various regiments and headquarters staff. He was ordered to hold a hilltop quarry.

We posted sentries, but nothing happened all night and we got some rest. Shortly before dawn we stood-to along the top edge of the quarry and as it got light we could see that it was very misty. Then figures started appearing out of the mist and we opened fire, but it was rather ineffective, because you could only see one or two men at a time and they loomed up out of the mist and were lost in it again before you could get a good shot at them. Then someone away on the left started shouting that we were being surrounded. The cry was taken up and everyone rushed away. I was glad there was no one in authority to see it, or I should have been blamed, though there wasn't really much I could do. In theory, I suppose, I should have shot one or two men, though that wouldn't have stopped any but perhaps half a dozen men close to me, if that. But it's pretty silly shooting your own men I think![44]

Lieutenant John Nettleton, 2nd Battalion, Rifle Brigade, 25th Brigade, 8th Division

Nettleton was left with only his servant and, recognising that they could do nothing, they too began to fall back to the next ridge. Here he caught up with the men and started to try and establish another line of resistance. Then he and a corporal explored along the ridge and into a wood on their right, trying to establish if there was anyone there capable of defending their open flank.

We had only gone about 100 yards into the wood when we suddenly saw a Boche patrol of six men in front of us, about 50 yards away. They saw us at the same time and we all stood staring at each other with our mouths open. The Boche recovered first. One of them dropped on his knee and aimed at us. That stirred me into action and I fell backwards down a bank I had just climbed, hauling the corporal after me by his collar. Unfortunately, this precipitate action made him let go of his rifle. That left the two of us, with only my revolver between us, against six Boche, and it didn't seem to me to be a very good idea to stay and fight it out. So we turned and ran – not the way we had come – but straight downhill through the wood. The whole place seemed to be alive with Germans, and we ran and dodged behind trees, and ran again, like enthusiastic Boy Scouts on a Saturday afternoon. Thinking it over, there was no real evidence that there was a single Boche in that wood other than the patrol we saw, but we thought there were and the thought lent wings to our feet. We didn't stop to enquire if the rustlings we heard were really only made by birds and squirrels.[45]

Lieutenant John Nettleton, 2nd Battalion, Rifle Brigade, 25th Brigade, 8th Division

After a while they out-distanced their pursuers, real and imagined. When they reached another amorphous group of British soldiers they tried hard to organise a line of resistance. But his next shock was a severe one.

A German field gun battery galloped up to the top of the ridge, unlimbered and opened fire on us. Being fired at by guns over open sights was a new experience – and a shattering one! The shells arrived with such a vicious 'whizz' and each one seemed to be aimed at you personally. I was not the only one who found it unnerving. Everyone did and the whole lot of us just broke and ran. This was the only time I saw a real rout. It is true that we had been retreating the whole day, but not, most of the time, on the run and we had had in mind the finding of a position where we could make a stand. But now it was just panic flight; with each man, including me, thinking of nothing but saving his own skin.[46]

Lieutenant John Nettleton, 2nd Battalion, Rifle Brigade, 25th Brigade, 8th Division

Once out of the German gun sights they began to recover their self-possession. Soon they were on yet another ridge. One more 'last stand'. But many of the men, effectively 'broken' by their experiences, were physically and mentally drained. The masses of new drafts that filled the ranks had no experience of war and the lessons of the training grounds were of little value. There was less willingness to expose themselves to more danger than was necessary.

We joined up with the rest of the troops stretched out in a long line right along the hill. They were, quite naturally, standing back from the crest of the hill, where they couldn't be reached by fire from the enemy below. But this meant that they also could not fire on the advancing Boche and it was necessary to advance the line until the men could see over the top and fire down the hillside. It only meant going forward 10 or 20 yards, but there was considerable reluctance to move that short distance. After all, if you put yourself in a position to fire at the enemy, you also put yourself in a position where he can fire at you – and most of the men had had enough of being shot at for the time being. You had to take small groups of half a dozen men and bring them forward inch by inch. Only those men who were almost within touch would come and they came forward slowly, step by step as though they had wooden legs. Kipling has expressed it exactly:

So, like a man in irons, which isn't glad to go,
They moves 'em off by companies, uncommon stiff and slow.

That is just how the men moved – 'uncommon stiff and slow'![47]

Lieutenant John Nettleton, 2nd Battalion, Rifle Brigade, 25th Brigade, 8th Division

The German offensive had been startlingly successful, ripping a hole some 35 miles wide and up to 12 miles deep on the first day. Next day the rout continued. Captain John Wedderburn-Maxwell was trying to hold back the Germans as part of the next viable line along the Vesle River.

I tried to get orders as to what I should do, but nobody had any orders to give me at all. I had these two guns and I took about sixty to seventy gunners mounted singly on a horse out of the teams, I destroyed the wagons and things I didn't want and with my two guns and unlimited ammunition I started my own private little retreat. I got right up onto the hills behind Vesle and I was above there on the first night of the retreat. It was a glorious moonlit night, the air was warm, the country was beautiful to look at. The fighting had died down and I had a couple of bottles of champagne. But I'd spent the day on my horse, with the hot sunshine with the bottles in each of my saddle wallets, when I took the cork out most of the champagne went with the cork! Then I had the most wonderful shooting because looking out across the valley you could see the German hordes, literally hordes, pouring from one wood to another. I was within comfortable range and I had the most tremendous shooting into these masses in the woods where they were all congregating. Suddenly the German batteries opened on me! They'd come up following their infantry, found them being beaten up by me, they saw my guns and in came their shells. I pulled my men away from the guns, ordered them out to the flank. After a bit the Germans stopped shooting at us, then at my signal, the drivers galloped up with the teams and away we went.[48]

Captain John Wedderburn-Maxwell, 36th Battery, 33rd Brigade, Royal Field Artillery

The Vesle Line was soon overrun. As far as the Germans were concerned they were on their way to the Marne River.

The French Army began to truly appreciate the trials Gough had experienced as it retreated towards various lines of defences that, although carefully drawn on the map – the Paris Line One and Paris Line Two – were conspicuous only by their absence on the ground. General Duchêne appealed to Pétain for help and Pétain went cap in hand to Foch. But the beauty of having Foch as Supreme Commander was then revealed, for Foch once again, as he had with Haig the previous month, stood back from the argument. It was Foch's considered opinion that the Aisne offensive made no strategic sense and therefore must be a diversion and he therefore decided to await events before releasing any of the Allied reserves. Of course, Foch was right – Ludendorff did ultimately intend to strike the 'real' blow in Flanders.

Yet strangely, while Foch retained his sense of perspective under pressure, Ludendorff made the cardinal error of abandoning a perfectly sound strategic plan to pursue the chimera of tactical advantage. As he gazed at his maps he became obsessed with the scale of the gains – perhaps if he reinforced the assaulting divisions then they could drive on across the Marne to Paris. Perhaps they could win the war at a stroke. Ludendorff fell for his own trap and started to move in reinforcing divisions – even from Flanders – to take advantage of the success of the Aisne offensive. Strategic imperatives were being subordinated to tactical success on the ground. At first the advance continued unabated, crushing the opposition as German troops swept forwards to the Marne. Yet the German tactics were unchanged so it should be no surprise that as the French reserves began to arrive the situation slowly began to stabilise. As the Germans grew weaker, so the French grew stronger. By 30 May the Germans had punched forward some 40 miles to reach the Marne and they had captured some 50,000 prisoners and 800 guns. But even as they invested ever more troops in the offensive, so the French resistance stiffened and the law of diminishing returns exerted its inimitable pressure. The Germans were thrashing around, entranced by visions of triumphal marches through Paris, but were slowly tied down by the French. In an ominous sign of the future two American divisions would be amongst those reinforcing the French at Château-Thierry. It would soon be over apart from the usual skirmishing, which would splutter on fitfully into early June.

In the meantime, what remained of the four British divisions of the IX Corps had been reduced to little more than a leaderless rabble.

They had been weak even before the German blow was struck, but now they had all but disintegrated.

> The 8th Division had ceased to exist as a division. There was no organisation and no orders. When you found men straggling about, you attached them to your little group and just wandered about the countryside, sitting on a hilltop till you were pushed off and then wandering back to the next one. The Army Service Corps left dumps of rations and ammunition at prominent points like crossroads and as you wandered by you helped yourself to what you needed.[49]
>
> Lieutenant John Nettleton, 2nd Battalion, Rifle Brigade, 25th Brigade, 8th Division

Eventually the division got away from the German pursuit, its units all but irrelevant to the main battle. Captain Philip Ledward found himself riding down a hill towards the town of Epernay on the Marne River.

> The battle was behind us and the city in front. The sun had gone down in a sky of brass. We kicked our weary gee-gees into an amble in order to get clear of Epernay before the nightly bombing began, crossed the Marne in a glorious still twilight and entered the Forest of Epernay. We got a last glimpse of the city, a silent purplish blur, with the pale streak of the Marne and the line of the hills opposite against a plain clear sky in which the stars were beginning to come out. Almost immediately afterwards we heard the German planes and bombing begin. Epernay Forest deserves its name! It is no country wood but something big and inspiring. On that glorious summer night we wandered and wandered in vain down the roads cut through the forest. I knew where I wanted to go and had a map that I kept consulting, but I was too tired to read it and kept going wrong. We passed a lake once, glittering silver under the moon. We never saw a living thing and never emerged from the unending trees.[50]
>
> Captain Philip Ledward, Headquarters, 23rd Brigade, 8th Division

For the British Army the worst was over. That did not mean that there was not a great deal of suffering ahead of them, but the corner had been turned. Soon it would be the British handing out the beatings: the British would show the Germans just how to attack – and win.

*

THE WIDELY ACCLAIMED 'tactical successes' of the three great German offensives had, in fact, brought the German Army almost to its knees. The windfall of extra divisions from the Eastern Front had been almost expended and those that remained lacked many of their best men. The absence of a consistent strategic focus in the German offensives was increasingly evident and the series of salients that Ludendorff had punched into the Allied lines merely stretched the German supply lines to their limit, elongated the length of the overall German front and left their troops hostage to the likelihood of either a devastating series of counter-attacks or a humiliating voluntary withdrawal in order to straighten and shorten a solid defensive line.

There was, of course, another perspective. The German attacks *had* rocked the Allies to their core. They had forced them to unify under Foch as the single commander-in-chief, they had even forced the British and French to assist each other directly by sending troops to threatened sectors. They had promoted near panic in Paris, helped by the shells from the long-range 'Paris' gun that had battered the city since 21 March 1918. The attack on the Aisne, which had brought the Germans appreciably nearer Paris, had shaken everyone. Unsurprisingly, French politicians began to lose their nerve. In the resulting hysterical outbreak everyone and everything about the military situation was questioned. Those individuals lacking resolve began to consider defeat and surrender; those determined to fight on took up their cudgels. Plans were made to evacuate the government to Bordeaux if the worst should happen and it has been estimated that up to one million Paris citizens had already taken matters into their own hands and moved out of the city since the spring.

It was in this atmosphere that the next Ludendorff offensive began. Operation Gneisenau was designed to widen the salient punched out by Operation Blücher, which stretched from the Aisne to the Marne Rivers. The front to be attacked extended from Noyon to Montdidier, but this time the German Eighteenth Army found that it was unable to disguise its preparations. The French Third Army holding the ground was fully aware of what was coming; even so, when the bombardment burst upon it at midnight on 8 June it was overwhelmed by its elemental force. When the infantry attacked on the morning of 9 June the French troops held in the Forward Zone were lost. The French

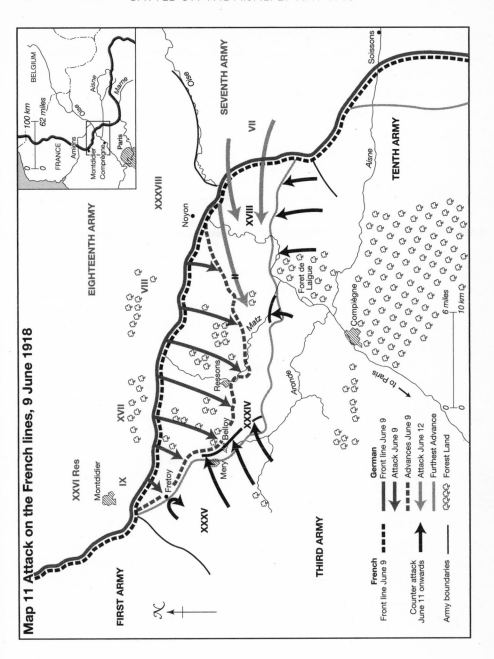

Map 11 Attack on the French lines, 9 June 1918

tumbled back up to 5 miles and the Germans got across the Matz River on that first day. For a couple of days the situation hung in the balance, but the French did not panic and soon the situation stabilised.

Then a new development – on 11 June the French counter-attacked hard, driving in from the western flank of the German salient. The offensive led by General Charles Mangin had several significant features. There was no preliminary bombardment, but a well-organised creeping barrage preceded the troops, who were given close support by tanks and low strafing aircraft. The fighting was bitter and the situation was complicated next day by a further attack from the German Seventh Army, driving westwards from the salient left by the Aisne battles. The Germans, however, had shot their bolt: the French artillery was present en masse, French aircraft swarmed all over the battlefield making a general nuisance of themselves and the French infantry seemed full of renewed confidence. In the end Ludendorff was forced to call off the offensive.

The Germans still had reserves to call upon, although each successive offensive brought them closer to complete exhaustion and every week seemed to bring news of new American divisions coming into the line. But the latest assault had also strained the still shaky unity of the Allied High Command, which had not yet fully bedded down. The French wanted the British to send reinforcement divisions to help them, but the British, who rightly feared that this was Ludendorff's plan, had resisted to the best of their ability. After a meeting between Haig and Foch the two sides once again recognised the necessity of working together: divided they would undoubtedly lose their way, together they were strong.

Ludendorff was now flailing. Operation Hagen in Flanders was postponed and his tactics for the next assault were just a rehash of previous plans. He would launch the Seventh, First and Third German Armies into what he unwisely called the *Friedensturm* – or Peace Offensive – and the French more prosaically would call the Second Battle of the Marne. The idea was to smash the French and then turn for the final battle in Flanders, optimistically scheduled for some five days later. Ludendorff's confidence now had more bluster than anything else about it. The Germans had some 207 divisions on the Western Front in mid-July 1918 and the Allies had 203. There was no longer any real numerical superiority. There was also no tactical surprise and the troops required to carry out the attack had been involved already in the Aisne and Matz battles. Worse still for the Germans, their methods were now thoroughly understood and the Allied air forces knew exactly what they were looking for. The German Air Service was both out-numbered and increasingly short of fuel, which greatly restricted its operations. There was no way that the Germans could prevent the Allied airmen from penetrating their front and monitoring the signs of imminent attacks. Reports from all sources poured into French intelli-gence and soon they had an accurate picture of the German plans. The French requested and duly received assistance from the British as the unified command structure worked relatively smoothly.

The Second Battle of the Marne was meant to have begun with the German bombardment at 0010 on 15 July, but the French defensive tactics worked far better than hitherto. Their front lines were evacuated to avoid troops being exposed to the horrors of the massed German trench-mortar fire, while the French artillery not only opened a deadly counter-battery barrage *before* the Germans had even started their own barrage, but were also well prepared to hit the massed German infantry as they moved forward some four hours later. The attack was on a tremendous scale, stretching from Servon to Château-Thierry. It was a titanic clash and deserves its own book, but it is enough to say here that the Germans were soundly defeated. Along huge areas of the front they could not pass the French Forward Zone, and where they did they were held in the Second Line or Battle Zone. The Allies knew what to do; the reserves moved up and soon stemmed any incipient German breakthrough.

Ludendorff may have taken brief hope from that very movement of British and French reserves to the area, inescapably weakening the Allied forces in Flanders where he planned the decisive assault. How-ever, unbeknownst to Ludendorff, control of events had already passed out of his hands. There would be no march through Paris in the summer of 1918. It was Foch and the French generals that would play the next hand: Mangin in particular symbolised the rebirth of the warrior instinct within the French Army. The French had amassed strong reserve forces in the threatened area with the very real intention of counter-attacking hard as they sensed the increasing German weakness. Their investment in tanks was beginning to pay dividends as there were nearly 750 of the light Renault tanks available to help punch home their point. The French planned to smash their Tenth and Sixth Armies into the exposed western shoulder of the great German salient between the Aisne and the Marne. By now almost everything was edging in the French Army's favour: it had large numbers of its own divisions outnumbering the Germans; it had the raw but enthusiastic troops of the large American divisions; it had the guns, the tanks and copious aircraft. By contrast, the German divisions were battle-weary and, whatever qualities they had had as fighting troops, they were now thoroughly degraded by their experiences in the German offensives that year.

The French bombardment crashed down at 0435 on 18 July. Now it was the Germans' turn to be on the defensive. When the infantry attacked they met little opposition and, although on the day they 'only' advanced 4 miles, the advance was significant. The French were once more on the front foot, pushing back the Germans and regaining French territory. On 19 July the French Fifth and Ninth Armies attacked the eastern flank of the salient. Soon French, British and American divisions were all attacking, and by 7 August much of the ground lost in the much-vaunted German offensive on the Aisne on 27 May had been regained. The planned war-winning Operation Hagen in Flanders had to be cancelled as Ludendorff assessed the revitalised Allied forces that faced him up and down the Western Front and realised that the Germans would have to be on the defensive for the foreseeable future.

CHAPTER NINE

Planning for the All Arms Battle

T HE BRITISH ARMY had for the most part a blessed relief during the early summer of 1918. The Allies were well aware that the Germans intended a massive attack in Flanders if they could manoeuvre a situation where the reserves had been sent south, but both Haig and Foch were too canny to give much of an opportunity to Ludendorff. In the end Ludendorff had run out of steam long before he could make his final push on the Channel ports. In the meantime, General Sir Henry Rawlinson, who had taken command of the Fourth Army in the Somme area, began to thoroughly reorganise his defences. The British had learnt their lessons. The Forward Zone would only be held by machine-gunners in the strongest possible posts, there would be no battalions held hostage to fortune in a blizzard of German shells and no desperate last stands to no real end. The artillery was kept back, away from the reach of the bulk of the German artillery and targeted at barrages hitting German troops just in front of the Forward Zone. Further back would be counter-attack formations, a Battle Zone and a Rear Zone. At last the British had grasped defence in depth. However, it was increasingly obvious that they might not need it.

As it consolidated its new defensive lines the British Army became slowly aware that the German Army in front of it was strangely inactive. The Germans would normally have devoted every effort to prepare a comprehensive defence system against British counter-attacks, but instead they seemed strangely lethargic. They organised a Forward Zone but it was weak, often just a single trench, with a conspicuous lack of the masses of barbed wire to channel the attackers into their machine guns. Perhaps the Germans realised that the British and French tanks made barbed wire almost redundant. Gone were the serried ranks of reinforced concrete pillboxes – the Germans lacked the time or the resources for such a construction programme. But if the Forward Zone could be considered almost an irrelevance, bound to be swept away in any real attack, then this only made more serious the lack of any properly defined Battle or Rear Zone behind it. The RAF zealously flew its photographic reconnaissance missions, seeking out the German fortifications and checking their progress day by day, and it soon became apparent that the German defences were badly disorganised. Of course, across much of the ground there was a multitude of old trenches dug and progressively abandoned in the frenetic fighting, and plenty of shell-hole lines all capable of being defended, but these did not represent a coherent system of defence to the Germans any more than they had to the British after 21 March. They were hardly state-of-the-art constructions, they lacked any defensive subtlety and, worst of all, what little barbed wire they possessed was erected on the wrong side! The Germans could no longer seriously expect to renew their much-cherished attack on Amiens or Paris, but at the same time they failed to address the probability of a British offensive in the near future. So they did nothing, in effect trusting their enemies to remain quiescent.

The defensive frailties of the Germans in the Somme area were just a symptom of a far more serious underlying malaise in the German Army. The root of the German problem was that their nation had reached the end of its long rope: the naval blockade was rotting Germany from the inside. Food shortages had not got any better while the *Kaiserslacht* battles were raging in the spring and summer of 1918. The raw materials of industry had all but run out. And the raw material of any army – young men – was in dreadfully short supply. There was nothing much to come but children, old men and the returning drafts of patched-up wounded. Worse still, these drafts were often unenthusiastic, lacking any martial spirit or air of common purpose. And worst of all they brought depressing news of the state of the 'Homeland' for whom they were fighting. Their arrival often lowered rather than improved the morale of soldiers at the front.

Another detachment of replacements arrived. Half of them were boys that appeared to be hardly16, others old men who looked quite sick.

They were able to describe the state of turmoil Germany was in. They told us that the present male population of Germany consisted of only cripples, deserters and war profiteers; the people were starving, even the babies underfed; that our navy was mutinous, the Austrian Army not to be depended on and the wish for peace uppermost in everyone's mind. The replacements that had come from the Eastern Front had fraternised with the Russians and were full of Bolshevistic ideas. Sullen and defiant, these men went about their duties showing open disapproval. Watching them I could well understand the rumours that dissatisfaction was spreading all through the German Army and the famous discipline was going to pieces.[1]

Unteroffizier Frederick Meisel, 371st Infantry Regiment, 43rd Ersatz Brigade, 10th Ersatz Division, Imperial German Army

The German divisions on the Somme front had been weakened by several factors. As we have seen, many had had their best men strained out for the elite stormtrooper formations. Then, of course, they had nearly all recently been through the mill of battle. The best divisions had been moved south to take part in the attacks on the French; those that remained were certainly of poor fighting strength. The German troops at the front were also gradually fading away from a simple shortage of food. They were well fed in contrast to the poor civilians back home, but that meant little. The rations they were given simply did not have the calories to keep body and soul together, particularly if hard physical labour was required.

The daily ration consisted of one-third of a loaf of dark bread, a half-filled mess tin of thin soup and a small piece of sausage. Our stomachs shrank – we were always hungry and grew leaner than ever. A delegation was sent to Major Rhine to complain, but the only answer it received was that he was sorry but he couldn't help it.[2]

Unteroffizier Frederick Meisel, 371st Infantry Regiment, 43rd Ersatz Brigade, 10th Ersatz Division, Imperial German Army

In battle situations the already hungry and physically weakened German infantry were often rendered desperate by the failure of their supply system.

We were like animals for we lived as such. At times we did not wash for days; our bodies were infested with vermin and most of us suffered from worms. Our clothes were torn and filthy, rags were used as socks. We ate anything that was barely edible and were content when they let us sleep without interruption. Our brains grew numb.[3]

Unteroffizier Frederick Meisel, 371st Infantry Regiment, 43rd Ersatz Brigade, 10th Ersatz Division, Imperial German Army

To the increasingly depressed German soldiers there seemed to be new life amongst the ranks of their enemies. In truth, their perspective may have been slightly warped, for the British, Australian and Canadian soldiers making up the British Fourth Army in the Somme area were not noticeably cheery, and their morale had not improved, but they were still resolute.

Something had put new life into our enemies, who seemed more confident, more determined. Had they really been reinforced by 2 million Americans? The Allied forces hadn't struck yet, but we sensed that they were merely feeling out our weakened position. Their aircraft filled the air, raking us with machine-gun fire and bombs from above, while artillery and trench mortars worked from every possible angle on the ground.[4]

Unteroffizier Frederick Meisel, 371st Infantry Regiment, 43rd Ersatz Brigade, 10th Ersatz Division, Imperial German Army

The German Army, the German High Command, the German soldiers and the German nation had all come to the same conclusion: the war was as good as lost.

I had been on leave of absence at home and I had seen how scarce food was and how depressed many people were at home because they saw all these attacks don't lead to a peace. People began to ask, 'What now?'[5]

Hartwig Pohlmann, 36th Division, Imperial German Army

Germany's energy and commitment were slowly leaching away.

Rawlinson soon became aware of the opportunities that lay before him in the combination of poor-quality German troops and their lack of properly constructed defences. The Australian Corps was still in the line and its vigorous raiding had systematically exposed the German weaknesses while at the same time the prisoners taken added greatly to British intelligence.

> These Huns belonged to a second-rate division and were very peaceable. No matter how our boys annoyed them they never retaliated – and of course we heaped it on thicker; what with trench mortars and bombs, the enemy's life was one long hell.[6]
>
> Lieutenant Edgar Rule, 14th Battalion, 4th Brigade, 4th Australian Division

Rawlinson resolved to test the water and asked the Australian Corps commander Major General Sir John Monash and Brigadier Anthony Courage of the 5th Brigade, Tank Corps to prepare a local attack to 'straighten the line' at the village of Hamel. The plans that emerged were to be a blueprint for the All Arms Battle that would mark the culmination of British offensive tactics in the Great War. In June 1918 Rawlinson had already expressed a belief that firepower would have to replace manpower as the dominant consideration in preparing an attack.

> All possible mechanical devices in order to increase the offensive power of our divisions. The only two directions in which such development can be reasonably expected are (1) the increase of machine guns, Lewis guns and automatic rifles, and (2) the increase of numbers and functions of tanks.[7]
>
> General Sir Henry Rawlinson, Headquarters, Fifth Army

His prescient remarks were made against a background of a serious manpower shortage. The British Army was a shrinking force. The replacement divisions and drafts rushed to the Western Front had not prevented a general shrinkage in the size of units due to the excessive rate of casualties suffered in the German offensives. The most obvious sign was in the strength of the average British division, reduced by design earlier in the year from twelve to nine battalions, but now the shortage of men had also reduced the average size of those battalions from around 800 (not the official size but what might have been expected in 1916) to nearer 650. Not counting its artillery and ancillary units the average British division had therefore shrunk from around 10,000 to nearer 6,000 rifles. Nevertheless, this was the essence of Rawlinson's point: the men were no longer just armed with rifles. They had ever-increasing numbers of the Lewis gun; they had copious hand grenades and rifle grenades; they had Vickers machine-gun battalions and mortar units embedded alongside them. Underpinning everything the army did was still the awesome power of the Royal Artillery. All the guns overrun and lost in the German offensives had already been more than replaced by a British heavy armaments industry that had been thoroughly harnessed to the ends of total war. There was no shell shortage in 1918 and the munitions industries had also excelled themselves in producing almost unlimited quantities of the gas shells required to suppress any German response in an attack.

The plan produced by Monash and Courage envisioned an attack by six Australian battalions armed with extra Lewis guns advancing on a wide front of 6,000 yards, supported by over 600 guns and accompanied by sixty tanks of the 8th and 13th Tank Battalions, whose approach would be covered by the sound of low-flying aircraft. There would be no preliminary bombardment as the guns would be pre-calibrated and then shoot from the map, just as they had done at Cambrai in November 1917. The combination of artillery and tanks was designed to reduce to the minimum the need for copious quantities of infantry. A thunderous barrage by the heavy artillery would crash down on all the previously identified German artillery batteries, strong points, headquarters and communications centres. At the same time the tanks and infantry would go over the top preceded by a creeping barrage of 60 per cent shrapnel, 30 per cent high explosive and 10 per cent smoke shells to suppress the fire of any surviving German machine-gunners lurking in shell holes. In addition, there were two further barrages of 4.5-in and 6-in howitzers falling on designated strongpoints. The planning process was meticulous with great attention to properly briefing the men. In particular, concentration was placed upon liaison and close-cooperation training between the infantry and the tanks to try and reduce the usual battlefield confusion.

The Battle of Hamel commenced at 0310 on 4 July 1918. It was to prove an outstanding success. The German troops in the area were swept aside. The British heavy artillery effectively silenced the German guns and the field artillery's 'creeping barrage' chaperoned the advancing infantry and tanks right up to and over the German defences. The marauding tanks or well-trained infantry sections deploying Lewis guns, rifle grenades and grenades dealt with any pockets of resistance. The village of Hamel was soon captured amidst an overall advance of up to 2,000 yards.

> As we got to our objective we found two dugouts. I happened to be there first and I heard movement in one of these shelters. When I yelled out to the occupants, out came two hands with a loaf of black bread in each, and presently a pair of terrified eyes took a glimpse at me. They must have been reassured by my look, because the Huns came out at once, and, when I sized them up, all thoughts of revenge vanished. We could not kill children and these looked to be barely that. If any of us had been asked how old they were, most of us would have said between 14 and 15, and that was giving them every day of their age. With a boot to help them along, they ran with their hands above their heads back to our lines.[8]
>
> Lieutenant Edgar Rule, 14th Battalion, 4th Brigade, 4th Australian Division

The demoralised Germans surrendered in droves and those that didn't were mostly killed or wounded. Allied casualties numbered 1,400; the Germans lost the best part of 3,500. These were good odds for attrition by any standards.

THE SUCCESS AT HAMEL further encouraged Rawlinson. The British lines were still far too close to the strategically significant railway centre at Amiens and there was a long-standing desire for a counter-attack to clear the Germans back. The Australians continued their policy of regular raids on the German lines and it was apparent that the Germans had still failed to address the issue of a proper defensive system. The British were weak, but they were not *that* weak. An attack on the Germans was a temptation that could not be, and was not, resisted. The conception of the scheme was surprisingly quick and Rawlinson duly submitted his plan to Haig on 17 July 1918. The overall outline was that the Fourth Army would attack in three stages: the first would overrun the German front-line system to a distance of about 2,500 yards at most; the second would be carried out by fresh divisions 'leapfrogging' to seize a further 3,000 yards; the third stage, after a brief pause, entailed the army pushing forward to capture the old Outer Amiens Defence Line running through Proyart. Consolidation to secure the new front and any exposed flanks would then follow. This plan was accepted by Haig, but Foch, as Supreme Commander, intervened to enlarge the general scope of the operation by including a simultaneous offensive by General Marie Debeney and the French First Army to the immediate south, which was placed under Haig's command for the duration of the attack.

When considering the Amiens attack planned for 8 August 1918 it is ironic that it was the same Fourth Army delivering the attack under the same general who had so conspicuously failed on 1 July 1916. But it was the same army in name only. For this offensive was to be characterised by the 'firepower not manpower' methods of the All Arms Battle as tested at the Battle of Hamel. The planning process was far more collegiate in the sense that the experts of the different supporting arms that made up the 'All Arms' whole were consulted at an early stage and indeed were an integral part of the preparations. Thus when Lieutenant Colonel John Fuller in temporary command of the Tank Corps saw that the tanks allotted to the assault were only some six tank battalions he at once recommended that the whole of the Tank Corps of ten heavy and two light battalions should be thrown into the pot, increasing the total number of tanks deployed at a stroke to 324 heavy tanks, 96 light Whippet tanks and 120 supply tanks.

This would be the biggest tank battle of the war. Although simple tank tactics had been worked out and practised, there were still manifold communications problems dogging the tanks at every level: it was difficult for the crew to hear each other inside the excessively noisy tanks, they could not effectively communicate with nearby tanks or infantry when in battle, and they could not maintain any kind of contact with the supporting artillery or the generals behind the lines. Tanks were still blunt-edged weapons, but their purpose was clear: first they would flatten any barbed wire defences that might slow up the advance and then they were to root out and destroy any machine-gun post or stronghold that was holding up the infantry. The main battle tank was the Mark V variant. The crew of eight consisted of the officer or NCO tank commander, driver, four gunners, a second replacement driver and one spare man to cover for casualties. The huge exterior of the tank was misleading for much of the interior was occupied with the huge engine, which not only leaked noxious gases but also heated the interior to an unbearable level. There were many other limitations in the Mark V that indicated clearly that this was a 'work in progress' and not the finished weapon.

Haig watched a demonstration of the latest infantry–tank co-operation tactics on 31 July and he was much encouraged.

> Remarkable progress had been made since Cambrai, not only in the pattern of tank, but also in the methods of using them. Tanks now go first, covered by shrapnel barrage, and break down all opposition. Enemy in strongpoints and machine-gun nests are then flattened out by the tanks. The latter then signal to infantry to 'come on', and these then advance in open order and mop up the remaining defenders, and collect the prisoners. During consolidation tanks zigzag in front to cover the operation. Australian infantry were used to demonstrate first of all, and then the onlookers from another battalion were put through similar exercises on the same course. The result of these methodical exercises has been to render a tank attack more effective and much less costly to us.[9]
>
> Field Marshal Sir Douglas Haig, General Headquarters, BEF

The tanks were a new weapon of war that had been fully integrated into the All Arms Battle by August 1918.

In contrast, the artillery experts had long had a complete theoretical and practical grip on the science of gunnery. Their contribution would be utterly crucial to any chances of real success. There was to be no preliminary bombardment by the batteries that Rawlinson had amassed. It was now evident that they did not have to destroy the German trenches before a successful attack could be launched. The main, if not the only, criterion was that the defenders' artillery and machine guns be suppressed. At the moment of the attack therefore a veritable torrent of gas shells and high explosives would descend from the heavens onto the German artillery batteries preventing them from firing onto the attacking infantry and tanks. At the same time a complex creeping barrage fired by the field artillery would 'creep' across No Man's Land with the attacking infantry as close to it as they dared. Many preferred to accept the risk of being hit by their own shells to the chance of letting the German machine-gunners emerge from their dugouts before they had been overrun. The British had not learnt this from Bruchmüller – they had their own superior techniques dating way back to 1917.

The artillery preparations were enormous. The surveyors had given the gunners the accurate maps they needed of the Somme battlefield. The thousands of guns had to be carefully and covertly moved in and camouflaged alongside the huge quantities of ammunition that would be needed. Every gun had recently been tested and adjusted on the army calibration range; all the gun sights would be tested again on the night before Zero Hour. The meteorological section, now taken incredibly seriously, would supply the data that would allow the gunners to adjust for changes in pressure, temperature and wind strength. Meanwhile, the position of every German artillery battery in the area was being slowly and methodically located. The RAF flew innumerable reconnaissance missions and the photographic interpretation experts, using every trick in the book, managed to see through many of the German gunners' best efforts to camouflage their battery positions. The sound-ranging teams with their complex system of microphones were identifying more and more German batteries. The experts of the Field Survey companies were also bringing into play their own techniques of flash spotting.

The system of observation posts was at fixed topographical points about 3 miles apart from north to south forming the base of any triangle when ruled out on the survey map, each post being connected by land telephone with each other and the headquarters. Using a survey director or theodolite our three angles of direction when plotted out on the map back at HQ became a very accurate triangulation of any object within our field of view. With the new maps printed by the Field Survey Department and constantly being checked by mobile topographers, the accuracy of the apex of our triangle was judged to be within 5 yards. While all visual information was sought for, the spotting of enemy guns was the main objective. This was most effective at night by flash spotting. On one observer seeing a particular flash being repeated from the same spot, he would report it to the other two and HQ. They in turn would observe for the same flash, which must synchronise with a buzzer the first observer uses as each flash is registered, until they

seeing the flash and using the buzzer eventually all buzz simultaneously. Meanwhile, the plotter at HQ receives not only a buzz but also a
flash of light from each post on a panel before him. Once he is satisfied
that all three are buzzing together accurately, he asks for our bearings.
We read these from the illuminated scale on which the director turns.
He then plots them by protractor and 'Hey Presto!' another German
gun is known to us and in due time will receive attention.[10]

Sapper Wilfred Cook, Field Survey Corps

By the means of these carefully applied modern techniques the location
of 504 of the 530 German guns in the area of operations was correctly
identified – 95 per cent in total. The German artillery would be almost
completely neutralised when the battle opened. The Royal Artillery in
the end deployed a total of 1,386 field guns and howitzers, with 684
heavy artillery pieces. The field artillery had between 500 and 600
shells per gun; the heavier pieces had mostly 400. There was plenty
here not only to saturate the German batteries but also to provide a
truly staggering 'creeping barrage'. The number of guns needed to
neutralise a given number of batteries or frontage of trenches had been
reduced to a mathematical formula. The requisite calculations were
made and the necessary guns were moved up ready for action. It may
not have been romantic or heroic, but it *was* war. And the Royal
Artillery was ready for war.

The RAF had also been brought right into the heart of the All Arms
Battle. It had been coming for well over a year now, but the mass use of
aircraft in ground strafing and interdiction bombing during the German offensives had pushed the aerial perspective much further forward
in the military panoply. The RAF must carry out its own reconnaissance work while at the same time its scouts must prevent the German
reconnaissance aircraft from penetrating the British rear – all this
without creating an abnormal level of air activity that would in itself
alert the Germans that an offensive was looming. This was a difficult
balancing act and it was perhaps fortunate that poor weather restricted
the flying of both sides in early August. The RAF also had the mundane
task of drowning the sound of the tanks as they moved into their
jumping-off positions. On the day itself aircraft would attack every
identified German airfield to try and neutralise the German air force.

As the assault started on the ground the RAF would fly contact patrols, monitoring the progress of the infantry, drawing attention to hold-ups and bringing down deadly concentrations of extra artillery fire wherever required. The scout squadrons dealt with any German aircraft appearing over the front and also engaged in low-level ground strafing along the line and back along the lines of communication. Bombers were trying to destroy the railway lines that would channel in the German reserves to cut off the battlefield from reinforcements at least in the short term.

All these multifarious aircraft had to be assembled within easy striking range of the Somme battlefield. By the late summer of 1918 the Allies were now so strong that they could amass a huge aerial Armada over the Somme without unduly, or at least obviously, weakening their strength elsewhere along the line. Indeed, some diversionary air activity was carried out over Mont Kemmel and in the Ypres area to draw German eyes there. In the end the RAF amassed no less than 800 army cooperation aircraft, scouts, day bombers, night bombers and long-range reconnaissance aircraft for the battle. To add to this was a further 1,104 French aircraft making a total of 1,904 Allied aircraft. The Germans had a mere 365 aircraft immediately available.

The central force of the All Arms Battle should never be either forgotten or underestimated – the infantry. The infantry soldier may be caricatured as a humble resource: a sweating, farting, moaning and cursing anachronism in the mechanical war, but he was still utterly irreplaceable in 1918. The soldiers were the ones that actually had to capture, occupy and retain the objective. No other force could do it. Infantry tactics had come a long way in a short time and the assault methods used by Rawlinson's Fourth Army in August 1918 were entirely different from those employed by his army on the Somme in July 1916. Gone were the long lines of infantrymen plodding forwards to endure unsuppressed German machine-gun and artillery fire as best as flesh and blood could manage. Now advance scouts would push forward some 150 yards or so, working close to the tanks and just behind the creeping barrage. These men were intended to work as 'beaters', identifying where possible surviving German machine-gun posts were so that the tanks could destroy them. Behind this screen would be the main body of the battalion attacking on a two-company front, with the men strung out in 'worms' of six to eight men moving forward in single file with between 30 and 60 yards between 'worms'. This was designed to minimise the effects of being caught in the open by either machine-gun or artillery fire. Behind the leading battalions the supporting battalion would advance in the artillery formation of platoons in file. All of the troops would be carrying the bare minimum of equipment required. The battalion was no longer the fighting unit – this had dropped to the company, then the platoon and was now the section. Although the infantry were still armed with the .303 Lee Enfield rifle, there were also now numerous Lewis gunners to provide concentrated support fire, Stokes mortars and rifle grenades to mimic artillery fire and hand grenades for clearing out enclosed spaces. In the last resort, or more frequently if the enemy had already surrendered, then they had their trusty bayonets. A flexible combination of these weapons could overcome obstacles that flummoxed their 1916 counterparts. When problems arose, then they had access to support: tanks were usually available to provide immediate assistance, while if a problem endured they could call for additional support from the Vickers machine guns, heavy mortars and even low-flying aircraft. The infantry were still at the centre of all of the battle tactics, they remained the pivotal force around which all the firepower was deployed.

The Cavalry Corps may have been an 'old' arm that was no longer of the first relevance, but it still had a theoretical role in Rawlinson's All Arms plan. If, and it was a big 'if', the Germans collapsed to create an exploitable 'gap', then the cavalry were to charge through, overrun the German artillery and then attack the neighbouring Germans from the rear. The 'modern cavalry' – the light Whippet tanks – were to be used alongside their predecessors in this frankly unlikely scenario. The cavalryman was still substantially faster-moving than the Whippet, while at the same time being considerably more vulnerable to machine-gun fire and barbed wire. The difficulties of effective coordination should have been fairly obvious.

Finally, there was one other specialist ingredient in the All Arms Battle, one that many would decry and try to forget: the general officers and their staff who coordinated the whole combined effort. The tactics to be employed on 8 August did not come from one fertile brain – a veritable army of staff officers hammered them out. The tactics in every attack over the previous years had been analysed, every technology closely evaluated and scrutinised in an effort to place them within the overall battle plan as defined in the Field Service Regulations. Specialists of every kind had bent their minds to refining and improving the killing power of weapons and their most effective methods of employment, whether it be aircraft, thermite bombs, gas shells, tanks or machine guns. Staff officers arranged everything for the coming battle: the maps, the roads, the railways, the complex movement plans, the accommodation of all the extra troops, the food and water supplies, the medical arrangements for the treatment of the wounded, the cages for German prisoners. And they had to do all this without in any way attracting the attention of the German Army.

Amongst the corps selected by Haig to form the bulk of the assaulting Fourth Army were the Australian Corps and the Canadian Corps. The Canadians and to a lesser extent the Australians had been carefully husbanded by Haig as a reserve of last resort or as the basis of a future counter-attacking force. They were still made up on the old twelve battalions per division scale and were thus numerically much stronger than the average British division. It was therefore a fair bet that if these two corps turned up in the same place an attack was intended. Fortunately, the Australians were already *in situ*, but the Canadian Corps was at the time part of the First Army in the Arras area and it was evident that much subterfuge would be required if the Germans were not to be forewarned. Two Canadian battalions, two casualty clearing stations and a wireless section were therefore visibly despatched to the Second Army in the Mont Kemmel sector to fool the Germans that an attempt was imminent to recapture the hill. Meanwhile, the 'real' move to the Amiens/Somme area was delayed to the last possible moment, and the corps did not take over its actual jumping off lines until just two hours before Zero Hour. The Germans were indeed fooled: the Canadian presence at Mont Kemmel, combined with the increased RAF activity there, made them slightly apprehensive of an attack in the north.

Throughout the whole of the planning secrecy was an obsession with Rawlinson and the staff. With preparations on this scale almost everyone gathered that something 'big' was brewing, but they were all urged to 'Keep your mouths shut'. In the diary of Signaller Sydney Fuller there is still a copy all these years later of the notice issued to every single officer and man to be pasted into their pay book.

> KEEP YOUR MOUTHS SHUT. The success of any operation we carry out depends chiefly on surprise. DO NOT TALK. When you know that your unit has been making preparations for an attack, don't talk about them to men in other units, or to strangers and keep your mouth shut, especially in public places. Do not be inquisitive about what other units are doing; if you hear or see anything, keep it to yourself. THE SUCCESS OF THE OPERATION AND THE LIVES OF YOUR COMRADES DEPEND ON YOUR SILENCE.[11]

The notice then went on to warn of the trickery employed by German interrogators should a soldier have the misfortune to be taken prisoner of war. Amiens had already been evacuated in the emergency of March and French civilians were forbidden to enter the Fourth Army area. There were even verbal tricks to help maintain the secrecy. Thus the preparations were always referred to as taking over more of the line from the French, while in the line the offensive was referred to as a raid. Simple really, but all adding to the overall security blanket.

The planning and concomitant arrangements proceeded smoothly. One complication was the decision by Haig to expand the scope of the operation at almost the last moment.

> I thought that the Fourth Army orders aimed too much at getting a *final* objective on the old Amiens defence line, and stopping counter-attacks on it. This is not *far* enough in my opinion, if we start by surprising the enemy! So I told Rawlinson (it had already been in my 'orders') to arrange to advance as rapidly as possible and capture the old Amiens line of defence, put it in state of defence; but not to delay – at once reserves must be pushed on to capture the line Chaulnes–Roye.[12]
>
> Field Marshal Sir Douglas Haig, General Headquarters, BEF

The general line of advance was to be towards Ham on the Somme River. Haig had mentioned it to Rawlinson before, although it was not in his first set of orders, but the aspiration to push further forwards had been given an urgency following a conference between Haig and Foch two days earlier on 3 August. Foch was pushing Haig hard. He wanted the operation to start as soon as possible and he wanted it to go as far as possible without becoming too vulnerable to counter-attack. Foch was increasingly of the opinion that the Germans were 'breaking up' and wanted to capitalise on that and keep up the momentum. Haig needed little urging; he was by nature a man that always took an optimistic view of the prospects of any offensive. Fortunately, this slightly rash last-minute extension of their objectives by the 20 miles up to Ham was to have little effect on the planning process of the operation. The artillery plans were not diluted by additional targets as the 7 miles to the original Amiens Defence Line objectives took the British front line well beyond the range of most of its artillery. The only real impact would be that if progress to the distant objectives stalled then the battle could degenerate in its later stages into an attritional stalemate as the Germans brought up their reserves and consolidated their front.

CHAPTER TEN

The Black Day:
Amiens, 8 August 1918

O N PAPER the two sides facing each other in the Battle of Amiens were of a relatively equal strength as far as a simplistic count of the immediately available divisions was concerned. Yet for all the manpower problems endemic amongst the British divisions the German divisions were in a far more parlous state, many being reduced to between 3,000 to 4,000 men. Overall there was a basic British superiority of three to two over the Germans. At first sight this was hardly convincing given the vast British numerical superiority on the Somme on 1 July 1916. But despite the clarion 'wake up call' of the Battle of Hamel the Germans had still failed to address the problems of their totally inadequate defence system in the recent gains. A few random trenches with bits and bobs of barbed wire may have stopped the British Army in the past, but this could not possibly stand up to the kind of modern All Arms offensive that Rawlinson was brewing.

The attack would be carried out by a combination of French, Canadian, Australian and British troops. On the right there was the French First Army which deployed its IX and XXXI Corps, although General Debeney had ordered his men to delay going over the top for forty-five minutes after their British neighbours, and even then they were only to push on if the British were successful. There was thus a discernable lack of confidence amongst the French generals, whatever urging they might receive from the impatient Foch. In essence their role would be that of an orthodox flank guard, covering the right of the advancing Fourth Army.

On the right of the British Fourth Army was the magnificent Canadian Corps commanded by Lieutenant General Sir Arthur Currie, which was attacking on the front between the Amiens–Roye road and the Amiens–Chaulnes railway. Since their grim experiences at the closing stages of the Third Battle of Ypres when they had captured Passchendaele Ridge the Canadians had been carefully handled by Haig, who was determined to retain them as a strike formation. Next in line was the Australian Corps, charged with attacking between the Amiens–Chaulnes railway and the Somme River. Finally, there was the III Corps under the command of Lieutenant General Sir Richard Butler, which had the daunting task of attacking over the valleys and spurs between the Somme and Ancre Rivers. Butler's corps was far more typical of the general state of the British Army. The divisions that made up his ranks had been through the mill since 21 March and it was thus unfortunate that they had by far the most difficult ground to overcome.

As part of the general arrangements prior to the attack the Australian troops extended their front by 7,000 yards to their right, taking over this part of the line from the French. They would hold this line thinly before the insertion of the Canadian Corps here at the last minute. As ever with the Australians it proved the opportunity for a well-placed anecdote.

> We got orders to take over part of the line south of Villers-Bretonneux, which was being held by the 2nd Tirailleurs, and Brigadier Herring and I went to see the French brigade to make arrangements for the relief. The French general was an oldish man with only one arm, but spry in spite of his disability. With the aid of his interpreter, who spoke very colloquial English, we studied their dispositions on the map and then went up on foot to look at the forward area. The Germans spotted our party and got on to us with whizz-bangs. One salvo burst right overhead and we all flattened ourselves on the ground. When I recovered my breath I said gallantly to the interpreter, 'I hope your old general will not be hit!' to which he replied ungallantly, 'Bugger him: I hope I don't get hit myself!'[1]
>
> Captain Thomas Louch, Headquarters, 13th Brigade, 4th Australian Division

There was a far bigger palaver about bringing forward the hundreds of tanks. The tanks did not have the reliability or endurance to travel under their own steam, but were instead entrained to Amiens. Getting the 30-ton monsters aboard the train was no easy matter and demanded considerable skill and nerve from the drivers.

> And so we went to the railway to entrain. Now this was a most difficult manoeuvre, the last truck on the train (or first) acted as a ramp, two wheels being taken away and replaced when all the 'buses' were on. So if you were the first to drive on, you had to go the full length of the trucks, and seeing their width was not quite so wide as our tracks, it was a most difficult operation and demanded great skill. Going at a snail's pace, the driver had to be dead on.[2]
>
> Private Charles Rowland, 14th Battalion, Tank Corps

When they had come as far as they could by rail, the tanks were then driven the last few miles to laager up close to the front. Aeroplanes droning over the Germans would cover the distinctive roar of the engines.

Captain Henry Smeddle was in command of a section of three of the special elongated Mark V* tanks that each carried teams of machine-gunners with all their guns and ammunition. Their planned role was to follow up the infantry until the second objective had been attained. There they would drop off the machine-gunners and then patrol up and down in front of the line to stop any possible German counter-attack. The presence of tanks so close to the front would give away the imminence of an attack so considerable care was required in concealing them in their temporary laager or 'Tankodrome', as it was known.

> Our Tankodrome consisted of a long line of elms on the banks of a canal and their leafy foliage aided by our camouflage nets amply protected our tanks from the prying eyes of any scouting aeroplane. As soon as all work in connection with the camouflage had been completed, the men were given hot tea and ordered to rest until midday. Needless to say they did not require any second bidding and were soon fast asleep, some sprawling on the grass, others inside the tanks.[3]
>
> Captain Henry Smeddle, 15th Battalion, Tank Corps

The noisy, fume-ridden, deafening environment within a tank in action was such that the men needed to be at their best to cope with it. There was no point in tiring them out; indeed, they needed time to recover from the physical strains of merely driving the tanks forward the previous night.

The tank units had to liaise closely with the infantry units that they were accompanying into battle. Delegated to this task for the 5th Battalion, Tank Corps, who were working with the 3rd Canadian Division, was their adjutant, Major J. G. Fitzmaurice who duly attended the divisional conference immediately prior to the battle.

> I only came in contact with the brigade commanders at a divisional conference before the battle. They were all Canadians. One of them, Brigadier General McDonald, I think, I do remember for two reasons. Firstly, he was not a believer in tanks and said so extremely bluntly. Secondly, when asked to expound his plan of attack, he began by saying, 'I know they call me, Bloody Mac!' and proceeded to justify the title by explaining that in each of his battalions one platoon was detailed to see that no prisoners were taken. He was careful to explain that there was a big difference between murdering prisoners after capture and refusing to capture them. He inclined to the latter plan, in order to save personnel required as escort and valuable rations expended in feeding the captured.[4]
>
> Major J. G. Fitzmaurice, 5th Battalion, Tank Corps

Inevitably, the process of briefing was somewhat complex, as the orders were passed down the whole elongated chain of command and with due regard to secrecy it was only a day or two before that the officers briefed their tank commanders. To assist them the battalion reconnaissance officer supplied them with detailed marked-up maps and aerial photographs, which allowed them to see the ground they would be travelling over, the nature of the obstacles to be encountered and the exact locations of suspected German strongpoints.

> On this day maps arrived for issue to tank commanders on a scale of about 3 inches to a mile, and showing a large amount of detail. Each tank also had an oblique aeroplane photograph, taken from a few hundred feet in the air above the point of each company's advance. I had to mark up the maps with the objectives and other information such as position of any anti-tank guns, etc., which I had been able to

320

locate or get information about. All this resulted in each tank having a pretty fair idea of what it was going to meet, at any rate in the earlier stages of the attack.[5]

Major Mark Dillon, 2nd Battalion, Tank Corps

With the maps and photographs to hand the tank commander would brief the crews. Private Charles Rowland was the gunner in the Mark V tank *Niveleur* – French for 'stone crusher' – which was commanded by Lieutenant Ronald Mould.

The main problem was to silence some guns, field guns, which were on the edge of a wood facing us, and inside as well. This we could see on the photographs quite plain, and we did not like the look of them, as they would, if not knocked out by the barrage, be firing point-blank at us on open sights, and we did not think we would have much chance. Then he set about with his plan, as how we should work the rota of the crew, driving in our turns to a certain point, then move around clockwise, so all got a share on the 6-pounders, machine guns and the observer next to the driving seat, who had also a machine gun firing straight forward (first time around allotted to me). And the attack was to be next morning at dawn – 4.20 a.m., allowing ten minutes for the barrage to lift from the front line and move to the next lot of trenches, and so creep through the defence. The point we were aiming at as our objective was on the top of a slight ridge, and to go 6 miles into this part had never been heard of before, and we thought someone had gone crackers to think of such a thing, but that was the orders, and we were all a bit worried. Sounded easy on paper![6]

Private Charles Rowland, 14th Battalion, Tank Corps

Then it was time for the final preparations: checking water levels, oil and petrol, then making sure that everything mechanical was in good working order. There was so much to go wrong.

I gave orders and final instructions for adjusting tracks, gears and various other details too numerous to repeat here, which were to be carried out right away. The remainder of the afternoon was spent in assisting the tank commanders to test their compasses, adjust and look over the machine guns, cartridge belts, 6-pounders etc. At 9 p.m. there was still much to be done, but as we had the whole of the next day to complete our preparations I decided to knock off, give the men a good night's rest.[7]

Captain Henry Smeddle, 15th Battalion, Tank Corps

Next day, while his men completed their work on the tanks' fixtures and fittings, Captain Smeddle was required to accompany the reconnaissance officer to plan his route forward that night. Tanks at night are blind, blundering monsters and everything that could be done to identify and learn the best available route would help to prevent them dropping out. Even so they still needed a guide walking in front.

I proceeded with the tank commanders to reconnoitre the route to our lying-up point, and from there to the front-line trenches, a total distance of about 3 miles. We had but little difficulty in finding a suitable route, which was along a road that ran right up to within 50 yards of the place selected, about 700 yards from the front line and situated on top of a high ridge from which we could plainly see the German front-line trenches. It was decided only to tape the route from where it left the road – white tape an inch wide is laid along the ground to indicate a route in the dark where no definite track exists.[8]

Captain Henry Smeddle, 15th Battalion, Tank Corps

On his return he found the tanks were duly reported as ready for action and his passengers had arrived. Smeddle now gave his final briefing to his men.

I gave orders relating to the time of departure and discipline during the approach march. There was to be no smoking or flashing of electric torches; no shouting, whistling or unnecessary noise during the march. Only tank commanders could be allowed to smoke: the glow from their cigarette was to be the method by which they would guide their tanks while walking in front without attracting undue attention. One might think that all these precautions were superfluous and unnecessary, when the noise of the tanks alone was sufficient to drown any lesser sound like talking or shouting, but it is astonishing how a single human voice when raised, will carry far beyond and above the dull mechanical roar of the tanks.[9]

Captain Henry Smeddle, 15th Battalion, Tank Corps

One special kind of vehicle introduced was the carrier tank, charged with taking forward the huge amounts of fuel and ammunition that would be needed to replenish the tanks and infantry units when they had reached their objectives. Loading these machines was a tricky matter for each was to carry 400 gallons of fuel, 20,000 rounds of small ammunition and 200 rounds of 6-pounder shells. This was easier said than done. There was also the prospect of running the overheating engines next to a dangerous combination of fuel and explosives. The risks were spelt out for all when a lucky German shell hit one concealed group of carrier tanks that night.

> On approaching Villers-Bretonneux we saw flames and smoke coming from an orchard just north of the village. This was Partington's carry-ing company, which had had a chance shell dropped amongst it, and as all twelve tanks were loaded to capacity with inflammables and materials for the battle, there was little hope of saving any, but I believe the guard over the tanks managed to get away one or two.[10]
>
> Major Mark Dillon, 2nd Battalion, Tank Corps

Smeddle's men were then ordered to rest until 0100 on 8 August when they would have to get the engines running ready to move off by 0120. In the last few minutes Smeddle attended to his personal battle kit: his gas mask, revolver, water bottle, trench maps, map case and binoculars. He found all his machines with engines running and ready to go. Off they trundled, a slow-motion process.

> The speed was not to exceed walking pace, as tanks make far less noise with the engines running slowly than when travelling at a high speed. The night was not dark and we had but little difficulty in following our route. The distance between the tanks was kept at 25 yards and the speed of the column was regulated by the speed of the slowest tank. As there were several stops to make small adjustments, it was quite 3 a.m. before we reached our laying-up point, where we had no difficulty in picking up the tapes and getting each tank man-oeuvred into its position. The men were now called together and served out with hot stew, which had been brought along in containers from the camp.[11]
>
> Captain Henry Smeddle, 15th Battalion, Tank Corps

After synchronising watches with his section commander and receiving comforting reports from his tank commanders that everything was still in order, there was nothing left for Smeddle to do. In their follow-up role they would only go forward an hour after the first wave of tanks had gone into the attack.

> I told them to get what rest they could during the time we had to spare. I selected a spot behind one of my tanks and using my haversack as a pillow, I lay down. But I had not been on the ground five minutes before I discovered that the place was simply alive with spiders – the long-legged, fat-bodied type – and they seemed to display a great liking for crawling over my face and neck.[12]
>
> Captain Henry Smeddle, 15th Battalion, Tank Corps

He could not sleep. A combination of mild arachnophobia and stultifying tension stifled all thoughts of sleep.

> I found that there were only three minutes to go before 'Zero'. The silence seemed like that preceding a storm. An occasional crackle of machine guns in the distance and a few far-off booms of heavy artillery were the only sounds that met the ear, and yet only three minutes to go before the commencement of one of the greatest battles of the war. I kept my watch in my hand and watched the luminous pointer getting gradually nearer the time, until just as it started to cover the little round glowing point denoting the four, the barrage started. It broke the silence with a terrific crashing roar, flashes were spurting up from all around where we were standing, it was still dark, but the flashes from the guns gave out sufficient light to distinguish the forms of gunners and guns, the nearest of which was only 25 yards from where I was standing. So quietly had everything been prepared that I was not aware of its presence until it started firing.[13]
>
> Captain Henry Smeddle, 15th Battalion, Tank Corps

All told, he was a satisfied man; it had been a thoroughly professional preparation and he was proud of his men.

The Royal Artillery also had good reason to be satisfied with the impressive results of its exhaustive preparations as the guns blared out in solid unison with the most enormous roar at the appointed Zero Hour of 0420.

Every gun shot together and the thing was off. I never heard anything like it in my life, neither had anyone else, as it was about the biggest show that has ever been staged on the Western Front. Several times I could not hear my own gunfire, and for half the series, I laid and fired the gun myself. After three hours, I was practically deaf. We fired our first shot at 4.20 a.m. at 800 yards and in three hours the enemy was out of our range (6,500 yards). Within ten minutes of the start, the tanks, by the hundreds, and cavalry, by the thousands, were passing our guns. It made an awful pretty picture to see the tanks and cavalry looming up in the mist, over the crest, just about dawn. The field guns began to pass us at a gallop, too, not to mention the infantry by the hundreds of thousands.[14]

Gunner Bertie Cox, 60th Battery, 14th Brigade, Royal Field Artillery

It was a stunning barrage, the distillation of all that had been learnt during the war.

And suddenly, with a mighty roar, more than a thousand guns begin the symphony. A great illumination lights up the eastern horizon: and instantly the whole complex organisation, extending far back to areas almost beyond earshot of the guns, begins to move forward; every man, every unit, every vehicle and every tank on the appointed tasks and to their designated goals, sweeping on relentlessly and irresistibly. Viewed from a high vantage point and in the glimmer of the breaking day, a great artillery barrage surely surpasses in dynamic splendour any other manifestation of collective human effort.[15]

Major General Sir John Monash, Headquarters, Australian Corps

The flash spotters took due satisfaction as they saw all their hard work reaping its reward as the German batteries were pelted with gas shells and high explosives.

We had seen bombardments before, but this was something new in its intensity, starting as if by a conductor's baton, breaking the silence like a knife. Not a gun seemed to be left to the Germans – they must have been caught with their 'pants down' and we congratulated ourselves that we had helped fix their positions in readiness for 'Der Tag', which was now ours.[16]

Sapper Wilfred Cook, Field Survey Corps

Meanwhile, the infantry were enduring the long wait for Zero Hour, lying for up to five hours on their starting-line tapes until at last the roar of the barrage sent shells skimming over their heads to crash down just in front of them in No Man's Land. As their 'creeping barrage' began it was their moment of truth.

> Then we were over the tape and away, me with my Lewis gun section. Off along with the tanks. But it was off in a fog as well, a fog that had been coming down all night, and was now so thick you could hardly see 20 yards in front of you. The tanks, unless one came very near to you, you could only place by sound. It was an eerie start. In no time Germans, ghostlike in the mists, were showing up all over the place, most with their hands up above their heads in surrender. But here and there a machine gun still firing at random at us.[17]
>
> Corporal William Kerr, 5th (Western Cavalry) Battalion, 2nd Brigade, 1st Canadian Division

Close by, the leading tanks were also in their positions ready to rumble forwards in synchronicity, almost blindly feeling their way ahead to crush the barbed wire.

> Mould looked at his watch, it was 4.20 a.m., time to move, and all of a sudden, a mist fell over the area, which pleased us but did not help the navigator. But it did not last long and we were on our way to the first line, with all the machine guns firing. Slowly moving towards that, we found that the barrage had not killed all the enemy troops, but what was left were coming out with their hands up. But it was the Canadians' job to see to them, and we started to crawl into and out of the trenches, being bumped here and there, sideways, all over the place.[18]
>
> Private Charles Rowland, 14th Battalion, Tank Corps

As a working environment the inside of a Mark V tank was simply atrocious. The crew were rendered deaf, dumb and blind as the ungainly beasts slowly lurched their way across the trenches and shell holes.

> The view for any member of the crew was confined to what could be picked up through pin-holes or through the sights of their guns. As the tank came under small arms fire, bullet splash penetrated through the

pin-holes and between the joints of the armour plate, and further restricted the view, often causing temporary blindness. Observation was very difficult under heavy fire. Splash through the gun ports caused a man's face to become covered in blood; after, when wiped, many fine specks of molten bullet could be seen under the skin. Steel horizontally fitted eyepieces with chain-mail protectors were issued, but were rarely used as they were difficult to see through and were very heavy and uncomfortable to wear. Splash was accentuated by the flaking of the armour plate inside the tank. Wet blankets were hung round the Hotchkiss gun mountings but, although they stopped some of the splash, got in the way and were generally discarded. Under such conditions it was usually impossible to see anything from the face of the tank, onto which the enemy directed his small arms fire, but it gave the tank commander an indication where to go in order to close with enemy machine guns. The noise was deafening whenever the engine ran, and speech next to impossible, and when under small arms fire it was like an inferno. The officer usually sat next to the driver and directed him by signs; he also fired the front Hotchkiss gun. Very little control was possible as regards the gunners. Various devices such as speaking tubes and directing arrows were tried, but the most satisfactory method was to attract the attention of the gunner required with a pick helve and shout the necessary orders in his ear.[19]

Captain Gerald Brooks, 15th Battalion, Tank Corps

The tanks and infantry were easy targets as they crossed No Man's Land, but the German counter-barrage was an utter failure. Hammered as they were by the British shells falling all around their battery positions they did not make any kind of a response onto the British front-line trenches until five minutes after Zero Hour. By that time they were far too late: the troops and tanks were well on their way across No Man's Land. Before their range corrections could be made the German guns were even more liberally doused by the thunderous British counter-battery fire.

At the same time the bulk of the field artillery was busy firing the ubiquitous 'creeping barrage', the truly great British tactical innovation of the war, gradually lengthening the range as the tanks and leading troops moved forwards.

After a time our range was increased by 50 yards and then again by 100 yards. On each side of us and to our rear, guns, light and heavy, were blazing away. The din was terrifying. After being deafened in previous bouts of firing the gun over a period, I had chewed part of a Woodbines cigarette packet and plugged my ears.[20]

Gunner Percy Creek, 'A' Battery, 104th Brigade, Royal Field Artillery

The tanks moved steadily forwards over the German Forward Zone trench system. Many of the tanks were slightly behind schedule but, all things considered, they were well pleased with their progress.

It took us some time to get over the three lines, what with the wire around our tracks, and failing to get out of holes first time, going back and trying another spot, but eventually we were clear, and by now it was broad daylight, and I changed over to the right-hand 6-pounder alongside of Mould. But what a sight met the eye: as far as we could see, tanks moving forward, infantry behind, taking shelter from them, hundreds of field guns following. The whole lot looked as if it was on parade, and we both smiled.[21]

Private Charles Rowland, 14th Battalion, Tank Corps

Things didn't always run smoothly. One of the greatest problems for the tank crews was the extraordinarily limited visibility as they lumbered forwards. Naturally, the fog made it even worse and, as ever, there were some embarrassing interludes when tanks got totally lost.

We walked on through the gun lines conversing by gestures, and as the dawn began to break could see occasional tanks through the mist in front of us. After walking for about fifteen minutes, during which period I had my prismatic compass glued to my nose, we struck the main road and walked on down it. The mist was very thick and any number of people were lost. We were amazed to see a tank coming towards us, closed down and looking very ugly. With some trepidation I approached and halted it, and learnt that Lieutenant Cornish, the commander, thought that he was approaching the German lines, and he gave me a few hot words about foolish bravado in exposing myself. I managed to convince him that half an hour spent in swinging his compass and correcting it would have saved him from an anti-climax, and turning him round on the road, I waved him on in front of me. He later ran over a tank mine, or more probably a dud shell, and sustained a broken track.[22]

Major Mark Dillon, 2nd Battalion, Tank Corps

The Canadian, Australian and British infantry knew that they had to keep in touch with the tanks and the barrage if they were not to find themselves isolated on the battlefield. Even a matter of minutes could see the Germans emerge from their hiding places to set up their machine guns and wreak an awful vengeance. But as long as they kept close there was little fight in the shell-shocked Germans.

We knew that we had to follow our tanks so kept along after them. Every now and then 'Fritzes' would come running back with their hands up, well 'souvenired', watches and pocket books all gone. One Hun came suddenly in sight of a tank that I was near. He was so scared that he bounded right at me and would have knocked me down, but I poked the old bayonet at him and he steadied up. Their main idea seemed to be to get taken prisoner and to get out of the line at the earliest.[23]

Private G. V. Rose, 30th Battalion, 8th Brigade, 5th Australian Division

Not all of the German soldiers managed to surrender without fatal consequences. Feelings and emotions were running high: some men had seen their friends killed, if not that day then in the recent past, and were in the mood for revenge no matter what convention dictated.

Enemy machine guns rattled and very soon some of our men were down. There was an indescribable noise and confusion. We became wrapped in the smoke and fog, and could only find our way by listening for the direction of our guns and keeping our backs to them. Units became mixed and isolated parties fought their way forward. Our barrage got well ahead of us and groups of prisoners stumbled towards us out of the mist. I felt sorry for them, they needed no guard to escort them back. When almost up to the men in front I saw one of them shoot four Germans one after the other as they climbed out of the end of a trench. Strange emotions possessed me.[24]

Private Edgar Morrow, 28th Battalion, 7th Brigade, 2nd Australian Division

Back at the gun lines they saw the surviving German prisoners streaming past into captivity. There was indeed little need for guards as they were desperate to get away from the shells, the gas and the glittering bayonets of the British infantry.

> By 5 a.m., the prisoners began to go by and this procession continued all day. The thing that struck me as being most funny was the way the prisoners would dangle right along by themselves, no escort, to the prison cage about a mile away. If there were thirty or forty together, they would have an escort, but they mostly passed in twos or threes, all alone or four would carry one of our wounded on a stretcher. We spent a considerable part of the day checking them over; getting souvenirs and talking to those who could speak English. They nearly cleaned us out of cigarettes and emptied our water bottles. They all seemed tickled to death to be taken prisoners. They said the attack was a complete surprise. They were used all day as stretcher bearers. The Major brought up some of them to watch us fire our guns. Must have given them an awful feeling to think those shells were going over to kill their own flesh and blood.[25]
>
> Gunner Bertie Cox, 60th Battery, 14th Brigade, Royal Field Artillery

Captain Smeddle was due to move forward as part of a second wave of tanks at 0520, carrying their passenger machine-gunners in their Mark V* tanks ready to drop them at the second-line objectives to help consolidate the ground gained. Just moments before he was due to give the order to move, Smeddle made a shattering discovery that essentially undermined all his careful preparations over the last two days.

> I went back to my own tanks and found one of my tank commanders hammering away at one of his tracks. On going up to investigate, he informed me that he had just discovered that during the approach march this track had got slack and come off the guide rails – and he had not noticed it until just then. All this had to be shouted out and repeated several times before I could hear, the roar of the artillery was so deafening. I shouted back orders to get on with the adjustments and to follow on, as we could not wait for one tank. I was disgusted with the man for being so careless as to overlook an important thing like his tracks, especially after having reported, 'All OK!' on his arrival.[26]
>
> Captain Henry Smeddle, 15th Battalion, Tank Corps

The concept of 'accidental-on-purpose sabotage' had not yet occurred to most officers of the Tank Corps who still trusted their men implicitly. Yet accidents of this sort were no coincidence. If an unscrupulous nervous crewman or tank commander let a track 'come off' or poured water 'in mistake' for petrol into the fuel tank, then the end result was that they would not have to go over the top. It was an 'honourable' way out, one not available to the poor infantry, who after all could hardly plead mechanical breakdown: a broken bootlace did not have the same legitimacy. However, on 8 August this case was definitely the exception that proved the rule as only five of the tanks failed to go into action. This was little compensation to Smeddle who found his own section reduced at a stroke by a third as he trundled off with his two remaining tanks.

The first part of his progress was easy, even though the light mists made an occasional quick reference to his pocket compass essential. The tanks passed over first the British and then the German trenches, until they caught up with the infantry and stopped to refuel as planned in the Warfusée valley.

We then proceeded on to the first objective, which we found occupied by the first wave of infantry. They had advanced with but little opposition and few casualties, most having been caused by shell fire. At this point one of the official cinema operators came along and filmed my tanks as they were moving along. Shortly after this the enemy shell fire got a little more intense and two of my men who were walking outside their tank got wounded by splinters from a 4.2 high explosive that had burst near by. Their injuries were not serious so I sent them back to the dressing station on foot. The nose cap from a shell struck the tank 2 feet off my face, a terrific smack and ricocheted into the air with a 'BIZZZZZZZ'. Batches of prisoners kept coming along in numbers varying from two to one hundred.[27]

Captain Henry Smeddle, 15th Battalion, Tank Corps

The German Army was rocking on its heels but it was still capable of cobbling together a response even in the midst of disaster. Its aircraft were swiftly called into action, diving low over the battlefield, harassing the infantry below them.

A German plane now appeared, flying low and shooting at anything that it could see. We got to any cover we could find. I have never felt more wormlike in my life. No matter how deep the shell hole, one was still in full view of the plane.[28]

Private G. V. Rose, 30th Battalion, 8th Brigade, 5th Australian Division

Second Lieutenant John Fleming of 'U' Battery, 16th Brigade, Royal Horse Artillery was also attacked by German scouts as he took forward a section of their 18-pounder guns with the intention of engaging any German artillery firing in an anti-tank role. He was acting as a forward observation officer accompanying the front wave of infantry while the guns were following up with the second wave.

Our contact planes were buzzing about busily overhead dropping messages and, where needed, cases of ammunition. Out of the blue to the south of the line appeared five German fighting scouts. We heard afterwards that they were all aces who had flung themselves desperately into the battle to do all they could to hinder our advance. They went for our poor old 'beetles' bald-headed and I saw some quite fantastic flying. Our own planes came down to just above the front line for cover only a few hundred feet up, but the Huns never checked. One Fokker singled out an RE8 just above me and forced him down and down and down, until at last he actually landed near where I was. A whole battalion of Aussies was lying on their backs shooting at the Hun, but I'm dashed if that Fokker didn't turn again and shoot the RE8 up again on the ground. He was so low that I was brassing off at him with a revolver and his wing tips almost touched the ground as he turned and twisted like a woodcock with a squib attached to his tail. I still take my hat off to those Huns.[29]

Second Lieutenant John Fleming, 'U' Battery, 16th Brigade, Royal Horse Artillery

In that short but vicious dogfight the Germans succeeded in forcing down, one way or another, all the British contact aircraft in that sector. It was a desperately confusing situation as the aircraft of various sides buzzed low over the trenches at over 100 mph. Identification was often difficult with inevitable mistakes occurring on both sides.

Fritz had cleared out, but had left machine guns posted at intervals along the east–west road. Whenever these opened up we had to lie down. Herb Heathcote got a hit in the thigh. The stretcher bearers tied him up and wished him a safe trip to 'Blighty'. The tanks soon settled the machine guns. One would waddle over: a few vicious spits from the Hotchkiss and – finish Fritz's gun. They were game, those Fritzie gunners. They would fire their gun to the bitter end. No sign of our planes yet. Suddenly we saw a plane flying low coming right at us, about 20 feet up. We started firing, but discovered it was a Camel – one of ours![30]

Private G. V. Rose, 30th Battalion, 8th Brigade, 5th Australian Division

Meanwhile, having reached their second objectives Captain Smeddle found that the infantry had already pushed ahead without them, sensibly choosing to remain close to the creeping barrage rather than wait for the tanks. On they went trying to catch up. It was shortly afterwards that they came upon one of the best target opportunities of the whole war.

The enemy were evidently quite unaware of the rapidity of our advance for just as we were about opposite Harbonnières we saw an ammunition train steaming into the station as if nothing was the matter. It was immediately shelled by all the 6-pounder guns of the approaching tanks, and one must have struck a powder van for suddenly the whole train burst into one great sheet of flame reaching to a height of not less than 150 feet. Needless to say that train was stopped. It was followed by another, a passenger train rushing up fresh troops; this was running on another rail and ran right into our lines – it was captured complete with personnel.[31]

Captain Henry Smeddle, 15th Battalion, Tank Corps

However, in some sectors of the wide front the tanks had met serious opposition from concealed German batteries that had either not been identified before the battle or were unsuppressed for one reason or another by the blanket counter-battery fire. The *Niveleur* under the command of Lieutenant Mould and the other tanks of 14th Battalion, Tank Corps ran into severe difficulties in this fashion.

Then the trouble started; we had come in range of the German field guns in the wood. Shells started to fall all around us and so, according to our plan, the driver started to zigzag. He turned left and the gunners on that side started firing the 6-pounders, then he swung right and we

333

pumped some into the front of the wood; he turned left again and we looked to our right, and just then a huge blaze shot up into the air. It was one of our section tanks that had got a direct hit, and we knew they would have all gone west. It happened to be Mould's friend who was the officer of that bus and you could tell he was upset. Then further along the line another one went up. We were being blasted from all sides by now and the shells kept dropping and rocking the bus as they burst, but somehow missing us. We were getting nearer and nearer and could even see the gunners, but we had the advantage as we knew it is hard to hit a target with a field gun using open sights and we zigzagged on. Then all of a sudden they stopped firing and started to run away. Our guns had taken their toll and we left them to the Canadians to mop up, plastering the wood as we passed by with the left-hand gun.[32]

Private Charles Rowland, 14th Battalion, Tank Corps

Major Dillon, the reconnaissance officer of the 2nd Battalion, Tank Corps, was still advancing on foot when he ran into his own spot of bother from the German artillery.

There seemed to be very little hostile retaliation going on, so we hurried on in the hopes of seeing the war from a front seat. Unfortunately, a 77-mm field battery at about Warfusée had not been overrun and was cracking off any ammunition it could find. One of these, a shrapnel shell, burst on percussion between my legs, and that is all I know of the battle of 8 August in person. I was carried down the road by four German prisoners who were more anxious to get out of the battle than even I was. I remember seeing a very beautiful sight in Villers-Bretonneux on my way through – two or three very dirty and heavily bearded soldiers clad in camisoles and ladies panties and nothing much else. They had had their clothing saturated with mustard gas and the local dressing station had nothing but what they could find on the spot to clothe them with. From there, I was evacuated to hospital, and thence to England.[33]

Major Mark Dillon, 2nd Battalion, Tank Corps

In a sense, although he was wounded, Dillon was fortunate, for by this time every tank was a veritable hell on earth for the crews sweating buckets inside them.

It was like Dante's *Inferno* in the bus. You could hardly put a foot down for spent shell cases and cartridge cases, and could hardly breathe for the fumes of the engine, which was red hot by now, steam from the boiling water, and even the oil in the return tank was boiling over. Sweat was pouring out of us and we kept having a swig of water out of a petrol tin, when there was a chance, and the cordite fumes from the 6-pounders was nearly choking us; but we could do nothing about it.[34]

Private Charles Rowland, 14th Battalion, Tank Corps

The deadly carbon monoxide gas coupled with the noxious petrol fumes emanating from the engine and blended with the acrid cordite smoke from the guns, created a cocktail of misery for the crews in their randomly heaving tanks. The men were often nauseous, felt faint, suffered blinding headaches and were thoroughly deafened by the relentless noise. Lieutenant Mould's men alternated between tasks, pushing on, and at the same time pushing themselves to the very limits of human physical endurance.

We passed the wood into a cornfield; by this time I was in the driving seat again, and as we kept meeting machine-gun fire, we had to resort to the old zigzag again. We passed hundreds of Germans with their hands up, these we left for the Canadians to deal with, and in the late afternoon we reached our objective on the top of the ridge. The infantry came up and started to dig in, and at last we were able to open the doors and get out, only to fall in a heap on the ground on top of each other, out to the world. Gradually we came round and out came the bottle of rum, and we came to. We could not believe our eyes – in the valley below we could see the enemy piling stuff onto trucks on a train, men pulling out guns to get them away, and they were hauling in the observation balloons and trying to put them on their trucks. Utter chaos.[35]

Private Charles Rowland, 14th Battalion, Tank Corps

As they rested, there was an unpleasant scene. Many officers did not recognise that just a few hours fighting in a tank made a man unfit for duty for several days afterwards.

Captain Gilmour came up to congratulate us and *asked* Mould if he would take the 'bus' down into the valley. Note: he *asked*, did not order,

335

or else there might have been trouble later. After a heated argument, Mould told him straight, 'We are not going another bloody inch; my crew are absolutely exhausted being in nearly ten to twelve hours, and we are not capable of doing any more!' Gilmour replied, 'I will see you and your crew don't get any honours!' And he did just that. But that did not worry us, we had survived so far. It was late afternoon by now.[36]

Private Charles Rowland, 14th Battalion, Tank Corps

Their job was done, but before they moved back to laager up they saw the cavalry once again fail to make an impact. The situation might have seemed tailor-made for *L'Arme Blanche* but there were still problems in deploying the cavalry. The arrangements for them to work in conjunction with the Whippets often fell apart as the optimistic 7–8 mph claimed by the light tanks was reduced to about 3 mph across open country, even without shell holes and trenches. This left them miles behind the faster cavalry. They were also vulnerable. Private Eric Potten had been injured in an accident and was missing when his usual Whippet was hit by a shell during the fighting. The consequences were stomach turning.

I had to go up and see what we could manage to save from the tank. We had to get the instruments out, the guns, had to salvage anything we could. The tank was completely smashed up, it had had a direct hit right at the front. I never ate any bully beef after that for years. They were splashed all over the inside of the tank. Blast and fire. Terrible! Awful![37]

Private Eric Potten, 6th Battalion, Tank Corps

Nevertheless, there was some deft exploitation work carried out by individual Whippets. Of these the most famous was the *Musical Box* commanded by Lieutenant Clement Arnold of the 6th Battalion, Tank Corps. At first there was some mystery as to what had happened to Arnold and his crew as their Whippet was last seen in hot pursuit of the Germans east of Harbonnières. Their abandoned burnt-out tank was found surrounded by German corpses and nearby Australian infantry told a tale of a valiant derring-do. Lieutenant Arnold and his crew of two (Driver William Carnie and Gunner Christopher Ribbans) were reported missing, and there the matter would rest until after the war when he returned from a prisoner-of-war camp in Germany. Arnold and his crew had moved 2,000 yards cross-country to the south of the railway line at Villers-Bretonneux. Here they ran into their first trouble from the German artillery.

> We came under direct shell fire from a four-gun field battery, of which I could see the flashes, between Abancourt and Bayonvillers. Two Mark V tanks, 150 yards away on my right front, were knocked out. I saw clouds of smoke coming out of these machines and the crews evacuate them. The infantry following the heavy machines were suffering casualties from this battery. I turned half left and ran diagonally across the front of the battery, at a distance of about 600 yards. Both my guns were able to fire on the battery, in spite of which they got off about 8 rounds at me without damage, but sufficiently close to be audible inside the cab, and I could see the flash of each gun as it fired.[38]
>
> Lieutenant Clement Arnold, 6th Battalion, Tank Corps

This was not a fair fight: normally a Whippet would have been a reasonably easy target for a battery of guns manned by determined crews. But something was wrong with the German gunners that day and they just kept missing their target.

> From the nearness with which the shells were dropping it was evident that we had been spotted. By driving a curving zigzag course we made it difficult for the enemy battery to get anything like good shooting. At first we could not locate the exact position of the guns, but on getting to a slight rise in the ground, we could see them through the slight mist. We altered our course slightly to the left and succeeded in getting alongside the guns.[39]
>
> Gunner Christopher Ribbans, 6th Battalion, Tank Corps

Once they were behind and in amidst the guns the Germans were utterly helpless.

> By this time I had passed behind a belt of trees running along the roadside. I ran along this belt until level with the battery, when I turned full right and engaged the battery from the rear. On observing our appearance from the belt of trees, the gunners, some thirty in number,

abandoned their guns and tried to get away. Gunner Ribbans and I accounted for the whole lot.[40]

Lieutenant Clement Arnold, 6th Battalion, Tank Corps

This had been a significant action and undoubtedly saved lives amongst both the Australian infantry and other tank crews. After a short while Arnold pushed on, briefly linking up with cavalry patrols. He then attacked an area of German billet huts in a valley located between Bayonvillers and Harbonnières. Here he caught a large number of German troops engaged in packing their kits to make their escape.

> On our opening fire on the nearest, many others appeared from the huts, making for the end of the valley, their object being to get over the embankment and so out of sight. We accounted for many of these. I cruised around, Ribbans went into one of the huts and returned, and we counted about sixty dead and wounded. There were evidences of shell fire amongst the huts, but we certainly accounted for most of the casualties counted there. I turned left from the railway and cruised across country, as lines of enemy infantry could be seen retiring. We fired at these many times at a range of 200 yards to 600 yards. These targets were fleeting, owing to the enemy getting down into the corn when fired upon. In spite of this, many casualties must have been inflicted, for we cruised up and down for at least an hour.[41]

Lieutenant Clement Arnold, 6th Battalion, Tank Corps

The *Musical Box* was badly isolated by this time and began to come under escalating amounts of heavy machine-gun fire, which raked across the tank seeking out a weakness. Eventually it found one.

> The enemy machine-gunners kept up a fairly constant hailstorm of bullets on the cabin walls. We discovered that the spare tins of petrol on top of the 'bus' had been perforated and the petrol began to run down the inside of the tank. Naturally, as soon as the liquid came in contact with the hot air inside the machine, it began to vaporise and we soon began to feel sick and light-headed. Lieutenant Arnold had the great presence of mind to order, 'Gas masks on!' This action undoubtedly saved us from being gassed. The fire from the machine guns became more and more intense, and, in one part of the cabin, the armoured plating appeared to be red hot from the concentrated fire of explosive

bullets. Splinters were coming through every crack and every loophole.[42]

Gunner Christopher Ribbans, 6th Battalion, Tank Corps

They were lucky the Whippet did not catch fire. The combination of the fumes, the excessive heat from the engine and the copious amounts of bullet splash whipping all across the interior of the Whippet, made conditions almost unbearable. Nevertheless, Arnold pushed on, launching a solo attack on a mass of German motor and horse transport. Arnold and Ribbans fired to their hearts' content, causing considerable carnage and even more panic as the roads were blocked.

We met the most intense rifle and machine-gun fire imaginable, from all sides. When at all possible we returned the fire, until the left-hand revolver port cover was shot away. I withdrew the forward gun, locked the mounting and held the body of the gun against the hole. Petrol was still running down the inside of the back door. Fumes and heat combined were very bad. We were still moving forward and I was shouting to Driver Carnie to turn about as it was impossible to continue the action, when two heavy concussions closely followed one other. And the cab burst into flames.[43]

Lieutenant Clement Arnold, 6th Battalion, Tank Corps

Their incredible run of luck had come to an abrupt end.

A tremendous explosion! The vaporised petrol inside the tank had been ignited. I was thrown onto the floor and became unconscious for a few seconds. When I came to I found my clothing on fire and everything around me. My face and hands were badly burnt. I immediately jumped from the burning tank, only to be received by a hail of machine-gun bullets. I dropped to the ground.[44]

Gunner Christopher Ribbans, 6th Battalion, Tank Corps

In fact, in the total confusion and panic of the burning Whippet, the impressively cool Arnold seems to have got his semi-conscious crew through the door.

Carnie and Ribbans got to the door and collapsed. I was almost overcome, but managed to get the door open and fell out on the ground and was able to drag out the other two men. Burning petrol was running out onto the ground where we were lying. The fresh air revived us and we all got up and made a short rush to get away from the burning petrol. In this rush Carnie was shot in the stomach and killed. We rolled over and over to try to extinguish the flames. I saw numbers of the enemy approaching from all round. The first arrival came for me with rifle and bayonet. I got hold of this and the point of the bayonet entered my right forearm. The second man struck at my head with the butt end of his rifle, hit my shoulder and neck, and knocked me down. When I came to, there were dozens all around me, and anyone who could reach me did so, and I was well kicked; they were furious.[45]

Lieutenant Clement Arnold, 6th Battalion, Tank Corps

Lieutenant Clement Arnold and Gunner Christopher Ribbans were taken prisoner and duly marched off. Their driver, William Carnie, had indeed been killed.

This courageous episode may reflect great credit on the three individuals concerned, but although subsequently much publicised post-war, this was the exception that proved the rule as far as the overall effectiveness of Whippets in action was concerned. They were useful but few had the run of sustained luck that enabled *Musical Box* to avoid being knocked out as it should logically have been by the first German battery of guns it encountered, avoid mechanical breakdown, avoid a bullet hitting something vital and, most of all, avoid bursting into flames rather earlier. To some the episode created a vision of marauding tanks penetrating deep behind the German lines and causing mayhem, but the Whippet was not that weapon of war. It, too, was a work in progress. Yet the Whippets seemed to have more of a future than the cavalry. They may have been slower, but when they encountered the Germans they were far more bullet-proof than men on horseback. When the cavalry went it alone they were dreadfully vulnerable to machine guns and suffered heavy casualties.

Despite this, the British achievements so far in the battle had been considerable. The German artillery had been rendered largely inoperative and irrelevant to the battle as their crews were for the most part killed or neutralised before being overrun by the advancing tanks and infantry. The Canadian and Australian Corps had an unalloyed success. There was hard fighting in places, but they achieved nearly all their objectives along the old Amiens Defence Line. Even when they had outrun the range of their own field artillery the absence of German artillery was critical. Without their lethal intervention the new British tank and infantry tactics combined with the intelligent use of Lewis guns, rifle grenades and Stokes mortars meant that German machine-gun posts and strongpoints were overwhelmed by the sheer firepower deployed against them.

The advance of the III Corps north of the Somme had been far less pronounced and with good reason. This was not a fresh formation preserved by special design for an offensive. It was an ordinary British corps and as such was made up of divisions that had been through the mill several times already in 1918. The ranks were therefore not only denuded of experienced officers and NCOs but also made up of young drafts fresh from home and with no practical experience to guide them. On top of this a coincidental local German attack on 6 August un-knowingly acted as an effective spoiler to their preparations. The hard fighting that stretched into 7 August, the day before the British were due to attack, had further drained the strength and vigour from two of the intended assault divisions. Geography was also against them, as the ground between the Somme and the Ancre was a narrow plateau cut by a series of gullies and spurs, that were most helpful to the defence. Perhaps because of this terrain, III Corps had only thirty-six tanks deployed in its sector. So it was not terribly surprising that the results achieved by the III Corps were nowhere near as dramatic as those achieved by the Australian and Canadian Corps to the south. In particular, the Chipilly Spur reached out into the Somme valley to provide both excellent observation and a gun platform beyond the range of the British field artillery.

We had to attack the ridge. It was a fairly long ridge. Unknown to us there were from ten to twenty heavy German machine guns in emplacements. My God, he really opened up! He let us have it. He just swept us. I looked round as I was advancing and you could see the numbers of our people melting away, just dropping all around you. Those that fell were still shot over again. There were no orders – nothing! There was nothing you could do. It was getting so bad, as I took my steps I thought, 'The next one will be it!' But, of course, you didn't know what being hit was. I jumped for this big shell hole. Fortunately, it was empty, no water in it. I wouldn't have minded if it had, I'd have gone in! I knew there was no hope of getting any orders because there was nobody to give any. The bullets were hitting the back of the shell hole; it was raining bullets.[46]

Private Bill Gillman, 2/2nd Battalion, London Regiment, 173rd Brigade, 58th Division

The attacks, not unnaturally in the circumstances, failed. Flesh and blood was not, and never would be, proof against machine-gun bullets. Even in the All Arms Battle mistakes could be made and the threat of the ridge had not been adequately allowed for in the plans. The III Corps was generally held up on its first objectives – although there was still an advance of up to 2,500 yards, which might in previous battles have been regarded as a reasonable accomplishment.

Overall, by any standards the Battle of Amiens was still an incredible success: in a single day the bulk of the Fourth Army advanced some 8 miles on a 10-mile front with the French conforming to the south. The Germans had suffered 27,700 casualties, of which over 15,000 were prisoners of war. They had lost over 400 guns and large numbers of mortars and machine guns. This was a disaster and Ludendorff summed it up quite pithily: 'August 8 was the black day of the German Army in the history of this war.'[47]

All this had been achieved at the loss of 'only' 9,000 British casualties and relatively light French casualties. One strange element of this was to be found in an Australian unit not directly involved – they were jealous.

It might have been expected that our men of the 13th Brigade had had enough fighting of recent weeks, and would have been content to sit back and let others have a go. But that was not the way they looked at it. Seeing hundreds of prisoners coming back, and hearing from their guards that the battle had been a cake-walk, they felt aggrieved that having done more than their share of the dirty work when things were hard, others were now getting all the fun when the going was good. But there was no need for them to worry – they were soon called upon to take a hand.[48]

Captain Thomas Louch, Headquarters, 13th Brigade, 4th Australian Division

There would indeed be plenty of fighting left for the men of the 13th Australian Brigade over the next few months.

One worrying feature was the heavy wastage in tanks. The Mark V was not really fit for purpose. It broke down with incredible frequency and if the machine endured, then frequently the half-poisoned crews could not. The slow-moving monstrosities were also an easy target if they did happen to run into any surviving German field artillery. For one reason or another, of the 415 tanks that went into action on 8 August only 145 were ready to resume the attack next morning. One of those still fit for action was the *Niveleur*, which was laid up at the rallying point.

We were getting news of the losses from various crews. They had been heavy. We had lost two out of four in our section alone, and all this made one very depressed. There were lads in the crews who we had trained with in England, and we knew more or less all of them. Our two tanks had received direct hits and they would have had no chance to get out, and were burned alive. But we had no time to ponder on this. Our orders now were 'Get your "buses" ready for action!' And so, although pretty exhausted, we set about, as there was not a lot of daylight left. First we cleared out all the 6-pounder spent cases and the spent cartridge cases from the machine guns, so we could move inside. The chief mechanic set about the engine, cleaning all spark plugs, carburettors, starting gear, seeing to the tappits, going all over, he made sure his 'baby' was in perfect order. What an asset he was to the crew. He was marvellous. While other crews had all sorts of trouble with the engine ours was running sweetly, and we all realised that meant life or death, and we appreciated his craftsmanship. We were outside tightening up the tracks, which was a hefty job, done with a spanner some 14–16 inches long with a tube attachment fitted on, so two men could get some leverage on. We did not seem to have much strength for this, but we had to do it. All the grease points on the track had to be filled up by the grease gun. Machine guns taken to pieces and oiled. The 6-pounder guns cleaned and oiled. Petrol and oil and water to be put in; the 6-pounder shells, in racks to be filled up; the strips for the machine guns replaced; drinking water tank to be refilled – endless jobs to do. All the stuff we required had to be brought up by supply tanks and lorries, following us as we advanced, So it went on until dusk when we went inside, put the lights on and finished off in there. When we had decided that we could do no more at the bus, we were told to snatch a few hours sleep, so we just picked a spot on the ground outside and lay down, tired out.[49]

Private Charles Rowland, 14th Battalion, Tank Corps

The vulnerability of tanks to concealed field artillery operating in anti-tank mode was such that in future battles 8 Squadron RAF whose army cooperation aircraft were assigned to liaise with the tanks, would be augmented by a scout squadron in an effort to identify, strafe and bomb anti-tank positions from the air. The tank, like the infantry and the artillery, was not a stand-alone weapon and had clear weaknesses as well as strengths. It could not operate alone and when bereft of the right kind of support it was all but useless. The tank's value lay in what it brought to the All Arms equation. Amiens, not Cambrai, was when the tank was fully integrated into the British All Arms Battle.

THE BATTLE OF AMIENS had achieved the initial objectives as defined by Rawlinson, but the expansion by Haig and Foch of the scope of the operation to aim at the Chaulnes–Roye Line and even Ham meant that the Fourth Army was by no means done yet. The advance of 8 miles engendered its own problems for the British. Firstly, and most importantly, the artillery was left miles behind and although the field artillery was swiftly on the move, the heavy artillery so important for counter-battery fire would take days to bring forward and prepare for action. Secondly, the logistical problems were also intense. The British lines of communications now effectively ended some 8 miles behind the new front line and all the ammunition, shells, fuel, food, water and ancillary supplies that the infantry, artillery and tanks would need had to be got forward. No one knew exactly where all the units or their headquarters were located, telephone lines were being pushed forwards at a pace, but there was still a general air of confusion and a huge dislocation of command and control. These, of course, were the kind of endemic problems that had dogged the Germans during their advances earlier in the year. Technology had made rapid advances during the

Great War but the complex communications required by an army on the move were still haphazard or non-existent. As military operations in 1918 could be defined by their necessity for complete control, it is obvious in retrospect that a continued successful advance on 9 August would be extremely problematic. Orders were issued at various levels of command: some contradictory, some countermanded, some late and some that never arrived. No one knew what the units on their flanks were doing, few could be sure that they would have the tank and artillery support they needed if they were to avoid heavy casualties. They also had no idea of what the Germans were up to, an important consideration for generals with the highest respect for German defensive fighting skills. Finally, the left flank of the Australian Corps was potentially exposed by the failure of the III Corps to keep pace on the other side of the Somme River. The end result was chaos: units attacked independently with a variety of random Zero Hours spread across the day, unsupported on their flanks and usually lacking either artillery or tank support. The troops on the ground were exposed to both artillery and machine-gun fire from the Germans. It should have been a disaster, a tale of hopeless heroism, dreadful casualties and perhaps a devastating German counter-attack. But miraculously it wasn't.

It was hard fighting and there were increasing casualties, but on 9 August the Fourth Army managed to advance 3 miles. The reason was simple. While the British were disorganised the Germans were in a far worse situation. They had no well-organised defence lines or Battle Zone behind them. Just like the British on 22 March the badly smashed-up divisions holding the line fell back in chaos and the reserve units moving forwards were sucked into a vortex of confusion. For that in essence was the point – there was no line to coalesce upon, nothing concrete that they could cling to. Most of the German divisions rushing to the front had left their artillery to follow on and, in many cases, they were already exhausted by the relentless demands of the German offensives in 1918.

The British troops certainly noticed that the fighting that day was an altogether tougher proposition. The *Niveleur* was involved in intensive fighting in the battle to take the town of Rosières. To add to the crew's difficulties they were ordered to take with them into the attack two infantrymen and their Lewis gun to help consolidate ground gained until the rest of the infantry could get forward. This may have seemed a good idea but this was not an elongated Mark V* and there was barely any room for the usual crew let alone passengers.

We could see other tanks moving at the same time and with the infantry close behind. The terrain was awful; one minute the nose of the bus was in a deep shell hole and the next minute the nose was high up in the air. And when one was driving, trying to avoid as many bumps as possible, when the point of balance was reached, slithering here and there, lop-sided sometimes, and the failure to get out of the holes first time, so we tried this way and that. And now we ran into shell fire pretty heavy, with the machine-gun bullets rattling on both sides. Then we came to a level piece of ground. Mould ordered us to put all guns in action, to blaze our way forward. The noise was terrific: two 6-pounders going and our machine guns. The atmosphere was starting to cloud with the fumes from the guns, and the engine was getting very hot by now. The two infantrymen who were trying to keep their feet, trying not to get in our way, they were sweltered and being sick all over the place, which was a shambles! We had run right into the opposition and they were giving us hell. Slowly going forward, zigzagging when we could, we had to get over his trenches and drive him out, but we seemed to make no impression and just crawled forward, hoping we would not get hit. We had just started on a level keel, when one of the infantrymen shouted, 'We're on fire!'[50]

Private Charles Rowland, 14th Battalion, Tank Corps

Burning alive in a mass of flames and exploding ammunition was not a pleasant prospect. But as they bailed out they found themselves right in the middle of the intense battle, with Germans all around them.

You only get one warning like that in a tank and you make for the door. Everyone dropped everything, and what a scramble there was for the two doors, not the easiest of doors to open, undoing the bolts (to keep out the enemy) and the very weight of them to push open – seemed ages before the first man was out. Mould shouted, 'Get to the back! Draw your revolvers!' and this is where we made for. We knew we would collapse as usual, meeting the air, so nobody stood, and with subconscious mind crawled one by one to the back of the bus. It seemed a mile. There we were all eight of us crouched down, dazed and pretty hopeless, and we could not believe our eyes when we looked around. We had dropped out right among the Germans, so close we could even see their faces, and we guessed our number was up. And what surprised us most after a minute or two, they never fired a shot at us; we were a supreme target. Whether they thought it was a trick or not we never knew. But what confidence a revolver gives you, although it was no earthly use in these circumstances. After about five minutes Mould said, 'I am going to crawl back and see, and will give you a knock on the shell of the bus if you can return.' He crawled back and got in. We waited, and then the knocking came, and we decided to go in, using both doors. The first one got in safely, but when the Germans saw what was happening, they opened fire. Never did that few yards seem like miles. I hugged the ground and dived in head first, with the bullets hitting the side of the tank as I did so, but missing me. One by one the remainder crawled into safety, all without being hit, except the last man, the Yorkshireman in the crew. Blood was streaming down his face. He must have been hit in his head.[51]

Private Charles Rowland, 14th Battalion, Tank Corps

It had all been a false alarm as one of the soldiers had obviously panicked as the machine-gun and rifle fire hitting the tank sides caused white hot flecks of molten splash to spatter over the crew or perhaps he had just found the engine fumes and thickening cordite smoke too much to bear. Back in the tank they were still under heavy fire. By now everyone was panicking to some extent.

Mould was shouting and getting the engine running, 'Open fire with everything!' so we started to blast away. We had not time to think about Firth who was wounded. The two infantrymen had passed out and we were scrambling over them. Steam was starting to fill the place, and the cordite fumes were choking you. Then one of the Scotch lads noticed Firth was firing a machine gun, with the barrel facing our incoming infantry, our own soldiers. He tried to pull him off, but could not. He had gone berserk with the wound in his head, so he gave him a left and knocked him out. The only thing to do and with a struggle we dumped him out (as we had in fun promised to do previously), but not before our own infantry had come up, and somebody would look after him (which we heard later they had done). Mould decided after cruising and zigzagging that we had done what we set out to do, so we dropped the two men with the machine gun, as the infantry had caught up with us and were digging in, and about-turned, still being pounded all round with shells, which kept bursting too close for comfort. And when we thought we could get out, we did just that; stopped and collapsed, recovered slightly, and then Mould got out the hard stuff. After a good swig we started talking, something we had not been able to do for hours, as it was now past noon and we had been in action since 4 a.m., and were beat.[52]

Private Charles Rowland, 14th Battalion, Tank Corps

Meanwhile, for the infantry it was altogether a more chaotic affair. The Canadians moved forwards the most and were still somewhat inclined not to take prisoners following the unambivalent orders of Major General Sir Archibald Macdonell commanding the 1st Canadian Division.

The Major General's next order of battle came as a bit of a surprise as it was passed along from man to man, 'Advance will recommence at 2 p.m. Prisoners are a nuisance.' That was the latest view of the Hun – who had been slaughtering us for over four years on the Western Front, whose deadly submarines had hardly left us with a bite to eat, and who, in spite of the beating he had taken the day before, was still holding out on us. I never heard a single man question, 'Prisoners are a nuisance' and as far as I was concerned I wholeheartedly agreed.[53]

Corporal William Kerr, 5th (Western Cavalry) Battalion, 2nd Brigade, 1st Canadian Division

So did the civilised rules of warfare gradually break down under the pressure of total war. It is noticeable that there is no mention of tanks in many of the accounts.

Zero Hour was set for one-thirty in the afternoon when the slow and deliberate attack was continued and the 'jumping off' place for the 2nd Battalion was at Gentiles Wood. 'Heinie' had evidently recovered sufficiently to round up some of his artillery judging by the barrage that greeted us. He sent over a varied assortment of pepper gas, tear gas, poison gas, machine guns, whizz-bangs and 'five nines'. And by the careless manner in which those things were falling in our midst, it was quite evident that we were going to spend a very merry afternoon. No sooner had we got nicely under way than the boys began to drop, and yet, no matter how many got knocked out there were always the lucky few to carry on to the end. Poor old Lieutenant Ferguson, absolutely fearless and exceedingly popular among the boys of No. 2 Company. I can picture him now as he was that day, so unlike his natural self. He had a sort of dejected look about him and told us that he was going to 'get his' that day. How he knew is something we don't quite understand. He got it all right, a piece of shrapnel through the head. I was *with* him at the time; just another 'C-R-R-UMP' and he slumped to the ground – dying instantly. And so it was for the remainder of that afternoon – just one after another – many of them out for good, some writhing in agony, perhaps breathing their last, with the more fortunate ones able to navigate back to some field dressing station. All tremendously eager with the thought of a possible trip to 'Blighty' to spur them on.[54]

Lance Corporal Kenneth Foster, 2nd (Eastern Ontario) Battalion, 1st Brigade, 1st Canadian Division

When they took a trench many of the Canadians took a swift and bloody revenge for their losses in accordance with their orders. Consolidation was important, but they had no time to waste on the niceties.

They were hiding down in their deep dugouts. I could hardly believe our luck. The trench was ours, but we had to make sure. With barely a minute to get on with it, and still thinking of the men I had just seen mown down, I flung a Mills bomb down the steps of three of their dugouts and heard them explode as I leapt out of the trench to continue the advance. 'Orders is orders!' I thought.[55]

Corporal William Kerr, 5th (Western Cavalry) Battalion, 2nd Brigade, 1st Canadian Division

Kerr and his men had gone another 200 yards or so towards a small orchard. Then he became aware of a succession of near misses as bullets flew past him.

I felt sure some blighter was aiming at me personally. I tried hard to spot where the shots were coming from, but it was not until we got a bit

further and had taken some evading action, that I spotted a small
pillbox with its black mouth and the shots coming from it. I had my
Lewis gunner cover it until I got just behind it, in time to see a German
soldier coming out of the entrance and holding a small flag with a red
cross in front of him. 'You bloody twister!' I thought and aimed my rifle
at his chest to let him have it. But the sight was covering the cross and
at the last moment I hesitated. But so sure was I that he was the man
who had been firing at us, I was not going to let him get away with it. I
lowered the barrel and shot him in the calf of the leg. You could have
heard his screams a mile away. 'Put a bomb in the pillbox!' I called over
to one of my men, 'To make sure it is out of action!'[56]

Corporal William Kerr, 5th (Western Cavalry) Battalion, 2nd Brigade, 1st Canadian
Division

The Canadians had long ago learnt the importance of making sure that
there were no Germans left lurking behind them. Mopping up was
an important part of battlefield tactics that was ignored at their peril.
They were helped over the next section by a couple of Whippet tanks but
shortly after they had wandered off on another mission. The Canadians'
progress was then stymied by a well-sited German machine-gun post.

The whole line of advance was completely held up by a kind of hamlet
by a machine gun 300 yards away pouring its bullets into the low road
bank that gave the only cover. The tanks, which had been flitting about
from one part of the advance to another, had gone and would not be
back with us for fifteen minutes. There came a hurried getting together
of officers and they right away came up with the answer! 'Corporal
Kerr,' ordered Captain Lloyd, 'you will take your Lewis gun section
and disperse that machine gun!' 'My God!' I thought! Just like that. No
time to plan a best way or give this dangerous task a single thought. Just
up section and at them. 'Very good, Sir!' I replied and spread my
section with myself on the left, the Lewis gunner with the gun towards
the right and the men with the magazines in between, 'Right, now!' I
shouted and over the open field we went. We set off in bursts of 50
yards and then, 'Down!' but had only managed a couple of dashes
when the machine gun opened up with a vengeance and one man got
hit. At the next burst the brave machine-gunner fell, never to rise again.
I noticed that the German trench – apparently now deserted except

350

where the machine-gunners were operating – was much nearer me than the machine-gun position. So when the next dash was made, I made double the distance, lobbed a grenade into the trench and jumped in behind the explosion. I ran along the trench and lobbed another bomb ahead of me to make sure, and by the time I had gone another 50 yards, what was left of my section was dropping in beside me, one after the other. The enemy gunners appeared now to have gone and in no time the advance was up with us. It was not long before we came upon the Germans, two lots of three – and one way or another they paid for it, all of them.[57]

Corporal William Kerr, 5th (Western Cavalry) Battalion, 2nd Brigade, 1st Canadian Division

Kerr was amply rewarded, being promoted in the field to acting sergeant and awarded the Military Medal. Shortly after he was given a task that clearly indicated that the penalty of failure in battle was often far more prosaic.

I was ordered to take my section and search for dead bodies and bury them wherever found. There was neither men nor time to do anything else with them until later, when they would be dug up again and properly buried elsewhere. The order also stipulated that their identity discs be removed and handed in, and markers put up at the spots where the dead were buried. Some seven or eight were thus put out of sight for the time being, but none without at least a couple of words of sympathy from their still-alive mates, whose own turn it might be next.[58]

Corporal William Kerr, 5th (Western Cavalry) Battalion, 2nd Brigade, 1st Canadian Division

Some of the battlefield burials carried out by the troops were even more functional. One grave dug by the Australians aroused the subsequent mirth of Second Lieutenant John Fleming when he moved forward later in the battle.

Some of the graves dotting a battlefield had inscriptions, often macabre as in the case of one I saw – that of a German killed during an Australian advance. To the man's rifle had been pinned a sheet of cardboard on which was scrawled in chalk:

Here you lie, brother Boche

Your Pals won't bury you, Hindenburg won't bury you,

   your Kaiser won't bury you; they can't.

But the poor bloody Aussie will bury you, because YOU STINK![59]

Second Lieutenant John Fleming, 'U' Battery, 16th Brigade, Royal Horse Artillery

This was the brutal reality of war in 1918. Little scope here for romantic ideals of death and imperishable glory.

The final dimension of the Battle of Amiens was that of the air. The RAF had been charged with a distinct interdiction role in cutting off the battlefield so that the Germans would have difficulty in bringing forward reserves. The relative success of these operations had led to a decision to try and cut the bridges over the Somme River with a series of determined bombing raids. The idea was not only to prevent the arrival of the reserves but also to trap the bulk of the German Second Army on the west side of the Somme. As the Fourth Army fought its way forward the RAF was engaged in a desperate series of bombing raids, while the equally desperate and determined German Air Service tried to fend it off. The aerial fighting was intense with over 700 bombing missions flown and 57 tons of bombs dropped on the bridges. For three days the RAF tried its very best, accepting dreadful casualties that trimmed the day bomber squadrons, in particular, to the bone. But, here again, there was a weapon that was not yet powerful enough to achieve ambitious aspirations. Bridges are small targets difficult to hit from high altitudes and were well protected by massed anti-aircraft guns and machine guns if the bombers flew low. Most of the bombs exploded harmlessly in the Somme River where only the fish suffered. Even when the bridges were hit the 112-lb bombs were simply too small to do much more than superficial damage that could be quickly repaired. Finally, in concentrating on such a small, localised target they were helping the hard-pressed German scouts and anti-aircraft defences who knew where they were going – which was, of course, half the battle. The RAF would have been far better off concentrating on the railway system that was funnelling the reserve divisions into the area. Railways were easier targets and had the great benefit of being easily damaged and indeed from 10 August the focus of the bombing attacks was duly widened.

*

BY 10 AUGUST the law of diminishing returns was exerting its inevitable pressure on the British ground offensive. The Fourth Army was weakening as it fought its way forward, with just one fresh British division being added to its strength, while the Germans were being steadily reinforced despite the best efforts of the RAF. On 8 August six new German divisions were moved up, three more appeared on 9 August and another four on 10 August. The Allied superiority of numbers had disappeared. In addition, none of the British command, control or communications problems of the previous day had been resolved. Indeed, the extra 3-mile advance on 9 August had only added to the overall sense of confusion and a general chaos. Once again there were different start times, units attacked without support from the flanks and there was a lack of properly planned artillery work. The advances made were nowhere near as spectacular with the best achievement being made by the Canadian Corps, which managed to get forward another 2 miles. The French had the best of the day, as their First Army pushed forward level with the Canadians and occupied the town of Montdidier. They also widened the frontage of the attack by a further 10 miles by throwing into action the French Third Army. All these advances came to an abrupt end when they encountered a German line that was offering a serious level of resistance. The Germans were occupying the copious trenches that had formed the front lines back in February 1917 before they had voluntarily withdrawn to the fastness of the Hindenburg Line. These would not have been a problem to the new British All Arms tactics, but as we have seen the Fourth Army was in no fit state to deploy these tactics. With the artillery in chaos and the tanks mostly out of action it was an old-style confused battle, with old-style casualties.

It was by then a rarity, but the Mark V tank *Niveleur* was still capable of going into action after its exertions over the previous two days. Only sixty or so of the original armada of tanks were still in action on the morning of 10 August. The night before the tank crews had prepared for battle, but this time their preparations were much more rudimentary. There were no photographs of the ground to study this time and no arrangements for a supporting artillery barrage

We set off with the infantry following us for shelter. The terrain was terrible, driving was difficult, we were a man short in the crew and this meant longer spells at any one job. We got a worse reception from the Germans than the day before. How we escaped a direct hit, I never knew. We kept all our guns blazing away when we were on an even keel, and it was hell again. Moving forward at a crawl, in and out of trenches and shell holes, we were getting knocked about, to add to our already black and blue bodies. We made progress, then an infantry officer stopped the tank, to tell us some infantry were held up in the ruins of what was once a village; the Germans were in the cellars and causing havoc among his men. Would we go through and blast them out? It was on our right so Mould told the driver to switch in that direction and we made for the rubble, and decided to go up what was once the main street. With all guns going at both sides, we blasted the cellars, going through and back again, and never saw any Germans. With that the infantry followed as we once more blasted the place, and they got through, and we set off again, zigzagging trying to miss the shell fire. By this time the air in the bus was non-existent, and we were sweltered, and after cruising around, Mould decided, seeing we had got the infantry through to their objective, to about-turn and leave them to it. And we made our journey back to a new rallying point, which we reached just after noon, we had been in the tank since dawn, about nine hours, and as usual we collapsed and it was quite some time before we could pull ourselves together, to brew up and have something to eat, and then to clean up the tank and ourselves. Then the word came through we were to pull out of action for a refit and rest. We greeted this with glee. We had been in action three days non-stop, and beaten to the world physically.[60]

Private Charles Rowland, 14th Battalion, Tank Corps

Lieutenant William Tobey of the 16th Lancashire Fusiliers was advancing along the Amiens road towards the battalion's objective of Roye.

We came under machine-gun fire and the platoons closed up and lined a thick hedge. We could hear machine-gun bullets thudding into the hedge and passing overhead. I was enormously pleased that I could stick it; I felt enormously braced. I felt that I was at the spear point of history being made. I felt we had to go forward, if they taught you one thing at Sandhurst it was that if you tried to get forward, you couldn't go far wrong! So I said to my company commander, 'Should I take my platoon forward?' He said rather hesitatingly, 'Yes, all right!' I jumped through the hedge, called to my men to follow and I ran forward. I felt something hit me on the thigh and at the same time I saw great numbers of Germans getting up and running away up the valley opposite to us. My batman Booth was with me and I said to him, 'I think I've been hit!' He and I got into a big shell hole and thought things over. The machine gun was traversing, playing over our heads, you could hear the bullets. Then the machine gun relented and I looked out. Over to the right I saw a squadron of French cuirassiers charging. They were mown down, I saw them all fall. I had a thought, 'Well this lets me off, if they can't get forward, I'm justified in being in my shell hole!' I don't know to this day whether they were real dragoons or a hallucination brought on by my excited and tired state![61]

Second Lieutenant William Tobey, 16th Battalion, Lancashire Fusiliers, 96th Brigade, 32nd Division

Tobey and his men occupied an old trench that had been part of the German front line way back in July 1916. As they took a breather they became aware that ground to air cooperation still required some refining.

An RAF plane came over, circled round and began to bomb us. They threw several bombs, I got a piece in the arm and my men said to me, 'Won't you let us shoot the bugger down?' I said, 'No, not on any account!' My men were carrying little shiny tin discs and we were supposed to catch the reflection of the sun and shine up at any plane that was playing these tricks. This we did and the RAF bloke sheered off.[62]

Second Lieutenant William Tobey, 16th Battalion, Lancashire Fusiliers, 96th Brigade, 32nd Division

The next arrival was to be a tank. It, too, failed to materially assist the infantry.

A solitary tank came up. It stopped and the commander came out and said, 'What's going on here?' We said, 'Well, we're held up by a machine gun on the left and if you go forward and attack him, we'll come after you!' In this trench there was a wide causeway put there by the Germans and he could have crossed by it. But instead the tank commander drove the tank straight forward at the trench. It tipped into it but it then hadn't got the power to pull itself out, the tracks simply slipped: it couldn't climb out. The tank commander and the crew came out and we were left there with this tank with its nose sticking up in the air. We realised it was going to be a very dangerous thing to be near, so we moved away. It attracted an absolute hail of machine-gun fire and an anti-tank gun. It was soon set on fire and its innards poured out in the shape of ball bearings and molten metal – it was red hot.[63]

Second Lieutenant William Tobey, 16th Battalion, Lancashire Fusiliers, 96th Brigade, 32nd Division

Tobey and his men stood by to await the inevitable German counter-attack. It was evident that they were not going to receive any worth-while support in the near future.

On the left of the causeway I had a section of my platoon and they came under a terrible enfilade fire from a small anti-tank gun. One of the men was hit in the chest and split open like a herring. It was the first man I had seen killed in action. I thought it was better to get the man behind the causeway. Corporal Cave had broken a leg, couldn't move and was left behind. As we went away he said, 'Don't leave me behind, Sir!' I said, 'I won't, I'll come for you!' The rest of us crossed the causeway and settled into the other part of the trench. Then we could see a bombing attack developing along the trench to the left. I said to the men, 'I want three volunteers to go and carry Corporal Cave back here!' Three men stepped forward, one of which was the only black man in the battalion. I said, 'You go and I'll give you covering fire!' I got up on the top of the causeway with a Lewis gun and as my men went into the trench I fired over their heads at where the bombing was coming from. After a few rounds the gun jammed with dirty ammuni-tion – I put it down and took a rifle. At any rate the bombers didn't come forward any more and we got the corporal safely away and down the line on a stretcher.[64]

Second Lieutenant William Tobey, 16th Battalion, Lancashire Fusiliers, 96th Brigade, 32nd Division

Tobey and his men couldn't possibly get any further. They set about consolidating the trench ready for whatever the Germans could throw at them.

> We beat off a counter-attack with a classical, 'At the enemy in front: 5 rounds rapid, FIRE!' Our company sergeant major, who was an old soldier, he'd been to the School of Musketry in Hythe, and he said, 'Stand your ground and give fire!' That generally does the trick; that's what's done the trick in the British Army ever since the Peninsula War![65]
>
> Second Lieutenant William Tobey, 16th Battalion, Lancashire Fusiliers, 96th Brigade, 32nd Division

Tobey stayed with his men all night but next day was evacuated with his wound, which turned out to be a serious bullet wound in the left thigh.

On 10 August the Canadian Corps had fought well, thoroughly justifying its status as an elite force. But there was to be an unpleasant coda for Lance Corporal Kenneth Foster when, fresh out of battle, he was selected to form part of a firing squad on 12 August 1918.

> During our rest period we were given instructions in a certain drill that was entirely new to me. For several days we went through the same performance. It was a sort of target practice and guard of honour combined. However, it was not for us to ask questions, they were orders and we had to obey orders. Finally we were pronounced OK for whatever our task might be and the officer in charge politely informed us that the following morning at dawn we were to act in the capacity of an official firing party when one of our own men was to be shot for desertion. He was court martialled on two previous occasions and was let off on some pretext or other. The third time he met his doom and the execution was carried out in this manner. The prisoner was placed in a chair, tied and blindfolded, with a piece of paper over his heart. The rifles, previously loaded with half live rounds and half blanks were placed on the ground about 30 feet away. The firing party then marched in, for it took place in an old farmyard. No verbal command was given, the party acting on the blast of the officer's whistle. We were first reminded that failure to carry out instructions would mean the

same fate. In the event of no one hitting the mark the officer in charge would carry out the ghastly deed. As I remember it the whole thing only took about a minute. In fact, it seems more like a dream now than something that really happened. It is with some effort that I recall the facts that transpired on that eventful August morning. Not being murderously inclined, it can be readily understood when I say that it was some time before I could get the disagreeable subject off my mind. Such is war. The ways of mankind are strange. At war, the penalty for not killing is death; in peace, the penalty for killing is death.[66]

Lance Corporal Kenneth Foster, 2nd (Eastern Ontario) Battalion, 1st Brigade, 1st Canadian Division

The man executed would appear to have been Private Norman Ling who was 22 years old. He was the last Canadian soldier to be executed in the Great War.

FOR A WHILE THE FOURTH ARMY teetered on the edge of repeating the mistakes of the past. On 11 August things got no better. The amount of ground gained was small and the Germans made some small but significant counter-attacks. Rawlinson recognised that the Fourth Army had lost its momentum and that further attacks would be to no avail. It was his opinion that they should close down the offensive in its area and allow the neighbouring Third Army to pick up the baton. This was the key step forward, for by constantly switching the place of attack the British would not let the Germans settle. At first it appeared that nothing had changed. Foch issued directives requiring a continuation of the advance by Fourth Army, which Haig at first seemed to accept. However, after a series of meetings, not only with Rawlinson but also with Currie and Monash, Haig changed his mind and proposed the alternative of a thrust by the neighbouring Third Army to the north. The Fourth Army would only attack again when it had properly prepared and could deploy the full panoply of the new British battle tactics. At first this was to be only a few days ahead on 15 August, but reality soon intruded. There was simply too much to be done, far too many preparations to be made by the Royal Artillery to give such an early resumption any chance of success. Their guns would not be ready, the German batteries would not be located and therefore could not be neutralised properly. The German defences were strong enough to render any makeshift measure inadequate and the casualties would without doubt be high. Once again Rawlinson and Currie protested and this time Haig saw the full sense of what they were saying.

> At 10 a.m. Sir Henry Rawlinson came to see me and brought photographs showing the state of the enemy's defences on the front Roye–Chaulnes. He also showed me a letter which he had received from General Currie commanding the Canadian Corps stating that to capture the position in question would be a very costly matter. He (Currie) was opposed to attempting it. I accordingly ordered the date of this attack to be postponed, but preparations to be continued with vigour combined with wire cutting and counter-battery work.[67]
>
> Field Marshal Sir Douglas Haig, General Headquarters, BEF

One way or another Haig had the final piece in the jigsaw of battle tactics that were to win the war. This was not only how to prepare an attack but also when to stop attacking and attack elsewhere, while at the same time properly prepare a renewed assault for when the time was right for the British and wrong for the Germans. Next day, with the issue clear in his head, Haig went to confront Foch, who took considerable umbrage at what he considered backsliding. Irascible as ever, Foch first tried to bully and then *order* Haig to make the attack at once.

> Foch pressed me to attack the positions held by the enemy on the front Chaulnes-Roye. I declined to do so because they could only be taken after heavy casualties in men and tanks. I had ordered the First French and Fourth (British) Armies to postpone their attacks, but to keep up pressure on that front so as to make the enemy expect an attack on this front, while I transferred my reserves to Third Army. Foch now wanted to know what orders I had issued for attack: when I proposed to attack? Where? And with what troops? I think he really wanted a written statement to this effect from me for his records! I told Foch of my instructions to Byng and Horne; and that Rawlinson would also cooperate with his left between the Somme and the Ancre when Third Army had advanced and withdrawn some of the pressure which was still strong in that sector. I spoke to Foch quite straightly, and let him

understand that I was responsible for the handling of the British forces. Foch's attitude at once changed and he said all he wanted was early information of my intentions, so that he might coordinate the operations of the other armies, and that he thought I was quite correct in my decision not to attack the enemy in his prepared position.[68]

Field Marshal Sir Douglas Haig, General Headquarters, BEF

The Supreme Commander had learnt a valuable lesson: he did not *command* Haig, his powers were by agreement and Haig still answered first of all to the British government. But on the other hand Haig, by launching an attack with the Third Army, was in a sense falling in with Foch's higher agenda: to relentlessly hound the German Army until it fell apart at the seams. More to the point the Fourth Army had been rescued from a futile attack, the failure of which could only have damaged the Allied cause and given the Germans new heart. So it was that the Battle of Amiens came to an end on 11 August 1918. The British had made a total advance of about 12 miles but it is crucial to grasp that the real importance lay in the damage done to the German Army rather than the acquisition of meaningless land. And there was no doubt about the harm the German Army had suffered: although the British had lost some 22,000 casualties and the French around 24,000, the Germans have been estimated to have lost between 48,000 and 75,000 casualties, of which 18,550 were taken prisoner by the British and a further 11,373 by the French. The British and French Armies were suffering heavy casualties but the German Army was bleeding to death.

The German High Command badly needed some good news as it was increasingly afflicted by a sense of total despair. In particular, Ludendorff was close to mental collapse. On 11 August he had requested a meeting with the Kaiser and told him frankly that the war was lost.

Everything I had feared and of which I had so often given warning, had here, in one place, become a reality. Our war machine was no longer efficient. Our fighting power had suffered, even though the great majority of divisions still fought heroically. August 8 put the decline of that fighting power beyond all doubt, and in such a situation, as regards reserves, I had no hope of finding a strategic expedient whereby to turn

19. Two of the 8th Londons examining captured German machine guns
on 8 August 1918. (IWM Q 6920)

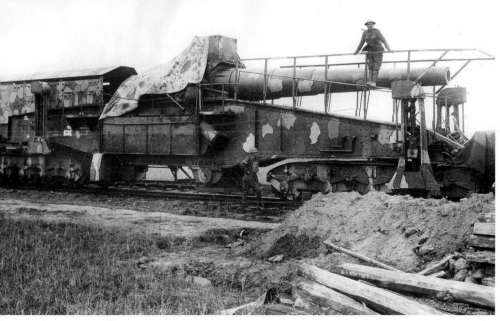

20. A 14cm German naval gun captured near Harbonniers, 9 August 1918.
(E(AUS) 2780)

21. A massed crowd of German prisoners taken by Fourth Army, 27 August 1918. (Q 9271)

22. Australian and German wounded sheltering under the Whippet tank 'Musical Box' near Harbonniers, 9 August 1918. (E(AUS) 2880)

23. A photograph of the scene at a German cookhouse which triggered rumours of a German corpse factory in the Bellicourt Tunnel, October 1918. (E(AUS) 3491)

24. Australian troops attacking the Hindenburg outpost line on 18 September 1918.
(E(AUS) 3260)

25. A 60-pdr gun firing as part of the dawn barrage towards Canal du Nord,
27 September 1918. (Q 9333)

26. German prisoners carrying a stretcher with a backdrop of tanks advancing on Bellicourt, 29 September 1918. (Q 9370)

27. Troops near Joncourt, 9 October 1918. (Q 9529)

28. The victorious men of the 137th Brigade, 46th Division collected on the banks of St Quentin Canal and being addressed by Brigadier General J. C. Campbell from the Riqueval Bridge, 2 October 1918. (Q 9534)

29. French child gazing at a smashed piano at Denain, 25 October 1918. (Q 3308)

30. French women and children cheering the arrival of 57th Division at Lille, 18 October 1918. (Q 9589)

the situation to our advantage. On the contrary, I became convinced that we were now without that safe foundation for the plans of General Headquarters, on which I had hitherto been able to build, at least so far as possible in war. Leadership now assumed, as I then stated, the character of an irresponsible game of chance, a thing I have always considered fatal. The fate of the German people was to me too high a stake. The war must be ended.[69]

Quartermaster General Erich Ludendorff, General Headquarters, Imperial German Army

Ludendorff offered to resign, but was kept in place. The German Army was faltering at every level. The Battle of Amiens was over, but the Battle of Albert on the Third Army front was just about to begin.

CHAPTER ELEVEN

Advance to the Somme

IT IS TRADITIONAL to swiftly dismiss the fighting that followed the Battle of Amiens as some kind of orderly or prosaic procession to an inevitable victory, not worthy of either analysis or detail. Yet the Germans fought hard every step of the way and at the time few people believed that the war could possibly come to an end in 1918. The German Army may have been in trouble, its leadership may have conceded ultimate defeat, but it still remained a formidable fighting machine. Indeed, the German Army in a damaged or wounded state was still substantially better than most national armies in the peak of condition. It was for this reason that Henry Wilson, Chief of the Imperial General Staff back in London, was firmly of the belief that Germany would not be beaten until 1919. He had expressed his appreciation of the situation in a long memorandum on British military preparations on 25 July 1918.

> A period of preparation should ensue during which all the Allied resources should be husbanded, organised and trained for the culminating military effort at the decisive moment. This will not be a period of passive defence, far from it, but it will be a period during which no final decision is attempted. The first question that arises is – when is this decisive effort to be made? That is to say, will it be possible to accomplish it in 1919, or must we wait until 1920.[1]
> General Sir Henry Wilson, Imperial General Staff, London

Wilson even suggested a date by which the preparations for the decisive thrust should be made: 1 July 1919.

Someone else imbued with a total misunderstanding of the situation and therefore resolutely planning for 1919 was Lieutenant Colonel John Fuller as senior staff officer with the Tank Corps. With the monocular view of the extremist he considered that he alone had the answer to the conundrum of winning the war on the Western Front. He envisioned a combination of tanks and aircraft concentrating their attack on the German headquarters and supply chain in an effort to put a bullet through the brain of the German Army. His plan for a new kind of mobile warfare was not without merit, although it relied on a type of tank not yet available. In reality the grim scientists of the chemical industry already had a far more realistic alternative for a radical new kind of warfare if the war had lasted into 1919: the DM gas that could penetrate all existing German gas masks.

Another individual who can be regarded as a pessimist, an unaccustomed characteristic for him, was the Minister for Munitions Winston Churchill. He visited the Western Front on 21 August, just as the Battle of Albert was beginning. Here he encountered the one unbending individual who recognised that there was a chance to finish the war in 1918 – the indomitable Field Marshal Sir Douglas Haig, who found himself slightly bemused by Churchill's negative assessment of the British chances of imminent victory.

> He is most anxious to help in every way, and is hurrying up the supply of '10 calibre head' shells, gas, tanks, etc. His schemes are all timed for completion in next June! I told him we ought to do our utmost to get a decision this autumn. We are engaged in a 'wearing out battle' and are outlasting the enemy. If we have a period of quiet, he will recover, and the 'wearing out' process must be re-commenced. In reply I was told that the General Staff in London calculate that the decisive period of the war cannot arrive until next July.[2]
>
> Field Marshal Sir Douglas Haig, General Headquarters, BEF

Behind Haig was the equally determined figure of Foch, who continued to prod the British forwards in no uncertain terms: 'After your brilliant successes of the 8th, 9th and 10th, any timidity on their part would hardly be justified in view of the enemy's situation and the moral ascendancy you have gained over him.'[3] Having got the shift of front and delay that he wanted, Haig was in full agreement. He recognised that now the Allies had established an ascendancy over the Germans they must take advantage of every chance to rub their noses in it.

Tragically the fighting that lay ahead of the British soldiers that made up Haig's armies would be some of the worst of the war. Many of his men were exhausted by the campaigns they had already fought in 1918, but for them it had truly only just begun. What faced them was probably the hardest campaign ever fought by the British armed forces. On the Somme in 1916, or at Passchendaele in 1917, units had generally gone into the line, fought a two- or three-day battle and then been withdrawn into support or reserve, whereas in 1918 the pressure was simply unrelenting. There was such a shortage of manpower that those units who *could* keep going were repeatedly used until their ranks were eroded away and the survivors' nerves worn to shreds. Men were caught in an awful trap where they could see victory approaching but also knew that as things stood they might not live to see it, yet they fought on. This was self-sacrifice on a grand scale.

In the two weeks after Amiens the fighting never really stopped, although the next major assault was not until 21 August. It was launched by the thirteen divisions of General Sir Julian Byng's Third Army on the front between the Scarpe and Ancre Rivers. Byng's first plan contemplated an initial advance of 6,000 yards with a secondary ill-defined exploitation phase. Haig was insistent that Byng must aim higher. This was par for the course with Haig: throughout his career as commander-in-chief he had always been an optimistic general who sought to maximise any possible gain from the 'investment' of men, guns, tanks and all the other paraphernalia and exorbitant effort entailed in an offensive. In the past this had led to overreaching and to failure, but now he was right. Haig urged Byng to break the German front line, thrust forwards as quickly as possible as far as Bapaume, with the flanks covered by the neighbouring First and Fourth Armies, who would launch near-simultaneous attacks. As usual, he also ordered up his cavalry divisions: for all their limitations in modern war they were still his fastest-moving exploitation force. In addition, as a further threat and distraction to the Germans, the French Tenth Army would launch its own attack to the south of the Fourth Army, starting on 20 August.

The ground lying in front of the Third Army provoked evil memories for both the British and the Germans as they grimly fought

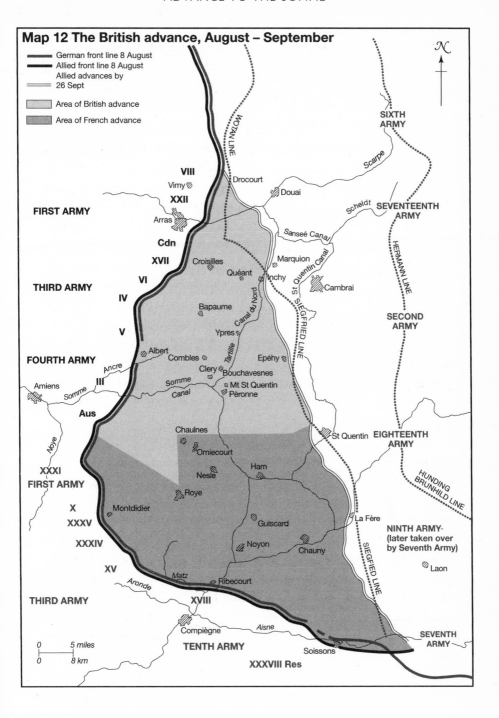

Map 12 The British advance, August – September

- German front line 8 August
- Allied front line 8 August
- Allied advances by 26 Sept
- ▨ Area of British advance
- ▨ Area of French advance

N

SIXTH ARMY

WOTAN LINE

Scarpe

VIII

Vimy ◈

Drocourt

Douai ◈

XXII

FIRST ARMY

Arras ◈

Scheldt

Sanseé Canal

SEVENTEENTH ARMY

Cdn

HERMANN LINE

XVII

Croisilles ◈

Marquion

St Quentin Canal

VI

Quéant ◈

Inchy

IV

THIRD ARMY

Cambrai ◈

Bapaume ◈

Canal du Nord

SECOND ARMY

V

Ypres ◈

ST SIEGFRIED LINE

Albert ◈

Combles ◈

Epéhy ◈

FOURTH ARMY

Clery ◈

Bouchavesnes

Ancre

Tartille

III

Somme

Mt St Quentin

Amiens ◈

Somme

Canal

Pèronne ◈

Aus

Chaulnes ◈

St Quentin ◈

EIGHTEENTH ARMY

Noye

Omiecourt ◈

HUNDING BRUNHILD LINE

XXXI

Nesle ◈

Ham ◈

FIRST ARMY

Roye ◈

X

Montdidier ◈

La Fère

XXXV

Guiscard ◈

NINTH ARMY
(later taken over
by Seventh Army)

XXXIV

Noyon ◈

Chauny ◈

XV

Matz

Ribecourt ◈

Laon ◈

SIEGFIED LINE

Aronde

THIRD ARMY

XVIII

Compiègne ◈

Aisne

SEVENTH ARMY

| 0 | 5 miles |
| 0 | 8 km |

TENTH ARMY

Soissons ◈

XXXVIII Res

over all the blasted valleys, ridges, villages and woods of the 1916 Somme battlegrounds. The whole area was covered in old entrenchments of every shape and size; there was barbed wire everywhere and the communications had been smashed and painstakingly restored on numerous occasions. The preparations made by the Third Army mirrored the preparations for 8 August. A successful methodology had been established and although there was some inevitable tinkering to meet local conditions the fundamentals remained the same.

As the numbers of British guns ballooned on the Western Front every one of its armies had a staggering amount of artillery to deploy by late August 1918, with a corresponding reduction in the logistical preparations required for any specific attack. Thus, although after its recent efforts the Fourth Army still had the most guns at 1,756, the Third Army could deploy 1,294, the Second Army 1,218 and the First Army 1,216. Nevertheless, there was still much to do and as part of this general effort the Londoners of 109th Battery, Royal Field Artillery had taken up their gun positions by an old railway track passing by the ruins of Boisleux-au-Mont. Here they worked all day bringing up 400 rounds per gun and digging in as best they could. Around them they could see the rest of the army preparing for the attack.

> The utmost activity was going on all around us. Files of infantry, the assaulting troops, supports and reserves, kept winding past, laden with their rifles, entrenching tools, haversacks, water bottles and other paraphernalia for battle. Countless ammunition wagons, small arms carts and pack mules were still moving along the dry earth tracks eastwards. And then the tanks appeared. Our men lent on their spades and peered down the track as the quaint churring creatures came, one following the other thrusting resolutely eastwards. Leading them came an officer, walking quietly out of the gloom, ash stick in hand, revolver on hip, as though he was taking his pack for an early morning walk.[4]
>
> Lieutenant John Capron, 109th Battery, 281st Brigade, Royal Field Artillery

The usual tension gripped every man of the gun detachments during the countdown to the barrage. Perhaps God had changed side over the last couple of months, for now it was the British last-minute preparations that were wreathed in a morning mist.

But now Zero Hour was close upon us: 4.55 a.m. Digging stopped and gun crews manned their guns. 4.52 – 4.53 – 4.54 – 4.55!! The shrill of the whistles drowns in the crack and whicker of the first salvo. But the near at hand slamming of our own 18-pounders is caught up and lost as it is carried away in the great hollow reverberating roar that shatters the morning as the massed artillery gets into its stride.[5]

Lieutenant John Capron, 109th Battery, 281st Brigade, Royal Field Artillery

The tanks and infantry started forward from their jumping-off positions. The sheer pulverising horror of a British bombardment, utilising every form of death-dealing ordnance was to them a thoroughly welcome and marvellous sight. Every high explosive, gas or shrapnel shell, every thermite bomb, every smoke shell was killing or blinding Germans that might have killed them when they went over the top.

As we approached our front lines our own creeping barrage opened and a more wonderful sight I have never seen. Just breaking dawn, streams of liquid fire falling from the very heavens, high velocity mixed with smoke to screen us, TNT, thermite. Oh, it was a sight never to be forgotten. Our infantry were waving to us as we passed and cheering vociferously. We ran over Boche: we machine-gunned him, he came out, falling on his knees and praying to be taken prisoner. One Boche sergeant major offered me his revolver, his watch, his money, fell on his knees and would not leave me, his nerves and morale were shattered to shreds by our barrage and the tanks. It was great fun – those who would not surrender we ran over, very few of those. My 'bus' was hit by a 9″ shell and set on fire, but all my crew and myself escaped. We had a great time and if my engines had been in good trim I should never have been hit.[6]

Captain James Humphries, 6th Battalion, Tank Corps

Once again the assault divisions that took their first objectives were required to consolidate while fresh divisions charged through them and into the attack. In one such second wave was Captain Lionel Ferguson of the 1st Cheshires who were pushing through Bucquoy.

In the centre of Bucquoy we met a large tank that had just captured a prisoner. They asked me direction and handed the captive over. I found he could speak English and he told me he had seen a number of our troops go by while he was hiding in a sniper's post. He also asked me if this was our 'Big Show' as, if so, the opinion of his countrymen was that the war would be over in a month. I was unable to bother with him and as he was quite willing to go back by himself we left him. He being the first German many had seen, he was robbed of all his belongings, even to his buttons![7]

Captain Lionel Ferguson, 1st Battalion, Cheshire Regiment, 15th Brigade, 5th Division

Back in the artillery lines the gunners saw the German prisoners streaming towards them in total disarray. Here in these shuffling, defeated crowds was concrete evidence of the jaw-dropping power of their guns.

As the light strengthened, over the skyline poured a body of men in the field grey of the German Army – prisoners! Curious indeed to see them stumble past our guns with dull dazed faces – real live enemy seen for the first time unobscured by wire and trench works. They were lucky to come alive out of that inferno that we had helped create.[8]

Lieutenant John Capron, 109th Battery, 281st Brigade, Royal Field Artillery

Meanwhile, the 1st Cheshires had pushed on into the fog and soon came across another tank that had lost its way in the overall confusion. Given the misty conditions and the awful visibility from inside a tank this was not surprising. Captain Ferguson then had the opportunity to see at first hand the awesome power of the tanks *if* they could be got into action.

The officer in charge was inclined to let the fog clear, but I informed him a number of our troops were ahead of us and that we must press on. So, after directing him to the road, he waddled along with us. An enemy machine gun opened up on our right at that moment and the old tank went right for it, firing a round as it advanced. We stopped to watch the scrap, a sight for all the world like a big dog going for a rat. The machine gun was firing and before the Boche gunners had time to escape, the huge monster was upon them, finishing them forever. It was the first blood we had seen that morning.[9]

Captain Lionel Ferguson, 1st Battalion, Cheshire Regiment, 15th Brigade, 5th Division

As the fog began to slowly lift the Cheshires pushed on through heavy machine-gun fire, past Achiet-le-Petit and pausing to take shelter beneath the railway embankment. Although they did not know it this would be typical of the fighting of this period. Despite the numerous trenches, the Germans were not occupying lines as such. Instead, they relied on a defence in depth, willingly surrendering up to 4,000 yards at a time and using artillery fire and concealed machine-gun posts to slow down and break up attacks. The machine guns were exceptionally difficult to locate in the wilderness of trenches and shell holes that offered a million hiding places. The creeping barrage, sweeping methodically across the ground was the best weapon against these machine guns; the problem came for the British, as the Germans had realised, when they had moved beyond the range of the field artillery that fired the bulk of the shells. The Royal Artillery had made arrangements to move forward specially designated batteries to provide local support to the infantry, while the bulk of the guns would move forward as soon the creeping barrage had finished. Nevertheless, the inevitable delays in crossing a recent battlefield, the crowded roads, the strafing from German aircraft and the all-round confusion meant that the guns could not resume work in time to properly support the advancing divisions. If the infantry and their supporting tanks went too far, then they could be severely exposed to small-scale German counter-attacks.

> Three Whippet tanks were now with me sheltering under the embankment. I pointed out to their officer in charge a large number of the enemy marching in the direction of Achiet-le-Petit and well to our left rear. I took these to be prisoners, but discovered with my glasses they all carried arms! The next moment they extended over the ground we had just advanced over and opened fire on us. The situation had become ugly. The tanks had by this time run right into the enemy attacking my rear, but all were very soon put out of action and two, if not three, caught fire. I could see a large tank on the ridge in front firing away with the enemy all around it; it was out of action and could not move. My only way of escape was to retire to my right. So I endeavoured to get my men to form a flank and retire in stages. I found this difficult as at such a time, the men were dumbfounded and would offer small resistance. I got the machine-gunners to fix up their gun, but before it was in action the sergeant and corporal were both hit, and the enemy was now about 30 yards away. I gave the order to move and take up a

position about 100 yards back. This order was taken by what men I had left as an excuse to get right back and nothing could stop them. We could find no cover or trench of any kind and were walking through a hailstorm of machine-gun bullets. Men fell left and right.[10]

Captain Lionel Ferguson, 1st Battalion, Cheshire Regiment, 15th Brigade, 5th Division

Here the line solidified again. But it had been a painful experience. Overall, the Third Army attack had been a success with the most difficulty being experienced on the right by the Ancre River.

Next day the Third Army stood fast while it made all the myriad preparations necessary for its next great leap forward. General von Below, the commander of the German Seventeenth Army that opposed it, had so little grasp of the overall situation that he thought that the British had shot their bolt and might be vulnerable to a counter-attack – which he duly launched. Unsurprisingly, there was a distinct lack of enthusiasm amongst the German troops and in places the British hardly noticed the attacks due to their half-hearted nature.

I got up this morning before four and soon after the Hun attacked. It was a carefully prepared operation. He gassed all the ground that he didn't want to take and bombarded all that which he did. But when it comes to asking the final question of his infantry, they are not equal to the task. We drove them back everywhere.[11]

Brigadier General Anthony Henley, 127th Brigade, 42nd Division

Strangely, despite this success, Brigadier Henley was almost killed that very day, not by the Germans but by one of his own men.

Seven Hun planes came over, flying very low: very rare. Nobody looked to see whose they were but I, then I bawled out orders to shoot to everybody who had a rifle. And they very sedately began. The second man to fire let off his piece 6 feet away – into a bank within exactly 1½ barleycorns of the back of my head, so that chalk jumped all over me in a shower. I was aware of a violent desire to punch his head and did, in fact, shout much concentrated abuse in his ear and shook him – he was a frail little fellow. My last cry was, 'Shoot at the bloody aeroplane and not at the Brigadier!'[12]

Brigadier General Anthony Henley, 127th Brigade, 42nd Division

It was an excellent illustration of the inexperience and declining level of military skills of the ordinary British soldier in the line; that, or the valiant Brigadier was a tad more unpopular than he thought!

MEANWHILE, ON 22 AUGUST the baton had once again been passed to Rawlinson's Fourth Army. His III Corps was charged with overwhelming the German salient that stretched from Bray-sur-Somme in the south, passing through Dernancourt and round to Albert. This involved an advance along the ridge of high ground between the Ancre and Somme Rivers, the very area that had thwarted the III Corps on 8 August. One of the worst problems faced the 47th Division, which was advancing across the spurs running down from the ridge to the Somme. The Londoners had had a hard war, a hard year and now August was proving a hard month. There was an incredible strain on individuals within tired battalions, a strain that they tried their best not to reveal to their worried families back home in 'Blighty'. One such dutiful son was Private Albert Fereday of the 1/15th Londons, who wrote home to his mother the day before the big attack.

> My dearest mother, I did not have the opportunity of posting the letter I wrote yesterday so that these two will arrive together. At present I am in a very comfortable trench about 5 miles from the front line, so of course I am as 'safe as houses'. I am only here for a few hours though as I am going a good way further back to a little village where I intend to have a good rest.[13]
> Private Albert Fereday, 1/15th Battalion, London Regiment, 140th Brigade, 47th Division

Historians beware: anyone relying on that letter for 'historical truth' as to Fereday's state of mind that night would be severely embarrassed. On the same day he wrote a far more revealing letter to one of his best friends.

> I cannot settle down to write a good letter this week as I have had such a horrible shaking and have not quite got over it. The anticipated stunt over the top did not come off for some reason or other but this battalion had to hold some of the ground taken in the recent push (left flank) and

Fritz gave us a warm time. Naturally, the ground has not yet been consolidated so that there was very little protection to be had. On Sunday morning (early hours) I was digging a communication trench near the front line when Fritz got wind of it. For three hours he shelled us with very heavy stuff – 5.9s etc., high explosive and gas. It was impossible for us to go back to our dugouts as we should have had to go about 300 yards in the open under fire and at the time no shelter was known in that trench sector. Unfortunately, there were one or two direct hits, which killed two of our boys and wounded several – one of them, Cansick, was a chum of mine; he was killed. After some time a dugout was found and with some difficulty a few of us left behind managed to get the wounded in safely. I found that while my mind was occupied with the work of bandaging up the chaps I was in charge of I seemed to forget the danger and scarcely noticed the hostile shells. It was hell! How I came through without a scratch I don't know. It must have been that God thought fit to answer many prayers; but I hope I never have to go through such an awful ordeal again. We get shelled pretty heavily each day so that very little work could be done. While in reserve in this sector I was able to explore the battlefield, the scene of the recent fighting. Even if I wanted to describe all I saw I could never do justice to the scene but I don't want to. If ever I was sick of this war it was when I first saw this place. If only everyone knew of the horrors of this war it wouldn't last another five minutes. But until it's over we have got to 'stick it'; the only reward I desire is to come out alive – not so much for my own sake but for others. Happily Mother didn't know I was even in the trenches, and you are the only one I shall ever tell the little I have of the experiences of the last week. After all they are dead and buried so far as I am concerned altho' they have left their mark; I don't feel I could face the same again with the same fortitude or steady nerve. But by prayer all things are possible and what better assurance of anything do I want than that. A rumour has just been circulating that we are going up the line again and that there is to be a push I am practically sure. What part I shall play in it I don't know but I hope I do my best. This letter is quite 'off colour', but never mind – it is an expression of love from your affectionate chum.[14]

Private Albert Fereday, 1/15th Battalion, London Regiment, 140th Brigade, 47th Division

Albert Fereday was killed the next day. He has no known grave, although he is commemorated on the Vis-en-Artois memorial.

The attack on 22 August was business as usual. Despite the usual secrecy and precautions the Germans had been standing to since midnight and were distinctly twitchy. All that night the German artillery fired various harassing barrages and there was an enormous feeling of satisfaction for the assaulting troops when the British barrage finally roared into life at 0445.

Suddenly at 4.45, with an enormous roar of guns, the British artillery opened fire from behind us. It was the most terrific bombardment imaginable – one continuous, gigantic roar of guns, extending over a front of many miles. For days afterwards we were partially deaf. But at the time we were filled yet again with the savage satisfaction at the power of our guns after the shelling we had just endured. Ten minutes later, in response to wild gesticulations, for no human voice was audible in such uproar, we scrambled most awkwardly out of the trench. I say awkwardly; to me personally it was a moment of anguish, because each time I jumped up the bank I slipped back into the trench. My pals had disappeared when I had the inspiration of running further along and trying again. This time I was successful, and soon caught up with the others, all of whom, like myself, were heavily loaded with ammunition. It was just getting light and the first thing was to get into correct formation: little groups of six men placed 25 yards apart, the whole platoon being about 100 yards from the next. We proceeded at walking pace with that mighty roof of shells hissing and screaming over our heads. We could see a few German shells falling here and there, but could not distinguish their noise, so great was our own. We could talk only by intense bawling at each other, and *then* could not be heard! Before proceeding far over the rough ground, stumbling and jumping trenches, we saw some Germans running towards us in a state of terror, their hands flying above their heads, one old man wept aloud. These fugitives were allowed to pass though our ranks.[15]

Private Roland Fisher, 1/24th Battalion, London Regiment, 142nd Brigade, 47th Division

Ten tanks supported the 47th Division and this and the creeping barrage were too much for the German defenders. German morale was definitely friable and troops were once again surrendering in circumstances where in the past they could have been expected to either fight to the death or at least carry out a fighting withdrawal. The attack was a success all along the front, although the cavalry had been unable to perform their exploitation role after being faced by machine-gun fire from the ridges ahead. Nevertheless, this was a new world: that very morning Haig issued a note to his army commanders clearly indicating the latest offensive creed designed to take the maximum advantage of the German frailties. After all, who knew how long they might last?

> To turn the present situation to account, the most resolute offensive is everywhere desirable. Risks, which a month ago would have been criminal to incur, ought now to be incurred as a duty. It is no longer necessary to advance in regular lines and step by step. On the contrary, each division should be given a distant objective which must be reached independently of its neighbour, and even if one's flank is thereby exposed for the time being. Reinforcements must be directed on the points where our troops are gaining ground, not where they are checked. A vigorous offensive against the sectors where the enemy is weak will cause hostile strongpoints to fall, and in due course our whole army will be able to continue its advance. The situation is most favourable; let each one of us act energetically and without hesitation push forward to our objective.[16]
>
> Field Marshal Sir Douglas Haig, General Headquarters, BEF

These orders were entirely sensible, but in their aggressive philosophy they were also, undeniably, a death sentence for thousands of British troops. Pushing forwards independently and paying no attention to unprotected flanks was the best way of making the most of the situation, but it still exposed troops on the ground to severe risks at the sharp end of the advance.

Thus it was that elements of the 1/24th Londons found themselves somewhat isolated in a former German trench. At first they felt perfectly secure and, indeed, they took considerable pleasure in comprehensively 'souveniring' the immediate locality.

> The Germans must have quitted in a hurry for we discovered many of their private possessions and filled our pockets with souvenirs – hats,

helmets, razors, field glasses etc. There was a quantity of black bread and large tins full of coffee with which we proceeded to refresh ourselves, drinking considerably more than was good for us, to our later discomfort! Our searching was frequently interrupted by the sound of shots from the further end of the trench, which we had not explored.[17]

Private Roland Fisher, 1/24th Battalion, London Regiment, 142nd Brigade, 47th Division

This was not the first time that looting had come before grim military efficiency. Unfortunately, such slackness often has a price. It was not long before Fisher and his comrades realised that they were in desperate trouble.

One of the sentries had seen Germans approaching our trench on three sides. There were only ten men in this part of the trench: one of them was sent immediately to report to company headquarters – he did not return and was not seen again. The Germans were closing in, so our Sergeant took it on himself to order our retreat, but not before we had fired upon the enemy with our Lewis guns, below which I happened to be standing, and as it fired several of the ejected nearly red-hot cartridges fell inside my open collar, severely burning my neck. Carrying the gun and ammunition we all ran up the trench and out into the open. As we dashed back across the field the bullets from the Germans were hitting the ground all around our feet, sending up little clouds of dust. We found that being so full of coffee, we could hardly run! I don't believe anyone of us expected to escape. Loads were dropped and in a state of inner despair we kept on. I found myself at the tail-end of a string of awkwardly running men. Across the field ran a raised road built on a bank 4 or 5 feet high. I never thought I should cross over the road, but with feet and body that seemed to weigh a ton, I at last ran up the bank, made myself a prominent target for a few seconds and then, to my utter astonishment, ran down the other side to shelter. Then on we dashed, covered by the raised road, and came to a line of holes in which were men of the 19th London Regiment. Our men went rushing by, until it came to the two slow boys, Hill and myself, who were only too glad to obey an officer who had been calling to us to stand with them. Both of us were completely out of breath and most grateful to accept a vacant hole![18]

Private Roland Fisher, 1/24th Battalion, London Regiment, 142nd Brigade, 47th Division

The 142nd Brigade had been forced back under the pressure. The 1/15th Londons were moved forward to help fill the gaps opening up in the over-stretched 47th Division front line.

The company crossed the road and shook out into diamond formation, small blobs of men, to make a more difficult target as we traversed the completely open ground. Almost at once a heavy barrage of shells was put down on us and one of the blobs got a direct hit. I ran to the spot with Holmes, another stretcher bearer, and found only one man unhurt, but he was so badly shocked that he was firing his rifle indiscriminately in all directions. Having disarmed him, we took stock of the situation. The section had been blown into two widely separated bodies. Two mates: Stansfield and Lance Corporal Wilson were dead. Another 'Big' Wilson, a Lewis gunner, was breathing stertorously with a wound in the throat and Lance Corporal Barber had been hit in the stomach. We did what we could for them and I sent Holmes away with the shocked man and another who was only lightly wounded, to try and find the aid post, and to bring back some help to carry the others. It was nearly dark when he left me. The shelling had died away and the battalion had disappeared forward. As night fell it got very cold. 'Big' Wilson died soon after Holmes had gone and Barber was complaining of the cold. I lay close beside him, trying to get some warmth into him. He was delirious and was talking to the dead men around us. After what seemed to be hours in a completely deserted world, I heard Holmes voice calling for me. He had found the aid post of another unit in a quarry on the road and had brought two men with him. With their help we got Barber onto a stretcher and set off back to the road. The others we left lying where they had fallen. They were only just over 19 years old. I remembered that Lance Corporal Wilson's parents had sent him a bullet-proof waistcoat, which had caused a lot of leg-pulling. It hadn't helped him much. Four men crossing rough ground in the dark with a stretcher made slow progress and the night was well advanced before Holmes found the aid post again. Here the medical officer pronounced Barber dead. After all the strain and effort of the last few hours, my light-headed thought was that it was just the sort of thing he would do to me whom he had never shown any signs of liking![19]

Stretcher Bearer Lance Corporal Robert Angel, 1/15th Battalion, London Regiment, 140th Brigade, 47th Division

On rejoining his unit Lance Corporal Angel then gave way to temptation and began scouting around for battlefield trophies.

Wandering around looking for souvenirs during an idle moment, I found a German soldier lying wounded and while attending to him, I was hailed in English by a German officer, a major, who was propped up on a pack with a bayonet wound in the thigh. I told him that I must get the soldier away as I had spotted him first, but would send a party for him. He shrugged philosophically and remarked that having been there two days another hour or so would be of no account. I got some headquarters fellows to fetch him in, including the orderly room corporal, to whom he gave his automatic pistol as a souvenir. The corporal, delighted with his present, but unfamiliar with pistols, promptly shot himself through the hand while examining it![20]

Stretcher Bearer Lance Corporal Robert Angel, 1/15th Battalion, London Regiment, 140th Brigade, 47th Division

The attack of the 18th Division on the left of the III Corps had been a success, although it had hard fighting in its task of crossing the Ancre and also retaking Albert. The 36th Brigade had been lent from the 12th Division especially for this attack, but unfortunately its men had no time to familiarise themselves with the ground. Amongst them was Lieutenant Jim Davies.

We arrived there at night, short of officers again. We got into position and I didn't know quite what was going to happen, what my objective was now. There was quite a barrage going on from us and one tank came out and went on. An SOS went up from the Boche I presumed so I made up my mind. I went forward and I suppose I'd been going forward for about ten minutes. It was dark and I'd never seen that part of the line before. The Boche had got light machine guns out in the front and one of those got me! It got me through both legs, I went down and the bloke next to me was killed, he was lying about 4 feet away from me. I took my scarf off, put a tourniquet on my left leg with my pistol through and tightened up. I was lying there, day broke, then I saw about thirty or forty men coming back. I couldn't see anybody in command of them and I called out, 'Who are you?' They were West Kents. 'What are you coming back for?' They said, 'He's too strong for us!' I said, 'He's not too strong, my troops are forward, go forward!' They didn't take any notice of me; I couldn't do anything! A sergeant and about four Fusiliers appeared, not my company, but I had a shrewd guess that they were 'shell-hole droppers': they go over in the attack but they've got no loyalties and they would drop down into a shell hole. I had been wounded again, a piece of shrapnel through the knee, and I told them to move me to a shell hole. They tried to move me, but by then it was painful, I couldn't move. One of the boys went off with a stretcher with only three handles on it! There were some prisoners coming down the road, and he came back with four prisoners including two German stretcher bearers. They started to look at my legs, there were little bits of bone all sticking out. The knee was completely shattered. I didn't try to move it; it was bloody painful! I said, 'It's hopeless, leave it alone!' All they'd got was paper bandages. They lifted me up on their shoulders and took me down. They started to run when there was shelling and I shouted out to a corporal to stop these Boches from running! My stretcher was saturated with blood.[21]

Lieutenant Jim Davies, 9th Battalion, Royal Fusiliers, 36th Brigade, 12th Division

He eventually reached the casualty clearing station but his instinctive diagnosis as to the seriousness of his wounds was correct. One of his legs was utterly hopeless, hanging by a thread and it had to come off.

I don't remember being undressed, I don't remember going into the operating theatre. But I do remember coming to and seeing a table with a chap with his side all open. There was a sister giving anaesthetics and she said, 'Somebody come and help me hold this officer down!' And that was it! I didn't know any more till about nine o'clock the next morning. I was all bandaged up and the first thing I did was reach down and I felt a stump. The sister said, 'Anything you want?' I said, 'Yes, I want to be sick!' She brought a kidney bowl and there was lot of brown stuff I brought up. She said, 'Anything else you want?' 'Yes, can I have a drink of whisky?' She brought me a large whisky. It had been a guillotine amputation, straight through, plug the bone marrow and bind it all up.[22]

Lieutenant Jim Davies, 9th Battalion, Royal Fusiliers, 36th Brigade, 12th Division

The Battle of Albert continued on 23 August when a general advance was ordered all along the French and British fronts from Soissons in the south to Arras in the north. One omen to the superstitious was that the leaning statue of the Virgin Mary had at last toppled from the church tower of Albert. As this was supposed to herald the imminent end of the war the news was widely celebrated. But the show had to go on and 'the Fourth and Third Armies moved forward to great effect. In the south the Australians broke through towards Chuignes: by this time they were a truly formidable fighting machine. But the 'ordinary' British divisions played a full part. This time the men of the 56th Division went into the attack with the 1/13th Londons attacking towards the villages of Boyelles and Boiry-Becquerelle, the men going over the top at 0507.

In the first light of dawn we silently lined up in the quarry and marched up the sunken road to the front line. Part of the way up, two Scottish pipers appeared from nowhere and piped us on our way. I'm not sure the gesture did us much good. Those wailing pipes sounded weird and melancholy in that desolate landscape. We stood to in the trench and waited. A rum ration was distributed and I tried to chew a biscuit. Watches were synchronised. We were ordered to fix bayonets. One or two tried feeble jokes, but they fell flat. The officers crouched with whistles in their lips. At 5 a.m. on the tick, a gun behind us fired a single shell. A red Very light sailed into the sky. Immediately all pandemonium was let loose. The noise was absolutely deafening. Some of the guns seemed to be only a few yards from us. Shells and bullets whistled, sang and shrieked over our heads. There was smoke everywhere, stabbed by vicious red and white flashes. Hundreds of machine guns kept up a gigantic continuous chatter. The earth shook. This was a real bombardment – the only one I was ever in. I was stunned by the suddenness of it. Captain Smith waved his arms – the whistles were useless – and we clambered out of the trench. We were over the top. I felt naked.[23]

Private T. H. Holmes, 1/13th Battalion, London Regiment, 168th Brigade, 56th Division

Holmes was a signaller and his heavy signal light bumped against his legs as the men gingerly moved forward in a long line some 10 to 20 yards apart across a flat area fringed by low hills. They had gone about 100 yards before the Germans burst into life. Now Holmes witnessed a superb example of infantry–tank cooperation.

> A machine gun rat-tatted in front of us and bullets swished near. It was incredible that anyone could have been left alive to fire at us. Mr Smith dropped flat into a shell hole and we dropped into another close to him. He yelled to me to make my first signal. I trained my lamp onto a winking light in the rear, while Vic Wells sent a code letter meaning, 'Machine-gun post active!' Soon a new sound struck our ears: a deep chug-chugging. Out of the smoke giant shapes dramatically loomed up, lurching along like ungainly prehistoric monsters. They were tanks. I cheered, which was rather a waste of precious breath. They clattered past and we followed a respectful distance behind them. One of them swivelled awkwardly towards the sparks of the machine gun and churned right over it. I saw a ghastly mass of crushed heads and limbs tangled up in twisted iron.[24]
>
> Private T. H. Holmes, 1/13th Battalion, London Regiment, 168th Brigade, 56th Division

The way ahead was clear again. But there always seemed to be far more than one string to the German bow. The sheer press of events had rushed the British preparations and their counter-battery work had not been thorough enough. Far too many German batteries remained unsubdued.

> Shells began to land around us. The enemy artillery had been roused. Mr Smith doubled from shell hole to shell hole and we perforce had to follow him. I secretly wished he wasn't such a gallant soldier! Once or twice he would tell me to send back the code for, 'Artillery support wanted!' and in a few minutes a salvo or two would scream over our heads.[25]
>
> Private T. H. Holmes, 1/13th Battalion, London Regiment, 168th Brigade, 56th Division

The Royal Artillery was always ready to respond to such direct requests as best it could. As the 1/13th Londons pushed forward the Germans found themselves unable to resist the multi-faceted assault on their minds and bodies.

Crouching figures in strange green uniforms with their hands held up loomed up out of the smoke. They were Germans. They were a pitiful sight. Their senses must have been pounded out of them by the bombardment, but they had enough instinct to realise that their lives hung on the slender thread of what happened to them in the next ten minutes. They were grey with fear. Some held watches and army caps and cried, '*Souvenir, Tommy, souvenir!*' Others cried, '*Kamerad, Tommy, Kamerad! Me piccanin!*' and raised the palms of their hands 1 foot, 2 feet, 3 feet off the ground to indicate their parental responsibilities. One or two dragged a wounded figure in khaki along with them, on the reasonable assumption that this act of mercy would save them from being shot dead. We prodded them all on, waved them to the rear and they staggered on to the 'moppers up'.[26]

Private T. H. Holmes, 1/13th Battalion, London Regiment, 168th Brigade, 56th Division

The German front-line troops may have given up hope, but the German gunners were still active. They began to send over a heavy barrage of gas shells.

Some of the smoke began to take on a yellowish tinge and made the eyes and throat smart. Captain Smith put on his gas mask and signalled to us to do the same. Any sort of activity for more than quarter of an hour was irksome in a gas mask. The goggles became clouded and the space inside the mask warm and wet. Signalling was particularly murderous. But you dare not remove them while there was gas about. The only thing to do, apart from staying still and letting the fumes disperse, which was a long job, was to hurry through the shelling to a clear area. But the cunning enemy was as aware of this as we were, so he 'crept' his barrage of gas shells slowly forward at approximately the same rate as a man could walk and you might be in the gas cloud for hours.[27]

Private T. H. Holmes, 1/13th Battalion, London Regiment, 168th Brigade, 56th Division

Holmes was finally caught out when, after an hour or so, the harassing bombardment of gas shells seemed to peter out. At the same time a welcome slight breeze got up and the gas seemed at last to be dispersing. Seizing their opportunity Holmes and his fellow signallers began to take off their gas masks while they sheltered in a large shell crater. It was to prove a fatal error.

Bill slipped his fingers under the rubber, pulled the face-piece away and gulped in deep breaths. Vic Wells followed suit and had just about let go of his mouthpiece and released the straps from his scalp. I was last and had only slipped my head straps, but still sucked the mouthpiece. At that moment a stray gas shell dropped smack on the edge of the crater. There was a zoooop and a clonk, a cloud of yellow choking gas and we were in the middle of it. I often visualised the scene in the German lines: 'Hey, Fritz we've got one gas shell left over, what should we do, hein?' And Fritz says, 'Ach, might as well send it over to the British schwein!' And so they poop it off and one Englishman dies, one gets permanent bronchitis and the other nearly goes blind. Viv and I frantically pulled our masks on again. Bill lay gasping and clutching his throat. We pulled him out somehow. It was just about noon. I was 19½ years of age.[28]

Private T. H. Holmes, 1/13th Battalion, London Regiment, 168th Brigade, 56th Division

Bill never got his mask back on and died in the casualty clearing station. The last Holmes heard of his gassed friend, Viv, he was having treatment for his damaged lungs ensconced in a sanatorium back in England. Holmes himself found his eyes closed up completely, painfully red and swollen while a constant stream of mucus poured from his nose and mouth. His lungs had also been affected and he wheezed like a concertina, but he was alive and would eventually make a complete recovery. If the German gunners had waited another second or two before firing then his mask would have been right off his face.

Sergeant Sam Lane, also of the 1/13th Londons, had broken right through the German lines and found himself isolated with about six men from his platoon. While he pondered what to do next they took what cover they could in a drainage ditch alongside the road. Sergeant Lane had been used to the blasted battlefields of trench warfare and found it strange to be surrounded by the luxuriant foliage of bushes and trees in full bloom.

Suddenly there came a sound of talking and, believe it or not, laughter. Six or eight Germans carrying a machine gun broke through the bushes not 40 yards away. Instantly my men, still in the ditch, raised their rifles to fire, but, thinking fast, I touched their arms and shook my head, and they lowered their rifles. It was a tempting target, but we could not have hit more than half of them, and they had a machine gun, which we did not. They could have made short work of us and the fight would have aroused any other Germans in the vicinity. So we let them go and they disappeared not knowing how near to death some of them had been.[29]

Sergeant Sam Lane, 1/13th Battalion, London Regiment, 168th Brigade, 56th Division

There were no other British troops in the locality, but Lane decided that he must push on a little further at least.

The enemy was obviously retiring. Noise, except in the distance, had ceased. Giving the signal, I scrambled up the bank, followed by my boys. As we burst through the bushes a sight met our eyes I shall not forget. For there, about 100 yards ahead, was a battery of German field guns, their barrels pointing straight at us. Still running forward, a glance showed me guns pulled by teams of horses racing to the rear through a gap in the wood behind, with another team already limbering up. It is probable that the battery had no knowledge of the real state of affairs in front of them, but the arrival of their machine-gun party had warned them it was time to retire quickly. I had spotted a trench just in front of the guns. Astonishment was mutual. At the sight of us, the German officers and NCOs pulled out their revolvers and began firing wildly at us. Still running forward, I had no option but to go on, and the thought came instantly, 'This is VCs or nothing!' I shouted, 'Come on, chaps!' and we charged forward. The revolvers must have been in shaky hands, or perhaps the distance was a little too far, for we were not hit. Suddenly, as we came forward, down came the muzzles of the two remaining guns, and they fired point-blank at us at a range of 40 yards: shells, long tongues of flame, blast and smoke belched from the guns straight at us. The shells sailed between and over us, to explode a short distance behind, and the gun flashes, although intense, did not reach us. We were shaken but we still ran forward. The trench was just in front of the battery. If we could make that, we should be able to do something, but I could not capture a battery with half a dozen men. For all I knew, there might be a crowd of infantry in the nearby wood. When we came to the trench, we would have to cross it to get at them. We jumped in: immediately both guns pounded the top of the trench, or as near as they could get to it, with shells. It was obvious they could not depress the muzzles sufficiently to hit the trench, but the thud and vibration as they hit the ground a little to the rear, certainly kept our heads down. Raising three or four bombs between us, I slung them over the top, hoping for the best, for when we jumped in, I had noticed there still seemed to be a crowd of the enemy milling around – and we used our rifles when possible to some effect. Suddenly things seemed to go quiet. The enemy gunners had managed to retire with their wounded, but had been forced to leave both their guns, and there they were, a few yards from us: deserted and silent. Our prize – two German field guns.[30]

Sergeant Sam Lane, 1/13th Battalion, London Regiment, 168th Brigade, 56th Division

Now their course of action was clear: they would defend their glittering prizes. It was still only early afternoon and it would be about four hours later that the Guards Division arrived to help consolidate the new front line.

The actions fought by the Londoners of the 56th Division must stand as a tribute to the fighting of all the dozens of British divisions on the 23 August and the days that followed it, as the British Third and Fourth Armies smashed their way across the old 1916 battlefields on the Somme. The Germans had only taken a couple of days to gain this ground in March 1918, and now they were being paid back in kind, as they were swiftly turfed out of their defensive positions. Of course mistakes were made, local attacks still sometimes failed with heavy casualties, German counter-attacks still caused temporary chaos and, most of all, copious numbers of men died, were wounded or worn to shadows by physical and mental exhaustion.

How I wished we could have had a photo taken this morning. We have not had a shave or a wash for six days; nor have I used a knife or fork with my meals. My tunic is badly torn and my trousers have no seat left in them. Yet I am a dandy compared to many of the men: few have got puttees and many have hardly got any clothes left.[31]

Captain Lionel Ferguson, 1st Battalion, Cheshire Regiment, 15th Brigade, 5th Division

However, most of them could see the point of what they were doing and why it was necessary that they had to collectively keep hammering at the Germans.

We shall be at it again tonight, I expect. Of course, about a week's rest with baths and clean clothes is what we should like, but it is everything to keep Fritz running while he is out of breath.[32]

Brigadier General Anthony Henley, 127th Brigade, 42nd Division

In essence, what they were enduring was as nothing to the trauma they were inflicting on the German Army. More and more German divisions were being thrown into the battle but they were arriving piecemeal, often without their artillery, and the Allies allowed them no time to settle in. In some sectors the British made progress even though the Germans had an ostensible superiority in numbers. But many of their reinforcement formations had already been sucked dry. The post-war history of just one German unit gives us an illustration of what they were up against.

The hostile brigades rolled forward behind a mighty curtain of fire and thoroughly smothered the very mixed up German combatants, who had to defend themselves simultaneously against infantry, squadrons of tanks, cavalry and aircraft. What did it matter if here and there our guns blew up a tank, if our machine guns shot an attacking cavalry detachment to pieces, if our fighter aeroplanes shot down several hostile machines? The enemy filled the gaps in the twinkling of an eye, but the brave body of Württembergers and their helpers got weaker hour by hour.[33]

History of 120th Württemberg Regiment, Imperial German Army

After four days of frenetic action the battered Württemberg Regiment was left with just 250 out of a theoretical 3,000 soldiers. The rest were dead, wounded, prisoners of war, or just generally cast to the four winds and missing on the chaotic battlefield. The British never seemed to leave the Germans alone, the Royal Artillery never seemed to sleep and there were ever-increasing small-scale night operations intended to seize advantageous tactical features for the next 'bound'.

The enemy tried by every method to work forward close to the front, especially by night, and there were some stiff bomb fights. Even if one's own front was quiet; that of one's neighbour was seething. Consequently we were eternally on the qui vive and in a perpetual state of being alarmed and standing to. Nearly all the available effectives were required for reconnaissance and outpost duties. Company commanders had to exercise much skill to enable them to give their men at any rate the sleep that was necessary for them. Every morning it could be seen that the enemy had got closer.[34]

History of 22nd Fusilier Regiment, Imperial German Army

The overall morale of the British troops fluctuated depending on whether their unit was in action or not. It was difficult to remain cheerful when one's friends were being killed left, right and centre. But those out of the front line could see that there were real signs that the Germans might be nearly finished.

Well, what do you think of the war news now, it almost looks as if we had Fritz on the run, believe me the troops feel fine about it, the morale is excellent and from what I saw of the German prisoners we captured in our show, their morale is certainly going to pieces. Well sweetheart, am looking forward to being with you before long, I wonder if you could borrow, hire or steal a bicycle for me when I get back so that we could be able to ride around to see our friends.[35]

Captain James Evans, 5th (Western Cavalry) Battalion, 2nd Brigade, 1st Canadian Division

But even on the run the Germans, as we have seen times without number, were dangerous. Certainly no individuals could 'count their chickens' with regard to their personal survival or look forward to a life post-war until the last shot was fired. Unfortunately, Captain James Evans would be killed within just a week when he was hit by a German sniper on 1 September.

The generals in charge necessarily had to be hard-hearted as they sent their tired men into action day after day. That was after all their responsibility as commanders. But the men of 'D' Battery, 310th Brigade, Royal Field Artillery were given a rare sign of the human face behind the 'mask' of Douglas Haig. The battery had suffered a good deal from prematurely bursting shrapnel shells fired from a battery behind it and shrapnel balls scattering randomly across its gun positions. Major Richard Foot had been particularly upset when one of his subalterns Jack Massy-Beresford was killed by this 'friendly fire'. As they moved out of their gun positions the gunners took with them the corpse of this popular young officer wrapped in a blanket and carried on the trail of the leading gun.

> On the march, I was called to the head of the battery to find no less a person than the Commander-in-Chief himself by the roadside – Sir Douglas Haig. He was alone, except for a sergeant of 7th Hussars carrying his union flag as a lance pennon. I had known Haig in his pre-war days at my home – he was a contemporary of my father's at Royal Military College, Sandhurst. When I reported, as was customary, my name, rank and unit, he at once remembered me. He was a very taciturn man, but as the battery filed by on the road and saluted him, he asked about the body on the leading gun. I told him about Jack's death, complaining rather bitterly and brashly no doubt, about our day's troubles with faulty ammunition. After the battery had passed, he fell in behind them on the road with me, got out a notebook and made a note of Jack's name. Later I heard that he had indeed taken the trouble to write a personal note of condolence in his own hand to Jack's family. His kindly sympathy, communicated later to the battery, did a lot to cheer us up after a horrid day.[36]
>
> Major Richard Foot, 'D' Battery, 310th Brigade, Royal Field Artillery

Despite his taciturn aloofness, Douglas Haig was demonstrably not the embodiment of heartless iniquity that some popular commentators would have us believe.

As August drew to a close Haig sought to expand the front of the offensive. He therefore ordered the First Army, commanded by General Sir Henry Horne, to launch the Battle of the Scarpe, effectively a partial replay of the Battle of Arras it had fought in April 1917. Hence on 26 August 1918, the First Army attacked hard pushing forward some 4 miles towards Monchy-le-Preux. Ludendorff now had six British and French Armies battering away along his increasingly beleaguered front. Something had to give – so the German Army deliberately set in motion a staged withdrawal behind the Somme River. The new line would run from Noyon in the south, along the east bank of the Canal du Nord to Nesle, then following the Somme River to beyond Péronne. The line would then run via Le Transloy and Vraucourt through to join the Drocourt-Quéant Switch Line of the Hindenburg Line near Arras.

The German retreat began on 27 August. As is the way of things the Germans claimed it was a voluntary manoeuvre carried out for entirely tactical reasons, thereby shortening the line and securing a superior tactical position. Of course, the Allies believed that it was an involuntary retreat and the Germans were just bending with the prevailing wind. As one might expect, the retirement was carried out with considerable skill. The German tactics were simple but effective: a ferocious bombardment would be fired from their massed field artillery and they would then withdraw as the barrage was taken up by the longer-ranged guns. Meanwhile, single field guns or trench mortars were left behind to 'ambush' the advancing British infantry in conjunction with the ubiquitous concealed machine-gun posts.

On and on the British pushed forward. Private Mick Burke of the 8th Manchesters was one of many who found that the German resistance was well capable of destroying men both physically and mentally. On 29 August, they were pushing forward towards Riencourt when they came under sustained heavy fire.

> A big shell came over and burst about 25 yards in front of me, making a big crater. I said, 'Let's make for that. He'll not put another there.' I placed the Lewis gun on top and everybody got nicely settled in, but the next shell didn't burst on the ground, it burst in the air and dropped all the shrapnel on top of us! It took my left hand off and came down through my steel helmet, scarring my face. I picked myself up and ran back to the trench, leaving behind my gun and equipment. My hand was held by a piece of flesh and it banged and slapped as I ran. Blood was pumping all down my face and onto my uniform.[37]
> Private Michael Burke, 1/8th Battalion, Manchester Regiment, 126th Brigade, 42nd Division

He collapsed back into the trench where he was tended to by two stretcher bearers. They competently bandaged the remnants of his hand and then placed him on a stretcher lying on the bottom of the trench. But his saviours had other things on their mind.

> One of them asked, 'Can you keep a secret, Mick? We're going to do ourselves in!' 'Are you?' I said. 'Well, move me further down the trench then, away from where you are!' After they had moved me I was facing

them and saw all that happened. They couldn't use British weapons because they would have been found out and charged with self-inflicted wounds, so they got a German rifle, put a bullet in the breech and the first one had his in the leg just above the ankle. The blood shot out as from a hosepipe for a second or two, then it stopped. He whipped his puttee off and placed a bandage round it, put another round in the breech and said, 'Right mate, where do you want yours?' 'I'll have mine in the arm!' was the reply. 'Keep your arm still then!' and he duly obliged. They told me it was the only way out.[38]

Private Michael Burke, 1/8th Battalion, Manchester Regiment, 126th Brigade, 42nd Division

Shortly afterwards an officer arrived and Burke was safely evacuated. Collectively and individually men on both sides were coming to the end of their tether. There never seemed to be a respite and if men survived one attack, it seemed a near certainty that they would be hit in the next. Yet still the British were regaining ground and by 30 August the town of Bapaume was captured.

In the later stages of this advance tanks were becoming a rare sight on the battlefield as they gave way to mechanical fatigue and their casualties in the recurring actions mounted. On 31 August, Private Charles Brown was part of Lieutenant Vivian Staub's crew of a now obsolescent Mark IV tank of the 12th Battalion, Tank Corps. As they moved forward into the attack in the Vaulx-Vraucourt sector in support of the 3rd Division they had a horrific battle experience that Brown would never forget.

At the Zero Hour, our barrage opened. Mr Staub, our officer, kept pressing to push forward, but I pointed out we were practically in the range of our own barrage. As the shells burst just a few yards in front of us all the colours of the rainbow could be seen, especially as it was still dark with dawn just breaking. The Germans were using tear gas shells, so I drove with my gas mask on nearly all the time. I also had a visor on, a metal mask with slots and a steel chain below to cover the lower part of my face. In directing the tank I had to look through a kind of periscope to prevent direct hits coming through the aperture. Following behind the barrage the first thing we saw was a trench full of Germans. The machine guns on the left had jammed, so I turned round to give the other gunners a chance, but they were just as unlucky. When the

Germans saw that we were more or less impotent, they started to pepper us with machine-gun fire and anti-tank bullets. The noise reminded me of the riveters at the shipyard in Belfast. Finally the anti-tank bullets came through, knocking out our engine. One bullet tore through the arm of Smithers, the gunner right behind me, severing an artery and sending a stream of blood on my neck. One of the chaps in the tank got the wind up and shouted, 'Surrender, or we will all be killed!' He got hold of a white signalling flag, lifted the flap in the roof and started waving it. Lieutenant Staub, who was on my left, said, 'Take your revolver and shoot him!' I replied, 'Why don't you do it?' I got out of my seat, got to the back and pulled the fellow in, giving him a rap on the head to quieten him. Four or five of the crew were wounded, and as the engine had been knocked out, Mr Staub ordered us to evacuate the tank and form a machine-gun post in a shell hole on the lee side of the tank. There we were – a sitting duck in the middle of No Man's Land. Mr Staub crawled to the trench behind us and found it occupied by the Gordons. The rest of the crew crawled to the trench some 150 yards away. Mr Staub and I stayed with the tank and dressed the two badly wounded. I had a lot of bullet splinters in my right knee but was more or less mobile. Smithers was unconscious, in a bad shape and could not be moved. Green, the other badly wounded, was conscious, but not mobile. The machine-gun fire and sniping was so heavy that carrying Green was out of the question, so we all had to be flat with Lieutenant Staub at the head and me at the feet, with a push and a pull. We were constantly being sniped on and it was dangerous to even lift one's head. It took us over two hours to get to the trench.[39]

Private Charles Brown, 12th Battalion, Tank Corps

As soon as they had got Green to safety Staub and Brown made to go and fetch Smithers but were stopped by an officer of the Gordons who pointed out that the Germans had overrun the tank. Lieutenant Vivian Staub was awarded the Military Cross for his courage in rescuing Green, while Brown received the Military Medal.

By the end of August, the Fourth Army was but a shell of its former self. It had lost the Canadian Corps, which had long ago been returned to its parent First Army, and now consisted of just the III and Australian Corps. As the battle progressed it was evident that the Australian commander Lieutenant General Sir John Monash was assuming an increasingly influential role. Both Haig and Rawlinson had intended the Fourth Army to ease back in its offensive operations, following up advances made elsewhere and acting as a flank guard rather than actively driving forward. Yet Monash was convinced that the Germans in front of him were ready for the taking and believed that if the force kept going it could use its gathering momentum to 'leap' across the Somme. Both Rawlinson and Haig had the good sense to accept the judgement of the 'man on the spot' and Monash was allowed to continue his relentless pursuit. The result was one of the most amazing battles of the Great War; one that cemented the reputation of the Australian Corps as perhaps the finest attacking formation in the entire British Army.

The key position to be taken if the Australian Corps was to get across the Somme River was Mont St Quentin, which lay just a mile to the north of the old bastion town of Péronne. In itself it was not that intimidating, rising just 140 feet or so above the overall ground level, but it and the adjoining Bouchavesnes Spur had been turned into formidable strongpoints stuffed with machine guns and covering the various west–east Somme crossings at Cléry and Péronne. When Monash ordered his depleted, exhausted ranks to take a running jump at such a fortress he was lucky in their response. At 0500 on 31 August the 5th Brigade, 2nd Australian Division attacked with a combined strength that has been estimated at around 1,320 of all ranks – not much more than a single augmented battalion. They used everything they had learnt during the whole war: the trickery and ruses typical of Gallipoli, the tightly focused creeping barrages, the Lewis gun fire-power and above all the individual fighting skills that had made them the best troops on the Western Front. By 0800 that morning they had taken the mound and were sending back some 700 bemused German prisoners. It had been a military achievement of the highest order, but this was just the start of what would be a dreadful slogging match. The Germans reacted sharply and their storming counter-attacks soon swept the 5th Brigade from its hard-won gains and tumbled it off the hill. Next day, 1 September, the Australian Corps tried again. The men simply would not be beaten. This time the 6th Brigade would have the pleasure of attacking Mont St Quentin, while the 14th Brigade from the

5th Australian Division attacked Péronne itself and the 3rd Australian Division attacked Bouchavesnes Spur.

The actual assault was carried out by the 23rd and 24th Battalions of the 6th Brigade. Although they were outnumbered by the German garrison, they forced their way forward until they were held up by German troops holding a large crater near the top of the hill. The impasse endured for several hours, both sides trying to gain the advantage.

Behind the front line was Major Donald Coutts, a medical officer attached to the 24th Battalion. He had set up a regimental aid post in the 'Lost Ravine'. This was a canal working that had not been completed when the war started. It was 900 feet long, some 60 feet across and 20 feet deep. There were some imposing former German dugouts and tunnels but they all had their entrances facing the German lines on Mont St Quentin and were thus highly vulnerable to well-directed shelling.

Everyone thought the tunnel was unsafe as there were no supports. It was in a very dirty condition – Hun blankets and bedding lying everywhere. About 6 p.m. there were hundreds of men in the ravine and the 5th Division were passing though it on their way to Péronne. The Hun shelled all around us during the afternoon, and just about dark he began to concentrate on the ravine with 4.2″ and 5.9″ shells. Casualties were coming in all the time, most of them 5th Division men. We were kept dressing wounds continually. Most of the shells were just passing over us, but occasionally he would get one into the ravine. We were kept going continuously all night. About 10.30 p.m. two men were brought in, and I had to amputate one man's arm at the shoulder and the other man's leg through the right thigh – I had to use a razor for this. I put his other leg in a splint, as it was badly wounded, nearly severed at the knee joint. We sent this man on about one hour afterwards and he was in fair condition. Just before daylight, when our barrage opened, the Hun put down an intense barrage on the ravine. One shell came in through the entrance to our tunnel and burst inside, wounding Syd Oke who was standing beside me helping to splint a broken thigh. The tunnel filled with smoke and dust, and we couldn't see for some time. Got Syd onto my stretcher and found a large wound in the back. The piece had evidently gone into his abdomen. A few minutes afterwards a shell hit the other entrance to our dugout and burst in the doorway. The place was filled with phosphorous fumes and smoke. We were afraid that a 5.9″ would hit the roof of the dugout and the whole place would fall in on us.[40]

Medical Officer Major Donald Coutts, 24th Battalion, 6th Brigade, 2nd Australian Division

Eventually the Australians somehow carried the day and in bitter fighting won no less than six VCs. The Australians were now beyond exhaustion but were still kept in the line. Private Rose and his section of men from 30th Battalion were sheltering in their shallow dugout when the Germans started shelling.

I looked out to see what he was up to and got a mouthful of vile gas – a dirty yellow colour. I retched immediately before I was able to get my gas mask on. I got it on and warned the others. The company orderly corporal came running down the trench calling out and spewing violently. He was so bad that he could not keep his mask on. The idea of this sort of gas is to make one vomit so much that the gas mask could not be kept on as protection.[41]

Private G. V. Rose, 30th Battalion, 8th Brigade, 5th Australian Division

Men of the 57th Battalion crossed the Somme River in the dark on a mission to relieve their comrades in the 58th Battalion. The precarious passage was made even worse by the power of imagination.

A shattered bridge sloped into the water, its broken back deep beneath the surface. We crossed on two planks that swayed with our footsteps in the dark. The stream rushed and whirled and beat against the shattered masonry and twisted iron, roaring over the sunken blocks, raising itself in a crested wave whose whiteness was seen beneath, faintly in the gloom, as we shuffled carefully on that frail pathway, laden as we were.[42]

Sergeant William Downing, 57th Battalion, 15th Brigade, 5th Division, Australian Corps

They probed into the town of Péronne, which by this time had caught alight and was burning fiercely.

A beam fell amid a shore of sparks, and something burst into flame; then, as the walls within were lit by its yellow glare we heard a scream in the gutted rooms and a voice that babbled in German. We hurried on, for our mates in front were hard beset: but we still heard with horror that shrieking wretch behind us.[43]

Sergeant William Downing, 57th Battalion, 15th Brigade, 5th Australian Division

In the final stages the fighting degenerated into the most vicious scrap imaginable, as illustrated by the street fighting during an attack on Allaines just north of Péronne on 2 September.

The Huns who had now properly got the wind up were racing through the broken-down buildings trying to make their escape with our lads in close pursuit. On turning corners in their mad flight they were just as likely to run into an Aussie as not and then – their number was up.[44]

Lieutenant J. T. Blair, 28th Battalion, 7th Brigade, 2nd Australian Division

After several hours of desperate fighting Péronne duly fell. The Somme Line had been broken and the Germans once again would have to retreat.

MEANWHILE, THE EQUALLY RENOWNED CANADIAN CORPS of Horne's First Army was also trying to achieve a difficult task when it attacked the much-vaunted Drocourt-Quéant Switch Line, which was a northerly extension of the Hindenburg Line, on 2 September. It was a strong position consisting of two trench systems, stiffened with the usual reinforced concrete machine-gun posts and masses of barbed wire. Although not quite as formidable as the Hindenburg Line proper it certainly still represented a severe obstacle. Supporting Lieutenant General Sir Arthur Currie's Canadian Corps was the XXII Corps to the north and the XVII Corps of Byng's Third Army, which was attacking to the immediate south. The Canadians, however, were the key to the success of the whole operation. And what a success it was. When the Canadian 1st and 4th Divisions pushed forward they met with minimal resistance, to a degree that would have been simply unbelievable a year before.

Before we reached the Drocourt-Quéant Line we were abreast of the 50th Battalion and had become practically one wave. Here the barrage was scheduled to play for some time so we took what shelter we could.

We were as close to the roaring barrage as we could possibly approach. Presently it lifted and we went forward preceded by a few tanks. It was next to impossible to crawl through the wire so we had to use the paths which the enemy had left for his own convenience. Many were shot by enemy machine gun and snipers as we passed through, but we retaliated in the same way. A number of them tried to run back. Of course they had to use paths, so they were huddled together. One of our machine-gunners dropped with his gun and opened fire. They went down in a heap, all but one. He turned and surrendered.[45]

Sergeant George Kentner, 46th (South Saskatchewan) Battalion, 10th Brigade, 4th Canadian Division

The Canadians got through the front-line system with relative ease and began to push on past the support system. The 46th Battalion was moving on to the village of Dury. Here there was a strange mixture of wholesale surrender and bitter resistance.

Our party of about twelve men took off under artillery and machine-gun fire from the enemy. After a while we came to the right of the village and got onto a sunken road. Over to the right was a bunch of Heinies beating it from an old windmill. We potted at them with rifles and machine guns and caused some casualties. Advancing along the sunken road, we completely surprised and outflanked two machine-gun posts simply swarming with men. After we fired a few shots we took the whole bunch of prisoners, about 100–150 of them. Proceeding up the sunken road to help with the prisoners, I happened to look over to my left. I saw there another thickly manned machine-gun post of Heinies shooting over to the left from an embankment. I dropped down on the bank of this sunken road and fired at the man operating the machine gun. He fell over backwards and the machine gun with him. Some more of the boys arrived and joined in the firing. We got many others, but soon the remainder put up their hands to surrender.[46]

Private Morley Timberlake, 46th (South Saskatchewan) Battalion, 10th Brigade, 4th Canadian Division

Once Dury was captured the Canadians settled down to await the German counter-attack. Sure enough it came at 1200, signalled as usual by an artillery barrage crashing down around them. Sergeant Kentner was in an outpost established forward of the village and it soon became untenable.

> Evidently our machine-gun post on our right had been overrun as the Hun seemed rather close to us. We saw a couple of our men run madly back. One was struck in the leg and fell in a shell hole. He reappeared in a moment, less equipment, and completed his dash. We were entirely alone with only our grenade section in view. Our only escape was over open ground, which was now being swept by machine-gun fire.[47]
>
> Sergeant George Kentner, 46th (South Saskatchewan) Battalion, 10th Brigade, 4th Canadian Division

To stay meant capture, so they ran back in pairs and Kentner was lucky enough to get back unscathed to Dury. He then found that it was by no means the end of his ordeal as the battalion was peremptorily ordered to retrieve the lost ground.

> I was personally convinced that we would never succeed in reaching and capturing the position. We worked our way up and waited for the signal. Finally it came. There was a short pause at the end of the third whistle blast and then Corporal McVeety shouted, 'Come on, boys!' and leaped over the top. In an instant we were all over, racing forward, yelling and screeching and cursing as wildly as men ever did. The sight of us charging across the open ground with fixed bayonets and our weird, wild, almost insane cries disheartened Fritz. His front posts ran back to their machine guns, but here they stayed. Seconds later the whole ground was swept by machine-gun fire and men began to drop. McVeety was among the first to be killed. Never have I faced such a terrific storm of machine-gun bullets. We piled into his first line of posts and those who had not run back remained there forever. The enemy's nerve was broken. They began to run but our bullets were cutting them down. We were bent on their destruction and had no thought of mercy.[48]
>
> Sergeant George Kentner, 46th (South Saskatchewan) Battalion, 10th Brigade, 4th Canadian Division

Dury was secured, although at the cost of a battlefield littered with the corpses of both sides.

Further to the south the 16th Battalion of the 1st Canadian Division was held up in front of Cagnicourt by a mass of uncut wire in four or five thick belts some 8–10 feet wide. The men had tried to rush it without success and were sheltering in the shell holes pitting the ground when they saw a tank coming forward to their rescue. At this point one of their number leapt into heroic action.

> When the tank came to within 300 feet of the German wire a heavy machine-gun fire was opened upon it from the front trench. Corporal Metcalfe jumped up from the shell hole where he was and with his flags pointing towards the enemy's trench, led the tank towards it and then along it. The enemy kept a heavy machine-gun fire on the tank and as it got close to the trench commenced to throw at it clusters of bombs tied together.[49]
>
> Private J. H. Riehl, 16th (Canadian Scottish) Battalion, 3rd Brigade, 1st Canadian Division

His companions were amazed and not a little inspired by Metcalfe's selfless actions.

> Suddenly a heavy fire started from the trench in front of us. We looked up to see what it was about and there we saw the tank with Lance Corporal Metcalfe walking beside it, a little to the right in front of it, pointing with his signal flags in our direction. The tank was coming on at an angle from the left flank. I saw Metcalfe walking about 30 yards and then we decided it was our turn to help. We made a dash for the trench and made it before the Germans got their guns on us.[50]
>
> Sergeant F. E. Earwaker, 16th (Canadian Scottish) Battalion, 3rd Brigade, 1st Canadian Division

The German machine-gunners had been distracted just long enough. When they captured the trench they found seventeen German machine guns in the 'nest' – Lance Corporal William Metcalfe's survival was seen as miraculous and he would be awarded the VC for his actions. But in general the German resistance was fragile. At the least reverse they seemed far more prone to surrendering. As Lieutenant Colonel Cyrus Peck commanding the battalion put it: 'I never saw the enemy so cowardly. Prisoners surrendered in shoals. They outnumbered us vastly, but they were in a demoralised condition.'[51] A short while later Peck himself was to win his own VC when German resistance once again fitfully spluttered into violent life. It was that kind of strange two-paced fight. When the dust had finally died down the Canadians had scored a notable success. On the 3 September the Germans resumed their retreat all the way back to the Canal du Nord, the next great obstacle to the Allied advance.

It is often forgotten that less exotic British divisions were also doing their bit, but they too were fighting hard. Just one battalion amongst hundreds was the 1st Cheshires of the 5th Division who were also attacking as part of the IV Corps, Third Army. The Cheshires were ordered to take the strongly held village of Beugny on 2 September. They had been drained by the hard fighting and were sorely in need of a large reinforcement draft that had been straining hard to catch them up during the recent rapid advance. In the end it was clear that they would have to go into the attack with their companies still very much under-strength. Their operational orders were skimpy. Indeed, there was no precision at all; they were merely to move forward, take up jumping-off positions and then launch the attack at 0515 with the village of Beugny as their objective. As they moved into the line in the dark there was considerable confusion with their guides soon losing their way and the constant threat and harassment of the German night bombers was a further nuisance. They knew that Beugny was some 500 yards ahead to the half-right but that was about all. Their barrage opened up and immediately provoked a vicious response from the German guns.

At 5 a.m. the enemy guns opened on our trench and in less time than it takes to write had just about blown us to hell. Great big shells fell right into the trench, causing at least 50 per cent casualties before we started. We also got sneezing gas and liquid fire mixed up with high explosive. I was uncertain what order to give, or rather how to give it, but it was certain if we stopped in the trench till 5.15 a.m. none of us would be left to do the attack. I noticed 'B' Company on my left leaving the trench, so I called to those who could hear me to get out and lie in No Man's Land till time was up. I saw them all start. Shells were now falling like hail and I saw a number of fellows blown to bits including two officers' batmen, who were just near me in the trench. A wounded runner came and gave me the company roll, telling me it was from Company

Sergeant Major Smith who was wounded. I was just mounting the parapet followed by my servant, two runners and signallers, when we were caught by a shell and I next found myself sheltering in the trench with my runners either dead or badly wounded beside me. One fellow, I think he was a Lewis gunner, was lying on top of me and was able to talk. He told me a shell had just caught the back of my headquarters section and that I had jumped back into the trench. As I now felt better, I came to the conclusion I was only suffering from shock, but soon found I was sitting in a pool of blood and my leg seemed stiff. The trench was a shambles and I could see at least twenty killed all around my position. Suddenly six or seven Huns came creeping along the trench and I at first thought we were being attacked, but on my covering them with my revolver they at once informed me they were prisoners.[52]

Captain Lionel Ferguson, 1st Battalion, Cheshire Regiment, 15th Brigade, 5th Division

Captain Ferguson was eventually evacuated back to 'Blighty' with his leg wound. The Cheshires' attack was a failure for although Beugny was surrounded on three sides it was not taken that day. Yet they were just a tiny part of the huge offensive along the front. In essence, Ferguson and his men had simply been unlucky to have been in the wrong place at the wrong time. Beugny would fall without a fight next day as the Germans quietly pulled out during the night. In the end the advance continued regardless.

Another unit that had been up to its collective neck in the fighting for months was to run into serious trouble on 3 September. Major Richard Foot had tucked his battery into a convenient hollow just behind the infantry support line. It was to prove a painful mistake.

We had orders to fire a set-piece barrage at first light, including the carrying and preparation of 200 or more rounds for each gun. But it proved to be a trap because the German gunners, seeking no doubt to deny the ground to assembling infantry, drenched the whole battery position area with mustard gas shell all night. As we unpacked our shells from their boxes there was a steady plop-plop-plop of the enemy gas shells around us, some so close that all of us got sprayed with the liquid gas on our clothes. Working in respirators is never easy and always exhausting. But the work was there to be done; we did it – and fired our barrage. When it was over and in full daylight, nearly all of us

399

were badly blistered on arms and hands. Even those who had kept their respirators on all the time had their eyelids so swollen that they could scarcely see. Some forty of us, myself among them, formed a 'crocodile' of walking wounded, each man with a hand on the shoulder of the man in front of him, to the nearest dressing station. The pain and irritation of these enormous blister wounds are frantic in their effect. Yet it was quite a cheerful procession: someone would make some silly joke, and a ripple of laughter, stopped often by the cracking of blistered lips, would run from front to rear as we stumbled along.[53]

Major Richard Foot, 'D' Battery 310th Brigade, Royal Field Artillery

This is a very different picture from the atmosphere evoked by the famous painting *Gassed* by John Singer Sargent. Major Foot and the worst cases spent a couple of weeks in the field hospital and were then sent back to their units. Better discomfort than death any day.

There were great variations in the severity of the German opposition but overall there were more good days than bad days for the British and Canadian troops. Experienced officers also found that the Germans were becoming overly reliant on their machine guns.

The surprising bit is the number of prisoners. You will see in the Hun communiqués that he covers his retreat with rearguards of machine guns, and that is just what you would think if you saw and heard the fight. All his fire seems to come from machine guns, and yet there are these frequent considerable bags of infantry in exposed positions. If they knew how to use their rifles, they could produce a most withering volume of fire, but I can only conclude that they don't understand the weapon. That is borne out by the promptitude with which they throw them away. The ground everywhere is littered with Boche rifles and steel helmets.[54]

Brigadier General Anthony Henley, 127th Brigade, 42nd Division

Of course, the British Army was also feeling the strain and, in the very nature of things, those officers and units with a proven record of delivering success on the battlefield were called on again and again to lead the way.

Several men were killed during this short period and our nerves began to feel frayed at the edges. I myself remember standing in a trench in an abstracted state of mind when an officer approached noiselessly from behind and tapped me on the back. Naturally, I turned round with a jerk. 'What, nervous?' he exclaimed. For seven weeks we had moved about continually, had attacked three times, had seen much that filled us with hatred of the whole affair; moreover, our numbers had dwindled terribly, and our own company had dropped to no more than thirty men – it was once about 175. The continual marching so told upon us that our spirits seemed to sink lower even than March.[55]

Private Roland Fisher, 1/24th Battalion, London Regiment, 142nd Brigade, 47th Division

Simply put, there seemed to be no way out for the ordinary soldier other than the blind lottery of death or a 'Blighty' wound. For those that fell in battle a macabre fate could sometimes await them.

One thing I saw then which I had not previously seen in France was the spoiling of the dead by night. People, I must assume they were human, we never saw them and never knew, prowled the fields at night after a battle and relieved the dead of anything valuable, a ring, a watch, money, a pair of boots, but not uniform or military equipment. If a ring did not come off easily, the finger was cut off, if someone was lying out wounded, he did not remain wounded long, but died quickly. I made a point of leaving my signet ring with the adjutant.[56]

Captain Charles Brett, 5th Battalion, Connaught Rangers, 199th Brigade, 66th Division

The German Army finally completed its retreat to the Hindenburg Line fastness on 11 September. They had also pulled back from the Lys Salient with the intent of shortening the line and allowing divisions to move south to join the main battle. Back and back the troops went, abandoning all the gains of April 1918 and returning to their former front lines. All they managed to keep was Armentières and the Messines Ridge. The bulk of the ground was useless; the salient 'won' had proved nothing but a potential trap for the German garrison. The British followed up the retreating Germans with cautious advance guards, feeling their way forward and in a sense monitoring and shepherding the German retreat rather than launching outright attacks. The intention was to conserve the fading energy of the troops, allowing thereby as many divisions as possible to be moved out of the line during the brief lull to be restocked by drafts. It was hoped they would be revitalised by rest and training. At the same time the logistical demands of improving the communications right across the former battlefield were addressed as best as possible with the prevailing manpower shortages. Railways were pushed forward, roads and bridges repaired and the depots were moved up closer to the new lines. This was the calm before the storm that Haig was determined to unleash on the Germans before the month was out. The question now was whether the Allies could crack the Hindenburg Line and win the war at a stroke, or whether the Germans would hold out for another year. Serious campaigning would be all but impossible once winter proper set in during November. Time was running out if the war was to end in 1918.

CHAPTER TWELVE

With Our American Friends at the Front

T HE AMERICAN ARMY has barely featured in this history of the Western Front in 1918, and with good reason – until the autumn of 1918 its contribution had been negligible. Some line hold-ing, one or two minor attacks: this all faded into insignificance against the awesome backdrop of whole nations at war on the Western Front. The importance of the American Expeditionary Force (AEF) was its potential rather than its ability as a real player. The Regular Army had numbered around 25,000 men when its war began in April 1917 and its first concern had been to manage the massive expansion of its forces. The British Regular Army had been small in 1914 – around 250,000 men – but the Americans had only a tenth of that miniscule force. Where were they to find the men, the NCOs, the officers and the High Command with the experience of commanding large formations? How were they to feed, clothe and house a mass army? Where would the weapons come from? How could the nascent American armaments and munitions industry supply all the ammunition, shells, guns, tanks and aircraft they would need?

The British and the French knew the answer: they wanted to use the Americans as a vast pool of potential soldiers that they would train and incorporate into their own armies, replenishing units that had been ground down to the bare bones by battle. From a military perspective this had considerable merit in that the systems had already been established in Britain and France to take in raw recruits and turn out fully equipped, trained soldiers with all that they needed in battle.

They were offering to process the raw manpower of the United States. Yet this military solution to the problem was completely impractical on political grounds. The Americans could not subordinate their entire military capability to foreign powers and any president that suggested it would be committing political suicide, as Woodrow Wilson was well aware. The self-interest of their existing military commanders also mitigated against such a subjugation of the AEF to the common Allied interest. The British made a compromise proposal whereby an American battalion would be included in British brigades, then as experience was gained, American brigades would serve in British divisions, divisions in corps, corps in armies until they were ready to form an American Army of their own. This, too, was rejected out of hand. The American body politic and military were united: the Americans would raise, equip and train their own independent army under their own leadership, organised in a distinctive fashion, to operate in its own right on their own allotted sector of the Western Front. This was easier said than done.

The recruitment went well. Hundreds of thousands flocked voluntarily to serve in the AEF and the introduction of national conscription was then managed without any great opposition welling up. Indeed, by the end of the war millions of men had been conscripted into the army. But many of the other problems proved far more difficult to solve. The Americans simply did not have the time to build up the heavy munitions industry base to produce their own artillery, aircraft and tanks. For these they would in the end have to rely on their Allies. They also found that they did not have the experienced officers and NCOs to train the teeming numbers of raw recruits. They could manage to imbue them with the basic military skills but for the more complex skills and arcane disciplines required in trench warfare they had to call in help from the British and French Armies.

One matter on which they remained obdurate was their insistence on retaining American leadership of their units in battle. The problems of this were represented in the limited combat and command experience of General John Pershing, who had been selected as the commander-in-chief of the AEF. John Pershing was born on 13 September 1860. He attended the US Military Academy at West Point where he did well before graduating in 1886. He served with the 6th and 10th

US Cavalry where he was in action in some of the last Indian uprisings. Promotion came slowly, but he was appointed to the post of instructor at West Point in 1897. He had then fought with some distinction in the colonial wars conducted against the Spanish in 1898 and the Philippines in 1899–1902. He was still only a captain, but in 1905 he made a wise career move by marrying the daughter of a senior Republican senator. After a stint as military attaché in Japan he was promoted by President Theodore Roosevelt to brigadier general in 1906, thereby leapfrogging over 800 officers who were technically senior to him. His career was blossoming. In 1914 he was given command of the brigade responsible for the Mexican border and duly led the American forces into action during the punitive expedition that abortively chased the revolutionary Francisco Villa around Mexico from 1916 to 1917. Despite this chastening failure, Pershing impressed President Woodrow Wilson and was duly promoted from major general to general and given command of the American Expeditionary Force in May 1917.

The American staff officers and Pershing had taken an intense professional interest in observing, and indeed assessing, the conduct of the Great War in the opening years of the war. Unfortunately, they observed but did not see. Like so many generals before him, Pershing thought that the imperatives of trench warfare did not apply to his men. Not having experienced himself the effect of massed German artillery raining shells down on No Man's Land, ignorant of the reality of the firepower generated by massed machine guns, Pershing believed that the indomitable character, superior morale and individual fighting skills of his soldiers rendered them above such considerations. In particular, their skills with the rifle and bold battlefield tactics would allow them to circumvent the restrictions of trench warfare and secure a breakthrough. Through lack of experience, Pershing was ready to make all the same mistakes that the British had made in the early years of the war, and who was to gainsay him? He was the commander of the AEF and as such his opinions carried the day.

The Americans found it exceptionally difficult to get complete trained divisions despatched to the Western Front. Although they made a good start by despatching the 1st Division as early as June 1917, it had been hastily thrown together and was in no way ready for real operational use: it was more a political gesture of commitment than anything else.

After that the sheer scale of their task meant that by March 1918 they had only managed to get four divisions across the Atlantic. The pressure of events then to some extent disturbed the purity of Pershing's vision for an independent American Army. Out of necessity units and personnel were attached to British and French units for experience in quiet parts of the line.

There was often a real culture clash between the American troops and their European allies. The 'doughboys' were not just from another continent, they might as well have been from another planet as far as the exhausted British and French troops were concerned.

> The *poilus* are amazed at my happy state of my mind. I tell them that all the Americans feel the same way, and they absolutely shake their heads in pity, I guess, at our imbecility. But it is true that everybody is very happy all the time, taking the hardships as a sort of game. Obviously the novelty of everything wears off after three years of it, and I don't blame them. I am really enjoying myself immensely. The physical discomforts you experience occasionally are a part of the game and you can stand anything for a while. The shells that you hear switching toward you in a great crescendo, are fairly terrifying if they are close – but there is a splendid feeling when you see they missed you![1]
>
> Lieutenant Kenneth Walser, 101st Field Artillery, 51st Brigade, 26th Division, AEF

The hard-bitten British troops looked on them with a jaded eye. The older campaigners amongst them could remember when they had felt the enthusiasm and optimism of raw recruits, before the reality of war had left its mark.

> The Americans were green – greener than the greenest grass. They knew this and they knew our men were old hands and they wanted to hear about the war from people who knew it from personal experience. But the stories they wanted to hear were stories out of *Boy's Own Paper*: gallant officers waving gleaming swords as they led their brave men in glorious charges; noble soldiers cradling their dying comrades in their arms as they listened to the last whispered message to mother – and so on. They had just no shadow of an idea what war was like. As for our men: they had struggled and lived in everlasting mud; they had been gassed, blown up and wounded; the war had been going on since the

beginning of time and appeared to be going on for ever and ever; they had given up all hope of it ever ending and it was beyond their understanding that anyone should want to talk about it! The Americans couldn't understand this utter weariness about the war and the two sides never got on together – they just didn't speak the same language and the incomprehension was mutual.[2]

Lieutenant John Nettleton, 2nd Battalion, Rifle Brigade, 25th Brigade, 8th Division

One irritation caused by a trivial cultural difference – the frequency of spitting – was greatly magnified within the cramped communal environment in the trenches.

They had the most extraordinary habit, I don't know whether it's part of their military manual, but to be a really good soldier you had to expectorate long and frequently! Whereas we had to treat our trench as a dining room, bedroom, drawing room and everything else combined, they just looked on it as one big spittoon! That was extraordinarily unpleasant and our fellows didn't like it, because you never knew what you would find when you sat down. I had to have pails put at intervals with quite a big poster over each of them, 'If you must spit; spit here!'[3]

Lieutenant Colonel Edward Cawston, 2/10th Battalion, London Regiment, 175th Brigade, 58th Division

The arrogant confidence of men who had never been in combat grated against the sensibilities of those who had experienced the full horrors of war far too often. There is no doubt that both sides took pleasure in amplifying perceived cultural differences to irritate their opposite numbers. Americans played the rescuing heroes, but British officers frequently gave advice in a deliberately superior manner and then were infuriated when Americans ignored it; indeed, sometimes they took a mordant satisfaction in witnessing their come-uppance at the hand of the Germans.

I have never found myself able to forgive the American nation for the unforgivable words and attitude of one of their cocky infantry officers. A long column of men hove in sight, infantry, all wearing very broad-brimmed hats and marching in a very sloppy manner along the road from Poperinghe. We sat up and gawped at them. They presently drew level with us, and of all damn silly things to do, halted, fell out on the left side of the road and took a rest – lighting up fags and so forth. A little group of officers strolled over to us; I greeted them with a 'Good morning, gentlemen!' It had dawned upon us who they might be – and they certainly were – Americans! The senior among them said, 'Say, buddy, how far is it to this l'il old shootin' gallery of yours?' I had no idea of this idiot's rank, but I was shaken to my foundations by this question. My hackles rose, despite myself. I disliked this guy (all Americans are guys, are they not?) instantaneously – obviously a coarse-grained insensitive lout. I replied as politely as I could, albeit with a certain coolness in my manner, 'If you mean the Ypres Salient, Sir, you will be in it in about five minutes from here – and I strongly advise you to move your troops away as quickly as you can, because', I glanced at my wristwatch, 'it is now three minutes to eleven, and at eleven precisely Jerry puts down a carefully bracketed shoot of high velocity shells upon that stretch of road you have halted upon.' The idiot had the nerve to grin. He extracted the cigar from between his teeth and said, 'Oh, I guess that'll be OK!' That was the besetting sin of the Americans: you could always tell an American, but you couldn't tell him much, because he already knew it all![4]

Lieutenant Richard Dixon, 251st Siege Battery, 53rd Brigade, Royal Garrison Artillery

The aftermath was inevitable, the shells crashed down just as predicted and the inexperienced American troops duly panicked and ran for it, spreading themselves far and wide across the flat Flanders fields.

I fear we laughed and laughed, but, lest you think us brutally callous, let me assure you that, so far as we could see, and judging by the agility displayed by Uncle Sam's boys, no one got hurt, or badly hurt, anyway. If anyone did get a shell splinter anywhere in his New World anatomy, it didn't interfere with his movement across the landscape.[5]

Lieutenant Richard Dixon, 251st Siege Battery, 53rd Brigade, Royal Garrison Artillery

The American units had been organised at Pershing's behest into huge divisions totalling 28,000 men. Each of these divisions consisted of two strong infantry brigades (which in turn were made up of two regiments of three battalions each), a battalion of engineers, three machine gun battalions and supporting artillery units. This was well over twice the size of the average British, French or German division and reflected

Pershing's desire for a formation with heavy firepower coupled with an ability to withstand casualties from within its own resources. However, these divisions also proved unwieldy beasts, difficult to command and control, especially for their major generals who, of course, had scant experience at this level.

When the German offensives began the Americans at first played a purely peripheral role. A few of their engineers attached to the Fifth Army had played a part within Carey's Force in the defence of Amiens. But the British and French wanted much more. As the German offensives bit they campaigned to have American troops sent across the Atlantic, not as fully formed complete divisions, but as purely infantry formations. This would allow them to rapidly build up the raw numbers of the AEF on the Western Front. The Allies also began to use the American divisions, with Pershing's grudging acquiescence, to relieve French divisions in rather more threatened sectors than the quiet backwaters they had previously occupied.

One notable early incident occurred when nearly 2,800 German stormtroopers attacked the 102nd Infantry Regiment of the 26th Division in the Seicheprey sector on 20 April 1918. When Sergeant Charles Boucher had been briefed the previous day the regiment had been told that an attack was imminent and had been ordered to fight to the last man. That night the German barrage raged down on their post. It was to be a terrible introduction to war on the Western Front.

> The barrage lasted till dawn began to show and our first casualty was discovered. He was almost completely covered with earth and the blood was pumping from his mouth, ears, and eyes. Nothing could be done for him so he just choked up and passed on. We all knew what we could expect after such a heavy barrage and, since we were short of ammunition, I ordered our men to hold their fire till the Prussian shock troops hit the barbed wire. We hadn't long to wait and, just as they arrived at the barbed wire, we opened up on them. They advanced in close formation and soon the wire and the ground in front of us was covered with their dead and wounded. They then crawled over each other only to be mowed down by our deadly fire. The shouting and screaming of the wounded and dying wasn't easy to listen to and very hard to forget. A platoon had been captured on our right and another

on our left so, now, we were surrounded on all sides and our casualties began to pile up on us. I had been wounded early in the morning by a hunk of shrapnel, so I used a shoelace and a piece of wood I cut from a duckboard in the trench to make a tourniquet and stop the bleeding and hobbled about the rest of the day, as best I could. Corporal Gritzback was in charge of a machine gun squad and his gunner, Private Lilley, was hit on the head and killed so, Dodi Gritzback lifted his body off the gun and took over. He mowed them down as they kept on coming in on us and, finally, he was hit just below the brim of his helmet. The helmet was scooped off his head and hit one of his men on the face opening up his cheek. Then, Corporal Coe got a bullet in the guts and we lain him on the parados. He kept hollering, 'Charlie! Oh! Charlie! For God's sake, do something for me.' I gave him some water from my canteen. Then, I ripped open his shirt and there was a hole in his belly. Then a piece of shell hit him in the neck and decapitated him completely so his misery was over.[6]

Sergeant Charles Leo Boucher, 102nd Infantry Regiment, 26th Division, AEF

When night fell they crawled out, most of them badly wounded. The Americans, on balance, showed considerable promise as individual soldiers, but had proved hopelessly disorganised in their response to the situation. There were considerable delays in sending forward re-inforcements or in launching a counter-attack. Officers had rather prematurely given up hope, knowing the front-line posts to be sur-rounded; they had presumed them to have been wiped out. They nearly were, as just eight of Boucher's platoon of sixty survived and in total the Americans suffered 669 casualties.

A further test of the American military capabilities came when the 1st Division, AEF, that had been attached to the French VI Corps, was tasked with making an attack on the village of Cantigny in the Montdidier sector on 28 May 1918. Supported by French artillery and tanks, the Americans swept forward and soon overran the village. Then the problems began.

Taking Cantigny was nothing compared to holding it after we got it. The Germans made nine counter-attacks and nine times they failed. We didn't know what sleep was as we had to stand to all the time. Every little while this order would come down the trench: 'Pass it on, stand to, they're coming!' 'They're coming! They're going to flank us on the left!' This kept up for three days: one continuous rain of shells, no sleep, no eats, and all the water we got was what we took off the dead men by crawling out on the top and taking their canteens. Men were being picked off to the right of us and to the left of us. Still the wounded who were not able to get back were lying about us in the trench, besides several who had some strength left were crawling down the trench and working their way to the rear as best they could. Some got back and some never did, as we found several dead on the way out. Some were blown to bits and others had just died. It was common to walk near a man or roll him over or give him a touch with the foot to see if he was asleep or dead. Three full days passed with nothing to eat.[7]

Private Frank Last, 18th Infantry Regiment, 1st Division, AEF

Nonetheless, despite all the pressure, they held out. More than a year after they had nominally entered the war, the AEF was in proper action at last: they too were now men at war.

The next battle was far more significant as it occurred as the late May German offensive was sweeping towards the Marne River. Foch appealed to Pershing for help and this time Pershing did respond, despatching his 2nd and 3rd Divisions to the front. The machine guns of the 3rd Division helped stop the German advance in its tracks by defending the bridges at Château-Thierry. Meanwhile, the 2nd Division took up a defensive line not far to the west with the intention of underpinning the French units who were still falling back in some chaos. This gave Captain Lloyd Williams of the Marine Corps the golden opportunity to utter the immortal words to his local French commander, 'Retreat? Hell – we only just got here!' This somehow summed up not only a traditional American insensitivity, but also their very real determination to perform well and make the difference. They did indeed stand fast, but the French had already lost Belleau Wood that lay in front of their positions. On 6 June the 2nd Division was ordered to recover the woods and the US Marine Brigade was committed into a frontal attack. It advanced in training ground 'waves' with minimal artillery preparation over the open fields towards Belleau Wood and the neighbouring Bouresches village. As a demonstration of raw courage it was undeniable and the attacks have passed into legend, sent into action as the men were by Colonel Albertus Catlin with the pithy, 'Give 'em hell boys!'[8], while the less exalted, but equally inspirational, Sergeant Dan Daly's battle cry of, 'Come on you sons of bitches, do you want to live forever?'[9] has a refreshingly contemporary feel. Yet their tactical naivety was also transparent.

> I say they went in as if on parade and that is literally true. There was no yell and wild rush, but a deliberate forward march, with lines at dress right. They walked at regulation pace, because a man is little use in a hand-to-hand bayonet struggle after a 100 yard dash.[10]
>
> Colonel Albertus Catlin, 6th Marine Regiment, 4th Brigade, 2nd Division, AEF

Unfortunately, they were even less use if they were already dead, shot down by German machine guns. Colonel Catlin was wounded that day and was undoubtedly a brave man, but he was hopelessly naive as far as assault tactics were concerned. And the Marines suffered accordingly, losing over 1,000 casualties in the first day.

The battle for that inconsequential wood went on for most of June. It became a focus of attention: both sides fought for it, but few men could have said why – the fact that the other side wanted it was enough. In this it strongly resembled the often pointless, local battles for obscure copses and villages on the Somme where the British Army had learnt its trade nearly two years previously. Now the Americans too were learning the hard way: constant heavy shelling, gas shells, lashings of small arms fire, splintered trees, non-existent communications, total confusion and an absence of All Arms coordination.

> We got into the edge of the wood, dug in and took position ready for an advance or a defence against a counter-attack. This was the kind of fighting that many Americans knew, not trench warfare but open warfare, the way that their ancestors had fought on the frontiers and in all the wars of our country. But the difficulty with Belleau Wood was you never knew where the front was! Little groups of Americans, little groups of Germans got together to fight each other, and while you were fighting in one direction, all of a sudden without any warning you would find that there were some Germans to the rear of you and they had to be mopped up. Clean up, mop up and move ahead with the unyielding determination to enforce your will on the enemy. That was Belleau

Wood: fighting hand to hand, from position to position, not knowing where the next attack would come, but the steady moving forward in the wood of the Marines until they cleared the entire woods. All over the terrain in the rocky crevices and the foxholes we found the German dead, not only from the day before but from four or five days before.[11]

Sergeant Melvin Krulewitch, 2nd Division, AEF

The Marines endured vicious fighting, a starvation diet and utter exhaustion while surrounded by nameless putrescent corpses. This was war. Yet when they were relieved the new arrivals once again exuded innocence.

We are in a place made immortal by Americans – and they are not unusual or extraordinary supermen, but simply Americans. I am with the infantry in the line and if the Boche gets this place back, it will be because none of us is left alive. You would be very proud of America if you could see the things that are here now. I am very glad you can't though. Squads lying where they fell, charging in perfect formation against a Boche machine gun – pitiful shattered helmets, letters from home, bayonets no longer shiny near the end – everything bloody and stained.[12]

Lieutenant Kenneth Walser, 101st Field Artillery, 51st Brigade, 26th Division, AEF

Walser seemed to have learnt little from the evidence of the slaughter in front of him. Instead he symbolised the optimism of countless young Americans arriving on the Western Front.

I hope I may take part in the push that will come then we shall crush them to pieces. The Boches are bewildered at the Americans and hate to fight them. They take Americans prisoner and the Americans turn on them with their fists and bring back their captors as prisoners. Every American knows that he is good for half a dozen of them, and none of us is war weary yet.[13]

Lieutenant Kenneth Walser, 101st Field Artillery, 51st Brigade, 26th Division, AEF

Here in a nutshell were all the same old half-truths, the myths and downright propaganda – the complete confidence in a racial super-iority that simply did not exist. They would soon learn, as so many had before them, that self-belief and élan are not enough: firepower, training and tactics were the foundations of success in modern warfare. Nevertheless, their blind optimism was in itself a potent weapon against the increasingly despondent Germans.

When the Germans attacked again on 15 July the Americans were entrusted with a 7-mile section of the line along the Marne from Château-Thierry to Varennes. They did well, matching the performance of the French divisions around them and although the Germans penetrated their forward positions the Rear Zone defences held firm.

> At 3.30 a.m. the general fire ceased and their creeping barrage started – behind which at 40 yards only, mind you, they came – with more machine guns than I thought the German Army owned. The enemy had to battle their way through the first platoon on the riverbank – then they took on the second platoon on the forward edge of the railway where we had a thousand times the best of it – but the Germans gradually wiped it out. My third platoon took its place in desperate hand-to-hand fighting, in which some got through only to be picked up by the fourth platoon, which was deployed simultaneously with the third. By the time they struck the fourth platoon they were all in and easy prey. It's God's truth that one company of American soldiers beat and routed a full regiment of picked shock troops of the German Army.[14]
>
> Captain Jesse Woolridge, 38th Infantry Regiment, 3rd Division, AEF

The Americans were developing their defensive skills apace.

When the French counter-attacked on 18 July the 1st and 2nd American Divisions (part of the French XX Corps) were in the forefront of the attack on the Soissons heights. The Americans did well, attacking three days in succession across difficult terrain, but took heavy casualties – partially, at least, due to their inexperience.

> We had the Americans as neighbours and I had a close-up view of them. Everyone says the same: they're first-rate troops, fighting with intense *individual* passion (concentrated on the enemy) and wonderful courage. The only complaint one would make about them is that they don't take sufficient care; they're too apt to get themselves killed.[15]
>
> Stretcher Bearer Pierre Teilhard de Chardin, Moroccan Division, XX Corps, French Army

As the fighting continued deep into August, the American contribution grew exponentially, until finally two American corps fought side by side in the line. It is fair to say that they were still continuing to learn the hard way. One typical learning experience was suffered by the men of the 305th Machine Gun Battalion of the 77th Division, who were pinned down in a makeshift trench position after having crossed the Vesle River on 22 August. Short of food, drinking polluted shell-hole water and under constant fire, they began to see the real horrors of war for the first time. Not everyone could be a hero when the chips were down. Sometimes there were no Germans visible to fight man to man; sometimes it was just a matter of endurance.

> Dunbar cried most all day. He figured these were his last days on earth. Every time a shell burst the poor fellow prayed aloud. The heavies were busy all day and the detonation was nerve-racking. Jerry kept the skies lit up with star shells and the snipers' bullets were just skimming the parapet. At 1.30 a.m. Jerry laid down a terrific barrage and he threw over everything from 1-pounder to *minenwerfers*. Had to wear our gas masks all night. Some of the shells knocked the banks down and almost buried us. His whizz-bangs were timed perfect and were bursting right over our heads. Timothy received a bad wound in the leg from the flying shrapnel and I bandaged the wound – but couldn't see what I was doing. Dunbar and Darcy were praying for a happy death – and Shannley wanted to open up. It was hell on earth in that hole and to make matters worse Bates tore his mask off. He was like a madman for a minute and I knocked him cold and tied his hands with my belt. The barrage lifted at 4 a.m. and when day broke it was some sight. All the trees were cut down and the ground was torn up with shell holes – all sizes. The gas was bad all day. Bates was in bad shape but we kept him bound up. We all thanked our lucky stars we pulled through the night.[16]

Private Thomas Grady, 'B' Company, 305th Machine Gun Battalion, 77th Division, AEF

Trials like these lasted for days and nights on end. Men could see no end to the torment and it was inevitable that some broke under the strain, although many more stood up to the challenge and endured. In the end the Germans, pressed also by the French, would fall back to the Aisne River in late August.

*

THE AEF WAS BECOMING A REALITY in the field at last. By this time the Americans had some five divisions training alongside the British and Haig had hoped to throw these units into the pot for the series of attacks planned following the success of the Fourth Army assault on 8 August. Haig was to be bitterly disappointed, but in the argument that followed both sides just about managed to retain their dignity.

> General Pershing came to see me. He stated that he might have to withdraw the five American divisions now with the British. I pointed out to him that I had done everything to equip and help the American Army, and to provide them with horses. So far, I have had no help from these troops (except the three battalions which were used in the battle near Chipilly in error). If he now withdraws the five American divisions, he must expect some criticism of his action not only from British troops in the field but also from the British Government. All I wanted to know was definitely whether I could prepare to use the American troops for an attack (along with the British) at the end of September against Kemmel. Now I know I cannot do so. Pershing said he would not withdraw his divisions as long as the present battle was in progress.[17]
>
> Field Marshal Sir Douglas Haig, General Headquarters, BEF

Pershing had his own long-cherished plans that reached fruition with the formation of the First Army and its use in an American-led offensive on the St Mihiel Salient, which was set for 12 September 1918. This was a pronounced arrow-headed salient some 32 miles deep and tipped by the village of St Mihiel, which gave it its name. It had long been a thorn in the French side, threatening and disrupting their communications.

The Battle of St Mihiel marked the moment when the AEF truly came of age. Its officers had to prepare realistic plans and its staff officers needed to make them happen: all the logistical functions of an army would be well and truly tested. Pershing and his staff made every effort to try and ensure success and when the artillery barrage (much of it contributed by the French) commenced it did not disappoint the expectant troops.

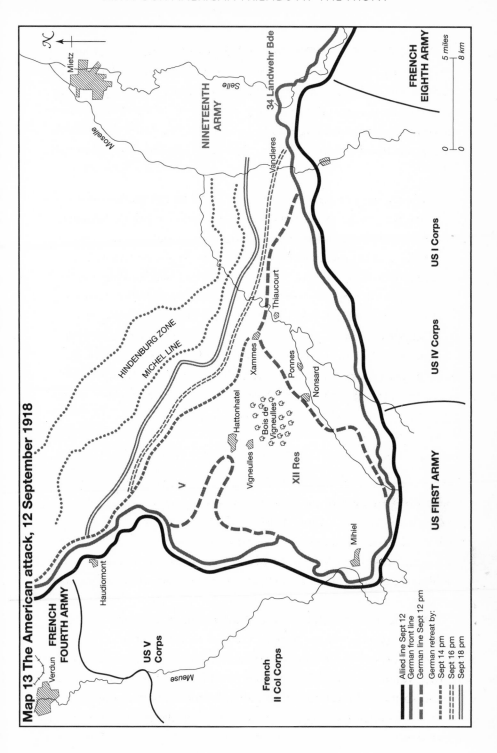

Map 13 The American attack, 12 September 1918

FRENCH EIGHTH ARMY

5 miles
8 km

34 Landwehr Bde

NINETEENTH ARMY

Selle

Mietz

Moselle

Vandieres

Thiaucourt

US I Corps

US IV Corps

HINDENBURG ZONE

MICHEL LINE

Xammes

Ponnes

Nonsard

Hattonhatel

Bois de Vigneulles

Vigneulles

XII Res

US FIRST ARMY

Mihiel

Haudiomont

FRENCH FOURTH ARMY

Verdun

Meuse

US V Corps

French II Col Corps

Allied line Sept 12
German front line
German line Sept 12 pm
German retreat by:
Sept 14 pm
Sept 16 pm
Sept 18 pm

At exactly 1 a.m. the artillery cut loose and for four hours it hammered the Boche lines, batteries and back areas. It seemed as if all the artillery in France had suddenly opened up, for we really did have an unusual amount of it. The sky was red with big flashes, the air seemed full of 'Empire State Expresses' and the explosion of the heavier shells made the ground tremble. That's not a poetical expression: the ground shook pretty steadily all night. It was a wonderful and awe-inspiring sight.[18]

Second Lieutenant Phelps Harding, 165th Infantry Regiment, 42nd Division, AEF

As the moment neared for the troops and tanks to go over the top at 0500, the barrage swelled up still further into a swirling crescendo of deafening sound and fury.

Machine-gun fire was added, and shells containing liquid fire and other illuminating material were used. No 4th of July display ever equalled this deadly display. I waited for a while after they went over the top, then, gathering the crew together, we sauntered along after them. Reaching the jumping-off place, we started across No Man's Land. This was a mass of wire, which had been somewhat torn up by shell fire, and further opened up by wire cutters, previous to going over the top. The second battalion was taking a support position at the beginning of the attack, so we soon caught up with them. On our right and left I could see other troops in formation moving forward in the attack. As we passed over the German front lines, I wondered how anyone could live through such a bombardment. The trenches and all the earth were utterly blown up. The shell holes were so numerous that we had to walk carefully in order to keep from falling into them. I did not see a single dead German until well up in the forenoon. We had no wounded to carry. German prisoners were being used to carry our wounded back. Prisoners were coming back in large numbers.[19]

Private Clarence Richmond, 5th Marine Regiment, US Marine Corps, 2nd Division, AEF

The advance was a great success. But something else was happening: while the First Army had been building up for the attack the Germans had been making their preparations for withdrawal and it was largely rearguards that the Americans encountered. To all intents and purposes it proved a walkover. Nevertheless, the experience had been valuable: staff officers have to learn their trade as much as gunners and infantry.

> On the night of 13 September we and one of the infantry regiments went over in the St Mihiel Salient to cut off and clean up the so-called 'pocket'. We bussed and marched for three days and nights, and in our wanderings practically crossed the upper end of the salient, but as a fight it was a joke, for we never fired a shot and all we saw were many destroyed Boche trenches and dugouts, and any quantity of hungry Austrians who were anxious to do anything in the world but fight and whose favourite form of sport was eating![20]
> Colonel Leland Garretson, 315th Machine Gun Battalion, 80th Division, AEF

And, of course, the success improved American morale: already no shrinking violets they now considered themselves ready for anything.

> The Boche may not have had much respect for the American Army a few months ago, but from what the prisoners say now, we are about as welcome as the proverbial skunk at a lawn party.[21]
> Second Lieutenant Phelps Harding, 165th Infantry Regiment, 42nd Division, AEF

The AEF had proved it was capable of mounting a large-scale offensive. Greater challenges would lie ahead. Once again the learning curve would prove a painful one to climb, but the Americans had numbers and boundless enthusiasm: they would not fail.

CHAPTER THIRTEEN

Breaking the Hindenburg Line

IN SEPTEMBER 1916 the German Army had begun the construction of the Hindenburg Line (known to the Germans as the Siegfried Stellung), intended as a general fall-back position as the British Army battered its way forward on the rolling downland of the Somme. It stretched from Arras, down via St Quentin to near Vailly, right down on the Aisne River. As the Germans' tactical position deteriorated in the later stages of the battle it was decided to withdraw the 30 or so miles back to their newly built fortress. Work had continued until the line consisted of multiple lines of trenches 6,000–8,000 yards deep, dotted with strongpoints and concrete machine-gun posts and all covered by copious belts of barbed wire – a formidable Battle Zone by any standards. Destabilised by the final desperate months of fighting in the Battle of the Somme, the Germans had fallen back to the fastness of the Hindenburg Line in February/March of 1917 to remain there until they had burst out on 21 March 1918. Now they were back.

The Germans had not, however, been idle. The main Hindenburg Line had been built to take advantage of reverse slopes to try and diffuse the destructive power of the British artillery. However, the presence of the St Quentin Canal along a stretch of the front had been too much of a temptation: it was 35 feet wide and up to 6 feet deep, and a formidable obstacle in its own right. As a result, a substantial section of the main positions here were located immediately behind the canal and hence in a valley potentially overlooked from the ridge in front. The Germans were fully aware of this and had developed a strong outpost line all along the ridge. But the capture of the British lines in

March 1918 offered a more radical solution. All the labour that could be spared was utilised to convert the former British positions into the German pattern by fortifying villages, erecting ever more barbed wire and providing 'proper' reinforced deep dugouts in contrast to the usual British 'scrapes'. The end result was the Hindenburg Line that faced the British in September 1918: the three old British lines, the ridge outpost line, the Hindenburg Line proper, the Hindenburg Support Line and finally, the Hindenburg Reserve Line.

As can be readily imagined the very idea that Haig was about to attack this formidable fortress complex promoted a substantial degree of concern from politicians, amongst which one could certainly include the Chief of the Imperial General Staff General Sir Henry Wilson. In the run-up to the attack Haig received a telegram in which his superior tried to distance himself from the plans.

> The following telegram from Wilson reached me this morning. It is marked 'H.W. Personal' and was sent off yesterday:
>> Just a word of caution in regard to incurring heavy losses in attacks on the Hindenburg Line as opposed to losses when driving the enemy back to that line. I do not mean to say that you have incurred such losses, but I know the War Cabinet would become anxious if we received heavy punishment in attacking the Hindenburg Line WITHOUT SUCCESS.
>> Wilson
>
> It is impossible for a CIGS to send a telegram of this nature to a C-in-C in the field as a 'personal' one. The Cabinet are ready to meddle and interfere in my plans in an underhand way, but do not dare openly to say that they do not mean to take the responsibility for any failure though ready to take credit for every success! The object of this telegram is, no doubt, to save the Prime Minister in case of any failure. So I read it to mean that I can attack the Hindenburg Line if I think it right to do so. The CIGS and the Cabinet already know that my arrangements are being made to that end. If my attack is successful I will remain on as C-in-C. If we fail, or our losses are excessive, I can hope for no mercy. What a wretched lot of weaklings we have in high places at the present time.[1]
>
> Field Marshal Sir Douglas Haig, General Headquarters, BEF

Haig wrote back to the egregious Wilson; he may have been fairly inarticulate but he certainly could express himself on paper when sufficiently riled. No one receiving Haig's telegram could be under any doubt as to his scorn.

> With reference to your wire *re.* casualties in attacking the Hindenburg Line. What a wretched lot! And how well they mean to support me!! What confidence![2]
>
> Field Marshal Sir Douglas Haig, General Headquarters, BEF

When Wilson replied, pleading that the ongoing police strike in England made the Cabinet sensitive to heavy losses, Haig must have regretted the loss of the clear-thinking previous CIGS. There is no doubt that Robertson would have grasped the situation far quicker and with less need for personal manoeuvring.

> How ignorant these people are of war! In my opinion it is much less costly in lives to press the enemy after a victorious battle than to give him time to recover and organise afresh his defence of a position! The later must then be attacked in the face of hostile artillery and machine guns, all carefully sited.[3]
>
> Field Marshal Sir Douglas Haig, General Headquarters, BEF

Haig was entirely correct in wanting a decision as soon as possible while the Germans were thoroughly disorganised. To pause would simply waste momentum and time. The winter was coming and no one in his right mind would want to attack the selfsame Hindenburg Line in the spring of 1919. Both Foch and Haig were determined not to allow the Germans the time to improve the defences all winter, to work out new defensive tactics and to garrison the line with fresh or revitalised divisions. Such a situation would be a real test of the All Arms Battle tactics.

On 10 September, during a brief visit back to London, Haig rammed home his message into the ears of Lord Milner, the War Minister.

> Within the last four weeks we had captured 77,000 prisoners and nearly 800 guns! There has never been such a victory in the annals of Britain, and its effects are not yet apparent. The German prisoners now taken will not obey their officers or NCOs. The discipline of the German

Army is quickly going, and the German officer is no longer what he was. It seems to me to be the beginning of the end. From these and other facts I draw the conclusion that the enemy's troops will not await our attacks in even the strongest positions. Briefly, in my opinion, the character of the war has changed. What is wanted now at once is to provide the means to exploit our recent successes to the full. Reserves in England should be regarded as reserves for the French front and all yeomanry, cyclists etc. now kept for civil defence should be sent to France at once. If we act with energy now, a decision can be obtained in the very near future.[4]

Field Marshal Sir Douglas Haig, General Headquarters, BEF

Back in France plans were afoot to obtain that decision sooner rather than later.

Foch was convinced that the moment had come for a frenzy of blows stretching along the Western Front, striking here, there and everywhere, allowing the Germans no chance to rest, concentrate their forces or move their reserves. The French and the Americans would be first into the attack in the south on 26 September when they would push deep into the Meuse-Argonne area. While the Germans were trying to cope with this assault, the following day on 27 September the First and Third Armies would lunge forward across the Hindenburg Line towards Cambrai. Another day, another massive offensive, as on 28 September the French, Belgians and Plumer's Second Army would launch a Fourth Battle of Ypres by crashing forward in Flanders. Finally, on 29 September, the Fourth Army was also to be launched at the Hindenburg Line. The Fourth Army in particular had a lot to do before it could even consider attacking its objectives. Each attack meant a world of planning, preparations beyond the conception of most civilians and logistical feats on such a scale that they seemed to defy logic. Separately each offensive was a mighty undertaking; taken together they were one of the most sustained assaults in the history of warfare.

Defensive systems have been planned and constructed throughout the centuries. I suppose the Great Wall of China and Hadrian's Wall are the classic examples of successful ones. But had the Picts possessed the resources of the Romans, very possibly the wall would have proved no barrier. Such defences are valid against primitive opponents, but against the full mechanical resources of a well-equipped army seem to be, in the end, futile. And Germany was now up against a mighty concentration of power built up over four years by Britain and her Dominions. Masses of artillery and tanks were ready to go into action to smash through the famous Hindenburg Line and we in the 53rd Brigade were a small part of that huge and – as it proved – irresistible concentration.[5]

Lieutenant Richard Dixon, 251st Siege Battery, 53rd Brigade, Royal Garrison Artillery

Unfortunately, the brief rest and retraining interval before the assaults began had by no means cured the British divisions of the after-effects of six months' hellish warfare. Although they were winning, the state of morale was not conventionally good. Men were exhausted by the trials they had undergone and were fully aware that there was much more to endure in the near future. Private Edward Williamson of the 17th Royal Scots was safely back in the rear areas where his unit had been training hard to master the new techniques required in open warfare, but it was soon apparent that not everyone was ready to go into the attack for real.

It was early evening, our meal finished and we sat in the candlelight adjusting equipment, chatting or writing last-minute letters before the 'Fall in!' The peace was suddenly shattered by a loud report, magnified by the hut's confined space. I slithered to the floor off the form I reclined on, startled and amazed to find the cause of the shock was the fellow who had been sitting with his back to me, apparently cleaning his rifle, had suddenly decided to give himself a self-inflicted wound. 'Fetch the Sergeant!' someone called. The man was on the floor, moaning and holding the injured foot as I with others gathered round. I looked in his face: it was Private McTaggert, late of the cookhouse and now back in the platoon. He had panicked, could not face the ordeal and hardship that lay ahead for us all and plugged his left foot as the easiest way out, though in great pain. Poor devil! We watched him being carried out by the first-aid men, knowing that when fit again he would be court-martialled and discharged with ignominy.[6]

Private Edward Williamson, 17th Battalion, Royal Scots, 106th Brigade, 35th Division

Very few men went to this kind of desperate extreme, but most of McTaggert's comrades well understood what had made him do it. The German defences were a terrifying prospect that could turn any normal man's knees to water.

Of all the attacking armies the Fourth Army was faced with the greatest problems. To have a real chance of vaulting the Hindenburg Line they desperately needed to overrun the former British lines and, if possible, the German outpost line that lay in front of the main positions. A preliminary operation was planned for 18 September, but in the preceding days there were a series of 'minor' operations to secure the best possible jumping-off positions. One such was made by the 11th Essex in the Savy Wood area. It may have been a trifling attack in the overall scheme of things, but there were to be major personal repercussions for the unfortunate Private Leslie Sherwood.

My mates were dropping either side of me in the trench and suddenly I 'copped a packet' as we used to say. A shell exploded above me and to the right. A lump of white-hot steel shattered my right ankle. My back and elbows were peppered with splinters of steel. After the first hammering impact my foot went dead. I went deaf and from then on the bursting shells sounded like taps on cardboard boxes. Now came a problem. I was fully conscious and wanted to lie down in the trench, but the floor was under 18 inches of very liquid mud. Hopping a little on one leg, I gathered up haversacks, water bottles etc. of the dead and built up a pier in the mud on which to rest my wounds. But the device was unsatisfactory and gradually collapsed in the mud. I was too weak to make any further attempt, so my wounds sank deeper and ever deeper into the mud. I prayed that the barrage would soon ease up enough to let the stretcher bearers collect us up while there was still life in some of us. Half a dozen lads were beyond human help. After three or four hours of the punishing strafe there was complete silence and along came the stretcher bearers, four men to a stretcher, to pick up what was left. Then followed the perilous, almost impossible, quarter-mile journey – four men slipping and sliding with a stretcher over their shoulders to the first-aid post, a quickly erected tent with a doctor up to his eyes in mud.[7]

Private Leslie Sherwood, 11th Battalion, Essex Regiment, 18th Brigade, 6th Division

After a quick glance from the doctor and that inevitable panacea for all ills – a cup of tea – Sherwood was taken in an ambulance back to a huge tented casualty clearing station at Albert. Next morning he was taken to the operating tent and 'put under', ready for the surgeon's knife.

> Cosily tucked up in bed, I awoke about midday to the usual after-effects of chloroform. I was treated to a drink of champagne and soon felt ready for my first meal of Bovril and some fruit jelly. Fine! But I wished the Sister would ease the vice-like grip round my shin, it was much too tight. 'Shush!' says the Sister, 'There is no grip there, relax!' Later on she came round to check on the various wounds and appropriate dressings. Turning back my blankets I then noticed it – only one foot standing up, the other missing! 'Strange!' I thought to myself. 'Here, Sister, is my foot off?' She replied, 'Yes, laddie, don't worry you will be on the train for "Blighty" in another hour.'[8]
>
> Private Leslie Sherwood, 11th Battalion, Essex Regiment, 18th Brigade, 6th Division

At this his darkest hour, Sherwood was grateful for his memories of an old Boys' Brigade friend who had lost a leg much earlier in the war and was now 'dashing around' on an artificial leg.

> During the healing period there was no great pain, apart from the dreaded daily cleansing and dressing of the wound. But like all who have lost limbs, I became distressed at the phenomenon of 'phantom limbs'. That is the feeling and movement of one's missing parts: foot and toes. When recovering from the shock of amputation, the nerves of the missing members gradually awaken and have the sense of being twisted and confused, rather like plaited tresses of hair. The harder one might try to straighten out those toes to the normal position, the more they become confused.[9]
>
> Private Leslie Sherwood, 11th Battalion, Essex Regiment, 18th Brigade, 6th Division

Sherwood would never get the chance to forget that trivial line-straightening operation of 17 September.

On 18 September the Fourth Army attack went in on the German defences running along the western heights overlooking the Hindenburg Line, stretching from St Quentin in the south through Ronssoy right along to Épéhy, which would be attacked by the V Corps of the

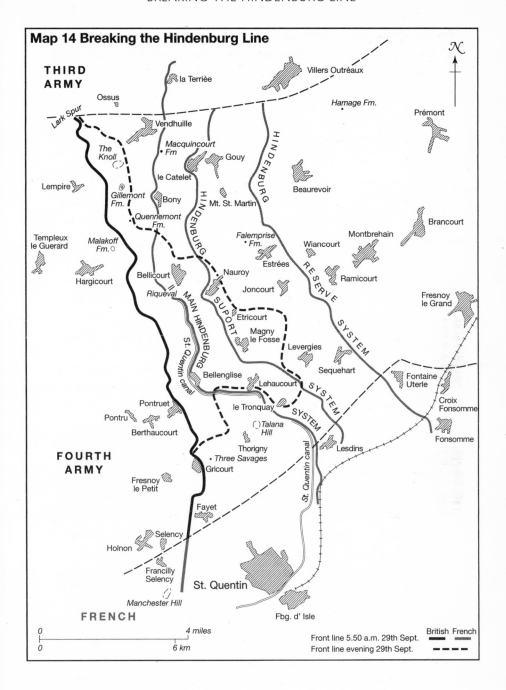

Map 14 Breaking the Hindenburg Line

N

THIRD
ARMY

la Terrière

Villers Outréaux

Ossus

Hamage Fm.

Prémont

Lark Spur

Vendhuille

Macquincourt
Fm.

Gouy

The
Knoll

le Catelet

Beaurevoir

Lempire

Gillemont
Fm.

Bony

Mt. St. Martin

Brancourt

Quennemont
Fm.

Falemprise
Fm.

Montbrehain

Templeux
le Guerard

Malakoff
Fm.

Wiancourt

Estrées

Bellicourt

Nauroy

Ramicourt

Hargicourt

Riqueval

Joncourt

Fresnoy
le Grand

Etricourt

Magny
le Fosse

Levergies

Bellenglise

Sequehart

Fontaine
Uterle

Pontruet

Lehaucourt

Croix
Fonsomme

Pontru

le Tronquay

Berthaucourt

Talana
Hill

Fonsomme

Thorigny

FOURTH
ARMY

Three Savages

Gricourt

Lesdins

Fresnoy
le Petit

Fayet

Selency

Holnon

Francilly
Selency

St. Quentin

Manchester Hill

FRENCH

Fbg. d' Isle

HINDENBURG

HINDENBURG

SUPORT

MAIN HINDENBURG

St. Quentin canal

RESERVE

SYSTEM

SYSTEM

SYSTEM

St. Quentin canal

0 ———————— 4 miles
0 ———————— 6 km

Front line 5.50 a.m. 29th Sept. ▬▬▬
Front line evening 29th Sept. ▬ ▬ ▬

British French

427

Third Army. It was the intention to take all the old British defences and if possible to push on and overrun the German outpost line. It is worth remarking that in this endeavour the Fourth Army was therefore intent on attacking strong defensive positions despite the fact that they were held by a German garrison that was of roughly equal strength. There were definite tinges of over-confidence discernible here in the whole planning process. In essence, the advance would have to rely on surprise and the all-embracing power of the guns, for there were only twenty tanks in total available for the attack as the remainder were being reserved for the assault on the Hindenburg Line itself later in the month.

Many of the experienced Australian officers were worried by the sheer scale of what they were trying to achieve. The 14th Battalion was to make the final leap from the old British lines to the well-fortified and wired German outpost line, making the approach across a mile of open ground, and by then it would be beyond the support of a good proportion of the field artillery. In effect, the plan relied on the fractured morale of the German Army.

> We were to take thirty dummy tanks with us to put the wind up the Huns – these things were made of canvas, and from a little distance were the real thing to look at. Those of us who were at Bullecourt in 1917, and had tinkered about the Hindenburg Line there, saw disaster staring us in the face. All the officers, though not the men, knew they were being put onto the altar in this experiment. But our orders were clear and that was sufficient; we would do our best and trust to luck, or the Higher Command.[10]
>
> Lieutenant Edgar Rule, 14th Battalion, 4th Brigade, 4th Australian Division

The first stages of the operations went in under a fantastic barrage as 1,488 guns and howitzers opened up at 0520: the counter-barrage flayed the German artillery batteries, then the creeping barrage began moving slowly forwards supplemented by massed Vickers machine guns firing just over the advancing infantry's heads in an effort to make up for the lack of tank support. Once again the Australian Corps cut through the German lines like butter, smashing right through the former British lines. The Australians operated on the very heels of the creeping barrage; they would rather take casualties from the occasional shell dropping short than risk the German machine-gunners collecting their scrambled wits and opening fire. Lieutenant Edgar Rule and his men moved forward at 0700. The weather did not improve his mood.

> We formed up in artillery formation and moved off. It was still raining and the mud underfoot made it very heavy going. It would have been bad enough without our load, which consisted of either a pick or a shovel, 220 rounds of ammunition, three bombs and iron rations, while the Lewis gunners had their guns and panniers. It was the most exhausting day I've ever endured. How the lads kept up I don't know, for they carried far more than I did. We were wet outside and steaming inside our clothes.[11]

Lieutenant Edgar Rule, 14th Battalion, 4th Brigade, 4th Australian Division

Rule and his men had a terrible time pushing on to the outpost line and he was slightly wounded by pieces of shrapnel from a hand grenade driving into his back. On and on they went, feeling their way forward. They were still attacking long after it had gone dark. By then they were exhausted and just desperate to get it all over with.

> At 11 p.m. I crawled onto the parapet just as the barrage lifted onto the support line and endeavoured to get the men out of the trench. Just then the Huns put up a flare and at the same time opened on us with their machine guns. Their fire was so close that I scrambled into the trench again with despair gripping my heart. The machine guns were firing phosphorus bullets and we could plainly make out three that were firing on us. In despair I turned to Tom Griffith, an officer of 'A' Company, and told him that it was madness to attempt it. To my surprise he yelled out as he started bombing up the sap, 'Have a bloody go at them!' This pulled me together and out on the top the bombing section and I clambered. We must have gone about 100 yards, with 40 still to go, when these guns opened again. I looked around and my heart sank. Here was the whole company bunched in a heap. On account of the lead that was flying, we all got down flat on the ground. Bullets were licking up the dirt all around us. I heard a man yell just behind me and then he lay quiet. What to do was past me; I was just on the point of ordering a bolt, when one of the boys with a Lewis gun crawled up alongside me, and in a second opened fire along their

trench – and to our surprise silenced the Huns. A little further along another of the lads took his cue and opened fire. After each burst these gunners would yell, 'Now's your time; rush them!' They did this several times before anyone moved, but at last it sank in and several of the men moved, NCOs started to go forward. Even then I was very dubious, but these lads set the pace. We all upped and ran for dear life towards those Huns, yelling like lunatics.[12]

Lieutenant Edgar Rule, 14th Battalion, 4th Brigade, 4th Australian Division

The Germans fired for a few moments, then bolted for their lives. Despite it all, they had achieved their objectives. Next day the Australians could look right down into the German positions of the Hindenburg Line behind the St Quentin Canal in the valley below, between Bellenglise and Bellicourt. The achievement of the Australian Corps was quite spectacular: 4,243 German prisoners, 76 guns and over 300 machine guns had been surgically excised from the war, all for a cost of 'only' 1,260 Australian casualties.

The III and the newly reconstituted IX Corps advancing on either side of the Australians did not fare so well, partly because they faced an even more severe task. The Germans were absolutely determined to cling on to fortified villages such as Épéhy and Ronssoy, and there were also complications in the lack of support from the French on the southern flank, but for all that it was evident that some of the British divisions had not yet entirely grasped the subtleties of the All Arms Battle. In the absence of British tanks the Germans were still capable of putting up a meaningful opposition. In the village of Épéhy the 2/2nd Londons engaged in some vicious street fighting.

You couldn't see what you were doing. Your mind was on like a razor edge, every move, even the swirling mist used to seem like something human. You could see about 3 or 4 yards clear as a bell and then it would come swirling round again. You were trigger happy then! That saved me, this fog opened and there was couple or three Jerries with a machine gun in a front garden and the bloody gun was pointing at me! I opened up fire first; it was split-second stuff, swung the Lewis gun round automatically and that was it – I'd saved me life! If they'd opened up just a fraction before, me and my tea would have gone – I wouldn't have known anything about it! I took a quick glance and they were finished.[13]

Private Bill Gillman, 2/2nd Battalion, London Regiment, 173rd Brigade, 58th Division

Nonetheless, along the whole front the Germans still lost a total of 9,000 prisoners. Over the next ten days before the main assault on the Hindenburg Line small-scale attacks chipped away at the German positions until the III and IX Corps had drawn level with the Australians.

The ambivalent attitude of the authorities back in Britain can be judged by the outrageous letter of 'congratulations' sent by Wilson to Haig the day after the attack on the outpost line: 'Well done, you must be a famous general.' Haig slapped him down with a neat blend of sarcasm and truth.

> Very many thanks for your kind little note of yesterday. No, certainly not! I am not, nor am I likely to be, a *famous* general. For that must we not have pandered to Repington and the gutter press? But we have a surprisingly large number of *very capable* generals. Thanks to these gentlemen, and to their 'sound military knowledge built up of study and practice until it has become an instinct'; and to a steady adherence to the principle of our Field Service Regulations Part 1 are our successes to be chiefly attributed.[14]

Field Marshal Sir Douglas Haig, General Headquarters, BEF

THE ASSAULT OF THE American First Army and the French Fourth Army on a 44-mile front between the Meuse and Reims commenced at 0530 on 26 September. It was to prove the start of a harrowing experience for the still relatively inexperienced American troops. Ahead of them lay numerous well-sited German defence lines and the depths of the Argonne Forest: a tangled mass of hills, valleys, hidden gullies all covered in trees and dense undergrowth. This would be a real test for the American doughboys.

> Only five minutes more for a great many of the boys to live. Four minutes, three minutes, two, then one. 'Ready? Let's go!' The instant we started climbing out of the trench the artillery cut loose on the

Germans. At the same instant the Germans cut loose with artillery and machine guns. Immediately men began to drop. Cries and moans, yells and screams rent the air, and could be heard even above the roaring of cannon and bursting shells of the enemy. Shells were bursting overhead and underfoot. The very air was exploding in our faces. The ground was moving, rolling under our feet. Enemy machine-gun bullets were tearing through our soldiers like so much hail and taking a great toll. It was a roaring furnace, all fire, smoke, hot lead and shrapnel in which it seemed we were all trapped and must perish, but some of us went on and on. A large swamp lay between our lines and the Germans. In order to get us across this our engineers had built some walks under cover of the night. We soon found that crossing on these was much too slow and as we were losing troops heavily, Captain McCormack, our company commander, took the lead and plunged into the swamp. We all followed, holding our rifles over our heads. Breaking through the scum and water up to our armpits, we crossed the swamp. On the other side, the ground was marshy and would not hold our weight. Unless we could step on a bunch of water grass, we were continually pulling each other out of the mire. This condition of the ground probably saved a lot of men from getting hit by shrapnel. As the shells lit here, although their detonation was instantaneous, they would bury in the mud and then explode. We got through the marsh, then came the German wire entanglement. We walked on top of the wires instead of trying to wade through it, but a lot of us broke through several times and got entangled. It was tough going. Soldiers everywhere were tearing their clothes in frantic efforts to extricate themselves and get to the trench and at the Germans.[15]

Private Charles Dermody, 132nd Infantry Regiment, 33rd Division, AEF

Amongst the second wave Corporal Thomas Grady went over with his machine guns in support of the leading troops of 77th Division.

Received a shot of rum at 6.20 and over we went with the 75s still banging away. Brought up against the enemy wire and it was a mess. The trenches were completely demolished and the trees were cut down like wheat. The footing was bad owing to the shell craters and we couldn't keep up with the infantry. The prisoners began to roll in and we found 'em carrying their wounded. We had to cut our way through barbed wire every few hundred feet and the hills and grades were the toughest ever. Reached his second line trench and was showered with shrapnel and machine-gun fire. Mounted our guns and fired a few bursts of harassing fire into the thickets, and the doughboys went over. Before we could dismount and catch up they plunged ahead regardless. We finally caught up to them in the third line where they captured five machine guns and about fifty prisoners. *Beaucoup* dead and wounded lying around.[16]

Corporal Thomas Grady, 'B' Company, 305th Machine Gun Battalion, 77th Division, AEF

Although on the first two days the Americans advanced some 7 miles, progress soon ground almost to a halt. The fighting in the Argonne was to prove hard-grafting work. The rough, wooded terrain, criss-crossed by ridges, was highly suited to defence and there was a great potential for deadly German ambushes.

These damned woods are full of hills and ravines and I guess the French knew it too! Cleaned up a couple of machine-gun nests and had some trouble with snipers. Bullets were whistling over our heads and we had to take cover from shrapnel – lost a few men here. We got ahead of our objective for the day and ran into our own artillery fire – had to fall back. Our divisional plane flew over and we displayed our panels. Scout came back and reported machine-gun nest to our left. So we crawled out – 10-yard intervals – and mounted the guns. Set the sights 900 and 1,100 metres and I checked up. Waited for him to open up again and then we gave him a few bursts – searching – and I saw two of 'em go down. A few minutes later the infantry rushed the position and captured five prisoners. Our best job to date.[17]

Corporal Thomas Grady, 'B' Company, 305th Machine Gun Battalion, 77th Division, AEF

The intense fighting would continue right through October. One of the most famous incidents occurred when the so-called 'Lost Battalion' of the 77th Division found itself cut off behind the German lines after an attack made on 2 October. The battalion had accidentally penetrated deep behind the German lines with no support. Digging in where they stood, the men would hold out in a heroic defence for six

days. On 8 October, as part of the ultimately successful relief operations, the men of the 328th Infantry Regiment were ordered forward.
Amongst them was Corporal Alvin York, who had already formed a
grim view of the situation in the Argonne.

> God would never be cruel enough to create a cyclone as terrible as that
> Argonne battle. Only man would ever think of doing an awful thing like
> that. It looked like what 'the abomination of desolation' must look like.
> And all through the long night those big guns flashed and growled just
> like the lightning and the thunder when it storms in the mountains at
> home. And, oh my, we had to pass the wounded. And some of them
> were on stretchers going back to the dressing stations, and some of
> them were lying around, moaning and twitching. And the dead were all
> along the road. And it was wet and cold. And it all made me think of
> the Bible and the story of the anti-Christ and Armageddon. And I'm
> telling you, the little log cabin in Wolf Valley in old Tennessee seemed
> a long, long way off.[18]

Corporal Alvin York, 328th Infantry Regiment, 82nd Division, AEF

As they moved on their objective the attack was thwarted by a line of
German machine guns along a ridge. York and some seventeen other
men were feeling for the left flank of the German position and soon
found themselves behind the German lines and effectively lost. After his
sergeant was wounded, York took command and led the nine survivors
into frenetic action – Tennessee frontier style.

> Those machine guns were spitting fire and cutting down the under-
> growth all around me something awful. And the Germans were yelling
> orders. You never heard such a racket in all of your life. I didn't have
> time to dodge behind a tree or dive into the brush, I didn't even have
> time to kneel or lie down. I don't know what the other boys were doing.
> They claim they didn't fire a shot. They said afterwards they were on
> the right, guarding the prisoners. And the prisoners were lying down
> and the machine guns had to shoot over them to get me. As soon as the
> machine guns opened fire on me, I began to exchange shots with them.
> I had no time to do nothing but watch them there German machine-
> gunners and give them the best I had. Every time I saw a German I just
> teched him off. At first I was shooting from a prone position – that is,

lying down – just like we often shoot at the targets in the shooting matches in the mountains of Tennessee, and it was just about the same distance. But the targets here were bigger. I just couldn't miss a German's head or body at that distance.[19]

Corporal Alvin York, 328th Infantry Regiment, 82nd Division, AEF

Suddenly the nearest Germans made a desperate frontal bayonet charge on York.

A German officer and five men done jumped out of a trench and charged me with fixed bayonets. They had about 25 yards to come and they were coming right smart. I only had about half a clip left in my rifle, but I had my pistol ready. I done flipped it out fast and teched them off, too. I teched off the sixth man first; then the fifth; then the fourth; then the third; and so on. That's the way we shoot wild turkeys at home. You see, we don't want the front ones to know that we're getting the back ones, and then they keep on coming until we get them all.[20]

Corporal Alvin York, 328th Infantry Regiment, 82nd Division, AEF

York was now confident that he had the situation under control. All the courage just seemed to ooze out of the Germans and they began to surrender.

I knowed now that if I done kept my head and didn't run out of ammunition I had them. So I done hollered to them to come down and give up. I didn't want to kill any more 'n I had to. I would tech a couple of them off and holler again. But I guess they couldn't understand my language, or else they couldn't hear me in the awful racket that was going on all around. I got hold of the German major. He said, 'If you won't shoot any more I will make them give up.' So he blew a little whistle and they came down and began to gather around and throw down their guns and belts. All but one of them came off the hill with their hands up, and just before that one got to me he threw a little hand grenade, which burst in the air in front of me. I had to tech him off. The rest surrendered without any more trouble.[21]

Corporal Alvin York, 328th Infantry Regiment, 82nd Division, AEF

In the end York and his squad took some 132 German prisoners and captured thirty-five machine guns. Although the exact details of his exploit can, and have, been disputed, it was nevertheless a tremendous achievement and Corporal Alvin York was duly awarded the Congressional Medal of Honor.

The Lost Battalion was eventually relieved, but many other far less celebrated incidents occurred as scattered groups of men found themselves playing a deadly game of cowboys and Indians in the thick woods. Private Mathew Chopin was serving with the Mortar Platoon of the 356th Infantry Regiment, 89th Division, when the platoon found itself utterly lost and separated from its regiment.

> Machine guns were barking in the dark forest on all sides, lending their echoing sounds to Argonne's forest hills! All around us the gaunt, grey sky was dense with smoke, while hanging mists grew thick beneath the forest's boughs. Nearer and nearer came the sound of the sharp cracks of the Boche snipers' rifles sending their thrills through our very bones! There was no time to lose and we were soon busy filling sandbags and piling them up in a large square to form a barricade. I had just unbuckled my belt from my pack when our boys on the barricade opened fire! I dropped on my knees with my '30-30' and emptied it as fast as I could! Again and again bullets hummed and whizzed around my head. I saw my partner drop, getting it in the forehead, while another turned over moaning with blood pouring from above his heart. I didn't know where I was going to get mine! I lay flat on the ground, using a Stoke's mortar base-plate for protection. All around the automatics were cracking and popping as fast as they could blaze away. To add to the terror and discomfort of the situation, German bullets were clipping the leaves and branches of the forest trees, while shells, through dense clouds of smoke and gas burst all around us. I lived an age in ten minutes and began to have a sickly, nervous feeling of uneasiness whether I would ever live through all of this hell![22]
>
> Private Mathew Chopin, 356th Infantry Regiment, 89th Division, AEF

The men found out soon enough that they were trapped behind the German lines. Worse still, none of them knew where they were and there was little prospect of rescue.

> Exhausted, hungry and thirsty, we kept up the fight for four days and nights, without rest or food and drinking only seeping water from shell

holes to quench our feverish thirst. Our incessant efforts to endure
fatigue and hunger were on the wane. All hopes of getting help seemed
in vain. Tired in mind and body and with a strain on heart and nerve,
we continued to fell the Hun! We sent out three runners on the third
day. None of them ever returned. Doomed to either surrender or fight
to a bitter end![23]

Private Mathew Chopin, 356th Infantry Regiment, 89th Division, AEF

They also came under threat from the creeping barrage of their
own guns, which seemed to be moving inexorably towards them, until
by sheer good fortune a passing Allied aircraft noticed their desperate
signals. Shortly afterwards, on the fourth day they were relieved.

How any of us came out of this hell I don't know, for we had gone
through about all that a human being could possibly stand. Back
through mud and water, over seas of shell craters, across hills and
swamps, we hiked. All along the way, here and there, strewed bodies of
our dead heroes, all stiff and smeared with blood! Other loathsome
sights were bodies of German officers, with their heads cut off entirely
from their bodies and lying upward in a decomposed condition. As we
passed a truck, I begged a soldier in it to give me just anything to eat.
He pulled out a piece of dry bread that I ate like a starved dog and filled
my pockets with the remaining crumbs. We soon halted on a hillside
and were told to rest up a day. Too tired to unroll my pack, I sank to
the ground, falling fast asleep.[24]

Private Mathew Chopin, 356th Infantry Regiment, 89th Division, AEF

Many of the American soldiers were experiencing 'real' action for
the first time. Most would have to fight a long, lonely personal battle
with their own terrors.

Fear is a man's biggest individual enemy. Not in the battle when there
is action and movement and sport and excitement, but in the recesses of
his little pit that he dug by dint of scratching maybe with his jack-knife
and mess pan using them as pick and shovel, when the damp, misting,
whistling wind is blowing through the shattered trees around and the
groaning of the wounded becomes unbearable, and hunger and thirst
seem to drag vitality from you inch by inch, and the shells big and little
are pulling one more from among the few men you have left, and you

437

shiver from cold and the thoughts of some horrible death you've seen some fellow die that day, his one game hand trying to stuff his entrails back into his belly, maybe some of his brains in his helmet and the pain from a shinbone bent double, toe touching knee, spasmodically making his last breath a gurgled curse of pent-up hatred! God in heaven knows that if it doesn't cast a spell of fear over you I don't know what will.[25]

Lieutenant Eugene West, 5th Marine Regiment, 2nd Division, AEF

Although the Americans continued to advance they were still losing far too many men. It was due to a combination of reasons: their simplistic tactics, poor communications, sometimes inadequate leadership, the thoroughly hostile terrain – and, of course, the German Army.

The continuing lack of American tactical sophistication was demonstrated by the lessons that Major General Robert Alexander chose to draw from his post-battle assessment of his division's experience in the Argonne fighting. His comments betrayed a near-mystical belief in the powers attributed to the rifle.

I thought I noticed that there was a disinclination to utilise to its full potential power the infantry rifle. Whether this disinclination came from lack of proper training, I am not prepared to say, but dependence seemed to be made upon machine guns, grenades and the other auxiliaries to the partial exclusion of rifle fire. I am quite convinced that we cannot too strongly insist upon our desire to bring about the full utilisation of this fire. The other auxiliaries, machine guns, hand grenades, 37 mm, are useful in their way, but they are merely auxiliaries, and intelligent use of the infantry rifle wins battles when no other instrumentality will suffice.[26]

Major General Robert Alexander, Headquarters, 77th Division, AEF

And there it was: a totally misconceived analysis. Alexander was not stupid, but he had nowhere near enough experience of the reality of either trench or open warfare. Like his commander-in-chief Pershing, his military experience had been gleaned in skirmishes against native Americans, and Spain in the Philippines and Mexico. These were the same sort of minor colonial conflicts that had informed the early thoughts of British generals. And indeed, his ideas are all too redolent of the expressions of pious intent issued by British and French generals in the first years of the war. By 1918 it should have been evident to anyone that naked firepower was all-important and although rifle fire could be a useful adjunct it was all too often easily suppressed by machine-gun fire. The idea of individual marksmen working together using accurate aimed fire to pick off their enemies is one of near fantasy. Aimed, accurate rifle fire (the two are not synonymous as you can aim and more often than not miss) was extremely rare, especially if the riflemen were under fire from artillery, machine guns and trench mortars. In these circumstances then the wise rifleman tends not to fire at all if he wants to survive. The incredible luck and marksmanship of Corporal Alvin York were not a sound basis for divisional infantry tactics.

And yet when all was said and done, the Americans did fight hard in the closing months of the war. Their huge new armies were now not only theoretically depressing the German morale as a future threat, but they had joined the British and French in battering away at the over-stretched and doomed German defences.

THE NEXT GREAT ALLIED ASSAULT was made on 27 September by the First and Third Armies. The First Army would capture the brooding heights of Bourlon Ridge before securing its left flank and operating to protect the left flank of the Third Army as it advanced on the general line of Le Cateau to Solesmes. The hardest task was faced by the Canadian Corps, which would have to force the crossing of the Canal du Nord on a narrow frontage of 2,500 yards. The canal was mainly dry, for construction had been rudely interrupted by the outbreak of war in 1914. It was, however, a serious obstacle to movement, being some 30–60 feet deep and 90–120 feet wide depending on the particular area. Revetted banks were up to 12 feet high and the canal was often filled with barbed wire. Some 300 yards behind this was the actual Canal du Nord Line, and 4 miles behind that the Marquion and Marcoing Lines, by which time the front under attack by the Canadians would have expanded to 9,500 yards.

The plans drawn up by Lieutenant General Sir Arthur Currie were textbook examples of modern warfare. The Canadian 4th and 1st Divisions would once again lead the way before being joined by the 3rd Canadian and 11th British Divisions on either side. Currie set his heavy artillery wire cutting as early as 18 September, but there was to be no preliminary bombardment per se and absolute secrecy prevailed to try and conceal Allied intentions. When the infantry went over the top at 0520 the massed artillery would fire powerful creeping barrages to suppress the German opposition using a potent combination of 50 per cent shrapnel shell, 40 per cent high explosive and 10 per cent smoke shell to blind the Germans as to the Canadian approach. To this was added the massed Vickers machine guns and mortars.

For all the preparations the troops were distinctly nervous.

> I had to take the platoon over that morning. It was raining, it was cold and dirty and it was my first experience of taking over thirty-odd men and I was worried, really worried about it. The canal was ahead of us and we didn't know if there was water in it or not. Each section was given a rope. If there was water in there, somebody in the section had to get out and pull the rest out, but I don't know how it was going to be done![27]
>
> Sergeant Don McKerchar, 46th (South Saskatchewan) Battalion, 10th Brigade, 4th Canadian Division

He had good reason to worry for when the attack went in he hadn't gone 10 feet before he was badly hit by no less than seven pieces of shrapnel in his right arm and was also knocked out by a glancing head wound. It was a neat matter of judgement how close to the barrage the troops should be. Too close and the casualties might be excessive, too far away and the Germans would emerge from their bolt-holes to create havoc. Experience was all-important.

> Sergeant Major Rogers kept a lot of us young fellows from getting killed by our own barrage. He wouldn't let us advance until our barrage lifted. We had to carry scaling ladders as the canal was very deep where we crossed over. Myself and a pal named Brown, we carried the ladder so we were the first up and we had gone a little way when a shell exploded right behind us. It hit us like a giant fist in the small of the back. I thought I was blown in two: I was all numb. I asked Brown if he was okay. He said he thought so! The screams behind us I will never forget. Brown and I were fine, but that shell wiped out our whole section.[28]
>
> Private Stan Colbeck, 46th (South Saskatchewan) Battalion, 10th Brigade, 4th Canadian Division

For all these personal and small-scale disasters to sections and platoons, the Canadian attack overall was a triumph. The Canadian engineers did a fantastic job in erecting various footbridges and more substantial bridges capable of carrying road traffic early that morning. As every hour passed they were strengthened and augmented and this greatly facilitated the enormous task of getting thousands of support troops through the gap to spread out and push ever forward. The creeping barrage had done its work and supported by tanks the men captured all their objectives. It had been a splendid achievement.

Alongside the Canadians the XVII, VI and IV Corps of the Third Army were also attacking all the way down the front. They, too, made progress but were generally stopped short of their final objectives. In the centre the VI Corps did well where the Guards Division was not only assaulting the Canal du Nord, but also had to deal with the Hindenburg Line proper. Amongst its ranks was Guardsman Horace Calvert. He had joined up underage in 1914 – he was still only 18; indeed, he had just refused promotion to avoid giving orders to men much older than himself. By 1918 he was an experienced soldier who had grown up on the battlefields. But he had never experienced anything like this.

> The 18-pounders were wheel to wheel. I've never seen as many guns at the front. The ammunition was stacked up. The gunners who were busy getting ready told us that they were going to put a shell on every 3 yards of trench – and then keep it up! They said, 'You won't have any difficulty if we can keep that up!'[29]
> Guardsman Horace Calvert, 2nd Battalion, Grenadier Guards, 1st Guards Brigade, Guards Division

Close by was Captain Wilfred Tatham of the 1st Coldstream Guards, who was given the task of improving the canal crossing.

> It was quite silent; no one was letting off a gun within hearing distance. A few seconds before Zero Hour one machine gun went 'Pop-Pop-Pop!' And then, suddenly, hell let loose. Guns every 15 yards. We stumbled along the trench; I remember laughing with the excitement – the guns made such a din. When we reached the front line all was confusion; there usually is with men like Christmas trees trying to pass

each other in narrow trenches. In time we sorted ourselves out, but it is difficult to give commands in the dark when you can only just hear a man shouting in your ear! We scrambled on top and strolled down to the canal. What an innocent I was, I imagined our front companies far in front, whereas there were Germans still holding out only a few hundred yards or so to our left. My job was easy and pretty safe on the floor of the 20-foot canal. Just on our left there was a bridge over the canal. It had been blown up and one half had collapsed on the German side. Behind a tangle of girders and concrete were two machine-gun posts. They were called 'Rat' and 'Mouse'. It was thought they had been abandoned – they had not! Imagine the problem of crossing a dry canal fixed with barbed wire, entailing scrambling or sliding down a 20-foot sloping brick wall, fighting through the wire and climbing up the other side with machine guns not more than 30 yards away! Was it surprising the front troops hesitated? But the company commander, Captain Cyril Frisby, didn't hesitate! He knew that the whole of the operation depended on the kernel of the nut being crushed; he immediately called for volunteers, leapt up himself and slid down the bank followed by three equally brave men. Somehow they got through the wire and up the other side – the gunners surrendered. The company commander was an old man – he was 33! Not one of those reckless unthinking youths who do not understand fear. This is the greatest type of courage.[30]

Second Lieutenant Wilfred Tatham, 1st Battalion, Coldstream Guards, 2nd Guards Brigade, Guards Division

As the casualties mounted, Tatham was soon sent forward right into the thick of the action.

I was sent up to command one of the front companies, which had lost all of its officers and sergeants. There were fifty men left. I arrived to find no war – the corporal in charge handed over his command and 240 Germans standing in line. His first comment surprised me: he asked permission to shoot down all the prisoners. Curiously un-English! His story was that the Germans had surrendered and hoisted a white flag. His company commander had gone over to the Germans and been shot dead by a sniper. It was probably a mistake, but this corporal, who had been through a really hellish time and had just seen the conventions of war flagrantly flouted, had lost his normal balance.[31]

Second Lieutenant Wilfred Tatham, 1st Battalion, Coldstream Guards, 2nd Guards Brigade, Guards Division

In the second wave came the 2nd Grenadier Guards, who were required to swing left and establish a firm left flank to the main advance.

There was this big concrete lined empty canal, about 20 feet deep. There were scaling ladders, we had to go down and then climb up the other side with full equipment. The Coldstreams had done a good job because there was no opposition to us. We got into the Hindenburg Trench and we had to turn to the flank to face any attack from the left. We looked towards Bourlon Wood. In the distance we could see the German artillery being pulled out of the outskirts of the wood. They were galloping on the road with their guns, but we couldn't do anything, it was too far off for effective rifle fire, so they got away. I went across an open field, there were no hedges it was just open. Right in the centre was a big sunken emplacement for a gun – you couldn't see it till you got on top of it nearly. It had never been fired, it was one of the defences of the Hindenburg Line only to be used in case of an attack, but they failed, we were too quick![32]

Guardsman Horace Calvert, 2nd Battalion, Grenadier Guards, 1st Guards Brigade, Guards Division

In view of the scale of the obstacles laid in front of them both the First and Third Armies had performed well. Once again it was apparent that they were more than capable of breaking through anything the German Army could put in front of them.

THE THIRD ASSAULT was launched on 28 September by the Army Group commanded, at least nominally, by Albert I, King of the Belgians. Plumer's Second Army, assisted by the French and the Belgians, was to drive forward across the old Ypres Salient abandoned back in April 1918 and surge over the Passchendaele Ridge. And that was only the start. The usual careful preparations were put into train: the guns gathered, targets noted, maps and models studied and strict secrecy observed. For the troops, though, it was business as usual: over the top to who knows what fate.

> We thought that there might be a lot of casualties this time. At half past five we lined up in pouring rain, torrential rain. In the rank behind me a boy started crying, a boy I had taken back for shell shock on the Somme, he was removed there and then. What they did with him I don't know but he didn't take part in the advance, he would just have been a menace.[33]
>
> Private Alexander Jamieson, 11th Battalion, Royal Scots, 27th Brigade, 9th Division

Some of these men had served for several years at the front; others had only just arrived. Yet, however experienced they were, going over the top in the Ypres Salient could never be routine. The risks were too great, the history of slaughter too recent for it not to be imprinted on their minds. Yet the events of recent weeks had given them some hope that this time it might be different.

> I glanced at my immediate neighbours: George was less voluble than usual and appeared loaded down with additional bombs to carry. Ted Burroughs close behind him with his tin hat at a jaunty angle, a little further along the traverse was Gillogley towering over his protégé 'Pop' Hopkins. We had been through so much together, that I broke position for a moment to shake hands with each of them and wish them luck in spite of scowls from an NCO. The warmth was mutual. The minutes ticked away and the atmosphere was tense. But spirits were high for this must be the final goodbye to trench warfare at last. It was exactly 5.30 a.m. when the whistles shrilled and we leapt over the top in pouring rain and fanned out in extended order.[34]
>
> Private Edward Williamson, 17th Battalion, Royal Scots, 106th Brigade, 35th Division

What happened then would have seemed an unbelievable dream just a year before during the Third Battle of Ypres. The attacking divisions stormed to success almost everywhere. The German artillery was cowed into submission by the effective counter-battery fire; the once-feared pillboxes were picked off with relative ease using firepower rather than flesh and blood. With one bound in one day the British had achieved more than they had in four months of misery the year before. Most of the 'heights' of the Passchendaele–Gheluvelt–Messines

Ridge had fallen and the brooding menace of Houthulst Forest had been largely overrun.

> That first day we didn't suffer a great many casualties. I saw the terrible state of the Ypres Salient in daylight, I'd usually seen it in darkness: the wrecked tanks from 1917, dead horses and mules, shell holes every-where. By the end of the first day we were clear of that on a ridge where we could look ahead and see trees and all the rest of it that had never been affected by war. It was just unbelievable; we knew then that things were going well![35]
>
> Private Alexander Jamieson, 11th Battalion, Royal Scots, 27th Brigade, 9th Division

Next day the advance if anything gained pace. It was so successful that one of the main tasks of the sappers lay in removing the various booby traps left by the retreating Germans.

> The common booby traps took the form of a tin filled with explosive, a spring-loaded lid with a plunger and detonator fitted inside. They were planted in shallow holes in the road surface and covered over. The mule's feet would not explode them, but immediately the wheels and the 'piece' came onto the lid, up they all went. It was particularly dangerous to remove these traps when corroded, as any movement might explode them. The traps were always dealt with by the Royal Engineer officer. I had another tricky problem concerning the removal of some 10 cwt of liquid perdite in jars placed in a culvert on the only main road leading to the front, over which the division would have to move in its advance. The detonators were much rusted and I was relieved when they were disconnected and the explosive dumped in nearby shell holes by my sappers. Immediately I reported all clear, the guns and wagons began to roar up the road towards the enemy positions.[36]
>
> Lieutenant Godefroi Skelton, 205th Field Company, Royal Engineers

This problem was being encountered up and down the whole Allied line. The Germans were masters at creating booby traps. The only safe attitude was to presume that everything was booby-trapped until it had been checked by the sappers.

> A bloke got blown up at the piano in my company. He could play – he was our best pianist – that's what upset us! The place was deserted,

Jerry was a way back and of course the first thing he did when he saw the bloody piano was he lifts the lid of the piano and away he went – with the piano as well! He never got a chance to bang a note! A couple of his mates who'd hardly got in the front door heard the explosion and went in – they saw what was there – nothing practically, with the piano smashed open. They rushed out and told us, 'Keep your hands off everything!' It was a good lesson – he saved a lot of lives probably![37]

Private Bill Gillman, 2/2nd Battalion, London Regiment, 173rd Brigade, 58th Division

However, not all of the sappers were equally careful: the cautious Lieutenant Godefroi Skelton would certainly not have approved of the robust methods employed by a Canadian sapper further along the front.

I was sent to explore some dugouts in a big railway embankment in front of Quiéry-la-Motte with a Canadian Royal Engineer sergeant, to see if they were safe for the battalion to use. This Canadian's methods of testing for booby traps were most alarming. He would go up to any suspicious-looking object, e.g. a wire sticking out of a wall, and give it a tug – while I stood outside the doorway and implored him to be careful. I presume he knew what he was doing, since he did not blow us up, but it did not look like it and I found going round with him a nerve-racking experience.[38]

Lieutenant John Nettleton, 2nd Battalion, Rifle Brigade, 25th Brigade, 8th Division

THE FINAL STAGE in the swirling series of offensives was to be made by Rawlinson's Fourth Army on 29 September. The main thrust would be made by the Australian Corps, augmented this time by the American II Corps (the 27th and 30th Divisions) who had been placed under the overall command of Lieutenant General Sir John Monash. They were to attack the Hindenburg Line where the St Quentin Canal ran underground for 3½ miles between Bellicourt and Vendhuile. The Americans would go first and the Australians would sweep through to exploit any breakthrough. The raw American troops were getting copious advice from their boisterous Australian comrades. Some of it was of genuine merit, some more intended as a 'wind up' than anything else.

Australians and Americans get along fine. We talk to them and they tell us lots of things that are important to a soldier who has not been in a battle. The Aussies advise us never to be taken prisoners, for they say the Huns torture their prisoners. We believe them, for they have been in the war long enough to know. These are the words our Lieutenant used in telling us we were to go into battle soon: 'You are going into your first real battle soon and I expect every man of you to do your share. Don't stop if your buddy is killed or wounded, but say, "Tough Luck!" and pass on.' We are all full of cheer and anxiously waiting for the shelling to start. The infantrymen are as full of cheer as we. They are anxious to get a whack at Fritz. At last we are at the beginning of a real battle between Prussianism and Democracy! And we are to fight on the side of Democracy that the world may forever be free from the Prussian peril! That never again will we have to leave our peaceful pursuits and cross an ocean to fight such barbarians.[39]

Private Willard Newton, 'F' Company, 105th Engineers, 30th Division, AEF

There was little of this fetching innocence and idealism amongst the hardened and war-weary troops of the British Army. Four years of war had ground down those individuals fortunate enough to have survived such trials. They were willing enough if they were given a chance, but there was no enthusiasm for the battle or, indeed, for the cause in which they were presumed to be fighting. The Americans had a lot to learn about the reality of war. And the Germans were more than willing to teach them.

There is no doubt that the Australians needed help for they were very near to their breaking point. Despite their extraordinary achievements their morale was in a febrile state. There was no conscription in Australia and their depots were almost empty as the numbers of drafts from home had almost petered out. Many of the reinforcements that arrived were wounded men who had only just recovered and now found themselves once more required to put their bodies in the line at the front. Monash had refused the opportunity to withdraw them from the line as he considered that the Germans were almost finished and that his men were 'on top'. Yet the inevitable result was that the Australian battalions were being rapidly drained away in August and September. A battalion that should have had nearly a thousand men

447

was often reduced to its bare bones of just a few hundred and as a result the infrastructure of the Australian formations was beginning to fall apart. In a couple of worrying incidents many of the men of the 1st and 59th Battalions refused to obey orders when ordered back to the line. But even worse was the widespread refusal to enforce the orders issued on 23 September that finally reduced the Australian brigades to the three-battalion organisation. The disbanded battalions would be broken up and used to reinforce the others.

> It started with the 3rd Division down in the village of Doingt. There was a movement to do away with a battalion in each brigade, to reinforce the others. All very well in theory, but it meant breaking up all the treasured associations that had grown up around each battalion, and also, seeing that they were to cease to exist, their traditions would disappear with them. The men resented it, refused to be broken up and would not go to their new battalions. As they had ceased to exist officially they could not draw rations. So the men of the other battalions of their brigade used to feed them. The movement soon spread to our division. One of the 14th Brigade battalions was put on parade and told off to march to its new battalions. The men refused to move, so the officers and NCOs reported to their new units, while the men carried on, on their own, appointing their own officers. They used to come across to us for tucker and they used to raid the ration trains that went near their camp.[40]
>
> Private G. V. Rose, 30th Battalion, 8th Brigade, 5th Australian Division

As Monash desperately needed his men back in the line for the assault on the Hindenburg Line on 29 September the order was temporarily rescinded. As a result the officer and NCOs duly returned to their former battalions and they and their men went into action as usual.

The highly regarded Monash was given the honour of planning the bulk of the operation although Rawlinson certainly tweaked the plans to allow for an assault by the neighbouring IX Corps across the St Quentin Canal. This was meant to widen the frontage assaulted, to reach from Bellicourt right down to Bellenglise in the south, and thereby reduce the impact of German fire from the flanks. The overall strength of the German Hindenburg Line main defences, coupled with the ongoing shortage of tanks, meant that the battle plan had to allow for a prolonged bombardment by the massed guns of the Royal Artillery. There was just too much barbed wire and too many deep dugouts and concrete reinforced machine-gun posts to allow a predicted barrage to deal with everything at once. Surprise was important but on this occasion it had to be surrendered for hard practical reasons. The Royal Artillery also had one splendid advantage in that a detailed map of the entire layout of the German defences had been captured on 8 August. It knew where its particular targets were and could direct onto them the appropriate amount of high explosive to destroy them. In particular, the gunners must have had great pleasure in deluging the German artillery with mustard gas shells for the first time. The British chemical industry had not covered itself in glory in its speed of response to the first German use of mustard gas back in the summer of 1917. But now, at last, 30,000 mustard gas shells had arrived at the front and the British could not wait a moment longer to use them. Then, when Zero Hour came, the Royal Artillery could return to its usual role of suppressing all forms of German resistance by drenching them with shells even as the assaulting infantry were emerging from their jumping-off trenches.

There is no doubt that the Hindenburg Line was a fearsome prospect all along its length, but the task of the men of the 46th Division was by far the most intimidating prospect. A Lewis gunner pondered on what lay before him.

> The canal at some points had drained to a few feet owing to burst banks. But where we were going the water was about 8 to 10 feet deep. Overnight we were dished out with lifebuoys stuffed with kapok. The idea was to part swim, part wade across, rifles held above our heads, machine-gunners ditto. When one realises that the gun alone weighs over 90 lb and Jerry is firing at you all the time from the opposite bank, one can see what a picnic it would be! The other members of your team are loaded up with ammunition and a canvas bucket of Mills grenades, so, all set for a real good time![41]
>
> Corporal George Parker, 1/8th Battalion, Sherwood Foresters, 139th Brigade, 46th Division

The canal was not particularly deep, but heavily laden infantrymen under fire need all the help they can get in crossing water obstacles. The sappers were soon deeply involved in the preparations.

The engineer work for the attack consisted almost entirely of the preparation and forwarding of bridging material of all kinds. Collapsible boats, cork rafts, rafts made of empty petrol tanks lashed to wood bearers, mud mats, lines and pulleys for getting men and ammunition across the water, and a 101 other things, including timber for making bridges suitable for artillery. All these had to be prepared and taken forward, as near to the line as possible.[42]

Captain John Marshall, Headquarters, Royal Engineers, 46th Division

They even managed to procure 3,000 lifebelts from cross-Channel steamers. Many of the men of the 46th Division were convinced that their role in the attack was more in the nature of a sacrificial stunt or diversion than anything else. They might gain a foothold on the far bank but they felt sure it would cost the best part of the division to achieve it. Perhaps some of the older ones could remember the awful failed diversion at Gommecourt on 1 July 1916. This had the potential to be far worse. In the circumstances it was essential that the men should be given the confidence that they did have a chance to get across the canal and that it was not a lost cause.

The troops had to be got across the canal somehow and, if all else failed, it was suggested that they should swim it. So some genius thought of the life belts used on the leave boats, and a lorry-load of them was brought in from Boulogne. Experiments were tried in the Somme to convince the battalions participating in the attack that a fully armed man, with no knowledge of swimming, was safe from drowning while wearing one of these belts. Lieutenant Page was in charge of this exhibition by non-swimmers, and the result was most successful, giving the men perfect confidence.[43]

Captain John Marshall, Headquarters, Royal Engineers, 46th Division

The one thing the troops had increasing assurance in was the power of their own guns. They could see them pounding the German strongpoints and they knew that when the moment came the massed guns would open their mouths and belch forth every kind of shell. At 0550 on 29 September the troops went over the top, charging down the slope towards the canal as fast as they could.

An enormous barrage opened. It was tremendous. Everything possible was rained on the rear of the canal to prevent their reserves being brought up. The other side knew something was on by the intensity of our barrage, so, up went their flares, green and gold, and over came the counter-barrage. The racket was awe-inspiring; it was impossible to hear, even if orders were given. Over we went, slipping and sliding down the canal bank to the cold water below. The opposite bank was pitted with machine-gun nests, in tunnels dug into the 30-feet-high sloping bank. How any of us even reached the water beats me, but a surprising number did. The water was up to armpits, and holding that gun above my head was bad enough without being machine-gunned as well. Clawing our way onto the bank we were underneath some of the machine guns making it more difficult to hit us, so my team and many others flung Mills grenades into the various tunnels nearest to us, while clinging for dear life to any scrap of projection on the bank. After many years I still don't know how we got away with it.[44]

Corporal George Parker, 1/8th Battalion, Sherwood Foresters, 139th Brigade, 46th Division

The 1/8th Sherwood Foresters had been given the responsibility for capturing Bellenglise. As the German fire died down the men clambered up the bank and began the grim business of consolidation. The British Army had learnt many lessons of the necessity of rooting out all resistance to avoid Germans emerging from their hiding places deep underground to pepper them from the rear.

The practice was to shout down the mouths of tunnels to the occupants to throw out their weapons and come out. Some did, but ignoring the order meant a Mills thrown in, so in the end most surrendered. The Hindenburg Line was a marvellous piece of fortification. The bank was drilled with an amazing amount of skill into a complete underground fort. Wooden stairs led down, some twenty of them, to huge rooms, all supported by beams and struts. Wire bunks surrounded some walls, blankets still on them. Quite a lot of personal belongings had been left in their hurried departure. In one large chamber, 'Officers' quarters!' I thought, there were tables, chairs and a PIANO – taken from French houses of course, but considering the conditions we had existed in for years, you can guess what we said![45]

Corporal George Parker, 1/8th Battalion, Sherwood Foresters, 139th Brigade, 46th Division

The various tunnel and dugout complexes would have to be cleared one by one. The biggest, known as the Bellenglise Tunnel, was an enormous construction able to keep a whole battalion or more in relative safety. The gunners had succeeded in blasting down the western entrance and the occupants were so stunned that they surrendered meekly when the British bombing teams arrived.

> The huge dugout, or system of tunnels and dugouts, which ran from Bellenglise to a point near Magny-la-Fosse, was found to contain nearly 2,000 nerve-shattered men who surrendered in haste, the more especially as all exits were stopped by squads of bombers, and my old friend Captain Teeton and his men had dragged a German howitzer to the Magny end of the tunnel and were cheerfully firing it down the opening. The shell bursts in the narrow tunnel cannot have been very comforting to our Boche friends. The tunnel was fitted with a complete electric light system. Lieutenant Read, the divisional intelligence officer, informed me of this, stating that the electrical staff had been taken prisoner. I asked him where they were and was told that they were on their way to the nearest prisoners' camp. On this I suggested he should try and get hold of them again, as if the tunnel, which we, naturally, were making use of, was mined, the men would be sure to know it. Within a few hours he had retrieved them, and on being put to run their engine again, they made haste to point out the changeover switch by which it had been arranged that the mines should be fired automatically on the restarting of the engine. The positions of the charges were pointed out with alacrity![46]
>
> Captain John Marshall, Headquarters, Royal Engineers, 46th Division

Marshall's inspired suggestion was referred to with considerable understatement by Captain Raymond Priestley in his book *Breaking the Hindenburg Line* as 'A happy thought!'[47]

Not everyone was overly energetic about pushing forward and certainly many of the men of the assault battalions of the Staffordshires of the 137th Brigade probably considered that they had done enough in actually forcing the passage of the canal.

> There was a dense fog hanging over the low-lying ground round the canal; some of it probably true fog and some of it smoke shells. One

could not see many yards ahead and the company became split up. It took several minutes to collect together again before attempting to cross the canal. The fog lifted gradually. The canal here was in a fairly deep cutting. The bank down which we picked our way was a mass of undergrowth, which concealed barbed wire, and which was very difficult to negotiate. We were lucky enough to find a plank bridge to cross by. The far end had been destroyed but the water was only about knee deep. On the far side, on the towpath, three or four Staffords were drinking tea with an equal number of German prisoners. We met a Stafford major with quite a number of men. They had not reached their objective, but seemed determined not to advance any further. The Stafford major had the wind up badly – when two unarmed Germans advanced through the lifting fog he ordered his troops to line the canal bank! Our morale would have been affected had we stayed near him, so we left him to capture the two willing prisoners. Actually, I doubt if any Staffords advanced any further than this in our immediate vicinity. On the slope up from the canal we saw in a trench a lot of arms waving above the parapet. On reaching the trench we found the occupants unarmed, all their belongings packed up and ready to be marched back. One ancient officer's servant was deemed sufficient escort for them. We appeared to have nobody on either flank, but I thought the rest of the battalion must have reached the Brown Line. By some miracle we were going in exactly the right direction and when we reached the Brown Line we were in our correct position.[48]

Captain Arthur Pick, 1/4th Battalion, Leicestershire Regiment, 138th Brigade, 46th Division

Bickering between regiments aside, the 46th Division had performed one of the great military feats of the war. It had been well supported by the artillery – indeed, almost the whole of the IX Corps artillery had supported it in the attack – but it was not the guns that had to get across the canal under fire that morning. That was the role of the infantry and it was an incredible achievement: the last great German defence work was comprehensively breached.

Suddenly the mist rose and the sun of our 'Austerlitz' appeared, strong and refulgent. Over the brow of the rise opposite to us came a great grey column. Never had we seen such a thing! We counted the files –

there were nearly a thousand prisoners in the column. Half an hour later a similar column appeared, and then another, and another – we had broken the Hindenburg Line.[49]

Captain John Marshall, Headquarters, Royal Engineers, 46th Division

In all, the men of the 46th Division claimed 4,200 prisoners, 70 guns and more than 1,000 machine guns for their day's work.

Our brigade commander gave us a speech in a quiet spell, patting us on the back, as one might say. 'You boys have made history!' he said. 'Your deed today will never be forgotten!' I wonder?[50]

Corporal George Parker, 1/8th Battalion, Sherwood Foresters, 139th Brigade, 46th Division

To be fair to Brigadier J. Harrington nearly ninety years have now passed and still the deeds of the 46th Division are regarded as a pinnacle of achievement by an 'ordinary' British infantry division. The memory of those deeds is also preserved by a peculiarly evocative picture, which shows the men lining the steep banks at the scene of their triumph.

Meanwhile, the main attack was being made by the 27th and 30th American Divisions, with the Australians moving up behind them to exploit any breakthrough. They had a slightly easier task in that they were attacking in the sector where the canal was safely tucked away in a tunnel. Nevertheless, in the north the 27th American Division and the 3rd Australian Division that followed them had a terrible time. They had not yet reached the designated start lines and thus the effectiveness of the supporting bombardment had been badly diluted. They were also not well served by their tank support. As ever, up and down the front that day, the tanks were part of the equation rather than the whole. If they were ever exposed without proper infantry and artillery support in front of their nemesis – the German artillery – then they were surely doomed.

If anyone evoked my real sympathy it was the Tank Corps with its lumbering tanks doing about 2 miles an hour. I watched them going forward with infantry following, being able to see myself over the rising ground as they went blindly on. If only we had had wireless or some communications with them we could have saved hundreds of casualties.

They would lumber up a slope, we being able to see the German guns waiting just over the crest – waiting for the target they knew was coming. At point-blank range they could not miss and no armour then known could have saved them; a burst of flame, perhaps one man might escape, but very rarely – another tank gone and its crew. The Germans wait for the next one, horses standing by, another direct hit and with horses harnessed they are off – it was not fighting, it was 'murder'. Two of us watched this for hours, reporting continuously to headquarters, but there was nothing else we could do.[51]

Sapper Wilfred Cook, Field Survey Corps

One young officer who had a torrid time of it was Lieutenant Ralph Polk Buell commanding 'C' Company of the 107th Regiment AEF, which was attacking on the northern flank of the 27th Division. He soon became aware that if he did not actually lead his men from the front then they would not go forward. This was not the ideal place to try and execute control of a company in action, as was soon evident.

All of a sudden I saw in front of me a trench manned by three Germans with a machine gun, perhaps 40 yards away and at the back of them, in an angle in the trench, a group of about fifteen more Germans, with what appeared to be two machine guns. The ground between us was being heavily swept by machine-gun fire from the left, and the one gun in front of me was just commencing to fire to my left. The Germans apparently had not seen me, as there was some haze. My first impulse was to drop down, let the line come up and flank this position; but I was afraid that my men might stop if I did, all along the line, and might also mistake my motive, lose their confidence in me, and with it much of their morale. So I decided that the best thing to do was to go right at it, hoping that if I could get through the enfilading fire the Germans would be disturbed by the show of force and quit. It took me perhaps half a minute to come to this conclusion, and I started to run toward the trench. Just at this time one of my men yelled to me, 'Look out, Lieutenant, it's a trap!' The Germans apparently heard this, because they turned in my direction. The man with the machine gun swept it around towards me and one of his companions covered me with his rifle. Seeing that I had no chance to get to the post by myself, I shouted to the man nearest me, 'Tell them to charge!' The Germans were

455

apparently confused and made no effort to fire until I had gotten within 20 feet of them, when they opened up on me. I did not want to shoot until I was closer, but I found I would have to, so I took a shot at the man with the rifle and put him out of action. I later saw him dead in the trench. Just at this moment I was hit in the shoulder and nearly knocked off my feet. I did not realise that I was badly hit, and tried to keep going, taking several steps and bringing me probably 10 feet away from the machine gun, which was spitting all the time, but for some unknown reason was not hitting me. I tried to shoot the gunner, but had apparently exhausted the clip in my automatic, for it would not go off, and as I was vomiting blood and apparently about to go down I tried to throw my automatic at the man, hoping to put him out of business. My recollection is that just as I got my arm back I spun around and went down on my back. I do not remember anything more until I came to a few minutes later, lying there with a very vigorous fight going on over me. In a few minutes my men managed to clean the position out and went on.[52]

Lieutenant Ralph Polk Buell, 107th Infantry Regiment, 54th Brigade, 27th Division, AEF

Lieutenant Buell would be awarded the Distinguished Service Cross for his courage.

Further south the 30th American Division started well and managed to break through the German defences. As an engineer, Private Willard Newton of the 105th Engineers was following up behind as the infantry advanced on Bellicourt. All around him was copious evidence of the fighting.

Scores of dead Americans, Australians and Germans can be seen lying here and there, some covered in overcoats, others lying just as they fell. Walking wounded are going back in twos and threes, while those unable to walk are being carried off the field as rapidly as possible under the circumstances. Men with arms shot off, men with slight shrapnel wounds and gassed victims are being helped to the rear by German prisoners and by other men similarly wounded. Dead horses are lying about the field. Packs, rifles, cartridge belts, wrecked ammunition wagons, hand grenades and ammunition of every size and kind are scattered everywhere in great quantities.[53]

Private Willard Newton, 'F' Company, 105th Engineers, 30th Division, AEF

The company was meant to construct a road across the wilderness areas of the front line but constant German shrapnel fire disrupted its efforts. Their officer ordered the men to help evacuate some of the wounded but as they struggled back there was another example of their inexperience that could have been fatal.

> As we are crossing a wide depth of barbed wire entanglement, a gas shell falls near by. But we are unaware of it until we noticed the sergeant in charge of the detail a few feet ahead of us put on his mask. We thought at first it was the powder from the guns that made our eyes, noses and throats burn. When we find out the difference it is too late, for when we put on our masks we have to take them off, being unable to wear them. The gas makes our eyes run water, while the burning in our throats makes us spit continually.[54]
>
> Private Willard Newton, 'F' Company, 105th Engineers, 30th Division, AEF

Meanwhile, the 5th Australian Division had been tasked with leap-frogging the Americans and pushing forward towards the Hindenburg Support Line.

> They had about one and a half hours start on us. As we got nearer to the line we came into a fog, which became more dense every minute. It was partly artificial and partly natural. The ground was well churned up with shell fire and there were no trees about. The direction we travelled must have been up towards Hargicourt. Odd batches of prisoners appeared occasionally through the fog, escorted by Yanks, and there were a fair number of dead lying about. Fritz was shelling pretty persistently, but owing to the fog it was impossible for him to see what he was aiming at. A shell landed right next to the party in front of us – a Lewis gun crew. The whole of them, about eight men, went over like ninepins. To my surprise they all got up again and walked on. They had only been blown over by the concussion. An occasional machine gun opened out on us and this puzzled us, as we knew the Yanks were on ahead, till we discovered that they had not mopped up the dugouts. Some of the Huns had just laid low till the Yanks passed, then popped up again and carried on. We now struck a railway line and advanced along it. We passed through the Yanks, who seemed rather dis-organised. They had lost a lot of their officers and NCOs, and being

fresh to the line did not know what to do. About 150 of them attached themselves to our company and stayed with us for that day and the next. They said they wanted to see where the big war was! Fritz made things very willing during the afternoon, but as we were well scattered and so used to fighting, he did not do much damage. The poor Yanks, on the other hand, were so close together and so unused to fighting that they suffered rather heavily.[55]

Private G. V. Rose, 30th Battalion, 8th Brigade, 5th Australian Division

The following remarks by an experienced Australian officer sound a strange echo of the kind of sceptical comments frequently made by British officers about the Australian performance in battle during 1915 and 1916.

It was tragic to observe the state of disintegration that existed among the American troops. Probably as individuals they were not to be blamed, but their behaviour under fire showed clearly that in modern warfare it was of little avail to launch an attack with men untrained in war, even though the bravery of the individual men may not be questioned. In effect, so far as the Americans were concerned, it was a case of a mob let loose, all plans forgotten and no definite objective in view. No wonder the German machine-gunners had a field day. They must have felt like poor sportsmen shooting sitting game.[56]

Captain Oliver Woodward, 1st Australian Tunnelling Company

The absence of any proper 'mopping up' was the most serious omission by the Americans. The absolute necessity for a proper search of all dug-outs for concealed Germans had been cruelly impressed on the British consciousness back on the Somme in 1916. Now it was the Americans' turn to learn the hard way.

Evidently they had been too busy in Paris to learn the lessons that their instructors tried to teach them – they entirely omitted the important item of 'mopping up' the dugouts. At divisional headquarters I heard the candid opinion of Sir John Monash upon their prowess. Never have I heard such an elegant flow of language, either in the army or out. He called them all the names under the sun – nothing was too bad for them. These two American divisions marched first in the parade in

New York with the numbers of their killed on banners. They ought to have had the figures stencilled on the seats of their trousers.[57]

Captain John Marshall, Headquarters, Royal Engineers, 46th Division

When the Bellicourt entrance to the long canal tunnel was captured it seemed at first to provide proof-positive of one of the most enduring myths of the Great War.

Above the arch at the entrance to the Bellicourt Tunnel, where the canal passes underground, a most extraordinary chamber was found, approached by a stair from the canal path inside the tunnel. It contained three large cauldrons: one empty; one with a few inches of filthy grease at the bottom, from which emerged a blackened human hand; while the third held the cut-up portions of several human bodies. On the floor were a dozen other bodies, while a row of tins containing a disgusting-looking grease were ranged along a back wall. An appalling stench pervaded the whole place. A sort of trolley-way led down to this place from the trenches above. All who saw this at once rushed to the conclusion that they were beholding one of the much talked of German 'corpse factories' in which bodies were said to be melted down for their grease. It takes something to make an Australian soldier sick, but this sight turned some of them up. There was a small opening in the brickwork near the top of the chamber and we were informed after-wards by a prisoner that a small shell had come through this, killing all these men and throwing some bodies into the coppers. The place was actually a kitchen supplying the trenches above.[58]

Captain John Marshall, Headquarters, Royal Engineers, 46th Division

Despite having secured the Hindenburg Line, the area was still not safe: the Germans were determined to resist in every way possible. As such, bombing was becoming an increasing threat to life behind the front line.

We still had a bottle of whisky left. Evening was falling, and we had just made a table out of an old packing case and were sitting down in the trench preparing to open our treasured bottle, when a huge bombing aeroplane, flying low down, came right over us. Colonel Garforth and Combemale tried to crawl under the improvised table – I stuck to the bottle, which was in serious danger of being upset. About 70 yards from us the aeroplane dropped its first bomb on a gang of prisoners who were coming down the road, killing fifty-three men, thirteen of whom were British. Feet, hands and half-faces were blown all over the place. A hand, burnt perfectly black, alighted on our parapet, while the horse of the trooper who was escorting the prisoners was spread out, like jam, on the embankment of the roadway.[59]

Captain John Marshall, Headquarters, Royal Engineers, 46th Division

The aircraft continued up the road dropping its bombs and causing numerous casualties. One of the bombs fortunately failed to explode, but for Captain Marshall this bomb represented a whole new raft of dangers when it was drawn to his attention by the Assistant Provost Marshal of the 46th Division.

It had passed right through the granite pavé in the gutter of the main road and only its 'tail' projected above the surface of the roadway. Ammunition wagons were passing over the tail and had bent it flat with the road. I tried to pull the bomb out, but could not shift it. The Assistant Provost Marshal stood at a respectful distance during this operation! He told me later that he would not have done it himself for a million pounds after what he had seen. With two sappers I dug it out. It was 6 feet long and had failed to explode owing to the striker pin having bent on contact with the pavé.[60]

Captain John Marshall, Headquarters, Royal Engineers, 46th Division

THE FOURTH ARMY HAD crashed through the Hindenburg Line and in addition taken the Support Line. Only the Reserve Line, known to the British as the Beaurevoir Line, lay ahead and that was by no means the finished article as a defence work. It would not hold up the British for more than a few days. They were winning, that was clear, but for the infantry on the ground the war went on.

The 32nd Division was tasked with capitalising on the gains of the magnificent 46th Division. For one young officer, Lieutenant Clifford Platt, it was already his fourth visit to France and he had been wounded on two previous occasions. On 1 October he and his men were committed into a battalion attack on the village of Joncourt, which was reputedly held in strength by the Germans as an outpost in front of their main positions. Losses to officers meant that for the first time he was in charge of a company attack. He had acted as the consummate professional soldier: the situation was clear to him, his men had been fully briefed and the correct approach formations and tactics had been dutifully applied during the attack. In the end it made little difference as far as he himself was concerned.

Thump! A bullet hit me, spun me round and hurled me to the ground. Burning pains shot up my back and, although for the moment paralysed, I found myself studying alternatively the sky and the grass by my nose. Sensations are so numerous and so crowded at such a time, that it is utterly impossible to disentangle them. The superstitions inherited from generations of ancestors operated unconsciously but forcibly: I remember wondering if I had been killed and my ego was just taking a last look at the thing it had inhabited for so long. Then my commonsense reasserted itself and I thought about getting back to the trench. I wriggled round to face that way and it hurt like the deuce. Just then a man crawled out of the trench and started running towards me. A whizz-bang pitched under him and he collapsed about 5 yards away from me. I saw the blood streaming from his leg and a horrible gash in his face. Then I started to try and crawl, but found it a bit too much for me. Another man appeared out of the trench, ran and flung himself down about a yard in front of me. He refused to go and pull the other man in, but caught hold of my wrists and somehow started crawling backwards, pulling me along with him. I worked, as far as I could, with my toes. And after about 5 minutes we successfully dropped into the trench. Vandyne, the man who had pulled me in, a bullet-headed criminal of Dutch extraction from South Africa, at once went over again with another man and pulled into the trench the man who had first tried to get to me. He was a Royal Scot named Foy and later, on my recommendation, received a bar to his Military Medal, while Vandyne was released from imprisonment under which he was awaiting a court martial. A military criminal in action is nearly always wonderful.[61]

Lieutenant Clifford Platt, 15th Battalion, Lancashire Fusiliers, 96th Brigade, 32nd Division

Foy would lose his leg as a result of his impetuous courage; Vandyne was wounded in the foot. The war went on.

On 3 October the remnants of the once mighty Australian Corps advanced past Joncourt and on to the next village of Wiancourt.

> A machine gun from Wiancourt opened up on us, chipping up the dirt all around. We hopped in behind a hedge and lay down – some of the more sensible took shelter behind a barn. Fritz saw us go and fired through the hedge. A 32nd Battalion man was lying immediately behind me. I heard him give a queer cough and looking round saw that he had been shot in the stomach or near it. He died almost immediately. It was quite enough for me. I picked up my rifle and did a duck for the barn. There was a 32nd man there with a black eye. He and his cobber had just had a barney about something or other, and had come to blows. I think the cobber had two black eyes! Rather queer to be settling a private quarrel in the middle of a stunt.[62]
>
> Private G. V. Rose, 30th Battalion, 8th Brigade, 5th Australian Division

Once they had managed to force themselves through the Beaurevoir Line and, as a finale, to capture the strongly held town of Montbrehain the Australians could go no further, they were exhausted. At last they were pulled out of the line.

> The subtlety of the 'heads' now showed itself. The battalions had refused to be broken up while in the line. Now, in the darkness, various companies were marched off in different directions and handed over to other battalions in the brigade. It was no use kicking. Tucker was not so plentiful here as in the Forward Zone and striking troops would only starve – the brigade being distributed over a fair-sized area.[63]
>
> Private G. V. Rose, 30th Battalion, 8th Brigade, 5th Australian Division

The Australians had become one of the most effective assault forces in the entire war. They had always nibbled at the German lines, cutting out forward posts and seizing prisoners. But since 8 August they had been biting out huge chunks, attacking without rest for two whole months. Their achievements were a roll-call of honour for their country: they had captured nearly 23,000 prisoners from around thirty German divisions that had tried to stand against them. They had taken 332 guns, but had also suffered over 25,000 casualties themselves. They were exceptionally well led by Monash and had a superb cadre of officers, gritty NCOs and tough-as-nails ordinary 'diggers'. Together they and the Canadians had set a benchmark for the whole BEF. There was now nothing left to give: their work was done. The Hindenburg Line had been comprehensively ruptured; the road to Germany was open at last.

CHAPTER FOURTEEN

Germany Falling

OCTOBER SAW THE GERMAN ARMY locked in freefall. Attacked from end to end of the Western Front it was giving ground everywhere. Its reserves, such as they were, were dispersed along the entire front. Behind them there were no great defensive trench systems, no great wastelands: the Allies had broken through into open country. This was a new form of warfare. The Germans would fight on but it was evident to everyone that it was only in their power to harass and irritate the Allies as they advanced; they could not stop them. Germany lacked the men, the guns and the resources to stem the Allied advance and gain the time to prepare a new series of defence works. German casualties in 1918 had been simply unbearable: in prisoners alone they had lost 250,000 German soldiers. And this was not the start of a war: it was the end. The youth of the nation had been dying year in and year out for more than four long years. Young men were a scarce resource in Germany. But then everything in Germany was scarce: raw materials, food and fuel. Most debilitating of all, there was now no hope of ultimate victory. The Americans may have been inexperienced, but they were present in huge numbers and were prepared for the long haul. Behind the German Army lay the Rhine and perhaps that was a chance to hold up the Allies, but there was nothing in the situation to suggest that the massed guns of its enemies could not blast their way across even that mighty river. Haig had predicted it in the autumn of 1916; he had gambled on it in the swamps of the Ypres Salient a year later; now his day had dawned. The German Army was beaten.

Ludendorff certainly knew it. He had just received news from the

Balkans that Germany's Bulgarian allies were seeking an armistice. He was also fully aware that the Austro–Hungarian Empire was almost on its knees. The Turks, too, were in retreat everywhere. Whether looked at from the perspective of any individual battlefield, the Western Front or globally the answer was the same: Germany was doomed to defeat. Ludendorff himself was close to collapse and seems to have undergone some mild psychiatric treatment to calm his nerves. He and Hindenburg met to discuss the situation and both knew that something drastic had to be done. By now Ludendorff inhabited a strange fantasy world, based on the shaky foundations of wish-fulfilment laced with a denial of personal responsibility. He wanted an armistice, yes, but he still had visions of continuing the struggle.

> Our one task now was to act clearly and firmly, without delay. The Field Marshal listened to me with emotion. He answered that he had intended to say the same to me in the evening; that he had considered the whole situation carefully and thought the step necessary. We were also at one in the view that the armistice conditions would have to provide for controlled and orderly evacuation of the occupied territory and the possible resumption of hostilities on our own borders. We did not consider any abandonment of territory in the east, thinking that the Entente would be fully conscious of the dangers threatening them as well as ourselves from Bolshevism.[1]
>
> Quartermaster General Erich Ludendorff, General Headquarters, Imperial German Army

Ludendorff and Hindenburg were underestimating the hardened resolve of bitter opponents such as Clemenceau, Lloyd George, Haig and Foch. These were not men to let the Germans get away with anything whatsoever. And indeed, the German warlords were emphatically not men to be trusted. They possessed the madness to plan to resume the war at the first opportunity if they could only be given the chance to breathe.

> The Armistice is militarily necessary to us. We shall soon be at the end of our strength. If the peace does not follow, then we have at least disengaged ourselves from the enemy, rested ourselves and won time. Then we shall be more fit to fight than now, if that is necessary.[2]
>
> Field Marshal Paul von Hindenburg, General Headquarters, Imperial German Army

Hindenburg and Ludendorff shared a confidence that the German Army would be reinvigorated if it was charged with defending its own country.

> If the war should approach our own territory, if the feeling that he was protecting home and all that word meant, entered into the heart of each man at the front, who knew full well the meaning of such terms as 'theatre of war', 'battlefield' and 'lines of communication', if the war with all its destruction threatened German soil, then I felt our seventy million Germans would stand like one man, determined and ready to sacrifice for their country all the mighty strength that still remained to them. Whether France herself, bled white and suffering worse than we were, would remain in the field for long after her territory was evacuated, also was doubtful.[3]
>
> Quartermaster General Erich Ludendorff, General Headquarters, Imperial German Army

Ludendorff's fantasies of resuming the war once the Germans were back within their own borders was also entirely missing the point of the militarily crippling conditions that the Allies would surely impose in return for an armistice. And what of the political situation in Germany? There the heady breath of revolution was in the air. A stopgap chancellor, Prince Max von Baden, the second cousin of Kaiser Wilhelm II, had been appointed on 3 October, but this was hardly the radical step needed to defuse the simmering political unrest that was sweeping through German society. Although he introduced some moderate, liberalising constitutional changes and even appointed some socialist delegates as ministers, he soon found that he could not control the surging rise of the forces of the left or placate the stubborn, unchanging establishment of the right. Germany remained firmly in the grip of political crisis.

IT IS ALMOST IMPOSSIBLE to give a coherent narrative of the advances made on all fronts by the British, French and American Armies. Maps are no help; they show only a morass of arrows denoting the unrelenting assaults. Freed by the conditions of open warfare of the necessity to advance and maintain an unbroken front, individual

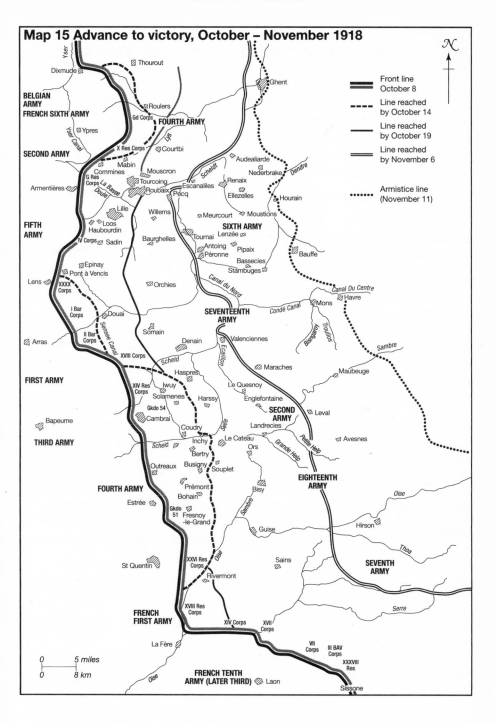

Map 15 Advance to victory, October – November 1918

Legend	
━━━	Front line October 8
╌╌╌	Line reached by October 14
───	Line reached by October 19
═══	Line reached by November 6
⋯⋯⋯	Armistice line (November 11)

0 5 miles
0 8 km

divisions planned their own battles, set their own objectives and pushed on in the attack. Even brigades or battalions sought to exploit opportunities with little regard to whether their flanks were properly covered or they would have sufficient support backing them up. This would have been suicide just a few months earlier. The attacks would have been defeated in detail, swamped by the mass firepower of the German artillery. There were disasters: occasions where units bit off more than they could chew, where the Germans turned and savaged their pursuers. Casualties were appalling, open warfare meant what it said and German machine-gunners sold their lives dearly.

The British infantry were also becoming increasingly exhausted and found that they were going to the well rather too often. On 8 October the men of the 13th Royal Fusiliers were ordered forward as part of the 37th Division attack on the Beaurevoir Line in the Third Army area.

> Somebody said, 'That farm has got to be taken!' It was called Hurtebise Farm. A tank came along and 'Chick' Edgar and I, we went behind this tank. It was easy, walking along, hardly anything happening. On the other side of the valley we could see three Germans and they'd just come out of a trench. Old 'Chick' Edgar he puts his rifle up and he has a go. One of these fellows dropped. Then these bloody bullets got me in the leg! It went straight through my leg and blew a great big hole in the back. It didn't hurt! I was really thankful that I'd got hit. I said to 'Chick', 'I've got one!' He'd gone white, he wasn't looking very well; he knew he'd killed or hit somebody. Off I went. I sat down for a bit and six Germans helped me down – I robbed them – I got another six watches from these fellows who helped me down! I put them in a sandbag. When we got to this first aid post, the officer said, 'What have you got in there?' I said, 'Oh I've got a few watches!' He said, 'Well give me one!' By the time I finished I gave them all away![4]
>
> Corporal Donald Price, 13th Battalion, Royal Fusiliers, 112th Brigade, 37th Division

By this time Corporal Price had been on the Western Front for three years and when he found himself hospitalised in Boulogne he was determined to postpone, if possible, his return to active service. In his view his wound had earned him a decent rest and he did not want his body letting him down by an over-fast recovery.

There was only a little bullet wound at the front, it was the back that was the trouble; there was a great hole. It had gone right smack in the middle of the leg and the bullet had gone right round the bone and blew a hole right out of the back, it didn't even crack the bone! I was a very, very healthy lad and my wounds were healing too quickly! So I decided to keep the wound open. I tried to keep the back open, knocked the scab off once or twice and used my toothbrush to rub the scab off. But I healed very quickly; the whole thing was healed. I was limping a bit about the 10 November and that was about all! Then I went to Etaples.[5]

Corporal Donald Price, 13th Battalion, Royal Fusiliers, 112th Brigade, 37th Division

The artillery had its work cut out keeping up with the pace of the advance as the Third Army closed in on the town of Cambrai. It wasn't just a matter of moving the heavy guns and limbers forward, it was also the hundreds, indeed thousands, of shells that a battery needed if it was not to fall impotently silent. The motor lorries brought the bulk of the shells forward and dumped them off at convenient locations, often on crossroads. Here they were stacked up and the drivers of the various artillery units could come back to pick up the shells they needed. There was little time for complicated camouflage and the arrangements had to be fairly transparent. This also could be a disadvantage. The guns were moving forward fast and as they dropped into new positions they often found themselves under severe pressure. They rarely had the time to dig in properly and they were therefore excruciatingly vulnerable to any German counter-battery fire.

In the gun position there was still plenty to be done before we could be ready for the bombardment. On the guns themselves the men were feverishly busy unloading ammunition, arranging stores and fusing shells. Under such shelter from the rain as a neighbouring tree afforded and by the capricious light of a torch, the Major was to be seen trying to plot the exact position to within 5 yards of each gun on the map – no easy task even in daylight. Other officers were doing their best to lay their guns on the correct line, and the battery command assistants struggled with their gun calculations for the actual targets to be engaged. Finally as Zero Hour approached the German shell fire increased in intensity and added a further complication. Evidently suspecting some stunt their gunners began sweeping wildly up and down the length and breadth of Cantaing and of the canal valley, which did not encourage mathematical thinking. However, somehow or other, our last gun opened fire only a few moments late and not, let us hope, *too* wide of the target![6]

Lieutenant Brian Bradnack, 122nd Siege Battery, 66th Brigade, Royal Garrison Artillery

When at last they were ready, his guns began to join the hundreds of others in pounding the German positions in and around Cambrai.

Half-left, hovering over Cambrai, a huge column of smoke stood up motionless into the darkness, glowing bright crimson at the base and changing colour upwards through orange and yellow till it finally lost itself in a dark and shapeless mass in the upper blackness, which only revealed itself by blotting out the stars. In the foreground, the valley gleamed with hoar frost thick as snow. In the moonlight, against the shadows of the woods that ringed the canal, every gun and every gunner stood silhouetted stark and clear against the whiteness. Soon after the barrage opened, the smoke of the guns settled down on the valley like a sea of cotton wool, sliding gently downwind, except where a gun fired and the pall just there eddied and swirled in the concussion. In the 'sea' men waded about on their guns, immersed to their waists, silently amid the echoing din that filled the valley. Gradually the column of smoke, that for us was Cambrai, began to shine silvery at the top, and, as the sun rose higher, the silver light crept down and down, engulfing first the yellow and then the orange, while as yet the valley was in darkness but for the flashes of the guns. Finally as dawn appeared the red glow about the base disappeared, vanquished by the sunlight. And all at once the bombardment had ceased.[7]

Lieutenant Brian Bradnack, 122nd Siege Battery, 66th Brigade, Royal Garrison Artillery

On 6 October Unteroffizier Frederick Meisel of the 371st Infantry Regiment was moving back through the suburbs of Cambrai. The Germans felt the hot breath of the British guns down their necks.

Our division passed through Cambrai. British shells had set it on fire. The air was acrid with black smoke, the heat intense. Our pace increased as the danger from falling timbers became evident. Scurrying down the endless streets, Otto tried to light a cigarette, 'Anybody got a match?' Pointing to a smouldering telegraph pole, Paul replied, 'There, help yourself!' Eyes and throats were beginning to burn, lips becoming parched with the heat. Just as I thought we were doomed to be burned alive, the outskirts of the town were reached. A short rest was ordered while we filled our lungs with sweet fresh air. A wind had sprung up, driving away the thick clouds of smoke, showing the burning city clearly, the flames lighting the landscape.[8]

Unteroffizier Frederick Meisel, 371st Infantry Regiment, 43rd Ersatz Brigade, 10th Ersatz Division, Imperial German Army

When some of the British gunners entered the town following its capture on 9 October, they rather perversely blamed the Germans for the fires and general destruction rather than their own artillery.

Visited the town of Cambrai and found it practically impossible to take the car into the centre of the town as the Boche had exploded mines at all the approaches, causing huge craters that even tanks couldn't pass, although the advance had been too rapid for him to cut down trees. The damage done was the result of incendiary bombs left behind by the enemy and fires deliberately caused when the Hun saw he would have to retreat – for days past we had watched huge fires burning in different parts of the town. All bridges were destroyed, but the main portion of the town was practically intact until bombed and shelled by the Huns after their evacuation. Most of the houses were full of furniture, but everything had been turned upside down. The Huns fully kept up their reputation by placing booby traps all over the place. One 'Tommy' who tried to play a pianola had his arm blown off, and other casualties were caused by bombs attached to wires in dugouts or to rifles and souvenirs placed in conspicuous places. Later it was found that the whole neighbourhood was infested with a new kind of bomb, which did not operate until the acid it contained had eaten through certain wires.[9]

Captain Ernest Boon, 306th Siege Battery, Royal Garrison Artillery

On 10 October the 5th Connaught Rangers reached the outskirts of Le Cateau, scene of an early battle in August 1914. They could see that it was held in strength by the Germans and soon realised that they were rather exposed, situated as they were at the very apex of the advance.

They began to shell us unmercifully. I will never forget the look of horror on the face of one of my men, as a splinter of shell disembowelled him, in the seconds, or moments, before he died. Another had one of his legs almost amputated just at his knee, and I, with my penknife, severed the few scraps of flesh and sinew which held it together before tying him up and sending him back on a stretcher. It was really most unpleasant, especially as we were all completely worn out. We dug little holes in the earth, sat in them and hoped that we would not get a direct hit.[10]

Captain Charles Brett, 5th Battalion, Connaught Rangers, 199th Brigade, 66th Division

Then, just as they were reaching the end of their tether, orders came up that they were to make a new attack at 1700. For Captain Brett and his exhausted men this was the last straw. They had made their first attack, after no sleep the night before, some three days earlier. Since then they had been in near-continuous action, harassed by shell fire, with no sustaining hot food or drink; in fact, they hadn't had much food at all. As for sleep they had to manage with nothing more substantial than the occasional disturbed nap.

At 5 p.m. exactly we got out of the holes and set off down the road that led downhill into Le Cateau. We had no support whatever from our artillery. I was leading the company and with me was the officer commanding No. 1 Platoon; the other three platoons following at intervals. We had got about 100 yards when the German guns opened up, they had an observation post in the church tower in Le Cateau that spotted us. The shells were coming over my head, less than 10 feet above me and were bursting on the roadway about 30 yards behind me. The following platoons suffered very heavy casualties indeed, but I, and those with me, pressed on – there are circumstances in which it is not wise to look behind you.[11]

Captain Charles Brett, 5th Battalion, Connaught Rangers, 199th Brigade, 66th Division

Three of the Connaught Rangers companies were ordered forward, the fourth being charged with mopping up duties. Sometimes it was the leading platoon that was caught by the bursting shells, sometimes those following – it really was just a matter of luck who lived and died.

On the road into the town the Germans kept up a concentrated barrage – it sounded as if express trains were crashing through space and blowing the roadway into a ceaseless fountain of dust, smoke and blazing light. The leading platoon was almost destroyed by one of these shells and the dead bodies came rolling down the high banks at the side of the road.[12]

Second Lieutenant Alan McPeake, 5th Battalion, Connaught Rangers, 199th Brigade, 66th Division

The survivors pushed on and penetrated into the town itself. By then it was dark and the empty streets took on a threatening appearance.

As the men rushed on through the deserted streets, the strain of waiting for something to happen and the menace of the yawning doorways made the first contact with the Germans almost welcome. Owing to the barrage and the smoke, contact between companies was altogether lost, and later, platoons, sections and even individuals were fighting on their own.[13]

Second Lieutenant Alan McPeake, 5th Battalion, Connaught Rangers, 199th Brigade, 66th Division

One such small isolated group was led by Captain Brett. He had crossed the then undamaged main bridge across the Selle River and was creeping cautiously through the streets looking for the railway embankment on the far side of the town that represented their ultimate objective.

I discovered that our party was eight strong – two officers and six men. A machine gun opened up on us, from the top of what appeared to be an obstacle across the road, 50 or 60 yards away, and the bullets made bright sparks as they hit the granite setts of the roadway. We all took cover in doorways and the machine gun stopped. My subaltern said, 'Come on, we can't stop here!' and we all started up the street. A German shouted, '*Wie geht?*' to which I replied, in elementary school-boy German, '*Was ist das?*' which apparently satisfied the German who replied, '*Gans recht!*' So we went on and found the obstacle across the street to be an iron railway bridge, which had been blown up and tipped sideways. On top were several Germans with the machine gun – we climbed up and disposed of them. Having done so, we looked down into the roadway on the German side of the bridge and saw below us fifty to a hundred German soldiers standing and looking up at the top of the bridge to see what it was all about. It was pretty dark but one could see the serried rows of white faces looking up. At my command we leapt down among them, killed and wounded several, and captured two, all the rest turned tail and fled. It was well for us that they were very poor-class troops.[14]

Captain Charles Brett, 5th Battalion, Connaught Rangers, 199th Brigade, 66th Division

There was no sign of any kind of support and Brett decided that he did not have enough troops to hold the embankment and that he must withdraw. He fell back through the town towards another bridge that he hoped would not be being watched. This bridge had been demolished, but he was optimistic that he could find a way across.

It had been an iron footbridge, which had disappeared – but the iron handrail still ran across, several feet above the water. I handed my rifle to the man immediately behind me and set off across the river on the handrail. It was a bit wobbly, but bore my weight all right, so I ordered the others to come over one at a time. The first man over handed me back my rifle and I was interested to see that he was one of our German prisoners! We staggered back to the place we had started from. I collapsed into one of the little holes we had dug, utterly exhausted and went to sleep at once. When I woke next morning I found there was something with me in the hole – it turned out to be the leg I had cut off the evening before, with its boot and puttee complete! It is remarkable how long it takes to get anywhere near normal again after complete exhaustion. It was several days before any of us was fit to lift his head or take the slightest interest in anything except food and sleep.[15]

Captain Charles Brett, 5th Battalion, Connaught Rangers, 199th Brigade, 66th Division

The bulk of Le Cateau remained in German hands.

When the troops moved into some captured towns and villages they found that the Germans had not had time to clear the French away and there was a welcome reception for the Allies. Captain Oliver Woodward, an Australian sapper officer, was received with joy as he moved towards the town of Busigny on 10 October.

Crowds of civilian refugees began to come back from Busigny, as the enemy were driven out of the town. Out of general kindness our men offered bread, margarine and jam to the children, and before long our breakfast had vanished. Many of the children up to five years of age had never tasted butter or jam or white bread, and never before was a meal so happily eaten. The look of pure astonishment and joy on the faces of the kiddies was so wonderful that no member of our party regretted that his morning's breakfast consisted of tightening up another hole in his belt. The adults were so overjoyed at the action of our men that they insisted on kissing one and all in the usual French manner. This rather detracted from what was otherwise a pleasing interlude![16]

Captain Oliver Woodward, 1st Australian Tunnelling Company

The Germans fell back and occupied various hastily taken up positions along the eastern bank of the Selle River facing the Third and Fourth Armies. Although the defences were not in the same league as the Hindenburg Line, they still had to be approached carefully. Before an attack could be made a decent start line had to be secured and the guns brought up. All this would stall progress.

On 11 October the Third Army generally had a frustrating day as it approached to 'nibble' at the Selle Line and its outposts. For the men on the ground however, it was less frustrating than terrifying. Lance Corporal Alfred Abraham and his men of 'A' Company, 8th Queens Royal West Surreys were sent forward without the support of a creeping barrage across the shallow valley lying in front of the village of Rieux. The ominous signs of recent fighting surrounded them: dead horses, abandoned equipment and fresh shell holes. They passed through Rieux and Abraham shook his section out into open order as the men found themselves under heavy machine-gun fire. They were crossing open country denuded of any cover and rising gently to a low ridge some 250 yards ahead.

Jerry made a point of shooting officers first, then the NCOs. It was easy for them to distinguish officers because their uniforms were quite different from ours and they did not carry rifles. An NCO's stripes were lighter and more distinguishable from a distance than those in use today. Our open order drill involved giving hand signals and using the whistle, both of which could be easily spotted by a man behind a machine gun. I immediately found a stream of machine-gun bullets whistling past me. I dropped to the ground and lay there for a few seconds while bullets thudded into the ground all round me. I felt thankful that I had that shovel on my back and I slithered the butt of my rifle in front of my head. As soon as the storm of bullets moved away from me, I got up and started to go forward again. I found myself walking a little in advance of Sergeant Cole of another platoon. By this time we were totally mixed up and I had lost touch with my platoon officer and sergeant. I was about 10 feet from Cole when a stream of bullets came tearing round my head. Instinctively I ducked and the sergeant said, 'What the fuckin' 'ell are you creeping along like that for?' Those were the last words he ever spoke: before I could reply a machine-gunner got him in his sights and his head just disintegrated.[17]

Lance Corporal Alfred Abraham, 8th Battalion, Queens Royal West Surrey Regiment, 17th Brigade, 24th Division

They could make no further progress and were forced to dig in where they were.

Next day they were part of a major assault by the Third Army across the Selle River, which generally failed. After the fighting had died down, Lance Corporal Abraham and his men took shelter for the night in shallow dugouts scraped into the side of a roadside ditch. They had lost a lot of men over the last two days and were suffering the cumulative effects of their recent experiences.

There was a hell of a row going on not far in front of us and all around us. We were very tired by now and dimly I heard someone say, 'Gas?' Someone else said, 'Fuck the gas!' and then I must have fallen asleep. We were all so exhausted that even nearby shell bursts went unnoticed and I had lost all count of time. I woke just as the sky was beginning to lighten, feeling pretty rough. Cornell and I climbed out of our hole and both vomited on the road. Cornell looked at me and said, 'Christ, you look a mess!' I took a look at him and replied, 'Well, you're no bloody oil painting!' Our eyes looked like oysters in buckets of blood and it was obvious that we had been gassed. Jerry had been mixing mustard gas shells with his HE and one had burst on the road not more than 6 feet from where we had slept.[18]

Lance Corporal Alfred Abraham, 8th Battalion, Royal West Surrey Regiment, 17th Brigade, 24th Division

All of the men of the section were soon vomiting, while their eyes, noses, throats, lungs, stomachs and exposed parts were all blistered or scorched by the effects of the mustard gas. With their eyelids stuck together, coughing and retching, they had to be evacuated from the line. Soon a classic scenario was underway.

> We set off in a long crocodile for the casualty clearing station and had gone a long way like this, when we heard a horseman approaching. The rider pulled up and said, 'Who the hell is responsible for sending these men like this?' Our guide told him where we had come from and where we were bound for and he said, 'Fall the men out at once and I will see they have transport!' As the owner of the voice galloped away the Quartermaster said, 'Well boys, that was the General!' It was not long before a fleet of motor ambulances rattled up.[19]
>
> Lance Corporal Alfred Abraham, 8th Battalion, Royal West Surrey Regiment, 17th Brigade, 24th Division

Soon they had reached the casualty clearing station and now the relative benefits of being gassed became apparent. They were not dead or mutilated. The Germans had removed them from the battlefield but their prognosis for recovery was excellent.

> The CCS by the sound of things was in a marquee. We were given little bags to put all our personal possessions into; then we stripped and were led to tepid baths in what felt like galvanised washtubs, where we endeavoured to get ourselves clean. The orderlies were very helpful and when we had finished bathing we were given a towel, socks and pyjamas and from now on we were stretcher cases. I was able to lie down clean, warm and comforted by the knowledge that I had been through hell and survived. Although no one with medical knowledge gave me any advice on the matter, I think at no time did I believe I was permanently blinded. All I had to do was to rest and get better. Just to lie there and rest was sheer bliss.[20]
>
> Lance Corporal Alfred Abraham, 8th Battalion, Royal West Surrey Regiment, 17th Brigade, 24th Division

It is worth noting that just as the Third Army was beginning to be seriously held up, so too in the north the Second Army launched another huge attack in Flanders on 14 October and began a series of advances accompanied by the neighbouring Fifth Army. If the Germans managed to hold in one place they were surely giving way elsewhere in the line.

Open warfare was still a new thing to most of the Second Army and Major Philip Neame VC, a pre-war regular who had fought with the 'Old Contemptibles' of 1914, was shocked to find that the years of trench warfare, where the infantry placed much of their faith in machine guns and hand grenades, had eroded their ability to use the Lee-Enfield .303 rifle.

> What I did notice was the failure of the infantry to use their rifles. They'd either shout for a Lewis gun or the nearest machine gun; you see we had machine-gun companies then. They got out of the habit of using their rifles. We'd reached the River Schelde and there were some Germans on the other bank – they were retreating fairly fast. I'd ridden up to it and some of our infantry were there with their rifles, there was no Lewis gun, and they weren't firing. I said, 'Go on, have a shot at them!' I seized a fellow's rifle and started shooting myself at Germans just across the river – it was only 100 yards wide.[21]
>
> Major Philip Neame VC, Headquarters, 30th Division

Of course, in this case they should have fired. But in a sense his men were right; if they *could* get access to support fire from machine guns, Stokes mortars, rifle grenades and all the other paraphernalia of the mechanical warfare that drove the All Arms Battle then they were right to do so. They could generate a far higher firepower than their inaccurately aimed rifles ever could.

On 17 October the First Army also pushed forward onto Douai and the reconstituted 8th Division at last found itself going forwards rather than back. There were still shocks in modern warfare: many horrible, but others amusing in their release of pent-up tension. Lieutenant John Nettleton had crossed a canal and was cautiously exploring down the towpath to check the immediate sector was clear of Germans.

> I was pretty sure the Boche had withdrawn, but, even so, I got the fright of my life when, as we were passing a cottage we heard the clatter of breaking crockery. My runner unslung his rifle and I drew my revolver. In great trepidation we crept up the garden path as quietly as we could.

Then we flung open the door and rushed in – to be confronted with a tiny kitten who was crawling about on the dresser from which he had knocked down a cup. The relief was so great that we both burst out laughing.[22]

Lieutenant John Nettleton, 2nd Battalion, Rifle Brigade, 25th Brigade, 8th Division

Later he was amongst one of the first parties to enter Douai, which had indeed been abandoned by the Germans without a fight. They had, however, left their mark.

As far as the buildings were concerned the town was more or less intact. But inside the buildings everything of value had been removed and everything else wantonly smashed and destroyed. Not only things that might have been of use to us, but everything: mirrors, furniture, pictures, crockery, even the organ in the cathedral – all smashed to atoms. Mattresses were ripped open and the stuffing scattered; even children's toys were broken up in a senseless orgy of destruction. I saw a French gendarme weeping openly as he looked at the wreck of his home and held in his hands the remains of a broken doll. The damage done by modern warfare is appalling enough – there was absolutely no point in going to so much trouble to make it worse.[23]

Lieutenant John Nettleton, 2nd Battalion, Rifle Brigade, 25th Brigade, 8th Division

On the same day the Fourth Army burst back into life after its quiescent period facing the German line along the Selle River. This time, after the appropriate preparations, there was to be no mistake. Zero Hour was fixed at 0520 on 17 October. The men of the 1/8th Sherwood Foresters were leading the attack and managed to cross the river before running into real trouble from the ridge line occupied by the Germans in front of them.

We managed, with great loss, to get over some pontoon bridges that the engineers and pioneers had miraculously rigged up overnight, cleared some trenches there, with bayonets and grenades, took more prisoners, mostly boys younger than me. In front of us across a flat area was a ridge, which as we approached erupted with tremendous machine-gun fire. Our officers were killed in getting to that ridge and by the time we reached its shelter all NCOs but myself and another corporal were either dead or wounded. My team, now only three, and I set up our

Lewis gun on the top of the ridge, keeping heads well down. Suddenly
lines of grey figures swarmed over towards the ridge, they were putting
in a counter-attack! I opened up with my gun, traversing left and right
over the plain. I could actually see men falling like ninepins, but still
they came on, reinforced by more and more waves of field grey. I
thought we had had it.[24]

Corporal George Parker, 1/8th Battalion, Sherwood Foresters, 139th Brigade, 46th
Division

At this inauspicious moment the sole surviving officer tapped Parker on
the shoulder and promoted him 'in the field' to sergeant!

So, there I was, made sergeant, in the middle of a battle, all of us
looking like finishing any minute; most likely never to have the
opportunity to wear the chevrons, anyway! Suddenly firing started to
come from the side of our position, then almost at the back of us. It
didn't need brains to know what that meant: we were a few men on a
bit of a hill, being gradually surrounded – we hadn't a hope in hell of
getting out of it. We kept up our fire, and our artillery opened out on
the rear of the German hordes, but it was too late, no one could get to
us in time to help. Leaving my No. 2 firing the gun, I tried to edge
along to the Lieutenant, 50 yards along, to ask him if he agreed to us
trying to crawl back before the encirclement was complete. It seemed as
though I had been kicked by a horse on the left knee; it gave way and
down I went, rolling down the bank. The only thing I thought of then,
was to get out of it, before the only gap in the circle closed. I crawled;
dragging that blasted leg, in between hundreds of our dead, towards
what I hoped was the right way. I was more scared then than when I
was behind my gun – so helpless. Even then Jerry gave me a parting gift
– a bullet in my hip – I don't think he liked me![25]

Corporal George Parker, 1/8th Battalion, Sherwood Foresters, 139th Brigade, 46th
Division

As he crawled back he met other wounded men, desperately trying to
get back to safety.

I met a man from the 5th Sherwoods who had one eye shot out. We
were both bleeding like hell, but there wasn't time to think about it. We
crawled along together, coming across an officer, lying in a hole

groaning. He had been shot through a lung and had struggled so far before giving up. Poor devil, every time he breathed, blood and foam bubbled from holes in his chest. There was no hope for him, nothing I could do. He asked for water. I still had some in my water bottle and gave him the bottle to keep. He asked me to take his wallet and identity discs. We stopped with him until he died, his last words were to thank us, what for poor chap, I don't know, we couldn't do anything for him![26]

Corporal George Parker, 1/8th Battalion, Sherwood Foresters, 139th Brigade, 46th Division

Once again, while individuals suffered, the attack as a whole was a victory. The Fourth Army had broken through the Selle Line and occupied defensible positions along the ridge between the Selle and the Sambre Rivers, which would clearly be the next German defence line. Up and down the line German troops were making desperate counter-attacks and although they may on occasions have succeeded they also lost far too many men. Unteroffizier Frederick Meisel was in one such venture and soon found that success turned to ashes.

A British machine gun left behind by its crew stood in the field ready for us. Richard and I reached it at the same time. We turned it round and brought their own gun into action against them. I fired several shots; then the belt jammed. Richard leaned over and adjusted it; then he was hit. With a gurgling noise he slumped over. Death was instant: the bullet pierced the helmet, the blood running from his nose and mouth, while the brains oozed out in a thick yellowish mass from the back of his head. His body lay squarely on the ammunition belt. A hatred flared up in me against the English. Jerking his body aside to free the belt, I automatically resumed firing, when it jammed again. I was raging and for a moment forgot where I was.[27]

Unteroffizier Frederick Meisel, 371st Infantry Regiment, 43rd Ersatz Brigade, 10th Ersatz Division, Imperial German Army

Another German veteran was dead: his experience lost, his comrades at first infuriated and then, in the cold light of dawn, disheartened. They had no future in this war.

*

FUTILITY IS A WORD often used to describe the Great War. This depends on one's perspective as to whether German militarism had to be stopped in its tracks and indeed, whether the preservation of a balance of the great powers in Europe was really necessary to British security. Was the neutrality of Belgium really important? Did the British have to fight to keep the Germans back from the Channel ports or even to preserve Britain's naval supremacy – and if they did what long-term good did it do them? Could anything be worth all the lost lives? These issues can still be debated today. Yet there is no doubt that the last couple of weeks of the war *were* futile. For the greatest questions had long been answered: the Allies would win the war, Germany would be humiliatingly defeated and the Allies would use that defeat to extract every ounce of retribution. Yet the war was like a runaway train: it could not be stopped easily. The German politicians and High Command twisted in the breeze, trying to do their best for their country while not attracting the opprobrium of blame for the inevitable surrender. Ludendorff was finished. He changed his position on a daily basis: now convinced Germany had lost and calling for an armistice, next convinced they could regroup and defend the German borders, then outraged by the Allied armistice conditions. The end came after a vigorous exchange of views with the Kaiser. Ludendorff, like his army, was defeated and he resigned on 26 October. His replacement as Hindenburg's chief of staff was a hard, practical man, General Wilhelm Groener, who swiftly analysed the situation and found it utterly hopeless.

At the front there had been another pause, a period of relative calm extending along most of the front between 26 October and 1 November. Fighting continued in some sectors but there was an absence of great offensives. The Allied armies all needed a chance to reorganise, juggle their units, move up the guns and replenish their ammunition supplies, which were running low under the pressure of continuous fighting for the best part of three months. The men had been out in the open, mostly living rough, finding what accommodation they could: abandoned dugouts, wrecked houses or a scrape in the ground.

> We pulled into a field one evening. By the time we had tended to the horses and guns it was dark. We had a warm drink and some iron rations: hard biscuits and bully beef. The field had seen quite a lot of

action and the stench of death was around. I dropped to the ground behind the gun and, exhausted as I was, I could only sleep fitfully. It was just getting light and on getting to my feet I looked down and saw that I had been lying alongside a dead German. He was just a boy and maggots were crawling from his nose. The sergeant saw him too and exclaimed, 'Christ almighty – poor bugger!' I turned away and vomited. I always had a squeamish stomach.[28]

Gunner Percy Creek, 'A' Battery, 104th Brigade, Royal Field Artillery

The troops' food, water and rum supplies usually reached them, but there were, of course, hiccups and occasional shortages to contend with. And it was now winter: cold penetrated their bones, sapping their strength. As November loomed there was nowhere to dry clothes, nowhere to get warm and if soaked in the rain they could be damp for days. But worst of all was the accumulating effect of the casualties: the fighting was relentless and the men were draining away. Between August and November a staggering 360,000 of the 1.2 million men of the BEF had become casualties of one sort or another. Every one of them an individual, every one a story to be told. Reinforcements had made up the numbers to some extent but the newcomers were bound to be young and inexperienced. They would not have long to learn.

PRELIMINARY OPERATIONS began on 1 November prior to the offensive planned for 4 November. Thus the Third Army made a series of attacks in the Valenciennes sector. Sergeant John Stephenson, a Lewis gunner with 'A' Company, 1/6th Duke of Wellington's, found himself as part of the first wave going over at 0515 in a desperate attack to rush the German front line, cross the Rhonelle River, then advance to seize a sunken road running along the ridge in front.

We went 'over the top' at 5 a.m. and three of my team were killed right away. Just a little way out, we found some hidden machine-gun posts fully manned. We dealt with them promptly. There were no barbed entanglements. Our next obstruction was the Rhonelle River, which we crossed by means of the trees that the Lancashire Fusiliers felled for us. We caught up to the barrage in which there was a break, but my team were all knocked out except Smailes and myself. We went through that break in the barrage and were now ahead of it. We got to the sunken road before the barrage and found it full of Germans. We jumped straight into the trench-like road. The Germans who first saw us looked bewildered, but others started grabbing their rifles and grenades. I swung my Lewis into action from the hip, while Smailes let off a few telling shots with his rifle – at which they flung down their weapons and raised their arms in surrender, many crying out, '*Mercy, Kamerad!*' I continued using the Lewis gun where any groups of opposition formed. Some of them started running across the road to the rear and I had then to let them know quickly that what I said I meant.[29]

Sergeant John Stephenson, 1/6th Battalion, Duke of Wellington's Regiment, 147th Brigade, 49th Division

Once the situation had calmed down to his satisfaction, Stephenson, who was to be awarded a bar to his existing Military Medal for courage and initiative under fire, came across a temptation that few soldiers could resist.

I saw a German soldier wearing the Iron Cross and I thought, 'What a souvenir to take back home!' I went over to him and showed him that I wanted it as a war trophy. He did not seem to want to part with it, but I suppose that under the conditions and my appearance with itching trigger finger – he thought it best to let me have it. I intended keeping it, but in a very short time I thought I would object very strongly if they tried to take my war decoration from me. So I called him over, fastened it back on his tunic and told him in my halting German to look after it and keep it. How relieved he seemed to be.[30]

Sergeant John Stephenson, 1/6th Battalion, Duke of Wellington's Regiment, 147th Brigade, 49th Division

To their south a strong German counter-attack had thrown the 61st Division back out of the village of Maresches and the 2/5th Gloucesters were ordered to retake it that night. Captain R. S. B. Sinclair was in command of 'A' Company, which was to seize the crossroads east of Maresches assisted by a creeping barrage. The action that followed summed up the sheer confusion of open warfare in the dark.

We moved forward into a void of darkness – our only means of keeping direction was by compass, except for the bursting of the star shells. We were unable to keep up with the barrage; moreover we lost touch with one another. We moved through the advanced line of our divisional troops, over a field of turnips, in what was supposed to be diamond formation. I remember plunging through a hedge with the men and landing in an orchard, where we came under enemy fire. We rallied the men, fixed bayonets and charged into the darkness. We were certainly very far short of our official objective. Forms of Germans loomed up at us; some of us got in front of our own Lewis guns; some succeeded in bayoneting a few Germans. I deflected a German thrust with an ash stick – my revolver was clogged with mud – and things seemed to be in a pretty state of chaos. Things quietened down and we dug ourselves in, having not the foggiest notion where we were, or who was on our flanks, or where the enemy was, or what had happened to the rest of the battalion. We were very much 'in the air'.[31]

Captain R. S. B. Sinclair, 2/5th Battalion, Gloucestershire Regiment, 184th Brigade, 61st Division

Open warfare was above all confusing and the slightest mistake could mean heavy casualties. Next day the attack was renewed and Maresches finally fell into British hands.

German resistance was increasingly variable. Sometimes they fought like demons; sometimes they seemed to be actively seeking the opportunity to surrender. Most common of all was a dull acceptance of their fate. They would fight on, but they no longer believed in their cause. They had no hope of victory.

Laid down were some wounded German soldiers and they were none too happy. They told me – in English – that they belonged to the Württemberg Regiment. What huge fellows they were! They looked weary of the war and said, 'Why are we fighting each other? We have never seen you before and you have never seen us! We do not want to kill you; why do you want to kill us?' They were questions to which I knew no answer.[32]

Sergeant John Stephenson, 1/6th Battalion, Duke of Wellington's Regiment, 147th Brigade, 49th Division

The Allies used their increasing control of the skies to drop thousands of propaganda leaflets over the German lines, trying to spread the message that Germany was doomed to defeat.

Enemy aircraft circled above the city, dropping instead of bombs pamphlets written in German telling us that the Bulgarian and Turkish Armies had quit, and the Austrians were asking for a separate peace. The pamphlets urged us furthermore to lay down our arms and to go home as the Allies were making war on the German government only and had no grudge against the people themselves. As soon as an armistice was accepted, they promised to remove the blockade and send food to our starving families.[33]

Unteroffizier Frederick Meisel, 371st Infantry Regiment, 43rd Ersatz Brigade, 10th Ersatz Division, Imperial German Army

Everywhere the exhausted Germans went the same miserable message was rammed down their throats. Even the French civilians dared to cock a snook at their once mighty conquerors as they fell back.

Wearied by long marches, weakened from scanty rations, often with communications so disorganised that for days supplies could not reach us, as a rearguard we tracked behind the retreating army. A worn and footsore band, moving through a landscape of sombre forests and infertile fields. Fog and cold weather were settling in, making things more difficult. Already we were entering territory that was occupied by the civilian population. Standing in groups in the streets they mocked us openly, '*À Paris! Ha! Ha! Jamais Paris!*'[34]

Unteroffizier Frederick Meisel, 371st Infantry Regiment, 43rd Ersatz Brigade, 10th Ersatz Division, Imperial German Army

Elsewhere, the hatred engendered by four years of war was not easily put aside. Gunner Percy Cheek was an appalled spectator to an act of wanton murder.

We had drawn up on the side of a road waiting for ammunition. Coming from the front was a line of prisoners. One of our gunners rushed to the column wielding a shovel, which he crashed down on a prisoner's head splitting the skull – he was only a boy and he dropped like a log. The gunner was seized by NCOs and led away. Stretcher bearers took away the dead German. Sergeant Britton told us that the gunner had just received word that his brother had been killed on active service. War begets hate and hate leads men to commit atrocities.[35]

Gunner Percy Creek, 'A' Battery, 104th Brigade, Royal Field Artillery

*

THE LAST GREAT OFFENSIVE began on 4 November. The Fourth, Third and First Armies were to attack on a front of 40 miles. It would not be easy: in front of them lay the Sambre-Oise Canal, the canalised Sambre River, and various tributaries. The dense woodland fastness of the Forest of Mormal also loomed up ahead of them. One of the most difficult tasks befell the men of the 1st Division who were facing the Sambre-Oise Canal. The men peered forward and pondered on the task that lay before them. They would have been fools were they not afraid.

> The autumn leaves and the hedges, it was like an English countryside – it was pouring with rain too. We had a smoke and a chatter. We knew the end was very near and the Germans were on the run. We were thinking to ourselves, 'Well is this our exodus?' Dawn was just breaking when it was Zero Hour. We could see the outline of the canal and the trees. We knew what we were up against because we knew the Germans had a machine gun in the lock house.[36]
>
> Private Walter Grover, 2nd Battalion, Royal Sussex Regiment, 2nd Brigade, 1st Division

Close by was Captain Oliver Woodward and his men of the 1st Australian Tunnelling Company, which had been attached to the 409th Field Company of the Royal Engineers. They were collectively charged with the task of getting a bridge strong enough to carry a tank across the 17-foot-wide lock at Rejet-de-Beaulieu. Just getting the bridge components up to the canal banks was in itself a major undertaking that strained the men to their utmost.

> Try to picture the task. A pitch-black night with a steady fall of rain, an area of country on which none of us had even set foot, filled with shell holes. And about 5 tons of rolled steel joists in 20-foot lengths to be transported over a quarter of a mile before midnight, at which hour all troops were expected to be at their assembly position. Each of the girders weighed about 800 lb and they were carried by ten men, five on each side. At this hour the area through which we had to pass was being continually swept by artillery fire and occasional bursts of machine gun. The men had to march slowly forward, ensuring that

each step was on firm ground before taking the next. There could be no flinching when a shell burst, no matter how close. With an 800-lb girder carried on the shoulders a false step or a faltering when a shell burst could easily cause as much damage by broken limbs as a bursting shell would inflict. Under all these disadvantages the men worked without a sign of faltering and just before midnight we had carried all our material to the forward assembly point.[37]

Captain Oliver Woodward, 1st Australian Tunnelling Company

This was made the more creditable as his men were fully aware that the war was at last approaching an end. As Woodward ruefully put it, 'We had weathered the storm and just when we seemed about to enter the harbour, the cry of "breakers ahead" was sounded!'[38] Whatever their inner fears they had carried out their task.

Still in the dark of night at the Zero Hour of 0545, the men of the 2nd Royal Sussex Regiment charged forward towards the dank canal. When the first wave got to the canal banks they found that somebody had blundered and their careful rehearsals behind the lines had a rather crucial failing.

Before we got onto the canal itself we had to get across a dyke and they had duckboard bridges that we were supposed to cross on, but they were too short when the first chaps got there. So they were waiting for the next lot of duckboards to come up all bunched up. They were all piled up on the bank. We were the second line. Over came a salvo of shells amongst us; that's where we lost a lot of men. Then at last the engineers managed to get these longer boards and we got across. Then they threw the bigger ones across the lock itself. We had a bullet go right through our Lewis gun that I was carrying. As we were going across I heard a 'Ping!' but during all the rattle of machine guns and shells I didn't take much notice. I always carried something in front of me and that bullet would have gone through me if it hadn't been for the Lewis gun. They found out where the strong point was and they put two or three shells through it and the Germans gave up.[39]

Private Walter Grover, 2nd Battalion, Royal Sussex Regiment, 2nd Brigade, 1st Division

Woodward had watched all agog as the British sappers of the 409th Field Company went into furious action covered to some extent by the fire of the Sussex men lining the canal bank.

> At Zero plus 15 minutes, I went forward with Sergeant Hutchinson just in time to see Major Findlay, commanding officer of the 409th Field Company, brilliantly lead his men across the lock by jumping across on the partly opened lock gates. With bombs he stormed an enemy machine-gun crew who were located in the boiler house. It was a magnificent sight.[40]
>
> Captain Oliver Woodward, 1st Australian Tunnelling Company

The gallant Major G. de C. E. Findlay would later be awarded the VC for his leadership and courage, as was Lieutenant Colonel Dudley Johnson commanding the 2nd Royal Sussex, who also led his men across the canal.

Woodward and his men had to move forward to help install the bridge across the lock. Although the German machine gun had now been silenced their artillery was still actively dropping shells all around them.

> I crossed the lock and we prised off the coping stone. The launching of the first 20-foot girder across this 17-foot span was a slow job and we had just got it across when the enemy dropped a shell practically at our feet. It was a small high velocity shell – of the seven of us on the enemy side of the canal, three were wounded. Once the first girder was safely across, the work was much easier, as we were able to slide the other girders across this one. The tank bridge was eventually completed four and a half hours after Zero.[41]
>
> Captain Oliver Woodward, 1st Australian Tunnelling Company

The Fourth Army had managed to jump the Sambre-Oise Canal Line to establish a healthy bridgehead some 15 miles long and between 2 and 3½ miles deep. Some 4,000 Germans and eighty guns had been captured. Yet this was not all, for on the same day the Third Army had crashed forwards some 5 miles while the First Army continued the advance it had begun on 1 November. There was no doubt that the German retreat was slowly turning into what might best be characterised as a rout.

In this hugely successful attack, however, a single life was lost that has blighted much of the modern perspective of not only the fighting on 4 November, but also the conduct of the whole war. It was just one death amongst many, but on that freezing cold, miserable morning of 4 November Lieutenant Wilfred Owen was killed as the 2nd Manchesters attempted to cross the Sambre Canal near the small village of Ors. Owen had a burgeoning reputation as a poet and his brilliant compositions 'Anthem for Doomed Youth', 'Strange Meeting' and 'Dulce et Decorum Est' have since come to define the popular view of the tragic futility of the Great War. Although he had been suffering from the after-effects of shell shock he had recovered sufficiently to return to the front in August 1918 where he had already won a Military Cross for his courage in action. Now, as the Royal Engineers struggled to put together a passable bridge from floats linked together by wire, he was shot down by German machine guns even as he urged his men on. His heart-rending death so very late in the war cemented his place at the head of the pantheon of war poets. He is buried in the civilian cemetery in the village of Ors.

THE GERMANS FELL BACK under the cover of the grim, dark November nights, nights that seemed to sum up the prevailing depression as the rain poured down, only to be alleviated by periods of drizzle. The British were winning but there was little around them to lighten their mood. The wet conditions meant that the roads and tracks they relied on were turning to deep mud before their eyes. They were also hampered by the German demolition of all bridges and culverts, cratering roads and felling trees to block them; anything to slow down the Allied advance. Their use of booby traps increased, while a clever, new delayed-action fuse fitted to the ordinary 5.9" shell caused scores of casualties long after the battlefield was supposedly safe. The German infantry seemed to have vanished leaving only machine-gun posts and groupings of artillery to ambush any pursuers. Even if the roads had been intact the Allies had too few cavalry, almost no tanks or armoured cars still working and no real concept of motorised troops to permit a rapid 'view halloo' pursuit. As the advance continued and the line of communications lengthened, the difficulties in supplying sufficient food and munitions turned into major problems. All these factors together conspired to slow the pace of the advance radically, although the RAF bombers and low-flying scouts took their toll of the retreating German columns whenever the clouds lifted for a moment.

As the Allies moved forward they were increasingly finding large numbers of French civilians who had been caught up in war as their homes and villages became a battlefield around them. Major Thomas Westmacott found several civilians hiding in their cellars on entering the village of St Waast.

> As the enemy were still in the village no one had had time to visit the poor things, and they were delighted to see us. They all made us drink coffee made of oats, and in one place insisted on giving us chip potatoes. Then they sang the Marseillaise with tears in their eyes. I almost tried to sing it myself, but I had a lump in my throat like a pigeon's egg. All the time the enemy were pouring a tornado of shells all round. Two little girls, of about 10 or 13, were like monkeys, trying to run out and look at the shells. They sang a parody of the Marseillaise made up by French and Belgian prisoners of war, not very complimentary to the Boches. Their mother told me that she was always in hot water because the smallest girl would sing it in front of the enemy. It is quite impossible to describe their courage, but one realises why and how the French people have set their teeth and stuck it all through these years. I asked the little girl for a kiss, and I felt honoured to get it.[42]
>
> Major Thomas Westmacott, Headquarters, 24th Division

He found even more excitement when he entered into the town of Ravay. Here there was a real crowd gathering to welcome their liberators.

> As we rode in people began to run out of their houses, regardless of the shelling. By the time we reached the Grand Place we were surrounded by a seething crowd of people simply delirious with joy. I had a little chocolate for the children, but it did not go very far. Luneau was dragged off his horse and smothered with kisses. I was almost dragged off but I managed to stick on. They kissed my boots and lifted up their babies to be kissed, all laughing, sobbing and shouting, '*Vive la France!*

Vive l'Angleterre!' They fished out French flags from somewhere and
hung them out of the window. They begged for French newspapers and
any news we could give them. And all the time the Boche was shelling
the place and nobody cared a damn! As we dismounted at the house of
the Maire, a shell hit it and a splinter passed between Luneau and me –
rotten luck if I get done in with the end in view.[43]

Major Thomas Westmacott, Headquarters, 24th Division

The people were undoubtedly friendly, but not all the component
parts of the British Army were entirely safe from their culinary attentions. One mascot paid an awful price to satisfy their appetite for fresh
meat.

Another casualty in the Mormal Forest was the loss of the battery pet, a
fine fat billy goat. He had been on a wagon that got ditched and, in the
subsequent confusion, slipped his halter and disappeared into the
wood. He was quite a character that goat, the pet of the wagon lines for
more than a year, waxing plump on the plentiful supply of hay and oats
for the horses. He had a mania for tobacco and would rear up and put
his forefeet on a smoker's shoulders, snatch a lighted cigarette from the
astonished man's lips and eat it with evident enjoyment. He could also
be relied upon to butt an unpopular visitor, and his horns hurt with his
full weight behind them! We never found him again, though search
parties looked for him in the forest for several days. We could only
imagine that he had been found, killed and eaten by the local French
civilians, who were very short of meat.[44]

Major Richard Foot, 'D' Battery, 310th Brigade, Royal Field Artillery

EACH DAY MIGHT HAVE been the last day of the war, but
wasn't. Anti-climax became a way of life. But let there be no mistake:
the troops may have wanted the war to end as soon as possible, but the
overall mood, certainly amongst the British officers, was that they were
determined to finish the 'job' properly.

I hope no terms will be granted that don't make the Huns absolutely
grovel. We have the Boche so beat that if he won't grovel now, it is only
a matter of hanging on a little bit more, when he positively won't be

able to help himself. What one has seen and heard makes one hate and loathe the Boche just more than ever as the most unutterable of all brute beasts.[45]

Brigadier General George Stevens, Headquarters, 90th Brigade, 30th Division

Their American counterparts had an equally stern attitude, as expressed here by Colonel Garretson in a comforting homespun manner.

Our job is to make the miserable Boche climb on his chair and be a good boy. So far as we can see he has not as yet shown any very wholesome haste to get on the chair without a considerable amount of assistance from our part, so I guess we will carry on for a bit yet.[46]

Colonel Leland Garretson, 315th Machine Gun Battalion, 80th Division, AEF

This was the overall perspective; there was no sense of magnanimity, just a grim determination to crush the German Army to a degree that it could never arise to threaten the peace of Europe again.

We had all got our tails well up. The end of the war was at last in sight and well in sight! It must come soon now. The general fear was that Germany would unconditionally surrender on our terms, before we absolutely smashed her. Then a day came when news was received that the Kaiser had abdicated! This was an occasion for great rejoicing and every drop in the battery of an alcoholic nature was consumed on the strength of it. Great days, these! Anything might happen now! Things had got to such a pitch that whenever a telephonist came into the mess with a telephone message, all eyes were scrutinising his face to see if the news he brought could be there read.[47]

Lieutenant Edward Allfree, 111th Siege Battery, Royal Garrison Artillery

The troops would not have long to wait for the glorious end, but some would still fall just short of victory. These deaths were unforgettable to the men that witnessed them.

One of our men received a terrible stomach wound – I don't think I'll say what I saw. But I do remember this poor wretch rolling over and over and the steam from his blood rising up. It was obvious he was not going to live. From the first to the last days of the war men were dying. But those who so nearly finished the course and fell at the last fence, these are the ones we most feel sorry for. To think another day and he should have been safe. But it wasn't to be.[48]

Private Harold Bashford, 2nd Battalion, Bedfordshire Regiment, 54th Brigade, 18th Division

As the Allies advanced in most sectors the fighting continued, but it was of a minor nature: clashes between the German rearguards and the advance guards of the British. Slowly but steadily they pushed forward. There was no let up until the German Seventeenth Army turned at bay, intent on buying time for the other armies to retreat, and made a brief stand in front of Mons on 10 November. The Canadian troops pinned the defenders from the front and advanced on the flanks, threatening the garrison of Mons with capture if it stood. At about 1700 the main force began to pull out and next morning at 0230 the Canadian advance patrols attacked to finally liquidate the last remaining machine-gun posts in the town two hours later. The date was 11 November 1918. Here the war had begun for the BEF in August 1914. Here it would finally end.

CHAPTER FIFTEEN

This is the End:
11 November 1918

WHEN THE END CAME it arrived relatively quickly for the troops on the ground, although there was much frenetic activity going on behind the scenes in the final month of the war. While the soldiers continued to fight and die, behind the scenes the Allied politicians were conducting a fraught series of meetings to hammer out the terms they would be willing to accept in return for peace. The framework for their discussions was President Woodrow Wilson's Fourteen Points, which he had first promulgated in Congress on 8 January 1918 in response to cynical German peace overtures – and hence before his country had managed to take an active role in the war. In essence, these set out a blueprint as to how the nations of the world could live together in harmony. Yet this was a complacent wish list that reeked of hypocrisy, and some of the points displayed a jaw-dropping naivety: 'Open covenants of peace, openly arrived at, after which there shall be no private international understandings of any kind but diplomacy shall proceed always frankly and in the public view.' Nevertheless, the overall tenor was hard enough on the Germans to be acceptable as a starting point for negotiations for the Allied leaders. Under the terms of the Wilson plan the Germans were to surrender all their Russian and Romanian gains in the East, an independent Poland was to be created, Belgium evacuated and Alsace-Lorraine surrendered. This, as far as Lloyd George and Clemenceau were concerned, was all good stuff, although they also insisted that the Germans should make reparations for all war damage suffered by the Allies.

The problem, and sticking point, as far as Britain was concerned, lay with Point II: 'Absolute freedom of navigation upon the seas, outside territorial waters, alike in peace and in war.' This would outlaw the key weapon of war that had underpinned British Grand Strategy for centuries: the blockade. A bitter exchange ensued, featuring threats from the American diplomatic representative, Colonel Edward House, that America would make a separate peace, which the British and French countered sharply by threatening to fight on alone. This, however, was mere posturing on all sides. Eventually, on 4 November, a compromise was reached when the Supreme War Council agreed to offer peace on the basis of the Fourteen Points, with the British expressly reserving their right to negotiate on the subject of freedom of the seas at the ultimate peace conference. Wilson passed this acceptance to the German government next day, but there was to be a sting in the tail, for at the same time he announced that it would be General Ferdinand Foch who would receive any German representatives sent to negotiate the armistice pending a peace conference. There could have been no better choice as far as the Allied military leaders were concerned.

The Allied commanders had also been meeting to discuss their military demands: Foch himself, Haig, Pétain and Pershing. This was a cold-eyed grouping, these were the men who had dealt day to day with Germany's armed might over the past years and they were utterly determined that this was to be a true knockout blow – that the Germans were not going to be able to get up from the canvas any time soon. Just to get an armistice the Germans would have to cripple themselves as a military force: Belgium, France and Alsace-Lorraine would have to be fully evacuated within fourteen days and 5,000 guns, 30,000 machine guns, 3,000 trench mortars and 2,000 aircraft would have to be handed over. The transport system was to be crippled by handing over 5,000 locomotives, 150,000 railway coaches and 5,000 lorries. German naval power was to be neutered by the surrender of six dreadnoughts, 160 U-boats and eight light cruisers, while what remained of the High Seas Fleet was to be held and monitored in Allied harbours. To add injury to insult, the British naval blockade would continue. Finally, the Allied commanders wanted the occupation of the west bank of the Rhineland, with bridgeheads and a neutral zone all along the eastern bank of the Rhine. There would be no impregnable Rhine Line fortress available should the war reignite and no German dreams of emerging refreshed from the ashes of defeat to renew the war. And all this would secure the Germans only a temporary armistice!

Meanwhile, the German government was in a state of flux. The socialists were fast gaining in power, revolution was in the air and the Allies were utterly intransigent. For a while the chancellor, Prince Max von Baden, threshed around trying to resolve the question of what to do about Kaiser Wilhelm II, whom the British were none to cheerfully threatening to hang. Ludendorff's replacement, Quartermaster General Wilhelm Groener, had one solution when he bluntly suggested that the Kaiser kill himself by leading his troops into battle. When the Kaiser declined that option it became obvious that wholesale change was required: the Kaiser must abdicate and at the same time, on 9 November 1918, Max von Baden resigned in favour of the Socialist leader in his cabinet coalition: Friedrich Ebert.

Max von Baden had already sent off the German armistice delegation consisting of the Centre Party politician Matthias Erzberger and two relatively junior generals. They had the thankless task of negotiating with Ferdinand Foch. They passed through the French lines and the two sides met in a railway carriage in the Forest of Compiègne. Erzberger tried his best, but as he had been instructed to secure the cessation of hostilities at any price, he was unable to extract anything but the most trivial of concessions. Finally, at 0515 on the morning of 11 November, he signed the armistice document. Awash with mortification and humiliation, Erzberger read out a statement: 'A people of 70 million men are suffering, but they are not dead.' Foch's reply summed up the style of his negotiations: '*Très bien!*' The Armistice would commence with wonderful symmetry at the eleventh hour of the eleventh day of the eleventh month.

IT WAS TOWARDS THE END of 10 November that the first rumour of the imminent armistice began to circulate at the front. In some cases the news was garbled in transmission and troops prematurely celebrated peace.

We moved into billets in Harlebeke and on the evening of 10 November it was confidently rumoured that an armistice had been signed. The rumour was of course incorrect, but the town went mad! Two of the three field companies were in the town that night and we made 'whoopee'. We dined together and there was much hilarity, then went to see what was happening outside. The troops had raided a petrol dump and taken hundreds of 2-gallon tins of petrol and a supply of cotton waste. They had placed the tins at intervals in the main streets, taken off the caps and inserted the cotton waste as a wick. Then on a signal given by Very light, all the tins were ignited and the previously dark town became a blaze of light. One accident marred the fun: a man accidentally fired a Very light pistol when it was pointed at another man's head and he was killed.[1]

Captain John March, 90th Field Company, Royal Engineers, 9th Division

The lowered value of human life encouraged by four years of war was evident in the casual acceptance of one more death. But Lieutenant March and the premature celebrants were perhaps lucky that the Germans had not shelled them.

Meanwhile, that same night the exhausted Lieutenant Richard Dixon and Captain Brown had just jolted their way into Boulogne on a packed leave train. Their boat would not leave until next morning so they made their way to the Officers' Club for a good wash and brush up, a drink and bed, in no particular order.

We were tired, rather dirty and we were in war kit. We had our tin hats and gas masks slung from our shoulders, I was wearing a trench coat stained with blood and had in my Sam Browne belt a German Luger pistol in its holster. We entered a large bar room, filled with smoke and lots of Australian officers, most of whom were exceedingly tight. We thrust our way through to the bar counter, where some boozy loons roared at us in mock terror. 'Jesus!' they howled. 'Look lads! There's a bloody war on somewhere!' Captain Brown swore at them in English and Hindustani, and I gave them the benefit of certain French oaths, which would have caused mortal offence had they comprehended the meaning. But as Australians seemed constitutionally incapable of learning any other language but their own, and only about a couple of thousand words of that, it didn't matter. They were bonny fighters, but intellectually a dead loss.[2]

Lieutenant Richard Dixon, 251st Siege Battery, 53rd Brigade, Royal Garrison Artillery

Early next morning they awoke and caught their morning leave boat still unaware that the end was nigh.

As we began to enter Folkestone Harbour about midday, every craft in there possessing a siren began to let it off. We on board that leave ship were at first astounded by the noise – what was all the fuss about? But as it went on and on and we steamed slowly and majestically to our appointed birth, and beheld the crews of several ships cheering and waving at us, we tumbled to it. 'Dickie,' said Captain Brown, 'the bloody war's over! It's over!' And it was. No more slaughter, no more maiming, no more mud and blood, no more killing and dis-embowelling of horses and mules. No more of those hopeless dawns, with the rain chilling the spirits, no more crouching in inadequate dugouts scooped out of trench walls, no more dodging snipers' bullets, no more of that terrible shell fire. No more shovelling up of bits of men's bodies and dumping them into sandbags, no more cries of, 'Stretcher bearers!' No more of those beastly gas masks and the odious smell of pear drops that was deadly to the lungs. And no more writing of those dreadfully difficult letters to the next of kin of the dead.[3]

Lieutenant Richard Dixon, 251st Siege Battery, 53rd Brigade, Royal Garrison Artillery

Lieutenant John Nettleton was already back in England on leave. He had a double cause for celebration.

11 November was my birthday and the Armistice was the best birthday present any man ever had. I went down to the Promenade at Chelten-ham and saw all the people milling about the streets singing and dancing, but, even so, it was impossible to realise that the war that had been going on since the beginning of time was really over. I don't think I did realise it till I got on the leave train at Victoria to go back to France and found that it was just another railway journey. Always before, at seven o'clock in the morning, Victoria station had been a very grim place, with people wrapped up in their own private griefs and

nobody taking any notice of anyone else. Now it was just a railway station and the goodbyes were '*Au revoirs*' not '*Adieux*'![4]

Lieutenant John Nettleton, 2nd Battalion, Rifle Brigade, 25th Brigade, 8th Division

At the front the news spread relatively slowly. There had been too many rumours masquerading as news for men to completely trust what they heard.

We had just had breakfast when we heard shouts of '*La guerre fini!*' A party of French cavalry were passing, cheering, and again the cries of '*La guerre fini, la guerre fini ce matin, onze heures, les Allemands partis, napoo, fini!*' or something like that – we could scarcely believe our ears. Parfitt, our motorcyclist despatch rider, came riding up. 'It's true lads!' he said. 'It's all over, there is an armistice at eleven o'clock, it is all posted up for you to read at headquarters!' All trooped down to read for ourselves the official message. It was hard to believe. Only one man looked disappointed. Corporal Coverton had finished the job he loved – chasing the Hun. He had been a tower of strength to us all, but, if ever a man enjoyed himself in a way foreign to others, it was him. We had actually to cheer him up until he became reconciled to the idleness now ours![5]

Sapper Wilfred Cook, Field Survey Corps

As the hours and minutes ticked away that fateful morning was marked by an increasing tension. No one wanted to be the last corpse, the last man crippled by the Great War. And the danger facing them was still very real.

You don't know the feeling you have. Everybody had the wind up. Really afraid, really windy! When ten to eleven came I was really windy! He started shelling, one or two long-range stuff, expending his shells instead of carrying it back, getting rid of it. I just threw myself under an embankment; all of a sudden I felt a crack on my steel helmet – shrapnel! It jerked my head a bit, gave me a bit of a headache, but it didn't penetrate the helmet itself. I looked up and there was a girl at the side of me, I thought, 'My God, I've gone mad now! A damned girl beside me in the midst of a war!' Anyhow it seems this girl was in a local farmhouse, heard the shelling, saw me dart under this embankment and she'd come out and done likewise! The shelling finished right on the dot at eleven o'clock! Not another thing![6]

Private Bill Smedley, 14th Battalion, Worcestershire Regiment, 63rd Division

Private Smedley had been a lucky man, but men were still dying right up to the very end.

At about ten o'clock a shell came down and killed a sergeant of ours that had been out since 1915. Killed by the shrapnel. We thought that was very unlucky – to think he'd served nearly four years and then to be killed within an hour of the Armistice.[7]

Private Jim Fox, 11th Battalion, Durham Light Infantry, 20th Division

These last casualties took on an emotional significance that would have been lacking just a day or so before.

Stood by all night and it was a hot place. One of my guns knocked out of action by shrapnel and I found one of the new men – Jones – dead in his dugout. Cold and raining. Runner in at 10.30 with order to cease firing at 11 a.m. Firing continued and we 'stood by'. The 306th Machine Gun Company on my right lost twelve men at 10.55 when a high explosive shell landed in their position. I reported Jones's death and marked his grave. The captain conducted a prayer and cried like a baby.[8]

Corporal Thomas Grady, 'B' Company, 305th Machine Gun Battalion, 77th Division, AEF

On both sides of the wire the gunners were faced with real questions of personal morality – should they continue to fire their guns when they *knew* that peace was only a matter of minutes away? Or should they carry on blazing away killing a last few Germans? Second Lieutenant Cyril Dennys and his men took what might be called the humanitarian option and tried hard to avoid causing futile deaths.

We were overlooking the Scheldt River, terribly exposed position, and it seemed to us that if there was a battle we were going to have a pretty rough time of it. But before it could come we had this news that at 11 a.m. hostilities were going to cease and that there was to be no firing from then onwards. We just bloody well couldn't believe it! It didn't seem that this could be really happening. Just before 11 a.m. it occurred to us that it would be very annoying to be left with loaded guns that we couldn't fire! Because unloading is an awful nuisance with big guns and you have to be jolly careful what you do! What we did was to cock our guns up to an angle that we felt made it certain that no one was going to get killed because I think everybody at the final moment didn't want to slay somebody in the last few minutes.[9]

Second Lieutenant Cyril Dennys, 212th Siege Battery, Royal Garrison Artillery

Other batteries sought to commemorate their last few rounds at their soon-to-be erstwhile enemies. Thus the officers of the 109th Battery formed an impromptu elite gun detachment amongst themselves to man one of their 18-pounders for the final shots of their war.

At five minutes to the hour we fired two rounds 'for luck'. Thinking that our last shots would be historic we took pains to fire them with solemnity. Birch, who had ridden up to see what was afoot, set the fuses, I loaded and Powell fired the gun. Our Belgian host, whom we had airily told that '*La guerre est fini*!', stood an interested spectator. But the Hun retaliated by sending back twelve 4.2s, which landed in the very orchard in Bougnies in which the teams were waiting. When the retaliatory shells whistled back and screamed overhead, the Belgian dived, indignant, back down his cellar steps, calling as he went with querulous veracity, '*La guerre no fini*!' Luckily there were no casualties.[10]

Lieutenant John Capron, 109th Battery, 281st Brigade, Royal Field Artillery

Even at the eleventh hour, defeated they may have been but it was evident that the Germans were not men to be trifled with. These final exchanges can be given a humorous characterisation but not when tragedy struck. High explosive shells were *never* funny.

The battle raged until exactly 11 a.m. and all of a sudden a 'big freeze' set in. One had a feeling it was a dream and unbelievable. The sudden stillness was interrupted by a single heavy shell, which exploded on a trail near our battery among a platoon of infantry and killed four and wounded about a dozen. Having seen so many tragedies this made us sad and mad. Some joker on the other side probably wanted to fire the 'last' shot.[11]

Anton Lang, 2nd Battery, 2nd Bavarian Foot Artillery Regiment, Imperial German Army

When the moment finally came that they had been waiting for and dreaming about, for many it was almost an anti-climax.

I was supervising the work of checking and cleaning our guns and equipment, refilling all our ammunition belts etc., ready for our next advance, when a runner from headquarters arrived, saluted our officer and handed him a message. He read it, looked at his watch, then called me over to him. He said in a most matter-of-fact, unemotional tone, 'Corporal, hostilities cease in seven minutes time!' I saluted him and said, 'Very good, Sir!' in the same tone of voice. When I passed the news on to my team it was received in the same nonchalant manner and they just carried on with what they were doing, without comment, except for saying, 'OK, Corp!' It seems absolutely extraordinary that none of us, at that stage, felt the slightest sense of relief or jubilation at the news. News that we had all looked forward to for four and a half years, and hoped to hear one day, but often thought that we would never live to hear. And now it had actually arrived it just did not sink in at once. It was just like water on a duck's back![12]

Corporal Arthur Atkins, 14th Battalion, Machine Gun Corps, 14th Division

The fighting had continued right up to the end and now just minutes later it was suddenly all over. Men did not know how to react; they had never felt such an enormous relief in their whole lives. The news was often too much to take in and most men seem to have found it nigh on impossible to articulate the jumbled emotions running through their heads.

Every man had a grin from ear to ear on his face. Nobody yelled or showed uncontained enthusiasm – everybody just grinned – and I think the cause was that the men couldn't find words to express themselves. I think of the man who every day has his life in danger and who dreams of home more than heaven itself and suddenly finds that the danger is past and that his return is practically assumed, that he has won after personally risking his life. No wonder they couldn't say much – they simply grinned.[13]

Captain Cecil Gray Frost, 'L' Battery, 6th Company, 2nd Machine Gun Battalion, Canadian Machine Gun Corps

Their joy was inevitably tempered by grief. Few men had not lost family or friends in the Great War. Their loss weighed upon the survivors now that it was finally all over.

> One would have expected that at this stage the field would have been filled with men carried away in a paroxysm of joy, but it was not so. Instead officers and men moved quietly about from one group to another, giving and receiving a handshake amongst comrades. It was an occasion too great for words. The artificial barriers of rank were temporarily cast aside, and we felt to the full the real comradeship of war and the realisation that the distasteful task had ended. In our mind we called to memory those of our comrades who had made the supreme sacrifice.[14]
>
> Captain Oliver Woodward, 1st Australian Tunnelling Company

There also still remained for many men a deep and abiding hatred for the Germans whom they blamed for all they had suffered. Men could not immediately release the pent-up emotions that had dominated their every waking hour during nearly five protracted years of suffering and fear.

> When eleven o'clock came, all was silent: not a gun to be heard, nor any other sign of war. It seemed almost uncanny. The war – that long and bloody and ghastly war – was over! Not only over, but it had been won – decisively won – by us and our Allies! The Germans were defeated, crushed! The boastful, bragging Hun who had started and brought this bloody war on the world, was beaten and in the dust! How entirely comforting! How satisfactory![15]
>
> Lieutenant Edward Allfree, 111th Siege Battery, Royal Garrison Artillery

There were, of course, minor infringements of the truce on both sides. It was difficult to ensure that everyone knew what was happening. Indeed, there may have been elements that simply wished to carry on killing for as long as possible.

> One of our big guns in some wood nearby continued to fire until 12.30 – a wireless message came from the Germans complaining of its activities. We thought the explosions were those of some of the road mines, which occurred about every five minutes. The Germans also

very politely wirelessed that their huge dump of shells at Trélon was mined, and that it was timed to go up in fourteen days![16]

Captain John Marshall, Headquarters, Royal Engineers, 46th Division

On both sides the majority had had more than enough of killing and 'played fair'. As the guns were finally stilled and the unaccustomed silence fell over the battered countryside, men rejoiced in the sheer luxury of being free from danger.

Windy work was over: no more shelling, no more gas, no more forward observation stunts with the infantry, no more casualties! In fact, the rest of life a holiday, that's what it seemed like then! With the war over, what else mattered? Why worry again about anything? Life without war should be blissful happiness – one long leave with no return to war at the end of it! So it seemed to me that day. The holiday spirit was upon us![17]

Lieutenant Edward Allfree, 111th Siege Battery, Royal Garrison Artillery

Yet hard upon the feelings of freedom came the thoughts of what were they going to do now. Many had simply presumed that they would not live to see the end of the war. Part of their mental defence was the idea that they had nothing to look forward to and that as doomed men they did not have much to lose if they were killed. Their mental landscape had changed in a flash.

An unreal thought was running through my mind. I had a future. It took some getting used to – this knowledge. There was a future ahead for me, something that I had not imagined for some years. All that mattered was that the war was over and by a miracle I had come through it when so many better men had not – and that I was going to see Babs![18]

Lieutenant Richard Dixon, 251st Siege Battery, 53rd Brigade, Royal Garrison Artillery

The armistice appeared to offer a wonderful template for a painless, fairy-tale future where they would live happily ever after.

Yet the world had not really changed. The same underlying problems still existed around the globe. Germany was defeated but international tensions, class warfare, racial hatreds, economic imperatives and religious fanaticism all still remained to torment humanity. One ludicrous example of how nothing had really changed occurred right in front of Private Charles Brown's disbelieving eyes.

> At night, in our hut, two Irishmen, after a few drinks, started quarrelling as to whether the Protestants or the Catholics of Ireland had contributed most to the winning of the war. The argument became quite heated and revolvers were drawn. I happened to be in the line of fire, so after a little persuasion I got hold of their revolvers and peace was restored.[19]
>
> Private Charles Brown, 12th Battalion, Tank Corps

There were different realities of life to confront as Sergeant John Stephenson, freshly garlanded with a bar to his Military Medal, had reaffirmed when he was called before his officer a few days later.

> He told me the sad news that my mother had died and I must get ready to go home on leave. What a homecoming. I thought that I had got home before the funeral and I looked into each room to see mother. She had been buried two days before I got home. This was something I had not thought of. There was one consolation, and that was mother was alive on Armistice Day. She knew that I was still alive, the fighting had ended and that was a crumb of comfort. I felt that a very large part of my life had vanished.[20]
>
> Sergeant John Stephenson, 1/6th Battalion, Duke of Wellington's Regiment, 147th Brigade, 49th Division

The German soldiers, of course, were pleased that the war was over. But they had the numbing sensation of total defeat to contend with. Many took refuge in a simple patriotic optimism that assured them that no matter how bad the situation was their country surely would rise again.

> Back to the Rhine – back, back without a stop. The highways were crammed with moving men, endless lines of men, war equipment, guns, pack trains, lorries and horses. Through France and Belgium, the grey columns moved. Nobody knew what the future held, but everybody's mind formed a belief of better days to come. Back to build up what was wrecked; back to a country proud even in defeat. We crossed the border and were again on German soil. Our road took us over German

fields, through German villages and towns. Flags were out in the buildings and signs decorated with late autumn flowers carried the inscriptions, 'Welcome Home'. German faces greeted us smilingly, blond and blue-eyed girls waved their handkerchiefs in glee, boys ran alongside us, eager to carry the rifles or equipment. Speeches were made and through it all the church bells chimed, 'Peace at Last'.[21]

Unteroffizier Frederick Meisel, 371st Infantry Regiment, 43rd Ersatz Brigade, 10th Ersatz Division, Imperial German Army

As they marched back, a few of his compatriots took the chance to show that as a race the Germans were not entirely devoid of a sense of humour. Lance Corporal Harry Hopthrow was amused by one example as he was passing through a small French town.

We met a little bit of psychological warfare, because two or three of us went into a *estaminet* to get a cup of coffee while we were waiting and there was a quite good-looking girl there. '*Bonjour mam'zelle*!' 'You can kiss my bottom, Sir!' The Germans had taught them to say this as a suitable greeting.[22]

Lance Corporal Harry Hopthrow, Signal Service, Royal Engineers attached to Headquarters, 30th Division

The British followed the Germans step by step, right back into Germany, moving forward to take over the western Rhineland and crossing the Rhine River to take up the allotted bridgehead at Cologne. One senior staff officer of the 24th Division found his heart bursting with pride in his men, his division, his corps and the whole British Army, as he watched them march across the three Rhine bridges into Cologne.

I have seen a sight today that I shall never forget. Our infantry began to cross the Rhine at 9.15 a.m. So as to do things really well, the German police were told to see that no wheeled German traffic was allowed on the streets and they obeyed their orders to the letter. There were big crowds of Germans looking on in spite of the rain, but they seemed more curious than anything else. I saw one woman in tears, poor soul, but bar that it might have been almost an English crowd. General Jacobs, my corps commander, stood under the Union Jack by a big statue of the Kaiser and took the salute. The men marched with fixed bayonets, wearing their steel helmets and carrying their packs. I wish you could have seen them, each man making the most of himself, full of pride and élan. Then came the guns, turned out as our gunners always turn themselves out. Mind you, the division was fighting hard all through the last battle, and they have been marching steadily through Belgium and Germany for the last thirty days, but the horses were all fit and hard as nails, and the buckles of the harness were all burnished like silver. The mules were as fit as the horses and went by waggling their old ears as if they crossed the Rhine every day of the week. A German looking on said that the division must have just come fresh from England. It is difficult to remember what we were like last March and April during the retreat of the Fifth Army – and to find ourselves here as conquerors in one of the proudest cities of Germany.[23]

Major Thomas Westmacott, Headquarters, 24th Division

THEY HAD WON THE WAR but most of the men serving in the British Army now merely wanted to get out of khaki and be safely back in civilian life as soon as was humanly possible. This, though, would be a staggering administrative task. Millions of men would have to be returned to their former employments and, if this was not strictly controlled, then utter chaos and mass unemployment was inevitable.

I was put in charge of our demobilisation branch, to prepare arrange-ments for the demobilisation of the BEF. This was an important and serious matter and I was fortunate in being able to collect an efficient staff to help. A War Office staff had been working for many months on the general problem of demobilisation for all theatres of war in huts erected in the lake of St James's Park, which had been drained. This was under the command of General Burnett-Stuart and, after much study, two most comprehensive volumes of Demobilisation Regulations had been prepared. After studying them, I came to the conclusion that few officers would have either the time or the inclination to concentrate on these voluminous tomes and extract such parts as applied to them and their men. I decided therefore that we must write our own Demobilisation Instructions for the BEF. This we did, and thereby incurred the wrath of General Burnett-Stuart. I did not mind this. In the event we were justified, for the arrangements made worked smoothly and with the least possible trouble to officers and men.[24]

Assistant Adjutant General James Whitehead, General Headquarters, BEF

The details of their proposals were staggeringly boring, as details usually are, but one thing was certain: the demobilisation system had to be transparently fair and carried out as soon as was feasible. Any abuse of the rules would provoke mass dissent from men who were now only serving King and Country on sufferance.

The scheme was based on the priority release of 'key' men needed to start up industry and such men received from home green cards, on receipt of which they were sent home. I soon heard rumours that things were not going well in this respect: two cases which I recollect being that a green card had been received for the release of the mace bearer of a mayor and the other for the release of someone's butler. I arranged for the proper scrutiny of green cards and soon stopped that racket.[25]

Assistant Adjutant General James Whitehead, General Headquarters, BEF

Amongst thousands of bored men, chafing under a discipline that now seemed redundant, there were many disturbances that could have been easily characterised as mutiny if the bulk of officers, NCOs and men had not kept their heads while the hot-heads railed and kicked against the traces. Guardsman Horace Calvert witnessed a typical 'spot of bother' at the Le Havre Base Camp in December.

I was going to the canteen and when I got there it had been raided! Other buildings were ransacked! They were going to attack the officers' mess! I saw staff officers surrounded by a lot of troops and they were telling them they wanted money paid every week, they hadn't been paid for weeks; they wanted the right to go into Le Havre; and they wanted the Military Police easing up a bit on them! They shouted at them, one of them was a staff brigadier! I was on the outskirts, I didn't join in, I listened! I thought, 'I'm not getting mixed up in that lot!' The discipline I'd received was that you accept orders without question. I knew that these men were trying to give their demands in an improper way. There were two or three ringleaders, they were doing all the talking and waving everyone around to come and join them, there was two or three hundred there. It wasn't a mutiny – I would call it a disturbance! They managed to disperse them eventually, they told them they couldn't do anything, they'd have to take up this matter with the senior officers above them. What happened was they got everybody out of that camp – in 24 hours they were all lining up, getting into trains and off! Sending them all over the place, they cleared the lot out![26]

Guardsman Horace Calvert, 2nd Battalion, Grenadier Guards, 1st Guards Brigade, Guards Division

Not unnaturally the biggest problems occurred over Christmas. Here the military arrangements that had been proceeding slowly, but reasonably efficiently, were comprehensively undermined at a stroke by Lloyd George. It was a classic political intervention that in seeking to cut corners instead threw a lighted match into an inflammable situation.

The slow rate of demobilisation was being much criticised at home and the Prime Minister suddenly ordered that all men at home at that time were to be demobilised at once. This put the fat into the fire, but was persisted with in spite of the protests of the army authorities. The results were unfortunate. We had, with much pain, made elaborate arrangements in the BEF that those men last on the list for demobilisation were to be given that Christmas leave. Directly it became known that those men had been demobilised, mutinies were widespread, chiefly in the leave camps among the men who had just returned from home leave and therefore just missed this demobilisation. One of the most serious was at Calais, where there were some thousands of men. They took charge and refused all orders. The Commander-in-Chief gave me full authority to interrogate the men and demobilise any hard cases on the spot. I motored at once to Calais with two of my officers, and having reached the camp and asking for the commanding officer, was told that he had been deposed. I said that if that was the case it was of no use for us to remain, but we were told that we could not leave. I then met the 'delegates' to whom I spoke in no unmeasured terms. They then let us leave, but just at that moment the camp was found to have been surrounded by a division led personally by Lord Byng and the trouble ended. The ringleaders were tried by court martial and several sentenced to death, which sentences were commuted to terms of penal servitude. A perfect example of the ill effects of a thoroughly bad order from on high.[27]

Assistant Adjutant General James Whitehead, General Headquarters, BEF

Men were still serving deep into 1919. Of course, the 'real' peace had not been signed but the Armistice conditions had removed the German capacity to wage war in anything but the most token manner. It was not unnatural that men chafed at their continued service, especially as the army soon returned to its default state: a peacetime regime redolent of 'spit and polish' where 'brasso' ruled. But these men were not 'natural' soldiers. They had joined for the duration of the war and for no longer. The system may have been fair enough in principle, but it was inevitable that thousands of individual cases fell through the net. In the end everyone seemed to have some reason or other to be dissatisfied with a demobilisation process that seemed to be going on forever. Thus Private Alex Jamieson considered that he had been placed in the wrong group, as his friend, also an apprentice, had joined up at the same time but was demobilised months earlier in March 1919.

In spite of my firm and my father at home applying to the War Office I wasn't demobilised until November 1919 – a year after the Armistice. There was a lot of dissatisfaction. During the summer of 1919 we had a military tattoo and Churchill was suddenly introduced, and was greeted with loud booing because he had a great deal to do with drawing up the arrangements for demobilisation.[28]

Private Alexander Jamieson, 11th Battalion, Royal Scots, 27th Brigade, 9th Division

Eventually they would all get home. Free to try and pick up the traces of their civilian lives that many found had ceased to have much meaning. Too much had changed: the world had changed while they were away; *they* had changed – in many cases, beyond all recognition from the callow boys that had gone to war.

THE GREAT WAR was indeed over at last. Vast empires had fallen and the world had surely altered forever. Millions of men had died; millions more were crippled or maimed. The war had flared right across the globe, soared up to the heavens, reached across and under the seas. The young men who had survived this modern Armageddon knew they were lucky, but their lives had still been irrevocably changed – usually not for the better. Millions of men returned home from the war to their homes, families and girlfriends. Most coped well and against all the odds managed to live reasonably happy and contented lives. Yet many others found themselves alone in a crowd. No one had really defined the nature of combat fatigue or post-traumatic stress disorder in the 1920s and there was little psychological help available until it was too late. Some soldiers back from the front had simply seen too much and experienced too many horrors to go quietly into the tranquillity of civilian life. The collation of symptoms known as shell shock was common, but barely commented on in public life. A hidden world of suffering existed: a starched array of stiff upper lips, with a dark unspoken undercurrent of men failing to cope with the diverse pressures of civilian life and far too often resorting to casual violence. For many families the Great War did not end in 1918 – thousands of battered women and children bore physical and mental scars that really originated in the traumas of the battlefields.

The badly wounded were the obvious victims. One such was Joseph Pickard who had been smashed up by a shell on Easter Sunday, 31 March 1918. He knew his leg wounds and pelvic injuries were serious, but he was determined to remove the bandages and see the state of his facial wounds – in particular, what was left of his nose. He had felt enough before he lapsed into unconsciousness to know that it would be bad.

> I said, 'Have you got a mirror, Sister?' She said, 'Yes'. I said, 'Do you mind if I have a loan of it?' 'Aye, you can see.' I cut all the blinking bandages off to have a look at it. The nose was off to about halfway up the bridge. She was a bit dubious and said, 'What do you think?' 'Well!' I said. 'What can I think, its off, its gone – you don't think I'm going to travel up the line to look for it!' She said, 'You'll get better!'[29]
>
> Private Joseph Pickard, 1/5th Battalion, Northumberland Fusiliers, 149th Brigade, 50th Division

But he could never really forget the loss of most of his nose when the disfiguring evidence stared back at him every time he looked in the mirror. And of course, everywhere he went people stared: children were the worst.

> Can you ever imagine being without one? I never put the bandages back on; I got a piece of plastic to put across the hole, I just covered it, I didn't have any nose. All the kids in the blinking neighbourhood had gathered: talking, looking, gawping at you. I still had this little bit of plastic stuff as a nose. I could have taken the crutch and hit the whole lot of them! I knew what they were looking at. So I turned round and went back to the hospital. Talk about confidence. I was sitting one day and I thought, 'Well, it's no good, I can stop like this for the rest of my life – I've got to face it sometime!' So I went out again – people staring – I used to turn round and look at them![30]
>
> Private Joseph Pickard, 1/5th Battalion, Northumberland Fusiliers, 149th Brigade, 50th Division

In the end Pickard had an early form of plastic surgery when a piece of his rib cartilage was used to rebuild his nose in 1921. It would never look *quite* right but it was a good deal better than nothing. There were many far worse off than him – and he knew it.

Thousands suffered the phantom pains of missing limbs, the crippling disabilities, the callous jeers from children in the street, the irreparable rending wounds that reduced life to painful torture, wounds that could not be looked at without a shudder of horror-filled empathy. They inhabited a world of pain and suffering beyond comprehension: a world of tetraplegics, paraplegics, multiple amputations, wrecked lungs, mutilations, emasculation and blindness.

Perhaps in truth there was no happy ever after for anyone returning from the Great War, no land fit for heroes. Not for the British people at any rate. The world economy had been severely over-strained and Great Britain found itself chained to an enormous national debt. Individual profiteers may have made millions out of the war but every bullet and shell; every rifle, machine gun and howitzer; every tank, ship and aircraft; every uniform and every one of those millions of rations had to be paid for eventually with real money. A worldwide depression was utterly foreseeable and as economies teetered on the brink of utter collapse, so it was once again that ordinary individuals suffered most in wave after wave of wage cuts, temporary lay-offs and redundancies.

Politics took a messianic turn as radical new 'solutions' were proposed by 'strong' leaders promising an end to all problems. And as a grim backdrop, bubbling away was the prospect of renewed conflict. The Great War was never really a war to end war – that was just a catchy slogan dreamed up after the deluge had begun.

> We were told that this was 'the war to end war' and some of us at least believed it. It may sound extraordinarily naive, but I think one had to believe it. All the mud, blood and bestiality only made sense on the assumption that it was the last time civilised man would ever have to suffer it. I could not believe that anyone who had been through it could ever allow it to happen again. I thought that the ordinary man on both sides would rise up as one and kick any politician in the teeth who even mentioned the possibility of war.[31]
>
> Lieutenant John Nettleton, 2nd Battalion, Rifle Brigade, 25th Brigade, 8th Division

But in reality it *was* just another war. Bigger than any that had preceded it perhaps, but in essence no different. It had causes and underlying tensions between the nations, and one thing was certain – these pressures had not suddenly evaporated on 11 November 1918. After the Treaty of Versailles brought a formal end to the war in 1919 the world was, if anything, an even more dangerous place. The old conflicts remained resolutely unresolved and many new ones had been created as the pre-war world order shattered. It is no coincidence that the great, escapist Walt Disney fairy tales with their slightly dark hinterland originated in the late 1930s when it had become apparent that another war loomed.

Britain and its empire finished the war with the most efficient and deadly army in the world. The British Army was not the best in the sense of the individual quality of its soldiers; these were not supermen, just ordinary men doing their duty as best they could while trying their very best not to get killed. It was certainly not the biggest army and, thanks to civilian politicians and the endless Easterner campaigns, much of its potential strength had been dissipated in pointless side-shows. But it was a huge, modern, mechanised army that had truly grasped the art of war as far as it existed in 1918. It had mastered all the deadly technology and tactics of contemporary warfare within the overall umbrella provided by the awesome power of the Royal

Artillery – the guns, that in the final analysis, had won the war. The plans for warfare in 1919 were truly chilling: from the armoured fantasies of the tank theorists to the murderous chemists who were all set to poison a whole generation of German soldiers. The British Army seemed to stand on a mountain of productive capacity that generated ad infinitum the guns, howitzers, mortars, tanks, machine guns and noxious chemicals that made modern warfare a hell on earth for its enemies.

There was a touch of 'last man standing' about the British Army as well: the Russians and Austrians had been undone by the weaknesses lurking deep within their own despotic states; the French had been worn down to the bare bones by four murderous years of war and casualties that no nation could absorb without a savagely depressive effect on morale; the Serbians had been quickly defeated; the Bulgarians and Turks had lacked the resources to equip a modern army; and finally, the Americans, who were all prospects and promises but achieved little on the ground. And the Germans? The Germans had finally been overcome, ground down over the years by their huge casualties, economically and politically undermined by the long-term effects of the Royal Navy blockade and, crucially, utterly defeated face to face on the Western Front. In those final battles the British Army had been the spearhead of the Allies, driving time and time again into the vitals of the German Army. Now it was the victor and, when combined with the traditional strength of the Royal Navy, the British Empire truly seemed to rule the world.

It was, of course, an illusion, existing only for a brief moment in time. When weighed on the scales of twentieth-century super-powers Britain was nothing but a small island bolstered by the resources of its empire. Its huge Great War army was soon demobilised and the British as a whole had to face up to the reality of their fast-fading economy crippled by the costs of war. The inevitable peacetime economies and a sensible desire to avoid conflict with the rising naval powers of America and Japan even ripped the guts, if not the heart, from the Royal Navy. The hard-learnt lessons of the Great War were soon forgotten, rendered immaterial by technology or twisted away from their pragmatic genesis into irrelevance or, worse, downright misconceptions. In the 1920s and 1930s the British Empire was soon nothing but a play-actor posturing in an emperor's clothes; Britain was once again vulnerable to those who would challenge its world position.

Acknowledgements

THE OFFICIAL HISTORY of 1918 on the Western Front is five weighty volumes long: it does not skimp on the facts, but it certainly does not give any detailed individual accounts of fighting and, as might be expected, concentrates on the BEF. It should therefore be of no surprise that out of concern for the welfare of the reader's trembling wrist something had to go in this single volume. I have tried to give a flavour of the American contribution, but inevitably those seeking a detailed description of the French battles will be disappointed; any German analysis is also limited by the same considerations. The result is an impressionistic approach, weaving analysis of the overall position with brief outlines of the course of events during the campaign. This then has layered across it hundreds of personal stories that illustrate the nature of the fighting and how individuals responded to some of the worst fighting of the war. I have seized upon certain incidents that I use to represent thousands of similar occasions on those teeming battlefields. How to choose? Well, I have selfishly followed my own interests and what excites me. In the discovery of sources I have unashamedly also to allow serendipity a due weight in the selection process. Some well-known incidents are difficult to omit without leaving a vague feeling of 'something missing', but I have tried to throw new light on these oft-told stories, seeking new witnesses or different perspectives.

In writing this book I am fully aware that I am less of an original author and more a sort of conduit (or as my friends would have it, drain). The hundreds of personal experience accounts and recordings that I quote are the real heart of this book and I have merely linked them together with a narrative to explain what was happening around them. The veterans' original words have a real immediacy and power that can't be beaten. Nevertheless, it should be noted that these original quotations have been, where necessary, very lightly edited for readability. Thus punctuation and spellings have been largely standardised, material has occasionally been reordered and irrelevant or confusing material has been omitted without any indication in the text. However, changes in the actual words in original sources have been avoided. I have tried to contact the original copyright owners wherever possible and I hope that those I failed to find will be tolerant. I thank you *all* for your kind permissions and indulgence.

I have also been in the debt of some fine historians who have shaped my pattern of thinking on the Great War. First of these is the late, great John Terraine, but I am also grateful to Correlli Barnett, John Bourne, Len Carlyon, Gordon Corrigan, Bryn Hammond, John Lee, Chris McCarthy, Charles Messenger, Martin Middlebrook, Albert Palazzo, Professor Gary Sheffield, Pete Simkins, Andy Simpson, Nigel Steel and Rob Thompson. I hope I have learnt from all of them, but I would particularly like to thank Robin Prior and Trevor Wilson whose book *Command and Control on the Western Front* I have found tremendously influential over the last ten years. I would also make special mention of Paddy Griffith and his seminal *Battle Tactics of the Western Front: The British Army's Art of Attack, 1916–18.* Collectively these historians have dug Great War military history out from the deep abyss of maudlin sentiment. We may not all agree with each other all the time – in fact, we manifestly don't – but the underlying respect for historical argument and debate rather than journalistic pointing and shouting is common to all.

I would also wish to express my thanks to James McWilliams and R. James Steel whose book *The Suicide Battalion* is a marvellous source of Canadian personal accounts for the 46th Canadian Battalion. Also thanks to the copyright owners of W. H. Downing, whose book *To the Last Ridge* (London: Grub Street, 2005) is a vivid Australian account that I could not resist using. The excellent Doughboy Centre hosted by the Great War Society was invaluable in guiding me to numerous American accounts. The equally wonderful Canadian Letters & Images Project is also a fine internet source (www.canadianletters.ca).

As ever, for the personal experience sources I owe a great debt to the Sound Archive at the IWM and I cannot thank enough our Keeper, Margaret Brooks. I am also grateful to my colleagues James Atkinson, Richard Hughes, Richard McDonough and the towering glory that is John Stopford-Pickering. Originating back in the early 1970s, the archive has been added to year by year, until its assortment of detailed and genuinely unsentimental interviews is second to none. The Sound Archive collections are so wide in scope that almost every author could benefit from immersing themselves in our copious recordings for a week or so. But few do, indeed some prefer to scribble platitudes about the sanctity of contemporary sources. Yet there are problems with all forms of historical evidence. We all cheerfully quote from heavily edited memoirs that were often written down years after the fact, contemporary diaries can be works of pure fantasy or merely reflect transient feelings and impressions, while letters reflect all the news that is appropriate to the mothers, friends or girlfriends who were their intended audience, rather than the grim reality of life on the Western Front. And of course, the first purpose of war diaries and official reports is always to exculpate the colonel and adjutant of the battalion or unit from all blame for any reverse in the field – after all, it was always the unit on the right (always the right!) that gave way and never, *ever* their own men.

The stance of authors who believe everything they read and nothing that they hear can leave their books incomplete and lacking a hard-edged focus as a direct consequence. Of course, oral history has to be treated with exceptional care – battle stories are often garbled under the manifold effects of stress or distance in time since the event – but it excels in the mundane, the crude realities and the minutiae that no one in their right mind would ever write down. If we ignore oral history interviews lasting up to twenty hours that meticulously chart an individual's progress before, during and after the war, then we miss out much of the nitty-gritty detail and 'real' personal feelings that are simply not recorded in diaries and letters home or in the slightly self-conscious post-war memoirs. In some cases this results in a literal sanitation of war: the crude horrors of war are omitted as unsavoury, the 'men' fear nothing, the 'chaps' are always dreadfully disappointed not to be going over the top and everyone *always* fought to the very last round before even considering surrender. All sources need to be treated with care and all authors make mistakes in judging evidence – in the end it is down to a matter of personal judgement whether to believe an account or not. But like the British generals of the Great War, historians needs to use 'all arms' at their disposal and cannot ignore any valid sources if they are to get the whole raw picture of men at war.

The IWM Department of Documents collection is the single most important resource in researching the history of the Great War. Thanks to its Keeper, Rod Suddaby, and the dedicated work of his staff the voices, long stilled, of thousands of veterans are still preserved – not forgotten as some would have it but, *au contraire*, lovingly catalogued and conserved for future generations who want to know what the war was like for those who actually experienced it. I would particularly like to thank Tony Richards, Wendy Luttorloch and Simon Offord for all their patient help and encouragement. Three work experience students Anna Blackwell, Daniel Crewes and Chidozie Orji were of particular help. I would also like to thank the IWM Photographic Archive for their assistance in supplying the photographs, particularly Rose Gerrard and Alan Wakefield and all the 'backroom boys' who they tell me do all the real work! Elsewhere in the IWM I would like to thank Chris McCarthy who knows where *all* the bodies are buried, Alan Jeffries is a diamond, Bryn Hammond has never been anything but a true pal over the years, and how could I forget my old *compadre* Nigel Steel who is currently bringing a much-needed touch of sheer class to the backwaters of the Australian War Memorial.

The Tank Museum at Bovington is another fantastic resource made available by a cheerful and efficient staff led by the incomparable David Fletcher. I owe them a great deal.

The Western Front Association has been tremendously helpful over the years and I think it is right at the centre of the recent surge in interest in the Great War. Active branches exist all over the country and long may they continue – indeed, I am proud to be a member of one of the few organisations that seems to genuinely welcome my membership! The equally splendid Great War Forum set up by the remarkable Chris Baker is a constant source of both freely shared expertise and innocent amusement.

On a more personal level I would thank my lovely wife Polly

Napper and our two 'little smashers', Lily and Ruby, who are growing slowly older without, I fear, growing up much. Long may it continue! My oldest chum, John Paylor, read the text and is therefore, in my view, solely responsible for any remaining errors. Finally, I come to my editor, Keith Lowe. Now a distinguished historian in his own right he still finds time to burnish my hackneyed prose while writing his own works of genius. Without his whole editorial and production team this book would not exist. I would particularly thank my patient copy editor Jo Murray and my eagle-eyed proofreaders Alex and Linda Revell.

If this book has a theme it is that war is always dirty, murderous and frightening, rarely in any way glorious or inspiring. I began in my late twenties interviewing First World War veterans; then in my thirties and forties I interviewed veterans from the Second World War and Korea; now edging reluctantly into my fifties, I'm interviewing boys in their twenties just back from service in Iraq and Afghanistan. *Plus ça change* . . .

Notes to the Text

1 Of Mice and Men

1 E. Ludendorff, *Ludendorff's Own Story: August 1914 – November 1918* (New York & London: Harper & Bros, 1919), p.158

2 Ibid., pp.160–61

3 IWM DOCS: K. E. Walser, Transcript letter, 5/1917

4 W. Robertson, quoted in J. E. Edmonds, *History of the Great War: Military Operations, France and Belgium, 1918, Vol. I* (London: Macmillan & Co Ltd, 1935), p.2

5 IWM SOUND: M. Rymer Jones, AC 10699, Reel 2

6 IWM DOCS: R. G. Dixon, Typescript account, 'The Wheels of Darkness', p.133

7 INTERNET SOURCE: H. D. Bolster, Letter, 24/3/1918, Canadian Letters & Images Project, http://www.canadianletters.ca/media.php?collectionid=106&docid=3& warid=3

8 IWM DOCS: D. L. Rowlands, Transcript letter, 5/2/1918

9 IWM DOCS: K. W. Mealing, Transcript account, p.35

10 IWM DOCS: R. A. Backhurst, Manuscript account, p.7

11 INTERNET SOURCE: J. L. Evans, Letter, 24/4/1918, Canadian Letters & Images Project, http://www.canadianletters.ca/collectionsSoldier.php?warid=3&collectionid=201

12 W. Robertson, *From Private to Field Marshal* (London: Constable, 1921), pp.319–20

13 Ibid., p.329

14 H. Gough, *The Fifth Army* (London: Hodder and Stoughton, 1931), p.241–2

15 IWM DOCS: I. M. Hedley, Manuscript diary, 21/1/1918

16 W. Robertson, *From Private to Field Marshal*, pp.335 & 336–7

17 IWM DOCS: I. M. Hedley, Manuscript diary, 26/1/1918

2 The Best-laid Schemes

1 GHQ Staff, quoted in J.E. Edmonds, *History of the Great War: Military Operations, France and Belgium, 1918, Appendices 6*, p.23

2 Ibid.

3 Ibid., pp.23–4

4 Ibid., p.24

5 Ibid., p.27

6 H. Gough, quoted in J.E. Edmonds, *History of the Great War: Military Operations, France and Belgium, 1918, Appendices II*, p.46

7 IWM DOCS: C. C. Miller, Transcript account, 'A Letter from India to my daughters in England', p.29

8 Ibid., p.30

9 Ibid., pp.30–31

10 IWM DOCS: R. F. Petschler, Manuscript account, pp.23–4

11 IWM DOCS: J. E. March, Typescript account, p.35

12 H. Gough, *The Fifth Army*, p.246

13 Ibid., p.245

14 IWM SOUND: N. M. Dillon, AC 9752, Reel 12

15 IWM DOCS: G. D. J. McMurtrie, Typescript account, p.55

16 IWM DOCS: L. R. Ward, Manuscript lecture notes, pp.2–3

17 IWM DOCS: B. O. Bradnack, Typescript account, p.49

18 IWM DOCS: E. C. Allfree, Typescript account, p.307

19 Ibid., pp.310–11

20 IWM DOCS: B. O. Bradnack, Typescript account, p.50

21 Ibid., p.55

22 F. C. Stanley, *The History of the 89th Brigade, 1914–1918* (Liverpool: Daily Post, 1919), pp.250–51

23 IWM SOUND: E. G. Williams, AC 10604, Reel 21

24 F. S. G. Piggott, quoted in H. Gough, *The Fifth Army*, p.251

25 H. Gough, *The Fifth Army*, pp.251–2 (Edited)

26 IWM SOUND: H. Pohlmann, AC 4197, Reel 1

27 IWM DOCS: F. Meisel, Transcript account, p.19

28 IWM DOCS: E.V. Kühns, Transcript account, p.25

29 IWM SOUND: H. Pohlmann, AC 4197, Reel 1

30 IWM DOCS: B. O. Bradnack, Typescript account, p.51

31 IWM SOUND: A. F. Behrend, AC 4017, Reel 1

32 IWM DOCS: C. C. Miller, Transcript account, 'A Letter from India to my daughters in England', pp.31 & 33

33 IWM DOCS: J. Brady, Typescript account, p.129

34 B. H. L Prior, quoted in F. Loraine Petre, *History of the Norfolk Regiment, 1685–1918* (Norwich: Jarrold & Sons, 1919), p.282

35 IWM DOCS: D. J. Polley, Transcript account and also 'The Mudhook Machine Gunner'

3 21 March 1918

1 H. Sulzbach, *With the German Guns* (London: Frederick Warne, 1981), p.150

2 IWM SOUND: W. A. Rappolt, AC 12414, Reel 9

3 IWM DOCS: E.V. Kühns, Transcript account, pp.25–6

4 E. Jünger, *Storm of Steel* (London: Chatto & Windus, 1929), p.250

5 IWM DOCS: B. O. Bradnack, Typescript account, p.56

6 I WM SOUND: A. F. Behrend, AC 4017, Reel 1

7 IWM DOCS: B. O. Bradnack, Typescript account, p.56

8 IWM DOCS: J. F. Fleming-Bernard, Typescript account, p.18

9 IWM DOCS: E. C. Allfree, Typescript account, pp.319–20

10 IWM SOUND: C. G. Dennys, AC 9976, Reel 10

11 IWM DOCS: B. Chaney, Typescript account, pp.131–2

12 H. Gough, *The Fifth Army*, p.260

13 Ibid., p.261

14 E. Jünger, *Storm of Steel*, pp.254–5

15 IWM SOUND: H. Pohlmann, AC 4197, Reel 1

16 IWM DOCS: M. L. Harper, Typescript account, pp.1–2

17 IWM DOCS: J. Brady, Typescript account, p.131

18 Ibid., pp.131–2

19 IWM DOCS: C. C. Miller, Transcript account, 'A Letter from India to my daughters in England', p.33

20 Ibid., pp.33–4

21 W. Elstob, quoted in R. Bonner, *Wilfrith Elstob VC DSO MC* (Knutsford: Fleur de Lys Publishing, 1998), p. 14; and H. C. E. Westropp, *Sixteenth, Seventeenth, Eighteenth, Nineteenth Battalions The Manchester Regiment: A Record, 1914–1918* (Manchester: Sherratt & Hughes, 1923), p.48

22 H. C. E. Westropp, *Sixteenth, Seventeenth, Eighteenth, Nineteenth Battalions The Manchester Regiment*, p.48

23 Anon Staff Officer, quoted in H. C. E. Westropp, *Sixteenth, Seventeenth, Eighteenth, Nineteenth Battalions The Manchester Regiment*, p.51

24 IWM DOCS: H. R. Hardman, Typescript account, p.1

25 IWM DOCS: R. F. Petschler, Manuscript account, p.29

26 Ibid., pp.30–31

27 IWM SOUND: H. Hopthrow, AC 11581, Reel 11

28 Ibid.

29 IWM DOCS: B. O. Bradnack, Typescript account, p.57

30 IWM DOCS: P. Creek, Manuscript account, p.42

31 IWM SOUND: C. G. Dennys, AC 9976, Reel 10–11

32 IWM DOCS: E. C. Allfree, Typescript account, pp.323–4

33 IWM DOCS: W. F. Pressey, Typescript account, p.132

34 IWM DOCS: E. C. Allfree, Typescript account, pp.326–7

35 IWM DOCS: W. F. Pressey, Typescript account, pp.132–3

36 IWM DOCS: E. C. Allfree, Typescript account, pp.327–8

37 Ibid., pp.332–3

38 IWM DOCS: B. O. Bradnack, Typescript account, p.58

39 IWM DOCS: R. A. Backhurst, Manuscript account, p.11

40 Ibid., pp.11–12

41 IWM SOUND: J. Fitzpatrick, AC 10767, Reel 13

42 IWM DOCS: J. Brady, Typescript account, pp.133–4

43 Ibid.

44 Ibid., p.138

45 H. Sulzbach, *With the German Guns*, p.151

46 IWM SOUND: D. N. Wimberley, AC 4266, Reel 1

47 IWM DOCS: R. W. F. Johnston, Transcript account, p.99

48 Ibid.

49 Ibid., p.100

50 Ibid., pp.101–2

51 Ibid., p.103

52 IWM DOCS: F. Warren, Transcript diary, 21/3/1918

53 IWM DOCS: A. W. Bradbury, Typescript account, p.44

54 IWM DOCS: F. Warren, Transcript diary, 21/3/1918

55 Ibid.

56 D. Haig, quoted in G. Sheffield and J. Bourne (eds), *Douglas Haig: War Diaries and Letters 1914–1918* (London: Weidenfeld & Nicolson, 2005), p.390

4 Retreat to the Somme

1 H. Gough, *The Fifth Army*, p.264

2 H. Gough, quoted in J. E. Edmonds, *History of the Great War: Military Operations, France and Belgium, 1918, Vol. I*, p.265

3 IWM SOUND: E. G. Williams, AC 10604, Reel 22

4 Ibid.

5 Ibid.

6 Ibid.

7 Ibid.

8 Ibid.

9 Ibid.

10 IWM DOCS: J. F. Fleming-Bernard, Typescript account, p.22

11 IWM DOCS: W. F. Pressey, Typescript account, p.137–8

12 IWM DOCS: L. R. Ward, Manuscript lecture notes, p.5

13 IWM DOCS: J. F. Fleming-Bernard, Typescript account, pp.23–4 & 28

14 IWM DOCS: H. C. Rees, Typescript diary, 22/3/1918

15 IWM DOCS: M. L. Harper, Transcript account, pp.2–3

16 E. Jünger, *Storm of Steel*, pp.271–2

17 IWM DOCS: G. E. V. Thompson, Transcript account, pp.46–7

18 IWM DOCS: G. A. Brett, Typescript account

19 Ibid.

20 IWM DOCS: R. D. Fisher, Manuscript account, p.54

21 IWM DOCS: G. A. Brett, Typescript account

22 IWM DOCS: L. J. Wells, Manuscript account pp.2–3

23 P. G. Grant, quoted in R. U. H. Buckland, *Demolitions, Fifth Army, 1918* (Pamphlet reprinted from Royal Engineers Journal, 3/1933, 6/1933 & 9/1933), p.31

24 F. C. Stanley, *The History of the 89th Brigade, 1914–1918*, p.258

25 IWM SOUND: E. E. Bryan, AC 4042, Reel 1

26 IWM DOCS: R. F. Petschler, Manuscript account, p.35–6

27 Ibid., p.36

28 Ibid., pp.36–7

29 Ibid., pp.37–8

30 IWM DOCS: W. J. Parkin, Typescript account, pp.51–2

31 IWM DOCS: R. F. Petschler, Manuscript account, p.38

32 IWM DOCS: G. D. J. McMurtrie, Typescript account, p.55

33 IWM DOCS: F. Warren, Transcript diary, 23/3/1918

34 Ibid.

35 Ibid.

36 IWM DOCS: E. C. Allfree, Typescript account, pp.343–4

37 IWM DOCS: F. Warren, Transcript diary, 23/3/1918

38 Ibid.

39 IWM DOCS: E. C. Allfree, Typescript account, pp.347–9

40 Ibid., p.349

41 Ibid., pp.354–5

42 IWM DOCS: F. Warren, Transcript diary, 23/3/1918

43 Ibid.

44 Ibid.

45 IWM DOCS: P. R. Hall, Typescript account, p.21

5 Desperate Measures

1 J. E. Edmonds, *History of the Great War: Military Operations, France and Belgium, 1918, Appendices 26*, p.142

2 D. Haig, quoted in G. Sheffield and J. Bourne (eds), *Douglas Haig: War Diaries and Letters 1914–1918*, p.391

3 IWM DOCS: P. R. Hall, Typescript account, pp.21–2

4 IWM DOCS: H. E. L. Mellersh, Transcript account, 'Schoolboy into War', pp.205–6

5 IWM DOCS: G. D. J. McMurtrie, Typescript account, p.62

6 IWM DOCS: J. E. March, Typescript account, pp.37–9

7 Ibid., p.39

8 IWM DOCS: J. G. Laithwaite, Typescript account, p.38

9 Ibid.

10 IWM DOCS: F. J. Whaley, Manuscript account, p.3

11 Ibid., p.5

12 TANK MUSEUM BOVINGTON: G. Brown, 'Some Reminiscences of Cambrai and the German March Offensive'

13 Ibid.

14 IWM DOCS: W. J. A. Hahn, Transcript account, '*Kriegsgefangwher*, 1918', p.2

15 Ibid., p.4

16 IWM DOCS: P. E. Williamson, Typescript account, pp.36–7

17 IWM DOCS: W. F. Pressey, Typescript account, p.143

18 IWM DOCS: S. Bradbury, Typescript account, p.95

19 IWM DOCS: A. W. Bradbury, Typescript account, pp.53–4

20 IWM DOCS: R. F. Petschler, Manuscript account, p.42

21 IWM DOCS: P. A. Ledward, Manuscript account, pp.57–8

22 IWM DOCS: S. Bradbury, Typescript account, pp.96–7

23 IWM DOCS: T. H. Westmacott, Typescript account, 'Retreat of the Fifth Army'

24 Ibid.

25 IWM DOCS: H. C. Rees, Typescript diary, 25/3/1918

26 H. Gough, *The Fifth Army*, p.286

27 D. Haig, quoted in G. Sheffield and J. Bourne (eds), *Douglas Haig: War Diaries and Letters 1914–1918*, p.392

28 IWM DOCS: P. R. Hall, Typescript account, p.22

29 Ibid., pp.22–3

30 IWM DOCS: F. R. Curtis, Manuscript account, pp.1–2

31 Ibid., p. 2

32 IWM DOCS: E. C. Allfree, Typescript account, pp. 357–9

33 TANK MUSEUM BOVINGTON: H. Thompson, Typescript letter, 19/7/1919

34 H. D. de Pree, quoted in D. Jerrold, *The Royal Naval Division* (London: Hutchinson & Co, 1923), p.287

35 Ibid., p.291

36 IWM SOUND: R. H. Tobin, AC 4242, Reel 1

37 IWM DOCS: E. C. Allfree, Typescript account, pp.359–60

38 N. Fraser-Tytler, *Field Guns in France*, (London: Hutchinson & Co, 1922), p.232

39 Ibid., pp.233–4

40 IWM DOCS: D. J. Polley, Transcript account

41 Ibid.

42 IWM DOCS: J. F. Fleming-Bernard, Typescript account, pp.42–3

43 IWM DOCS: P. E. Williamson, Typescript account, pp.39–40

44 IWM DOCS: A. W. Bradbury, Typescript account, p.50

45 IWM DOCS: F. P. Cook, Transcript account, p.59

46 IWM DOCS: E.V. Kühns, Transcript account, pp.25–6

47 IWM SOUND: W. A. Rappolt, AC 12414, Reel 9

6 Turning the Tide

1 D. Haig, quoted in G. Sheffield and J. Bourne (eds), *Douglas Haig: War Diaries and Letters 1914–1918*, pp.393–4

2 IWM DOCS: F. Warren, Transcript diary, 26/3/1918

3 IWM DOCS: A. Cousins, Transcript account, pp.72–3

4 IWM DOCS: F. Warren, Transcript diary, 26/3/1918

5 Ibid.

6 IWM DOCS: F. R. Curtis, Manuscript account, p.3

7 IWM DOCS: F. Warren, Transcript diary, 26/3/1918

8 IWM DOCS: W. J. Parkin, Typescript account, p.54

9 IWM DOCS: R. Foot, Typescript account, 'Once a Gunner'. p.87

10 Ibid., p.121

11 IWM DOCS: A. Hollis, Typescript account, p.1

12 Ibid.

13 Ibid., p.3

14 IWM DOCS: H. A. Rigby, quoted in A. Hollis, Typescript account, pp.2–3

15 IWM DOCS: A. Hollis, Typescript account, p.3

16 F. Nagel, *Fritz: The World War I Memoirs of a German Lieutenant*

(Huntingdon, West Virginia: Der Angriff Publications, 1981), p.95

17 IWM SOUND: J. C. F. Hopkins, AC 21, Reel 3

18 IWM DOCS: F. P. Cook, Transcript account, p.57

19 IWM DOCS: F. Warren, Transcript diary, 27/3/1918

20 Ibid.

21 Ibid.

22 Ibid.

23 IWM DOCS: H. C. Rees, Typescript diary, 26/3/1918

24 Ibid.

25 IWM DOCS: P. Creek, Manuscript account, p.44

26 IWM DOCS: B. Chaney, Typescript account, pp.135–6

27 Ibid., pp.136–7

28 IWM DOCS: H. C. Rees, Typescript diary, 27/3/1918

29 IWM DOCS: J. T. Capron, Typescript account, p.30

30 Ibid., pp.30–31

31 Ibid., p.31

32 INTERNET SOURCE: G. F. Dose, German Infantry Regiment 187 in Flanders, at Arras and Cambrai, 1917–1918, http://wwi.lib.byu.edu/index.php/Diaries,_Memorials,_Personal_Reminiscences

33 IWM DOCS: T. A. Bickerton, Transcript account, pp.18–20

34 INTERNET SOURCE: G. F. Dose, German Infantry Regiment 187 in Flanders, at Arras and Cambrai, 1917–1918, http://wwi.lib.byu.edu/index.php/Diaries,_Memorials,_Personal_Reminiscences

35 E. Ludendorf, *Ludendorff's Own Story: August 1914 – November 1918*, pp.237–8

36 IWM DOCS: F. Warren, Transcript diary, 28/3/1918

37 Ibid.

38 Ibid.

39 IWM DOCS: J. F. Fleming-Bernard, Typescript account, pp.57 & 62–3

40 Ibid., p.61

41 IWM DOCS: L. E. Humphreys, Typescript account, p.6

42 IWM DOCS: T. H. Westmacott, Typescript account, 'Retreat of the Fifth Army'

43 D. Haig, quoted in G. Sheffield and J. Bourne (eds), *Douglas Haig: War Diaries and Letters 1914–1918*, p.396

44 IWM DOCS: H. C. Rees, Typescript diary, 29/3/1918

45 IWM DOCS: F. Warren, Transcript diary, 30/3/1918

46 Ibid.

47 IWM SOUND: J. Pickard, AC 8946, Reels 16 & 17

48 IWM DOCS: G. Skelton, Typescript account, p.9

49 IWM DOCS: R. M. Luther, Typescript account, p.44

50 IWM SOUND: J. Davies, AC 9750, Reel 13

51 IWM DOCS: T. S. Louch, Typescript account, pp.20–21

52 IWM DOCS: E.V. Kühns, Transcript account, pp.27–8

53 IWM DOCS: W. F. Pressey, Typescript account, p.145

54 IWM DOCS: I. M. Hedley, Manuscript diary, 4/4/1918

55 IWM DOCS: W. H. Harris, Transcript account, p.56

56 Colonel Wetzell, quoted in J. E. Edmonds, *History of the Great War: Military Operations, France and Belgium, 1918, Appendices 20*, p.131

7 Battle for Flanders

1 IWM DOCS: H. J. C. Marshall, Transcript account, pp.21–2

2 IWM DOCS: C. E. L. Lyne, Typescript account, p.22

3 Ibid.

4 Ibid., pp.22–3

5 Ibid., pp.24–5

6 IWM DOCS: A. E. Bagley, Transcript account, pp.2–3

7 Ibid., pp3–4

8 IWM DOCS: F. Meisel, Transcript account, pp.21–2

9 IWM DOCS: J. W. Stephenson, Typescript account, p.34

10 IWM DOCS: C. E. L. Lyne, Typescript letter, 28/4/1918

11 IWM DOCS: F. Meisel, Transcript account, pp.22–3

12 Ibid., pp.23–4

13 IWM SOUND: P. Ostreicher, AC 4192, Reel 1

14 IWM DOCS: W. House, Typescript account, '1914–1918 War Memoirs' p.28. Estate of H. W. House, 1983.

15 IWM DOCS: C. Uren, Typescript account, pp.4–5

16 IWM DOCS: W. House, Typescript account, '1914–1918 War Memoirs', pp.29–30

17 Ibid., p.31

18 IWM SOUND: P. Neame, AC 48, Reel 14

19 D. Haig, quoted in J. E. Edmonds, *History of the Great War: Military Operations, France and Belgium, 1918, Vol. II* (London: Macmillan & Co Ltd, 1937), p.512

20 IWM DOCS: H. C. Rees, Typescript Diary, 11/4/1918

21 Ibid.

22 IWM DOCS: A. Thompson, Transcript POW debriefing report, 20/6/1919

23 IWM DOCS: A. E. Bagley, Transcript account, pp.6–7

24 Ibid., p.10

25 Ibid., pp.12–13

26 Ibid., p.27

27 Ibid., pp.27–8

28 Ibid.

29 IWM DOCS: A. Thompson, Transcript POW debriefing report, 20/6/1919

30 Ibid.

31 IWM DOCS: A. E. Bagley, Transcript account, p.30

32 IWM DOCS: F. Meisel, Transcript account, pp.24–6

33 Ibid., pp.27–8

34 Ibid., pp.28–9

35 IWM DOCS: H. J. C. Marshall, Transcript account, pp.23–4

36 Ibid., p.24

37 G. S. Hutchison, *Footslogger: An Autobiography* (London: Hutchinson & Co, 1931), p. 210

38 Ibid.

39 Ibid., pp.210–11

40 Ibid., pp. 211–12

41 Ibid., p. 211

42 IWM DOCS: I. M. Hedley, Manuscript diary, 13/4/1918

43 Ibid., 14/4/1918 & 15/4/1918

44 C. Harington, 'The Ypres Salient in 1918', (*The Ypres Times*, Vol. 2, No. 2, 4/1924), p.36

45 IWM DOCS: F. J. Whaley, Manuscript account, pp.4–5

46 Ibid., p.5

47 IWM DOCS: R. F. Petschler, Manuscript account, pp.49–50

48 IWM DOCS: F. Meisel, Transcript account, p.30

49 Ibid., p.31

50 Ibid., pp.31–2

51 Ibid., p.32

52 IWM DOCS: P. A. Ledward, Manuscript account, pp.72–3

53 Ibid., p.77

54 IWM SOUND: M. S. Esler, AC 378, Reel 3

55 Ibid.

56 F. Mitchell, *Tank Warfare: The Story of the Tanks in the Great War* (London: Thomas Nelson, 1935), p.189

57 Ibid., pp.189–90

58 Ibid., p.191

59 Ibid., p.192

60 IWM DOCS: T. S. Louch, Typescript account, pp.20–21

61 R. A. Fynch, quoted in C. E. W. Bean, *The Australian Imperial Force in France: During the Main German Offensive, 1918* (Sydney: Angus & Robertson, 1940), p.603

62 Edited from W. H. Downing, *To the Last Ridge* (London: Grub Street, 2005), pp.118–19

63 J. C. Christian, quoted in C. E. W. Bean, *The Australian Imperial Force in France: During the Main German Offensive, 1918*, fn. p.604

8 Battle on the Aisne

1 IWM DOCS: E.V. Kühns, Transcript account, p.30

2 IWM SOUND: S. Rogerson, AC 4214, Reel 1

3 IWM DOCS: P. A. Ledward, Manuscript account, pp.81 & 82

4 IWM DOCS: W. H. Harris, Transcript account, p.57

5 IWM DOCS: H. C. Rees, Typescript diary, 26/5/1918

6 IWM SOUND: S. Rogerson, AC 4214, Reel 1

7 IWM DOCS: W. J. Parkin, Typescript account, p.67

8 IWM DOCS: P. A. Ledward, Manuscript account, p.83

9 IWM SOUND: S. Rogerson, AC 4214, Reel 1

10 IWM DOCS: P. H. B. Lyon, Manuscript diary, 26/5/1918

11 Ibid.

12 IWM DOCS: H. C. Rees, Typescript diary, 27/5/1918

13 IWM DOCS: P. A. Ledward, Manuscript account, pp.83–4

14 S. Rogerson, quoted in E. Wyrall, *The Diehards in the Great War* (London: Harrison & Sons, 1930), p.235; and J. H. Boraston and C. E. O. Bax, *The Eighth Division in War, 1914–1918* (London: Medici Society, 1926), p.222

15 S. Rogerson, quoted in J. H.

Boraston and C. E. O. Bax, *The Eighth Division in War, 1914–1918*, pp.222–3

16 IWM DOCS: P. H. B. Lyon, Manuscript diary, 27/5/1918

17 INTERNET SOURCE: E. Riddell, 50th Division Website, http://www.fairmile.fsbusiness.co.uk/riddell.htm

18 IWM DOCS: M. S. Esler, Typescript account, pp.77–8

19 Ibid., p.78

20 Ibid., p.79

21 IWM DOCS: A. Boyle, Typescript diary, 27/5/1918

22 IWM DOCS: P. H. B. Lyon, Manuscript diary, 27/5/1918

23 IWM DOCS: C. W. Taylor, Typescript account

24 IWM DOCS: W. H. Harris, Transcript account, p.57

25 Ibid., pp.57–8

26 IWM DOCS: H. C. Rees, Typescript diary, 27/5/1918

27 IWM SOUND: G. Cole, AC 9535, Reel 12

28 IWM DOCS: H. C. Rees, Typescript diary, 27/5/1918

29 Ibid.

30 Ibid.

31 Ibid.

32 IWM DOCS: W. H. Harris, Transcript account, p.58

33 IWM DOCS: P. H. B. Lyon, Manuscript diary, 27/5/1918

34 IWM DOCS: J. Nettleton, Typescript account, p.143

35 IWM SOUND: S. Rogerson, AC 4214, Reel 1

36 IWM SOUND: U. Burke, AC 569, Reel 17

37 L. Leat, quoted in R. A. Colwill, *Through Hell to Victory: From Passchendaele to Mons with the 2nd Devons in 1918* (Uckfield: Naval & Military Press, 2007) pp.195–6

38 A. J. Borne, quoted in R. A. Colwill, *Through Hell to Victory*, p.196

39 Col. Anderson-Morshead, quoted in R. A. Colwill, *Through Hell to Victory*, p.215

40 IWM SOUND: U. Burke, AC 569, Reel 17

41 IWM DOCS: P. A. Ledward, Manuscript account, pp.90–2

42 IWM DOCS: W. J. Parkin, Typescript account, p.70

43 IWM DOCS: P. A. Ledward, Manuscript account, pp.95–6

44 IWM DOCS: J. Nettleton, Typescript account, pp.144–5

45 Ibid., p.147

46 Ibid., pp. 148–9

47 Ibid., pp.150–51

48 IWM SOUND: J. Wedderburn-Maxwell, AC 9146, Reel 8

49 IWM DOCS: J. Nettleton, Typescript account, pp.152–3

50 IWM DOCS: P. A. Ledward, Manuscript account, pp.98–9

9 Planning for the All Arms Battle

1 IWM DOCS: F. Meisel, Transcript account, p.58

2 Ibid., p.42

3 Ibid., p.51

4 Ibid., p.60–61

5 IWM SOUND: H. Pohlmann, AC 4197, Reel 1

6 E. J. Rule, *Jacka's Mob: A Narrative of the Great War by Edgar John Rule* (Melbourne: Military Melbourne, 1999), p.125

7 NATIONAL ARMY MUSEUM: Rawlinson Papers, 'Increase in our Offensive Power by additions of Machine and Lewis Guns'

8 E. J. Rule, *Jacka's Mob*, p.133

9 D. Haig, quoted in G. Sheffield and J. Bourne (eds), *Douglas Haig: War Diaries and Letters 1914–1918*, p.436

10 IWM DOCS: W. Cook, Transcript account, 'The Lengthened Shadow', pp.199–200

11 IWM DOCS: S. T. Fuller, Diary, 2/1918

12 D. Haig, quoted in G. Sheffield and J. Bourne (eds), *Douglas Haig: War Diaries and Letters 1914–1918*, p.438

10 The Black Day

1 IWM DOCS: T. S. Louch, Typescript account, pp.32–3

2 TANK MUSEUM BOVINGTON: C. Rowland, Typescript account

3 IWM DOCS: H. Smeddle, Manuscript account, 'The attack on Aug 8th 1918'

4 TANK MUSEUM BOVINGTON: J. G. Fitzmaurice, Transcript account, 'The experiences of an Adjutant'

5 TANK MUSEUM BOVINGTON: N. M. Dillon, Transcript account, 'The Recollections of a Battalion Reconnaissance Officer'

6 TANK MUSEUM BOVINGTON: C. Rowland, Typescript account

7 IWM DOCS: H. Smeddle, Manuscript account, 'The attack on Aug 8th 1918'

8 Ibid.

9 Ibid.

10 TANK MUSEUM BOVINGTON: N. M. Dillon, Transcript account, 'The Recollections of a Battalion Reconnaissance Officer'

11 IWM DOCS: H. Smeddle, Manuscript account, 'The attack on Aug 8th 1918'

12 Ibid.

13 Ibid.

14 INTERNET SOURCE: B. H. Cox, Letter, 13/8/1918, Canadian Letters & Images Project, http://www.canadianletters.ca/letters.phpletterid=1012&docid=1&collectionid=115&warid=3

15 J. Monash, quoted in N. Browning, *The Blue & White Diamond: The History of the 28th Battalion, 1915–1919* (Bassendean, W.A.: Advance Press, 2002), p.412

16 IWM DOCS: W. Cook, Transcript account, 'The Lengthened Shadow', pp.211–12

17 IWM DOCS: W. Kerr, Transcript account, pp.106–7

18 TANK MUSEUM BOVINGTON: C. Rowland, Typescript account

19 TANK MUSEUM BOVINGTON: G. H. Brooks, Transcript account, 'Tank Actions in France: The Section Commander and the Tank Commander'

20 IWM DOCS: P. Creek, Manuscript account, p.51

21 TANK MUSEUM BOVINGTON: C. Rowland, Typescript account

22 TANK MUSEUM BOVINGTON: N. M. Dillon, Transcript account, 'The Recollections of a Battalion Reconnaissance Officer'

23 IWM DOCS: G. V. Rose, Typescript account, 'Three Years and a Day', p.119

24 E. Morrow, quoted in N. Browning, *The Blue & White Diamond: The History of the 28th Battalion*, p. 412–13

25 INTERNET SOURCE: B. H. Cox, Letter, 13/8/1918, Canadian Letters & Images Project, http://www.canadianletters.ca/letters.phpletterid=1012&docid=1&collectionid=115&warid=3

26 IWM DOCS: H. Smeddle, Manuscript account, 'The attack on Aug 8th 1918'

27 Ibid.

28 IWM DOCS: G. V. Rose, Typescript account, 'Three Years and a Day', p.120

29 IWM DOCS: J. F. Fleming-Bernard, Typescript Account, p.27

30 IWM DOCS: G. V. Rose, Typescript account, 'Three Years and a Day', p.121

31 IWM DOCS: H. Smeddle, Manuscript account, 'The attack on Aug 8th 1918'

32 TANK MUSEUM BOVINGTON: C. Rowland, Typescript account

33 TANK MUSEUM BOVINGTON: N. M. Dillon, Transcript account, 'The Recollections of a Battalion Reconnaissance Officer'

34 TANK MUSEUM BOVINGTON: C. Rowland, Typescript account

35 Ibid.

36 Ibid.

37 IWM SOUND: E. Potten, AC 11042, Reel 6

38 C. B. Arnold, quoted in J. F. C. Fuller, *Tanks in the Great War, 1914–1918* (London: John Murray, 1920), p.231

39 TANK MUSEUM BOVINGTON: C. Ribbans, Letter, 17/1/1919

40 C. B. Arnold, quoted in J. F. C. Fuller, *Tanks in the Great War, 1914–1918*, p.231

41 Ibid., pp.232–3

42 TANK MUSEUM BOVINGTON: C. Ribbans, Letter, 17/1/1919

43 C. B. Arnold, quoted in J. F. C. Fuller, *Tanks in the Great War, 1914–1918*, p.234

44 TANK MUSEUM BOVINGTON: C. Ribbans, Letter, 17/1/1919

45 C. B. Arnold, quoted in J. F. C. Fuller, *Tanks in the Great War, 1914–1918*, p.234

46 IWM SOUND: W. A. Gillman, AC 9420, Reel 11

47 E. Ludendorff, *Ludendorff's Own Story: August 1914 – November 1918*, p.326

48 IWM DOCS: T. S. Louch, Typescript account, p.34

49 TANK MUSEUM BOVINGTON: C. Rowland, Typescript account

50 Ibid.

51 Ibid.

52 Ibid.

53 IWM DOCS: W. Kerr, Transcript account, pp.108–9

54 INTERNET SOURCE: K. W. Foster, Typescript memoir, Canadian Letters & Images Project, http://www.canadianletters.ca/letters.php?etterid=4502&warid=3&docid=5&collectionid=274

55 IWM DOCS: W. Kerr, Transcript account, p.109

56 Ibid., pp.109–10

57 Ibid., pp.110–11

58 Ibid., p.112

59 IWM DOCS: J. F. Fleming-Bernard, Typescript account, p.62

60 TANK MUSEUM BOVINGTON: C. Rowland, Typescript account

61 IWM SOUND: W. Tobey, AC 567, Reel 3

62 Ibid.

63 Ibid.

64 Ibid.

65 Ibid.

66 INTERNET SOURCE: K. W. Foster, Typescript memoir, Canadian Letters & Images Project, http://www.canadianletters.ca/letters.php?letterid=4502&warid=3&docid=5&collectionid=274

67 D. Haig, quoted in G. Sheffield and J. Bourne (eds), *Douglas Haig: War Diaries and Letters 1914–1918*, p.445

68 Ibid., pp.445–6

69 E. Ludendorff, *Ludendorff's Own Story: August 1914–November 1918*, p.332

11 Advance to the Somme

1 H. Wilson, quoted in J. E. Edmonds, *History of the Great War: Military Operations, France and Belgium, 1918, Vol. IV* (Nashville: Battery Press, 1993), p.532

2 D. Haig, quoted in G. Sheffield and J. Bourne (eds), *Douglas Haig: War Diaries and Letters 1914–1918*, p.448

3 F. Foch, quoted in J. E. Edmonds, *History of the Great War: Military Operations, France and Belgium, 1918, Vol. IV*, p.173

4 IWM DOCS: J. T. Capron, Typescript account, p.37

5 Ibid.

6 TANK MUSEUM: J. Humphries, Letter, 23/8/1918

7 IWM DOCS: L. I. L. Ferguson, Manuscript diary, 21/8/1918

8 IWM DOCS: J. T. Capron, Typescript account, p.37

9 IWM DOCS: L. I. L. Ferguson, Manuscript diary, 15/4/1918

10 Ibid., 21/8/1918

11 IWM DOCS: A. M. Henley, Typescript diary, 22/8/1918

12 Ibid.

13 INTERNET SOURCE: A. Fereday, Letter, 21/8/1918, Canadian Letters & Images Project, http://www.canadianletters.ca/letters.php?letterid=1264&docid=1&warid=3&collectionid=119

14 Ibid.

15 IWM DOCS: R. D. Fisher, Manuscript account, pp.74–5

16 D. Haig, quoted in J. E. Edmonds, *History of the Great War: Military*

Operations, France and Belgium, 1918, Vol. IV, Appendix XX, p.588

17 IWM DOCS: R. D. Fisher, Manuscript account, p.76

18 Ibid., pp.76–7

19 IWM DOCS: R. L. Angel, Typescript account, p.22

20 Ibid., p.25

21 IWM SOUND: J. Davies, AC 9750, Reel 13

22 Ibid.

23 IWM DOCS: T. H. Holmes, Typescript account

24 Ibid.

25 Ibid.

26 Ibid.

27 Ibid.

28 Ibid.

29 IWM DOCS: S. Lane, Typescript account, 'Battle of the Albert, Boyelles, August 1918'

30 Ibid.

31 IWM DOCS: L. I. L. Ferguson, Manuscript diary, 26/8/1918

32 IWM DOCS: A. M. Henley, Typescript diary, 27/8/1918

33 J. E. Edmonds, *History of the Great War: Military Operations, France and Belgium, 1918, Vol. IV*, p.260

34 Ibid., p.296

35 INTERNET SOURCE: J. L. Evans, Letter, 25/8/1918, Canadian Letters & Images Project, http://www.canadianletters.ca/collections Soldier.php?warid=3& collectionid=201

36 IWM DOCS: R. Foot, Typescript account, 'Once a Gunner', pp.97–8

37 M. Burke and F. Heaton, *Ancoats Lad: The Recollections of Mick Burke* (Manchester: Privately published by Neil Richardson, 1996), p.30

38 Ibid.

39 IWM DOCS: C. B. Brown, Typescript account, p.292–4

40 IWM DOCS: D. D. Coutts, Typescript account, pp.91–2

41 IWM DOCS: G. V. Rose, Typescript account, 'Three Years and a Day', p.132

42 W. H. Downing, *To the Last Ridge*, p.160

43 Ibid.

44 J. T. Blair, quoted in N. Browning, *The Blue & White Diamond: The History of the 28th Battalion, 1915–1919*, p.445

45 G. Kentner, quoted in J. L. McWilliams and R. James Steel, *The Suicide Battalion* (Stevenage: Spa Books, 1990), p.162

46 M. Timberlake, quoted in J. L. McWilliams and R. James Steel, *The Suicide Battalion*, p.163

47 G. Kentner, quoted in J. L. McWilliams and R. James Steel, *The Suicide Battalion*, p.164

48 Ibid., pp.164–5

49 J. H. Riehl, quoted in H. M. Urquhart, *The History of the 16th Battalion (The Canadian Scottish), Canadian Expeditionary Force, in the Great War* (Toronto: Macmillan, 1932), p.296

50 F. E. Earwaker, quoted in H. M. Urquhart, *The History of the 16th Battalion*, pp.295–6

51 C. W. Peck, quoted in H. M. Urquhart, *The History of the 16th Battalion*, p.297

52 L. L. L. Ferguson, quoted in A.

Crookenden, *The History of the Cheshire Regiment in the Great War* (W. H. Evans, Chester, 1925), pp.158–9

53 IWM DOCS: R. Foot, Typescript account, 'Once a Gunner', pp.98 & 120–21

54 IWM DOCS: A. M. Henley, Typescript diary, 22/8/1918

55 IWM DOCS: R. D. Fisher, Manuscript account, p.82

56 IWM DOCS: C. Brett, Typescript account, p.38

12 With Our American Friends at the Front

1 IWM DOCS: K. E. Walser, Transcript letter, 4/3/1918

2 IWM DOCS: J. Nettleton, Typescript account, pp.155–6

3 IWM SOUND: E. Cawston, AC 4054, Reel 1

4 IWM DOCS: R. G. Dixon, Typescript account, 'The Wheels of Darkness', pp.63 & 65

5 Ibid., p.66

6 INTERNET SOURCE: Memoir of C. L. Boucher, transcribed and edited by C. E. Merrill, http://www.luckycharlie.com

7 INTERNET SOURCE: F. Last, 1918, La Deuxiéme Battaille del la Marne, http://batmarn2.club.fr/frk_last.htm

8 A. Catlin, quoted in D. Bonk, *Château Thierry and Belleau Wood 1918* (Oxford: Osprey Publishing, 2007), p.61

9 D. Daly, quoted in E. M. Coffman, *The War to End All Wars: The American Military Experience of World War I*

(Lexington: University of Kentucky, 1998), p.217

10 A. Catlin, quoted in D. Bonk, *Château Thierry and Belleau Wood 1918*, p.62

11 IWM SOUND: M. L. Krulewitch, AC 4149, Reel 1

12 IWM DOCS: K. E. Walser, Transcript letter, 8/7/1918

13 Ibid.

14 INTERNET SOURCE: J. Woolridge, Letter, In Their Own Words, Doughboy Centre, http://www.worldwar1.com/dbc/ow_5.htm

15 P. T de Chardin, quoted in E. M. Coffman, *The War to End All Wars: The American Military Experience of World War I*, p.246

16 IWM DOCS: T. F. Grady, Manuscript diary, 24/8/1918–25/8/1918

17 D. Haig, quoted in G. Sheffield and J. Bourne (eds), *Douglas Haig: War Diaries and Letters 1914–1918*, p.443

18 IWM DOCS: P. Harding, Typescript letter, 22/9/1918

19 INTERNET SOURCE: C. Richmond, 'Recollections of a Buck Private', Diary, 12/8/1918, http://www.robinrichmond.com/wardiary/

20 IWM DOCS: L. B. Garretson, Typescript letters, pp.43–4

21 IWM DOCS: P. Harding, Typescript letter, 22/9/1918

13 Breaking the Hindenburg Line

1 D. Haig, quoted in G. Sheffield and J. Bourne (eds), *Douglas Haig: War Diaries and Letters 1914–1918*, p.453

2 Ibid.

3 Ibid., p.456

4 Ibid., p.458

5 IWM DOCS: R. G. Dixon, Typescript account, 'The Wheels of Darkness', p.110

6 IWM DOCS: P. E. Williamson, Typescript account, p.46

7 IWM DOCS: L. J. S. Sherwood, Typescript account, p.15

8 Ibid., p.16

9 Ibid., p.17

10 E. J. Rule, *Jacka's Mob: A Narrative of the Great War by Edgar John Rule*, p.140

11 Ibid., p.141

12 Ibid., p.143

13 IWM SOUND: W. A. Gillman, AC 9420, Edited from Reel 11 & 12

14 D. Haig, quoted in G. Sheffield and J. Bourne (eds), *Douglas Haig: War Diaries and Letters 1914–1918*, p.462

15 INTERNET SOURCE: C. Dermody, 'A Yank in the First World War', transcribed by L. McCauley, http://www.htc.net/~dermody/yankww1.htm

16 IWM DOCS: T. F. Grady, Manuscript diary, 26/9/1918

17 Ibid.

18 INTERNET SOURCE: A. York, Diary, 7/10/1918, http://www.acacia.pair.com/Acacia.Vignettes/The.Diary.of.Alvin.York.html

19 Ibid.

20 Ibid.

21 Ibid.

22 INTERNET SOURCE: M. Chopin, 'Through the Valley of Death', transcribed by L. McCauley, http://www.geocities.com/louisiana_doughboy/index.htm

23 Ibid.

24 Ibid.

25 INTERNET SOURCE: E. West, Letter, 15/10/1918, transcribed by M. W. Beeman, http://www.worldwar1.com/dbc/ewmain.htm

26 R. Alexander, quoted in Anon, *History of the Seventy-Seventh Division, August 25th, 1917 –November 11th, 1918* (New York: 77th Division Association, 1919), p.155

27 D. McKerchar, quoted in J. L. McWilliams and R. James Steel, *The Suicide Battalion*, p.174

28 S. Colbeck, quoted in J. L. McWilliams and R. James Steel, *The Suicide Battalion*, p.175

29 IWM SOUND: H. Calvert, AC 9955, Reel 16

30 IWM SOUND: W. Tatham, AC 328, Reel 1

31 Ibid.

32 IWM SOUND: H. Calvert, AC 9955, Reel 16

33 IWM SOUND: A. J. Jamieson, AC 10434, Reel 2

34 IWM DOCS: P. E. Williamson, Typescript account, pp.46–7

35 IWM SOUND: A. J. Jamieson, AC 10434, Reel 3

36 IWM DOCS: G. Skelton, Typescript account, p.9

37 IWM SOUND: W. A. Gillman, AC 9420, Reel 11

38 IWM DOCS: J. Nettleton, Typescript account, pp.183–4

39 IWM DOCS: W. M. Newton, Typescript diary, 24/9/1918, 28/9/1918 & 29/9/1918

40 IWM DOCS: G. V. Rose, Typescript account, 'Three Years and a Day', pp.137–8

41 IWM DOCS: G. K. Parker, Typescript account, p.29

42 IWM DOCS: H. J. C. Marshall, Transcript account, p.5

43 IWM DOCS: ibid pp.2–3

44 IWM DOCS: G. K. Parker, Typescript account, p.29

45 Ibid.

46 IWM DOCS: H. J. C. Marshall, Transcript account, p.10

47 R. E. Priestley, *Breaking the Hindenburg Line: The Story of the 46th (North Midland) Division* (London: T. Fisher Unwin Ltd), p.68

48 IWM DOCS: A. B. Pick, Typescript account, pp.138–9

49 IWM DOCS: H. J. C. Marshall, Transcript account, p.9

50 IWM DOCS: G. K. Parker, Typescript account, p.29

51 IWM DOCS: W. Cook, Transcript account, 'The Lengthened Shadow', pp.216–17

52 INTERNET SOURCE: After-action report by R. P. Buell, provided by C. Doane for site run by M. H. Feldbin, http://www.oryansroughnecks.org/buell.html

53 IWM DOCS: W. M. Newton, Typescript diary, 29/9/1918

54 Ibid.

55 IWM DOCS: G. V. Rose, Typescript account, 'Three Years and a Day', pp.139–41

56 IWM DOCS: O. A. Woodward, Typescript account, pp.127–128

57 IWM DOCS: H. J. C. Marshall, Transcript account, p.15

58 Ibid. , p.12

59 Ibid., pp.13–14

60 Ibid., p.12

61 IWM DOCS: C. L Platt, Manuscript account, pp.11–13

62 IWM DOCS: G. V. Rose, Typescript account, 'Three Years and a Day', p.144

63 Ibid., p.147

14 Germany Falling

1 E. Ludendorff, *Ludendorff's Own Story: August 1914 – November 1918, Vol. II*, p.376

2 P. von Hindenburg, quoted in J. Lee, *The Warlords* (London: Weidenfeld & Nicolson, 1919), p.375–6

3 E. Ludendorff, *Ludendorff's Own Story: August 1914 – November 1918, Vol. II*, p.375–6

4 IWM SOUND: D. Price, AC 10168, Reel 14

5 Ibid.

6 IWM DOCS: B. O. Bradnack, Typescript account, p.105

7 Ibid., p.106

8 IWM DOCS: F. Meisel, Transcript account, p.66

9 IWM DOCS: E. Boon, Typescript account, pp.10–11

10 IWM DOCS: C. Brett, Typescript account, p.39

11 Ibid., pp.40–41

12 A. McPeake, quoted in H. F. N.

Jourdain and E. Fraser, *The Connaught Rangers, Vol. III* (County Cork: Schull Books, 1999), p.193

13 Ibid.

14 IWM DOCS: C. Brett, Typescript account, p.41

15 Ibid., p.42

16 IWM DOCS: O. A. Woodward, Typescript account, p.130

17 IWM DOCS: A. J. Abraham, Typescript account, pp.96–7

18 Ibid.

19 Ibid., pp.107–8

20 Ibid., pp.108–9

21 IWM SOUND: P. Neame, AC 48, Reel 15

22 IWM DOCS: J. Nettleton, Typescript account, p.187

23 Ibid., pp.187–8

24 IWM DOCS: G. K. Parker, Typescript account, p.30

25 Ibid., p.31

26 Ibid., p.30

27 IWM DOCS: F. Meisel, Transcript account, pp.72–3

28 IWM DOCS: P. Creek, Manuscript account, p.51

29 IWM DOCS: J. W. Stephenson, Typescript account, p.55

30 Ibid.

31 Captain R. S. B. Sinclair, quoted in A. F. Barnes, *The Story of the 2/5th Gloucestershire Regiment* (Gloucester: Crypt House Press, 1930), pp.141–2

32 IWM DOCS: J. W. Stephenson, Typescript account, p.56

33 IWM DOCS: F. Meisel, Transcript account, p.71

34 Ibid., p.76

35 IWM DOCS: P. Creek, Manuscript account, p.51

36 IWM SOUND: W. E. Grover, AC 10441, Reel 5

37 IWM DOCS: O. A. Woodward, Typescript account, p.136

38 Ibid., p.133

39 IWM SOUND: W. E. Grover, AC 10441, Reel 5

40 IWM DOCS: O. A. Woodward, Typescript account, p.137

41 Ibid., p.138

42 IWM DOCS: T. H. Westmacott, Typescript letter, 6/11/1918

43 Ibid., 7/11/1918

44 IWM DOCS: R. Foot, Typescript account, 'Once a Gunner', pp.104–5

45 IWM DOCS: G. A Stevens, Typescript letter, 7/11/1918

46 IWM DOCS: L. B. Garretson, Typescript letters, pp.43–4

47 IWM DOCS: E. C. Allfree, Typescript account, pp.445–7

48 IWM SOUND: H. Bashford, AC 9987, Reel 4

15 This is the End

1 IWM DOCS: J. E. March, Typescript account, p.39

2 IWM DOCS: R. G. Dixon, Typescript account, 'The Wheels of Darkness', p.99

3 Ibid., pp.138–9

4 IWM DOCS: J. Nettleton, Typescript account, p.192

5 IWM DOCS: W. Cook, Transcript account, 'The Lengthened Shadow', p.222

6 IWM SOUND: B. Smedley, AC10917, Reel 9

7 IWM SOUND: J. Fox, AC 9549, Reel 6

8 IWM DOCS: T. F. Grady, Manuscript diary, 10/11/1918–11/11/1918

9 IWM SOUND: C. G. Dennys, AC 9976, Reel 12

10 IWM DOCS: J. T. Capron, Typescript account, pp.48–9

11 TANK MUSEUM: Anton Lang, AC E1092.81.18/7/1973

12 IWM DOCS: A. L. Atkins, Typescript account, pp.66–7

13 TRENT UNIVERSITY ARCHIVES: C. G. Frost, Letter, 17/11/1918; Internet source: http://www.freepages.genealogy.rootsweb.com/~brett/cmgc/cmgc_cgf_letters.html

14 IWM DOCS: O. A. Woodward, Typescript account, pp.142–3

15 IWM DOCS: E. C. Allfree, Typescript account, pp.447–8

16 IWM DOCS: H. J. C. Marshall, Transcript account, pp.29–30

17 IWM DOCS: E. C. Allfree, Typescript account, pp.447–8

18 IWM DOCS: R. G. Dixon, Typescript account, 'The Wheels of Darkness', p.139

19 IWM DOCS: C. B. Brown, Typescript account, p.315

20 IWM DOCS: J. W. Stephenson, Typescript account, pp.60–61

21 IWM DOCS: F. Meisel, Transcript account, pp.78–9

22 IWM SOUND: H. Hopthrow, AC 11581, Reel 14

23 IWM DOCS: T. H. Westmacott, Typescript letter, 13/12/1918

24 IWM DOCS: J. Whitehead, Typescript account, p.19

25 Ibid., p.20

26 IWM SOUND: H. Calvert, AC 9955, Reel 17 & 19

27 IWM DOCS: J. Whitehead, Typescript account, p.20

28 IWM SOUND: A. J. Jamieson, AC 10434, Reel 2

29 IWM SOUND: J. Pickard, AC 8946, Reel 17

30 Ibid., Reel 18

31 IWM DOCS: J. Nettleton, Typescript account, p.197

Index

Abraham, Lance Corporal Alfred 475–7
Adcock, Sergeant 80
Ailette River 266
aircraft
  All Arms Battle tactics 311–12
  bombers 188–90
  ground-attack 37, 88–9, 186–8
  night flying 189
  reconnaissance 20
Aisne, Battle on the
  planning and preparations 264–5, 269
  British preparations 266–72
  artillery bombardment 272–4
  infantry assault, 27 May 274–93
  German assault slows 293–5
  German gains 294
  assessment 296
Albert 35, 192, 218, 426
Albert, Battle of
  planning and preparations 362–6
  Third Army assault 367–71
  Fourth Army assault 371–9
  assault, 23 August 379–87
Albert I, King of the Belgians 443
Alexander Major General Robert 438
All Arms Battle tactics 3–5, 18–21, 305–6,
  307–14
Allen, Private Stan 151–2
Allfree, Lieutenant Edward 54–5, 68–9,
  87, 88, 89–90, 134–5, 136–8, 165,
  169, 493, 504, 505
American Expeditionary Force 423
  action, 15 July 414
  arrival 405–8
  and the Battle of St Mihiel 416–19
  and the Battle on the Aisne 294
  at Belleau Wood 411–13

  casualties 410, 412
  confidence 413–14
  early actions 409–11
  and the Hindenburg Line 431–9, 446–7,
    454–9
  leadership 404–5
  the 'Lost Battalion' 433–6
  organisation 408–9
  spitting 407
  strength 13–14, 403–4, 464
American Expeditionary Force formations
  II Corps 446
  US Marine Corps 411–13, 418,
    437–8
  1st Division 405, 410–11, 414
  2nd Division 411–13, 414
  3rd Division 411, 414
  26th Division 413
  27th Division 454–6
  30th Division 447, 456–7
  77th Division 415, 432–3
  80th Division 419
  18th Infantry Regiment 410–11
  102nd Infantry Regiment 409–10
  107th Infantry Regiment 455–6
  132nd Infantry Regiment 431–2
  165th Infantry Regiment 418, 419
  328th infantry Regiment 433–6
  356th Infantry Regiment 436–7
Amiens 39, 183
Amiens, Battle of
  planning and preparations 307–16,
    317–24
  artillery deployment 309–11
  air support 311–12, 331–2, 352, 355
  tank deployment 318–24
  artillery barrage 324–7

tank assault 326–9, 330–1, 333–40, 345–8
infantry assault 326, 327, 329–30, 332–3, 348–50
gains 340–1, 344–5, 360
III Corps assault 341–2
assessment 342–4
casualties 342, 360
wastage of tanks 343–4
mopping up 350–2
operations, 10 August 353–8
end of 358–61
AEF involvement 409
Amiens Defence Line 195
Ancre River 218
Anderson-Morehead, Colonel Rupert 287
Angel, Stretcher Bearer Lance Corporal Robert 376–7
anti-aircraft batteries 24
Anzac Day 261–2
Argonne Forest 431–9
Armentières 230–3, 401
Armistice, the
negotiations 495–7
comes into force 497–508
Arnold, Lieutenant Clement 336–40
Arras 35, 199
Arras, Battle of, 1917 17
artillery 306; *see also* Royal Artillery
accuracy 19–20
advance, October 469–71
at Albert 366–7
ammunition shortages 4
anti-tank guns 51
and the Battle of Amiens 309–11
defence in depth 42–3, 53–6
German assault, 21 March 64–74
Numbers, British 366
numbers, German 36
power 514–15
rate of fire 66
tactics 3–5, 19–21, 36–7, 327–8, 369
Atkins, Corporal Arthur 503
atrocities 486
Australian Corps 209–10, 213–15, 218, 256–8, 304–5, 306, 314, 325, 340–1, 342–3, 345, 379, 390–1, 446–8, 462–3
2nd Australian Division 329, 391–3, 394
3rd Australian Division 454
4th Australian Division 215, 261, 305, 307, 318, 428–30
5th Australian Division 261–2, 329, 332, 393–4, 448, 457–8
8th Australian Division 262–3

1st Tunnelling Company 458, 474–5, 487–8, 489, 504
Austrian Army 303, 515

Bac St Maur 225–6, 227
Backhurst, Private Reginald 24, 91–2
Baden, Prince Max von 466, 497
Bagley, Private Albert 227–8, 239–42, 243–4
Bailey, Brigadier General Vivian 152–3
Bailleul 220, 250
Bapaume 150–2, 186–8, 364, 389
barbed wire 48–9, 50, 62, 301–2
Bashford, Private Harold 493–4
Beaurevoir Line 460–3, 468–9
Beauvais 178
Behrend, Captain Arthur 61, 67
Belleau Wood, Battle of 411–13
Bellenglise 451–3
Bellenglise Tunnel 452
Bellicourt Tunnel 459
Below, General Otto von 35, 45, 370
Berry-au-Bac 272
Béthencourt 145
Béthune 246–7, 253
Beugny 398–9
Bickerton, Private Thomas 202–3
Blair, Lieutenant J. T. 394
Boiry-Becquerelle 379–84
Bois des Buttes 285–8
Bolster, Private Herbert D'Alton 23
Bomfay Farm 169
booby traps 252, 445, 490
Borne, Private Alexander 287
Bouchavesnes Spur 391, 392
Boucher, Sergeant Charles Leo 409–10
Boulogne 498–9
Bourlon Ridge 439
Boyelles 379–84
Boyle, Medical Officer Captain Alan 277
Bradbury, Trooper Arthur 102, 156, 173
Bradbury, Sergeant Stanley 155–6, 157
Bradnack, Lieutenant Brian 53–4, 55–6, 60–1, 66–7, 86, 90–1, 469–70
Brady, Private James 62–3, 75, 77–8, 94–5
Bray-sur-Somme 371
Breaking the Hindenburg Line (Priestley) 452
Brett, Captain Charles 401
Brett, Captain George 122–3, 123–5, 472, 473–4
Brie 163
Bristol Bridge 139–40, 144–5
British Army
achievement 5–6

advance, October 466–81
and the AEF 406–8
ammunition shortages 4, 137
artillery strength 366
casualties 104, 191, 203, 219, 263, 266, 307, 342, 360, 430, 462, 483
command control 108, 169–74, 344–5
communications 70–1, 83–4, 113
condition, July 364
condition, October 482–3
conscription 24
consolidates new defensive lines, Somme area 301
defence in depth 39–43, 48–50, 53–6, 56–7, 222, 301
demobilisation 508–11, 515
deployment, Spring 38–9
Field Service Regulations 17
firepower 305–6, 478
high command failures 2–3
Labour Corps 47, 229
manpower restrictions 28–9
manpower shortage 56, 364
morale 206–8, 304, 386, 424–5
quality 514–15
replacements 263
and retreat 46–7
stores 174–5
strength 33, 229, 403
tanks 259–61, 308–9, 318–24
training 52–3, 57
British Army formations. *see also* Australian Corps; Canadian Corps; Royal Artillery
First Army 38, 202, 221, 235, 236, 366, 387–90, 423, 439, 443, 478–9, 487, 489
Second Army 38, 221, 235, 251, 314, 366, 423, 443, 477–8
Third Army 38, 141–2, 149–54, 184–5, 190, 191–2, 209–10, 359–60, 364–71, 384, 394, 398–9, 423, 428, 439–43, 475–7, 487, 489
Fourth Army 301, 304, 307–8, 314, 318, 342, 345, 353, 358–60, 366, 371–9, 384, 390–1, 423, 425–31, 446–60, 475, 479–81, 487, 489
Fifth Army 39, 45–50, 74, 105, 141–2, 142–9, 180–3, 190, 191–2, 210, 217, 478
III Corps 94; 96, 106, 190, 318, 341–2, 371, 390, 430–1
IV Corps 398–9, 441
V Corps 97, 104, 118–20, 122–6, 426

VI Corps 98–100, 199, 441
VII Corps 93, 97–8, 108, 132, 147, 190
IX Corps 233, 264, 294, 430–1, 448
XI Corps 221, 230
XIII Corps 199
XIX Corps 91–3, 96, 108, 190, 210
XV Corps 221
XVII Corps 199, 394, 441
XVIII Corps 58, 78–85, 96, 108, 190, 210
XXII Corps 394
Army Service Corps 137, 295
Field Survey Corps 310–11, 325, 454–5, 500
Guards Division 441–3
Royal Army Medical Corps 62–3, 75, 77–8, 94–5
Royal Engineers 50–1, 83–5, 106–7, 127–31, 147–8, 156, 173, 192, 214, 224, 237, 246–7, 253, 278, 445–6, 450, 452, 453–4, 458–60, 498, 504–5, 507
Tank Corps 51–2, 119–20, 150–2, 165–7, 259–61, 306, 308, 318–24, 326–9, 330–1, 333–40, 343–4, 345–8, 353–4, 363, 367, 389–90, 454–5, 506
1st Division 487
3rd Division 98
4th Division 278
5th Division 384, 398–9
6th Division 97
8th Division 156–7, 158–9, 256–9, 261, 262, 264, 266, 268–9, 269–70, 270–1, 273–4, 275–7, 278–80, 283–95, 295, 478–9
9th Division 93, 233
11th Division 439
12th Division 377–9
14th Division 74, 75, 77–8, 94–5, 217–18, 503
16th Division 93, 139
17th Division 97
18th Division 74, 75, 377–9
19th Division 97, 233–5
20th Division 58, 96
21st Division 93, 264
24th Division 91–2, 208–9, 491–2, 507–8
25th Division 97, 233, 264
29th Division 229, 237
30th Division 78, 80–5, 478, 492–3
32nd Division 460–1
34th Division 98–100, 233
36th Division 77, 78–80, 106

37th Division 468–9
40th Division 98, 224–7, 237, 266
42nd Division 370, 385, 400
46th Division 449–54
47th Division 97, 122–6, 152–3, 371–7
49th Division 229
50th Division 58, 96, 116, 130, 158–9,
    183, 211, 221, 227–8, 235, 237–44,
    264, 266, 269, 270, 271–2, 274–5,
    277–8, 280–4, 284, 288–9
51st Division 97, 154, 155–6, 157, 221,
    227, 235, 237
55th Division 221, 224, 228, 235
56th Division 379–84
58th Division 74–5
59th Division 98
61st Division 78, 484–5
63rd (Royal Naval) Division 63, , 168–9,
    171–2
66th Division 91–2, 92–3
77th Division 501
89th Brigade 56–7
Rifle Brigade 193, 217–18, 284, 290–3,
    295, 406–7, 446, 478–9, 499–500,
    514
Carey's Force 195–9, 210–11, 409
17th Lancers 30, 31, 162, 166, 216–17,
    249–50
Bedfordshire Regiment 493–4
Cheshire Regiment 367–8, 368–70,
    384, 398–9
Coldstream Guards 441–3
Connaught Rangers 401, 471–4
Devonshire Regiment 285–8
Duke of Cornwall's Light Infantry 146
Duke of Wellington's Regiment 230,
    483–4, 485, 506
Durham Light Infantry 23, 237, 238,
    271–2, 272, 274–5, 277–8, 284, 501
East Lancashire Regiment 145
Essex Regiment 202–3, 425–6
Gloucestershire Regiment 182, 484–5
Grenadier Guards 441, 443, 509–10
Hampshire Regiment 150, 251–3
Hertfordshire Regiment 193
King's Liverpool Regiment 110–13, 127
King's Royal Rifle Corps 101–2, 102–3,
    132–4, 135–6, 138–9, 183, 192–5,
    205–7, 211–12
Lancashire Fusiliers 149, 354–7, 461
Leicestershire Regiment 452–3
London Regiment 70–1, 74–5, 117–18,
    122–6, 152–3, 197–8, 341–2, 371–7,
    379–84, 400–1, 407, 430–1, 445–6

Manchester Regiment 80–3, 85, 92–3,
    139–40, 144–5, 161–2, 388–9
Middlesex Regiment 163, 182–3,
    258–9, 275–6, 286
Munster Fusiliers 194
Norfolk Regiment 63
Northumberland Fusiliers 212–13,
    227–8, 238–44, 275, 512–13
Queen's Royal West Surrey Regiment
    475–7
Royal Fusiliers 149, 214–15, 377–9,
    468–9
Royal Inniskilling Fusiliers 47, 48, 48–9,
    61–2, 78–80
Royal Scots 98–100, 154, 173, 424–5,
    444–5, 511
Royal Scots Greys 102, 156, 173
Royal Sussex Regiment 487, 488, 489
Royal West Kent Regiment 24, 91–2
Sherwood Foresters 449, 450–1, 454,
    479–81
Somerset Light Infantry 52–3, 131–2,
    146–7
West Yorkshire Regiment 286
Wiltshire Regiment 233–5
Worcestershire Regiment 500–1
Yorkshire Regiment 280
British Empire 515–16
Brooks, Captain Gerald 326–7
Brown, Private Charles 389–90, 506
Brown, Private George 151–2
Brown Quarry 81, 83
Bruchmüller, Oberstleutnant Georg 36,
    66
Bryan, Sergeant Ernest 127
Bucquoy 218, 367–8
Buell, Lieutenant Ralph Polk 455–6
Bulgaria 465, 515
burials 351–2
Burke, Private Michael 388–9
Burke, Captain Ulick 285–6, 287
Bus 124
Busigny 474–5
Butler, Lieutenant General Sir Richard 74,
    318
Butte de l'Edmonde 277
Byng, General Sir Julian 38, 118, 142, 364

Cagnicourt 397–8
Californie Plateau 266, 272, 280
Calvert, Guardsman Horace 441, 443,
    509–10
Cambrai 469–71
Cambrai, Battle of, 1917 18–21, 93, 118

Canadian Corps 23, 314, 318, 340–1, 353, 390, 446, 463, 494
  1st Canadian Division 24–5, 326, 348–51, 357–8, 386, 394, 396–8, 439
  3rd Canadian Division 320, 439
  4th Canadian Division 394–6, 439–41
  5th Canadian Division 325, 330
  Canadian Machine Gun Corps 503
Canal du Nord 398, 439–43
Cantigny 410–11
Capron, Lieutenant John 199–201, 366, 368, 502
Carey, Major General George 195–6, 210–11
Carnie, Driver William 336–40
Castel Bridge 208–9
casualties
  AEF 410, 412
  Amiens 342, 360
  Australian 430, 462
  British 104, 191, 203, 219, 263, 266, 307, 342, 360, 430, 462, 483
  French 219, 360
  German 6, 104, 219, 307, 342, 360, 464
  German assault, 21 March
  Hamel 307
  last 501–2
  Operation Mars 203
  Operation Michael 95, 97, 104, 191, 219
  post-war suffering 512–13
Catlin, Colonel Albertus 412
cavalry 21, 209, 210–11, 313, 340
Cawston, Lieutenant Colonel Edward 407
Chaney, Signaller Bert 70–1, 198
Chapman, Andy 62
Château-Thierry 294, 299, 411
Chemin des Dames Ridge 264, 265, 266, 268
Chipilly Spur 341–2
Chopin, Private Matthew 436–7
Christian, Lieutenant J. C. 262–3
Churchill, Winston 363
Clastres 55
Clemenceau, Georges 176–7, 178, 495
Cléry-sur-Somme 135–8, 391
Colbeck, Private Stan 440
Cole, Signaller George 280–1
Cologne 507–8
Combles 147–8
communications 43, 47, 70–1, 83–4, 113, 308, 345
Congreve, Lieutenant General Sir Walter 93, 132
Cook, Sapper Frederick 173, 192

Cook, Sapper Wilfred 310–11, 325, 454–5, 500
Corbie 215
corpse factories 459
Courage, Brigadier Anthony 305, 306
Cousins, Stretcher-Bearer Albert 180–1
Coutts, Major Donald 392–3
Cox, Gunner Bertie 325, 330
Craonne Plateau 280–1, 281
Creek, Gunner Percy 86, 197, 328, 482–3, 486
Crozat Canal 94, 96, 106, 108, 132, 142
Currie, Lieutenant General Sir Arthur 318, 358, 394, 439–40
Curtis, Private Frederick 163, 182–3

Daly, Sergeant Dan 412
Davies, Lieutenant Jim 214–15, 377–9
de Pree, Brigadier General H. D. 167–8
Debeney, General Marie 190, 308
defence in depth 39–43, 48–50, 53–6, 56–7, 222, 301
Delville Wood 152–3
Dennys, Second Lieutenant Cyril 69–70, 86–7, 501–2
depression, economic 513–14
Derby, Lord 30, 31
Dermody, Private Charles 431–2
Dillon, Major Mark 51–2, 320–1, 323, 328–9, 334
Dixon, Lieutenant Richard 22, 407–8, 423–4, 498–9, 505
Dose, Oberleutnant 201, 203–4
Douai 478–9
Downing, Private John 165–7
Downing, Sergeant William 262, 393–4
Drocourt-Quéant Line 394–8
Duchêne, General Denis 268, 294
Dury 395–6

Eastern Front 33
Ebert, Friedrich 497
Elliott, Brigadier General Pompey 215, 261
Ellis Redoubt 50
Elstob, Lieutenant Colonel Wilfrith 80–2
Epéhy 54, 90, 426, 430–1
Epernay 295
Epine de Dallon 56
Erzberger, Matthias 497
Esler, Medical Officer Captain Maberly 258–9, 275–6
Essigny 62, 94
Essigny Plateau 94–6, 104

Estaires 227, 237
Evans, Captain James 24–5, 386
executions 357–8

Fampoux 202–3
Fanshawe, Lieutenant General Sir Edward 97
Fayolle, General Émile 190
Fereday, Private Albert 371–3
Ferguson, Captain Lionel 367–8, 368–70, 384, 398–9
Findlay, Major G. de C. E. 489
Fisher, Private Roland 123, 373, 374–6, 400–1
Fitzmaurice, Major J. G. 320
Fitzpatrick, Sergeant Joe 92–3
Flanders 18, 34, 38, 477–8
Flanders, Battle of. *see* Operation Georgette
Fleming, Second Lieutenant John 68, 115, 172, 207, 332, 351–2
Flesquières Salient, the 35, 38, 96–7, 104, 118–20, 122–6, 263
flying pigs 144
Foch, Field Marshal Ferdinand 176–8, 191, 210, 221, 229, 237, 250, 256, 264, 294, 298, 299, 308, 315–16, 358–60, 363–4, 411, 422, 423, 496–7
fog 64, 72–3
Foot, Major Richard 184, 185, 386–7, 399–400, 492
Foster, Lance Corporal Kenneth 348–9, 357–8
Fox, Private Jim 501
Fraser-Tyler, Major Neil 170–1, 189
French, Field Marshal Sir John 16, 25
French Air Force 312
French Army 142
   and the AEF 406
   and the Battle of Albert 364
   and the Battle of Amiens 317, 342, 353
   and the Battle of St Mihiel 416
   and the Battle on the Aisne 268, 285, 293–4
   casualties 219, 360
   collapse, 1917 18
   and the Hindenburg Line 423, 431
   at Mont Kemmel 254–6
   and Operation Georgette 236–7, 250
   and Operation Michael 72, 101, 142, 145–6, 160–1, 176–8, 190–1, 205, 217
   and the Second Battle of the Marne 298–300

   strength 33
   tactics 299
   tanks 300
French Army formations
   First Army 190, 217, 308, 317, 359
   Third Army 190, 296, 298, 353
   Fifth Army 300
   Sixth Army 264, 265, 268, 300
   Ninth Army 300
   Tenth Army 300, 364
   V Corps 145–6
   IX Corps 317
   XI Corps 285
   XX Corps 414
   XXXI Corps 317
   Alpine Division 254
Freniches 52–3
Frost, Captain Cecil Gray 503
Fuller, Lieutenant Colonel John 308, 363
Fuller, Signaller Sydney 315
Fynch, Sergeant R. A. 262

Garretson, Colonel Leland 419, 493
gas 3, 5, 36, 68–9, 254, 255, 258, 260, 274, 363, 370, 381–2, 393, 400, 449, 476–7
Gassed (Sargent) 400
German Air Service 299, 312, 331–2
German army
   and the Armistice 506–7
   artillery concentration 36
   casualties 6, 104, 219, 307, 342, 360, 464
   cavalry 209
   collapse 5, 6
   condition, July 362
   defences, Somme area 301–2
   exhaustion 485–6
   morale 174–5, 183, 373–4
   planning, spring 33–4
   rations 303
   replacements 245, 302–3
   retreat, November 490–1
   retreat to Hindenburg Line 387–402
   shells Paris 296
   situation, October 464
   Stormtroopers 21, 37, 265
   strength 16, 33, 298–9
   tactics 2, 21, 36–8, 46, 117, 204, 294, 388
   tanks 50–1, 259–61
   weakened condition, Somme area 302–4

German army formations
Second Army 35, 120
Third Army 298
Fourth Army 220, 230
Sixth Army 220
Seventh Army 264–5, 298
Seventeenth Army 35, 45, 120,
199–205, 370
Eighteenth Army 35, 45, 74, 104–5,
120, 296, 298
36th Division 59, 60, 73–4, 304
1st Guards Foot Artillery Regiment 65,
175
2nd Bavarian Foot Artillery Regiment
502
22nd Fusilier Regiment 385–6
63rd Field Artillery Regiment 65, 96
73rd Hanoverian Fusiliers Regiment 66,
73, 118–19
120th Württemberg Regiment 385
187th Infantry Regiment 201, 203–4
371st Infantry Regiment 59, 230,
231–2, 244–6, 254–6, 302–4, 470–1,
481, 486, 506–7
1047th Telephone Unit 59–60, 66, 174,
216, 265
Nr. 82 K Flak 189
First Army 264–5, 298
Germany
blockade of 302, 496
British forces enter 507–8
economic situation, 1917 11–13
political unrest 466, 497
post-war situation 515
scarcities 464
Gheluvelt 444
Gillman, Private Bill 341–2, 430–1, 445–6
Gough, General Sir Herbert 29, 39, 45–6,
51, 58, 71–2, 96, 101, 107–8, 126,
141–2, 159–60, 190, 191, 195, 210
Grady, Private (later Corporal) Thomas
415, 432–3, 501
Grant, Major General P.G. 126–7
Groener, General Wilhelm 482, 497
Grogan, Brigadier General George 270,
273, 285, 288, 290
Grover, Private Walter 487, 488

Hahn, Corporal William 152–3
Haig, Field Marshal Sir Douglas
hatred of 2
background 15–17
and the Battle of the Somme 16–17
military doctrine 17

campaigns, 1917 17–19
political interference 25, 26–7, 28–31,
250
deployment, Spring 38–9
and Gough 46
and Operation Michael 105, 141–2
meetings with Pétain, March 160–1,
176–8
unifies command south of the Somme
190
and Foch 210, 298, 358–60, 363–4
cheerfulness 217
and Operation Georgette 220–1, 229,
236–7, 249–50
and the First Battle of Ypres 250
and the Battle of Amiens 307–8, 314,
315–16, 358–60
on tanks 309
and the Canadian Corps 318
and Churchill 363
and the Battle of Albert 364, 374, 386–7
and Monash 391
and the AEF 416
and the Hindenburg Line 421–3, 431
recognises German Army beaten 464
peace demands 496–7
Haldane, Lieutenant General Sir Aylmer
98
Hall, Private P. R. 139–40, 144–5, 161–2
Ham 127–9, 130–1, 315–16, 344
Hamel, Battle of 305–7, 317
Haplincourt Wood 151
Harding, Second Lieutenant Phelps 418,
419
Hardman, Private Horace 82
Hargreaves, Major Thomas 123–5
Harington, Brigadier Charles 251
Harper, Captain Maurice 74–5, 117–18
Harrington, Brigadier J. 454
Harris, Second Lieutenant Walter 217–18,
268–9, 278–80, 283–4
Havrincourt Wood 122
Hazebrouck 220, 236, 237, 247, 250, 256
Hedley, Major Ian 30, 31, 216–17, 249–50
Heneker, Major General William 261,
288, 400
Henin Hill 100
Henley, Brigadier General Anthony 370,
385
Hindenburg, Field Marshal Paul von
11–12, 465–6
Hindenburg Line
German retreat to 387–402
defence works 420–1, 423–4, 448–9

assault planning and preparations 421–6
Fourth Army assault, 18 September
    426–31
AEF assault, 26 September 431–9
assault, 27 September 439–43
Fourth Battle of Ypres 423, 443–6
Fourth Army assault, 29 September
    446–60
tanks on 454–5
fall of the Reserve Line 460–3
Hoegenmacker Mill 247–8
Hollis, Second Lieutenant Arthur 186–8
Holmes, Private T. H. 379–82
Hopkins, Second Lieutenant J. C. F. 189
Hopthrow, Lance Corporal Harry 83–4,
    507
Horne, General Sir Henry 38, 387
House, Colonel Edward 496
House, Major Wilfred 233, 234–5
Hughes Barney 155–6
Humphreys, Major Leonard 208
Humphries, Captain James 367
Hutchinson, Lieutenant Colonel Graham
    Seton 247–9
Hutier, General Oskar von 35, 45

Ignaucourt 206
intelligence 43–5, 57–8, 61, 269, 270
Italy 15

Jamieson, Private Alexander 444, 445, 511
Johnson, Lieutenant Colonel Dudley 489
Johnston, Captain Robert 98–100
Joncourt 460–2
Jünger, Leutnant Ernst 66, 73, 118–19

Kentner, Sergeant George 394–5, 395–6
Kerensky, Alexander 11
Kerr, Corporal William 326, 348, 349–51
Knox, Second Lieutenant Cecil 106–7
Krulewitch, Sergeant Melvin 412–13
Kühns, Signaller Edwin 59–60, 65–6, 174,
    216, 265

La Flaque Dump 170
Laithwaite, Second Lieutenant Gilbert 149
Lane, Sergeant Sam 382–4
Lang, Anton 502
Last, Private Frank 410–11
Laventie 221
Lavre River 235
Le Cateau 471–4
Le Havre Base Camp 509–10
Leat, Corporal L. 286–7

Léchelle 124
Ledward, Captain Philip 156–7, 256–8,
    268, 270–1, 273, 288, 289–90, 295
Lenin, Vladimir 11
Licourt 158–9
Ling, Private Norman 358
living conditions 22–5
Lloyd George, David 14–15, 17, 25–8,
    30–1, 105, 177, 191, 229, 495, 510
Longavesnes 132–3
looting 154–6, 214, 228, 244–5, 247
Lorette Ridge 38
Louch, Captain, Thomas 215, 261, 318
Ludendorff, Quartermaster General Erich
    role 11–12
    on the collapse of Russia 12
    on the AEF 13
    planning, spring 33–4
    and Operation Michael 34–5, 104–5,
        120, 122, 216, 219
    and Operation Mars 204
    loss of stepson 204–5
    and Operation Georgette 220
    Villers-Bretonneux attack 256
    and the Battle on the Aisne 264–5, 294,
        296
    and Operation Hagen 298–300
    and Amiens 342
    offer to resign 360–1
    and the retreat to the Hindenburg Line
        387
    recognises German Army beaten 464–6
    resignation 482
Luther, Driver Rowland 214
Lyne, Major John 224–7, 231
Lyon, Captain Hugh 271–2, 272, 274–5,
    277–8, 284
Lys river 222, 225–7, 235
Lys Salient 401

Macdonnell, Major General Sir Archibald
    348
McKerchar, Sergeant Don 440
McMurtie, Captain George 52–3, 132,
    146–7
McPeake, Second Lieutenant Alan 472–3
machine guns
    deployment 42
    Lewis 3, 202–3, 286, 306, 313
    Maxims 63
    Vickers 3, 63, 97–8, 243–4, 306
Magnin, General Charles 298
Manchester Hill 81–2
Manchester Redoubt 81–3

March, Captain John 50–1, 147–8, 498
Marchélepot 158–9
Maresches 484–5
Maricourt 154, 165, 169
Marne, Second Battle of the 298–300
Marne River 295
Marshall, Captain John 224, 246–7, 450, 452, 453–4, 458–60, 504–5
Marwitz, General Georg von der 35
Maxse, Lieutenant General Sir Ivor 78
Mealing, Lieutenant Kenneth 24
Meisel, Unteroffizier Frederick 59, 230, 231–2, 244–6, 254–6, 302–4, 470–1, 481, 486, 506–7
Mellersh, Second Lieutenant Harold 145
Mesopotamia 15
Messines Ridge 220, 222, 230, 250, 251, 401, 444–5
Metcalfe, Corporal William 397
Méteren 247–9
Metz Switch Line 122
Middle East campaigns 14–15
Miller, Captain Charles 47, 48, 48–9, 61–2, 78–80, 177
Milner, Lord 31, 176, 422–3
Mitchell, Lieutenant Frank 259–61
Monash, Major General Sir John 256–7, 305, 306, 325, 358–9, 391, 446, 448, 462
Monchy le Preux 387
Mons 494
Mont Kemmel 220, 253–6, 312, 314
Mont St Quentin 134–5, 391–3
Montbrehain 462
Montdidier 296, 353
Morrow, Private Edgar 329

Nagel, Leutnant Fritz 189
national debt 513
Neame, Major Philip, VC 236, 478
Nettleton, Lieutenant John 284, 290–3, 295, 406–7, 446, 478–9, 499–500, 514
Neuf-Berquin 238–9
Newton, Private Willard 447, 456–7
Nivelle, General Robert 17–18, 26–7
Nivelle Offensive, 1917 17–18, 26–7
Nobescourt Farm 115
Noyon 296

observation balloons 102
Oestreicher, Gunner Paul 232–3
Oise River and Canal 74
Operation Archangel 34

Operation Blücher. see Aisne, Battle on the
Operation George 34, 35
Operation Georgette
  planning and preparations 220–2
  assault, 9 April 222–9
  assault, 10 April 230–47
  German advance on Bailleul 247–50
  assessment 263
Operation Gneisenau 296, 298
Operation Hagen 265, 298–300
Operation Hector 34
Operation Mars 34, 35, 199–205
Operation Michael
  planning and preparations 34–8
  British intelligence gathering 43–5, 57–8, 61
  British preparations 45–50
  advance to launch positions 58–60
  British await assault 60–3
  preliminary bombardment, 21 March 64–74, 103
  infantry assault, 21 March 74–85, 87, 91–3
  British artillery in action, 21 March 85–91
  British retreat, 21 March 87–8, 89–91
  German advance, 21 March 93–101
  air support, 21 March 88–9, 102
  British reserves advance, 21 March 101–3
  assessment, 21 March 103–5
  withdrawal to Emergency Line 106–8, 115–16, 131–40
  Roupy counter-attack 110–13
  prisoners of war 112–13, 117–18, 125–6
  artillery withdrawal 113–15, 134–5, 135–8
  the Flesquières Salient 118–20, 122–6
  assault, 23 March 120–6
  Somme bridges demolished 126–31, 127–9, 130–1
  air support 136
  Haig intervenes, 24 March 141–2
  defence of Somme Line, 24 March 142–9, 159–60
  air support, 24 March 146
  Third Army withdrawal, 24 March 149–54
  British disciplinary lapses, 24 March 154–9
  25th March 161–9, 169–74, 174–5
  Haig's meeting with Pétain, 26 March 176–8
  withdrawal, 26 March 180–3, 191–2

artillery regroups, 26 March 184
German artillery breaks down, 26
March 184–5
air support, 26 March 185–90, 192
strategic situation, 26 March 190–2
French deployment, 26 March 190–1
27 March 192–9
28 March 199–205, 205–10
29 March 210–11
30 March 211–16
final actions 216–18
assessment of 218–19, 263
Ors 490
Owen, Wilfred 1, 6, 490

Page, Lieutenant Colonel C.A.S. 275–6
Palestine 15
Paris, shelling of 296
Parker, Corporal George 449, 450–1, 454,
479–81
Parkin, Private William 130, 183, 270,
288–9
Passchendaele 251–2
Passchendaele Ridge 221, 251, 318, 443,
444
Peck, Lieutenant Colonel Cyrus 397–8
Pernert, Leutnant Erich 204–5, 408–9
Péronne 35, 133–4, 135–6, 139–40, 161–2
Péronne, Battle of 391–4
Pershing, General John 404–5, 406, 411,
416, 496–7
Pétain, General Henri-Philippe 18, 101,
142, 160–1, 176–8, 294, 496–7
Petschler, Lieutenant Robert 50, 83–4,
127–9, 130–1, 156, 253
Phillips, Private Edgar 239
photographic reconnaissance 44, 53
Pick, Captain Arthur 452–3
Pickard, Private Joseph 212–13, 512–13
Piggott, Lieutenant Colonel F. S. G. 57–8
Pilckem Ridge 221, 253
pillboxes 43
Platt, Lieutenant Clifford 460–1
Plumer, General Sir John 38, 250–1
Pohlmann, Hartwig 59, 60, 73–4, 304
Poincaré, Raymond 176
Polley, Private David 63, 171–2
Pont de la Trompe 237
Pontavert bridge, action at 285–8
Portuguese Corps 221, 222, 224, 228
post-traumatic stress disorder 512
Potten, Private Eric 336
Pressey, Bombardier William 88, 89,
113–14, 155, 216

Price, Corporal Donald 468–9
Priestley, Captain Raymond 452
Prior, Lieutenant Colonel Bernard 63
prisoners of war
advance on the Somme 368, 391, 400
Battle of the Aisne 278, 279–80, 282–4,
294
Battle for Flanders 232–3
Battle of Amiens 329–30, 342, 348, 360
Battle of Sambre 489
the Hindenburg Line 430, 431
Hindenburg Line 454, 462
interrogation of 43–4
Operation Michael 85, 92–3, 94–5, 104,
112–13, 117–18, 125–6, 152, 153, 188
total German 6
propaganda 485–6
Proyart 308
psychological effects 22–3

Rappolt, Feldwebel Walter 65, 175
Ravay 491–2
Rawlinson, Lieutenant General Sir Henry
31, 210, 301, 304–6, 307–8, 309, 314,
315, 358–9, 391, 448
Rees, Brigadier General Hubert 116,
158–9, 195–9, 210–11, 227, 237–8,
266, 269, 272, 280, 281–3
refugees 206, 230–1, 474–5, 491–2
Rhine, the 464, 507–8
Rhonelle River 483–4
Ribbans, Gunner Christopher 336,
339–40
Richmond, Private Clarence 418
Riddell, Brigadier General Edward 275
Riehl, Private J. H. 397
Riencourt 388
Riga, battle of, 1917 36
Rigby, Lieutenant Harry 187–8
Robertson, General Sir William 14–15,
25–6, 27, 30–1
Rogerson, Captain Sydney 266, 268,
269–70, 271, 273–4, 285
Romania 13
Ronssoy 430
Rose, Private G. V. 329, 332, 393, 448,
457–8, 462
Rosières-en-Santerre 182–3, 345–8
Roucy Hill 288
Roulers 221
Roupy 110–13
Rowland, Private Charles 319, 321, 326,
328, 333–4, 335–6, 343–4, 346–8,
354